THE PARTY SYMBOL
Readings on Political Parties

EDITED BY

William Crotty
NORTHWESTERN UNIVERSITY

W. H. Freeman and Company
San Francisco

Sponsoring Editor: Richard J. Lamb
Project Editor: Pearl C. Vapnek
Copyeditor: Steven Dopkin
Designer: Marie Carluccio
Production Coordinator: Fran Mitchell
Illustration Coordinator: Cheryl Nufer
Compositor: Lehigh/Rocappi, Inc.
Printer and Binder: The Maple-Vail Book Manufacturing Group

Library of Congress Cataloging in Publication Data

Main entry under title:

The Party symbol.

Includes bibliographies.
1. Political parties—United States—Addresses,
essays, lectures. I. Crotty, William J.
JK2261.P316   329'.02   79-22945
ISBN 0-7167-1144-3
ISBN 0-7167-1145-1 pbk.

Printed in the United States of America

9 8 7 6 5 4 3 2 1

THE PARTY SYMBOL

CONTENTS

v

PREFACE

This book is intended for students concerned with the operations and contemporary health of political parties. Its principal audience will be in courses that deal with the American political parties and their contributions to a productive and vital social order. The assessments contained in this volume come at a critical time in the life of the parties.

Political parties are in a process of transition. Potentially, the changes are enormous. They could reorder party operations and redirect the energies of the parties from activities more important in an older day to those that anticipate directly the needs of a nation undergoing fundamental social change. Or the political parties could muddle along, much as they have through their long and colorful history. They could attempt to keep to the old ways and traditions; adapt poorly to the newer social demands placed upon them; and, consequently, progressively lose their once dominant position in American electoral affairs. Should the latter occur—and, judged by present standards, it is the more likely possibility of the two—it would be most unfortunate. Political parties in America are critically important agencies for representing and linking the individual to his government. If, in fact, the parties are faltering—as it appears they are—the institution that best represents the collective voice of similar social and policy-oriented groups will be gone. (More than likely, political parties would continue, but merely as names; their powers would be dissipated and their influence negated.) There is no substitute for the political parties. Undoubtedly, American society as a whole could get along with less efficient and less viable party organizations. But we would do so at a cost. We would all be the losers.

Because political parties are in a process of change, "the party symbol," as a standard of reference for voters and as a factor of consequence in elections and governing, is undergoing reassessment. The readings in this volume contribute to the understanding needed to make a reasonably informed judgment as to the place and contribution of political parties within the new political order of contemporary American society.

Political parties are extraordinarily complex institutions. They defy easy categorization or explanation even in the best of times. In periods of transition, the difficulties are compounded. The parties engage in a multiplicity of activities, relating to their clientele—the voters—in diverse and subtle ways. Their organizational structures are perversely unique. An understanding of these features is important for assessing the contributions of political parties to society. This is what this book is all about.

There are advantages, however, as well as difficulties, to studying an institution in transition. One is excitement. We know that political parties are experiencing fundamental change, and it is not too much to suggest that their very existence—at least as a viable and important force in American politics—may hang in the balance. The game is to appreciate what they have done, how they have organized to accomplish their goals, and what the significance of their activities is. Can the parties do better? How? Could some other social agency—the media, for example, or private interest or campaign groups—conduct the same activities with greater economy or efficiency? With what consequences? Are the parties adapting gracefully to the pressures being placed upon them? Can they change and grow, given their history and their present methods of operation?

A second major advantage of a book of readings on political parties during a period of stress involves learning. Many of the old ways and, to an extent, the old knowledge are not quite as applicable now as they once were. This affords both a challenge and an opportunity. It is possible, as many of the essays in this book proceed to do, to summarize the previous wisdom and then to push beyond it to chart new courses and test new explanations. If, for example, primaries are of increasing importance in presidential nominations, has the institution of the primary changed? Is it more representative of the party base than it had been previously, or than national conventions? Has participation in primaries increased, or has it continued to decline as many had predicted? Are the media assuming a dominant position of influence in presidential nominations and campaigns? Have state and national party organs modernized in line with the reform emphasis, developing competency as well as influence that capitalizes on the technological and political changes that have swept the nation? Have the ethnic and religious affiliations of voters continued to evolve in the ways assumed, with the consequences anticipated? How important are ideological, policy, or personal considerations in sustaining the electorate's involvement in the candidacy of a presidential contender (or in explaining the force of that challenge)? How relevant is ideology in motivating the individuals who contact the voters and run year-round the party organizations? And so on. Whatever the area, it can profit from a new look at its operations and the assumptions presumed to explain its functioning. Such concerns can be, and are, addressed in this book within a framework that allows for analyses that review and note the basic research findings on the topic and then proceed to supplement and extend these in light of more recent developments.

Overall, the selections in this volume are important attempts to present as accurate and helpful a picture of the political parties as present research capabilities and understanding allow. As a whole, the readings constitute a working introduction to a valuable, although sometimes maligned, institution during a sensitive period in its evolution.

As editor, I am grateful to a number of people. I am especially pleased that the authors of so many superior original essays agreed to have their work appear in this volume. The willingness of many of these researchers to redevelop their materials

in a manner conducive to their presentation in this book is particularly appreciated.

Richard J. Lamb, Political Science Editor of W. H. Freeman and Company, was a
constant source of good advice and good cheer. I thank him, Pearl C. Vapnek, who
supervised the book's production, and Steven Dopkin, who skillfully edited the
manuscript. To these people and all the others who have contributed to the production of this book, I am grateful.

October 1979   *William Crotty*

THE PARTY SYMBOL

OVERVIEW

The Party Symbol
and Its Changing Meaning

Political parties are crucial to the stable operations of a democratic society. They serve a variety of needs in representing the individual citizen—or at least those individuals who participate in the political process—in selecting the principal nominees for a variety of offices from president to mayor; in representing the opinions of people on major issues and concerns of the day; in giving a continuity and stability to governments and their actions over time; and in developing coalitions and policy directions, both within the electorate and, once in office, among the various branches of the government. Political parties link voters to their government. They give electors the chance to pass binding judgment on the issues and political leaders of the day. The parties help educate voters to the means for exercising political influence, and officeholders to the nature of their responsibilities and the limits of their power. With the backing of the voters, parties attempt to shape national policy and manage the society. That political parties are essential to a democratic society as we have known it, few would argue.

I

Background

It is important to realize that political parties developed out of necessity. They were not planned and they are not specified in the Constitution. In fact, they were resisted and distrusted by the Founding Fathers. Yet, parties developed because they were needed to master the chaos of a pure democratic system. The parties were based on coalitions of groups at the local level that held similar political

1

objectives. The parties were used to screen candidates who shared the views of the coalitions and then to mobilize support both to place representatives in office and, once in office, to support the party policies.

The party system first came into prominence in the 1790s. It worked well and, in time, came to be regarded as an ingenious and vital contribution to democratic performance. Since their early days, the parties continued, in their fashion, to serve the needs of the electorate and the nation. As time passed, the evolving parties developed new, and progressively more democratic, institutions to serve their constituents and to better harmonize their activities with those of a maturing democracy. The national nominating conventions, primaries, the national committees, the national-party structures and, more generally, the successive reform eras, have all helped to shape a party system that paralleled the equally uncertain and exploratory development of the nation's democratic tendencies. [1]

The coalitions of voters supporting the two main parties would shift and reshape with time and circumstance. The names of the parties would change, and the issues and personalities of one era would give way to those of the next. But the party system itself would continue, performing the duties that made it essential to the orderly exercise of democratic politics. Perseverance and adaptability, along with relevance, became the party system's distinguishing qualities.

Old, time-tested, needed, the handmaiden of democracy—if these characterizations are correct, then it must follow that political parties today are venerable institutions, honored for their contributions to the political enterprise and secure in their place in American life. Unfortunately, of course, this is not the case. Political parties in the United States have always been suspect. [2] Their past has been checkered and the publicity they receive often has more to do with what they do wrong than what they do right. More often than not, the parties have deserved the criticisms they have received. Their institutional and leadership failings and their actions, both in and out of office, have encouraged public disrespect and antipathy. Both parties have often been slow to realize their shortcomings and little inclined to do anything about them.

Today the parties' position is particularly vulnerable. Their weaknesses are evident. The parties have not been able to reverse the erosion of their popular support. They have failed to deal comfortably and meaningfully with an increasingly policy-oriented electorate. They have resisted adapting to, and coopting to their own ends, the technological and campaign-oriented communication developments. And they have proved reluctant to adapt antiquated and unrepresentative organizational forms to the exigencies of modern electoral politics.

The indictment is harsh. It may well be that the American parties are in decline. The peak of their influence and their most significant contributions may be past. If so, the results would be sad. America would be losing its most effective voice for the millions that form the base of society. Walter Dean Burnham was one of the first to call attention to the "long-term trend toward a politics without parties." He put this rather well:

> political parties with all their well known human and structural shortcomings, are the only device thus far unaided by the wit of Western man that can, with some effectiveness, generate countervailing collective power on behalf of the many individually powerless against the relatively few who are individually or organizationally powerful. [3]

The "unchallenged ascendancy of the already powerful," Burnham contended, would most likely result.[4] The prospect is not a pleasant one. Based on past experience, a strong, vital, and progressive party system would appear essential to the democratic order.

The Evil of Parties

The parties have had their crises, many of which they have not handled terribly well. In one sense, American political parties have been in a continual state of crisis. Their legitimacy, their values, and their integrity have been attacked from the very earliest days of the republic to the present.

Although needed, the concept of party was bitterly resisted. James Madison, in *Federalist No. 10*, apologized for the existence of party and sought ways to control its effects.[5] In his farewell address, George Washington was even more concerned and outspoken. The spirit of party, he warned:

> seems always to distract the public councils and enfeeble the public admin-istration. It agitates the community with ill-founded jealousies and false alarms, kindles the animosities of one part against another, foments occa-sionally riots and insurrection. It opens the door to foreign influence and corruption, which find a facilitated access to government through the chan-nels of party passions.[6]

Party warfare and factionalism, the outgoing president counseled, could lead to despotism.

The parties survived Madison's defensiveness and Washington's hostility be-cause their contributions were absolutely vital and basically unanticipated by those who wrote the Constitution. The parties tied the voters to their leaders in a grass-roots representative and elective effort that made operable the formal institutions of the government. Often it would seem, however, that Washington's warnings should have been heeded.

Interparty Competition

Many would argue that the strength of the two-party system lies in the competitive balance between the major parties. If elections are closely contested, the parties are likely to extend themselves to best represent the coalitional groups that identify with them. They expand the electorate, bringing in and representing new groups whose support they seek. They debate the issues aggressively, stand as a check on the government and its potential abuses, and generally perform as intended.

There are many periods of American history when one political party so domi-nated the allegiance of Americans that serious competition between parties for elective office was rare. In such cases the control exercised by one party—at na-tional, regional, or local levels or in different historical eras—virtually destroyed the competitiveness and value of a second party.

The Jeffersonian and Jacksonian Democratic parties overshadowed the sporadic opposition of the Federalists and the Whigs during the first three to four decades of the nineteenth century. The Republican Party, in turn, created in the mid-1850s, dominated American politics during most of the years between 1865 and the 1920s. The Great Depression of the late 1920s and 1930s led to the New Deal and the Franklin Roosevelt–Al Smith coalition of the big cities, labor unions, workers, ethnics, Southerners, blacks, and the less well-off. The new coalition proved a potent source of new strength and the Democratic coalition quickly emerged as the dominant party from the middle to the late years of the twentieth century.[7]

As the Democratic coalition prospered, the Republicans were reduced to a relatively small following that had trouble extending its membership beyond its traditional one-fourth to one-fifth of the electorate. The two-party system at this point may best be described as a "one and one-half" party system.

The 1960s witnessed a series of new dislocations—the civil-rights revolution, a changing life style, Vietnam, urban rioting—to which the parties found it difficult to adapt. The intensity of individual party commitments appeared to lessen and the party system entered a period of stagnation. The drift of the 1960s continued into the 1970s, evidenced among other things in a weakening of the New Deal coalition ties. The Republicans, who have their own problems, have yet to benefit from the seeming disarray of the Democratic coalition.

On the state level, the Democratic Party controlled politics from the close of the Civil War—or, more realistically, from the time of the compromise that was reached with Northern Republican Party leaders in the Hayes–Tilden dispute of 1876—until the 1960s. During the late 1950s and early 1960s, the civil-rights acts and a nation's changing priorities laid the groundwork for enfranchising blacks and building within the South a distinctive, issue-sensitive two-party system akin to the national model.[8] The Republican Party, meanwhile, enjoyed little power in influencing elections within the region. Blacks were effectively kept out of the political system and, on the national level, the Democrats—in formulating national party positions and in selecting presidential nominees—had to contend, in the Congress, with a powerful and unified regional bloc that had little in common with the Northern wing.

Traditionally, other regions, especially upper New England, the Midwest, and the Great Plains, had equally strong party traditions that favored the Republicans. In recent decades, and as part of the general Republican decline, the Democrats have been able to win seats in once solely Republican areas. Today, even Maine, once a bastion of Republican support, has become a Democratic state (based on the number of registered voters declaring for the two major parties).

Locally, many county and district races historically have been, and to this day continue to be, noncompetitive. Roughly 60 percent of the smaller cities cannot by law hold partisan elections, and other elections—for example, those involving school district and taxation questions—have been kept nonpartisan by statute or custom. Intense and sustained two-party competition at any level may well be the exception rather than the rule in the United States.

Ethical Behavior

Both political parties have known periods of rampant corruption when the party organizations and their leaders used the party machinery to further their own immediate economic ends. Historians like to point with a certain perverse pride to what they call the "age of boodle." Many consider it the clearest example of political corruption of some magnitude, and the exploits of the age have become legendary. The decisive role of the machine in using its insiders' knowledge for the following is well documented: to buy property and then resell it at a handsome profit to a city or state government for roads, parks, or public buildings; to modify zoning restrictions; to award contracts; to build roads; to authorize subways; and, in general, to do whatever it could to exploit public office to earn a few dollars. The abuses of the late 1800s, and the reaction to them, laid the basis for the Progressive era and the ambitious schedule of reforms it advocated.

A reading of the newspaper or a half-hour spent watching the evening news on television would indicate that economic abuse of public office is a consistent temptation. Mayors, legislators, and government officials accepting transportation, lodging, and vacations from lobbyists; contracts let without bid to friends and relatives; a corporation's law business directed to a congressperson's home-town firm; government buildings constructed at three times the cost of comparable private buildings; new highways, stadiums, repairs, and building contracts awarded to financial supporters; kickbacks on contracts to politicians; insurance, legal business, and special and lucrative court appointments steered to an alderman's law firm; "friends," whose businesses are regulated by the government, contributing trust funds to politicians and their families; stocks sold to legislators below market value; partnerships established specifically to receive designated federal contracts; city advertising and insurance contracts awarded to firms controlled by politicians; campaign funds used for personal expenses—these are just a few examples. The variety of, and opportunity for, graft, payoffs, kickbacks, and the like appear endless.

It may well be that the greatest potential for political corruption is present today. In terms of dollar amounts involved and the number of people and businesses that can benefit from legally borderline operations, it is difficult to believe that any past period exceeded the opportunities at present. At the federal level, courts, the media, the attorney general's office, and such regulatory agencies as the Securities and Exchange Commission appear to be involved in one case after another. It may be, of course, that the public tolerance for illegal activity is decreasing and that the incidents of bribery or unethical conduct that do surface receive a great deal of attention. Or it may be that the full airing of such cases—once hidden from the public's or media's view—is just beginning to come into the public domain.

The corruption of individual elective and party officials has done little to better the public perceptions of parties. Even more serious, however, are the political (as against economic) abuses of public office. Watergate represented the epitome of this strain. Personal financial gain was an aspect of the overall problem. Profiteering has been uncovered in the awarding of defense contracts; agreements for such things as work programs; the overall stimulus given to specified business developments; and the use of public funds to furnish, and increase the value of, private homes. The campaign funds—laundered through Mexican banks—some of which ended up with the Watergate break-in crew, were donated with a clear *quid pro quo* in mind.[9] Still, this was one of the more familiar, and even benign, aspects of the Watergate scandal.

The exploitation of the powers of office to silence dissent and to stifle opposition, the employment of the instruments and resources of government to punish adversaries, and the effort to place a public official above the normal restraints of the political system (whether these be political parties, the courts, the Congress, the media, or public opinion) went well beyond economic manipulations. They went to the very heart of the democratic system. Neither of the political parties were in any sense responsible for Watergate. But the parties, also, did little to check the exploitations of public office obvious even in the early years of the Nixon presidency. The contribution of either of the parties to resolving the difficulties encountered in a trying period of American history was marginal.

Watergate was a frightening low in American politics. If one were to compile a list of such low points, the worst for political parties might well have come during the years immediately preceding the Civil War. At this point, the party system, in effect, collapsed. It could not resolve the dominant social issues of the day. There were, however, extenuating circumstances. The United States was torn by controversies over the nature of the Union, the meaning of the Constitution, and the relative position of the states in the federal system. The issues were outgrowths of the slavery question and the sectional differences in values, economic developments, and priorities that had existed, unresolved, since the nation's birth. The issues far transcended the ability of the parties to deal with them. The collapse of the party system in the critical decade of the 1850s, in effect, foresaw the inability of the nation to resolve such fundamental differences amicably. In one sense, the rise of the new Republican coalition in the mid-1850s foreshadowed both the likely resolution of the conflicts and a new postwar party system more attuned to the social concerns of the coming age.

But despite their problems and their times of crisis, the parties have survived and, in their uncertain way, prospered. The longevity of the parties testifies to their utility. Political parties exist because they serve a variety of social and political needs better than any institution devised by man. The services they contribute are (or have been) necessary to the survival of a democratic order. To this point in American history, they have been critical to the sustained functioning of a broad-based democracy.

II

The Contemporary Scene

Whatever their past, political parties are in trouble today. At a time when their contributions on a general level are accepted and recognized as helpful, the parties themselves have entered a particularly trying period. The problems the parties must face have been brought on in large part by changes in the society. During the 1970s, both parties attempted in some manner to deal with the difficulties they were encountering. The reform movement that ensued had its principal impact on the large and more divided of the two parties, the Democrats. Reform may have introduced more problems than it resolved.

In this section, we will look at the principal areas of concern for the modern party. Both parties will have to arrive at some type of accommodation with the problems posed by a changing electorate, new campaign and communication technology, and the reforms initiated by the parties themselves.

The Electorate

The American electorate is in a period of change. The old party system was based on a process of accommodation. The major groups within the electorate viewed symbolic and economic rewards as returns for long-running party support. Negotiations and compromises were worked out among interest-group and party leaders at national conventions and in the Congress. In return for financial and electoral support, the party chose candidates who appealed to the main centers of strength within its coalition.

The process allowed for a good deal of flexibility at the top in negotiating policy commitments, and it tacitly excluded from consideration any group that did not vote in sufficient numbers to make its will felt. The influence of the grass-roots party membership was indirect; its role was to elect candidates and support issue positions agreed upon by the party and interest-group leaders. Even then, it was expected that the major groups in the coalition would vote loyally—election year after election year—for the party symbol. Defections to the other party on an issue because of a candidate were normally considered short-term aberrations.

The goal of the party was to win office. Should it win, all in the coalition were presumed to share in the rewards. The party's success, in turn, should reinforce the individual's commitment and thus help continue his (or her) loyal electoral support.

The party division was based on the issues and coalitions of the New Deal. The commitment to the party, in V. O. Key's words, was a "standing decision." It was made early in life based on economic and social forces and was reasserted during each election year.

The assumptions underlying this model came under attack in the 1960s. They had held up well during the 1940s and 1950s. The early voting studies, and specifically *The American Voter,* described an electorate that was relatively apathetic, psychologically committed to one of the two major parties, and loyal in supporting that party and its candidate.[10] The voters tended to have little issue information and few ideological predispositions. The party symbol was the chief factor explaining election results.

Turnout

Voter changes during the 1960s introduced an uncomfortable period for the parties. First, and least commented on, the proportion of voters participating in elections began to decline. From relatively stable levels in the 1950s and early 1960s, the proportion of the eligible voters began to decrease. The trend persevered, and in fact, was accelerated by the enfranchisement of the eighteen-year-olds.[11] Presidential elections in which roughly one-half of the legally eligible population does not participate are not uncommon. Congressional and state elections draw even lower turnout. A 30- to 40-percent turnout of those eligible can be found in many localities.

There is cause for alarm in these figures. One-half of the American adult population—seventy million people—find so little of interest in the issues, candidates, or parties during elections that they simply do not bother to vote. Neither political party is especially alarmed at the situation. Both are comfortable with electorates whose loyalties can be assured. A higher turnout might well mean a less predictable vote.

The parties aside, there is something troubling about a system in which tens of millions of people refuse to participate at even the most rudimentary level.

Perceptions

A second factor of consequence is the public view of parties and politics. It appears to be unusually harsh and negative and has become progressively more cynical since the early 1960s. Perhaps, this is not surprising. The public perception of the parties has never been very favorable. That it should worsen—and the negative view should encompass all of government—during a period that witnessed the escalation of the Vietnam War, the assassination of a number of prominent public figures, and the events of Watergate, is predictable. The problem is what to do about it. The sporadic reforms entertained by the Congress, successive administrations, and the parties themselves were meant to allay public suspicions. It is unlikely they have succeeded.

The perceptions the voters held of the parties in the early 1970s were anything but favorable. In 1972, well before the full dimensions of Watergate were even suspected, the Center for Political Studies asked a national cross section of Americans to rank political parties in relation to other governmental institutions (see Table 1). The electorate was unambivalent. Political parties were ranked the least powerful, the least trusted, and as doing the worst job. The parties won these dubious honors by extraordinarily large margins.

Professor Jack Dennis has been a continuing observer of the levels of support for the party system in the United States. His research indicates that respondents' rankings of the parties (and, for that matter, elections), vis-à-vis other political institutions, on the extent to which they are concerned with what the people want has declined precipitously over the period 1964–1972.[12] In his study, respondents in Wisconsin in 1972 and 1974 were asked to rank the various political institutions (the Congress, the Supreme Court, the president, etc.) in terms of the "good" that they have done people. The parties ranked last of the seven institutions tested in 1972 with a score of 3.9 on a 7-point scale. In 1974, in the aftermath of the Watergate scandal, the study's respondents ranked the parties even lower (3.5) and still dead last among the institutions examined. The presidency, for all its problems, still managed to do much better (a 4.1 ranking) than the parties.

The study is extensive. From it, Dennis concludes:

> First, these data show that public support for the parties, both in historical and cross-institutional perspectives is relatively weak. Attitudes toward the parties and the evaluations of the importance of the party institution show, with few exceptions, a general state of low public regard and legitimation. More importantly, even the areas . . . [that showed] relatively strong points of support a decade ago, have shown a significant decline since that time.[13]

The parties command little public respect. Dennis found the base of support especially weak in the early- to mid-1970s, and becoming weaker with each passing year.

Table 1 Voter Evaluation of Political Institutions: 1972 National Election Study

Government Institution Is:	Percentage of Response			
	Congress	Supreme Court	President	Political parties
Doing the best job in last couple years	33.1	16.1	47.0	3.8
Doing the second-best job	42.1	23.5	23.9	10.5
Doing the worst job	8.3	27.6	12.6	51.4
Most powerful	34.4	27.7	33.6	4.3
Second-most powerful	36.3	24.7	31.3	7.8
Least powerful	7.5	10.6	9.4	72.5
Most trusted	31.7	25.5	41.4	1.4
Second-most trusted	41.4	23.7	29.6	5.3
Least trusted	4.4	17.7	10.7	67.3

Source: Center for Political Studies, University of Michigan, 1972 Presidential Survey.

Party Loyalty

Party identification is a psychological measure used in voting studies to gauge the intensity (strong or weak) and the direction (Democrat or Republican) of individuals' support for the political parties. It is a powerful measure not given to random fluctuation and, once introduced in the 1950s, it proved the most significant of the three indices (candidate appeal and issue orientation being the other two) devised to explain election results.

The evidence demonstrates that party identification is becoming less important for voters. Data for the period 1952–1976 supplied by the Survey Research Center of the Center for Political Studies of the University of Michigan indicates that there is evidence of a decline in the number of voters identifying with each party. The Republican coalition is small, and its decline in partisan identification is modest but consistent. More worrisome, the proportion of "strong" Republican identifiers has decreased significantly and the proportion of "independent Republicans" has increased to where they now outnumber the strong identifiers. The modal (or most commonly found) group among Republicans are the "weak" identifiers.

The same pattern holds true for the Democrats. The number of party identifiers is down dramatically. The biggest drop is in the portion claiming to be "strong" Democratic identifiers; the decrease in this category is far steeper than for the Republicans. The number of "independent Democrats" has increased, and the party's modal group is the "weak" identifiers.

If this thumbnail sketch of the decline in party identification is relevant for elections, it is reasonable to expect that party would be less powerful in structuring the vote. This is exactly what happens. Voters, as noted, are inclined to turn out less, but when they do vote, they are considerably less likely to vote the party label for all offices on the ballot. Whereas straight-ticket voting was common in the 1950s, split-ticket voting appears to be the norm for more recent elections. The incidence of split-ticket voting, once below 20 percent, increased noticeably during the 1960s. Better than one-half the voters in the presidential elections of 1968, 1972, and 1976 split their vote between the parties. It seems extraordinary now, but in the 1950s, 70 percent of those sampled consistently voted a straight party ticket, and better than one-half reported voting for the same party's candidate for president in all elections for which they were eligible.

In the 1950s, party loyalty tended to anchor an electorate. Drastic changes in the vote from one election to the next were unlikely. If party support has become less important to the voter, then sharp swings in the proportion of the vote cast for each of the parties would be likely to result. This, again, is happening. It is not uncommon to move from close elections (1960, 1968, and 1976) to landslides (1964 and 1972); and, in a few short years, from a landslide victory in one party (1964) to one favoring the other party (1972). Election outcomes at successive levels (presidential, congressional, gubernatorial, local) can bear increasingly less relationship to each other, a result of the weakening bond of party affiliation.

Issue Voting

As party has become less important in structuring the individual's vote, policy questions have been assuming a new significance. Researchers have found a new coherence in voter evaluation of issues, and an increasing significance of the issues in voter decisionmaking. For example, Norman Nie and Kristi Andersen found, in a study of voting behavior for the period 1956–1972, an increased issue awareness and level of ideological constraint far exceeding anything found in the 1950s:

> the different levels of attitude constraint we encountered in 1945, 1964, and 1972 do not appear to be the result of either short-term fluctuations or of a gradual trend-like increase throughout the period. Rather, a very sharp shift appears to have occurred in the levels of ideological constraint between 1960 and 1964. . . . There is a major shift upward in levels of constraint in 1964, involving substantial increases in correlation between attitudes in almost all of the issue domains. [14]

Issues and their resolutions were becoming more important to people than support for a party:

> issue positions in 1964 displayed a consistency and a polarization which was in stark contrast to the situation found in 1956, '58, and '60. But the 1964 election, and the impetus it provided to citizens to structure their political beliefs into a coherent liberal/conservative ideology, was not merely a transient phenomenon. In the middle and late 1960s, Americans were bombarded with one social and political crisis after another: urban rioting, increased militancy within the civil-rights movement, campus demonstrations, political assassinations, deeper involvement in the quagmire of a distant war. Even though our data are essentially pre-Watergate, by the late 1960's the positive involvement of the early and mid-60's had turned decidedly sour. The war lingered on, the Great Society programs appeared to have failed, and it seemed as if the government was incapable of dealing with new problems such as crime, pollution, and inflation. The cynicism which arose from government's failure to deal with the society's problems by no means decreased the salience of politics—the feeling that what happens in Washington affects one's life persists—but, we believe, did cause many people to withdraw from politics in frustration. [15]

Whereas the individuals' party identification supplied the primary explanation for the outcome of presidential elections during the 1950s and early 1960s, the tide began turning in 1964. By 1972, the Survey Research Center of the Center for Political Studies of the University of Michigan was willing to concede that issues were at least as important as party identification in explaining election outcome.[16]

Party Image

A somewhat different measure of the party's role in voter decisionmaking is party image. This indicator is not as resistant to change as is party identification, and yet it does not vary wildly from one election to the next in response to short-term forces. Party image consists of the perceptions the people have of the parties—what they see the party as representing and whether their perceptions are positive or negative. Election analysts relate the party images held by the voters to the election results. Party image has proven an effective tool in explaining outcomes; it is also a fairly current indicator of exactly what issues respondents associate with the major parties. Concerns respondents do not relate to party stands can be as important in assessing the role and influence of the parties as those concerns that are associated with party stands.

Excluding the South, where the parties have been undergoing a realigning process, the party image associated with Democratic and Republican parties has remained relatively stable for presidential elections during the period 1952-1972.[17] This can be interpreted in optimistic terms as indicating the strength of the major parties and their hold on the population, but unfortunately, such an interpretation would be incomplete at best. The pre-Watergate Republican image was relatively stable and undynamic, relying on the party's abilities to manage the government and on its foreign policy programs. Overall, the party's image was not a strong and positive force on the voters.

Following the Depression, the Democratic Party's image generated favorable associations with economic issues. The Democrats became the party of "good times for average people" and the party of higher wages. The party has become favorably associated with issues and groups (social security, minimum wages, the working man) that help it electorally.

The problem is that to a degree both parties' images are outdated. Richard J. Trilling, the author of the study on party image on which these remarks are based, makes the point that the stability of party images masks the inability of both parties to respond in meaningful terms to the more recent concerns that have divided American society.[18] Issues that fail to become incorporated into the public's perceptions of the parties, then, do not serve to help clarify and define the parties and their positions for the voter. In effect, the parties are perceived as offering no solution and as being irrelevant to the resolution of the problems. If this assessment is accurate, American parties are indeed backward-looking.

Trilling writes:

On Vietnam and race, voters were unable to perceive meaningful differences—defining differences—between parties. . . . the ability of these issues to structure the vote apparently depends on the willingness of the parties to take opposing stands on the issues. . . . when parties fail to take opposite stands on critical issues these issues in turn seem to drop out of the party images of Americans, because Americans no longer see those issues as (potentially) defining the parties.[19]

The major issues of the 1960s and early 1970s did not become associated with either of the parties or their policies. The failure of the parties to offer meaningful, alternative responses to these social questions has to reflect adversely on the health and vitality of the entire party system.

Trilling believes the parties are in a period of declining "meaningfulness" for voters that

results in part from the growing irrelevancy of the themes that prompted the last realignment or from the failure of parties to take polarizing stands on those issues that have emerged in recent years as potentially realigning. Whatever its cause, [party] decomposition threatens to preclude the future ability of parties to structure politics and to influence policy.[20]

American parties, as they presently operate, are uncomfortable in dealing with an issue-oriented electorate. The parties prefer voting responses based on long-term assertions of loyalty and diffuse attachments built over decades. The electorate appears to be rejecting this basis for political support. It is becoming increasingly concerned about issues and it is forcing the parties to adapt to these changes or, in effect, acknowledge their own decreasing relevance. As we saw in the discussion of party identification, the attachments of the voters, particularly the youth, to the parties has weakened considerably.

Youth and the Parties

The Twenty-sixth Amendment, adopted in 1971, gave eighteen-year-olds the vote. The amendment had been a goal of reformers for decades. Yet the majority of young adults affected appeared uninterested. If anything, they seemed to be turned off by politics. The proportion not participating in the 1976 election was twice as great in the eighteen- to twenty-four-year-old category, and three times as great for the eighteen- to twenty-year-olds, as for the adult population on a whole. One-half of those who did not vote in 1976 were under thirty.

Beyond voting, the young are disproportionately represented among those not identifying with either of the major parties. The number of independents has increased rapidly during the last decade to where it equals (at about 40 percent of the electorate) the number of Democratic identifiers. Approximately one-half of the independents are under the age of thirty-five.

The figures suggest that a large portion of the newcomers to the electorate are not identifying with either party and that they are not participating in elections. They are remaining outside of the nation's political currents. The nonidentifiers introduce a potential volatility into American politics whose consequences cannot be predicted. They remove from politics the stability and continuity in identifications and attachments that characterized the four decades preceding the 1970s.

With new voters entering the electorate—about 8 percent are first-time voters in each presidential election—the problem can only worsen. [21]

It may be, as some contend, that when young people have to pay taxes, raise families, provide for education costs, encounter housing and medical expenses, and the like, that their political interest will ripen. It is unlikely, however, that if they have not developed an attachment for either party by the time they have become eligible to vote, they will develop one of any strength in later years. Meanwhile, the unaffiliated and the youthful nonvoter are cause for concern. They suggest that the appeal of the parties is concentrated among the older generations. →The parties appear to have little to offer the young.

The Revolution in Campaigning

A new technology of campaigns has evolved that is so pervasive and so influential that it has been called the "new politics." It is a politics that capitalizes on the communications and attitude measurement developments of the last generation. It is a politics built on the dollar bill. It is quite different from the traditional campaigns conducted by the party organizations and it has emerged, in fact, as a rival to the party supervision of a candidate's drive for election. It is a politics of fleeting images, personal style, and subconscious assumptions rather than one of substance. It is a politics of every candidate for himself, each with an individual campaign organization loyal only to the candidate and disbanded after the election. It is an antiparty politics of fragmentation and transitory candidate organizations. It is a politics with no core, no sense of collective effort. And, it should be added, it is a politics that has captured the political world.

There are three aspects to the new politics. First, it is based on technological achievements and breakthroughs that have been adapted to political use. Second, it requires money—a good deal of money. Third, it involves a whole cadre of hired guns—professionals in everything from media presentation to joke-writing. These "consultants" contract for a job, move in to execute it, and move on to the next account. The candidate, the issues of the campaign, and even the outcome of the election are secondary. The consultant has other clients and other responsibilities. Whatever its faults, this new politics has won the day. It is the voice of the present, so it is best to understand it.

Television

The new politics is one of media, image, and technology. Its evolution parallels the development of television as a potent campaign force. Television was first used extensively in the 1952 presidential election. At this point, it was a novelty. By the 1970s, however, television was *the* medium for presidential campaigns. It reached approximately 95 percent of the American households and it represented the voters' primary source of campaign news (see Table 2).

The age of television began in 1952. While Adlai Stevenson used television to present traditional political speeches delivered in cavernous halls, his opponent,

Table 2 Sources of Campaign Information: 1976
Presidential Campaign

Percentage of Voters Using Source			
Television	Radio	Newspapers	Magazines
89	45	73	48

Source: Center for Political Studies, University of Michigan,
1976 Presidential Survey.

Dwight Eisenhower, broke new ground. In both 1952 and 1956, Eisenhower's advisors attempted to show him as a warm and concerned human being. He was pictured, not always comfortably, taking tea with women's groups and discussing the economy with small gatherings of farmers and others. Eisenhower's media advisors also experimented with spot commercials, including one that had someone questioning Eisenhower on the high cost of living. He replied to the effect that every time Mamie went to the supermarket she was appalled. The commercial offered no solutions and the thought of Mrs. Eisenhower shopping in a suburban supermarket made one stop and think. The spot identified Eisenhower with the concerns of the voter, and it also gave ample warning of what to expect from such advertisements in the future.

One incident, not actually planned, demonstrated the enormous potential of the new medium. Richard Nixon, the Republican vice-presidential candidate, was under attack for maintaining a "slush fund" from contributors to pay expenses. Nixon took to television to vindicate himself. In an emotional, tear-filled presentation (the "Checkers" speech), Nixon managed both to defend himself and to turn public sentiment in his favor. Nixon survived the incident, was welcomed back to the ticket by Eisenhower, and went on to leave his own mark on American politics.

John Kennedy's 1960 presidential drive was one of the first to exploit fully all aspects of the new medium. Kennedy used television to develop an image as a dynamic and intelligent person capable of running the country. The Kennedy style and demeanor seemed particularly suited to television. His televised debates with Richard Nixon may well have provided the thin margin of victory in a close election. Since then, television has been fully utilized by those candidates who can afford it.

Television can make political careers overnight. It affords candidates the opportunity to speak on a one-to-one basis to prospective voters in their homes. The medium of political communication has become television.

Richard Nixon's campaign use of television in 1972, from the commercials stressing the grandeur of the presidency and Nixon's presidential accomplishments to the televised news conferences and bill signings, may have been the most adept to date. Television appears to have been extremely effective in associating Nixon with the office and image of the presidency, as well as in drawing an unfavorable image of his opponent.

In 1976, Gerald Ford made effective use of his admirable personal qualities in a televised blitz that helped make a race that seemed like an early runaway, close.

Many of the political commercials that appear on television do seem vapid. Take the following as an example. Senator Howard A. Cannon of Nevada was seeking reelection to the U.S. Senate. His polls showed that people saw him as bland and remote. The job was to humanize the Senator, personalize him, and make his liabilities appear as strengths. A script for a sixty-second televised commercial promoting Cannon addressed the problem as follows:

VIDEO	AUDIO
Cannon at Lake Tahoe—alone and seated on a rock.	He cares about the things that matter . . .
Close on bird.	He's been our Senator for 12 years now . . .
Close on Cannon offering food. *Cannon and chipmunk.* *Close on chipmunk.* *Cannon and chipmunk. Ease up camera to Cannon.*	His name is Howard Cannon. . . . Persistent, patient but determined, he's deeply concerned about the kind of world we're making for our children now. He's deeply involved in preserving the environment of man—it's natural beauty that makes living in Nevada great!
Long shot—view of Tahoe.	Let's keep it that way! Re-elect the man who cares! Vote for Howard Cannon on Nov. 3. [22]

Apparently the approach worked. Cannon was reelected.

It may be unfair to pick on Cannon, or any other campaigner. Television advertisements appear designed to satisfy the lowest common denominator among the public. Yet, they work and, as a consequence, they are used by those who can afford them.

Possibly, we may be underestimating television's broader contributions to American politics. Two political scientists, Robert McClure and Thomas Patterson, argue that television spots are not only effective—and few would dispute this—but they serve a valuable political function in providing the individual with political information. In fact, according to their thorough and important study of the impact of television on politics, *a viewer is more likely to pick up and retain political information from a commercial than he is from the televised news.* [23] Undoubtedly, this situation is explained in part by the bland mixture of televised news, its emphasis on process and movement rather than substance, and the fleeting attention given to the issues. Still, the conclusions of McClure and Patterson make one pause for thought.

Many prospective candidates do not have the funds needed for extensive television advertising. Some of them have tried to run campaigns through the use of free television coverage. Senator Eugene McCarthy, for example, was articulate and persuasive in his opposition to the Vietnam war in 1968. He was also telegenic and commanded a good deal of free television exposure that was important to his success. Other "new" candidates, like George McGovern in 1972 and Jimmy Carter in 1976, can gain television access. The exposure, however, can backfire on the unwary candidate, as it did for McGovern during the 1972 general election campaign and as it did four years earlier in the candidacy of George Romney for the Republican presidential nomination.

Another tactic, now used by all candidates to some degree, is to stage events for television consumption. The candidate alerts the media by engaging in an event that has visual and action impact—a motorcade or a visit to a fish market or a factory—and he schedules this event early enough to be filmed for the evening news. By appearing on the regularly scheduled news, he reaches more people than he ever could through more traditional campaigning methods.

Again, there are costs. One U.S. Senate candidate in New York gathered the television reporters and dove into the Hudson River to drum up support for his antipollution measures. He came up with an infection that almost took him out of the race.

Consultants

Effective television requires the services of professional media advisors. They are needed to plan the publicity campaign, buy the air time, supervise the production of the spot advertisements, determine and coordinate the campaign's media themes, and advise the candidate as to his image and how best to project it. The number of technical advisors required in this last area alone can be extensive.

The modern campaign needs more than media consultants, however. As Joseph Napolitan says, "If you want to be a candidate, let someone else be the campaign manager. Get someone who knows the business and let him set it up for you." [24] Napolitan would probably recommend a professional campaign consultant (like himself). All the candidate need bring is himself, his pocketbook, and an ambition for public office. The consultants can take it from there.

The services provided by the campaign consulting firms are impressive. Some specialize in campaign management or consulting in specified areas. Others are full-service operations, as they say. Bailey Deardourff & Bowen, the firm that managed Gerald Ford's election bid in 1976, promises its clients a step-by-step manual that may run as many as 150 pages. [25] The firm will find a campaign manager, a polling organization, and a mail order firm; it supplies the advertising expertise for the campaign itself and presumably, if needed, can contract for direct-mailing operations to raise funds and for professional campaign strategists and speechwriters as needed.

One of the first and best-known consulting agencies, Spencer and Roberts, advertises, "all-encompassing" services. [26] This includes everything from opening the campaign headquarters to coordinating the candidate's volunteer help and canvassing the votes. These little services, and others like them, are provided in addition, of course, to the media and advertising expertise the professional managers bring to the campaign. Spencer and Roberts is an old firm (in relative terms—established in 1960) within a new and expanding field. Their perspective on their role is interesting. They believe prospective candidates come to them so that "they won't make a lot of mistakes new candidates make because we already made them." [27] This is a nice description of the counseling services the political parties used to offer.

Spencer and Roberts became identified with Ronald Reagan's gubernatorial campaigns and efforts on behalf of conservative Republicans. Bailey, Deardourff & Bowen associated themselves with moderate Republicans primarily. Napolitan and some other consultants—Matthew Reese, Robert Squier, William Hamilton, and David Garth—tend to favor Democrats. The number of such management professionals and firms has expanded enormously. At the beginning of the 1970s, there were an estimated two hundred such agencies.

One consultant with an essential input into most contemporary campaigns is the pollster. Pollsters vary in the resources they offer, the sophistication of their work, the reliability of their findings, and the access to and impact they have on the campaign. Some perform specialized polling services at a set fee—nothing more. Others sit in the war council of the candidates, advising at each step of the campaign and maintaining a flexible approach to the number of polls and the purpose for which they can be used. This latter group performs the function of a campaign strategist, responding to candidate needs and to campaign emergencies: should the candidate speak out on an issue? should he or she take a firm and definable stand? The pollster assesses public reaction to televised campaign appearances, offers his personal views, and interprets his polling results for the candidate and his advisors.

The rewards for the pollster are impressive. A poll can cost from a minimum of $10,000 to $15,000 on upwards. Richard Nixon paid one firm alone (Opinion Research of Princeton, New Jersey) $450,000 for polls in 1968. The national Republican Congressional (Campaign) Committee in that year bought a $400,000 poll from a subsidiary of Spencer and Roberts. Such figures are becoming more common. Some more recent consultant arrangements are rumored to be in the vicinity of one million dollars. A person can become rich polling; and many have.

Beyond wealth, there is influence and status. Louis Harris came into prominence as the pollster of John Kennedy during his successful bid for the presidency. Harris received many government contracts after the election, and a newspaper column he began was carried nationally. Today, he rivals George Gallup as one of the nation's two best-known pollsters.

Patrick Caddell was a college student when he began polling for George McGovern. He received extensive publicity for his work in the 1972 campaign and went on to work for other Democratic candidates. He became Jimmy Carter's pollster and continued to advise Carter after he won the White House. Caddell's firm prospered, and he received many lucrative contracts from business concerns, and some even from foreign governments.

The value of good polling in campaigns, however, is uncontestable. William Hamilton, who polled for Edmund Muskie in his 1972 presidential bid, says a poll can tell a candidate which issues are important and which are strong enough to change voters' minds; whether such issues can be developed into a campaign theme; and how political conditions, including other candidates and their stands, will affect the race and its outcome.[28] Mervin Field, who runs the California Poll, points out that the use of polls goes beyond fact-gathering: polls become political weapons in a campaign. Polls can be "leaked" to the press to bolster a campaign or to discredit an opponent. They can also be employed "to convince financial backers, to encourage party workers, to bolster the confidence of the candidate, to freeze out potential opponents, and to support existing biases."[29] Polls and the pollster have become an integral part of the modern campaign.

Beyond polls and media advice, the range of what professional consultants can offer is impressive. Robert Agranoff, the leading academic expert on the new politics, has listed the various specialists available to the candidate. By area, these include:

Management	Information	Media
Campaign Management Consultant	Marketing Researcher	Journalist
	Public Opinion Pollster	Media Advance Person
Campaign Handler	Political Scientist	Radio and TV Writer
Public Relations Counselor	Social Psychologist	Radio and TV Producer
Advertising Agent	Computer Scientist	Film Documentary Producer
Advance Person	Psychologist	Radio- and TV-time Buyer
Fund Raiser	Computer Programmer	Newspaper-space Buyer
	Demographer	Television Coach
Management Scientist	Statistician	Radio and TV Actors
Industrial Engineer		Graphic Designer
Telephone Campaign Organizer		Direct Mail Advertiser
		Computer Printing Specialist
Accountant		Speech Coach
Election Legal Counselor		Speechwriter[30]

Source: From Robert Agranoff, *The New Style in Election Campaigns,* Second Edition. Copyright © 1976 by Holbrook Press, Inc. Reprinted by permission of Allyn and Bacon, Inc.

There appear to be consultants for every purpose imaginable. They can be very valuable in elections, of course, and perhaps in the broader area of the political system as a whole. John Saloma and Fred Sontag, after relating the rise of consulting and management firms to the decline of party organizations, go on to say:

> Political consultants now constitute one of the most important agents of change in the political system. They have become both innovators and brokers serving to bring new technologies, such as television and automatic data processing into politics. While many observers talk of the need to reform the parties or create new parallel structures in politics, the political consultants are in effect doing just those things.[31]

There is a faddish quality to the themes the consulting firms may hit on for any given election year—austerity, personal integrity, likability, pride, warmth, antiprofessionalism, trust, and so on—and there is an undeniable element of the huckster in some of the operations. As many of the more responsible consultants argue, entry criteria and ethical standards need to be developed and enforced. Exactly how that is to be done in such a fast-growing field is difficult to say. Napolitan and others have established the American Association of Political Consultants and the International Association of Political Consultants, a sign the field is being institutionalized at least.

The Consultants and the Campaign   Whatever the inherent difficulties, the impact of these management agencies can be great. The Bill Brock campaign for the U.S. Senate in Tennessee offers us one example. Brock was a candy manufacturer who, like many other wealthy people—Milton Shapp, Howard Metzenbaum, John Heinz III, Charles Percy, Nelson Rockefeller, Jack Eckerd, Howard Samuels, Norton Simon—wanted to enter public life at a high level. He engaged a New York campaign management firm, Treleaven and Associates. Harry Treleaven, the head of the company, assigned Brock a young aide, Ken Rietz, to run his campaign (both Treleaven and Rietz were to become prominent in the 1972 Nixon campaign). Treleaven, Rietz, and Brock hired an advertising company and a polling concern. They then developed their campaign organization (see Figure 1).

The Brock organization was impressive. It was thoroughly professional, comprehensive, and workable. Each division had its assigned duties. The advance sections worked with the scheduling and publicity assistants to ensure that the media and party officials were alerted before a Brock visit and that all rooms, meals, etc., were prearranged. The women's division held coffees and fundraising events and pressured other women's groups for endorsement. The canvassers processed 600,000 names through computers before the primary and supplied workers with printouts containing the names, addresses, telephone numbers, and voting preferences of prospective voters. The "Brockettes," a group of young girls comparable to football cheerleaders, appeared at rallies and supermarkets. Brock won the primary and the general election, but this is not the most important point here. What Brock and others like him have done through the use of consulting agencies was to create a miniature political party organization. Unfortunately, the expenditure of time and effort was wasted to a degree. The organization competed with the party for funds and workers during the campaign. After the campaign, it disappeared. Its only purpose was Brock's election, and its only commitment was to the candidate.

The Nixon reelection committee in 1972, the most elaborate in campaign history, had a staff of 500 and access to funds that were virtually unlimited. The President Ford Committee, formed to supervise the Ford reelection effort, had a staff of 200 and a field force of approximately 100. These workers were all paid. Additionally, the committee had access to 900 volunteers. [32] The Ford and Carter campaign budgets in 1976 were set by law at $25 million. The Ford, Carter, Brock, and Nixon campaigns staffs were dissolved after their respective elections. The same manpower, professionalized expertise, and financial resources evident in these campaigns, if plowed into the national or state party organizations, could well pay handsome dividends over the long run. Unfortunately, few politicians appear to share such concerns.

The Future for Professional Campaign Consultants   For better or worse, professional consultants are in vogue. They are firmly established, and any serious candidate for higher level office is likely to take advantage of one or more of their services. It appears they are here to stay.

Two reports can be called upon to make the point. A 1978 report on campaigns in Venezuela reveals such familiar names as John Deardourff, David Garth, Joseph

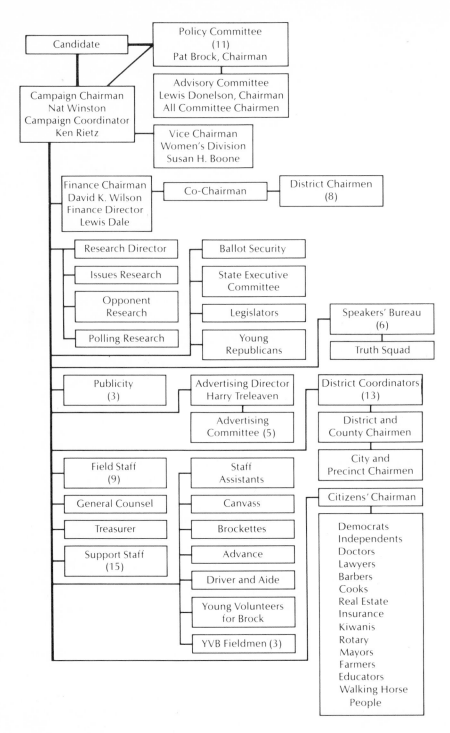

Figure 1 Brock campaign structure. (*Source:* "Professional Managers, Consultants Play Major Roles in 1970 Political Process," *National Journal,* September 26, 1970, p. 2082.)

Napolitan, David Squier, and Patrick Caddell working on behalf of the various candidates. The poses, smiling faces, carefully brushed hair, lovely families; the slogans ("the people come first"); the television commercials showing a candidate speaking, person-to-person, to farmers; the polling operations—all these aspects of U.S. campaigns are becoming staples of Venezuela's, and apparently, of the world's politics.[33] American consultants have been active in England, Canada, France, the Netherlands, West Germany, Spain, the Philippines, Japan, Italy, Mexico, and the Scandinavian countries. Consultants—like Coke and MacDonald's hamburgers— have become another American export.

Another report may be more disturbing. Bill Brock, defeated in 1976 for reelection to the Senate, was appointed Republican national chairperson. Brock proved to be dynamic and effective both in encouraging attractive candidates to run for office as Republicans and in making the Republican Party more attractive to groups not known to support it, such as blacks. As part of his overall strategy, Brock and the national party began to court Southern blacks. The manner in which he and the party chose to pursue this end is surely a sign of the times. Normally, developing long-range support within voting blocs is the type of activity for which national and state party organizations exist. Brock, however, awarded an $800,000 contract— financed partly by the Republican National Committee and partly by the Republican Congressional Campaign Committee—to a consulting firm headed by two blacks. The purpose of the investment was to help Southern Republicans receive a "fair share" of the black vote in the 1978 elections. In explaining the party's actions, Brock said: "I don't believe a party can truly be a national party unless it's inclusive."[34] Undoubtedly, this assessment is correct. The problem may be whether the parties will come to resemble anything beyond voting blocs within the electorate, mobilized at election time by the candidates for office—and their professional consultants.

Money

Not surprisingly, the new politics is expensive. It is predicated on having large sums to spend. Without money, the new politics would not be possible.

Campaign expenditures rose dramatically between 1952 and 1972, the last race before federal funding and severe campaign limits attempted to arrest the trend. According to the Citizens' Research Foundation, overall campaign expenses came to $140 million in 1952. By 1972, this figure had climbed to $425 million. A respectable presidential race could be run for between $2 million and $5 million up through 1948. In 1948, for example, the Democratic and Republican presidential contenders combined spent a total of $5 million. In 1952, this figure rose to $12 million, and the escalation of costs had begun in earnest. In 1972, it topped out: the two presidential contenders spent a combined total of roughly $100 million.[35]

The rising costs were directly associated with the new campaign technology. For example, a campaign consultant can charge anywhere from $500 per day, a fairly common figure, to $1,000 or more per day. Television time is expensive. The costs vary by market and time slot bought. Agranoff reports that rate structures for airing a thirty-second commercial on one station range from $3,000 in prime time to $50 in the after-midnight period. A comparable one-time showing of a spot commercial on a network can cost $25,000; a half-hour television show—if the networks will sell the time—comes to $75,000 to $80,000. The cost of air time to candidates for political programming in 1968 was estimated to be about $2,000 per minute. [36] The three U.S. Senate candidates in New York in 1970 spent an estimated $2.5 million on television in the general election. [37]

Production expenses can run as much as the time costs for a televised commercial or program, although they average about 20 percent of the time costs. The agencies that handle political advertising charge customers about 15 percent of the air-time outlay, plus travel, expenses, and creative costs.

Campaigns at all levels reflect the spiraling costs. Campaigns for the U.S. Senate costing $2 million dollars are no longer unthinkable. Nelson Rockefeller's now famous reelection efforts in New York have been estimated to cost between $6 million and $20 million each. George McGovern spent $500,000 for the media in a crucial showdown with Hubert Humphrey in the California primary in 1972. McGovern budgeted $900,000 for the meetings in New York State alone during the general election. U.S. House campaigns in a competitive district average about $100,000. In tightly contested, "show-case" races, the budgets can double.

The specific outlays for a campaign are difficult to pin down. Most consultants do not like to publicize what they charge. A professional manager in a congressional race might bill a client for $20,000 in a race budgeted at $100,000, or, in less expensive contests, a proportionate 20 percent of the cost estimates. A campaign organizer who charges $2,000 per week plus expenses is not out of line. A media consultant (not accounted for in the time or production cost estimates) can add another $10,000 to $25,000 to the campaign costs. Polls may be purchased for $10,000 to $50,000 (or more), depending on the area being sampled (congressional district, state, etc.) and the sophistication and depth of the interviewing. Computer firms that analyze voting and demographic patterns charge from $2,500 to $3,500 per congressional district. Direct-mail operations also can be expensive, costing as much as $150,000 per mailing. Direct-mail solicitation for funds can return from 10 cents to 80 cents on the dollar to a campaign, depending on who is doing the asking and the quality of the list being used.

The types of contracts that can be let are many. One consulting firm asked $175,000 to run Tennessee Senator Albert Gore's reelection campaign. [38] A political management firm was awarded a contract for $500,000 to canvass and identify the vote for a Boston mayoral candidate. [39]

With costs of this magnitude, serious candidacies are restricted to those who are wealthy or those who have access to wealth. The role of interest groups in the campaign process can also be magnified. For example, the AFL-CIO's Committee on Political Education (COPE) has long been active in funding Democratic candidates (primarily) who agree with organized labor's legislative objectives. Labor political action committees invested $6.3 million in congressional candidates in 1974. This figure rose to $8.2 million in 1976 and was expected to stay about the same for 1978.

The political action committee (PAC) of the American Medical Association (AMPAC) is indicative of the political work of the more ambitious conservative groups. AMPAC is very active in supporting conservative candidates for political office, particularly those who oppose such a measure as a national health-care plan. AMPAC provides funds, campaign expertise, and polls. In the period 1968-1970 alone, AMPAC spent more than $400,000 polling on behalf of Republicans. [40]

As parties have declined, ideological groups have become more important. These groups provide funds—on many occasions collected on a national basis—to support favored candidates. They can generate publicity and, in some cases, supply campaign technicians, volunteer workers, and such supplemental service as phone banks, firms for computer analyzing of demographic data, and so on.

The ideological interest groups have had a more profound impact on the parties than some of the limited-interest trade organizations. They have been more aggressive not only in funding selected candidates but in seeking out individuals to contest, in primaries, the more moderate members of the same party. The conservative ideological groups, for example, have sponsored candidates ranging from conservative to right-wing to run against centrist, incumbent Republicans. Senators Clifford Case in New Jersey and Edward Brooke in Massachusetts are examples of such candidates. The overall result has been a further splintering and fragmentation of the Republican and Democratic parties.

The ideological interest groups often depend on direct-mail techniques of solicitation. This method of fund raising was pioneered by the National Committee for an Effective Congress (a liberal nonpartisan group), but it has been employed most effectively by the right in recent elections. Richard Viquerie, in particular, formerly a fund-raiser for Alabama's governor, George Wallace, has come into prominence as the master of this particular technique. [41]

The mailing lists solicited by the direct-mail fund-raisers are political lists acquired from various candidates and policy-oriented committees. The fund-raising appeals conflict directly with attempts by the national and congressional parties to raise money. In head-to-head competition, the parties lose out to the more flamboyant ideological appeals of the right and left.

In the nonelection year of 1977, the National Conservative Action Committee raised one million dollars, and three other "new right" groups brought in between one-half and one million dollars. The money was to be used for lobbying and publicity purposes and in preparation for the 1978 congressional elections. In the latter regard, Viquerie promised to raise one-quarter of a million dollars for thirty races; he already had brought in $1.8 million for the U.S. Senate campaign of North Carolina's extremely conservative Jesse Helms (although the candidate only received $200,000 of this sum). [42]

The reform legislation of the 1970s made some notable gains in limiting soaring campaign costs. Enforceable standards regarding the limiting of expenditures and the disclosure of campaign costs in federal elections were put on the books. Individuals were restricted to donating no more than $5,000 to any one candidate or political committee and a total of no more than $25,000 in political contributions in any one year. Funding and campaign committees were required to register with the government and were made legally accountable for detailing income and expenditures. A regulatory body, the Federal Election Commission, was established to supervise compliance with the new laws and to compile and make available data on campaign costs. For the first time, the public was given an approximation of how much politics cost, where the money actually comes from, and what it is put into.

There have been several unanticipated, and less fortunate, results of the new campaign laws. The Supreme Court struck down part of the reform legislation limiting what an individual can invest in his own campaign. Wealthy individuals, as a consequence, have an even greater advantage than previously in subsidizing their own campaign efforts. Another unforeseen consequence of the new laws has been the emergence and proliferation of PACs. As the new campaign regulations were being considered by the Congress, organized labor became concerned that its ability to voluntarily collect funds from its members for use (by COPE, for example) in lobbying and in campaigns might be endangered. Labor pushed for, and won, explicit provisions safeguarding these practices. When the statutes passed, it soon became clear that the new laws guaranteed the same rights enjoyed by organized labor to all businesses and trade associations.

Business groups were at first wary. PACs were new and untried ground. When the Federal Election Commission sanctioned the right of corporations to form PACs in 1975, business began in earnest to exploit its opportunity. The number of business PACs increased from 89 in the days immediately after the new legislation was enacted to 538 entering the 1978 congressional-election year. Between 1974 and 1976 alone, the contributions of business PACs to congressional campaigns tripled, to where in 1976 their $6.9 million donations began to approach organized labor's. [43]

Most of the major corporations—Union Oil, Coca-Cola, General Electric, etc.— have established aggressive PACs. The money they contribute to candidates can be seen as a business investment. In this respect, it is different from the funds donated by the ideological groups. The business PACs put their money into incumbents— the people already in power within the Congress—with whom they feel comfortable. Failing that, PAC money usually goes to Republican challengers. In 1976, two-thirds of the funds from corporate PACs went to incumbents; 80 percent of the remainder went to Republican candidates.

Reform

The changes in the society, in the nature of campaigning, and in the values and orientation of the electorate have been accompanied by another trend. Pressure for widespread social and political reform mounted during the 1960s. In turn, the 1970s proved to be something of a reform decade. The exact consequences of the reform drives and the outcome for the political parties are not clear. Nonetheless, some early assessments can be made.

Reform has really taken place on two levels: (1) in relation to political and legal conditions, which, although outside the political parties, have a direct affect on the parties' operations; and (2) within the parties themselves.

In the first category, would be the changes in registration laws, which have increased the pool of eligible voters in the South, and the laws governing campaign funding already mentioned. Beginning with the Voting Rights Act of 1965 (and later through its successors), the franchise in effect was guaranteed to blacks in the South. The import of the Voting Rights Act was enormous. Blacks were included in Southern politics on a mass scale for the first time. Both major political parties in the South underwent a realignment and began to resemble, in policy and appeal, their national counterparts. The inclusion of blacks as a viable force in Southern politics transformed the nature of the South's politics and, among other things, helped contribute to the election of a moderate Southerner as president in 1976.

The Voting Rights Acts had an impact outside the South also. The results here have been more tentative. Efforts have been made to loosen registration requirements in an attempt to allow more people to vote. The results have not been encouraging. Registration barriers may not be what they were a decade ago, but they can still be formidable. Meanwhile, the proportion of the adult population participating in elections continues to shrink.

The advent of public financing for presidential elections has meant the realization of a long-held dream of reformers. The intention is to ensure that presidential elections—and eventually congressional elections—cannot be bought by those individuals, corporations, or unions with the funds to invest. The argument has been that elective officeholders belong to and should represent all of the people. They should not be beholden to or exclusive spokesmen for the handful of interests that hold the funds needed to successfully promote candidacies.

Raising campaign funds has always been troublesome, and it is subject to gross abuse. The problem is not new. What is new is the approach. Careful regulation of financial subsidies, coupled with full disclosure of receipts and expenditures, is intended to move the political parties and their candidates away from a perennially corrupting influence. The actual subsidizing of elective races has only been extended to date to presidential contests. Congressional campaigns are run much as in the past and, in fact, have benefited (as noted) from the unexpected infusion of large amounts of newly legalized corporate donations.

Public funding is a new experience for the party system. At this point, its long-term effects are unclear. Obviously, while meant to help the parties, it may contribute to their disintegration. As discussed before, public funding takes away from the parties a function they have traditionally fulfilled.

Finally, there is the reform movement within the political parties themselves. The Republican Party's reform efforts have led to little fundamental change. The Democrats, however, have rewritten the rules for participating in the party's affairs.[44] Beginning with the work of the most important of the reform agencies, the McGovern–Fraser Commission (1969–1972), these groups and their recommendations have dramatically changed the nature of Democratic politics and, not so incidentally, presidential-nomination practices. The rules by which candidates may contest for the party's presidential nomination have been redrawn. The Democrats also have attempted to change (perhaps with less success) the nature of representation within party councils and to update and modernize their national-convention and national-party structures. Overall, the goal has been to make the party more representative of and accountable to its base and to fashion a party more in concert with a changing electorate and a more demanding society. The extent to which the party has succeeded in achieving these objectives, and whether, in fact, the changes have served to help or hurt the party, remain subjects of controversy.

The selections in this volume address the questions raised regarding the responsibilities and levels of performance of the American party system in the closing decades of the twentieth century. The selections represent efforts to assess the American party system at a critical juncture in its evolution. They are intended to shed light on the party structure and its operations at a sensitive point in the debate over the value of political parties and their continuing role within a changing nation. Each of the essays is meant to provide a contemporary perspective that is necessary for an intelligent reevaluation of an extraordinarily important social institution.

The book is divided into four parts. The first deals with party structure. The second treats the most important of the party's activities, candidate selection. The third examines the nature of the electorate and the evolution of voting patterns, party identification, ethnic appeal, and communication patterns as they affect the political parties and their performance. The last part looks at aspects of the recent party reforms and their impact on the political parties at the local and national levels. Each section is preceded by a brief introduction to the specific essays that follow.

NOTES

1. These tendencies are developed in William Crotty, *Political Reform and the American Experiment* (New York: Crowell, 1977).

2. See Austin Ranney, *Curbing the Mischiefs of Faction* (Berkeley: University of California Press, 1975); Jack Dennis, "Changing Public Support for the American Party System," in *Paths to Political Reform,* ed. William Crotty (Lexington: Heath-Lexington, forthcoming); Dennis, "Trends in Public Support for the American Party System," *British Journal of Political Science,* 1975, pp. 187–230; and Dennis, "Support for the Party System by the Mass Public," *American Political Science Review* 60 (1966): 600–615.

3. Walter Dean Burnham, "The End of American Party Politics," in *Politics/America: The Cutting Edge of Change,* ed. W. D. Burnham (New York: Van Nostrand, 1973), p. 132. See also Burnham, *Critical Elections and the Mainspring of American Politics* (New York: Norton, 1970); and Gerald M. Pomper, "The Decline of the Party in American Elections," *Political Science Quarterly* 92, no. 1 (Spring 1977): 21–41.

4. Burnham, "End of American Party Politics," p. 132.

5. Roy P. Fairfield, ed., *The Federalist Papers,* 2nd ed. (Garden City, N.Y.: Anchor Doubleday, 1966), pp. 16–23.

6. Washington's quotation can be found in Edward M. Sait, *American Parties and Elections* (New York: Century, 1927), p. 169.

7. See Michael E. Good and Carl F. Pinkele, "The New Deal Coalition: A Reappraisal" (Paper presented at the Midwest Political Science Association Meeting, 1977; rev. 1978); Everett Carll Ladd, Jr., "Liberalism Upside Down: The Inversion of the New Deal Order," *Political Science Quarterly* 91, no. 4 (Winter 1976–1977): 576–600, and in this volume; Joan L. Fee, "Religion, Ethnicity, and Class in American Electoral Behavior," in this volume; James Sundquist, *Dynamics of the Party System* (Washington, D.C.: Brookings Institution, 1973); and S. M. Lipset, ed., *Emerging Coalitions in American Politics* (San Francisco: Institute for Contemporary Studies, 1978).

8. See Merle Black and George Rabinowitz, "American Electoral Change: 1952–1972 (With a Note on 1976)," in this volume; and Jack Bass and Walter De Vries, *The Transformation of Southern Politics* (New York: New American Library, 1977).

9. See Crotty, *Political Reform,* pp. 139–167.

10. The basic analyses are Angus Campbell, Philip Converse, Warren Miller, and Donald Stokes, *The American Voter* (New York: Wiley, 1960); and A. Campbell, et al., *Elections and the Political Order* (New York: Wiley, 1966). For more recent assessments, see Herbert Asher, *Presidential Elections and American Politics* (Homewood, Ill.: Dorsey, 1976); Gerald Pomper, *Voters' Choice* (New York: Dodd, Mead, 1975); Benjamin I. Page, *Choices and Echoes in Presidential Elections* (Chicago: University of Chicago Press, 1978); and Norman H. Nie, Sidney Verha, and John R. Petrocik, *The Changing American Voter* (Cambridge: Harvard University Press, 1976).

11. See Crotty, *Political Reform,* pp. 3–100; and Penn Kimball, *The Disconnected* (New York: Columbia University Press, 1972).

12. Dennis, "Trends in Public Support"; and for a more recent evaluation, Dennis, "Changing Public Support."

13. Dennis, "Trends in Public Support," p. 218.

14. Norman H. Nie and Kristi Andersen, "Mass Belief Systems Revisited: Political Change and Attitude Structure," in *Controversies in American Voting Behavior,* eds. Richard G. Niemi and Herbert F. Weisberg (San Francisco: Freeman, 1976), p. 105.

15. Ibid., p. 127.

16. Arthur H. Miller, Warren E. Miller, Alden S. Raine, and Thad A. Brown, "A Majority Party in Disarray: Policy Polarization in the 1972 Election," *American Political Science Review* 70 (1976): 753–758.

17. Richard J. Trilling, *Party Image and Electoral Behavior* (New York: Wiley–Interscience, 1976). See also Merle Black and George Rabinowitz, "American Electoral Change: 1952–1972 (With a Note on 1976)," in this volume; and Donald R. Mathews and James W. Prothro, *Negroes and the New Southern Politics* (New York: Harcourt Brace Jovanovich, 1966).

18. Trilling, *Party Image.*

19. Ibid., p. 87.

20. Ibid., p. 38. The term "party decomposition" and its present connotations were first developed by Burnham in *Critical Elections.*

21. See, on this topic, Nie et al., *Changing American Voter,* pp. 93–95, 350.

22. Richard Corrigan et al., "Big Money, Talent and Effort Devoted to Politicking on Television," *National Journal,* October 3, 1970, p. 2139.

23. See Thomas E. Patterson and Robert D. McClure, "Television and Voters' Issue Awareness," in this volume; and McClure and Patterson, *The Unseeing Eye* (New York: Putnam, 1976). On the institutional politics and marketing of television news more generally, see Ron Powers, *The Newscasters* (New York: St. Martin, 1978); and Gary Paul Gates, *Air Time* (New York: Harper and Row, 1978).

24. Richard Corrigan et al., "Professional Managers, Consultants Play Major Roles in 1970 Political Races," *National Journal,* September 26, 1970, p. 2077.

25. Ibid., p. 2078.

26. Ibid.

27. Ibid.

28. Andrew J. Glass, "Pollsters Prowl Nation as Candidates Use Opinion Surveys to Plan '72 Campaign," *National Journal,* August 14, 1971, p. 1702; and Charles W. Hucker, "Campaign Consultants Portray Candidates as Fiscal Watchdogs," *Congressional Quarterly,* July 22, 1978, pp. 1857–1860, and in this volume.

29. Glass, "Pollsters Prowl Nation," p. 1698.

30. Robert Agranoff, "The New Style of Campaigning: The Decline of Party and the Rise of Candidate-Centered Technology," in *The New Style in Election Campaigns,* 2nd ed., ed. Robert Agranoff (Boston: Holbrook, 1976), p. 25. See also Agranoff's comprehensive study, *The Management of Election Campaigns* (Boston: Holbrook, 1976).

31. John S. Saloma, III and Frederick H. Sontag, *Parties: The Real Opportunity for Effective Citizen Politics* (New York: Knopf, 1972), p. 283.

32. Dom Bonafede, "A Glimmer of Hope Burns in the Heart of the PFC," *National Journal,* October 2, 1976, p. 1379.

33. David Vidal "U.S. Image-Makers Put Stamp on Venezulian Campaign," *New York Times,* August 2, 1978, p. 2.

34. Howell Raines, "Republicans Courting Black Voters in South After Years of Inactivity," *New York Times,* August 8, 1978, p. B5.

35. See Crotty, *Political Reform,* pp. 103–190.

36. Agranoff, "New Style of Campaigning," pp. 28–36. Unless otherwise indicated, the cost estimates for media outlays in the text are taken from Agranoff.

37. Corrigan et al., "Big Money, Talent and Effort."

38. Corrigan et al., "Professional Managers, Consultants Play Major Roles," p. 2083.

39. Agranoff, "New Style of Campaigning," p. 32.

40. Glass, "Pollsters Prowl Nation," p. 1702.

41. Christopher Buchanan, "New Right: 'Many Times More Effective' Now," *Congressional Quarterly,* December 24, 1977, p. 265, and in this volume.

42. Ibid.

43. Charles W. Hucker, "Explosive Growth: Corporate Political Action Committees Are Less Oriented to Republicans Than Expected," *Congressional Quarterly,* April 8, 1978, pp. 849–850; and in this volume. See also Hucker, "Organized Labor Takes a Hard Look at Whom It Will Support This Fall," *Congressional Quarterly,* January 28, 1978, pp. 193–198, and in this volume.

44. For an overview of the reform movement and its implications, see Charles Longley, "Party Reform and Party Nationalization: The Case of the Democrats," in this volume; William Crotty, *Decision for the Democrats* (Baltimore: Johns Hopkins University Press, 1978); and Crotty, "Building a Philosophy of Party Reform" (Paper delivered at the American Political Science Association Annual Convention, New York, August 30–September 3, 1978). On reform and the proliferation of primaries and the change in their nature, see Richard L. Rubin, "Presidential Primaries: Continuities, Dimensions of Change, and Political Implications," in this volume. The institutional limitations of reform within the American party system are delineated by Kenneth Janda in "A Comparative Analysis of Party Organizations: The United States, Europe, and the World," in this volume. The Janda analysis is the first comparative view of American parties that systematically employs a variety of empirical indicators; it allows us to evaluate realistically in comparative perspective the strengths and shortcomings of the American parties. In this regard, see also the introduction to the final section of this book.

PART I

THE PARTY STRUCTURE

INTRODUCTION

Party structure is the most distinctive feature of the American parties, and it is appropriate that the book begin with analyses of this aspect of the party system. The first selection, "The National Committees as Grass-roots Vehicles of Representation," by William Crotty, deals with national-level party committees and party leadership. The essay reviews the powers, resources, and operations of the national committees. It goes on to pose, and answer, a series of basic questions: Whom do the national committees represent? Are they agents for the party's rank and file at the local level, trying to represent their views and give them some immediate stake in, and control over, the national parties and their policies? Or are they relatively ineffective agencies, easily bent to the will of an incumbent president (when of the same party)? In fact, when of the in-party, are they simply political extensions of the White House?

The second essay in this chapter, "The Role Orientations of State Party Chairmen," by Robert J. Huckshorn, draws upon the author's extensive analysis of the one hundred state parties and their leaders. Curiously, this is a political world seldom explored by political scientists. Huckshorn set forth three roles played by the state chairmen. These include acting as a "political agent" of a governor, often to the point of lobbying for the governor's policies. In this conception of the state chairman's job, the chairman sees himself as the political representative of the governor. His duty is to advance the governor's interest and to protect his flank. The next two roles deal with the "independent." The distinguishing characteristic is whether the chairman's party holds the governorship.

An in-party "independent" can serve for a fixed term of office and can, and often does represent, party interests and political concerns not necessarily shared by the governor. An out-party "independent" often has his own power base within the party or is the candidate of the party's defeated gubernatorial nominee. Many Republican state chairmen found themselves in this position at the time of the study. Overall, the state chairmen of both parties divide fairly evenly among the three roles.

In an important theoretical and empirical study of political-party operations at the local level, "Party Organizational Personnel and Electoral Democracy in Los Angeles, 1963-1972," Dwaine Marvick analyzes an imaginative longitudinal study, performed under his direction, of political party activists in one of the nation's largest metropolitan areas. Marvick discusses the ideological views of the middle-level party cadremen in relation to the representativeness and performance of the two major parties within an urban setting. In particular, he is concerned with the ideological and operational "symmetry" of the two parties. Basically, he argues that in a given locality it is reasonable to expect that activists of the two parties, when operating from the same resource base, will tend to develop the same general perceptions of political values as they affect competition and the same skills for organizing political contests, communicating relevant political information, and identifying, or mapping, if you will, political realities. He shows the significance of understanding the value structures and operational assumptions of the party representatives most directly in touch with the voters. The symmetries (when the activists of the two parties converge) and asymmetries in views and behavior of the cadremen within the major parties tell us much about what the parties do, what they represent, and why they perform as they do.

Marvick examines the demographic composition of the cadremen—both parties favor the middle class—and the ideological and policy preferences of the activists. In the latter regard, notable differences emerge. Both political parties are subdivided into ideological wings (liberal to moderate Democrats; moderate to conservative Republicans). There are substantial differences in policy commitments between the two parties as well as between the blocs within each of the two parties. Although each party's activists (and all party blocs) rank high on an index of ideological identification, their perception of the electorate and its policy concerns are approximately the same and realistic.

David L. Protess and Alan R. Gitelson in "Political Stability, Reform Clubs, and the Amateur Democrat," address concerns generally related to those that initiated Marvick's study. Writing about political-party activists in New York, Chicago, and Los Angeles in the late 1950s and early 1960s, James Q. Wilson originated the idea of the "amateur," a person who becomes active in politics for social reasons or because of a somewhat abstract commitment to the public good.[1] Contrasted with the amateur, was the "professional," an individual who makes his living from politics. The professional has a long-run obligation to politics, a deep commitment to winning elections, and a relatively low concern with ideology. Protess and Gitelson want to know if Wilson's characterizations of Chicago amateurs are still valid in the mid-1970s.

They find that while the latter-day amateurs and reformers have many of the same demographic traits as those of Wilson's sample, their views have changed. The amateurs of the study of Protess and Gitelson are more pragmatic and more sensitive to localized political concerns. The authors introduce a concept, "the logic of utility," to help explain the complex motivational patterns of political involvement. The conceptualization refines early contributions and helps to distinguish the two generations of political activists.

Part One concludes with Howard R. Penniman's incisive analysis of contemporary third-party movements in "Presidential Third Parties and the Modern American Two-Party System". The author reviews the history of third parties in the United States; the relationship of state party processes to third-party candidacies; the conditions that contribute to the appearance of third parties and the conditions that enable third parties to become influential; and the impact of third-party policy commitments on the nation's consciousness.

Penniman's study makes a major contribution to understanding the role and impact of third parties. He concludes, for example, that the direct primary has lessened the need for, and therefore the appearance of, third parties at the state and local level. Furthermore, and contrary to popular perceptions, third-party candidates do not want others at the state and local level to run on their party label. Third parties are primarily national-level devices intended to give the electorate a viable choice in issues on which the two major parties are in relatively close agreement or on which they take no clear stand. Third parties are avenues for political dissent. Penniman further argues that third parties have had less impact on national party programs than has been assumed and that they tend to depress, rather than stimulate, voter turnout.

NOTE

1. James Q. Wilson, *The Amateur Democrat* (Chicago: University of Chicago Press, 1962).

1 / The National Committees as Grass-Roots Vehicles of Representation

William Crotty

James Bryce, commenting in 1888 on party organization in America, wrote:

> The greatest discovery ever made in the art of war was when men began to perceive that organization and discipline count for more than numbers. . . . The Americans made a similar discovery in politics some fifty or sixty years ago. By degrees, for even in America great truths do not burst full-grown upon the world, it was perceived that the victories of the ballot-box, no less than of the sword, must be won by the cohesion and disciplined docility of the troops, and that these merits can only be secured by skilful organization and long-continued training. Both parties flung themselves into the task, and the result has been an extremely complicated system of party machinery, firm yet flexible, delicate yet quickly set up and capable of working well in the roughest communities. [1]

If Bryce's assessment is correct, it took the Americans an inordinate amount of time to extend their organizational ingenuity to constructing serviceable party structures at the national level. Almost as an afterthought, the Democrats institutionalized a limited national-level committee in the 1840s. The new Republican party followed suit in its first national campaign of 1856. Both national committees were restricted to coordinating the preparations for the quadrennial national conventions. Since their founding, and extending up to the modern era of politics, the national committees have had an uncertain tenure, an ambivalent influence on both national and state politics, and a curious life, well outside the mainstream of national concerns.

Overview

A few things are clear. Some type of national-party headquarters was virtually assured after the creation of the political parties in the 1790s. Nonetheless, the establishment of such an agency was resisted by the state parties that constituted the basic blocs in the national system. When the first semipermanent committee was finally established, it was done for convenience rather than for any new or aggressive conception of the party's role.

The National Committee and the Presidential Campaign

Until recently, coordinating, directing, and helping to finance the campaign of the party's presidential nominee every fourth year remained a major function—some would argue

The National Committee and the Presidential Campaign

Until recently, coordinating, directing, and helping to finance the campaign of the party's presidential nominee every fourth year remained a major function—some would argue the only major function—of the committee. The 1950s and to an even greater extent the 1960s witnessed a move away from the national committees as the fulcrum of the presidential campaign. The trend has been toward personalized structures of organization and decisionmaking created by the candidate and immediately responsible to him. In 1960, John Kennedy ran his presidential campaign through a personal organization loyal to him and well outside the regular party structure. Such candidate organizations have now become commonplace.

Possibly the most thorough development along those lines was in the 1972 presidential campaign of Richard Nixon. The Committee to Re-Elect the President (or CREEP, as its opponents referred to it) was established by Nixon, initially under the leadership of John Mitchell, to promote his reelection. The committee was lavishly financed and precisely organized. Decisionmaking was centralized in the national headquarters (or at the White House), and the scope of its organizational efforts surpassed those of the national party. The quality of the personnel contributing to the efforts of the Committee to Re-Elect the President; the campaign and budgetary resources available to its national, state, and local appendages; and the intensity and sophistication of its operations at all levels—these all far exceeded the capabilities of the national party and its state affiliates. [2]

Jimmy Carter was an outsider running for the presidency in 1976 with no particular ties to the national party or a national party constituency and, in fact, reportedly disdainful of national committee ties and the effectiveness and influence of its membership. Carter created his own structure of state-level supporters and, in effect, his own organization. Once elected, he chose to keep his loose personal organization intact and, adding insult, used the national committee's limited budget to subsidize such things as the mailing of Christmas cards to his personal network of workers. [3]

National committees have had few major accomplishments. They have provided a vehicle for supervising arrangements for the national conventions and, on occasion, they have been used by presidential candidates to coordinate their campaigns. Beyond these duties, the national committees have given critics who feared a strong central party precious little to worry about. In fact, for many years they, like the national conventions, sprang into existence only for the presidential campaign.

As one Democratic national committeeman explained in 1919:

> It was the custom of this body immediately after the presidential election had passed—and the custom seemed to prevail whether we succeeded, as we did in [President Grover] Cleveland's time [1884–1888, 1892–1892], or lost—of going out of business in a week or two, just as soon as we could pay up the bills, and indeed sometimes we went out of business before we did that. [4]

Funding

In some respects, things have not changed that much. The comments by the committee representative point up a continuing problem of the national party: acquiring adequate funding for national party activities. Along with a shaky political constituency, and limited duties, national committees have enjoyed no independent source of money. The struggle to meet expenses, however minimal they may be, or to pay off campaign debts, remained a constant irritation. Often a president or presidential candidate, in hopes of meeting the party's obligations, appointed as national chairperson a prominent fundraiser (John J. Rasrob, Mark Hanna, or Robert Strauss, for example) with ties to the nation's financial community. The tactic, like the national committees themselves, was intermittently successful.

The problem has been more acute for the Democrats, but both parties suffer under financial restraints. There are often severe limitations—not always appreciated by outsiders—as to what the parties can do. Furthermore, the national committees have been totally dependent on the willingness (not always manifest) of the president, when of the same party, to serve as a fund-raiser, on major interest groups, on wealthy contributors, or on the willingness of state parties to meet financial "quotas" intended to subsidize the operations of the national committees. The result, in addition to episodic and limited service capabilities, has been (and this is more true for the Democrats than the Republicans) an unusually shaky financial foundation, a limited capability to attract high-quality staff help (although there are a number of obvious exceptions to this generalization), rapid staff turnover at most levels, and most characteristic of all, frequent financial crises—at times met out of pocket by personal contributions of the party's treasurer or one of its more magnanimous and responsive supporters.

In more recent times, both Republican and Democratic national committees have attempted to implement more systematic and long-range funding of their operations. The Republicans have proven to be far more successful. In 1936 they created a National Finance Committee consisting of the finance chairpersons of the state parties and other influential fund-raisers, and headed by a chairperson designated by the national chairperson. The money collected was divided among the national committee, the National Republican Congressional Committee (a creature of House Republicans that funds House races), and the National Republican Senatorial Committee (a group that performs the same service for Senate Republicans). [5]

The Democrats have failed to coordinate their national fund raising. An attempt was made by Robert Strauss, while party treasurer and later national chairperson, to create a finance council modeled along the lines of the successful Republican venture. The committee was established, but never functioned with the skill and coordination of the Republican unit. As a result, House and Senate Democrats, as well as potential presidential candidates, continue to compete with each other for the limited financial resources of labor unions, interest lobbies, and the corporate and individual contributions that provide the lifeblood of national politics.

In general, the Republican National Committee has done well. The party was able to open a new national headquarters, named after former President Dwight Eisenhower, on Capitol Hill; it has avoided any indebtedness; and its annual operating budgets seem ample. The Democrats, on the other hand, still lack the continuity and professionalism in fund raising achieved by their Republican counterparts. Despite the best efforts of Strauss, their most skillful fund-raiser of recent years, the Democrats continue to operate with an uncertain annual budget and a party debt (following the election of 1976) of $3.8 million (down from $9.3 million in the wake of the 1968 presidential election). Despite these problems, in 1977 the Democratic National Committee spoke optimistically of raising $3.2 million for its 1978 operating budget (well above its $1.5 to $2.4 million average for the years 1969-1976), reducing its long-term indebtedness to $2 million, and raising an additional $1 million for distribution to House, Senate, and selected gubernatorial candidates during 1978. [6]

Should the Democratic National Committee succeed in realizing such ambitious targets, it would provide further testimony—should it be needed—to the powers of incumbency. Since a fair portion of the Democratic National Committee's budget (approximately $500,000 a year) goes directly to the White House to subsidize the political activities of its operatives, it would appear that a president—even one not sympathetic to the enhancement of national committee powers—would have a stake in reinvigorating national committee fund raising. [7] Still, the system appears so vulnerable to abuse that a president, and the national party, should be wary.

Speaking for a Grass-Roots Constituency

Although survival may be the principal distinguishing characteristic of the national committees, periodically there have been attempts toward more nationally representative and more active national organizations, for which the designation of national-level party committees is more appropriate. In different ways and under varying conditions, the Democrats (under Paul Butler, Senator Fred R. Harris, and Lawrence O'Brien) and the Republicans (under a succession of national chairpersons—and Dwight Eisenhower, once out of office) have initiated sporadic efforts to develop more assertive national bodies. A more consistent and cumulative set of institutional developments during the 1950s, 1960s, and 1970s attempted to fashion a national party headquarters actively servicing state and local organizations, candidates, and elected party officials, and speaking (hesitantly) for a national party constituency. The efforts to date have been indecisive.

The experimentation with policy committees (the Republicans' abortive All-Republican Conference in the early 1960s, the Democrats' Policy Council, 1969-1976, and Democratic Advisory Council, 1956-1960) can be seen in this light. These groups were intended to speak on policy matters in a way more representative of their respective party's mass membership. Their creation marked an implicit recognition that the national parties as constituted could not perform this task adequately and that the congressional parties, for whatever reason, did not.

The reform committees, popular since 1968, fall into this category also. They are presumed to speak for a wide, grass-roots constituency on organizational matters, including the selection of delegates for national conventions, the structure of the national party, adequate representation of principal party groups in party deliberations, and so on. The function of the reform committees, supposedly, is to achieve parties more open to influence by and representative of their mass constituencies.

There have been two other major innovations since the 1920s (one in each party) in efforts to make the parties more representative of and attuned to the needs of their diverse constituencies. Beginning with a rule adopted by the 1952 Republican National Convention, the party's national committee opened its membership to state chairpersons. The intentions were to represent the working arm of the party (an indirect acknowledgment of the awkward role of national committee members at the state level); to lessen the malapportionment of a body based entirely on equal state representation; and, most importantly, to represent Republican Party supporters by rewarding the areas of greatest Republican strength.

Curiously, the women opposed these reforms.[8] More substantial was the opposition from the small states, who enjoyed equal representation in the prevailing arrangement, and from the South, which also stood to lose influence if the change were adopted.[9]

The Party Charter

The McGovern-Fraser Commission and the O'Hara Commission (Commission on [Convention] Rules) toyed with efforts to change the Democratic National Committee structure. They did introduce a party charter—jointly, but belatedly (May 1972) endorsed by both commissions—to the 1972 national convention. The convention had been too torn by the South Carolina credentials fights over women, by the California "winner-take-all primary," and by the closed slate-making and the "quota" debate in Chicago to seriously consider any new reform proposals. It did authorize a new commission, eventually to be chaired by former North Carolina Governor Terry Sanford to write a new charter (very much like the old 1972 one as it turned out). The convention also provided for an off-year convention in 1974 to consider and vote on the new party charter to be proposed by the Sanford Commission, and it voted to add the state chairperson "and the next ranking officer of the opposite sex" within the state party to the national committee. The national committee would be enlarged to 234 votes divided among a body of 303 members.[10]

The 1974 midterm convention ratified the party charter presented to it. The charter included provisions for a national finance council, continued midterm party conferences, a judicial council to settle intraparty squabbles, and a national education and training council "responsible for the creation and implementation of education and training programs for the Democratic Party."[11] It also expanded the national committee to 363 members to be composed of the following: the chairperson and the highest-ranking state party officer of the opposite sex from each state; 200 other members apportioned to the states on the same basis as national convention delegates (a marked departure from previous practice); three governors selected by the Democratic Governors' Conference; the House and Senate leaders and one additional person from each chamber; three mayors chosen by the Conference of Democratic Mayors; the president of the Young Democrats; the ranking officers of the national party (chairperson, two vice-chairpersons, the treasurer and secretary); and twenty-five others selected in an unspecified way to allow representation for other party elements.[12] After resisting even modest change for generations, the Democrats had attempted to drastically recast their national committee. The old forms (the manner in which the national committees were constructed and the unrepresentativeness of the institutional, intraparty structures) and the old prejudices had proven in the past, as they likely would continue to do in the future, formidable barriers to fundamental change.

Limits on the National Committees

The slow and unspectacular evolution of the national committees, coupled with brief, basically unsuccessful flings at reformulating their objectives and perspectives, have resulted in something of an anomaly—at least when contrasted with the original intent of making the committees continually responsible to the party membership as represented by the national conventions. The national committees have come to depend on the will, interest, and foresight of their national chairperson at any given point in time, or, should there be a president in office of the same party, on the political objectives of the president in concert with the willingness of the national chairperson to present and defend the party's vital interests. The national committee becomes inescapably bound to the chairperson's initiative and abilities (or by the same token, the absence of these qualities). The national chairperson, in turn, is less subject to direction from the national committee membership per se than he is to the following external pressures:

1. The relationship between the national headquarters and the White House (when the party controls the presidency), and the president's concern (or lack of it) with party affairs.
2. The quality of interaction between the national party and state and local party organizations and leaders.
3. The continually sensitive association between the national party and the congressional party.
4. The concerns of the various interest blocs and their representatives who take an ongoing interest (at times supportive, in other cases less sympathetic) in the management of party affairs.

If a president has little interest in the party welfare—as manifested by the national committee—then the organization can atrophy. In an out-party situation (where the presidency is held by the opposition), factional rivalries, lack of funds, and accumulated debts can combine to stifle any national party activity. The relations between party leaders and officeholders, state parties, and the national committee and national chairperson are, at best, ambiguous.

The National Committees and the Congress

To compound the difficulties of the national committees, these bodies have often been perceived as enemies by powerful contenders for the party's presidential nomination and by party members in Congress. Any faction not in control of the national committee, given its unrestricted responsiveness to the will of the reigning chairperson, will view it with suspicion. At times, such an approach is highly realistic. The national chairperson can employ (and has done this) the resources of the national committee and its staff to forward the ambitions of a favored candidate. In defeat, the national committee and its chairperson normally are indebted to the losing presidential candidate and can be hostile to new voices within the party and to any potential new leadership.

The relationship between the national committee and the congressional party, in particular, has been marked by suspicion. The congressional parties have their own party and campaign committees that, as noted above, compete with the national committee for funds. In policy matters, the legislators are sensitive about "outside" (nonlegislative) agencies attempting to "tell them how to do their job" (i.e., trying to influence national legislation). Congressmen have been particularly resentful of national party organs infringing on their domain (as they perceive it), and this is the principal reason for their antipathy to such creations as the Democratic Advisory Council of the 1956-1960 period and the far less venturesome Democratic Policy Council of the years 1969-1976. Overall, legislators believe that the national committees provide them with few services (such as campaign help or funding) and have the potential to cause them a great deal of grief. Congresspersons' views concerning the national committees can be harsh ("a bunch of clerks," "represent no one but themselves").[13]

If one could sum up this experience with the national committees from the congresspersons' perspective, it would be that as presently constituted the national committees have provided them with little assistance—in some cases so little as to question any continuing need for the committees to exist.

The problem is that the congressional critics of the national committees have something to complain about. The national committees have been antagonistic to the Congress. They provide little assistance for congressional campaigns, and they have been the creature of presidents (when of the same party) to an extraordinary degree—in fact, to the virtual exclusion of anything else.

The National Chairperson

The national chairperson's role, given the sum of these factors, is curious. There are few, if any, constraints on his behavior exercised by the national committee (a varied and disorganized group that meets twice a year at most) or by the national headquarters staff, many of whom serve for only short periods of time and all of whom depend on the good will of the chairperson for their jobs. Conversely, the precarious position of the national chairperson—the vortex of extracommittee forces with which he must contend—coupled with the lack of any consensus or tangible support for national committee activities makes the chairperson's job an extremely difficult one. In general, committee activity and inactivity and the ambitious promotion of party objectives or the complete neglect of organizational concerns have depended, to a great extent, on the temperament of the chairperson. The pressure on the national chairperson can be enormous. The resulting effects on the party—the inability to sustain long-range planning and commitment or to offer the party an impartial and dependable reference point for its activities—would have to be described as debilitating.

The Chairperson's Job: Rule One

Although the chairperson's role is ambiguous—because it depends on political circumstance and individual initiative—a few strains are nonetheless clear. First, there is a demand implicit in the office for total subservience to the president, when he is of the same party. The tenures of Rogers Morton, Robert Dole, George Bush and Mary Louise Smith in the Republican Party, and John Bailey and Kenneth Curtis in the Democratic Party, illustrate the point. These chairpersons have been the servants, in the fullest sense of the term, of the White House. The national chairperson is picked by the president and his immediate political advisers, and he serves at their whim. The major personnel and organizational decisions are made in the White House. The activities the national committee staff will engage in are defined in the White House, as are the issues the national chairperson will address and even the nature of the remarks he will make.

Seldom is any detail of national committee operations too small to be overlooked by White House political operatives. The timing and even the agenda for national committee gatherings (and, of course, the eminently more important national convention meetings) are decided by those closest to the president.

Should a national chairperson forget the realities of politics, or should he begin to feel that he has obligations to a national party constituency that go beyond those to the immediate occupant of the White House, his career as national party leader will be short indeed. Two examples will serve to make this point.

Rogers Morton (1969–1971) was Richard Nixon's first appointment as national chairman. Morton, an experienced politician and former congressperson, was picked as an articulate and telegenic spokesman for moderate Republicanism. When Morton was promoted into the Nixon cabinet, he was replaced by Senator Robert Dole of Kansas, a sharp-tongued critic of liberal policies in the Senate and a strong Nixon supporter. Dole, while more stridently partisan than Morton, was also telegenic and media-oriented. He represented a willing and uncritical proponent of administration positions at a time the president felt a need for someone with such skills.

Dole, like Morton, was little concerned with and had few ties to any national party constituency. He did, however, have a sense of the party's long-run interests and, as the Watergate scandal began to gain momentum, his defense of the administration became less enthusiastic. In early 1973, Nixon replaced Dole after a meeting at Camp David. "I had a nice chat with the President," the outgoing chairperson told the Republican National Committee, "while the other fellows went out to get the rope." [14] Dole was replaced by George Bush, then Ambassador to the United Nations.

In his valedictory address to the national committee, Dole touched on one of the inherent problems of a national chairperson and of the national party when he said: "We understand our obligations to the country. We're not there to rubber stamp the President and we're sure he wouldn't want it any other way." [15] It was exactly this type of emerging concern that resulted in Dole's firing.

Following the election of Jimmy Carter as president, Robert Strauss, who had served as national chairperson for the period 1972–1976 and who assisted in the Carter campaign, was appointed as a cabinet-level trouble-shooter and trade negotiator for the new administration. He was replaced by Kenneth Curtis of Maine, a former governor and early supporter of Carter. Curtis, a moderate, had been a friend of Carter since the days when they both had served as governors of their respective states. Despite this friendship and an easy-going personality that stood him well with the media, party professionals, and the national headquarters' staff, Curtis was not to last long. Within a year of his appointment, he would be announcing his imminent retirement from what he termed a "lousy job." [16] Curtis got into trouble by complaining of what he saw as the day-to-day meddling in national committee operations by second-level White House personnel. When he complained, rumors quickly circulated that the White House was dissatified with his "weak" leadership. [17] By the end of the first year of the Carter administration, Curtis was on the way out.

Perhaps the handwriting was on the wall earlier than anyone cared to believe. The attitude of the new administration toward the national committee was being formed even before Carter was sworn in as president. A memo to the incoming president had been prepared in December 1976 by Patrick Caddell, Carter's young polister and, as it turned out, a continuing political adviser to the former Georgia governor. In his memo (later leaked to the press), Caddell advocated that the Democratic National Committee be made "an active, vibrant political arm of the Carter White House." [18] To do this, in

Caddell's terms to insure a "Carterized" national committee, it would be necessary to start with the national chairperson:

> It is clear that if the DNC [Democratic National Committee] is going to be "Carterized" and made a political wing of the White House, that requires a chairman who is a loyalist, and essentially a Carter insider. I suspect that any move that brings in someone who has an independent constituency and other political interests is going to result in an inability of the DNC to really carry out the functions we need. I think that the DNC chairman's selection be along the lines of someone who is both a loyalist, an insider, and a person who is willing to take direction from the Governor's [Carter's] political and personal staff. [19]

If Caddell's memo did not alarm national committee members (more than likely they were unaware of it), one of the new administration's first recommendations should have. Barely a month in office, Carter's principal political adviser, Hamilton Jordan, proposed in February 1976 the creation of a new eleven-member committee to be appointed by the White House to decide national party (and national committee) objectives and to monitor the activities of the national committee and its staff. The new committee, to be led by White House personnel, would include only three members of the Democratic National Committee. The angry reaction of national party representatives scuttled the plan. Nonetheless, the attitude of the new administration as to the status of the national committee and its perceived obligation (to serve, uncritically, the White House) was apparent enough. Curtis's failure to accommodate himself to such an arrangement led quickly to his downfall.

The lesson in both parties is clear: presidents expect national chairpersons and the national committee to do their bidding. The party chairpersons or the national committee appear to have no viable alternatives. Should a party chairperson resist, or simply be perceived to be not cooperating as fully as expected, he is quickly replaced.

The Chairperson's Job: Rule Two

If the implications of the first, and cardinal, rule of the chairperson's role are fully appreciated, the next two rules are quickly understood; to a large degree, they derive from the first. The uncertain nature of the chairperson's position is its chief characteristic when the president is not of the same party. As a consequence, radical, temporary shifts in the direction and concerns of the national party can follow one after another. There is no particular consistency in the programs, allocation of resources, priority concerns, activities engaged in, or even the nature of the personnel or the types of services available from the national party headquarters. Much depends on the personality, ambition, and vision of the chairperson. Often conditions over which he has no control determine the success of his incumbency. Can he command reasonably strong support from party factions? Is the party too split to permit anyone to be its spokesman? Is the chairperson a nationally recognized and respected figure? Do the media look to him to articulate the national party's position (or does it turn exclusively to potential presidential contenders or congressional leaders)? Are the funds available to hire a first-rate staff to provide the legislative and state parties with needed services? Does the chairperson, or the party more generally, have any specific goals (beyond winning the next presidential election)? Does the chairperson percieve his job as temporary or part-time (as many have, devoting their real efforts to their legislative duties, law practices, or home-state party concerns)?

Shifts in national-party orientations can be drastic. The conservative take-over of the Republican Party in the early 1960s formed the vanguard of the Goldwater movement, leading to its capture of the Republican Party nomination. William Miller, a conservative congressperson, was appointed as the Republican national chairperson from 1961 to 1964. Miller resigned to become Goldwater's vice-presidential running mate and was succeeded by a conservative ideologue and Goldwater campaign organizer, Dean Burch (1964–1965). The severe party losses in the 1964 presidential election led to the election of Ray Bliss of Ohio as chairperson. Bliss, a colorless technician unattuned to the needs of the media, had a reputation as a capable student of nuts-and-bolts politics. A man credited with rebuilding Ohio's Republican Party, he was given the job of revivifying the national organization of the devastated Republican Party.

The Democrats had two programmatically committed chairpersons during the 1950s, Stephen Mitchell (1952–1954) and Paul Butler (1955–1960)—reflections of the concerns of presidential candidate Adlai Stevenson. Following the Democrats' 1968 loss, Hubert Humphrey chose another issue-oriented Democrat, Senator Fred R. Harris of Oklahoma, to lead the party. Harris had been one of Humphrey's original two campaign managers (the other, Senator Edmund Muskie, was rewarded with the vice-presidential nomination). Harris's attempts to give a contemporary policy emphasis to national party deliberations soon hurt his relationships with party leaders, Humphrey included. Harris was unceremoniously replaced by a party regular, Lawrence O'Brien, who had briefly served a previous term as chairperson during the 1968 presidential campaign. O'Brien was more concerned with organizational questions, campaign services, and funding problems than had been Harris. O'Brien (1970–1972), in turn, was later replaced by Robert Strauss, a conservative Texan and an experienced fund-raiser. Beyond attempting to provide a stable basis for party funding, Strauss devoted his energies to returning old-line party professionals to dominant positions in the party hierarchy. In the process, he also attempted to reunite a factionally divided party and, with limited success, to reestablish cordial relations with such major political support groups as the AFL–CIO.

Democratic Party reform provides another example of the pivotal, if unpredictable, nature of the chairperson when the president is not of the same party. Reform efforts in the years following the 1968 Democratic National Convention were strongly supported by Harris. O'Brien was more cautious, although he did eventually back them and, in fact, his rulings at the 1972 national convention on reform-related questions earned him the enmity of organized labor, among others. Strauss had no sympathy for reform and, if it could be done without splitting the party, he would have preferred to scuttle it. The reform currents had their own individual roots of support. These proved too strong to roll back, and the reform emphasis eventually prevailed. Nonetheless, the unpredictability of support from the national chairpersons at critical junctures kept the outcome in doubt and resulted in continual battle-by-battle efforts during the years between 1968 and 1974.

The Chairperson's Job: Rule Three

Rule Three should be obvious. The national chairperson is *not* a representative of the national party's grass-roots membership and is not open to influence or control by it. Also, the national chairperson is *not* the creature of the national committee. He is accountable to neither the grass-roots party constituency nor its presumed representative, the national committee membership. Outside forces, somewhat intangible and very much shaped by the current political tides, define the chairperson's role and his responsibilities. Political necessities, coupled with the good will and political adeptness the chairperson brings to his position, determine to a great extent the success of his incumbency. The least important factor is the sentiments of the mass membership of the party. While the national chairperson may appear to speak for Democrats or Republicans (as the case may be) throughout the nation, in truth the reasons behind his selection and the corresponding constraints on his behavior guarantee his falling far short of being a spokesman for the national party constituency or its long-run interests.

National Committee Members

The national committeeman and the national committeewoman are selected by their state parties prior to the national convention and take their seats for a four-year term immediately after the convention. The committee members are chosen in a variety of ways—by state conventions, state primaries, the delegation to the national convention, and state committees.

Theoretically, national committee members supervise the conduct of national party affairs, the national chairperson's execution of his duties, and the operations of the national headquarters staff. In actuality, the national chairperson, as indicated above, is not answerable to the national committee representatives.

The national committee's headquarters staff is responsible only to the chairperson. Consequently, it is difficult, if not impossible, for one committee member (out of over 100 for the Republicans or 363 for the Democrats), speaking for a diversity of state interests, to have any significant impact on party operations. The structure of the national committee itself is too unwieldy to allow effective decisionmaking. The committee meets usually twice a year, primarily to hear the chairperson's report and to transact other business put before it. In the interim, it is the national chairperson's job to define and look after the party's interests.

The national committee member's role at the state level remains ill defined: he can make a constructive and dynamic contribution to state party affairs, and some do. He can also, by choice or through events, remove himself from the vicissitudes of state politics by staying beyond their tides. In some cases, the national committee member can represent an anachronism—a point of view, a set of values, or a faction in state parties whose time has past.

As an example, Jake Arvey, political boss of the Chicago machine, after guessing wrong in several elections, lost his position to a former protégé, Richard J. Daley. Daley effectively kicked Arvey upstairs by choosing him as national committee representative. Arvey continued as an elder statesman of the Democratic Party nationally and even headed its executive committee. At the same time, he had no power base within his own state and little influence on state politics.

In some circumstances, the national committee member may symbolize, to the discomfiture of all, a political faction opposed to those controlling the state machinery, or to the state chairperson, or even to the governor himself. Robert Vance of Alabama, for example, represented a national party faction within the state party that opposed Alabama Governor George Wallace. This took some courage and presented no particular problem during the 1960s when Wallace experimented with third-party candidacies. As Wallace moved back toward the Democratic Party in the 1970s, however, the party was confronted with the problem of winning him over (and thus coopting his constituency), while still not alienating the consistently loyal Vance faction. Politics being what it is, Vance's role in national party affairs was deemphasized as the party's leaders began to court the Wallace faction.

One thing is certain: the national committee officeholder seldom, if ever, represents the national party and its views—should it presume to have any—as they affect state party activities. Honor, visibility, and the generalized influence accorded formal position in the party hierarchy attach themselves to the position of committeeman. Any real political power, however, depends on the occupant: in state and, on a far more modest level, national politics, the burden is on the national committee member to fashion out of the position what he can.

There is some contrast between the two parties in how the talents of the committee members are used at the national level. The Republican Party employs its committee members more consistently and aggressively incorporates them whenever possible into the ongoing affairs of the national party (e.g., in systematically exploring possible rule changes to be recommended to the upcoming national convention). The approach has its merits. It fosters an *espirit de corps* as well as providing meaningful, continuing outlets for the committee members and their expertise. The orderly rules of procedure that characterize Republican national conventions represent, in effect, the outcome of a continual reassessment of convention forms by subcommittees of the national committee.

The Republican approach also has its liabilities. It does nothing about the anomalous position of the national committee member in the party organization. A reliance on committee members and the development of prerogatives in certain areas can delimit, for example, party exposure. The approach to party reform, and the publicity given the efforts of the two parties in this regard, provide a useful comparison. The first Republican reform group, the Development and Organization Committee, was composed of (and limited to) members of the Republican national committee familiar with convention procedures. It did a workmanlike, if unspectacular, job and published two reports; it received little public attention.

In an effort to match the Democrats in at least opening the committees to more segments of the party, and in hopes of capturing more publicity, the Republicans selected the membership of later reform groups from the Congress and, to a more limited extent, from the state parties. The resulting committees, and particularly the Rule 29 Committee (1972–1974), chaired by Congressman William Stieger of Wisconsin, proved somewhat more venturesome than its predecessors. The staff work and the resources of the Republican reform commissions continued to be controlled by the national committee, and the bulk of the members remained the relatively well-satisfied national committee representatives.

The Democratic Party has had a series of reform commissions. The first, and by far the most successful—the Commission on Party Structure and Delegate Selection (McGovern–Fraser Commission)—and its lesser-known cousin—the Rules Commission (O'Hara Commission)—set the pattern for those to follow. These drew their membership from as wide a spectrum of Democratic Party supporters as possible. In addition to national committee members, these commissions have included (in unequal proportions) state chairmen; academics; state legislators; county chairpersons; representatives of minority groups such as blacks, Mexican Americans, youth, and women; labor union officials (from both the dissident and AFL-CIO factions); congresspersons; U.S. Senators; governors and former governors; and party influentials without portfolio. One consequence has been a far greater visibility of Democratic Party reform efforts than otherwise could have been expected, and a greater legitimacy accorded the recommendations made to reform party processes by dissidents, regulars, and the press.

Powers of the National Committee

The national committees receive their powers directly from the national convention. These can be changed at will by the convention in any manner it deems proper, although normally this aspect of convention business elicits little debate. Even within the present jurisdictions of the national committees, the powers given these bodies are not inconsequential, although their potential is seldom exploited.

The *Rules of [the] Democratic National Committee* can serve as an example. Rules give the national committee a broad grant of power and state that the committee has "authority to take all appropriate action to promote the principles and programs of the Democratic Party in the interval prior to the next succeeding National Convention."

Rules further specify "the principal duties and powers of the National Committee" as follows:

- To maintain a national party headquarters.
- To conduct the national campaign for the party's presidential and vice-presidential nominees.
- To assist in the election of *all* Democratic candidates in any general elections.
- To promote party organization at all levels (which includes, according to *Rules*, political research, communications, media coverage, public relations, coordination of party levels and party and nonparty groups and leaders, speakers' activities, program initiation, performance of party mandates "and the discharge and fulfillment by the Party of its platform pledges and commitments publicly made").
- To encourage Democratic clubs.
- To finance party activities (through state quotas among other things).
- To arrange and manage the national committee.
- To implement the national convention platform.
- "To establish, maintain and sponsor such committees, groups, staffs or councils for the formulation of Party policy not inconsistent with the platform of the last National Convention".
- To maintain sustaining party memberships.
- "To do any and all other things reasonably incidental to the performance and exercise of the duties imposed and powers conferred by the National Convention and in promoting the principles and programs of the Democratic Party." [20]

Even a casual review of the points listed indicates that the national committee has a broad and potentially powerful mandate. It is interesting that these powers are not recent innovations. They rested in the national committee even before (for the Democrats) the adoption of their party charter. The latter simply reemphasized in this regard powers already resident in the national-level headquarters. It is fair to say that the potential in these grants of authority has never begun to be realized.

Future Prospects

The present, basically ineffectual, role of the national committees is not difficult to explain given the nature of their development, the demands of American politics, and the excessively decentralized and chaotic state of political parties in this country. The national committees are accidental developments created without forethought and intended to simplify a series of awkward problems concerning communication and coordination among dispersed state parties, candidates, and factions.

The national committees of the two major political parties have, like virtually all party institutions and practices, evolved from need. Little rational planning was invested in the agencies or their operations when instituted, and little has been subsequently. And, again like other party institutions, their utility and their contribution to representative democratic processes in the United States have been seriously questioned in the wake of the reforms that shook the party system in the 1970s.

The winds of change have at least brushed both parties. Both, for example, have had women chairpersons during the 1970s for the first time. Both national committees have, in their uncertain ways, overseen the development of a series of reform commissions. The fruits of such efforts are always unpredictable, but the Democrats, at least, have adopted a party charter intended to revitalize national party operations and have reconstituted their national committee in an effort to make it more representative of the diverse interests in the party's coalition. One of the Republican reform committees (the Rule 29 Commission), in an effort to prevent future Watergates, called on its national committee to authorize all future expenditures over $1,000 in any Republican presidential campaign (a proposal the national committee is ill equipped to enforce). Both national committees may be called upon in future years to introduce and enforce ethical standards of conduct in campaigns. The Democrats, in fact, already have such a provision in their party charter, although it is unlikely to have any real effect.

The introduction of public funding for presidential campaigns has meant that both national committees may receive as much as $2.2 million to subsidize their national conventions. The consequences of such federal largess are likely to be mixed. The intention, of course, is to reduce the reliance of the national parties on contributions to convention expenses by corporations, unions, and wealthy individuals seeking preferential access to the parties and their candidates. The achievement of such a goal, however, is problematic.

The grants should help the parties, and especially the Democrats, to stabilize their fund raising and to systematize their organizational efforts. More troublesome perhaps, both parties are likely to attempt to further exploit the role of federal subsidies in their operations. Already the Democratic Party is considering approaching the Federal Election Commission to permit the use of governmental monies to partially cover the costs of its "reform" committees (the groups deal with delegate selection). These overtures come at the very time the reform bodies have become less representative of the party nationally and more directly under the control of the administration.

Direct federal subsidies to the national parties serve to institutionalize the national agencies at a point in history when the legitimacy and contribution of the parties themselves have been brought into question. The national committee may well be in the process of being relieved of any necessity for justifying its existence or contributing to a more democratic and representative political system.

The problem is real enough. Meanwhile, business continues as usual, with the parties scraping up funds wherever and from whomever they can. Generally, the price for the body politic is steep. Watergate—and specifically the illegal investment of corporate and union funds to buy defense contracts, preferential government treatment, construction allocations, research developmental grants, exemptions from legal restrictions, relaxation of antitrust standards, dismissals of equal-rights and antipollution suits, and the like—demonstrated this in detail. Apparently, the system is vulnerable to much abuse, to the extent that the lesson has to be continually relearned.[21]

The national committees have their problems also. Both have ambiguous ties to youth at a time when it would appear in their interest to reverse the trend toward political independence by young people. The bonds are unlikely to improve. There is no easy solution to tension between the national and the congressional parties, although both the Republicans and the Democrats are attempting to include more legislators in their deliberations. The congressional representatives remain skeptical.

Both parties need stronger organizational ties to the state parties. Superficially, at least, these may be developing. There are now national governors', mayors', and state legislative conferences housed in the national committee headquarters. Both parties provide for regional organizations, and both, as noted above, now include state chairpersons on their national committees. The real need, however, is to provide a working tie-in to the state and local organizations and to better represent their continuing needs and interests in national party councils. Given the restrictions inherent in the role of the national chairperson and in the national committees, this type of vital relationship appears beyond the present party system.

Rightly or wrongly, policy concern will receive increasing attention from the national committees. Early policy-formulating bodies were meant to serve varying ends: they presented policies that contrasted (favorably, it was hoped) with those of the opposition; or they attempted to build a constituency for party wing or candidate; or they attempted to chart a party course through a difficult period; or they served simply to deflect serious controversy and to give the appearance of movement and concern. The policy bodies supervised by the national committees—in the case of the Democrats, from the Advisory Council of the 1950s to off-year conventions—have proven deficient in one respect or another as representative and policy-formulating bodies. Nevertheless, the tenor of the times is such that both national committees now schedule policy items as staples of their debate. The Republican National Committee, for example, irritated its titular leader, former President Gerald Ford, by rejecting his counsel and voting against support for the Carter administration's initiatives on the Panama Canal treaty. Similarly, the Democratic National Committee chose to water down (under prodding from its Canal Zone representative) a motion for support of the same treaty that had been introduced by the White House, an outcome that angered the Carter administration and colored its perception of the chairperson, Kenneth Curtis.[22]

The fundamental problems facing both national committees persist. The national chairpersons are national party leaders in only a limited sense. Often, they are little more than partisan spokespersons for a national administration. The national committees in their present form do not represent, and are not accountable to, any party-based grass-roots constituency.

Political parties are in ferment. The old ways are being reassessed and new ventures are being initiated. This much is certain. Less clear is whether the parties, and more specifically their national-level committees, will emerge any more compatible with a changing social order and a party constituency in transition. Their long and undistinguished history to date would argue against any such outcome.

NOTES

1. James Bryce, *The American Commonwealth,* vol. 1, ed. Louis M. Hacker (New York: Putnam, 1959), p. 178.

2. See the testimony by Robert C. Odle, Jr., before the Ervin Committee on the structure and operations of the Committee to Re-Elect the President, in *The Watergate Hearings,* by the *New York Times* (New York: Bantam, 1973), pp. 144-145 and, especially, pp. 746-747 in the unedited transcript of the Ervin Committee's hearings. The uses made of the Committee to Re-Elect's structure, of course, are another matter. These are well documented. See, as examples, *The Senate Watergate Report,* 2 vols. (New York: Dell, 1974); John Dean, *Blind Ambition* (New York: Simon and Schuster, 1976); and J. Anthony Lukas, *Nightmare: The Underside of the Nixon Years* (New York: Viking, 1976).

   The basic work on the national committees, and of particular help to this essay in developing the background material, is Cornelius P. Cotter and Bernard C. Hennessy, *Politics Without Power: The National Party Committees* (New York: Atherton, 1964). More limited in scope but also useful is Hugh A. Bone, *Party Committees and National Politics* (Seattle: University of Washington Press, 1958), and Bone's more recent "Political Party Management" (Morristown, N.J.: General Learning Press, 1973). Also of value are: Hugh A. Bone, *American Politics and the Party System,* 4th ed. (New York: McGraw-Hill, 1971). pp. 160-191; Cornelius P. Cotter, "The National Committees and Their Constituencies" in, *Practical Politics in the United States,* ed. C. P. Cotter (Boston: Allyn and Bacon, 1969), pp. 17-41; Joel Fisher, "The Role of the National Party Chairman" (Paper delivered at the American Political Science Association Convention, Washington, D.C., 1969); Edward M. Sait, *American Parties and Elections* (New York: Century. 1927); the *Proceedings* of the national committee sessions; and relevant issues of *Congressional Quarterly.*

   For membership characteristics of committee members during different time periods, see Wallace S. Sayre, "Personnel of Republican and Democratic National Committees," *American Political Science Review* 26 (April 1932). 360-362; Cotter and Hennessy, *Politics Without Power,* pp. 46-49; and Charles H. Longley, "Party Reform and Party Nationalization: The Case of the Democrats," in this volume.

3. Terence Smith, "It's Carter Folk vs. Regular Democrats," *New York Times,* December 11, 1977, p. E-3.

4. Sait, *American Parties and Elections,* p. 169.

5. Charles O. Jones, *The Republican Party in American Politics* (New York: Macmillan, 1965), pp. 29-30; and Alexander Heard, *The Costs of Democracy* (Chapel Hill: University of North Carolina Press, 1960), pp. 214-224.

6. *Proceedings of the Executive Committee Meeting of the Democratic National Committee, August 12, 1977* (Washington, D.C.: Democratic National Committee, 1977).

7. Smith, "It's Carter Folk vs. Regular Democrats."

8. William Goodman, *The Two-Party System in the United States,* 3rd ed. (Princeton N.J.: Van Nostrand, 1964), p. 168, n. 28.

9. Ibid.

10. *The Official Proceedings of the Democratic National Convention, 1972* (Washington, D.C.: Democratic National Committee, 1972), p. 406.

11. Party Charter as adopted by the 1974 Conference on Democratic Policy and Organization, Kansas City, Missouri, December 6-8, 1974.

12. Ibid.

13. Personal communications to the author. See also Charles L. Clapp, *The Congressman: His Work As He Sees It* (Garden City, N.Y.: Doubleday Anchor, 1963), pp. 403–405.

14. Lou Cannon, "Bush Takes Over as GOP Chairman," *Washington Post,* January 20, 1973, p. 20.

15. Ibid.

16. Terence Smith, "Democratic Leader Denies White House Forced Him to Quit," *New York Times,* December 9, 1977, p. 10.

17. Ibid. A Democratic National Committee staff member had another view: "He was just too decent, too democratic for the Democrats in the White House." See Terence Smith, "Curtis to Step Down as Democrats' Chief," *New York Times,* December 8, 1977, p. 19.

18. Patrick H. Caddell, "Initial Working Paper on Political Strategy," (Mimeo., December 10, 1976), p. 28.

19. Ibid., pp. 28–29. Excerpts from the memo did not appear in the media until May 1977.

20. *Rules of Democratic National Committee* (Washington D.C.: Democratic National Committee, n.d.), pp. 1–2.

21. See Bernard Weintraub, "A Carter Fund-Raiser Backs 2 Jet Fighters," *New York Times,* December 7, 1977, p. 17. On the funding abuses within the Nixon Adminstration and their consequences, see William J. Crotty, *Political Reform and the American Experiment* (New York: Crowell, 1977), pp. 139–167.

22. Smith, "Curtis to Step Down as Democrats' Chief."

2 / The Role Orientations of State Party Chairmen

Robert J. Huckshorn

The state party chairmanship has traditionally been viewed as an unimportant office occupied by faceless men serving at the will of powerful elected officials. Those anointed with the office were seldom recognized beyond the narrow confines of the party elite group that elected them. It was generally assumed that the state chairman performed one of two functions: he was the governor's liaison with the party or, if the party was out of power, he was a focal point for a miscellany of local party groups more interested in maintaining their independent integrity than in cooperating to strengthen the state party. Nowhere was the decentralized nature of the American party system more apparent.

A former governor of a Western state remarked during an interview four years after his defeat:

> In my opinion the state chairmanship is an anachronism and a holdover from earlier days when party organization was more important and when party leaders, such as the state chairman, had more grease in the form of patronage and jobs to keep the party machinery moving effectively. During my years as Governor the state chairman has always been my hand-picked man. I have had three of them. The first, Mr.———was my campaign manager and was the most effective because I trusted him and used him. The next two,———and———,were chosen because they would be ineffective and I wanted to be my own state chairman and have total control of the party organization in my office. To accomplish this, I built an infra-structure in the Governor's office, along with some selected political supporters from outside. These three or four staff men and political friends carried out my political chores for me. I truly believe that a strong governor must exercise control of his party and cannot leave that control to an individual elected by the county chair-

Based upon material previously published in *Party Leadership in the States* (Amherst: University of Massachusetts Press, 1976). Used with permission of the publisher.

A generous grant from the National Science Foundation enabled me to undertake a wide-ranging study of state party organizations with particular emphasis on the role of the state party chairman. Between 1969 and 1974 I interviewed 80 incumbent chairmen and chairwomen and over 100 additional national, state, and local party leaders including U.S. Senators and Congressmen, governors, former chairmen, and assorted other state and local party leaders.

Throughout the selection I have used the term "chairman" in its more traditional sense to include both men and women. I considered substituting alternate terminology such as "chairperson" but concluded that, while possibly more accurate, it was also more awkward and confusing. Furthermore, every female party leader was asked and preferred to be called "chairman" or "chairwoman."

men or the state committee, both made up of inactive amateurs in more cases than not.

Other party leaders in the state confirmed the governor's assessments of his state chairmen and the relationships he maintained with them. One of the state chairmen also confirmed the governor's assessments, but pointed out that the governor's subsequent defeat was, in his opinion, largely due to his reliance on close personal political operatives who were as removed from the organizational structure of the party as was the governor himself. It may be common practice for a governor to use the office of state chairman for personal political benefit, but the relationship is usually more complex than that. Unlike the dual in-party/out-party roles of the national chairmen, determined largely by the overwhelming presence of the presidential office, roles of the state chairmen tend to be defined by a variety of relationships—depending on the nature of the particular state party system—with other party and elected officials.

No effort has been expended by political scientists toward classifying state chairmanships, although considerable work has been done on party system classification. Party classification schemes have always been difficult because they encounter problems inherent in the comparison of dissimilar economic, social, and historical data. Differences among the states produce a whole series of varied party systems. Scholars, faced with rapidly changing state election laws, organizational structures, and political personnel, have often found it difficult to make lasting comparisons. [1]

State Party Chairmen Classified by Role

As used here, role means the way in which the political actor actually performs, as opposed to the normative description of what some think should be done in this job. The expectations associated with a particular role may change on the part of the actor and on the part of those who react to him. The passage of time brings changes in attitudes, goals, and relationships. A new state chairman must learn what his role is, but may choose not to confine himself to the traditional pattern of expectations. Role learning is a process of political socialization, but as the party leader becomes more familiar and comfortable with his role, subtle changes in performance often take place. Thus, at any given time the role conception may differ while the actors remain the same.

The classification by role presented in this selection relies extensively on in-depth interviews. In order to collect sufficient data for a classification scheme, a survey was conducted that included four open-ended questions, to be answered by each of the eighty men and chairwomen interviewed. A fairly consistent pattern of the role relationships between the party leaders, elected officials, and party organizations was apparent in sixty-nine of the eighty party systems. The exceptions were parties that had just elected a governor for the first time in many years, thus providing the chairman with a new role as in-party leader. In a few instances, internal stability had been shattered by the election of a particularly dynamic and activist chairman, whose appearance on the scene created tumultuous change in a relatively short time.

Three distinct types of role situation emerged from the analysis: the *political agent*, who serves as the partisan arm of an incumbent governor; the *in-party independent*, who exercises power in his own right and maintains his position regardless of who holds the governorship; and, the *out-party independent*, who served without an elected public leader and is recognized as *the* party leader (see Table 2-1).

Table 2-1 Roles of State Party Chairmen

Role	Democrat		Republican		Total	
	(N)	Percentage	(N)	Percentage	(N)	Percentage
Political agent	(13)	33.3	(13)	31.7	(26)	32.5
In-party independent	(11)	28.2	(13)	31.7	(24)	30.0
Out-party independent	(15)	38.5	(15)	36.6	(30)	37.5
Total	(39)	100.0	(41)	100.0	(80)	100.0

In-Party and Out-Party Chairmen

The literature on national parties has viewed the role of the national chairman on an in-party/out-party power dimension. Control of the presidency has been the crucial determinant. Cotter and Hennessy devote an entire chapter to the role differences between the in-party and out-party national chairmen. They note that, "how the national chairmen play their roles will be determined, in large part, by the presence or absence of a political superior in the White House." [2]

For the in-party, there is no ambiguity of leadership and the national chairman does as he is told. The out-party leader, on the other hand, gains recognition by virtue of his position, but may not exercise control simply by virtue of possessing the chairmanship. Even though he is the national chairman, he may have to contend with competing leaders on Capitol Hill, the defeated presidential candidate, or important officeholders in major states. Nevertheless, he occupies a vacuum in leadership, and has the possibility of becoming the "real" party leader.

Virtually nothing has been written regarding the in- and out-party variations in the state chairman's role. Most writers have assumed a direct parallel with the pattern of power that prevails in the national committees; that is, the in-party chairman is chosen by the governor and ratified by the state committee. His service to the party is indistinguishable from his service to the governor. The out-party chairman, on the other hand, might exercise more leadership in his party, serving as organizational supervisor, policymaker, campaign manager, fund-raiser, but opposition spokesman. These assumptions would be natural ones, but *they would not be accurate*.

In-party/out-party status is of considerable importance to establishing the role of the state chairman, but it is not necessarily the deciding factor in that determination. In many states, the governor is not considered the head of the political party. During recent years the Democratic Party of Illinois was more often than not under the domination of the late Mayor Richard Daley of Chicago. The late U.S. Senator Harry Byrd of Virginia dominated the Democratic Party of his state for decades despite his party's control of the gubernatorial office.

Some governors operate personal organizations that bypass the state party structure presided over by the state chairman. Others must work with a chairman who is elected independently of the governor's influence and operates as a free agent. In one-party factional states, governors control their own faction, but leave the state chairmen to preside over the coordination of other factions that are controlled by political competitors. In a few cases, a particular chairman, building upon different foundations, has been able to exercise long-term control over the party organization while serving several governors. A case in point is Connecticut's long-time Democratic state chairman, the late John Bailey.

During his quarter-century as state chairman, Bailey survived defeat and party infighting among nationally known political leaders. He established himself in the mid-1950s as the most powerful Democrat in the state, and his support was considered essential to nomination and election. He was responsible for the nomination and election of four of the state's governors. Bailey was also a legislative leader and served as a crucial communications link between his governors and the party apparatus.

In many states, the type of state chairman chosen is heavily dependent upon the wishes of the governor. Some governors want a chairman who will serve as their political lightning rod. One governor noted:

> I was elected in a hot factional fight and barely squeezed through. My first chairman was picked largely to take the heat off me. He did his best but survived less than two years. At that point, I decided that I had to lead the fight myself and I selected a different kind of chairman with a different mission the second time around.

Some governors recognize the importance of the party chairman to the success of their legislative programs and select, as a vehicle for control and direction of the legislative, a person capable of building and supervising a strong party organization. One such chairman described himself as the "Deputy Governor for political affairs." The decline in one-party states has brought with it a growth in the number of competitive minority legislative parties. Some governors have had to deal with an active legislative opposition for the first time in their state's history. Without precedents to work from, they have often used the state chairman as a means of accomplishing that purpose. Some chairmen have become, in fact, legislative lobbyists for their governors' programs.

Among the weakest chairmen in the nation are those of the dominant party in non-competitive states, particularly in the South. If candidates in one-party factional state can be elected to high office without regard to party organization, they are more likely to show their allegiance to the individual supporters who helped elect them than to the party per se. Several Republican state chairmen in Southern states contolled by Democratic governors are more active and more visible than are their Democratic counterparts.

The state party systems are constantly changing. The rise of Republicanism in the South, increased competition by Democrats in traditionally Republican states, shifting voter allegiances (including formal changes of party registration), widespread growth in the number of independent voters, and widespread reelection difficulties for incumbent officeholders have all combined to bring important shifts in party competition within the various states.

Some chairmen have been successful in developing considerable concentrations of power in the office by virtue of personal style and individual initiative. That is understandable in an in-party with a governor who, wishing to stamp his own brand on his party, carefully selects a chairman to help him wield the branding iron. More difficult to explain is such power in an out-party with minimal organizational machinery, few rewards, little enthusiasm, and a history of defeats. Yet there are numerous examples of out-party chairmen who turned their parties around by concentrating power in their office.

The implicit, if not the explicit, assumption underlying party classification schemes is that parties may be categorized by some established criteria. Classification by level of competition is one of the most widely used of these schemes and is relatively easy to accomplish through analysis of voting behavior and electoral success. Classification by party structure or organizational effectiveness is more difficult because of the lack of accepted criteria and because of the great diversity in party systems. The relationships interwoven by legal responsibilities, minority/majority status leadership, personality, political environment, and the impact of the gubernatorial office make it difficult to unravel the strands essential to arriving at any acceptable classification. It is easy to categorize parties as "in" or "out." That determination is based solely on possession of the governorship. The implication, however, that all in-party chairmen behave in the same way—as do all out-party leaders—is, of course, demonstrably untrue. Furthermore, some chairmen naturally fit more than one class. Those initially selected as political agent may, in time, become powers in their own right.

The State Chairman as Political Agent

The political agent serves as the partisan arm of an incumbent governor, or in a few cases, some other elected official who, by virtue of his position and in lieu of the governorship, is able to exercise party control. The political agent has organizational responsibilities and serves as manager for the party. He serves, in effect, as the governor's deputy for political affairs. He seldom exercises real control over the party apparatus, usually deferring to the governor whom he serves. In many states an incumbent governor is the recognized leader and spokesman for his political party. He has attained this position by virtue of his successful campaign for the gubernatorial office and, by winning, has assumed the burden of party leadership. This may not mean that he has a large personal following in the party, but only that he currently holds a position of power and of recognized leadership potential. His party leadership role may rank well down in the list of responsibilities that have come to him by virtue of his election. A governor who has defeated an organizational favorite in the primary election, or one presiding over a severely factionalized party, may be the party leader in name only. Yet he may seek to lead and to unite in order to bring order to the party and to exercise whatever party discipline is available to him in dealing with the legislature.

This fact was noted by Coleman Ransone, a leading scholar of state government and politics, when he stated:

> It is primarily because we do not really have party government at the state level that the governor must continue to play the role of politician even after his election. . . . The idea of disciplined parties in the legislature who work with the governor to execute a party program is largely a none-too-effective myth at the state level. The governor is elected in an atmosphere of factional politics and he continues to operate in that atmosphere in his dealings with the legislature, with his department heads, and with the other members of the executive branch.[3]

In those states where party discipline and unity are not very evident, the governor may wish to pull the contending factions together in order to accomplish his policy goals. In those states where more highly disciplined parties are the rule, the governor may want to exercise a more continuous control over party affairs in order to remain in personal command of his political forces or to meet the expectations of other party leaders.

Nevertheless, in most states the exercise of party leadership by governors has been difficult and sometimes impossible. The decentralization of party power permits county and local leaders to hold their positions regardless of who occupies the governor's chair. These leaders, of course, owe the governor nothing, leaving him with limited means to impose party discipline. State legislators, with whom the governor must work if he is to get his programs adopted, are elected separately, in limited constituencies and often at different times. Divided party control frequently forces the chief executive to bargain with factions of both his own party and the opposition party within the legislative and executive branches. Finally, the governor's use of the constitutional powers that he commands, such as the item veto, may create more enemies than friends. Combined with the growth of state civil-service systems, which undercut much of the patronage power, these negative factors have carved out party leadership roles that are difficult for the governor to carry out effectively.

The office of governor is important, and in somes cases omnipotent, in state politics because it is the office, and not the party, that is provided for in the constitution. The result is that the office often serves as the major *raison d'être* for the party itself, and the value the party places on control of the office may well be tied to the perceived role of the governor in the party's future.

With all of these considerations in mind it is hardly surprising that some governors feel the need for an agent to serve them in their dealings with the party organization. As one governor noted:

> I got elected largely in spite of the party organization. I am the first governor to represent the Democratic party in many years and I won the office without much party help. Nevertheless, my first year in office has convinced me that I must either take over the party and make it my own or reconcile myself to the fact that I will not be able to carry out my campaign promises. In order for me to function effectively I must be able to make the Democrates in the legislature see the light and go along with me. Otherwise, my political career is going to be short and the effectiveness of the party in this state will be destroyed.

Another, more fortunate governor in a Midwestern state described his relationship with the party in this way:

> I have been the recognized leader of the party for some years. I was approached by a group of the more powerful county leaders and asked to run. I checked with the legislative leadership of the party and received their support. I had strong party support from both of the major factions in the party and I won rather decisively. I have tried to treat everyone fairly and not to play favorites. I have sorted out those party leaders who are most reliable and who appear to have control of their people. I work with them closely and have had pretty good cooperation from them. Those who appear to me to be weak or who are not enthusiastic about my governship have either been replaced or have been coddled. The result has been a honeymoon of nearly two years duration. I believe that just about everyone will tell you that I am the party leader.

Both of these governors are served by state chairmen who have assumed the role of political agent. The chairmen were both handpicked by their governors and, in each case, had served as campaign manager. They are trusted advisers who maintain a close relationship based on long years of personal loyalty, political stewardship, friendship, faith, and trust. Neither chairman appears to be offended when the governor or his personal staff rejects his advice, but in both cases that seldom appears to happen. Chairmen serving these two governors have carved out for themselves an important role as political lightning rod.

One offered this explanation of his relationship with the chief executive:

> I am the Governor's agent in the party; he maintains his control of the party through me; that doesn't mean that I am a puppet; he listens to me; he takes my advice often, but sometimes we disagree on things and he then makes up his mind on the basis of what he personally wants to do. I have daily contact with the Governor, mostly on party matters. I help with the party officials throughout the state. If he needs someone called in the party in some county, I call them. We clear positions for appointment. I represent him at places when he can't be in two places at once. So that, in general, he either calls me or I call him, I would say, once a day. By the same token, I don't have veto power over anything. I can make suggestions and I can tell him what I think about things, but he has on occasion simply ignored me and gone on.

State chairmen as political agents occupy a peculiar role. Some are intentionally overshadowed by the governor and operate quietly behind the scenes, self-effacing to the point of political obscurity. Others are in the forefront of the political battle, taking the brunt of the partisan slings and arrows, and serving as a target to deflect attention from the governor when that appears to be politically advisable.

Of the eighty state chairmen interviewed, (32.5 percent)—thirteen in each party—can be identified as political agents. These men and women see themselves as different from other state chairmen. In fact, even though the term political agent is a typical example of academic jargon, a surprising number of respondents described their role in those very words.

Although not always the case, the assignment of an agent's role to the chairman is often signaled by the way in which his candidacy is announced and his election is carried out. In those parties in which it is customary for the governor to choose the chairman-designee, the media often provide easily recognized clues. Thus, in April 1970, the New York Times reported that the New Jersey Republican state chairman was "the personal choice of Governor William T. Cahill." [4] And, according to the Columbus Citizen-Journal, the "strong hand of Governor John J. Gilligan was in evidence Sunday as the Ohio Democratic Party executive committee named (the Democratic) state chairman." [5]

The duties of the political agent are varied. Although they differ from party to party, they normally include handling patronage matters and serving as party spokesman, legislative liaison, and political strategist.

In patronage matters the chairman usually serves as the acknowledged link between the party and the governor. He is almost always a member of the patronage committee and usually is the chairman of it. One of his principal roles is to prevent any job-related development from embarrassing the governor. Most chairmen consider patronage problems to be an undesirable but necessary part of their job. Patronage represents, after all, one of the few remaining bastions of party influence. Consequently, most political agents participate in every step of the patronage process, from the initial screening of applicants to the final selection process.

Many governors prefer to speak for themselves, especially when their pronouncement will be well received. In controversial matters, however, the chairman, as political agent, may be called upon as spokesman to draw partisan fire away from the chief executive.

Legislative liaison represents a major role for most of these chairmen. If the governor wishes to force action on the part of his legislative party, without alienating key legislators at the same time, he may call upon the chairman to handle such delicate matters for him. In general, the chairman's role as legislative spokesman for the governor is widely recognized and respected. Furthermore, a dozen state chairmen served concurrently as members of the state legislature, permitting them wide latitude in carrying out this phase of their duties.

Some chairmen consider themselves as lobbyists for the party (nee Governor's) program. Thus, a Midwestern Democratic chairman stated:

> I'm in constant contact with the Governor. I am his agent to the party and the legislature. During the session I am primarily a lobbyist. The Governor makes all policy statements and develops all policy without my help. I simply try to carry it out through the legislature. We have such strong majorities in the legislature that I usually am able to get our entire platform, which is really the Governor's platform, adopted.

Other chairmen who serve as agents meet daily or weekly with the chief executive to plan party strategy and to determine what action should be taken in delicate political matters. Most acknowledged that the governor sometimes does not follow their advice, but when important political decisions are made, the agent-chairman is usually a participant in the decision making process. Such decisions usually regard party matters such as fund raising, party reform, organizational problems, and the governor's speaking schedule.

A few chairmen are agents of officeholders other than governor. In each case the chairman's party did not control the governorship but did control another major elective office. One Democratic chairman acknowledged that he served at the pleasure of a big-city mayor and was the mayor's formal contact with the party hierarchy. Two others stated that their allegiance was to a U.S. Senator. In each case the senator was the only major statewide officeholder from the party, and in each state the senator's personal organization served, to a large extent, as the state party organization.

The governor's attitude toward the political party normally determines whether or not he is to be served by a chairman as political agent. Some governors wish to maintain control of the party because they view it as a crucial vehicle for political leadership. In the short run the party leadership can be helpful in bringing the governor's program to fruition. In the long run he may see his political future inextricably tied to that of the party. In either case it is important that he have a trusted surrogate formally in charge of party affairs.

The political agent need not be a lackey or a puppet. Some agents are among the most effective and successful state chairmen currently operating within the political system. The boundaries within which they operate, however, are drawn by the governor. If he wants to keep the reins of party control taut, he may arrange the election of a chairman who will do his bidding. Some chairmen are permitted no discretionary power at all. They are truly governors' men. They do what they are told and undertake nothing on their own. It might be said that they administer the party *for* the governor.

Other chairmen, also operating as political agents, enjoy an entirely different relationship with their chief executive. They, in fact, administer the party *with* the governor. They are encouraged to engage in forthright in-house discussion of party problems and plans, and their opinions are valued. They are loyal to the governor, but they are not subservient to him. Political agents come in many varieties. Some are integral members of the governor's team. They serve without being subservient. Others do as they are told and are permitted little flexibility. The key to identifying the political agent is understanding his relationship with the govenor. That normally means that the chairman is the governor's representative to the political party.

The In-Party Independent Chairman ·

The in-party independent chairman is one who serves the party that controls the gubernatorial governorship. However, the in-party chairman either won the election without the active support of the incumbent governor, perhaps defeating the governor's choice for the chairmanship, or he occupies a place of party power in his own right. He usually has a fixed term that antedates the governor's. Some chairmen have been in office for long periods of time and have seen several governors elected during their tenure. In a few instances the governor's support was important at the time of the chairman's election, but, once elected, the in-party independent serves independently of the governor.

Of the eighty state chairmen interviewed, twenty-four (30 percent)—thirteen Republicans and eleven Democrats—are classified as in-party independents (see Table 2-1). They represent states located in various regions of the country and having a variety of party systems. In four states, both chairmen are classed as in-party independents. One Midwestern state has a long tradition of political independence, and past efforts by governors to interfere in the selection of the party chairman have been counterproductive. As described by the state's in-party independent chairmen:

> You probably know that the leadership of both parties in——is separate from the governorship. Although we are in power now, the same is true when they are in power. There was one instance in the early 1960's when Governor——, even before he was inaugurated, announced his choice for state chairman and when the Committee met the man got only two votes. Our state committees, in both the Republican and Democratic parties, are very independent—to the point of being jackass stubborn.

Of the twenty-four in-party independents, four served in Southern parties, and three of them in traditional one-party Democratic states. Yet, even with the governorship guaranteed, they operate independently, either because of party factionalism or because the official organization is separated from the governor's personal organization. One Democratic Party in the South, long noted for personal factionalized politics, has enjoyed a tradition of independent party chairmen (and state central committees) since the late 1940s. That party decided years ago that the safest way to free the party organization from fratricidal political machinations was to maintain its absolute independence.

Factionalism, moreover, is not just a Southern phenomenon. In Indiana, John K. Snyder was elected Republican state chairman in 1970 despite the active opposition of Republican Governor Edgar Whitcomb. Snyder's election resulted from a long-standing feud in the Indiana Republican party between the former state chairman and the Republican National committeeman, an ally of Governor Whitcomb. Snyder's election came about through the votes of fourteen state central committeemen, including four who voted by proxy. The remaining eight boycotted the meeting by remaining in Governor Whitcomb's office across the street from Republican state headquarters.[6]

John M. Bailey was, mentioned above, Democratic state chairman of Connecticut for over a quarter of a century. He was also the best-known in-party independent chairman. Having played a major role in the election of four Democratic governors—Chester Bowles, Abraham Ribicoff, John Dempsey, and Ella Grasso—he continued to occupy his party chair during the two occasions when Republicans controlled the statehouse during his tenure. Never an autocratic boss in the tradition of Frank Hague, Bailey survived, and often thrived, on a combination of political allegiances and tough-mindedness. He was neither too proud to beg nor too timid to swing a big stick when the need was manifest.

The in-party independent chairman has considerably more flexibility in the exercise of his powers than the political agent has. He is not bound by the personal wishes of his governor, although he obviously must be interested in them. He operates on a different level, and his power derives from sources within the party organization itself—not from the temporary holder of the gubernatorial chair. His fortune is tied to the success of the party and his goal is *party* success. He is party-oriented rather than candidate-oriented. He often tends to be a "nuts and bolts" chairman, devoting many hours to organizational matters, candidate recruitment, and efforts to influence the nominating process. This does not mean that the in-party independent can ignore the governor. Success in the statehouse is inextricably tried to the continued success of the party. The in-party independent is, however, a political compatriot rather than a party retainer.

Many of the in-party independents considered their role to be a more comfortable one than that of their brethren serving as political agents, and a more rewarding one than that of out-party independents.

The Out-Party Independent Chairman

The third type of state chairman is the out-party independent, who presides over a party that does not control the governor's office. He usually emerges from a personal power base or is elected as the choice of an unsuccessful gubernatorial candidate. In some states the party seldom, if ever, holds the governorship and is always presided over by an out-party independent. This is the case for most Republican parties in the South. In other states the party may control one or more offices below the gubernatorial level or in the Congress. In still others the problems associated with factionalized parties bring about the election of chairmen who can mediate factional disputes while attempting to build a party organization.

Of the eighty state chairmen interviewed, thirty (37.5 percent of the total) are out-party independents. They are equally divided between the two major parties and represent states from all regional areas. They represent the only category without a governor.

An example was a Midwestern chairman who was elected to lead a party that had not controlled the governorship for over 20 years. Selected as chairman-designee by the most recent gubernatorial candidate, this man remained in office after the candidate's defeat. His most serious problem was the shortage of viable candidates for statewide races, and this, in turn, caused serious morale problems with the party hierarchy. The local organizations had deteriorated during the long office drought, and much of his effort was devoted to attempts to revive the substructure. This chairman was widely recognized as the *real* leader of the party. His major problem centered on re-creating a party to lead.

Other parties have traditions of electing chairmen with all the panoply and strategic infighting associated with an election campaign. Although the candidates for chairman sometimes are "sponsored" by leading public officials, they often win the position on the strength of personal support and by virtue of their own tactics.

Several chairmen noted that the role of the party leader in their respective states depends in large part on whether the party controls the governorship. The status of a party as "in" or "out" is a crucial one. A Midwestern chairman remarked:

> In————, the chairman must have the support of the governor and do pretty much what he says. Unfortunately, we lost the governorship two years ago and that casts us in a different situation. Without the governorship the chairman becomes the recognized political leader. We have both U.S. Senators but they have neither one ever shown any real interest in the party. They leave us alone and we leave them alone. I am expected to do all the things that you would normally expect a party leader to do. If we had the top office, I would simply be the political arm of the Governor.

It is quite true, as the chairman has noted, that the nature and importance of the chairmanship of the party that is out of power depends on the tradition of party government in the state, the availability of elected leadership (aside from the governor), the composition of the state committee, and the talent of the chairman. In some states the tradition of nonactivist chairmen is so strong as to preclude strengthening the office or even undertaking to strike out in new directions. Sometimes, the number of weak party identifiers who hold party office is virtually impossible to overcome.

Some state parties, notably those of the Southern Republicans, occupy no state offices and have few if any state legislative seats. The fact that there is no elected leadership in the state forces the chairman to assume the burden. Approximately one-half of the Southern Republican chairmen appear to have adopted for themselves a role as party spokesman, but most of them do little else. The other half, undismayed by their party's perpetual failure to win local and state offices, act as though they play a real part in a competitive two-party system. They work at party organization, make speeches, raise money, and issue policy statements. They often voice the intention of building a party apparatus that can serve to translate Southern Republican presidential votes into votes for state and local candidates. The attitude of the chairman toward his state committee is of considerable importance to his success. Most out-party independents maintained that they had a good relationship, but one that was dependent upon the chairman's good will toward the committee. The state committee appears to be of considerably more importance to the out-party chairman because it serves as his source of strength and because it often is most responsible for his election to the office. Even so, some state parties have traditional nonactivist state committees. The members are often those who have contributed their money in years past but have preferred to remain relatively inactive. The relationship to the chairman, once he is elected, is often perfunctory. One chairman stated:

> I have meetings twice a year although the by-laws don't require more than one annual meeting. I quickly discovered that the members have nothing to offer and even resent being asked to attend. I keep holding meetings, though, because it gives the party some semblance of life.

Another out-party chairman, in a state with strong two-party competition, argued that state committee participation is most important. He noted:

I am very active with the State Committee. It participates in all policy matters and meets monthly. We now have almost a full quota of members and although they give me a free hand to carry out the day to day activities of the organization, I would never take a major action without consulting them in advance. They respect me for that and they seldom ever go against my wishes. They know that I will respect their wishes or try to convince them to change their minds. I think it is a good system.

The final determinant of the out-party chairman's power is most subjective. The talent and enthusiasm of the chairman is not something that can be measured quantitatively, but it is a very important ingredient in determining the success of the party. One must talk with many chairmen before distinctions in style and ability become apparent. Even then there is great danger that an incumbent's true role may be misjudged. There are, nevertheless, marked distinctions between the abilities of out-party (as well as in-party) chairmen.

Some chairmen impress the observer as having taken to heart George Washington's warning to avoid the "baneful effects of the spirit of party." They have avoided those "baneful effects" by doing little or nothing to improve the out-party's fortunes. In some cases, and sometimes for legitimate reasons, they maintain no office, have no secretary, perform no duties, and carry out none of the responsibilities normally expected of a party leader. This is also true of some in-party chairmen, but in most cases, they merely are following the role assigned to them by an incumbent governor.

Subjectively, the more impressive out-party chairmen are those who have established goals for themselves, appear to have the native ability and experience to accomplish most of them, and work doggedly to succeed. As leaders of the party out of power, they would find few who would argue with their goals.

Role Types of State Party Chairmen

Each chairman must approach his office within the boundaries laid down by party tradition, party law, and the political exigencies of the moment. The right personality elected to office at the right time can overcome the mossiest of traditions and the hoariest of laws. To do so requires a goal-oriented, ambitious, dedicated, and talented person willing to devote himself to overcoming the obstacles placed in his path.

The three types of state chairmen play very different roles. Their power is often, but not always, a product of the type of party organization they represent. Control of the governorship is the key to their style and position. The power of a political agent may be as great as, or greater than, that of the in-party or out-party independent. The political agent who serves an activist governor can wield considerable power and influence.

The in-party independent is often viewed as the "organizational" leader, while his governor is looked upon as the "political" leader. This may appear to be a meaningless distinction, but it is one that is sometimes cited.

The out-party independent is usually recognized as the *real* party leader and, if the party is more than a rudimentary collection of individuals, can be powerful in his own right. The measurement of power, in other words, is relative. The degree of discretion enjoyed by the chairman may depend on his role as political agent, in-party independent, or, out-party independent—the political agent having the least authority and the out-party independent, the most. Examples can be found, however, in which the degree of discretion available to the chairman escalates in the opposite direction.

Most out-party independent chairmen view themselves as *the* party leader. As such they assume a great burden of responsibilities as party spokesman, mediator between party factions, and campaign strategist. In a sense, the role of the out-party independent is the easiest because he does not have to mesh the party organization to the governor's personal organization. Most chairmen in this category, however, would argue that their role is more difficult because they do not have an elected leader to rely on for advice and to provide leadership and focus for party affairs. Some chairmen play the role of out-party independent reluctantly and look forward to the day when they, or their successors, can become political agents or in-party independents.

NOTES

1. Some of the more useful classifications are presented in the following: Austin Ranney and Willmoore Kendall, *Democracy and the American Party System* (New York: Harcourt Brace Jovanovich, 1956), chap. 7; Joseph A. Schlesinger, "A Two-Dimensional Scheme for Classifying the States According to Degree of Inter-Party Competition," *American Political Science Review* 49 (December 1955): 1120; Coleman B. Ransone, Jr., *The Office of Governor in the United States* (University: University of Alabama Press, 1956), chaps. 2–4; V.O. Key, Jr., *American State Politics: An Introduction* (New York: Knopf, 1956), pp. 98–99; Richard Hofferbert, "Classifications of American Party Systems," *Journal of Politics* 26 (August 1964): 550–567; Richard E. Dawson and James A. Robinson, "Inter-party Competition, Economic Variables, and Welfare Politics in the American States," *Journal of Politics* 25 (May 1963): 265–289; Robert T. Golembiewski, "A Taxonomic Approach to State Political Party Strength," *Western Political Quarterly* 11 (1958): 494–513; and Austin Ranney, "Parties in State Politics," chap. 3 in *Politics in the American States*, eds. Herbert Jacobs and Kenneth N. Vines (Boston: Little, Brown, 1971).

2. Cornelius P. Cotter and Bernard C. Hennessy, *Politics Without Power: The National Party Committees* (New York: Atherton, 1964), chap. 5. See also William Crotty, "The National Committees as Grass-roots Vehicles of Representation," in this volume.

3. Ransone, *The Office of Governor*, p. 94. At the time Ransone was writing, this was probably a correct statement. Subsequent efforts to strengthen the state party organizations in many states may have softened it somewhat, although without comparable data from earlier years, it is impossible to measure party growth objectively.

4. *New York Times*, April 28, 1970.

5. *Columbus Citizen-Journal*, January 11, 1971, p. 1.

6. *Chicago Tribune*, November 27, 1970.

3 / Party Organizational Personnel and Electoral Democracy in Los Angeles, 1963-1972

Dwaine Marvick

The Los Angeles cadres project has, for twenty years, investigated the lives of party activists in Los Angeles. From the first major effort in 1956, the project has been systematically comparative, seeking each year to relate the campaign efforts and political perspectives found among a sample of active Democrates with those of a counterpart sample of active Republicans. The same interview forms have been used in parallell inquiries. In the subset analized here (1963, 1968, 1969, 1972), the samples of rival party cadres were matched to the apportionment formula used to establish county committee representation. Moreover, each year we were successful in obtaining consistently good response rates from ail thirty-one component district organizations in each party. The political circumstances of each wave were, of course, different—an interim springtime period in 1963, a primary campaign in 1968, an interim autumn period in 1969, and a general election campaign in 1972. By the same token, however, use of the county committee rosters as sample frames provided us each year with an equivalent set of localized peculiarities and, often, with the same participants.

The aims of this selection are the following:

1. To consider the implications of ideological asymmetry and well-matched rival parties for modern electoral democracy.

2. To suggest certain advantages of considering party phenomena from the viewpoint of participating observers (party organizational personnel).

3. To describe the Los Angeles situation in recent years, showing how well matched in equivalent resources the Republican and Democratic organizations have been.

4. To demonstrate the stability and substantive content of the ideological wings of rival major parties in Los Angeles.

5. To explore the implications of persistent ideological harmony (and dissonance) within each party's ranks.

This selection is a revised version of a research report prepared for delivery at the Ninth World Congress, International Political Science Association, Montreal, Canada, August 19-25, 1973. Since the report was delivered, two more waves of interviews (in 1974 and 1976) have been conducted with the same panel respondents in the Los Angeles area. The results, developing leads put forward in this paper, will appear in a forthcoming book, *Party Cadres and Electoral Democracy*.

6. To report the high level of political agreement among activists of both parties about where partisan voters stand on the issues and to demonstrate that such assessments are not substantially distorted by the policy preferences of those same activists.

Ideological Asymmetry and Well-Matched Rival Parties

In the study of politics, "party" is a key term. Yet there is a disturbing and pervasive ambiguity about what that term means and about the phenomena to which it refers. Parties are organizations whose activities are widely acknowledged to shape their host political systems in distintive ways. Parties are often characterized as primary mechanisms used for (1) leadership selection, (2) regime evaluation, (3) citizen participation, (4) group mediation, (5) political legitimization, and (6) mobilization of public support. Moreover, these and other functions are performed by entities called "parties" in what, by any judgment, would be considered sharply contrasting political order.[1]

Often these same functions are, in whole or part, carried out also by mechanisms that most participants and most analysts would want to call parties. Students of party phenomena have understandably backed off from functional definitions because of the Pandora's box thus opened. The complexity of party function is not merely related to the various forms of and labels for corporate organizational structures. The notion of "party" commonly refers to attitudes and belief structures as well. Partisanship is an integral part of the phenomena to be examined.

The functions attributed to political parties, seen as corporate structures, vary over time and vary by context. The domain within which partisanship operates as a guide for behavior is similarly diverse and changing. Under "movement regimes" that tolerate no organized opposition, parties emerge that espouse and champion revolutionary and subversive goals. In this context, partisanship carries the connotation of disciplined zeal.[2] Later, the same party apparatus may be used for bureaucratic surveillance—to guide and control the machinery of policy implementation and social change.

In the quite different context of stable electoral democracies, several parties all perform the parallel functions of sponsoring candidates for key leadership posts and formulating basic programs for government action. The point of permitting several parties to carry out the same functions is, of course, to vest the power to hire and fire in the electorate—and indirectly the power to choose between the programmatic alternatives for which rival men and parties stand—and to do so *whenever* the rival parties compete seriously from roughly equivalent resource positions.[3]

To be sure, each party's campaign problems will be different. In a given constituency, the electoral support base for rival parties is often unevenly distributed; realistically, each party's aims have to be tailored accordingly. Still, in many Los Angeles constituencies, competition has been serious and significant. Well-matched rival parties have, in different measure, tried (1) to mobilize loyal followings, (2) to recruit new voters, and (3) to convert the wavering backers of the rival party. In 1963, our informants were asked to indicate how they would rank those three campaign goals: 72 percent of the Democrats and only 58 percent of the Republicans gave top priority to recruiting new voters. Both sets of partisans gave second rank to mobilizing their loyal supporters, but, again, the Democrats were more in agreement (71 percent) than were the Republicans (55 percent). It is especially noteworthy that converting those who usually vote the other way was not considered a high-priority campaign goal: 79 percent of the Democrats and 68 percent of the Republicans ranked it lowest of the three campaign goals considered.

In any electoral democracy, there are reasons why rival party organizations in the same locality will look somewhat alike. There are functional grounds for expecting considerable *performance symmetry.*

The basic rivalry between party organizations means that one party's workers are likely to be preoccupied with the same electoral considerations that concern the other party's workers. What issue-publics are forming in the constituency? How can potential support be translated into real votes? What campaign tactics are feasible in this locality?

Moreover, those activists who are potentially instrumental in affecting the outcome of the election will tend to become professionalized; that is, they will come to value and to acquire the same skills concerning how to organize, how to communicate, and how to analyze political realities. This socialization process seems likely to go on regardless of the ideological leanings or group interests that may have initially prompted a person to join and work in a party. Insofar as the professional veneer overlays earlier predilections and sympathies, it may come to mute and transform an individual's outlook: an experienced activist may become a person quite different from the political enthusiast he was formerly. It is not clear, however, if the process of political professionalization encourages any attenuation of loyalty or of sensitivity to the earlier norms, aspirations, and ideological leanings of the group. It may, on the other hand, serve only to produce more formidable advocates.

Furthermore, those who work actively in an organization discuss, in addition to policy-relevant topics, a wide range of organizational problems. Inevitably, such discussions result in further homogenization of the participants frames of reference.

The prerequisites of democracy are not a set of readily defined characteristics of a "modal citizen" that need to be approximated by virtually all adults. Rather, modern democracy flourishes because of the diversity of roles and opportunties available to its citizens. It is evident that—within the political subculture, within the ranks of each party, within a given echelon of a party's organizational structure—party workers can be classified in various types, depending on their motives, skills, attitudes, and activities. To note the presence of diversity, however, does not preclude a search for distinctive modalities or significant forces straining toward polarity. [4]

To compete seriously, the rival organizations must be well matched, although, to be sure, one party may compensate for a lack of money by an abundance of voluntary help, or may seek to offset the opposition's attractive program for governmental action by choosing a candidate whose personal magnetism and stature are counterweights. Given these and other complications, something that can be called *performance symmetry* still seems necessary if electoral democracy, by vesting genuine power in the electorate, is to make the election-day outcome open to doubt.

But this still does not indicate whether the election-day choice will be meaningful. One may wonder whether the "in's" or the "out's" will be elected; once in, the former out's may, and sometimes do, behave much as did the former in's. It is necessary to ask whether the rival parties stand for alternative styles of governing, for alternative programs of public-policy implementation, and for the alternative notions of persistence and change.

In short, it is necessary to establish in what sense the rival parties are *asymmetrical.* In part, the answer calls for tracing the stable coalitions of support that back the winning and losing sides. Important lines of investigation have recently begun to clarify the lines of electoral division in Western democracies. If it is true that one party finds its core support in certain segments of the society while its rival champions the interests of other communities within the political system, then it seems likely that the social composition of each party would mirror its strong ties to certain geographic, ethnic, and social-status groupings. There might be considerable overlapping, of course. Eldersveld has noted how political parties seek to compensate for their deficiency in certain social credentials by bringing forward spokespersons with the appropriate speech habits, lifestyle, and community access. [5]

It has long been a commonplace in American politics that the Republican Party stands for the dominant status groups in the electorate while the Democratic Party champions the cause of the less privileged. In the samples of Los Angeles committee members, however, it is quite difficult to demonstrate that the volunteers who choose to work in the Republican cause are significantly more affluent, better educated, or more established than the cadres who form the Democratic ranks.

Insofar as the social credentials of cadres in clientele-oriented party structures are well matched, it can be argued rather persuasively that the support base of each party is likely to be uncertain, that traditional affinities will be weak, and that group-interested voters will implement their goals on election day by more calculated and more situationally defined considerations. Group-allegiance patterns are likely to fluctuate when each of the rival party organizations openly seeks to cater to a specific social group.

Often, in the Los Angeles area, the electoral rivalry has taken place between just such reasonably well-matched—with equivalent political resources and social credentials—adversary groups. In other areas, the campaigns waged by rival camps are unbalanced, and the result is a foregone conclusion. Still, in Los Angeles, political parties harnessed to electoral functions often compete seriously and hard. In these circumstances, party organizational personnel—by their efforts to shape the election-day choices available to voters—can be said to affect regularly and demonstrably the substance as well as intensity of political conflict within a modern society. [6]

When the substance of policy alternatives embodied in election-day choices are considered, the ideological dimensions of *asymmetry* emerge. It is quite possible, as we shall see, for rival parties to be well matched in campaign resources and in social credentials, and nevertheless to be heavily weighted in opposite directions when it comes to philosophies of public policy. Edmund Burke once characterized a political party as essentially made up of like-minded men: "Party is a body of men united, for promoting by their joint endeavors the national interest, upon some particular principle." [7]

It is not easy to see this as an accurate description of parties dominated by political machines or of party spokespersons negotiating a coalition of convenience with hard-headed interest-group leaders. At the same time, when we examine the ranks of party organizations in a context like Los Angeles, where participation is voluntary and the incentives are largely solidary and purposive rather than material, there is good reason to take Burke's definition as a statement with considerable descriptive accuracy. To study the role of ideology in the rival parties of modern electoral democracies requires more than inferences derived from reading party platforms or from analyzing candidate speeches. It calls for detailed and systematic data to clarify the patterned quality of the views held by consciously different types of party organizational personnel.

Participating Informants: A Conceptualization

There is need for a conception of party phenomena that will facilitate systematic study not only of tightly disciplined party structures but also of loosely knit apparatuses, and that will encourage attention to the attitude structures of partisanship as well as to the corporate structures manned by party cadres. What is here called a *participating-informant* approach to the study of party phenomena seems promising.

A participant-defined model starts with the view that political parties are at once extensive corporate structures ready to undertake joint efforts, and a network of shared attitudinal patterns that are invoked from time to time in the perspectives of people who are otherwise occupied in the interim. The participant-defined model emphasizes how to secure consciously coordinated efforts from participants who have only a few things in common; the model emphasizes how to obtain routine contributions from personnel who are assumed to share a reasoned commitment to a set of collective goals.

What are the hallmarks of a participating-informant approach? The first is attention to *communication patterns*—who sends messages and who listens; how easy it is (from a given location) to send a message, and how easy it is to hear what is communicated. The "acoustical" properties of the various sectors making up an extended party structure largely depend on the attitudinal predispositions of the participants themselves. This is so for both receptive partisans in the electorate and recalcitrant cadres in the organization proper. We can hope to build a better conception of the acoustical properties that prevail by studying the responses of informants. We should recognize, however, that the acoustical properties often characterize only certain effective structural extents of a party apparatus, rather than the whole, potentially operative, machine.

It may be hypothesized that group sensitivity to the acoustical limitations on communication within a loosely knit party apparatus is likely to make party activists relatively skeptical about the utility of printed messages and even of group conferences. Activists are likely to feel that nobody reads and nobody listens. Conversely, they are likely to put heavy trust on personal contacts, reports from eyewitnesses, and great reliance on individual messengers.

The second hallmark of a participating-informant approach is the attention it focuses on the *task-performance problems* that correspond to the manpower available for party work at the time and place in question. Many on-line campaign decisions are time-specific and irreversible. This is especially so at the grass-roots level, where quasi-autonomous party spokespersons must respond to voters who expect immediate answers. Again, it is those who participate who must inform us. It is not the competence or availability of individual activists that needs to be explained so much as it is the resulting party-unit performance in the immediate geographic locale. It is also critically important to study the constituencywide consequences of running a campaign in which grass-roots party units have markedly different performance records. [8]

It may be hypothesized that sensitivity to the "stratarchic" autonomy [9] of party units, which are only nominally coordinated by the constituency-wide apparatus, is likely to make a party activist skeptical about the workability of feedback mechanisms. In loosely knit, extended structures like political parties, it is probably more important to provide grass-roots personnel with stock answers to and fallbacks for electioneering problems (whenever these can be anticipated). It is probably rather futile to expect to steer a campaign effort from some remote vantage point in the organizational superstructure.

Moreover, attention to task performance by party units is important if we wish to map the organizational terrain. It is important to know which units are "hopeless," which are "improving," and which are "reliably good." Whatever these terms mean to the participants themselves becomes significant and the level of participant agreement can be studied. Near consensus from the participating informers about a particular party unit provides a warranted supposition about the objective facts; lack of consensus among those in a position to know about the performance of a particular party outpost or of a coordinating unit is evidence of an organizational situation in flux.

The third hallmark of a participating-informant approach to party life is the attention it calls to *substantive political views*. Participation is not simply measured by the amount of time contributed or the campaign tasks completed. It is important also to know who cares and who is relatively indifferent about a policy position or a campaign tactic. Obstacles to joint effort often result from finding out that colleagues hold odd opinions or disconcerting views about what is to be done.

In organizations loosely held together by the versatile performance of liaison personnel—and party apparatuses must rely especially upon such persons—considerations such as ambition, spite, embarrassment, and tactlessness can prove to be of pivotal weight. So can political opinions. If liaison figures adopt rigid ideological positions, or espouse policies that antagonize the party's outpost personnel with whom they must work, then the impediments thus introduced into a campaign effort—more than minor obstacles—can become systematic sources of distortion and sabotage for the whole party effort. [10]

Grass-roots personnel are indispensable to partisan campaign efforts. Local activists possess certain residual controls over how the campaign is waged in their locality. It is, after all, up to the active partisans and enthusiasts to carry the party messages into lukewarm or even hostile quarters. They personalize the standardized campaign appeals that are broadcast to mass-media audiences. Whether grass-roots personnel make speeches, contact voters systematically, or merely talk politics with their daily associates, they convey not only the basic campaign themes—insofar as they understand the desired emphasis—but also their own ethical and ideological commentary (through words and gestures) and the social and political credentials of their personal status.

Well-Matched Rival Parties in Los Angeles

Los Angeles is a sprawling metropolitan area. It exemplifies many of the sociopolitical conditions that are increasingly present as complicating factors in industrial nations. Population increases, high mobility rates, and growing demands for urban services have strained existing political structures and have undermined habitual sources of party support. The apparent advantage in numbers enjoyed by the dominant party is regularly challenged by serious competition. Each of the major parties, in its primaries as well as during general election periods, must engage in strenuous electioneering and voter-mobilization efforts.

Party organizations in Los Angeles are loosely knit structures. At the neighborhood level, voluntary political clubs flourish. There is a persistent nucleus of party organizational effort at the legislative district level, but there is virtually no direction or control exercised by the countywide structures of either party. In this kind of variegated pattern of overlapping constituency lines and municipal boundaries, there are frequent ticket splitters, maverick candidates, and hostile cliques in each party. A persistent appeal to nonpartisan and independent positions is made in all campaigns.

In California, the county committee is the lowest level of official party organization, as prescribed by statutes promulgated around 1910, during the Progressive era. Largely because of the nonpartisan nature of municipal and schoolboard elections, there are no statutory provisions for precinct, ward, or city party units. At primary election time, rank-and-file party voters, elect county central-committee members for two-year terms, either by assembly or supervisorial districts. Each of the thirty-one state assembly districts located within Los Angeles county is entitled to seven seats on each party's county committee. These district delegations are chosen at the June primary in even-numbered years. Often, rival slates are sponsored by intraparty factions. In both parties, it is not uncommon for ten to fifteen candidates to compete for these party-leadership posts. On the other hand, the typical primary voter pays little attention to selecting the county committee. Incumbency practically guarantees retention. Openings arise chiefly because substantial numbers of incumbents fail to file for reelection.

A California legislative report puts it succinctly: "Although the selection process of county committeemen appears to be inadequate, the responsibilities of the committee are commensurate." The statute defining the powers of these committees

> is ambiguous and gives the county committees no particular power except that which they can carve out for themselves. Limitations of funds, lack of political activity on a local level in which a county committee can participate, and lack of any patronage resources further limit the strength and vitality of the county committee. [11]

Individual members of a county committee may be influential within their party, but this is not necessarily true. Even when such influence is present, it is often due to factors such as social contacts, community status, or political experience, which do not stem from committee membership.

Although the resulting party conclave is virtually powerless as an authoritative control unit, it has provided a convenient and comprehensive sample frame for the periodic selection of matched samples of rival party cadres. In 1956, we used voluntary club rosters together with a snowball eligibility technique to select nearly 350 party activists, who represented about 90 percent of all those who were party activists in three selected assembly districts. In 1963, 1968, 1969, and 1972, we used the sample frame prescribed by law to ensure representativeness in county-level party deliberations. This legal grind ensures geographic diversity. Moreover, it reflects, with equivalent weight for each party, the actual degree of grass-roots competition and intramural struggle that exist in the thirty-one districts within the county. Even without technical weighting to reflect minor differences in our response rates, the completed interviews provide well-matched samples of Los Angeles "middlemen of politics": from those who, in four recent years, were significantly active in the Democratic and Republican party organizational structures to those who participated at the countywide level.

Like Herbert McClosky's 1956 use of each party's national convention roster of delegates as a sample frame to study what he termed "party leaders," the Los Angeles surveys here discussed are designed to get a cross section of party cadres. [12] These are party activists who work at the grass-roots level. Year by year, in both parties, about half of these people reported having been active in party work for at least 15 years. Clear majorities in both parties reported themselves as currently "very active" in both voluntary clubs and the county committee.

There is much overlap in membership between the county committee and the state committee. Nearly half of those listed on each party's roster in a given year had at some time been members of the state central committee. Although this committee is another official entity with little power, its composition reflects the manpower situation in each legislative district because its members are appointed by the party nominee thereof. Typically, candidates for state assembly, state senate, or the congress reward their most active campaign associates with appointment to the statewide committee.

Many county committee members are politically ambitious, though by no means all. Of those on the Los Angeles county committee, one in every four or five reported having held public office at some time, typically at the local level. When respondents were asked if they would consider taking "a responsible party position if the opportunity arose," each year approximately half of our Democratic and Republican informants responded, "definitely yes."

Using the county committee rosters as sample frames thus has resulted in obtaining good cross sections of party organizational personnel. Inevitably some committee members were only nominally active at the time of their interviews, but even these individuals reported that at earlier stages they too had held office and wielded influence in party circles. Most of the committee members were men and women whose commitment to party work, during and between campaigns, was unflagging, clearly engrossing to them, and extraordinarily time consuming.

Analysis of the social characteristics of Democratic and Republican Party committee members in the four surveys carried out between 1963 and 1972 brings out both similarities and differences between the parties. Evidently, the two parties both draw heavily upon the upper-middle-class strata of the community. At the same time, these recent studies do not support the conclusions of our 1956 study of campaign activists in Los Angeles, in which the Republican Party was shown to draw more heavily upon the dominant-status segments, while the Democratic Party was shown to recruit more often from aspiring strata within the middle class. Count for count, as Table 3-1 shows, the social characteristics of our matched samples of Democratic and Republican party activists are quite similar and quite stable through time.

A few trends can be discerned: the number of individuals under age thirty in the ranks of both parties is growing, and the modal income levels are steadily rising. But the typical party activist is no more likely to claim a more complete formal education in 1972 than he was in 1963. Another constant is sex and marital status. Both parties are heavily stocked with family men.

Still, there are some persistent differences that should be noted. The Republican Party is the party of Protestants, whereas a substantial part of the Democratic Party's ranks is represented by Jews. Businessmen and executives are more often to be found in Republican circles; lawyers and other professionals are more frequent among Democrats.

In reporting our 1956 findings, also, we stressed a difference in the *meaning* campaign participation seemed to have for activists in the rival parties. Our observations then were that Democrats were implicitly seeking to gain status through their organizational roles in party life, and that Republicans more often seemed to play similar roles in order to affirm status already possessed in the community. Analysis of these 1963-1972 data is not finished on these counts, but preliminary runs do not suggest a persistence into the 1960s of that finding from the Eisenhower period.

Despite differences, both parties were staffed primarily by upper-middle-class volunteers. Neither could really boast a roster that was a representative cross section of ethnic and nationality groupings, social classes, or occupational categories.

Table 3-1 Personal Characteristics of Los Angeles County Committee Members (in percentages)

(N)	Democratic Cadres				Republican Cadres			
	1972 (173)	1969 (223)	1968 (153)	1963 (146)	1972 (185)	1969 (214)	1968 (148)	1963 (165)
Age								
Up to 30	30	33	8	8	38	40	5	10
31 to 49	28	35	70	78	31	36	62	67
50 plus	42	32	22	14	31	24	33	23
Sex								
Male	78	79	74	83	68	80	79	79
Female	22	21	26	17	32	20	21	21
Married with Children	83	83	88	88	88	89	86	84
Occupation								
Professional								
Business	43	69	56	51	32	54	49	42
Administration	29	14	20	29	35	25	33	37
Other	28	17	24	20	33	21	18	21
Education								
No college	6	10	13	17	12	9	9	16
Some college	29	29	28	18	30	30	23	24
Full college	65	61	59	65	58	61	68	60
Income								
Lower	45	33	25	16	33	27	30	17
Middle	26	36	47	46	28	35	40	47
Upper	29	31	28	38	39	38	30	36
Religion								
Protestant	34	34	36	38	75	70	73	73
Catholic	18	20	22	26	16	12	12	17
Jewish	26	25	23	25	3	3	4	3
Other	4	8	7	4	3	9	5	5
None	18	13	12	7	3	6	6	2
Ethnicity								
Anglo	86	79	80	92	94	90	92	95
Black	10	9	8	8	6	7	6	5
Chicano	3	10	11	—	0	2	2	—
Other	1	2	1	0	0	1	0	—

Notes: 1963 age code is by decade of birth. Thus coding categories are "up to 33," "34 to 53," and "54 plus." The low-income threshold varies: maxima were $16,000 in 1972, $12,000 in 1969, $10,000 in 1968, $7,500 in 1963. Also, the high-income bracket begins at $24,000 in 1972, $21,000 in 1969 and 1968, $15,000 in 1963.

Party organizations that depend heavily on volunteers for their manpower tend to draw more heavily from the middle class than do party organizations that operate primarily on a spoils or patronage basis (e.g. the older Eastern and Midwestern urban machines). Early studies of Chicago, downstate Illinois, and upstate New York all indicated that party workers were uniformly drawn much more heavily from lower segments of the social structure. Formerly, politics was a career avenue neglected by the middle classes, so to speak. Recent West Coast studies in Seattle, the San Francisco area, and Los Angeles reverse this staffing picture. In Detroit, however, Eldersveld's data for 1956 show a dramatic difference between the working-class ranks of the Democratic Party and the middle-class composition of its Republican rival. [13]

That the two party organizations in Los Angeles should draw heavily from middle-class strata is not surprising, of course, in light of work showing how political participation is linked to social circumstances and rearing patterns. It does not follow, however, that the rival parties agitate for the same causes or champion the same subcommunity interests.

The Ideological Wings of Parties in Los Angeles

Ideology is not supposed to have much importance in American political life. It is one of the distinctive features of American politics that we have maintained a two-party system despite many changes in our social and economic order, and despite the political tensions thrown up by those fundamental changes. Europeans have often acknowledged the role of ideology as a force that maintains the identity of parties and sparks a competition between parties, making election-day choices more meaningful. Americans do not make equivalent claims. For a long time, American political parties have been seen as essentially nonideological in character. Support for this view has been widespread among serious scholars examing the American political system.

Typically, the primary characteristics of American parties are said to be (1) cooperation with certain enduring special interest groups, rather than reliance on political convictions about complex issues, and (2) emotional attachments to symbols of regional or ethnic origin, rather than concern with philosophies. These have been the basic party characteristics seen by observers of American parties. Edmund Burke's definition of party is often quoted to show what the American party system is not. Maurice Duverger, in his comparative study, *Political Parties*, discusses the nonprinciples character of American parties: "The two parties are rival teams, one occupying office and the other seeking to dislodge it. It is a struggle between the ins and the outs, which never becomes fanatical, and creates no deep cleavage in the country. [14] The result, he argues, is that elections cannot rightly be considered to represent a popular choice between policies.

Duverger's view is common to many political scientists and observers of the American party system. This view however, bears little relationship to the findings in our Los Angeles surveys. When party organizational personnel were asked why they joined their party and what differences they felt existed between parties, they regularly answered in rudimentary ideological terms. They were quite willing to characterize themselves as liberals, moderates, or conservatives. They found no difficulty in comparing their own ideological position with that of their friends, family, job associates, neighbors, or fellow party activists.

Asked to indicate their policy preferences on a set of current public issues, almost no one equivocated. Moreover, the policy preferences of liberal Democrats were manifestly and persistently different from those of moderate Democrats, and the preferences voiced by conservative Republicans were also strikingly different from those of moderate Republicans. Equally important is the finding that Democratic moderates are repeatedly found to have policy views quite different from those of Republican moderates. Evidently, these

Table 3-2 Ideological Self-Ratings by Los Angeles County Committee Members (in percentages)

Self-Ratings (N)	Democratic				Republican			
	1972	1969	1968	1963	1972	1969	1968	1963
Radical	7	6	—	—	—	—	—	—
Liberal	61	56	50	66	4	1	2	3
Moderate	28	30	43	25	38	31	34	32
Conservative	1	5	5	4	54	63	60	58
Unsure	3	3	2	5	4	5	4	7
	(175)	(224)	(164)	(146)	(185)	(215)	(148)	(165)

terms of ideological self-characterization are party-specific, at least in the data base generated by ten years of inquiry in Los Angeles county.

The set of eight interview samples analyzed here consists of four surveys of Democratic activists and four of Republicans. Responses of the Los Angeles county committee members interviewed in these surveys—which were conducted in 1963, 1968, 1969, and 1972—indicate quite asymmetric patterns of ideological self-description. Table 3-2 gives the details. In each of the Democratic samples, the modal term of self-description was "liberal," and the only widely chosen alternative was "moderate." A few self-styled "radicals" appeared; even fewer used the term "conservative" to describe themselves. Conversely, in each of the Republican samples, the modal term was "conservative"; again the alternative term was "moderate" rather than, in this case, "liberal" or "radical."

In the analysis that follows, Democratic radical cases that show up in 1969 and 1972 have not been discarded. Rather, they are grouped with the liberals. Similarly, Democrats who called themselves conservatives were too few to handle separately. They were not left out, however, but were merged with the party moderates. A few Republicans called themselves liberal, and they have been merged with the moderates of their party.

This is not an attempt to insist upon a common transpersonal meaning for the terms "conservative" or "liberal," and much less for "moderate." These are operative terms, used matter-of-factly by party activists. For a partisan to employ one of them as a term of self-description is an act of self discipline. The man or woman using such a term is invoking a touchstone for self-constraint. We are not concerned with the labels used by activists to characterize their ideological position. An assumption is made that something like a left-to-right continuum is operative in the self-characterization acts of our respondents. Radical is left of liberal; conservative is right of moderate. This elementary ordering principle is widely understood by American adults.

Party activists of both parties in Los Angeles showed in various ways their matter-of-fact acceptance of the fact that *meaningful differences in patterned political preferences* divided the activists into wings of their own party and sustained a clear basis for differentiating one party's ideological tendencies from those of its rival.

Ideological determinants of activity in politics were studied in two ways: first, by measuring, in various ways, the *issue content* of the ideologies espoused by active party workers; and second, by tracing the sense of *ideological harmony* felt by the party workers to

Table 3-3 Policy Preference Distances Within and Between Parties: Average Percentage-Point Differences on Six Liberal Policies

Liberal Democrat	⟷	Moderate Democrat	⟷	Moderate Republican	⟷	Conservative Republican
1972	21.6		30.8		18.3	
1969	18.2		19.9		18.0	
1968	14.0		21.0		15.3	

Table 3-4 1968 Ideological Self-Ratings and Policy Preferences of Los Angeles County Committee Members (in percentages) [a]

	Matched Samples		Ideological Types			
Federal Government Should: (N)	Dem. (160)	Rep. (142)	Lib. Dem. (82)	Mod. Dem. (78)	Mod. Rep. (54)	Con. Rep. (88)
Desegregate Schools and Houses						
Do more	74	19	83	63	31	12
Same as now	23	37	13	35	40	35
Do less	3	44	4	2	29	53
Expand Opportunities for Poor						
Do more	91	50	99	82	60	44
Same as now	9	20	1	18	24	18
Do less	0	30	0	0	16	38
Work for Nuclear Disarmament						
Do more	72	20	79	62	27	15
Same as now	22	34	18	27	44	28
Do less	6	46	3	11	29	57
Cut Government Spending						
Do more	44	94	32	58	91	96
Same as now	38	4	40	36	6	3
Do less	18	2	28	6	3	1
Control Cost of Living						
Do more	69	45	71	68	53	40
Same as now	26	13	25	26	14	13
Do less	5	42	4	6	33	47
Curb World Population Growth						
Do more	53	33	58	47	45	27
Same as now	33	40	32	34	37	41
Do less	14	27	20	19	18	32
Get Tough with Urban Violence						
Do more	34	80	18	53	83	79
Same as now	38	11	38	38	15	8
Do less	28	9	44	9	2	13

[a] The same data, reduced to Herbert McClosky's ratio-of-support scores, are reported for 1972 and 1969 in Table 3-9.

prevail between themselves and their friends, family, job associates, and neighbors, on the one hand, and their fellow party activists, on the other.

If we inquire about policy preferences of rival party cadres, as measured by their responses to seven policy preference questions common to the surveys of 1968,-1969,-and 1972, we find that the activists in each party divide predictably, and often dramatically, on issue after issue. Table 3-3 gives the summary information, and Table 3-4 shows the patterns.

Conservative Republicans are not like moderate Republicans; an average of 15 to 18 percentage points separate them year after year. Liberal Democrats are not like moderate Democrats; here indeed we find a mounting difference, from 14 points in 1968 to nearly 22 points in 1972, separating the two wings on a composite of six policies. Nor can it be assumed that moderate Democrats are like moderate Republicans either. In 1972, more than 30 percentage points separated them; using the same six-count average, a difference of 20 points prevailed in 1969 and 1968.

In a political system where parties draw from substantially the same overlapping segments of the social structure, these ideological factors may well play significant roles in separating persons of roughly the same social status into advocates of quite different philosophies:—on the one hand, defenders of the dominant interests, on the other hand, champions of subordinate status groups.

The Ideological Harmony of Party Cadres

Ideological convictions are important in activating people, especially when they acknowledge a sense of *ideological disharmony* with their daily associates. In each year, our participating informants were asked to characterize their political views and also to compare their outlook with those of friends, family members, neighbors, work associates, different kinds of voters, and fellow party cadres.

Republican and Democratic party activists are drawn from roughly the same occupational strata, income levels, and educational segments of Los Angeles society. It is in light of this underlying fact that the rather high levels of ideological disharmony acknowledged year after year by both Democrats and Republicans when talking about their daily associates must be interpreted. The importance of finding an ideologically compatible "home away from home" is a factor in leading people to work actively in the Democratic or Republican party organizations, as suggested by the evidence in Table 3-5.

Table 3-5 shows the substantial extent to which a sense of ideological harmony does exist with close friends. In each year of the survey, between one-half and three-fifths of those listed or both party rosters reported feeling "about the same" as their friends on most issues. Although there are gray areas in some years, there is generally a tendency for Republicans to report somewhat higher levels of ideological harmony with close friends than do Democrats.

Other aspects of Table 3-5 have to do with the direction of ideological tensions when close friends are not seen as holding the same views as the informant. Under such circumstances—that is, in about one-half of all cases—the percentage of the sample who see themselves as more liberal or more conservative conforms to the tendencies expected for both moderates and more militant ideologues within each party. Liberal Democrats overwhelmingly see themselves as more liberal, if any disharmony at all is admitted. By the

Table 3-5 Ideological Harmony With Close Friends Reported by Los Angeles County Committee Members (in percentages)

Informant Feels:	Matched Samples		Ideological Types			
	Dem.	Rep.	Lib. Dem.	Mod. Dem.	Mod. Rep.	Con. Rep.
(N)	(129)	(141)	(94)	(35)	(49)	(92)
1963						
More liberal	39	9	37	43	18	3
About the same	57	64	60	51	63	65
More conservative	5	27	3	6	19	32
(N)	(146)	(134)	(79)	(67)	(47)	(87)
1968						
More liberal	40	11	44	34	26	3
About the same	52	66	56	48	62	69
More conservative	8	23	0	18	13	28
(N)	(183)	(189)	(120)	(63)	(63)	(126)
1969						
More liberal	42	9	48	32	19	4
About the same	53	70	50	59	65	72
More conservative	5	21	2	10	16	24
(N)	(156)	(171)	(107)	(49)	(70)	(101)
1972						
More liberal	32	8	33	31	10	7
About the same	63	73	65	57	77	70
More conservative	5	19	2	12	13	23

same token, conservative Republicans, by a lopsided margin, see themselves as relatively more conservative, if any conflicts with friends over public policy matters is admitted at all.

Table 3-5 is especially interesting for the difference it reveals between moderate Democrats and moderate Republicans. When disharmony with friends is reported, the former are regularly more likely than the latter to see themselves as the liberal side of such a conflict.

In tabulations not reported here, comparable patterns emerge when party cadres compare themselves with other members of their immediate family. Moreover, committee members experienced a considerable heightening of ideological dissonance vis-a-vis their neighbors and work associates. Unlike the relationships one has with friends and family, these are substantially involuntary. Democrats, both moderate and liberal, are inclined to feel at odds on most policy questions with others living in the same upper-middle-class neighborhoods and with colleagues in the professional offices and business firms where they work. In the 1963 survey, there was a tendency for conservative Republicans to feel substantially more often than not that their neighbors were too liberal. By 1968 this feeling is no more pronounced for them than for moderate Republicans. Nearly one-half of the individuals in both wings of the Republican ranks manifest a sense of ideological harmony with both their neighbors and their work associates.

Once again, it is noteworthy that Democratic and Republican self-styled moderates are substantially different from each another. Whenever a sense of ideological dissonance

Table 3-6 Ideological Harmony With Fellow Party Cadres Reported by Los Angeles County Committee Members (in percentages)

Informant Feels:	Matched Samples		Ideological Types			
	Dem.	Rep.	Lib. Dem.	Mod. Dem.	Mod. Rep.	Con. Rep.
(N)	(125)	(136)	(91)	(34)	(46)	(90)
1963						
More liberal	17	16	22	3	41	3
About the same	68	64	69	65	57	68
More conservative	15	20	9	32	2	29
(N)	(144)	(137)	(77)	(67)	(50)	(87)
1968						
More liberal	24	20	40	6	44	7
About the same	58	67	57	58	50	77
More conservative	18	13	3	36	6	16
(N)	(180)	(192)	(118)	(62)	(65)	(127)
1969						
More liberal	30	18	42	6	40	7
About the same	49	60	53	42	54	63
More conservative	51	22	5	52	6	30
(N)	(156)	(169)	(107)	(49)	(69)	(100)
1972						
More liberal	27	14	30	22	23	7
About the same	60	63	63	53	62	64
More conservative	13	23	7	25	15	29

is acknowledged, the Democrat is virtually sure to explain that he is more liberal than his colleagues or neighbors. By comparison, the Republican moderate has been unpredictable on this count until 1969, when he was markedly inclined to explain such a sense of ideological disharmony by the fact that he was more conservative than those around him where he worked or lived.

These indications of the persistent, differentiated ways in which those in each ideological wing of the Democratic and Republican party cadre differ suggest the manner in which—quite apart from its intellectual rigor —the ideological self-conception of a person who has been moved to an active organizational role in party politics is relevant. In addition to the effect of ideological self-consciousness on party activism, the intramural consequences of ideological self-consciousness are worth noting. Table 3-6 analyzes ideological harmony among follow party cadres. [15]

Three marked and persistent patterns are evident. First, the level of ideological harmony is distinctively high for all ideological wings of both parties. Second, the direction of disharmony is quite predictable for the polar wings: Democratic liberals, if they acknowledge any ideological differences with fellow cadres, are overwhelmingly likely to view their colleagues as too conservative, Republican conservatives, on the other hand, if they admit any disharmony, usually attribute it to the fact their fellow workers are too liberal.

Third, Table 3-6 is further evidence of how different are the moderate wings of the rival parties. Note the intramural contrasts. Democratic moderates are a braking factor against the strain toward a leftist posture on public policies that is fostered by their liberal fellow workers. Republican moderates are a countervailing force to the rightist views of their more conservative fellows. Although none of this contradicts our expectations, the results do suggest, nevertheless, that the functional significance of self-espoused political ideologies is partly to be traced in the consequences of ideological dissonance and in the resultant dialogue among grass-roots activists in both political parties.

If measures of ideological harmony for those who work together in party organizations were available more generally, it is quite likely that some segments of an extended corporate structure like the Democratic or Republican party would be strikingly and persistently harmonious while other parts of the apparatus would regularly feature outspoken, substantive arguments. There is no reason to suppose that the sense of harmony does not vary along a considerable range. What is worth stressing, however, is the substantial empirical evidence that these kinds of sensitivities are persistent and predictable in both magnitude and direction.

Sizing Up the Electorate

In an influential article published in 1960, Herbert McClosky reported his findings from a complex investigation of issue conflict and consensus among party leaders and followers. [16] His data on leaders came from questionnaires administered to those who, in 1956, had been delegates to the Republican or Democratic national nominating conventions. Party followers, in his study, consisted of adult citizens—in a representative cross section of the American electorate—who indicated their partisan leanings when they were interviewed by a professional organization.

On a range of key policy issues of that year, both the delegates and the ordinary citizens were asked to state their own preferences concerning governmental action. McClosky's findings established in some detail: (1) that there were consistent, substantial, and predictable ideological differences between the rival party elites in the sample; (2) that, on many issues, Democratic voters held views that were rather close to those held by Republicans; and (3) that the views of the Democratic leadership group were quite close to the views of both Democratic and Republican voters, whereas the leadership group of Republicans was ideologically somewhat isolated. In short, the Republican leaders were out of touch with their own electoral following as well as with the "floating vote" also needed to carry closely contested elections. A question format similar to McClosky's was used in several recent years to ask party activists in Los Angeles to express their policy preferences for more, less, or the current level of federal action on various policy fronts. In both 1969 and 1972, the Los Angeles party cadres were also asked to estimate the views on those same issues held by most Democratic voters and by most Republican voters in their legislative district. Analysis of the data presented in this selection thus far has required no more than straightforward multivariate cross-tabulations. To simplify presentation of the data on cadre opinions of federal action on key policy issues, use is made of McClosky's ratio of support—a simple averaging procedure that assigns a weight of 1.0 to a preference for a leftist policy stand, a weight of 0.0 to a preference for a rightist stand, and a weight of 0.5 for satisfaction with the current level of federal action. On six of the seven policy issues posed, the leftist response was clearly one that favored more government action; calling for more federal action on the seventh policy—to "get tough with urban violence"—was considered a rightist preference, an assumption well substantiated each year of the survey.

For any group of respondents, the sum of the weighted scores on any given issue is divided by the number of participants, producing an average group score on the policy at issue. Scores above 0.75 are highly supportive of leftist government action; scores below 0.25 are manifestly negative about a leftist policy. McClosky suggested that scores between 0.46 and 0.55 might reasonably be interpreted as favorable to the status quo.

McClosky notes the prevalence of two sharply contrasting conceptions of American parties. One sees them as "brokerage organizations," with leaders whose views of policy tend to converge and become rather similar to those of their counterparts in the rival camp. His evidence from the mid-1950s, however, simply does not support this formulation of American parties. The other conception holds that rival parties, because their leaders strive for clearly distinguishable and logically defensible issue positions, become "rallying points" for electoral adherents also concerned about issues of public policy. His evidence from 1956 supports the second formulation; he also discovered that the Democratic leaders were apparently quite successful in rallying to their banner not only Democratic supporters, but Republicans as well. (It was, of course, a period of Republican ascendancy under Eisenhower.)

The data we are able to present for 1969 and 1972 scores cadre positions on seven policy issues. It also scores cadre perceptions of the stand taken by typical local voters of each party. The actual question posed was this:

In this Assembly District, would you say that *most* DEMOCRATIC VOTERS want the federal government to —— more, —— the same, or —— less?

A comparable question was posed concerning "most Republican voters."

This question, however, does not generate the same data configuration as McClosky generated. We have no direct information about how Los Angeles voters felt about the policy issues. However, the data do permit us to examine a number of related points.

First, as has already been established, the Democratic and Republican county committee members in Los Angeles—in surveys of three separate years—differ, in predictable ways, on the left-to-right policy preferences they hold on many issues—although not on all seven with equal force.

Second, it is further established that within each party, at this grass-roots organizational level, there is a persistent, readily identified, and substantial issue-position cleavage between a moderate faction and a more doctrinaire ideological wing—conservative among Republicans, liberal among Democrats.

Third, the data reported in Tables 3-7 and 3-8 show a truly impressive degree of agreement, among all ideological wings of both parties, in estimates of the modal policy preference of Democratic and Republican voters.

For example, conservative Republicans in 1972 register very low ratio-of-support-scores for the leftist proposal to cut defense spending; liberal Democrats score at the opposite extreme. When asked to say where they felt Democratic voters stood, the two groups registered support scores of 0.67 and 0.61. In locating Republican voters, the two groups were again in near agreement: 0.22 and 0.28 were the support scores given by the liberal Democrats and the conservative Republicans, respectively.

This is not an isolated example. On most issues, both types of Democrat and Republican cadres proved to be remarkably similar pollsters. To be sure, some differences emerged, but none compared to the spectrum of policy stands revealed when ratios of support indicating personal preferences were examined (see Table 3-9).

Table 3-7 Ideological Distance: Cadre Expectations About the Policy Preferences of Democratic Voters (in ratios of support)

Leftist Action:	Matched Samples		Ideological Types			
	Dem.	Rep.	Lib. Dem.	Mod. Dem.	Mod. Rep.	Con. Rep.
(N)	(169)	(174)	(119)	(50)	(75)	(99)
1972						
Desegregate schools and houses	.50	.59	.51	.49	.66	.55
Expand opportunities for poor	.72	.85	.69	.81	.86	.85
Work for nuclear disarmament	.79	.77	.79	.80	.74	.79
Cut defense spending	.67	.65	.67	.67	.68	.61
Control cost of living	.90	.79	.90	.90	.81	.78
Stop air and water pollution	.93	.88	.93	.93	.94	.84
Get tough with urban violence [a]	.19	.27	.18	.22	.24	.30
1969						
(N)	(217)	(205)	(139)	(78)	(71)	(134)
Desegregate schools and houses	.49	.67	.46	.55	.74	.63
Expand opportunities for poor	.68	.80	.66	.70	.85	.78
Work for nuclear disarmament	.64	.73	.68	.57	.75	.72
Cut defense spending	.60	.71	.60	.62	.75	.69
Control cost of living	.84	.79	.86	.81	.87	.76
Stop air and water pollution	.92	.89	.91	.94	.94	.87
Get tough with urban violence [a]	.23	.30	.23	.22	.35	.28

[a] Reverse scored to make comparable.

It is possible to use these data in order to measure the ideological distance between the views of a given type of ideological partisan activist and what he believes to be the typical stand taken by Democratic or Republican voters in his area. This can be done— as Table 3-10 shows—for the seven issues in each of the two survey years (1972 and 1969) and for the target reference voting blocs (Republicans and Democrats). Moreover, it can also be done for the seven-issue average. In each case, the formula used is simple:

$$ID = CLSS - VLSS$$

where ID = Ideological distance
CLSS = Leftist support score of cadre activist
VLSS = Leftist support score of voter bloc

The patterns revealed by this analysis are fascinating and would take much space to delineate. Here it is possible only to focus on the seven-issue average differentials:

Table 3-8 Ideological Distance: Cadre Expectations About the Policy Preferences of Republican Voters (in ratios of support)

Leftist Action:	Matched Samples		Ideological Types			
	Dem.	Rep.	Lib. Dem.	Mod. Dem.	Mod. Rep.	Con. Rep.
(N)	(169)	(174)	(119)	(59)	(75)	(99)
1972						
Desegregate schools and houses	.18	.28	.17	.21	.35	.22
Expand opportunities for poor	.20	.50	.18	.24	.50	.50
Work for nuclear disarmament	.42	.46	.40	.50	.53	.40
Cut defense spending	.24	.30	.22	.29	.33	.28
Control cost of living	.54	.60	.56	.50	.70	.53
Stop air and water pollution	.82	.74	.77	.84	.81	.69
Get tough with urban violence [a]	.17	.13	.08	.03	.08	.14
1969						
(N)	(217)	(205)	(139)	(78)	(71)	(134)
Desegregate schools and houses	.21	.35	.21	.21	.48	.28
Expand opportunities for poor	.22	.44	.20	.26	.55	.38
Work for nuclear disarmament	.36	.43	.35	.38	.49	.41
Cut defense spending	.36	.47	.30	.49	.57	.43
Control cost of living	.70	.71	.70	.68	.83	.64
Stop air and water pollution	.81	.84	.79	.84	.85	.84
Get tough with urban violence [a]	.8	.22	.07	.10	.19	.23

[a] Reverse scored to make comparable.

Three basic points emerge from study of Table 3-10. First, conservative Republicans stand close to where they feel the Republican voters stand on issue after issue, both in 1972 and 1969. Republican moderates are not far away, but they show a rather persistent tendency to locate themselves slightly to the left of Republican voters. Democratic moderates come next, and one might characterize them as standing on the far left of Republican voters. Liberal Democrats clearly and regularly place themselves on the extreme left relative to where they locate Republican voters. Essentially, the Republican conservatives represent the anchor point. They see almost eye to eye with (what they think are the views of) Republican voters. All other types fan out at a tangent that puts the liberal Democrats at a considerable distance from the particular reference group considered (Republican voters). The relationship, moreover, is linear, with the two sets of party moderates locating themselves at appropriate intermediate points.

Table 3-9 Policy Preferences of Party Cadres (ratios of support)

	Matched Samples		Ideological Types			
Leftist Action:	Dem.	Rep.	Lib. Dem.	Mod. Dem.	Mod. Rep.	Con. Rep.
(N)	(169)	(174)	(119)	(50)	(75)	(99)
1972						
Desegregate schools and houses	.86	.29	.95	.68	.39	.17
Expand opportunities for poor	.94	.53	.98	.85	.58	.44
Work for nuclear disarmament	.90	.49	.96	.81	.63	.36
Cut defense spending	.87	.33	.94	.76	.44	.21
Control cost of living	.89	.60	.91	.87	.71	.51
Stop air and water pollution	.98	.73	.98	.98	.81	.67
Get tough with urban violence [a]	.41	.18	.46	.30	.16	.20
1969						
(N)	(217)	(205)	(139)	(78)	(71)	(134)
Desegregate schools and houses	.87	.41	.91	.80	.64	.29
Expand opportunities for poor	.96	.53	.97	.93	.71	.44
Work for nuclear disarmament	.87	.46	.93	.75	.62	.49
Cut defense spending	.86	.54	.93	.74	.63	.49
Control cost of living	.86	.59	.89	.80	.74	.51
Stop air and water pollution	.99	.86	.99	.99	.88	.85
Get tough with urban violence [a]	.39	.19	.42	.31	.17	.20

[a] Reverse scored to make comparable.

Second, both sets of Republicans place themselves to the right of Democratic voters, whereas both sets of Democratic cadres locate themselves to the left of that voter bloc. Again, the militant extremes in either party place themselves farther from what they think ordinary Democratic voters want, on issue after issue, year after year, while the moderate wings in either party stand quite close to the position they attribute to ordinary Democratic voters. The pattern here is also linear. It is interesting to note that the reference group, Democratic voters, stands like a floating vote somewhere between the two parties, according to these data. Quite different is the ideological location as seen by all groups—of Republican voters.

Third, it is clear that both parties and, within each party, both wings (each in its different way), are active in articulating a rallying point of ideological consistency on the issues of the day, presumably as a basis for appeal to the voting blocs in their locality. Here we find a wrinkle on McClosky's finding, so to speak. It seems clear that all types of activists think of Republican voters as very conservative. This view fits well enough with the personal views of cadres who are conservative Republicans. But it also means that the

Table 3-10 Ideological Distance Between Cadres and Voters in 1972 and 1969: Where Cadres Stand and Where They Think Voters Stand (Differences in Ratios of Support for Seven Leftist Policies)

	1972 Party Cadres				1969 Party Cadres			
	Lib. Dem.	Mod. Dem.	Mod. Rep.	Con. Rep.	Lib. Dem.	Mod. Dem.	Mod. Rep.	Con. Rep.
	Party Cadre Score Minus Democratic Voter Score							
Desegregate schools and houses	+.44	+.19	−.27	−.38	+.44	+.25	−.10	−.34
Expand opportunities for poor	+.29	+.04	−.28	−.41	+.31	+.23	−.14	−.34
Work for nuclear disarmament	+.27	+.01	−.11	−.43	+.25	+.18	−.13	−.34
Cut defense spending	+.27	+.09	−.24	−.40	+.33	+.12	−.12	−.20
Control cost of living	+.01	−.03	−.10	−.27	+.03	−.01	−.13	−.25
Stop air and water pollution	+.05	+.05	−.13	−.17	+.08	+.05	−.06	−.02
Get tough with urban violence	+.24	+.08	−.08	−.10	+.44	+.23	−.12	+.05
Seven-issue average	+.22	+.06	−.17	−.31	+.27	+.15	−.11	−.21
	Party Cadre Score Minus Republican Voter Score							
Desegregate schools and houses	+.78	+.47	+.04	−.05	+.70	+.59	+.16	+.01
Expand opportunities for poor	+.80	+.61	+.08	−.06	+.77	+.67	+.16	+.06
Work for nuclear disarmament	+.56	+.31	+.10	−.04	+.58	+.27	+.13	−.03
Cut defense spending	+.72	+.48	+.11	−.07	+.63	+.25	+.06	+.06
Control cost of living	+.35	+.37	+.01	−.02	+.19	+.12	−.09	−.13
Stop air and water pollution	+.31	+.24	.00	−.02	+.20	+.15	+.03	+.01
Get tough with urban violence	+.34	+.27	+.08	+.07	+.60	+.35	+.04	+.10
Seven-issue average	+.55	+.39	+.06	−.03	+.52	+.36	+.07	+.01

Republican voting bloc is less and less a group to be seriously appealed to. As far as these data take us, it would appear that Republican voters are considered "way off in right field." Ironically, the only kind of party activist also "off in right field" is the self-styled Republican conservative.

Party as a Matrix of Corporate and Attitudinal Structures

Political parties are extended apparatuses that stretch across geographic and institutional lines. At any given time, some sections of the apparatus are likely to be preoccupied with objectives other than winning elections. They may resist attempts to mobilize cadre efforts for electioneering. Although party organizational personnel are expected to serve the needs of electoral competition, the actual performances of specific party units are seldom perfect. They vary from locale to locale, from contest to contest, from one party to its rivals.

Efforts made by rival party functionaries to coordinate the campaign efforts of party activists in the same constituency cannot be assumed to be great either. Some apparatuses are badly split by factionalism, have only limited resources, and face a rival organization in similarly bad shape. Other apparatuses, with electoral support bases that seem invulverable, are insensitive to public issues and group needs, and are preoccupied with the self-regarding demands of dues-paying members. Still other constituency-wide apparatuses are preoccupied with capturing or keeping a particular power base, and will only give token attention to capturing a distant state or national position.

Conclusion

Political parties are complex structures—attitudinal as well as corporate—for coordinating political efforts across extended domains. They are neither necessarily democratic, nor ideologically homogeneous, nor continuously operating in high gear, so far as their intramural processes go. In their extramural relationships with clientele groups, target publics, and rival organizations, they are similarly diverse. In basic ways, the activities undertaken by party units depend on the composition of the personnel roster and on the interaction patterns that ensue among those who must work together within the same "effective structural extent" of their party's apparatus. [17]

It is widely acknowledged that parties perform various important functions for the broader political system. Less clear, however, is the degree to which those who make the organized effort—the rival party activists and functionaries—comprehend those functions and consciously seek to carry them out. Yet the beliefs and attitudes of party cadres greatly affect the scope and continuity of their individual contributions. It is difficult to imagine a viable organization whose incentive system persistently manipulates its personnel into performing in functionally appropriate ways without their knowing it. The subjective meaning of political participation is not a minor factor in structuring the joint effectiveness of party units. It is the subjectively experienced reality of party life about which more needs to be known.

NOTES

1. An important analytical contribution is W. Crotty's "The Quest for Scientific Meaning in Analyses of Political Parties," in R. Golembiewski, W. Welsh, and W. Crotty, A Methodological Primer for Political Scientists (1968). See also the recent evaluation by W. E. Wright, "Comparative Party Models: Rational-Efficient and Party Democracy," in A Comparative Study of Party Organization, ed. W. E. Wright (1971). Earlier works of great importance in defining party phenomena are M. Duverger's Political Parties (1954 trans.) and A. Leiserson's rich and provocative essay, Parties and Politics (1958).

2. A useful, if polemical, discussion is Philip Selznick's The Organizational Weapon (1952). See also Z. Brzizinski and S. Huntington, "Cincinnatus and the Apparatchik," in World Politics 16 (October 1963): 52-78; and John W. Lewis, "Party Cadres in Communist China," in Education and Political Development, ed. James S. Coleman (1965).

3. This formulation of the problem is close to that of Joseph Schumpeter in Capitalism, Socialism, and Democracy (1939). See also R. Dahl's A Preface to Democratic Theory (1962) and a thorough and thoughtful examination of the resulting empirical evidence by Dennis F. Thompson, The Democratic Citizen (1970).

4. Harold D. Lasswell's long essay, "Democratic Character," in *The Political Writings of Harold D. Lasswell* (1951), is seminal. The extended treatment by B. Berelson in chap. 14 of the Elmira study of Berelson, et al., *Voting: A Study of Opinion Formation in a Presidential Campaign* (1954), explicitly argues against the necessity for a modal "basic democratic citizen," in light of empirical evidence from behavioral inquiries. See especially the lead article by the editors, S. Rokkan and S. M. Lipset, "Cleavage Structures, Party Systems and Voter Alignments," in their 1967 volume, *Party Systems and Voter Alignments: Cross National Perspectives*. A corresponding set of articles on American experience is W. N. Chambers and W. D. Burnham, eds., *The American Party Systems: Stages of Political Development* (1967).

5. S. J. Eldersveld, *Political Parties: A Behavioral Analysis* (1965), chaps. 3–5.

6. See the three-city comparisons in James Q. Wilson's *The Amateur Democrat* (1956).

7. Cited in F. Sorauf, *Party Politics in America*, 2nd ed., (1972), p. 8.

8. Surprisingly little work has been directed by academic investigators to this problem. See the suggested leads in case study analyses by S. Kelley, *Professional Public Relations and Political Power* (1956).

9. "Stratarchic" is used in the sense it is defined and employed in Eldersveld in *Political Parties: A Behavioral Analysis*, pp. 9–13.

10. See my evaluation of data for the 1967 India national elections, in "Party Cadres and Receptive Partisan Voters in the 1967 Indian National Election," *Asian Survey*, November 1970. An appraisal of the research problems arising from this perspective is in my "Communications in Political Parties," in *Handbook of Communications*, eds. W. Schramm, I. Pool, and F. Frye (1973).

11. California Assembly Interim Committee on Elections and Reapportionment, "Political Party Organization," January 1963, pp. 9–10.

12. The sequence of inquiries based at the University of California, Los Angeles, begins with a report by Dwaine Marvick and Charles Nixon, "Recruitment Contrasts in Rival Campaign Groups," in *Political Decision Makers: Recruitment and Performance*, ed. D. Marvick (1961). The 1963 surveys are reported in D. Marvick, "The Middlemen of Politics," in *Approaches to the Study of Party Organization*, ed. W. Crotty (1967). For symposium of studies based on the 1968 and 1969 surveys, see Marilyn Brookes et al., "Los Angeles Party Leaders and their Imagery of the Voters" (Paper presented at the 1970 Annual Meetings of the Western Political Science Association), University of California, Los Angeles.

13. By far the most sustained inquiry marshalling systematically gathered empirical data to clarify key aspects of American party organizational performance is Eldersveld's book-length study of Detroit in the mid-1950s, *Political Parties—A Behavioral Analysis*. See especially chaps. 3–5.

14. Duverger, *Political Parties*, p. 418.

15. Among the relevant work, the following should be noted: P. Converse, "The Nature of Belief Systems in Mass Politics," in *Ideology And Discontent*, ed. D. Apter (1964); J. O. Field and R. E. Anderson, "Ideology in the Public's Conceptualization of the 1964 Election," *Public Opinion Quarterly*, Fall 1969; H. McClosky, et al., "Issue Conflict and Consensus among Party Leaders and Followers," *American Political Science Review*, June 1960; Eldersveld, *Political Parties: A Behavioral Analysis*; E. Costantini, "Intraparty Attitude Conflict: Democratic Party Leadership in California," *Western Political Quarterly*, December 1963; W. Crotty, "The Party Organization and its Activities," in *Approaches*, ed. Crotty (1968); D. E. Stokes, "Spatial Models of Party Competition," *American Political Science Review*, June 1963; P. Converse, "The Problem of Party Distances in Models of Voting Change," in *The Electoral Process*, eds. K. Jennings and H. Zeigler (1966); Dennis Ippolito, "Political Perspectives of Suburban Party Leaders," *Social Science Quarterly*, March 1969; Allan Kornberg, "Some Differences in the Political Socialization Patterns of Canadian Party Officials," *Canadian Journal of Political Science*, March 1969. For a useful stocktaking plus important new evidence, see S. Verba and N. Nye, *Participation In America: Political Democracy And Social Equality* (1972).

16. McClosky et al., "Issue Conflict and Consensus."

17. Relevant empirical work on these performance aspects includes: Eldersveld, *Political Parties: A Behavioral Analysis;* L. Bowman and G. R. Boynton, "Activities and Role Definitions of Grassroots Party Officials"; *Journal of Politics,* February 1966; L. Bowman and G. R. Boynton, "Recruitment Patterns Among Local Party Officials: A Model and Some Preliminary Findings," *American Political Science Review,* September 1966; W. Crotty, "The Social Attributes of Party Organizational Activists in a Transitional Political System," *Western Political Quarterly,* September 1967; R. S. Hirschfield, et al., "A Profile of Political Activists in Manhattan," *Western Political Quarterly,* September 1962; S. Patterson, "Characteristics of Party Leaders," *Western Political Quarterly,* June 1963; G. Pomper, "New Jersey County Chairmen," *Western Political Quarterly,* March 1965; Robert Salisbury, "The Urban Party Organization Member," *Public Opinion Quarterly,* Winter 1965–1966; D. Ippolito and L. Bowman, "Goals and Activities of Party Officials in a Suburban Community," *Western Political Quarterly,* September 1969; P. Althoff and S. Patterson, "Political Activism in a Rural County," *Midwest Journal of Political Science,* February 1966; P. Clark and J. Q. Wilson, "Incentive Systems: A Theory of Organization," *Administrative Science Quarterly,* June 1961; T. Flinn and F. Wirt, "Local Party Leaders: Groups of Like Minded Men," *Midwest Journal of Political Science,* February 1966; L. Bowman, D. Ippolito, and W. Donaldson, "Incentives for the Maintenance of Grassroots Political Activism," *Midwest Journal of Political Science,* February 1969; M. Conway and F. Feigert, "Motivation, Incentive Systems and the Political Party Organization," *American Journal of Political Science,* December 1968.

Also useful in these regards are the following: Joseph Schlesinger, *Ambition in Politics: Political Careers In The United States* (1966) and his article "Political Party Organization" in *Handbook of Organizations,* ed. James March (1965); V. O. Key, *Politics Parties and Pressure Groups,* 5th ed. (1964); Austin Ranney and Willmore Kendall, *Democracy and The American Party System* (1956); Sorauf, *Political Parties in America;* Everett Ladd, *American Political Parties: Social Change and Political Response* (1970); William Keefe, *Parties, Politics and Public Policy In America* (1972); J. Kessel, *The Goldwater Coalition* (1968); W. D. Burnham, *Critical Elections and The Mainsprings Of American Politics* (1970); Gerald Pomper, *Elections In America* (1969); Eldersveld, *Political Parties;* J. Q. Wilson, *Amateur Democrat;* and J. M. Burns, *The Deadlock Of Democracy: Four Party Politics In America* (1963).

4 / Political Stability, Reform Clubs, and the Amateur Democrat

David L. Protess and Alan R. Gitelson

Introduction

Few political constructs have evoked more widespread discussion and further application than James Q. Wilson's concept of the amateur Democrat.[1] Since the publication of his study of Democratic reform clubs in New York, Chicago, and Los Angeles researchers have identified similar movements within the national Democratic[2] and Republican[3] parties. Other researchers have attempted to measure the operational validity of Wilson's construct by examining Democratic Party cleavage in urban communities different from those studied by Wilson.[4] Still others have reexamined the motivations for political participation in American party politics in light of Wilson's work.[5]

Despite the contributions of these efforts, several issues concerning the nature of reform club politics remain to be explored before the subject is exhausted. This study was undertaken to provide answers to two specific questions. First, is Wilson's theoretical construct of the amateur Democrat empirically validated by the membership composition of the contermporary reform club movement of Chicago? Second, to what extent and in what ways has Chicago's reform club movement managed to maintain and enhance its organizational interests in an environment of increasingly entrenched machine politics?

Amateur Versus Professional Politicians: Some Theoretical Considerations

Wilson's study, as he readily admits, was intended to be interesting rather than theoretical. Still, he does point to a number of variables that may be associated with a theoretical distinction between "amateur" and "professional" party activists.[6] In general, these variables form three categories: (1) ascriptive and other background variables, (2) political and social variables, and (3) motivational variables. These three categories of variables provide the framework for our analysis.

Authorship is equal and order of authors' names was randomly determined. This selection is based on a paper presented at the Annual Meeting of the Midwest Political Science Association, Chicago, April 1977. A revised edition of this paper was first published under the title "Political Stability, Reform Clubs, and the Amateur Democrat" in *Polity,* Vol. X, No. 4 (Summer 1978). By permission.

First, the amateur club member is said to be distinct from the professional or party regular in terms of sex, age, race, religion, and socioeconomic status. Wilson found a disproportionally high number of male, young, white, Jewish, upper-middle-income, professionals in the reform clubs he studied. Professional party activists were found to be more representative of the general composition of the urban community.

A second dimension on which the amateur and professional activists contrasted is their political and social orientations. Amateurs, Wilson suggests, manifest a broad ideological framework from which they evaluate candidates and issues. This means that amateurs not only have a stronger liberal inclination than their professional counterparts, but also that they tend to view political matters from a principled perspective. Thus, they are ideologues rather than pragmatists. Moreover, their ideological perspective permeates their lifestyle. While the professional has a parochial focus, with interests and organizational attachments that are essentially local, the amateur is portrayed as more nationally and internationally oriented. [7]

Finally, the amateur versus professional dichotomy is established in terms of the different factors that motivate individuals to become involved in politics. Wilson asserts that the amateur's initial participation responds to purposive incentives offered by the reform club movement. The activism of the amateur is rooted in a desire for politics to express the public interest. In contrast, Wilson's professional is more strongly attracted to the solidary and material incentives offered by regular party organizations. The prime motivating factor which precipitates the professional's political involvement is obtaining the perquisites that come from winning elections, rather than achieving the collective good. [8]

In practice, these two types of political activists can be identified by whether they belong to a local Democratic reform group or to a regular Democratic Party organization. But whether the three traits that comprise the amateur versus professional dichotomy are actually associated with this difference in affiliation has never been empirically ascertained. [9] Indeed, the literature on this subject vacillates between treating Wilson's construct as a stylistic tendency, i.e., a Weberian ideal type, and treating it as having discrete applicability. Two of the major purposes of this study are to determine the extent to which Wilson's construct has an operational reference and to delineate how that reference has evolved in the political world since the early 1960s.

Research Design: Method and Data

The data for this study were gathered by a mail survey during the month January 1975. Questionnaires were sent to a random sample of Chicago's major reform club, the Independent Voters of Illinois (IVI). [10] The sample included regular membership as well as officials designated as IVI leaders. Of the 135 questionnaires sent out, 100 were returned, yielding a response rate of 74 percent. Included among the 100 respondents were 22 who identified themselves as leaders, 71 who identified themselves as regular members, and 7 who could not be classified. [11]

A number of research propositions were generated for testing in this study. In accordance with the earlier Wilson study, we first hypothesized that IVI members would have high socioeconomic status. Next, based on recent increased activity and visibility of the IVI at the local level, we hypothesized that members would reflect a qualitatively higher degree of pragmatism regarding political objectives than was found in the Wilson study. Finally, we hypothesized that cognitive orientations of IVI members toward the community would reflect a more parochial outlook and orientation than Wilson found. In both the pragmatist and the parochial hypotheses, the assumption was made that with the growing visibility of the IVI in Cook County politics, the members would reflect a heightened interest in local affairs and a strong, pragmatic disposition toward winning local elections.

In order to test these hypotheses, IVI respondents were asked to complete a twenty-seven item questionnaire dealing with their background, their role as amateur politicians in Chicago, and their commitment to and endorsement of issues and candidates in recent elections. Specifically, the IVI members were asked to respond to questions dealing with their role in the political system vis-à-vis their membership in IVI.

Ascriptive and Other Background Traits

IVI members reflected an expected degree of upper-status homogeneity in their social characteristics. Previous descriptions of amateur Democrats by Wilson conformed to the data we collected on IVI members. [12] Several patterns evolved in our examination of background variables:

1. *Race.* Among IVI members interviewed, 90 percent were white, and the remainder either black or Asian.

2. *Religion.* Of the respondents, 49 percent classified themselves as Jewish, 27.6 percent as Protestants, and 11.2 percent as Catholics. [13]

3. *Education.* Of the sample, 84.7 percent had a college degree, and 42.9 percent had a graduate or professional degree.

4. *Income.* The modal income was $25,000 or more per year (49.5 percent of the sample), with only 9.5 percent of the respondents having an income of less than $10,000.

5. *Sex.* Distribution of sex was even (males 51 percent and females 49 percent), deviating somewhat from Wilson's sample of amateur politicians which showed a higher percentage of males. [14] Membership, then, was generally consistent with the social and economic composite developed by Wilson in his study 15 years earlier.

Political and Social Orientation

Two variables were critical in our evaluation of the IVI members' political and social profile: (1) goal orientation (idealistic versus pragmatic), and (2) cognitive orientation toward the community (cosmopolitan versus parochial). Wilson had earlier described the amateur politician as both cosmopolitan and idealistic in character. Along with his characterization of the independent as a liberal, these variables formed the basis for discriminating between amateur and professional political activists. We discarded any index for measuring a liberal versus conservative dichotomy as too broad and inconclusive. Indeed, Wilson's characterization of the amateur Democrat in Chicago as liberal was based on qualitative, not quantitative data. Although we found some members to have strong liberal ideas on domestic and foreign issues, there was no conclusive evidence that consistency in ideology was a trademark of the IVI member. [15]

Pragmatist Versus Idealist

For Wilson, the professional politician is the pragmatist

> preoccupied with the outcome of politics in terms of winning or losing. Politics . . . consists of concrete questions and specific persons who must be dealt with in a manner that will "keep everybody happy" and thus minimize the possibility of defeat at the next election. [16]

idealist

The professional politician's central interest lies in "gaining power and place for one's self and one's party." [17] For Wilson, the amateur's reward in politics is his "sense of having satisfied a felt obligation to 'participate.' The ideal amateur has a 'natural' response to politics," wheras the professional develops a certain "detachment toward politics and a certain immunity to its excitement and its outcomes." [18] At best, Wilson's description leads us to a rather vague and disjointed characterization of amateurs and professionals. Wilson admits this when he states that his description is "somewhat overdrawn." [19] Nevertheless, the pragmatist versus idealist dichotomy is one point from which to begin an examination of the role perception of the independent political activist.

Wilson's characterization of the independent political activist in Chicago in 1960 as amateur and by definition, idealistic, does not adequately define the role of the independent political activist in Chicago in 1975. IVI members, and particularly the leadership, appear to be more professionally oriented, while at the same time retaining some of the amateur characteristics outlined in the Wilson study.

Respondents were asked to choose from a list of six items those factors that were most critical in determining whom they would endorse for a political office. The six items were divided between pragmatic considerations (e.g., the candidates' abilities to generate money for their campaign) and non-pragmatic, or principled, considerations (e.g., the candidates' willingness, based on past performance, to sacrifice their political self-interest in order to achieve what they considered to be "the good of the community"). Of the factors that contribute to candidate endorsement by IVI members, 85 percent of the total is explained by nonpramatic, idealistic factors.

While this measure would suggest that the independent political activist is "public regarding" [20] and that winning an election is secondary, further evidence would seem to qualify that conclusion.

When asked to review their own perceptions of the probable success of the candidates they endorsed in past elections, 60 percent of the IVI respondents stated that in most of the contests in which they endorsed candidates, they felt those candidates had a better-than-average chance of winning their election. The ability of a candidate to win an election is, in itself, a conscious goal orientation of a majority of IVI members.

Data on the IVI endorsement record since 1960 bear directly on the amateur versus professional distinction. Between 1960 and 1974, 102 of the 211 candidates endorsed by IVI members were successful in their bid for public office. Obviously, it can be suggested that in any sequence of contests, IVI would have expected to endorse some winners. The 50 percent success rate, however, is above what might be expected for a strictly idealistic organization. IVI members do perceive their endorsed candidates often as potential winners and not simply as unsuccessful extensions of their personal "good government" philosophy. Interviews with IVI members revealed that the independent activist is aware that winning candidates will maximize the effectiveness of the independent movement in the political arena.

Parochial Versus Cosmopolitan

The parochial versus cosmopolitan model was employed by Wilson to distinguish between the professional politicians and the amateur independent political activists, respectively. According to Wilson, a parochial or local "from whose ranks most professional politicians are drawn, is a person who is preoccupied with the local community to the exclusion of affairs outside his community. He is 'parochial,' and has lived in his community for many years." [21] Wilson goes on to suggest that, "A cosmopolitan . . . is a person with minimal ties to the locality but a strong attachment to 'the Great Society' of national and international problems, ideas, movements, fashions, and culture. He is often a recent arrival to the community." [22]

Our examination of the Chicago parochial versus cosmopolitan distinction in 1975 suggests some interesting and conflicting comparisons with the 1960 Chicago analysis done by Wilson. IVI members in 1975 are more parochial than were Wilson's 1960 sample. Although IVI members do hold cosmopolitan views and are very interested in national affairs, they remain locally oriented, particularly vis-à-vis their membership in IVI.

Supporting this conclusion are data on organizational affiliations, which indicate that IVI members tend to join organizations with a local character and direction more often than they do organizations with a cosmopolitan character. Over 48 percent of the IVI membership belonged exclusively or almost exclusively to organizations in the Chicago metropolitan area focusing on local problems or issues. Only 39 percent of the membership belonged to predominantly nationally or internationally oriented organizations.

Another criterion used by Wilson to suggest parochial orientation was length of time lived in one's community. Wilson concluded that parochial professionals were likely to have more established ties to their community (as measured by length of time having lived in the community) than cosmopolitan amateurs, who were likely to be more transient. The 1975 data on this question indicate that 19 percent of the IVI sample have lived in the same neighborhood for over 25 years, 50 percent have lived in the same neighborhood for ten years or more, and 70 percent have lived in Chicago their entire lives. The long term residential plans of 85 percent of the respondents were to remain in Chicago.

Data on campaign involvement supported the parochial posture of the majority of IVI members questioned. Over 53 percent of the respondents indicated that they were more likely to participate in Chicago and Cook County election campaigns than in presidential campaigns. Preference for presidential campaigns was indicated by 39.6 percent of the sample.

The data do not suggest that independent political activists are more parochial than regular machine politicians in the city of Chicago. Qualitative evidence indicates that professional politicians in city and county government are more locally oriented than IVI activists. We would suggest, however, that a strict adherence to the parochial versus cosmopolitan dichotomy is misleading in any evaluation of the cognitive orientation of IVI members. A more realistic evaluation of IVI members would suggest that they have strong local attachments while holding cosmopolitan views.

Finally, we want to comment on the party identification of reform group activists in Chicago. We believe that the very title of Wilson's book belies the political attachments that members of the IVI have with the Democratic Party. While 57 percent of the IVI members considered themselves at least nominal Democrats, 5 percent of the sample are

Republicans, and 38 members perceive themselves as independent voters. Between 1960 and 1974, 47 percent (N-103) of the IVI endorsements were for Republican candidates, 27 percent (N-58) for independent candidates, and only 26 percent (N-57) were for Democratic candidates. Neither the perceived party identification of IVI members nor the endorsement record of the organization substantiates Wilson's characterization of reform group activists as amateur Democrats.

Our 1975 findings show, then, that some modifications must be made regarding Wilson's 1960 criteria for characterizing the amateur politician in Chicago. Although differences between the amateur and the professional political activists remain apparent, the amateur appears to be more parochial and pragmatic than Wilson suggests in his study.

Changes in the composition and attitudes of IVI members since the Wilson study may be explained from a variety of perspectives. It is possible that the changes result from the use of different methodological approaches and do not represent developmental changes. Thus, the more systematic approach of the present study may have simply tapped attitudes that were present when Wilson did his study, but went unnoticed at the time.

Given the general accuracy of Wilson's findings, however, a more likely explanation lies in the effect of time on actual changes in the organization between 1960 and 1976. Wilson studied the IVI at an early phase of its evolution, when the post-World War II reform club movement was in an experimental stage. It is quite possible that bureaucratizing forces, which developed in the organization during the 15-year period following Wilson's study, along with regular defeats by the machine, tempered the idealism of the amateur Democrat and created a mutant breed of reformer.

The Maintenance and Enhancement of the Reform Club Movement: A Paradoxical Phenomenon

To this point, the reform club activists have been examined in terms of their ascriptive and background traits as well as their political and social orientations. The motivations of reform club members for affiliating in the first place is the subject of the final section of this article. Because intensive interview data are not available for professionals, we shall focus on an evaluation of Wilson's assertion that purposive (as opposed to solidary or material) incentives precipitate the initial involvement of amateurs in reform club politics.[23] This question is explored in relation to the political environment in which Chicago's reform clubs attract their membership.

Perhaps the most remarkable trait of reform clubs in Chicago is their ability to survive. Since the publication of Wilson's book, the regular Democratic organization has increased its political control of the city. In 1963, Mayor Richard J. Daley (who was also the county Democratic Party chairman) barely won reelection, losing a majority of the city's predominantly white wards to his Republican challenger. Since that time, Daley won victories of increasing margins, and in 1975, he carried all fifty wards in his election victory.

The Chicago city council has also increased allegiance to regular party politics. There were more than ten independent aldermen 15 years ago. The number was reduced to seven in 1971, despite notable victories by reformers in two formerly machine-controlled wards. The 1975-1979 city council had only two independent Democrats, one independent, and a single Republican. In addition, party regulars are in control of every major city and county office with the exception of states' attorney.

Finally, intraparty struggles continue to be infrequent. Primary-election challenges for the post of ward committeeman—the post from which patronage jobs are distributed—are

Table 4-1 Membership Size of the IVI by Area

Year	Chicago	Chicago Suburbs	Statewide total
pre-1964[a]	ca. 600	ca. 150	ca. 1000
1964	572	141	775
1965	682	201	989
1966	1004	277	1452
1967	987	290	1422
1968	1021	270	1479
1969	1331	344	2569
1970	1403	409	2156
1971	1473	493	2327
1972	1523	611	2569
1973	1397	642	2468
1974	1131	565	2025
1975	1089	524	1852

[a] No precise membership figures exist for the period prior to 1964, but estimates by the organization's leaders indicate that membership size was fairly constant, at least between 1955 and 1963

uncommon and often based more on personal antagonism than on disagreements about machine politics. As of the 1976 primary election, only two of the eighty ward and township committeemen who comprise the decisionmaking apparatus of the regular party organization are classified as party reformers.

The regular Democratic organization has not, however, been undefeatable. The Democratic Party has recently suffered severe electoral losses at the state and national levels. The death of Mayor Daley in December 1976 has left the party with an uncertain future. Nonetheless, the machine's power base has always been primarily local. Within the city and Cook County many of the political institutions described by Wilson in his chapter on Chicago have become even more monolithic.[24] "Good government," as defined by the municipal reform movement, has not come to America's second largest city.

The continued, indeed increased, failure of the reform club movement to achieve its goals led us to hypothesize that organizations like the IVI would be beset with increased difficulties in attracting members and resources. Surprisingly, the opposite proved true. Accompanying the entrenchment of machine politics has been the veiled, but definite trend toward the enhancement of Chicago's reform club movement. This apparent paradox is indicated by growth in reform club organizations, activities, membership, and financial resources.

In the past few years, several new reform clubs have been organized in Chicago.[25] The most notable, the Independent Precinct Organization (IPO), was created in 1968 to provide a precinct-level, grass-roots challenge to the machine.[26] While IPO membership has only been about one-third of the IVI Chicago membership, it has been particularly successful in expanding the social base of the reform club movement to include nonwhites and young people. Together with the IVI, the IPO has increased the scope and number of challenges to the regular Democratic organization, if not materially affecting the overall success of the amateurs.

In addition to challenging more frequently Chicago's party regulars, reform clubs have increased their membership over the past decade. Table 4-1 indicates that IVI membership, after years of remaining fairly constant, grew almost continuously from 1966 to 1973, with the Chicago membership more than doubling since Wilson's study. It appears that continued frustration in the achievement of the IVI's major goal did not adversely affect the organization's recruitment of members.

We found the financial prosperity of the IVI unhindered by the entrenchment of the machine. While the IVI has traditionally operated at a deficit, the size of the deficit began to shrink in the late 1960s. In the IVI's 1975 fiscal year, the organization operated with a surplus for the first time.

Thus, while Chicago's reform club movement has suffered politically at the hands of its regular organization counterparts, it has gained in an organizational sense. The membership and financial growth of the IVI is particularly remarkable, given the development of functionally competitive organizations (e.g., the IPO and Common Cause) and the recent financial crisis of the nation, the latter of which would be expected to reduce contributions to voluntary associations. Given the predictable loss of some urban reformers to the suburbanization process, the increased number of Chicago IVI members is particularly surprising. An explanation of these phenomena must begin with a closer examination of organizational dynamics in general, and the motivations for affiliations with reform clubs in particular.

The Maintenance and Enhancement of the Reform Club Movement: Theoretical Considerations

It has been suggested by Wilson that incipient amateur Democrats are motivated to join reform clubs largely out of purposive, ideological considerations. [27] This is to be contrasted with potential professionals, whose involvement is triggered by more immediate, material inducements. Recently, research by Richard Hofstetter seriously questioned the operational validity of this distinction. [28] But even if Wilson's notion did in fact explain the motivational differences in initial organizational recruitment, it would hardly account for the varying degress of organizational strength of reform clubs. The explanation for increasing numbers of people within the pool of potential activists suddenly motivated to participate in reform club politics in the late 1960s and early 1970s must be found elsewhere.

If Hofstetter is correct in asserting that the growth of reform club movements may not explained in terms of the manifesting of ideological preferences by incipient reformers, it may alternatively be accounted for by the· political-economy model of organizational behavior. [29] Mancur Olson, for example, might suggest that an increasing number of persons are motivated to contribute to Chicago's reform clubs because of an expansion in the provision of selective inducements given by the clubs to those who join. [30] Specifically, the IVI might have increased its organizational resources by offering special inducements to new members such as low-cost charter flights to Europe, or other devices used by reform clubs elsewhere that appeal to the rational, self-interest of potential members.

Olson's definitions of the terms "rational" and "self-interest" are crucial to an understanding of the remainder of our argument. By rational behavior he means behavior that is directed toward achieving objectives by actions that are "efficient and effective." [31] Such actions, for Olson, will make a perceptible contribution to the attainment of the organization's objectives or to the "burden or benefit" of any other individual in the organization. [32]

Acting in one's self-interest is never clearly defined by Olson, but is generally used by political economists to refer to acts that maximize what is valued (usually things of economic value). The notions of rational self-interest lead Olson to conclude that the only way a political or economic organization that seeks nondivisible, collective goods—e.g., the IVI seeking "good government"—can attract members is to offer them selective inducements or to coerce them into joining. Such strategies are necessary because rational, self-interested individuals will realize that their contributions, taken individually, will have no perceptible effect on the achievement of such goods; they will, therefore, withhold their contributions in hopes of enjoying the benefits without incurring any individual costs. Thus, if Olson is correct, reform club growth might not reflect an increased desire to attain the collective benefit of "good government," but rather the availability of a new opportunity for incipient reformers to maximize their personal gain by contributing to a reform club.

Interviews with IVI leadership, however, revealed that no new selective inducements to join the organization were offered during the entire period of its expansion. Indeed, we found the organization itself to have changed remarkably little since its founding. Thus, Olson's argument is either irrelevant to organizations like reform clubs, or it requires modification in order to explain the particular growth of groups like the IVI.

One such modification of Olson's theory that does not abandon the political-economy model altogether has been prepared by Norman Frolich, Joseph A. Oppenheimer, and Oran R. Young.[33] They contend that with effective leadership, organizations that seek collective goods (e.g., the IVI seeking "good government") can induce potential members to join on a rational, self-interested basis. This may be accomplished when the leaders convince the potential member to weigh his individual contribution against the increased probability of the organization's subsequent success, rather than against the total contribution needed to attain its goals. In the case of Chicago's reform clubs, Frolich and his associates might explain organizational enhancement of the IVI in particular by its hiring of a charismatic, full-time fund-raiser and membership recruiter in the late 1960s. Thus, organizational resources increased more as a result of effective outreach than of increased selective inducements.

We would not deny that effective leadership is needed for an organization to attract members. Nevertheless, we doubt that effective leadership accounts for the particular growth that Chicago's reform club movement experienced in the late 1960s and early 1970s. Reform club resources were expanding at a time when the organization's political opposition, the machine, was becoming an increasingly accepted institution by Chicagoans. Given the failure of Chicago's reform clubs to begin to approximate their aim of "good government," it is unlikely that even the most effective leadership could convince a potential reform club activist to join the IVI or the IPO for reasons of rational, self-interest, i.e., in the expectation that his individual contribution might make a perceptible difference toward the achievement of reform.

The Maintenance and Enhancement of the Reform Club Movement

If Chicago's reform club activists are acting neither rationally nor ideologically by increasingly contributing to organizations like the IVI, on what basis are they acting? We believe that the answer lies in an understanding of the nature of the political machine. As many scholars have pointed out, a characteristic feature of machine politics is the attempt by policymakers to disaggregate and individualize urban public policies.[34] Olson states that there is an organized bias in machine cities against considering collective issues because the nondivisible nature of such issues reduces their political value. So, for instance, if Democrats get clean air, they cannot deny its use by Republicans or independents.[35] Thus, political machines are not set up to strive for collective goals, least of all those relating to "good government" issues.

Because the machine has limited perquisities to dispense, it must be selective in distributing them to particular individuals or groups. Not everyone—especially the upper-middle-class, liberal, intellectual independent—will be the beneficiary of public policy perquisites and services in a machine city. Consequently, the incipient reform activists may be among the most likely citizens in the polity to perceive themselves as excluded from Chicago's political process.

Thus, it is apparent that potential reform club members, often possessing the above characteristics, may become the most concerned about achieving their ends when a machine is at its maximum power. The IVI members in our sample, when questioned about their motivation for joining the reform club, frequently expressed a concern with becoming increasingly deprived of public benefits to themselves and their community. Follow-up interviews indicated three areas in which IVI members felt particular deprivations:

1. *Inequitable use of tax dollars.* Reform activists, who pay higher taxes due to their social class, believed they were paying the burden of cost of the mayor's pork barrel.

2. *Lack of adequate representation in city government.* As Wilson has commented: "Most important of all to the reformer. . . the Party was composed of the same old faces—mostly Irish faces."[36]

3. *Inadequate services to predominantly independent communities.* Reform activists, advancing the notion that communities receiving the best services are those that vote most strongly regular Democrat, expressed a concern about receiving inferior city services as punishment for their voting preferences.

Whether these concerns are objectively correct assessments is not the issue. What is relevant is that reform club activists often perceived themselves to be subjected to "taxation without representation" and were clearly motivated to join reform clubs as a result of their growing perception of this injustice.

However, as Olson suggests and as we concede, the reform club activist will not rationally contribute to the goal of good government because his contribution will have no perceptible effect on its achievement. We are suggesting that the concepts of "rationality" and "self-interest" are, at times, incompatible. (Political economists like Olson not only see them as basically compatible, but often use them together.) Although a person may rationally wish to withhold a contribution from an organization that exclusively seeks collective goods, he may contribute to such an organization anyway, despite the absence of selective inducements, out of self-interest or "personal utility."

The concept of self-interest must include more than monetary gain if it is to accurately describe the motivation for involvement in the reform club movement. A psychological definition of the term is more useful for explaining the data than a strictly economic one. Thus, we will use the term "personal utility" to denote an expanded definition of self-interest. Actions which maximize one's personal utility include the advancement of those things that person values, e.g., power, fame, and excitement, in addition to monetary gain.[37] In the 1975 study, reform activists increasingly perceived their personal utility to be minimized, in an economic and psychological sense, by the entrenchment of the machine.

This leads us to suggest that the more politically entrenched the machine becomes, the more the incipient political activist is likely to perceive himself as personally deprived. He is more likely to join an opposing organization out of personal utility (but not rationality). In short, rationality and personal utility may exist in an inverse relationship. The "logic of utility" dictates that the greater the political control of an organization denying the collective benefit, the greater the motivation to join an opposing group out of nonrational, personal utility.

Thus, the IVI could initially be formed in the absence of selective inducements due to the denial of the benefits of good government by the established party organization. Moreover, it could grow in recent times because of (not in spite of) the machine's further entrenchment.

We do not mean to suggest that all, or even most, IVI members join the organization out of self-interest or utility alone. We are merely suggesting that Olson's argument notwithstanding, there is a logical (calculated) basis for self-interest participation in reform club politics, in spite of the lack of rationality of such participation. We also suggest that self-interest, combined with effective political leadership, is the most compelling explanation for the rising resources of Chicago's reform club movement in recent years, despite a continued failure of reform club efforts to oust the machine from political control of the city.

The Future of the Reform Club Movement

Clearly, the growth of reform clubs in Chicago will not be unrestricted. "Rationality" functions as a barrier to unlimited growth of the organizations by causing incipient reform activists to weigh their potential contribution against the improbability of it having an appreciable effect on Chicago's political system. The variety of tactics employed by the machine to obtain compliance is another barrier. Chicago's regular Democratic organization has effectively frustrated the expression of even fully recognized self-interest, especially among segments of impoverished minority communities.

Wilson, in his discussion of the organizational problems of amateur Democrats, has pointed to organizational divisiveness as another limitation on organizational growth. [38] Chicago's reform club movement in particular has not only become organizationally fragmented, but faces intraorganizational dissension. The IVI has especially manifested a cleavage between those club members who favor the achievement of liberal goals—even at the expense of independence from the machine—and other club members who are willing to trade off liberalism for party autonomy where the two are incompatible. The division between these two factions has increased in recent years and clearly affects the level of organizational strength by hindering unified action on key issues and endorsements.

Finally, effective political leadership is necessary to convince the pool of potential reformers to act in their self-interest, if not rationally. Such leadership is difficult to obtain, given the paucity of organizational resources available to Chicago's reform clubs. Indeed, perhaps one major explanation for the membership decline of the IVI since 1972 is the frequent absense of its membership recruiter in attempts to organize the political campaigns of several independent candidates. Nevertheless, the tactics of this recruiter, along with those of the initial IPO organizers in the late 1960s, were probably more important than anything else in getting self-interested independents to take the plunge and join one of Chicago's reform clubs.

Summary

In the late 1950s and early 1960s, James Q. Wilson studied Democratic reform club politics in New York, Chicago, and Los Angeles. He found that professional activists could be distinguished from amateur activists in three major aspects: their ascriptive and other background traits, their political and social orientations, and their motivations for joining either regular party organizations or reform clubs. We reexamined Chicago's reform club movement more than a decade later in order to test the validity of Wilson's observations, and we examined more recent organizational developments in the movement.

Our findings supported some of Wilson's conclusions and contradicted others. The population of amateur activists examined in this study are characterized by the same basic background traits that Wilson found in 1962. Contrary to Wilson's conclusions regarding parochial and cosmopolitan traits, however, we found that IVI members in 1975 were more parochially oriented than indicated in the study conducted 15 years earlier. Moreover, we have concluded that Wilson's characterization of the independent political activists in Chicago in 1962 as amateur and, by definition, idealistic, does not adequately define the role of the independent political activist in Chicago in 1975. Our study indicates that amateur political activists are more pragmatic than Wilson indicated in his study. The divergence of our findings from Wilson's may be explained by the 15-year lapse as well as by the weak methodological tools we believe Wilson employed in his study.

In terms of motivational aspects, our findings are in agreement with Hofstetter's recent research, which refutes the incentives model devised Clark and Wilson to explain why people join reform clubs. We modify Hofstetter's alternative model by suggesting that self-interest and personal utility are the most persuasive explanations for the maintenance and enhancement of Chicago's reform club movement. We develop the concept of "logic of utility" as a heuristic concept that has moderate empirical support. This concept provides a rather marked departure from conventional wisdom, which claims that the motivation to join reform clubs is primarily ideological or purposive in nature. A further assessment of the explanatory value of the "logic of utility" in juxtaposition to the explanations of Wilson and others awaits additional methodological refinements and application to other situations in which similar conditions of organizational opposition exist.

NOTES

1. *The Amateur Democrat* (Chicago: University of Chicago Press, 1962).
2. John W. Soule and James W. Clarke, "Amateurs and Professionals: A Study of Delegates to the 1968 Democratic National Convention," *American Political Science Review* 64 (September 1970): 888–898.
3. Thomas H. Roback, "Amateurs and Professionals: Delegates to the 1972 Republican National Convention," *Journal of Politics* 37 (May 1975): 436–467. See also Roback's contribution to this volume.

4. For example, see C. Richard Hofstetter, "The Amateur Politician: A Problem in Construct Validation, " *Midwest Journal of Political Science* 15 (February 1971): 31–50.

5. Lewis Bowman, Dennis Ippolito, and William Donaldson, "Incentives for the Maintenance of Grassroots Political Activism," *Midwest Journal of Political Science* 13 (February 1969); and C. Richard Hofstetter, "Organizational Activists: The Bases of Participation in Amateur and Professional Groups," *American Politics Quarterly* 1 (April 1973): 244–276.

6. For a detailed description of the characteristics of amateur and professional party activists, see Wilson, *Amateur Democrat*, chaps. 1, 10, and 11.

7. Wilson is borrowing here a concept developed in Robert K. Merton's, "Patterns of Influence: Local and Cosmopolitan Influentials," in *Social Theory and Social Structure* (Glencoe, Ill.: Free Press, 1957), pp. 387–420.

8. For the most complete statement of Wilson's theory concerning organizational motivations, see Peter B. Clark and James Q. Wilson, "Incentive Systems: A Theory of Organization," *Administrative Science Quarterly* 6 (September 1961): 129–166.

9. Hofstetter has attempted to validate Wilson's construct but, by his own admission, his findings were somewhat inconclusive and suggestive of further examination. See Hofstetter, "Amateur Politician," pp. 31–50.

10. The IVI is Chicago's largest and oldest reform club organization. It was one of two Chicago reform club organizations examined by Wilson, the other of which no longer exists. Its basic goals have been threefold: endorsement, by active members, of candidates for public office; precinct work for the election of endorsed candidates; and lobbying for progressive causes. Few other reform club organizations besides the IVI exist in Chicago today. The Independent Precinct Organization (IPO) is a small, less influential club than the IVI. The IPO attracts a younger more activist membership than the IVI, but basically endorses the same "good government" candidates. The Better Government Association (BGA), the only other major reform group in Chicago, abandoned its policy of endorsing and working for candidates several years ago. The BGA concentrates on exposing corruption and inefficiency in Illinois government.

11. In addition to the IVI mail questionnaire, an effort was made to interview the eighty members of the regular Cook County Democratic Party Committee. Although Wilson avoids any systematic examination of regular Democrats in his study , his assumption was that the survey of these so-called professional politicians would serve as a useful data base from which to compare the sample of IVI members on a series of attitudinal, behavioral, political, and socioeconomic traits. After considerable effort, this aspect of the project was abandoned. Only a small portion of the committee's members were willing to cooperate with the researchers. We have concluded, however, that the base of the research—i. e., the study of role development and social and political orientations of amateur political activists—has given us the type of data necessary to suggest conclusions concerning the distinct nature of Chicago's reform club movement and its development since the 1960 study by Wilson.

12. Wilson, *Amateur Democrat*, pp. 1–31.

13. Percentages rounded off to the nearest tenth of a percent in the sample of one hundred are accounted for by a reduction in the sampe size due to missing data on a number of the survey items.

14. Of the sixty-eight members of IVI Board of Directors nineteen are women; no woman has served as chairperson of the organization.

15. Since the IVI is affiliated with the Americans for Democratic Action, we can assume a liberal orientation of IVI members.

16. Wilson, *Amateur Democrat*, p. 4.

17. Ibid., p. 4.

18. Ibid., p. 4.

19. Ibid., p. 4.

20. James Q. Wilson and Edward Banfield, "Public Regardingness as a Value Premise in Voting Behavior," *American Political Science Review* 58 (December 1964): 876–887.

21. Wilson, *Amateur Democrat*, pp. 10–11.

22. Ibid., pp. 10–11.

23. Ibid., chap. 6. See also Clark and Wilson, "Incentive Systems," pp. 129–166.

24. Wilson, *Amateur Democrat*, chap. 3.

25. For a somewhat journalistic account of the activities of these reform clubs, see Joe Mathewson, *Up Against Daley* (La Salle, Ill.: Open Court, 1974).

26. For an account of the activities of the IPO, see especially Greta Salem, "Participatory Politics," *Chicago's Future*, ed. Dick Simpson (Champaign, Ill.: Stripes, 1976), pp. 78–91.

27. Wilson, *Amateur Democrat*, chap. 6. See also Clark and Wilson, "Incentive Systems," pp. 129–166.

28. Hofstetter, "Organizational Activists," pp. 244–276.

29. The political economy model of organizational behavior suggests that organizational allegiance to political and economic associations flows from the calculation of one's self-interest (what political economists call "utility") rather than from ideological commitment. See especially Anthony Downs, *An Economic Theory of Democracy* (New York: Harper and Row, 1957); and Mancur Olson, *The Logic of Collective Action* (Cambridge: Harvard University Press, 1965).

30. Olson, *Collective Action*, passim.

31. Ibid., p. 65.

32. Ibid., p. 45.

33. Norman Frolich, Joseph A. Oppenheimer, and Oran R. Young, *Political Leadership and Collective Goods* (Princeton, N. J.: Princeton University Press, 1971).

34. See especially David L. Protess, "Banfield's Chicago Revisited: The Conditions for and Social Policy Implications of the Transformation of a Political Machine," *Social Service Review* (June 1974): 184–202.

35. Olson, *Collective Action*, pp. 164–165.

36. Wilson, *Amateur Democrat*, p. 73

37. Downs, *Economic Theory*, p. 24.

38. Wilson, *Amateur Democrat*, chap. 8.

5 / Presidential Third Parties and the Modern American Two-Party System

Howard R. Penniman

In 1964, Senator Barry Goldwater vowed that he would not be a "me-too" candidate. He promised that his policies would offer a real alternative to those of the Democratic administration. During the campaign, the Arizona senator proposed distinctly more conservative alternatives in foreign policy and in certain social and economic programs at home. The voters chose to reject his candidacy and his program and reelected President Lyndon B. Johnson by a wide margin. President Johnson received 61.1 percent and Senator Goldwater 38.5 percent of the total votes cast in the election.

Much was made of the magnitude of Senator Goldwater's defeat and of its importance to the party system. "The health of the two-party system," it was argued after the election, "depends on the capacity of the two parties to agree on most issues and, at the margins, to offer alternatives attractive to slightly different components of the population. This would make for disagreement on live issues—not on issues already settled and a part of an overriding national consensus."[1]

Agreement or near agreement between the major parties on issues that deeply divide the community, however, may also promote, at least temporarily, and imbalance within the political system. The fortunes of third parties may rise or fall in accordance with the degree of major party agreement on these divisive issues.

In the spring of 1964, the governor of Alabama, George C. Wallace, entered the Democratic presidential primaries in three states outside the South. In April, he won 34 percent of the votes cast in the Wisconsin primary. The following month, he won 30 percent of the Democratic vote in a presidential preference primary and a whopping 43 percent in the Maryland Democratic primary. In early June, he declared his readiness to enter the general election contest in the fall as a third-party candidate for president of the United States. He decided against the third party effort only after Senator Goldwater had voted against the civil rights bill pending in Congress in mid-June and had won the Republican nomination for president in mid-July.

In the election itself, President Johnson and Senator Goldwater together won 99.6 percent of the 70,307,672 votes cast. Of the remaining 336,838 votes, 210,732 were cast for the slate of unpledged Democratic electors in Alabama. (There was no Johnson–Humph-

This essay is based on papers delivered at the American Political Science Association National Convention in Los Angeles in September 1970 and at the Midwest Political Science Association Convention in Chicago in April 1976. The author wishes to thank the Earhart Foundation for financial assistance that made the research and writing of the two papers possible.

phrey slate of electors on the Alabama ballot.) This left a paltry 126,106 votes for the six minor-party candidates. Their share of the total vote amounted to 0.14 percent. Even with the great increase in the population, the third-party candidates received fewer votes in 1964 than in any national election since 1868 when, as in the Civil War election of 1864, there were no third-party candidates. The share of the vote gained by the six minor-party candidates in 1964 was less than the share received by third-party candidates in the whole history of popular voting for presidential candidates, again except for 1864 and 1868. [2]

Even before third-party support almost disappeared in 1964, the late V. O. Key had quoted students of third parties as seeming "to agree that the day of the third party, at least in presidential elections, is done." [3] After the 1964 election, others asserted that they too expected the early demise of presidential third parties and offered different reasons for their judgment. Not all political scientists were so sure. [4]

In 1968, George C. Wallace and his American Independent Party (AIP), running under various labels in the different states, received 9,908,141 votes (13.5 percent of the total popular vote) and 46 electoral notes. His nearly 10 million votes was the greatest number ever received by a third party. His 13.5 percent was larger than the share of the popular vote won by any other post–Civil War third-party candidate except Robert M. LaFollette in 1924 and Theodore Roosevelt in 1912. [5]

The margin of disagreement over issues that separated the major party candidates in 1964 may well have been responsible for the magnitude of the Johnson victory. It may also have been responsible for the striking paucity of voter support for the third parties. Four years later, when the major party candidates were generally thought to be much closer together, the majority of white voters in the deep South and a sizable minority outside the South joined Governor Wallace in finding no important policy differences between Nixon and Humphrey. Most of the deep South supporters of Goldwater in 1964 shifted their allegiance to Wallace in 1968.

In 1972, enough voters apparently felt that Senator George McGovern had moved so far from the center that only 37.5 percent of them supported him at the polls. Nixon won 60.7 percent and third-party candidates won 1.5 percent of the votes. The latter figure was down sharply from 1968 but well above the 1964 low.

It is generally true that in a two-party system a major party courts disaster if it appears to stray too far from the national political center on salient issues, though by doing so it may prevent the rise of any important protesting third party. On the other hand, when an emotional issue sharply divides the nation, but not the major parties, a third-party candidate who voices the view of those outside the major parties' consensus may win a large protest vote.

The rise of a strong third party only four years after the electoral low of 1964 provides ample justification for reexamining some traditional judgments about the nature of third parties, their leaders, and their place in the two-party system. This study will concentrate on five parties established after 1920. A number of basic changes that occurred around 1920 so modified the country's political environment that the post-1920 national third parties differed greatly from their predecessors. Women's suffrage became a reality in 1920. By 1920, the method of nominating most publis officials other than the president and the vice-president was changed from party convention to direct primary administered by the states. And in the mid-1920s, the first general restrictions on immigration greatly reduced the impact of immigrants on big-city politics.

Doctrinaire parties have been excluded from consideration not only because most of them were created before 1920, but also because they have been less closely related to the two-party system than the larger, temporary protest parties. Ideological parties, including the Communist Party and the Socialist Worker Party, sometimes have viewed themselves as outside the party system. At various times, they have advocated the destruction of the existing system rather than participation within it. These two parties have had an impact on the country's affairs during some of the period under discussion, but not as vehicles for seeking public electoral support. The Socialist Party and the Prohibition Party, on the other hand, while quite willing to work within the system to secure their goals, have seen their strength diminish since 1920 to the point where their nominees receive only a handful of votes and have little hope of any change for the better.

No distinction will be made in this paper between the "parties of protest" and the "bolters" or "secessionists" or "splinter" parties because (1) there is no agreement among political scientists about which parties fit into each category[6] and (2) because, as Professor Key pointed out, "in their role in the party system as a whole the two sorts of parties appear to be fundamentally similar."[7] The parties, then, whose nature and role will be looked to for evidence of the relationships between third parties and the party system are the Progressive Party in 1924, the Union Party in 1936, the Progressive Party and the States' Rights Party of 1948, and the American Independent Party of 1968.

Parenthetically, it may be noted that not only have the categories of third parties not always been useful, but most definitions of political parties in general would exclude all the parties under consideration here. Definitions that speak of such elements as stability and continuity and even membership (whether dues-paying or registered) would exclude every large third party since 1920.[8] Only an inclusive definition such as Leon D. Epstein's covers third parties. Epstein accepts as a party

> any group, however loosely organized, seeking to elect governmental office-holders under a given label. Having a label (which may or may not be on the ballot) rather than an organization is the crucial defining element. This allows the use of the word "party" for a group of aspiring office-holders who have no organized followers but merely decide to seek votes under a collective name in addition to their own personal names.[9]

Any group, in other words, that can get the names of its candidates on the ballot by meeting state legal arrangements is considered a party.

Direct Primaries and State Third Parties

Third parties of even passing importance are rarely found today at the state level. The last fully competitive state third parties—the Farmer-Labor Party of Minnesota and the Progressive Party of Wisconsin—disappeared more than 30 years ago.[10]

The institution of the direct primary as the accepted device for nominating candidates for every elective office from justice of the peace to governor accentuated the already decentralized character of American major parties. When the people choose the nominees of their party, the candidates are likely to reflect the views and the prejudices of the voters rather than of the party leaders.

Primary elections have sharply reduced the influence of national and state party leaders on nominations. In the populist areas, from Wisconsin west to the Rocky Mountains, all aspirants for office are more or less on their own in seeking their party's nomination. Candidates run their own campaigns, set up their own organization, and raise their own money. They make their appeal directly to the voters, who either accept or reject the candidacies. Only after their nomination, when its help often is unimportant, does the party support the candidates.

When any qualified citizen can seek the nomination of either major party to any office and voters are free to choose nominees who fit their views, there is no reason for either to turn to third parties as an outlet for their views about state and local issues. The Nonpartisan League in North Dakota in the 1920s made it clear in the state primaries that an organized effort can turn a conservative Republican Party into perhaps the most liberal state party in the country. The Independent Voters Association showed that the same party can be recaptured by conservatives.

Liberals George Norris and Robert M. LaFollette had no need to create third parties in Nebraska and Wisconsin because they could win by appealing directly to Republican voters against the conservative party leaders. [11] On the other side of the ideological street, neither Strom Thurmond nor George Wallace needed to go outside the Democratic Party in order to gain state office. The political views of each of these four candidates reflected more or less accurately the prevailing voter attitudes in their states while not necessarily reflecting either their national party's views or the views of the leaders of the state organization.

The extreme decentralization of American major parties has been an important reason that helps explain why the Congress has simultaneously housed liberals and conservatives, isolationists and interventionists, integrationists and separatists, supporters of labor and supporters of business, warmongers and pacifists. Whatever their views, all have been either Democrats or Republicans. Not since Vito Marcantonio of the American Labor Party (ALP) was defeated in New York in 1950 has there been a congressperson bearing any other label. [12] Douglas W. Rae, after studying legislative elections in the major democratic governments of the world for the period 1946 to 1964, found that the American House of Representatives was more thoroughly dominated by two parties than any other national legislative body. [13]

This two-party domination was not always true in the United States. The inability of third parties to elect members of the Congress in recent years contrasts strikingly with the situation in the nineteenth century. Between 1840 and 1860, some 165 third-party candidates were elected to the House of Representatives. Their success was neither a fluke of the early years of the "second American party system" nor a product of the divisions related to slavery. From 1870 to 1902, another 159 congresspersons were elected under labels other than Republican or Democratic. After that, the number of third-party congresspersons began to decline rapidly until they simply disappeared. [14]

Today the Liberal and Conservative parties in New York are the only remaining third parties of any importance at the state level. They are still relatively influential parties because New York state law, in effect, has given their executive committees the choice of running their own candidates for state and local offices or supporting candidates of one of the major parties. The 1967 New York law providing for the nomination of statewide candidates by direct primary did not alter this power of the third-party executive committees. The arrangements may benefit some candidates of the major parties, but it reduces the power of the major-party organizations.

Traditionalists in New York's major parties would be glad to change the law and reduce the attractiveness of these minority parties, but most Republican and Democratic legislators, not to mention governors, have profited from the support of either the Conservative or Liberal voters. Consequently, legislation to weaken these lesser parties cannot be enacted. [15] No other state legislature has been willing to encourage the rise of new parties at the expense of the major parties.

The direct primary and the decentralization of party authority, then, have virtually eliminated the need for third parties as instruments for expressing dissident views in state politics. This was made clear again by the citizens of Tennessee's eighth congressional district in a by-election in March 1969. This district, located just outside Memphis, had given Wallace a 25,505 vote plurality in 1968, nearly twice the combined vote of Nixon and Humphrey. Yet four months later, the American Independent Party congressional candidate in the same district, William J. Davis, won only 16,313 votes, or 23.8 percent of the total, while Democrat Edward Jones won 32,629 votes, or 47.6 percent of the total. [16] Wallace's campaign for Davis went largely unheeded. The case illustrates how easy it is for citizens to find one of their kind within a major party in contests below the presidential level. Since Jones, like Davis, was conservative on social issues, there was no reason for socially conservative voters to go outside the Democratic Party, no matter who urged them to do so. During the same period, Wallace's own popularity remained roughly at his 1968 vote level, never falling below 12 percent in either the Gallup or Harris polls.

Third Parties Are Presidential Parties

If the direct primary largely eliminates the need for third parties at the state level, no such development has occurred at the presidential level. Traditional major-party national conventions sought to name presidential candidates and write platforms that would appeal to the greatest number of their normal supporters and, at the same time, attract some so-called independents and maybe even a few voters from the opposition party. But a presidential nominee often must choose sides on divisive issues. On the race question, for example, he cannot simultaneously please voters in Chicago's South Side and voters in the third district of Mississippi. There are other issues that make it difficult for a candidate to be equally appealing to voters in Arizona and Rhode Island. If the party conventions name candidates and write platforms that are reasonably close to one another, as has normally been the case, then voters on one or both sides of the emotionally charged issues may find that neither candidate satisfactorily represents their views. Only if a third candidate presents himself can some voters outside the two-party consensus find a satisfactory candidate.

Direct primaries have made third parties unnecessary at the state level, but it may just be that the conditions of two-party competition at the presidential level make third parties essential. This would be particularly true when "gut" issues separate a regional minority from a national majority. Whether or not they are essential, however, third parties today are by the nature of American political institutions, presidential parties.

All of the parties considered here, except the Progressive Party in 1948, named candidates only for the nation's two top offices. The decision not to name or support candidates at the local or state level was not born of despair or of inability to find candidates to seek these lesser offices, as has sometimes been suggested. It was a conscious decision that the soundest way to secure the largest vote for presidential candidates was to avoid any conflict with congressional and state candidates who were sympathetic to the third party's goals but, nevertheless, ran under the auspices of a major party. It was also a decision not to intensify the problems of Republican and Democratic voters who might find it psychologically easier to cut the top off their party ticket than to reject the entire party slate. [17]

Robert M. LaFollette, in 1924, made it clear that he was not a third-party presidential candidate and refused even to speak of his supporters as a party. Philip LaFollette has quoted his father as saying:

> I stand for an honest realignment in American politics, confident that the people in November will take such action as will insure the creation of a new party in which all Progressives may unite. I would not, however, accept a nomination or an election to the Presidency if doing so meant, for Progressive Senators and Representatives and Progressive State Governments, the defeat which would inevitably result from placing complete third party tickets in the field at the present time. [18]

The view expressed by the elder LaFollette prevailed, but not all of his supporters agreed. Some viewed this statement as a means of appealing to both the "nonpartisans" in the labor movement (the AFL was supporting LaFollette) by not fielding a full slate of candidates and to the Socialists by speaking of the possibility of a new party at some future date. Neither LaFollette not the Conference for Progressive Political Action (CPPA) supported any Socialist candidates, although the Socialist Party officially endorsed LaFollette's bid for the presidency. The CPPA itself was not clear on its status. Its convention in July 1924 "instructed the executive [council] to call a national convention in January 1925, to consider the formation of a permanent independent political party." The Socialists were dismayed after the election to find that LaFollette had carried Socialist districts in New York while their own candidates for the state legislature had lost out to major-party competitors. [19]

The actions of LaFollette and the CPPA were no different from those of the other parties under consideration except the Progressives in 1948. The States' Rights Party had no reason to name candidates at the state and local levels in 1948. In four of the Southern states, the national candidates, Governors Thurmond and Wright, were on the ballot under the label of the Democratic Party. They carried all of these states (Alabama, Louisiana, Mississippi, and South Carolina). There was no slate of Truman electors on the Alabama ballot. In the remaining Southern states, Democratic congresspersons sometimes quietly supported Governor Thurmond rather than President Truman. The States' Rights Party was established to protest the strong civil-rights plank in the Democratic platform, and its founders had little to fear from Southern Democrats in the Congress who regularly opposed the president on civil rights. There was no policy advantage, therefore, in pressing the case for non-Democratic candidates.

The Henry Wallace Progressives, by contrast, attempted to establish state parties and to put up slates of candidates. The difference between the 1948 Progressives and the other parties may relate to the fact that the Progressives were more like the ideological parties than the other third parties under review. Communist activists played a role in the organizational planning of the party and the Communist Party endorsed the Wallace-Taylor ticket. [20] Progressive leaders may simply have seen so great a gulf between their purposes and those of the major parties—especially in foreign policy—that the creation of a separate party seemed the only reasonable course to pursue.

Whatever their reasons, the Wallace Progressives supported 123 candidates for the Congress in twenty-four states and senatorial candidates in ten states. They also supported gubernatorial and state legislative candidates in some states. A slate of candidates below the presidential level was ruled off the ballot in Georgia. [21] In New York, the Progressives supported 44 congressional candidates under the label American Labor Party (ALP)—some of whom were also on the Democratic ticket. ALP stalwart Vito Marcantonio was their only successful congressional candidate.

A serious effort was made to keep the Progressive Party in operation after the 1948 election. Wallace announced that he would be the Progressive candidate again in four years "if it would be the best thing for the Progressive Party." [22] Two years later, he broke with the left wing leadership over the issue of the Korean War, which the left wing asserted as the fault of the United States. By 1952, the Progressive Party's policy position was indistinguishable from that of the Communist Party, [23] but its candidate, Vincent Hallinan, received little popular support other than from the Communist Party, which worked hard in Hallinan's campaign. At this point, and perhaps in 1948 as well, the Progressives seemed to consider themselves outside the system.

A few candidates below the national level appeared under the American Independent Party label in 1968, but without the support of the head of the ticket. Some well-known independent candidates sought Wallace backing; their requests were ignored or refused. Even George P. Mahoney, the Democratic nominee for governor in Maryland in 1966, was denied Wallace endorsement when he ran, in 1968, as an independent candidate for the Senate who shared the Alabaman's political views. [24]

In sum, when third-party presidential candidates saw themselves as part of the larger political system, and when they expected to continue their political careers within a major party and anticipated some policy support from major party congresspersons—perhaps even quiet campaign assistance—they found no reason to name candidates for other offices. This reasoning was particularly persuasive when there was strong regional backing for the policies of the third-party presidential candidate and of the major-party congresspersons. Most third-party presidential candidates probably would prefer to prevent all candidates for lesser offices from using the new party label, but they cannot do so if the "usurpers" meet state legal provisions.

Third-Party Candidates

Who were the presidential candidates of the third parties? The simple answer is that they were successful politicians. All except Henry Wallace had won the support of the voters of their states before their unsuccessful bids for the presidency. They continued to win elections at home after their defeat. As noted elsewhere, William Lemke of North Dakota was elected to the Congress in 1936 even as he was losing the state as a presidential candidate. [25] The "extreme" views that drove these men to do battle with middle-of-the-road national Republican and Democratic candidates were sufficiently mainstream in state politics that the voters supported them again and again in primaries and in general elections.

LaFollette was elected on the Republican ticket in Wisconsin for 35 years. Lemke sat in Congress as a Republican off and on from 1930 until his death in 1950. Strom Thurmond moved to the Senate after his service as governor of South Carolina. Henry Wallace was elected vice-president with Franklin Roosevelt in 1940, although he won no elective office on his own either before or after his presidential campaign. George Wallace was elected governor in 1962, and his wife, Lurleen, was elected in 1966 when he was not eligible for another term. After a change in the state law, he was reelected in 1970 and 1974. Governor Strom Thurmond was the only candidate who did not have a national reputation at the time of his race for the presidency. The States' Rights party, however, was a regional, not a national party, and Thurmond was well-known regionally.

All these candidates had long been associated publicly with the issue or issues that helped to bring the third parties into existence. All the candidates for president were assured of the nominations well before they were announced.[26] Senator LaFollette's selection as the candidate of the combined forces of labor, democratic socialism, and western populism was a foregone conclusion from the moment a decision was made to name an alternative to the major-party candidates. For years, he had been the leader of the progressive wing of the Wisconsin Republican Party and the recognized leader of progressives of both parties in the Senate. He had campaigned for progressives of both parties in half the states of the Great Plains.[27]

Lemke, Republican congressperson from North Dakota, was less clearly a national symbol than most third-party nominees. He was not considered for this role until after the assassination of Senator Huey P. Long in 1935. Nevertheless, Lemke was a leader of the Nonpartisan League. He had pushed farm bankruptcy legislation through the House of Representatives in spite of the lack of support from President Roosevelt, and he was a widely known supporter of assistance for the elderly. Lemke was not nominated by a convention but by Father Charles E. Coughlin who headed the Union for Social Justice. Lemke's candidacy was announced to the forty-eight state chairpersons who Coughlin had appointed a few weeks earlier.[28]

Henry Wallace had been vice-president for one term under Franklin Roosevelt and had served in the cabinets of two presidents. He was generally identified with the left wing of the Democratic Party. Since early 1946, he had been the most prominent opponent of American foreign policy and particularly the policy toward the Soviet Union. He was fired from his cabinet post by President Truman for his criticism of administration foreign policies. Wallace became a probable third-party candidate from the day of his dismissal. He formally announced his candidacy in December 1947. His selection was ratified in Philadelphia in July 1948, after his name was already on the ballot in many states.

George Wallace was almost literally self-nominated. He found ready support to get his name on the ballot in all states.[29] Well before 1968, Wallace had become the major symbol of opposition to civil-rights legislation and to the desegregation of the schools growing out of the Supreme Court's decisions in 1954 and 1955. His campaign cry that there was not "a dime's worth of difference" between the major party candidates had obviously struck a responsive chord in the deep South and among some groups in the North.

Wallace voters agreed that there was very little difference between the positions of Richard Nixon and Hubert Humphrey. In Survey Research Center interviews in 1968, Wallace supporters generally agreed with the governor on the issues most closely associated with him—law and order, reduction of power in Washington, segregation, and victory in Vietnam. Some 80 percent of his supporters viewed Wallace as a conservative, and 57.5 percent also saw themselves as conservatives. By contrast, only 7.4 percent considered Nixon a conservative, and only 7.0 percent saw Humphrey in the same light. On the issue of the Vietnam war, 71.7 percent thought Wallace was a "hawk," and 60.0 percent identified themselves with the same position. [30] Only 18.7 percent of Wallace supporters rated Nixon, and 13.5 percent rated Humphrey, as hawkish. Far more Wallace voters than Nixon and Humphrey voters opposed open housing and national government handling of education and jobs. Only 7.3 percent of Wallace voters felt that the police had used "too much" force against demonstrators in Chicago at the time of the Democratic National Convention, while 49.5 percent thought they had used too little. By contrast, 20.3 percent of Nixon supporters and 34 percent of Humphrey supporters thought too much force had been used, while 30.1 percent of the Nixon voters and 23.9 percent of the Humphrey voters thought too little force had been employed. Of the Wallace voters, 70.4 percent said urban unrest, which they often associated with race, was either the "most important single thing" or "very important" in deciding how they would vote. Likewise, 63.8 percent placed Vietnam in those same categories. [31]

The Platforms of Third Parties

The substance of third-party platforms provides some clues to the level of their commitment to the political system as well as indicating the remedies they proposed for the problems of the day. Just as a major party's platform criticizes the other major party and its leaders, the third parties' platforms criticize both of the major parties against whom they are campaigning. However, their criticism ranges from complaints against the current views and activities of the major parties to denunciation of the whole system. The five parties being examined showed significant differences in the views they expressed concerning the integrity of the major parties and the morality of the system itself.

The Union Party made no comments about any other party or leaders or about the system itself. Its platform consisted simply of fifteen numbered proposals. The first asserted the need for an extreme isolationist position. The remaining fourteen generally began with the words "Congress shall . . ." The duties of the Congress, according to the platform, included regulating business and banks and helping farmers, the old, and the poor. There was none of the rabble-rousing style that was so often associated with Lemke's supporters, Gerald L. K. Smith and Father Coughlin. [32]

Senator LaFollette in his personal platform asserted that "monopoly has its representatives in the halls of Congress, on Federal benches, and in the executive departments." He criticized the Supreme Court for nullifying acts of the Congress and the bureaucracy for showing favoritism. He asked that the Congress be given the power to override the judicial veto. Elsewhere, he criticized the Congress's failure to act on proposals for the repeal of the Esch-Commins railroad law, a failure which he said was the result of "the joint action of reactionary leaders of the Democratic and Republican parties." [33] He directed no other criticism toward the parties or the system. His supporters in the CPPA called for an end to the "tyranny and usurpation of the courts" and proposed election of all federal judges. [34] In the then nonpartisan tradition of the AFL, the platform made no other statements critical of any party or of the system.

The States' Rights Party criticized the major parties and the national "Executive Department" for "promoting . . . [the] growth of a totalitarian state by domination and control of a politically minded Supreme Court." The platform opposed "the totalitarian, centralized, bureaucratic government and the police state called for by the platforms adopted by the Democratic and Republican conventions." Three more times the platform warned of the danger of "totalitarianism" or "the police state," the last time calling for public support to "ignominiously" defeat Truman and Dewey and "every other candidate for public office who would establish a police state in the United States." The party claimed to be the real representative of the Democratic Party tradition and denounced the Democratic National Convention for its civil-rights proposal. [35]

The Progressive Party of 1948 was by far the most critical of the major parties and of the political system. The platform in its preamble asserted that "private power has consti- tuted itself an invisible government which pulls the strings of its puppet Republican and Democratic parties." Under the general heading "Betrayal by the Old Parties," the platform stated, "the American people want peace, but the old parties obedient to the dictates of monopoly and the military, prepare for war in the name of peace." It specifi- cally denounced the financing and arming of corrupt "fascist governments in China, Greece and Turkey" and the protection of the "war-making industrial and financial barons of Nazi Germany and imperial Japan," and made ten other comparable charges.

Later the platform insisted that "the old parties, acting for the forces of special privi- lege, conspire to destroy traditional American freedoms," and thus "repeat the history of Nazi Germany, Fascist Italy, and Franco Spain." This assertion was followed by alleged instances of "conniving," "concocting," and "regimenting" by the two major parties work- ing together. Both parties were described as the "champions of big business," and refer- ence was made to the "bipartisan conspiracy in Congress . . . against adequate old-age pensions." As noted earlier, the United States and the West were charged with responsi- bility for militarism and imperialism. Further, the platform demanded the "repudiation of the Marshall Plan" and the repeal of "provisions of the National Security Act which are mobilizing the nation for war, preparing a labor draft, and organizing a monopoly- military dictatorship." [36]

The American Independent Party platform made reference to the national parties and their leaders, who were "inept" and "fearful," who "paid homage to the legions of dissent and disorder and worshipped at the shrine of political expediency." Their "inaction and subservience to illogical domestic policies" endangered labor's gains. The old parties, said the platform, had allowed the school system to deteriorate and had failed to handle the problems of Indians and Eskimos, the cities, and the farmers." [37] No criticisms were made of the political system itself.

In summary, the platform of the 1948 Progressive Party was so unrestrained in its criticism of the major parties and the government as to suggest that only the destruction of the system could solve the nation's problems. The second most critical party was the States' Rights party, with its warnings against the "totalitarianism" and the "police" state that would result from the proposed actions of the major parties against states' rights and for civil rights. It placed special emphasis on the sins of the Democratic Party, which it claimed had strayed from its heritage. Both the American Independent Party and Lafol- lette were critical of the leaders of the major parties, but not of the system. Finally, the Union Party criticized no one and pressed for only fifteen policy changes.

The Impact of Third Parties

The rise of third parties that draw enough votes to seem to threaten even temporarily the dominance of the two major parties in American politics raises questions about the impact of their brief flurry on the political scene. Any answers to these questions must be highly tentative. The parties that meet the above standard are: the Populist Party in 1892; the Progressive parties in 1912, 1924, and 1948; the States' Rights Party in 1948; and the American Independent Party in 1968.

Early in this paper, it was noted that there was a decline in the votes cast for third parties in 1964 when the major party candidates were perceived to be far apart on both foreign and domestic policy issues. Four years later, when the candidates and policies of the major parties were once more reasonably close together, there arose the third most powerful of the ad hoc parties in more than a century. The third-party vote jumped from 126,106 or 0.14 percent to 9,908,141 votes or 13.5 percent of the total votes cast. There is obviously no way of being certain that the proximity of the major party candidates will bring about a comparable development in any future elections. Still, the differences between 1964 and 1968 are so striking as to force speculation on the problem. The only parallel that comes to mind is the contrast between the elections of 1892 and 1896: in 1892, when the major parties were close together on major issues, the Populists won 1,029,960 votes, or 8.5 percent of the total; four years later, when the major parties were divided on major issues, the Populists virtually disappeared. Before too much is made of this point, it should be noted that since 1940, except in 1948 and in 1968, the major parties have been claiming a larger share of the vote than had traditionally been true for the elections between 1876 and 1936. In only six elections have the major parties received more than 99 percent of the vote, and all have taken place since 1940.

Third parties may also affect voter turnout. The turnout rate in 1892 was nearly 5 percentage points less than in either 1888 or 1896. The turnout in 1912 was 6.6 percentage points less than in 1908 and 2.9 percentage points below 1916. The turnout in 1924 was the lowest in the history of national popular voting for president. For special reasons, it was only slightly down from 1920 (0.3 percentage points), but it was a full 7 percentage points below the turnout in 1928.[38] The turnout in 1948 was 2.9 percentage points below 1944 and a full 10.3 percentage points less than in the first Eisenhower year, 1952.[39]

In 1968, the rate of turnout of voters was down only 1.1 percentage points, but this drop occurred in spite of an impressive increase in the rate of voting in the Southern states, which resulted primarily from the enfranchisement of blacks under the Voting Rights Act of 1965. Every state in the old Confederacy except Georgia showed an increase in the rate of turnout.[40] The turnout rate increased 19.2 percentage points in Mississippi, 16.7 percentage points in Alabama, 8.9 percentage points in Virginia, and 7.2 percentage points in South Carolina. Over 2.5 million more persons voted in the eleven southern states in 1968 than in 1964, which was almost exactly the total increase in votes for the whole country. Yet population growth was greater outside the South. The turnout of blacks in the South increased by 7 percentage points and that of whites went up about 2 percentage points. Many of the blacks who voted in 1968 had been legally or administratively prevented from voting in 1964.[41]

In the North, where voting rules were unchanged except to ease the literacy requirement in New York by allowing Puerto Ricans to take the test in Spanish, the voter turnout was down by about 4 percentage points—3 percentage points among whites and a striking 11 percentage points among blacks.[42] Outside the South, the turnout rate was down in every large industrial state. It increased in only four non-Southern states—Alaska by 5 percentage points, Hawaii by 0.9, Maine by 1.4, Maryland by 0.5.[43]

In the 1972 election, unlike previous elections that followed one in which a third party had won electoral votes, the turnout went down rather than up. A heavy drop in Southern voter turnout and the enfranchisement of the eighteen- to twenty-one-year-old citizens can account for some of the voting decline, but cannot explain a 5.3 percentage point slide.

Still, it is important to remember that in the five elections prior to third-party "successes," and in four of the five elections that followed them, the turnout was higher (and usually considerably higher) than in the year of the large third-party vote. The fact that voter turnout is unusually low when third parties are strong cannot be dismissed as pure coincidence. In the elections we have examined, there have been no obvious factors except the presence of third parties to explain the decline. The candidates have been as appealing as in most elections. In some instances, two or three of the candidates were famed for their ability to attract voters. In each election, important and relatively clear-cut issues were being argued. Yet voter participation went down.

It is easier to find symptoms than to explain diseases. Why should voters stay home when more than two parties earnestly seek their support? Perhaps large numbers of voters feel alienated from the system—which may, of course, be the reason for the strength of the third party. The Harris Poll reported after the 1968 election, "28 percent of adult Americans—over 33 million people—feel largely alienated from the mainstream of society." [44] It is also possible that the presence of more than two well-publicized candidates increases the heat of the debate without clarifying the issues. The numbers and the noise may merely confuse. The extra candidates may also create cross pressures that keep voters long identified with one of the major parties away from the polls. Whatever it may be, the explanation is not obvious.

Impact on Public Policy

Much has been written about the influence of third-party platforms and campaigns on the course of public policy and particularly on the programs advocated by one or both of the major parties. The example used by most analysts is that of the Populists and the Democrats in the 1890s. In 1892, the Populist platform, among other things, stated: "We demand free and unlimited coinage of silver and gold at the present legal ratio of 16-1." [45] Four years later, the Democratic Party, under the leadership of William Jennings Bryan, wrote into its platform: "We demand the free and unlimited coinage of both silver and gold at the present legal ratio of 16 to 1 without waiting for the aid or consent of any other nation. We demand that the standard silver dollar shall be a full legal tender, equally with gold . . ." [46]

The Populist Party decided not to nominate a candidate of its own for president in 1896 and instead joined the Democrats in backing Bryan. (The Populists named a different candidate for vice-president.) Although the party did not formally declare its demise until 1912, its support of Bryan, made possible by his position of silver, removed the major reason for citizens to vote for the Populists rather than for the Democrats. It is not unreasonable to assert, then, that a connection existed between Bryan's platform and the end of the Populists. It is less certain that the Democrats "stole" the issue or appropriated it in order to win the Populist vote. Still, this may have been at least one reason for the presence of the silver plank in the 1896 Democratic platform.

An examination of major-party and minor-party platforms since the 1890s produces very little evidence of so close a relationship between the Republican or Democratic politics and the policies proposed in the platforms of third parties. Aside from the Populists, no third party can make a very good case that it passed from the political scene because a major party adopted its program. On the other hand, it seems clear that third parties sometimes have disappeared because no one—neither the major parties nor the public—wanted their programs. The Wallace Progressives of 1948 won 1,157,326 votes. After Wallace left the party on the ground that the left wing had taken control, the party's candidate, Vincent Hallinan, managed to win only 140,023 votes. Both major parties denounced the Progressives, and neither borrowed anything significant from the Progressive platforms of 1948 and 1952.

Third-party platform planks that remain unadopted generations after they were first proposed and after the demise or decline of the sponsoring party, far out-number those that can be said—even with the greatest stretch of the imagination—to have been enacted into law. The policy proposals of third parties, to be sure, are part of the reservoir of ideas from which the whole community, including the major parties, may draw. Among the likely sources of platform ideas—interest groups, congresspersons and congressional staffs, the executive bureaucracy, the media, and so on—third parties must rank very low as contributors to the development of major-party programs.

Still, third parties may contribute to public support for or opposition to a particularly divisive policy by focusing public attention on the problem. When this happens, the major parties, as well as the press and the public, read the message written large in the election returns, and the parties react according to their judgment of political realities and their own political and moral commitments.

Summary

The findings of this limited inquiry into third parties support some widely shared views about the American party system and the place of third parties within the system. They raise questions about other frequently stated generalizations, and they suggest some hypotheses that seem to be worth further study. A summary of some of the findings follows.

1. Direct primaries, as noted by other political scientists, have helped to reduce the number of third parties established at the state and local levels. The primary has made it possible for any person or organized group interested in winning public office, for whatever reason, to seek support directly from the electorate. The primary has also increased the probability that candidates selected by this system will represent their constituencies' views on emotionally charged issues and not necessarily those of either the state or the national party organizations.

2. Third parties have generally been presidential parties in recent years. There is no obvious equivalent at the national level to the direct primary that allows regional differences to be represented when issues deeply divide the nation. The third party, then, becomes one means for voters to express dissent.

3. Presidential candidates of temporary third parties have generally been politicians who had succeeded in the competitive electoral politics of their home states, who had long been identified with the issue or issues that were at the center of their campaigns, and who were recognized as certain candidates if they were prepared to run.

4. Third-party presidential candidates, contrary to views expressed by some students of political parties, generally have not wanted to have candidates named on the new party ticket for state and local offices. This has been true for several reasons: because the presidential candidates themselves expected to continue to seek state or congressional office within one of the major parties; because they could expect support for their policy

proposals and possibly for their campaigns from congressional candidates remaining within the major parties; and because it is easier for voters to vote against the head of their party's ticket than to reject the entire ticket in favor of an entirely new slate.

5. The influence of third-party programs and platforms on the policies of the government and on the platforms of the major parties almost certainly has been exaggerated. There is little evidence from an examination of third-party platforms and those of the major parties to suggest that third parties have as much influence on policymaking as a number of other segments of the community.

6. There may be a relationship between the proximity of the major-party policy programs to one another on divisive national issues and the likelihood of a great increase in the size of the third-party vote. When the differences between the major parties are very slight, third parties may win a popular vote that is significantly above the average for the general time period.

7. When strong third parties are on the ballot, the voter turnout tends to be lower than in the elections immediately preceding and following. There are a number of possible reasons for this drop in participation, but the data examined for this paper offer no firm explanation.

There seems to be a relationship between the major policy problems of an era, the major-party response, and the status of third parties. The study of third parties can help illuminate the nature of the larger political system. For a better understanding of relationships within the system, more work is needed on phenomena suggested in this summary. Research is also needed on the recruitment of campaign workers by third parties, the financing of campaigns, the impact of rules regulating third-party candidates and their inclusion on the ballot, [47] the relationship (if any) between the rise of third parties and subsequent change in the relative strength of the major parties, and the relationship (again, if any) between the internal rules governing the major parties and the strength of third parties. The list could be expanded. Few areas of the study of the party system offer more interesting opportunities for inquiry. [48]

NOTES

1. Milton C. Cummings, Jr., *What 1964 Meant: The Elections in Retrospect* (Washington, D. C.: Brookings Institution, 1966), p. 4. Professor Cummings also edited a useful volume for Brookings, *The National Election of 1964.*

2. The figures for the elections used in this essay are taken from *Guide to U.S. Elections* (Washington, D. C.: Congressional Quarterly, 1975) and from Richard M. Scammon, *America Votes: A Handbook of Contemporary American Election Statistics,* vol. 12 (Washington, D. C.: Congressional Quarterly, 1977).

3. V.O. Key, *Politics, Parties and Pressure Groups* (New York: Crowell, 1964), p. 281. His excellent chapter on third parties is to be found on pp. 254–281.

4. Among those who were not sure of the demise of third parties were Allan Sindler, Hugh Bone, and Angus Campell.

5. In his subsequent career, Wallace was elected to two more gubernatorial terms in 1970 and 1974. After threatening to run again as a third-party candidate if Nixon failed to take the "proper" stance on school integration, Wallace sought the Democratic presidential nomination. At the time he was forced out of the campaign by a would-be assassin's bullet, he was leading all other candidates in popular votes. After the fifteenth primary election on May 16, 1972, Wallace had accumulated 3,354,360 votes, while Hubert

H. Humphrey had 2,647,676, and McGovern 2,202,804. Although Wallace led in popular votes, his organizations in Northern states were often so weak or inept that he lagged far behind Humphrey and McGovern in the number of elected delegates.

6. Key's *Politics, Parties, and Pressure Groups*, pp. 262–267, refers to both the 1912 Progressives and the Dixiecrats (States' Rights Party) as "secessionist" parties—a category into which Key also fits the 1872 Liberal Republicans. Walter Dean Burnham and John Sprague refer to the 1912 Progressives and the States' Rights Party as "organizational fractures," while they classify the 1924 Progressives, the Populists, and the American Independent Party as "insurgent movements" or "grass-roots phenomena." See their "Additive and Multiplicative Models of the Voting Universe: The Case of Pennsylvania, 1960–1968," *The American Political Science Review* 64 (June 1970): 489. Hugh Bone includes the States' Rights Party, the 1912 Progressives, and the National Democrats of 1896 as "bolters" in *American Politics and the Party System*, 3rd ed. (New York: McGraw-Hill, 1965), p. 132. Andrew M. Scott lists the Dixiecrats and the Progressives of 1924 and 1948 as "bolters" in *Competition in American Politics: An Economic Model* (New York: Holt, Rinehart and Winston, 1970), p. 30. These are merely examples of the varying classification schemes that have been used.

7. Key, *Politics, Parties, and Pressure Groups*, p. 263.

8. For a discussion of the problem of definitions, see Austin Ranney, "The Concept of 'Party,' " in *Political Research and Political Theory*, ed. Oliver Graceau (Cambridge: Harvard University Press, 1968), pp. 143–162. As we shall note later, some candidates of "third parties" did not think of their own organizations as parties. LaFollette made a great effort to retain his "independent" status.

9. Leon D. Epstein, *Political Parties in Western Democracies* (New York: Praeger, 1967), p. 9. Epstein suggests that if one person adopts a label, he qualifies as a party. Some modern third parties have had no organization and virtually no supporters.

10. For a classification of state third parties, see Howard R. Penniman, "Third Parties and the Politics of Tomorrow" (Paper presented at the 1976 Annual Meeting of the Midwest Political Science Association, Chicago, April 29 - May 1, 1976), p. 4. "Fully competitive parties" ran candidates at all levels within the state and frequently won.

11. After more than 30 successful years within the progressive wing of the Republican Party, Philip LaFollette led his faction out in 1934 to create the Progressive Party. He and Robert M. LaFollette, Jr., won two elections each under the new label. They and their followers returned to the Republican fold in 1946.

12. Frazier Reams won a seat in the House of Representatives as an independent from Ohio's ninth congressional district in 1950 and 1952. John Joseph Moakley, who had been a successful Democratic member of the state legislature of Massachusetts and of the city council in Boston, won a seat from the ninth district of Massachusetts in 1972 defeating Louise Day Hicks, who had won the Democratic Party nomination in the primary. Moakley was supported by most Boston Democratic leaders, who were disturbed by Hick's opposition to busing. In 1974 and 1976, Moakley was reelected to the Congress as the candidate of the Democratic Party.

13. Douglas W. Rae, *The Political Consequences of Electoral Law*, rev. ed. (New Haven: Yale University Press, 1971), Appendix F, p. 193.

14. U.S. Bureau of the Census, *Historical Statistics of the United States: Colonial Times to 1970*, Bicentennial Edition, Part 2 (Washington, D. C., 1975) p. 1083.

15. See Hugh A. Bone, "Political Parties in New York City," *The American Political Science Review*, 40 (April 1946): 272–283. Professor Bone recounts the story of the formation of the predecessor of the Liberal party, the ALP, which was created to provide organizational help for President Franklin Roosevelt in 1936 when Tammany was providing little support.

16. "Tennessee Election Results," *Congressional Quarterly* 27 (March 28, 1969): 440.

17. Philip E. Converse, Warren E. Miller, Jerrold G. Rusk, and Arthur C. Wolfe, "Continuity and Change in American Politics: Parties and Issues in the 1968 Election," *The American Political Science Review* 63 (December 1969): 1085. After noting great changes in presidential voting preferences between 1964 and 1968, the authors suggest that these changes "may be ironically juxtaposed against the serene stability of party identification in the

country . . . over the past twenty years." Most Wallace voters continued to identify themselves as Republicans, Democrats, or independents and all Wallace voters told Survey Research Center interviewers that they had cast ballots for either Republican or Democratic congressional candidates in 1968.

18. Philip LaFollette, *Adventures in Politics: The Memoirs of Philip LaFollette,* ed. Donald Young (New York: Holt, Rinehart and Winston, 1970), p. 91. In his memoirs, Philip LaFollette says that as early as December 1923, a family council "agreed that if Dad were to be a candidate, it would not be on a 'third party' ticket but as an independent. An independent candidacy might have more appeal to Progressive Republicans and Democrats than a third party" (p. 87).

19. Nathan Fine, *Labor and Farmer Parties in the United States, 1818 to 1928* (New York: Rand School of Social Science, 1928), pp. 409–416. Fine, himself a Socialist, expressed annoyance that the CPPA and LaFollette decided against a permanent party in 1925.

20. See Key, *Politics, Parties, and Pressure Groups,* pp. 272–273, and Bone, "Political Parties in New York City," pp. 138–139. See also K. M. Schmidt, *Wallace: Quixotic Crusade 1948* (Syracuse, N.Y.: Syracuse University Press, 1960), passim. Professor Schmidt seeks to minimize the importance of the Communist role in Progressive activities in 1948. Both the Socialist Party and the Socialist Workers Party denounced the Progressive Party and stressed the Communist Party role. See Kirk H. Porter and Donald Bruce Johnson, *National Party Platforms 1840-1948* (Urbana: University of Illinois Press, 1966), pp. 454–460 and 462–466.

21. Schmidt, *Wallace,* pp. 333–335.

22. Reported in *Facts-on-File Yearbook, 1948,* vol. VIII, no. 420, p. 372. The statement was made in Chicago on November 14, 1948.

23. Porter and Johnson, *National Party Platforms,* pp. 487–494.

24. Mahoney's segregationist views were an issue in both the Democratic primary and the general election. He repeated his slogan, "a man's home is his castle," in order to make his opposition to open housing clear to all. It was this opposition that drove many liberal Democrats, black and white, to support the Republican gubernatorial nominee, Spiro T. Agnew.

25. E. C. Blackorby, "William Lemke: Agrarian Radical and Union Party Candidate," *Mississippi Valley Historical Review* 49 (1962): 80. Lemke received only 12.8 percent of the presidential vote in North Dakota while winning his congressional seat by a comfortable 30,000 vote margin.

26. Vice-presidential candidates, like the major-party candidates for that office, were chosen by the presidential candidate or in consultation with him. Of the five candidates for the nation's second office, three were politicians, one was a union leader with no political experience, and one was a general.

27. LaFollette, *Adventures in Politics,* pp. 71–77. At one time or another, the senior LaFollette campaigned for Democrats, Republicans, and Farmer-Laborites who were considered progressives.

28. See Blackorby, "William Lemke," p. 76. Father Coughlin had written to his state chairpersons in early June promising that "in due course telegrams will be sent you containing, among other announcements, the names of the candidates for president and vice president."

29. It took a decision of the Supreme Court to get Wallace's name on the ballot in Ohio. See *Williams v. Rhodes,* 393 U.S. 23 (1968).

30. "Hawks," in this instance, were persons who wanted "complete military victory."

31. The data in this paragraph are taken from Charles R. Grezlak, "A Comprehensive Portrait of Wallace Voters in the 1968 Presidential Election" (unpublished paper).

32. Porter and Johnson, *National Party Platforms,* p. 375.

33. Ibid., pp. 252–255.

34. Ibid., pp. 255–256.

35. Ibid., pp. 466–468.

36. U.S. Bureau of the Census, *Historical Statistics*, pp. 1071–1072.

37. Porter and Johnson, *National Party Platforms*, Supplement 1968, pp. 2–20.

38. The Socialist Workers Party, in its platform, denounced the Communist Party for its servile support of the Stalin regime and also for its backing of the Progressive Party. Porter and Johnson, *National Party Platforms*, pp. 464–465. The Socialist Party's comments on Communist participation in the Progressive Party may be found in the Socialist platform (Porter and Johnson, pp. 454–455).

39. The turnout figures used here were taken from the U.S. Bureau of the Census, *Historical Statistics*, pp. 1071–1072. These figures were provided to the Bureau of the Census by Walter Dean Burnham and in some instances have been revised from his earlier figures that appeared in the report to the Freedom to Vote Task Force, *That All May Vote* Appendix III, (Democratic National Committee, December 16, 1969), pp. 2–4.

40. The turnout in 1924 was down only slightly from 1920, but the size of the change is misleading. Women had received the vote nationally in August 1920, and some of them simply had not had an opportunity to register to vote that year. More important, newly eligible voters historically have voted less frequently than any other potential voters. By 1924, however, more women had had an opportunity to register and to become accustomed to the processes of voting; the normal expectation, therefore, would have been a considerably larger vote than in 1920. Hence, the drop of 0.3 percentage points is more significant than at first appears.

41. Census Bureau figures show that the Georgia turnout dropped by 0.6 percentage points from 1964.

42. For a discussion of the Center's findings on turnout, see Converse, Miller, et al., "Continuity and Change," pp. 1088–1089. They use the Census Bureau definition of the "South," which includes fifteen states and the District of Columbia. Thus, the South appears less pro-Wallace than would be the case if only the eleven states of the Old Confederacy were included.

43. U.S. Bureau of the Census, *Historical Statistics*, pp. 1071–1072.

44. *Washington Post*, November 11, 1968.

45. Porter and Johnson, *National Party Platforms*, p. 91.

46. Ibid., p. 98.

47. Paul H. Blackman, *Third Party Presidents? An Analysis of State Election Laws* (Washington, D. C.: Heritage Foundation, 1976), passim. This book provides the most up-to-date discussion of the problems of third parties and the rules for receiving a place on the ballots.

48. For an interesting recent essay on the nature of third parties, see John William Ellwood, "A Model of the Life-Cycle of American Minor Parties: Supported by Data from the Rise and Decline of the Wallace Movement" (Paper presented at the 1977 Annual Meeting of the Southern Political Science Association, New Orleans, November 5, 1977).

PART **II**

CANDIDATE SELECTION

INTRODUCTION

Candidate selection is the single most important activity engaged in by a political party. Nowhere in the elaborate process of selecting elective officeholders do voters have a greater choice of contrasting appeals, policy views, and personalities than in the prenomination fights for party endorsement. It could be argued with some merit that this is the single most critical stage in the elective process. At this point, the political party, acting on behalf of its adherents, selects from potentially a multitude of able candidates (as in the presidential nominations, for example)—and the electoral coalitions and policy perspectives these contenders represent—the one it will support in the general election. From the variety of possibilities, representing enormous implications for the political system, the choice is reduced in the general elections to the two contenders chosen by the parties to represent their stands and to carry their hopes. When the voters in the general election begin to make their choice, the field has already undergone potentially its most significant reduction.

Not surprisingly, the procedures employed by the political parties to decide on nominees have been subjected to a great deal of examination. To an extent, in fact, they have begun to emerge as subjects of academic and party controversy. The most serious questions have been raised about the value and representativeness of primaries (as against caucus or convention systems) in nominating processes, and about the role of the media in deciding, or at least directly influencing, public attitudes and potential choices. As they relate to presidential nominations, in particular, both areas have begun to receive extensive attention. In the meantime, the national convention and its role in the choice of a nominee appear to be changing. The essays in Part II address these problems.

An important and thought-provoking contribution to the debate over the value and representativeness of primaries in presidential selection is Richard L. Rubin's "Presidential Primaries: Continuities, Dimensions of Change, and Political Implications." Rubin focuses on three important areas: the changing role of primaries and the nature of participation in primaries for the period 1912–1976; an intensive analysis of primaries over the last decade, with particular emphasis on turnout; and the relationship between primary and general election voter characteristics. In the process of analyzing these topics, the author asks such questions as: How many party members participate in primaries? Are the numbers of people involved at this stage of candidate selection increasing or decreasing? How representative are the primary voters of the party membership more generally? How representative are they of the voters who participate in general elections? Do primaries give certain blocs of voters increased influence in presidential nominations at the expense of other, perhaps more significant, groups in the electorate? Is the new emphasis on primaries in the best long-run interests of the party?

The questions are important. To answer them, the author has accumulated a storehouse of data not previously available. His analysis calls into question many assumptions that political scientists have been making concerning the representativeness and utility of primary elections.

Rubin shows, for example, that primary turnout has increased over the years. This is particularly important in light of current arguments over the inclusiveness of primaries. In fact, the author illustrates that primary participation jumped substantially with the reform of nominating processes in 1972, and that in 1976, despite a less intense prenomination contest, primary participation remained high (at a little over 60 percent of the potentially eligible Democrats). He concludes that a high primary turnout may have become institutionalized and, all things being equal, may well continue at these high levels.

As a consequence of recent developments, the influence of prereform (pre-1972) party elites on presidential nominations has declined. The role of the media may well have increased in importance as well as the influence of prenomination contests on general election results.

Rubin also finds, despite contentions to the contrary, that the representativeness of key groups within primary electorates compared favorably to the general election turnout. Also, and again this finding differs from previous arguments, labor-union families turned out in large numbers in Democratic primaries. The author concludes that the rank-and-file influence over presidential nominations has been increased through the institution of the primary and that the politics of today, as a consequence, are dramatically different from those of even a decade ago.

Others have explored the concerns that intrigue Rubin.[1] The general belief has been that primary electorates are unrepresentative of a political party's broader coalition. There are degrees of emphasis in this type of argument, and on some policy or demographic dimensions primary voters may indeed be close to the broader body of people who identify with a party and vote for it in the general election. It is generally felt, however, that the activists who vote in the primary tend to be more politically interested and alert; generally middle class, and therefore with higher educational achievements and a higher socioeconomic status; and strongly motivated over policy concerns or by support for a particular candidate, e.g., Jimmy Carter and Ronald Reagan in 1976; George McGovern in 1972; Eugene

McCarthy, Robert Kennedy, and George Wallace in 1968. These attributes of the types of activists who tend to participate more actively in the nominating politics of a given election year would make the primaries (and caucuses) generally unrepresentative of the broader party identifiers.

It is this type of characterization that Rubin begins to question. Rubin's analysis receives some support from the research of Herbert M. Kritzer, presented in his selection, "The Representativeness of the 1972 Presidential Primaries." This piece adds perspective to the issues addressed by Rubin. Kritzer's analysis compares those who participated in the 1972 Democratic presidential primaries (the Republican incumbent, Richard Nixon, was basically uncontested in his bid for renomination) with both Democratic Party supporters in the general election and those who failed to participate in the prenominations stage. Based on previous research, the expectation was that these Democrats who became involved in primary elections would be unrepresentative of Democrats more generally. This is not what Kritzer found. Comparing the different groups on three sets of measures—demographic variables, indices of political involvement, and attitudes on political issues—the author concludes that those who participate in primaries differ from Democrats in general only in the extent of their partisanship and their concern with political processes. He argues that primary voters are representative of the party rank and file and that when the choice among candidates is both meaningful and broad enough to cover the major concerns of the party's coalition, such a representative turnout may not be unusual.

Change in the composition and inclusiveness of primaries may be in the wind. It may be that primaries will come to reflect reasonably well the motivating concerns and major groupings within a party's coalition. It seems clear that the primaries (and, to a lesser extent, the party caucuses) have taken over the role of the national conventions as the principal battlegrounds on which presidential nominations will be fought and decided. [2]

If this is true, then the next question—the media coverage of and influence over presidential nominating contests—becomes all the more important. Two articles deal with this problem. [3] The first, by Rhodes Cook, "Media Coverage of the 1976 Nominating Process," provides a good introduction to the institutional and interpretative complexities of prenomination processes. Cook is concerned, in particular, with the media's role in structuring the attitudes of potential voters to conform to the results of prenomination contests.

The author looks in depth at four stages in the prenomination schedule: the first-in-the-nation Iowa precinct caucus; the first-in-the-nation New Hampshire primary; the Wisconsin and New York primaries in early April and the media's response to them; and the closing brace of primaries in early June and the media's selective interpretation of the major races in California, New Jersey, and Ohio at that time.

The essay conveys well the complexities of the overall process and the reasons that media representatives attempt to simplify both the procedures and the outcomes for broader public consumption. Indications of what is happening and of who won precisely what are most often far from clear. By simplifying outcomes, the media, of course, channels public attention toward and influences support for those "winners" they choose to emphasize in their unbalanced coverage of selected primary or caucus contests. Such a process is bound to direct attention to some candidates and away from others. The process of instant media interpretation also has a show-business quality to it. It is meant to entertain, as well as inform, and it often reduces political communications to something close to the lowest common denominator. At least, this is what the critics of the media's role in interpreting prenomination results claim. These critics believe the media have not served the political system well in this regard. The critics would like to see the media's role diminished and their influence restricted. Just how this could be done—much less how beneficial it would be—is far from clear.

The media do have their faults. They badly overplayed the results of the Iowa and New Hampshire contest, simply because these primaries were the first of their kind in the nominating season. The media chose to emphasize the Wisconsin outcome over that of an electorally far more important state, New York. The Wisconsin results were easy to interpret. The New York primary, in contrast, suffered from complex rules and its outcome was far less obvious. Such a selective interpretation can help one candidate over another. Jimmy Carter, for example, benefited from good early showings in Iowa and New Hampshire and, in fact, as a result of these contests and the media coverage they spawned, became the acknowledged front-runner. President Ford similarly benefited on the Republican side. Poor showings by Carter in New York and, at the close of the primary season, in California and New Jersey, attracted little attention. The media, in this case, found the Ohio race, where Carter won, more significant.

The problems that Cook outlines find added emphasis in the essay by Michael J. Robinson, "Media Coverage in the Primary Campaign of 1976: Implications for Voters, Candidates and Parties". Robinson is concerned with the differences between, and impact of, newspapers and television coverage of the first three months of the 1976 presidential nominating campaign. A particular emphasis is placed on the media's coverage of New Hampshire, a state that assumes an importance in the process far outweighing its political significance. The author also compares the emphasis in the media's coverage to the public's perceptions of the evolving campaigns.

The study is unique. The author monitored major dailies (including the *New York Times* and the *Washington Post*) as well as a large selection of news programs, including ABC's, CBS's, and NBC's nightly newscasts. The themes in these newspapers and television news programs were then compared with the information and attitudes of a random public opinion sample of Washington, D.C. residents.

The media emphasis on the New Hampshire results is extraordinary. This much is clear. Ronald Reagan claimed in 1976, as Robinson explains, that the media's interpretation of the New Hampshire results may have cost him the Republican presidential nomination. Be that as it may, of 616 news stories dealing with the nomination politics of all the states during the seventy days covered in the study, 41 percent of the reports were on New Hampshire. The results of the New Hampshire primary were spotlighted on the news and received extended analysis. As a comparison, the decisions of New Hampshire's 82,000 primary voters received more than three times the attention given in the network news to the later results from New York's 3.7 million primary voters.

There are differences between the print and the electronic media in coverage. Nonetheless, both highlighted the contests in New Hampshire. It is fair to ask if such coverage and such an emphasis on one of the nation's least electorally powerful states is justified? Potential voters interviewed in the study tended to give the early New Hampshire results undue emphasis. They, as did the media, saw the New Hampshire primary winners as front-runners. The "reality" of the media became the "reality" of the voter. The more attention given to this small New England state and its choices, the more voters tended to assume these outcomes must be of enormous significance. One might ask, as the author does, what the implications of such biases in emphasis have for the totality of the nominating process as well as for the long-run interests of the political parties.

The final essays in this section deal with the national conventions and the nature and factional alignments of the party elites represented there. In "Recruitment and Motives for National Convention Activism: Republican Delegates in 1972 and 1976," Thomas H. Roback examines the delegates to the 1972 and 1976 Repubican national conventions. The author finds that the delegates in both convention years are relatively well-off (with the greatest number having incomes in the range of $25,000 to $50,000) and that although the characteristics of the delegates do not change from one convention year to the next, the actual number of 1976 delegates who attended the 1972 convention was low (10 percent). Three out of four delegates had never been to a previous convention.

Roback analyzes the differences between Reagan delegates on the one hand and Ford (in 1976) and Nixon (in 1972) delegates on the other. Although the supporters of all three candidacies share many demographic characteristics, their ideological and attitudinal commitments are quite different. The Reagan delegates tended to be strongly committed on ideological grounds to their candidate and to the causes with which he was identified. Their continuance in politics also was based on ideological and policy-oriented motivations. In fact, a significant bloc of policy conservatives that supported Reagan could trace their ideological commitment back to 1964 and the Goldwater candidacy.

The "regulars," those supporting Ford in 1976 and the balance of Nixon supporters in the 1972 convention, had more diversified socialization ties to the party and motivational reasons for supporting their candidate and the Republican Party. Many had become involved in Republican Party politics through a traditional, family-oriented learning pattern. The intensity of their commitments differed from the issue-based partisanship of the Reagan delegates. As 1976 (and 1964) demonstrated in the Republican Party, and 1972 in the Democratic Party, the appeal to a committed bloc of policy-oriented constituents within a party can enable a candidate to mount a strong challenge for his party's presidential nomination.

The analysis by John S. Jackson, III, Jesse C. Brown, and Barbara L. Brown "Recruitment, Representation, and Political Values: The 1976 Democratic National Convention Delegates," complements that by Roback. The focus this time is on the 1976 Democratic National Convention. The authors are concerned with much the same type of questions that intrigued Roback, specifically the demographic and attitudinal characteristics of the 1976 delegates and the extent to which these compare with those of delegates to earlier Democratic conventions (1972 and 1976). The authors also examine the influence that the new delegate-selection rules—a product of the reform movement within the Democratic Party—have in changing the national convention's composition or in favoring one presidential contender over another. Finally, they attempt to explain the nature of Jimmy Carter's coalition and why he, an outsider in Democratic Party politics, was able to win the nomination.

The demographic characteristics of the Democratic convention delegates rival those of the Republicans. The new delegate-selection rules appear to have had a marginal impact on the 1976 national convention's composition, although as the authors indicate, it is difficult to draw any direct relationship between the two. The authors speak with more confidence about Carter's winning coalition, for the primaries did produce most of the Carter delegates. More importantly, however, Carter was able to demonstrate wide support within the party, which cut across factional and ideological lines. This broad appeal to the diverse groups within the Democratic coalition, more than any institutional or reform-initiated explanations, helps account for Carter's success. The new rules may have lessened the control over convention nominations once exercised by the state and big-city party leaders, party regulars, and major interest groups such as organized labor. If such is the case, the party's nomination is open and goes to the contender most skillful in mobilizing electoral support in the primaries and caucuses, and in dramatizing these successes through the media, during the election year. Such nominations are a far cry from those sponsored and awarded by the party regulars in the prereform era. Any candidate, whether a newcomer to the national scene or not, has a reasonable chance to demonstrate his political acumen and, with luck, to capture the party's nomination. This, perhaps more than anything else, is what the Carter nomination illustrated.

NOTES

1. Of direct relevance to Rubin's argument would be: Austin Ranney, "The Representativeness of Primary Electorates," *Midwest Journal of Political Science* 12 (May 1968): 224-238; Austin Ranney and Leon Epstein, "The Two Electorates: Voters and Nonvoters in a Wisconsin Primary," *Journal of Politics* 28 (August 1966): 598-616; Ranney, "Turnout and Representation in Presidential Primary Elections,"*American Political Science Review* 66 (March 1972): 21-37; Ranney, *Participation in American Presidential Nominations, 1976* (Washington, D.C.: American Enterprise Institute for Public Policy Research, 1977); David W. Moore and C. Richard Hofstetter, "The Representativeness of Primary Elections: Ohio, 1968," *Polity* 6 (Winter 1973): 196-222; Andrew DiNitto and William Smithers, "The Representativeness of the Direct Primary: A Further Test of V. O. Key's Work," *Polity* 5 (Winter 1972): 209-224: Harvey Zeidenstein, "Presidential Primaries—Reflections of 'the People's Choice'?" *Journal of Politics* 32 (November 1970): 856-874; William Cavala, "Changing the Rules Changes the Game: Party Reform and the 1972 California Delegation to the Democratic National Convention," *American Political Science Review* 68 (March 1974): 21-37; and James I. Lengle and Byron Shaffer, "Primary Rules, Political Power and Social Change," *American Political Science Review* 70 (March 1976): 27-42.

   On primaries and presidential selection more generally, see: Donald R. Matthews and William Keech, *The Party's Choice* (Washington, D.C.: Brookings Institution, 1976); James D. Barber, ed., *Choosing the President* (Englewood Cliffs, N.J.: Prentice-Hall, 1974); Gerald Pomper, *Nominating the President* (Evanston, Ill.: Northwestern University Press, 1966); James W. Davis, *Presidential Primaries* (New York: Crowell, 1967); V. O. Key, Jr., *American States Politics* (New York: Knopf, 1956); and William Crotty, *Political Reform and the American Experiment* (New York: Crowell, 1977), chaps. 1-3.

2. William Crotty, *Decision for the Democrats: Reforming the Party Structure* (Baltimore: Johns Hopkins University Press 1978): and Crotty, "Party Reform and Democratic Performance" (Paper presented at the Conference on the Future of the American Political System, Center for the Study of Democratic Politics, University of Pennsylvania, Philadelphia, 1979).

3. See also Thomas E. Patterson and Robert D. McClure, "Television and Voters' Issue Awareness," in this volume.

6 / Presidential Primaries: Continuities, Dimensions of Change, and Political Implications

Richard L. Rubin

The ambivalence of Americans toward their political parties is a recurring theme of our political history. In a recent book, Austin Ranney underscored the curious combination of organized partisanship and antiparty spirit:

> [In] the long and convoluted epic that is the story of party reform in America, one leitmotiv appears more often than any other. This is the tendency of Americans to deal uneasily with the necessities of partisan political organization because of their widespread belief that political parties are, at best, unavoidable evils whose propensities for divisiveness, oligarchy, and corruption must be closely watched and sternly controlled. [1]

In no other democracy has the utilization of party mechanisms and antiorganizational spirit been more fully and uniquely combined than in the development of presidential primary elections in the United States. While there have been some small-scale parallels to the direct primaries in the selection of legislative members in certain Western nations such as West Germany and Belgium, at the executive level the presidential primary system is unique. [2] In no other democracy have party mechanisms themselves been used to expresss essentially "antiparty" feelings.

Overall, presidential primaries have received relatively little attention by political scientists and historians; [3] thus, as presidential primaries take on increasing importance in the selection of the candidates of the major parties, scholars find few sources on which to build. The "hard" data base, in particular, contains gaps as well as some suspect state party registration statistics. With the exception of the continuing efforts of Ranney, and some interesting but intermittent contributions from others, significant contributions in the field, such as those by Morris and Davis, and Lengle and Shafer, have only recently reached publication. [4]

This article focuses on three areas of research that are still seriously undernourished. First, secular trends in presidential primaries will be examined through the analysis of aggregate election statistics. The extent of participation in presidential primaries, and the changing types and number of primaries offered, will be studied in relation to the history of presidential primaries from their beginning in 1912 through 1976. [5] Second, an assessment of changes in the scope and intensity of presidential primaries taking place in the last decade will be made. It will include a critical analysis of some of the seminal work in the field, incorporating new data on the electoral impact of certain primary rules on urban, suburban, and rural constituencies. The extent and durability of step-level change in presidential primary turnout also will be included in the assessment.

Third, the relationship between the presidential *primary* electorate and the presidential *general* electorate will be examined. By analyzing research data from large national surveys taken in 1976, the validity of earlier theories that have come from smaller and narrower samples of the primary population will be tested. In addition, key-group voting shall be extracted to see if certain speculations on group participation in the primaries (e.g., low participation by labor union members and more active participation by those with high socioeconomic status [SES]) hold up when tested by national survey data. Such an examination permits a new assessment of the relative "turnout power" of different coalitional partners and allows for some informed speculation on the probable outcome of future primary conflict for the presidential nomination.

A Historical Overview

The importance of presidential primaries is greatly magnified by the critical importance of nominations in the overall presidential selection process, as Donald Matthews points out:

> Nominations are the most critical stage of the entire process of presidential choice. Once the major parties have made their nominations only two out of the millions of persons meeting the constitutional requirements of the office have a realistic chance of entering the White House: More eligible persons are eliminated from the presidential contest at this early stage of the process than at any other. [6]

While presidential nominations in a two-party system have always been a crucial feature of the selection process, presidential primaries have not. As a technique of delegate selection in nomination politics, presidential primaries first appeared in Florida in 1904 and rapidly became a popular method of state selection by 1912—some 80 years after the beginnings of a mass two-party system. The early history of presidential primaries has been dealt with elsewhere, and we shall not dwell on the origins of primaries beyond reaffirming their deep roots in the reformist politics of the late nineteenth and early twentieth centuries. [7] Instead, we shall analyze the behavioral changes that have occurred in the presidential primaries during the seventeen two-party nomination campaigns between 1912 and 1976.

Figure 6-1 shows the broad dimensions of change over time by comparing the total primary votes cast by each party in every presidential election year from 1912 to the present.

Although the increase in total primary votes is accentuated by the absolute growth of the American population in the twentieth century, the upward trend of primary voting is disproportionate to this growth and is clearly a feature of nonpopulation factors. (These factors are treated specifically in Figures 6-1 and 6-2 and in Table 6-1). The broad outlines of Figure 6-1 do suggest that internal participation at the mass level of a political party is greater in the majority party—particularly in the later stages of its dominance in an alignment. For example, the impact of the Progressive movement on the (majority)

Republican Party is reflected in the higher level of Republican primary voting between 1912 and 1928, and is similarly evident in the greater level of primary voting among (majority) Democrats in the 1960s and 1970s (a combination of George Wallace supporters, antiwar groups, party reform groups, and party "regulars").[8] These data lend support to Lubell's thesis that whatever the principal causes of political conflict may be, they are played out first in the conflict of groups, candidates, and issues in the majority political party.[9]

A more precise examination of the relationship of internal competition to rates of primary election turnout must await later discussion; but for the present analysis it is of interest to note the significant rise in Democratic Party turnout in 1936, which, occurring as it did at the peak of New Deal strength, appears anomalous. Looking behind the aggregate figures to the specific content of the elevated Democratic primary vote yields data that suggest an explanation of this apparent insurgent vote in the 1936 primaries. When the nature of the Democratic presidential candidacies is analyzed, certain features become clear. The large Democratic primary vote was not antiorganization or insurgent in its thrust as it was, for example, in 1968 and 1972. An incumbent, Franklin Roosevelt, actually won 93 percent of all primary votes, and no other candidate won as much as 6 percent of the total vote—hardly a manifestation of intense internal conflict. In this particular case, the increase in primary turnout was a result of an incumbent president joining forces with some organizational leaders to swamp any budding opposition.[10]

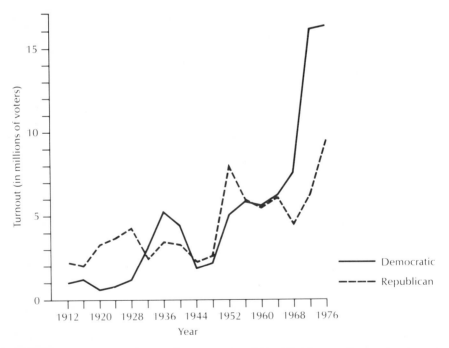

Figure 6-1 Turnout in all presidential primaries, 1912-1976. (*Source: Congressional Quarterly's Guide to United States Elections* and *Congressional Quarterly Weekly Report,* 1976.)

In Figure 6-2, the number of states holding presidential preference primaries in each election year is plotted by individual party over time. A presidential preference primary is one in which voters may indicate a preference for a potential nominee either by voting for delegates whose preference is indicated on the ballot or where the names of the

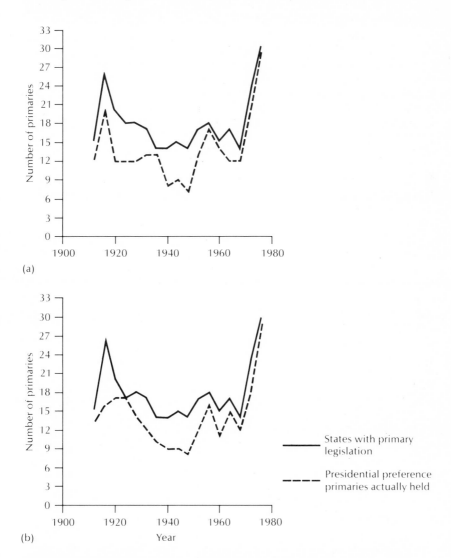

(a)

(b)

Year

States with primary legislation

Presidential preference primaries actually held

Figure 6-2 Presidential primaries, 1912-1976, excluding the District of Columbia: legislated (includes all types of presidential primaries) and actually held (includes only presidential preference primaries). (a) Democratic. (b) Republican. (*Source: Congressional Quarterly's Guide to United States Elections;* James W. Davis, *Presidential Primaries: Road to the White House;* Library of Congress, *The Nomination and Election of the President and Vice President of the United States, 1952-1976.*)

potential nominees are offered for voters' selection. The figure illustrates the sharp impact of progressive reforms and the following long period of decline (relative to 1916) in the number of states legally able to hold presidential primaries. Moreover, the number of states actually holding preference primaries during the period from the 1920s to the 1940s when compared to the number having the state-granted legal authority to conduct any type of presidential primary, is very low. In general, the greatest differences between the legal sanction to hold primaries and the actual occurrence of them were evident between 1928 and 1948 in the Republican Party and between 1920 and 1948 in the Democratic Party. [11]

From the 1920s through the post–World War II period, party organizational control by Republican and Democratic elites was seemingly able to contain the number of challenges brought through the medium of preference primary elections. In the Republican Party, progressivism and other insurgent pressures had dwindled as challenging forces to conservative organizational power; in the Democratic Party the success of the New Deal realignment and Roosevelt's close working relationship with certain party "bosses" effectively choked off serious challenges from inside the party. [12]

As noted earlier, the increased vote in the Democratic primaries was the result of a popular Roosevelt running with the support of organization leaders in most states. In the Republican Party, the declining importance of the primary in the nomination process was evidenced by the fact that a depression-trapped President, Herbert Hoover, lost seven of eight primaries (five uncontested) and still received the nomination with ease. [13] The New Deal and The Fair Deal periods did not revive the "party reform" spirit of the Progressives because reform of party organizations was crowded off the political agenda by the sharp social and political cleavages that developed between the two parties. Thus, as sharper lines of conflict were drawn between the two parties on issues critical to the well-being of large numbers of Americans, the issue of party reform became subordinate to the dominant cleavages—it became a victim of the conflict of conflicts. [14]

While there were important individual primary battles in the Republican Party in the 1944, 1948, and 1952 campaigns, the number of primaries remained relatively low, holding at a level well below that of the 1912 to 1920 reform period. The first major escalation in the total number of states selecting delegates by primaries (over the highs of the Progressive era) came in 1972, when twenty-one states and the District of Columbia held presidential primaries. In that same year, as F. Christopher Arterton has shown, a major increase in the percentage of convention delegates from primary states occurred, breaking a long stable pattern of selection. [15] This was followed by an explosion of presidential preference primaries in 1976, when twenty-nine states and the District of Columbia utilized presidential primaries of one kind or another in the nomination process.

Presidential Primaries in the Period After World War II

In studying presidential primaries in the period after World War II scholars have the advantage of more reliable sources of state primary data. The improved quality of the registration statistics in the postwar period gives us an opportunity to accurately measure participation rates over time in order to see if we can locate any step-level quantitative changes in primary turnout within this period.

Analysis of the individual party's preference primaries in Figure 6–3 points to several features of turnout that otherwise tend to be obscured when turnout in both parties is averaged in a presidential year. [16] Analysis of Republican Party data identifies high turn-out in the Taft-Eisenhower contest of 1952 (54 percent turnout), followed by a long period of lower primary turnout (and limited primary competition), and then a new, moderately higher peak over 1952 in the 1976 Ford-Reagan contest (55 percent turnout). The data show that until 1964 Republicans tended to turn out at a higher rate than Democrats in closed primaries, which is not an unexpected finding in light of the traditional relation-ship of higher SES among Republicans to higher rates of electoral participation.

Democrats, conversely, turned out at consistently lower rates in the primaries until 1968, the only exception occurring in 1956 when Stevenson and Kefauver battled through the primaries. Although Eisenhower, the Republican incumbent, was unopposed in 1956, Democratic turnout (42 percent) barely exceeded Republican turnout (41 percent). After 1964, Democratic turnout made successive leaps over preceding levels, reaching a post–World War II high of 52 percent in 1968 (up from 37 percent in Kennedy's 1960 cam-paign), and a new high of over 60 percent turnout in 1972, before leveling off at what appears to be a slightly lower level in 1976. [17]

The party-by-party analysis of Morris and Davis has documented the fact that compe-tition within the Democratic Party was a clear factor in escalating turnout. [18] Historically higher levels of turnout were, in fact, reached by the Democrats in 1972, forming a plateau of participation unequaled in over a half-century of primary competition. For,

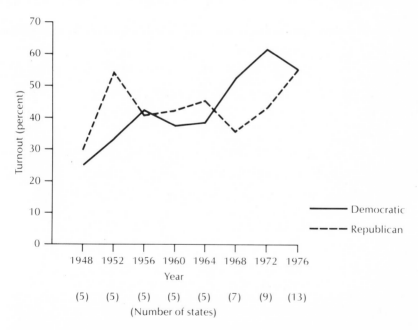

Figure 6-3 Turnout of registered voters by party in closed presidential preference primaries, 1948–1976. (*Source:* Secretaries of State for each state provided registration and turnout figures from 1948 to 1972; 1976 figures were taken from Austin Ranney, *Participation in American Presidential Nominations,* 1976.)

even though the intensity of competition among Democrats decreased with the apparently less divisive issues and personalities in 1976, turnout remained at a high level. [19]

The small apparent drop in Democratic turnout in 1976 is especially modest in significance if one considers that the Democrats did not have a close challenger to Carter in the competition for delegates after the Pennsylvania primary (the ninth of thirty primaries). This circumstance limited the extent to which the nomination appeared closely contested, particularly when compared to the two-man contest between Ford and Reagan in the Republican primaries. A small drop in turnout among the Democrats, therefore, may well be more than explained by other factors (for example, the reduction in overall campaign expenditures). In fact, Ranney's analysis of the 1976 campaign found a correlation of .40 between campaign spending and primary turnout. [20]

Bringing together certain old and new data, we can observe the following:

1. Competition brought out a significant escalation in turnout of primary-eligible voters —particulary the less-likely-vote Democrats—in the late 1960s and in the 1970s.

2. Turnout among Democrats, who are historically inclined to lower levels of participation in primaries, remained at a relatively high level in 1976 despite a less intense set of primaries.

3. Levels of campaign spending proved a strongly related source of higher primary turnout in 1976.

We might tentatively conclude from the above findings that what has occurred, at least for large numbers of rank-and-file Democrats, is the *institutionalization of high levels of primary turnout.* It appears that many voters have been socialized into new and higher levels of primary participation, levels that are now perhaps less directly dependent on the factors that precipitated the increase in turnout during the late 1960s and the 1970s. [21] The impact of massive television coverage, a new-found interest in the primary process itself, and, perhaps, new self-sustaining voting habits all seem to have contributed to the formation of a stronger base of mass participation in the selection of a presidential nominee.

Not only the events of the 1964–1972 period, but the *treatment* of those events by the television news media must be more fully considered in formulating any tentative theories of the cause of higher levels of participation in primaries. Michael Robinson, for example, has attempted to develop just such a linkage between changes in television journalism in the early 1960s (including the doubling of time devoted by the networks to evening news), new candidate strategies, and mass public response to the nomination process. [22] Speaking of the dynamics of this period, Robinson noted:

The greatest change was the shift toward a more plebiscitary process of electing leaders—in which television journalism provided a more direct link between the public and the candidates than had ever existed. The direct contact between electorate and elected was obviously little more than an illusion, but it was, for the first time since the colonial period, unfettered and unmediated by party or any large political organization. [23]

Several other considerations suggest a linkage between the major escalation of primary turnout and television journalism in this same period. It has been found that the television news audience is disproportionately drawn from the lower-middle and low end of the socioeconomic spectrum. [24] The data previously presented identified a major increase in primary turnout in that party (Democrats) which houses in its coalition a disporportionate percentage of individuals from these social classes. Robinson speculates that this stable and passive body of Americans was sharply aroused by a combination of both the events of the period and the television coverage of them.[25] And it stands to reason, if this was indeed the case, that these potential voters would more likely find their way to the polls in the Democratic primaries.

This interpretation of why Democratic participation sharply increased from its relatively low levels is, of course, speculative. But it touches upon important questions governing the nature and significance of the change in the behavior of the American voter—as well as the relative influence of the political and nonpolitical institutions on voter attitudes and behavior.

Some scholars have not found the same degree of change in the behavior of partisan masses as the above discussion would indicate, seeing continuity rather than change as the dominant mode of mass behavior among primary voters. Therefore, in the next section we shall address the question of the accuracy of measurements of change, the durability of such change, and the significance of our findings for the future study of electoral politics.

Studying Change in the Presidential Primary System

From a combination of the preceding discussion and the tables following shortly, a different interpretation of primary election dynamics is presented from that developed by the field's most noted scholar, Austin Ranney. Ranney's recent report, *Participation in American Presidential Nominations, 1976*, and his earlier works have made him deservedly the most respected scholar working in the field of primary elections.[26] He has been, in fact, the only scholar who has maintained a continuous interest in primary elections and, at the same time, developed a sufficient body of research to be confronted on an overall basis. And confront we must, for although much of Ranney's work will surely stand the test of time, certain of his perspectives, and the methodology supporting his views, need to be critically reexamined.

The reexamination of certain research is necessary because the predominant tendencies of his work seemingly obscure the elements of change that are to be found in the development of the primary system over the last, dramatic decade. As a result, evidence of significant change in the primary system is not fully developed, and major changes in the nomination system remain inadequately linked to long-term change in the interparty system.[27] In his most recent work, Ranney offers some variation in his methodological techniques but inevitably comes up with conclusions that do not quite fit primary turnout data that are extended over a time dimension. The continuation of generally low levels of turnout by partisans in the primaries is the picture that Ranney draws. He does not see traditionally low rates of participation up to 1964 followed by a step-level and durable increase in partisan turnout that may be of major electoral significance for American politics.

Here are some recent remarks of Ranney that tend to play down the extent, endurance, and significance of changes in primary turnout:

> So, while turnout in presidential general elections may be a respectable stream (if not a mighty river), turnout in presidential primaries is a small brook.[28]

Accordingly, while in 1976 the nation had far more presidential primaries—and far more closely contested ones—than ever before, there was a sharp drop-off in turnout. That drop, moreover, was larger than the much discussed drop-off in turnout in presidential general elections. [29]

Part of this author's difference with Ranney stems simply from a difference in perspective—is a glass half empty or half full? Is the turnout of more than half the eligible voters in the 1976 primaries a "small brook" or, rather, an impressively large percentage of the rank and file when viewed historically? In addition, some of the differences with Ranney stem from his methodology, which tends consistently to underestimate and depress turnout trends.

For example, Ranney determines the mean turnout in 1976 for Democrats to be 50.3 percent, and for Republicans, 50.6 percent, by taking the turnout of registered voters in each of thirteen closed-primary states and averaging them. By averaging state turnouts, rather than finding the percent turnout of all primary voters in these thirteen states, Ranney understates primary turnout in the states by approximately 4 percent. [30] By his method, a turnout of 28 percent in Kentucky is given equal averaging weight with the 72 percent turnout in a major primary state such as California—despite the disparity in populations and the fact that only 306,006 voted in Kentucky and over ten times that number, 3,373,732, voted in California.

Ranney's conclusion about the 1976 primary—that the "drop (from 1972), moreover, was larger than the much discussed drop-off in turnout in presidential general elections"—is in a certain sense misleading. A number of states relatively new to primary competition in 1976 (with lower turnout in their initial years) are counted in with those that have held closed primary elections regularly over the years. Thus, the lack of socialization to the primary process among unhabituated first-time voters could automatically decrease average primary turnout simply because the potential primary voting universe was, unlike the general electorate universe, suddenly expanded. [31] To measure turnout trends accurately (particularly when the number of states holding primaries doubled as it did from 1968 to 1976), turnout averages must be adjusted for "new" and "old" primary states in order to be a genuinely meaningful figure by which to judge changes in participation.

By making a controlled comparison over a time dimension, a behavioral pattern different from Ranney's may be drawn. Such a comparison would eliminate the variable of socialization in primary voting. Table 6-1 computes the primary turnout among the only five states that: (1) have continuously held closed preference primary elections from 1948 to 1976 and maintained registration records and (2) had prior experience (i.e., before 1948) with presidential preference primaries.

Table 6-1 brings into sharper focus the actual trends in primary participation and measures the present level of turnout independently of the socialization factor. Taking the Democrats first, we find the removal of the socialization factor clearly shows the sharp upward trend of turnout from a low of 25 percent in 1948 to 62 percent in 1972—with turnout fractionally higher, not lower, in 1976. [32] Despite the reduction of Democratic candidate campaign funds, the decreased expenditures on television, the absence of the stridency and divisiveness of 1972, and the lack of a strong second challenger for the nomination, the new high levels of turnout reached in 1972 were, in fact, maintained in 1976.

Table 6-1 Percent Turnout in Selected Presidential Primaries, 1948-1976[a]

	1948	1952	1956	1960	1964	1968	1972	1976
California								
Democratic	30	55	60	54	62	73	72	72
Republican	44	71	60	60	75	48	72	78
Massachusetts								
Democratic	8	7	7	12	8	22	52	57
Republican	12	50	8	9	14	19	23	42
Oregon								
Democratic	50	56	43	68	60	68	62	60
Republican	89	79	59	62	74	73	61	64
Pennsylvania								
Democratic	20	9	31	10	10	23	49	49
Republican	10	41	37	38	17	11	7	36
West Virginia						no		
Democratic	24	28	17	58	19	primary	55	53
Republican	30	40	27	31	31	22	27	46
Total[b]								
Democratic	25	33	42	37	37	49	62	62
Republican	29	54	41	42	45	32	42	58

[a]Selected were the five states having continuous registration figures and holding presidential preference primaries in each year from 1948 to 1972.
[b]Total turnouts computed using weighted means (weight = number of registered voters).
Source: Vote totals provided by Secretaries of State from the five states indicated.

When we examine the states individually, several interesting features are illuminated. First, the two traditionally antiorganization, "progressive" states, California and Oregon, share a similar history of much higher levels of turnout than the two urbanized "organization" states, Pennsylvania and Massachusetts. While turnout in California sharply increased in 1968 and held at the same high level in 1972 and 1976, the turnout increases in the two major "organization" states were much greater. In those states, turnout doubled from 1964 to 1968, doubled again between 1968 and 1972, and actually increased from 1972 to 1976. These findings, which in effect locate the greatest part of primary increases in large, urbanized "organization" states, add further weight to the thesis that the sharp increases in primary voting have come disproportionately from hitherto less mobilized groups in the Democratic electorate.

Data on the Republicans in Table 6-1 reinforces the findings already discussed in Figure 6-3, namely, that Republican turnout was traditionally higher than Democratic turnout up to 1964 but that after 1964 it was generally lower. Both of the "progressive" states again demonstrated higher levels of turnout than the traditional "organization" states. At the same time, the organization states, Massachusetts and Pennsylvania, had sharply higher turnout in 1976 despite the fact that Reagan did not contest Ford in these primaries.[33] This fact suggests that the trend toward higher levels of turnout may well be beginning to affect the Republicans, who, since the early 1960s, have been less primary-prone.

Overall, the evidence presented emphasizes the major upward thrust in primary-election participation, which, all else remaining the same, will continue as the populations of the states new to primaries become more familiar with the process. Unlike general election voting, primary turnout has actually increased significantly; therefore, the new, high levels of turnout deserve more and varied study with respect to their relationships to other institutions (like the media) and their significance for the individual parties, the party system, and the future of American electoral politics.

Primary Rules: Some Strategic Implications

The political environment in which candidates, activist groups, and primary voters meet is not as clear to the participants as it appears to be to political scientists and historians who view it in retrospect. Candidates in primary elections do not have the "cue" value of a party label that distinguishes one candidate from another as in a general election. As a result, they face a strategic environment that is far less stable in terms of expected behavior. Without the party loyalty factor (whatever its remaining power), and without the constraints of a two-candidate field that are typical of competition *between* the parties, intraparty elections become relatively more dependent on such factors as the number of candidates seeking similar constituencies, "hot" issues, and the personal qualities of the candidate.

Although broad historical themes can be used to account for change in American politics, change itself occurs as a result of a series of personal interactions in a politically strategic environment. As Lengle and Shafer have noted,

> American political history wells up out of the situational calculations of candidates, activists, and voters. If any given tendency is to be judged, retrospectively, to have dominated the politics of our own era, it must reach that domination through the decisions which these actors make in order to influence public policy, and especially through the decisions which individual politicians make in order to gain and hold public office. [34]

In the unstable, rough and tumble conflict for the presidential nomination, the strategic environment always has been important in defining the kind of candidate selected and, consequently, the range of choice offered to the electorate. Each party's rules, whether covering primary election or nonprimary matters, are an important part of the strategic environment and, as such, influence the many personal decisions made by each candidate.

> If the rules of politics reliably cause [individual politicians] to seek votes in certain ways, to stress certain issues, and to address a certain clientele, these rules far from being rolled over by the "current of history" may be crucial in determining how that current will run. [35]

Taking the 1972 Democratic presidential nomination as an example, Lengle and Shafer "replayed" the primaries using each of the three different types of primary rules: winner-take-all, districted, and proportional. They found that the same voting patterns would have brought about a different distribution of delegate strength under each set of rules. [36] Although their analysis did not include any discussion of adaptive candidate strategies aimed at countering rule changes (which might nullify some of the impact of rule changes), a good case was made that primary rules had a major impact on determining which candidate would be more likely to succeed, which blocs would be more or less influential, and which causes might be supported or ignored.

The analysis that follows deals with some of the questions explored by Lengle and Shafer, but from a somewhat different perspective. Lengle and Shafer analyze the impact of primary rules with respect to the power of *each state* to influence the convention's decision on a presidential nominee. Comparing and contrasting the states by their size and internal competitiveness, they conclude that

> A Districted system takes the final step by fragmenting the delegations of the big states, but not those of their less populous counterparts—in effect maximizing the power of the smaller and less competitive states. [37]

To a nation with its heavily populated and largely Democratic cities under great financial strain and starved for resources, the above analysis of the district system for Democratic primaries would seem to offer little hope for the future. The political power of urban groups would be attenuated, it appears, by the relative weakness of the large urban state vis-à-vis other states. The evidence of 1976 does, in fact, lend support to a thesis of this kind inasmuch as Carter fared badly in the Northern urbanized states as a whole. [38]

The outlook for the Northern cities (most of which are in states that use the district system) [39] is not, however, as bleak as Lengle and Shafer would indicate. When *intrastate* voting "clout" (i.e., votes per delegate) in Democratic primaries is analyzed vis-à-vis the apportionment of the "voting power" within the large states, as in Table 6-2, it appears that *rural and suburban groups—not urban groups—are underrepresented.*

When areas determined to be over 75 percent urban, suburban, or rural are isolated and examined, an interesting pattern emerges,—one that could potentially counteract the negative effects of districted primaries on large urban states. As can be seen in Table 6-2, urban areas were apportioned the most delegates per vote in all three states examined. Urban areas were consistently overrepresented as compared with other types of communities and with the overall statewide average. Rural voters in California and Ohio were clearly the most underrepresented, and in Michigan, suburban voters received the fewest delegates per vote.

The lower turnout of primary voters in the cities actually resulted in the overrepresentation of urban voters. This tendency serves as a potential counter to some of the adverse effects of districted primaries on a state versus state basis. The three states included in Table 6-2 each utilized different methods of delegate selection; despite their differences, all overrepresented the urban voters within their states. [40] As a result, a given number of urban voters gained a significantly greater number of delegates than the same number of suburban or rural voters. Black voters, for example, heavily concentrated as they are in urban areas, benefited from this intrastate distribution of delegate selection "clout."

Whereas Lengle and Shafer, basing their analysis on an interstate comparison, underscored the diminution of urban influence over the selection of a Democratic nominee, this examination suggests that urban input may still be strong if we look beneath the statewide figures. Because intrastate delegate apportionment formulas are generally based on Democratic turnout in the general election, urban areas (heavily Democratic in most general elections) receive more delegates than the less Democratic suburban and rural areas. [41]

Table 6-2 Votes Per Delegate by Community Type
in Three 1976 Democratic Primaries

Location[a]	Number	Votes/ delegates[b]
Michigan		
Urban	2	5,900
Suburban	3	9,819
Rural	3	6,984
Statewide	19	7,087
Ohio		
Urban	2	5,924
Suburban	2	8,114
Rural	4	10,114
Statewide	23	8,922
California		
Urban	5	14,761
Suburban	11	16,052
Rural	1	16,884
Statewide	43	16,236

[a]The definition of urban, suburban, and rural areas is based on the *Congressional District Data Books,* published by the United States Department of the Census. An urban district is one in which 75 percent or more of the population resides in the central cities of a standard metropolitan sampling area (SMSA); a suburban district is one in which 75 percent or more of the population resides outside the central cities but within the urban area of an SMSA; a rural district is one in which 75 percent or more of the population resides in a rural or non-SMSA area. Other districts were excluded from all but the statewide figures.

[b]Votes per delegate $= \dfrac{\text{number of votes cast in delegate selection unit}}{\text{number of delegates apportioned to that unit}}$

Source: Vote totals provided by the Secretaries of State from the three states indicated. The State Democratic Headquarters of each state provided delegate apportionment numbers.

The underrepresentation of suburban voters stems from their higher level of turnout in the primaries—a phenomenon that is understandable in light of the general correlation of higher SES with higher turnout. What is less easily understandable is why rural primary voters should be underrepresented in heavily populated states. This group, of the three demographic categories, tends to have the lowest level of income, education, and socioeconomic status. In support of this finding, Alan Monroe found a similar pattern of higher rural turnout in his examination of intrastate general election patterns in a large, heavily populated northern state (Illinois)—although he too was unable to offer a rigorous explanation. [42]

Whatever the reasons, Table 6-2 indicates an intrastate counterweight to the growing strength of medium, small, and less urbanized noncompetitive states in the battle for nomination influence. The data uncovered in Table 6-2 suggest some interesting strategic possibilities that may well influence future nomination politics, particularly within the Democratic Party. Because of turnout factors in urban primaries, a candidate with "urban appeal" could gain more delegates per vote than candidates who appeal to rural or suburban communities.

Carter's 1976 campaign benefited from the absence, in the early primaries, of any Democratic candidate from a large urbanized state. When a candidate from a major urban state (Brown, of California) finally entered the primary competition late in the game, he managed to outpoll Carter in most of the states they both entered.[43] Thus a Brown, Kennedy, or any other candidate with strong appeal to urban groups could gain a greater number of delegates per vote simply by competing favorably in urban Democratic strongholds.

The Primary Electorate, 1976

The 1976 primaries wer historically unique in that twenty-nine states and the District of Columbia actually held primary elections. In addition, both of the major parties' nominations were vigorously contested. Vast numbers of voters, many voting in primaries for the first time, went to the polls to render their decisions on the candidates. An obvious question is whether or not this large primary electorate that registered the final decision in November. In Table 6–3, an answer is suggested by an analysis of a CBS News national survey of general-election-day voters who reported that they had also voted in their state's primary.[44]

When categories of voters are compared, the data show that primary voters differed very little from general election voters in sex, age, race, and income. One of the larger differences within an otherwise narrow range of disparities was found among union voters,[45] who formed a relatively larger share of the primary electorate (32 percent) than they did of the general electorate (28 percent). These findings indicate that, contrary to conventional wisdom, rank-and-file union families were not weak participants in the 1976 presidential primary elections.

The importance of these findings is accentuated when combined with a post–election-day survey.[46] Table 6–4 defines the turnout of all citizens of voting age (the column furthest left), and then, separately, the turnout by partisan identification or independent status.

Analysis of age categories shows nothing unexpected, indicating the usual increases in turnout as age increases—although the usual drop-off after age sixty seems largely confined to Democrats. When variations in behavior by income are examined, both expected and unexpected findings are uncovered. The lowest level of turnout was found to be among the families whose annual income was $8,000 or less—and this was true in both the primary and in the general election. The most surprising finding, however, and one of major significance in terms of potential *intraparty* power, comes from an analysis of the primary voters with the highest income. While high-income (over $20,000 annually Republican and independent voters turned out at higher rates than middle-income Republican and independent voters, *high-income Democrats turned out at much lower rates than did middle-income Democratic voters.*

These findings might, in part, be explained as the result of cross pressures, i.e., high-income Democrats would be likely to find their own political values in conflict with those of their own socioeconomic environment.[47] But whether or not the cross-pressure concept can account for the relatively low turnout of high-income Democrats, the evidence from

Table 6-3 Distribution of 1976 Primary and General-Election Voters by Socioeconomic Characteristics (in percentage)

	Primary Voters in Primary States	All General Election Voters in Primary States
Sex		
Male	52	50
Female	48	50
Age		
18–21	6	8
22–29	20	22
30–44	30	29
45–59	27	26
60 and over	16	15
Race		
White	89	89
Black	9	9
Spanish	2	2
Family Income		
Under $8,000	17	17
$8,000–12,000	22	23
$12,001–20,000	36	35
Over $20,000	25	25
Union Membership		
Union household	32	28
Nonunion household	68	72
	(N = 6,248)	(N = 11,392)

Source: CBS News 1976 General Election Day Survey.

Table 6-4 suggests that attempts to build a top/bottom coalition among Democrats might well founder on the lower levels of participation by *both* bottom- and top-income groups in primary elections.

When union voting behavior is subjected to detailed analysis in Table 6-4, more unexpected findings are uncovered. Whereas at the most general level (percent turnout of all voters), union and nonunion households turned out at approximately the same rate in the primaries (41 percent and 40 percent respectively), when union behavior is controlled for party identification, large differences are revealed. Among Democrats, primary turnout by union members (56 percent) is much higher than among nonmembers (36 percent). Union turnout is not only exceptionally high (considering the reference is voting-age population and not registered voters), but contrasts sharply with the much lower turnout among high-income Democrats. The data clearly indicate that speculations to the effect that declining union influence in nomination politics is simply due to low turnout by the rank and file in primaries are unfounded.

Among union independents and union Republicans, on the other hand, turnout is much lower. In addition, while union independents turned out at approximately the same level as nonunion independents, union Republicans turned out at a markedly lower level (43 percent) than nonunion Republicans (56 percent)—possibly another indication of cross pressures at work.

Table 6-4 Percent Turnout by Party[a] and Socioeconomic Characteristics in the 1976 Primaries and General Election[b] (in percentage)

	Total		Democrats		Independents		Republicans	
Group	Primary turnout	General-election turnout	Primary turnout	General-election turnout	Primary turnout	General-election turnout	Primary turnout	General-election turnout
Age								
18–21	20	30	20	29	16	25	31	50
22–29	29	43	34	42	24	39	45	58
30–44	45	49	49	55	41	55	50	61
45–59	52	68	59	62	47	69	57	71
60 and over	55	64	47	52	50	64	65	73
Family Income								
Under $8,000	34	45	31	36	30	43	49	62
$8,000–12,000	36	46	49	56	26	37	46	58
$12,001–20,000	46	59	52	58	38	54	60	73
Over $20,000	48	66	43	47	46	72	62	73
Union Membership								
Union household	41	54	56	63	33	48	43	56
Nonunion household	40	53	36	42	35	51	56	69

[a]The question used to determine party identification was: "Do you usually think of yourself as a (1) Republican, (2) Democrat, or (3) independent?"
[b]To compute turnout rates for eligible voters, we multiplied the group's turnout rate in the general election by the percentage of the general election voters from that group who reported voting in the presidential primary. For our purposes, those who reported having voted in the primary will constitute a representative sample of primary voters, though we offer two caveats: (1) there was, as expected, considerable overreporting of primary turnout and (2) we necessarily missed those few persons who voted in the primary but not in the general election (see Note 44). Those not living in primary states were excluded from all figures.
Source: CBS News 1976 General Election Day Survey.

The relative size of the union turnout among Democratic identifiers strongly suggests that it is not low rank-and-file participation in primaries that has weakened labor influence on Democratic nomination politics, but rather the inability of labor elites to organize and structure the direction of the vote. It would appear that labor leadership's strategic choices and internal divisions were more responsible for the decline of labor influence in Democratic nomination politics than was the shift of the party to a format of primary elections.

The labor vote in the 1976 primaries, unique as it was in its level of turnout, was indistinguishable from that of nonunion Democrats in terms of candidates choices. Labor unionists voted for Democratic candidates in the primaries in almost the same proportions as other Democrats did.[48] These results can be interpreted from two perspectives: one view is that union families behave, in fact, just like other Democrats; the other perspective is that union leadership made little impact in organizing and focusing the rank-and-file labor vote.

It is doubtful that labor unionists are simply just like the other Democrats, particularly when labor defections in 1968 and 1972 are compared to the patterns of other Democrats.[49] Leadership failures, whatever the nature and causes, seem to better explain the data developed in this research. These findings also suggest the enormous potential of the labor vote in Democratic primary politics and a possible direction for candidate strategies in the future. Should one candidate gain the organized support of both the labor leadership and the rank and file, a major bloc of primary voters, far greater than any other, would be assured. Labor may well have reached its low point in intraparty influence; and the strategic implications of these findings suggest that a renewed effort by future Democratic primary candidates will be made for the unified backing not only of labor leaders, but of the powerful rank and file as well.

Conclusion

In this analysis we sought to uncover both continuities and major changes in the presidential-primary system. Aggregate data on primary elections were used to trace long-term trends from 1912 to 1976. The data revealed sharp rises in majority-party turnout in the latter stages of party alignment. The sharp increases in participation suggest that dissatisfied partisans tended to move into intraparty politics at the mature phase of the alignment, possibly because interparty dynamics did not shape suitable alternatives of expression for these voters. The identity of these new voters at this phase of interparty alignment and the role specific candidates and critical issues played in bringing about higher levels of intraparty participation remain important areas for future research.

The analysis of post–World War II primary turnout identified the step-level change in participation among traditionally low-turnout Democrats. By holding the "socialization factor" constant (Table 6-1), turnout among Democrats was found to increase from 37 percent in 1960 to 49 percent in 1968. In 1972, it again turned up sharply to a high of 62 percent, *where it remained in 1976 despite a less intensely fought campaign.* These findings, unlike Ranney's, prompted the tentative conclusion that a *durable institutionalization of high primary turnout has occurred* and that, all else remaining the same, turnout will continue at these higher levels.

A series of triggering events in the 1960s, and the changing scope of television journalism, seem to have combined with other factors to socialize previously passive groups into greater primary participation. These circumstances would seem to (1) further limit the role of party elites in shaping the choice of the party's nominee, (2) increase the influence of elites from nonparty institutions such as the media, and (3) enlarge the impact of nomination politics on general election outcomes. In every election since 1964, the party that experienced the greatest increase in primary turnout over the previous primary election has met defeat in the subsequent general election.

The identification by Lengle and Shafer of the relative weakness of large urban states vis-à-vis less populous (and less competitive) states was examined from a different perspective. While the analysis in Table 6-2 does not refute any of their theoretical claims regarding interstate competition, it does point to at least partially offsetting advantages for candidates appealing to urban constituencies in the primaries. It was found that, contrary to conventional wisdom, urban districts received relatively more Democratic delegates per voter than either suburban or rural districts. This circumstance, partially brought about by the use of interparty turnout as a basis of intraparty delegate apportionment, suggests that, within many large states, a candidate with urban appeal can gain a larger number of delegates with relatively fewer votes than can competitors with rural or suburban appeal.

The relationship of the primary electorate to the general electorate was analyzed, and it was found that, when key groups were compared, primary voters differed very little from general election voters. More startling findings were developed from an analysis of primary voters by partisan preference. Union Democrats turned out at very high levels, far exceeding the turnout among nonunion Democrats. Union Republicans, on the other hand, turned out at a level far below nonunion Republicans.

The most striking aspect of labor voting in the primaries, however, was that, among Democrats, the turnout of labor union families in the primaries (56 percent) was substantially greater than the turnout among the highest income (over $20,000 annually) Democrats (43 percent). The substantial turnout by labor in the primaries forces a reassessment of the primary-oriented Democratic Party and undermines the potential of a top/bottom coalition to control the nomination.

There is no doubt that the labor leadership greatly influenced Democratic nomination politics before the explosion of primary elections, but the weakness of labor influence in 1972 and 1976 should not be misinterpreted. In 1976, at least, it appears that strategic miscalculations of the leadership, rather than rank-and-file disinterest in primary voting, was the prime reason that labor's influence was so limited in the nomination campaign. Whatever the reasons, labor-union families turned out for the 1976 primaries in disproportionate numbers—and then voted for the different candidates in approximately the same proportions as nonunion families. It seems clear that labor elites were not able to guide the rank-and-file vote, even in such states as Pennsylvania, which had a strong organizational apparatus. Elite misjudgments, rather than rank-and-file disinterest in primary elections, would seem to better explain the weakening of labor influence on the present-day Democratic Party.

Overall, the emphasis of the research has been on the nature and extent of change in the primary process. The conclusion that the continuance of high levels of mass participation is likely in future primaries is especially important when the impact of intraparty dynamics is linked to interparty politics. Should high levels of mass participation continue in the primary process, what will be the consequences for the two parties that have served as vehicles of electoral realignment? Are the large swings from one election to the next between the two parties' candidates—at least in part a result of new intraparty dynamics—indicative of a new kind of presidential party system only minimally influenced by partisan leadership?

Although the primaries themselves are in part responsible for weakening the parties, the primaries are not only a "cause" but also an "effect," produced in part by a powerful demand by the American people for more influence on the choice of the presidential nominee. As a result, the role of party leaders in shaping the two major choices presented to the American people has been greatly diminished in favor of rank-and-file influence through primary politics. It is still unclear whether the new combination of mass partisan participation and media influence will serve better or worse than the old combination of a few "proving-ground" primaries coupled with "brokerage" by party elites. What is already clear is that present-day presidential politics is profoundly different from that practiced only a decade ago. The eventual impact of this change on both the style and the substance of politics remains uncertain.

NOTES

1. Austin Ranney, *Curing the Mischiefs of Faction: Party Reform in America* (Berkeley: University of California Press, 1975), p. 22.

2. For an analysis of cross-national similarities and differences in the primary process, see Leon D. Epstein, *Political Parties in Western Democracies* (New York: Praeger, 1967), pp. 201-232.

3. After the initial explosion of articles and books published following the establishment of the direct primary process, scholarly interest on the subject waned. The first major contributions to the study of the direct primary were Charles E. Merriam and Louise Overacker, *Primary Elections* (University of Chicago Press, 1908, 1928) and Louise Overacker, *The Presidential Primary* (New York: Macmillan, 1926). Also see Arthur Wallace Dunn, "The Direct Primary: Promise and Performance," *Review of Reviews* 46 (October 1912); C. E. Fanning, *Selected Articles on Direct Primaries* (New York: Wilson, 1918); and Henry Jones Ford, "The Direct Primary," *North American Review* 190 (July 1910).

   In recent years, Austin Ranney has been the most prolific writer on the primaries. See also Austin Ranney, "Turnout and Representation in Presidential Primaries," *American Political Science Review* 66 (June 1972): 21-37, and Austin Ranney, *Participation in American Presidential Nominations, 1976* (Washington, D. C.: American Enterprise Institute for Public Policy Research, 1977). Other recent articles include William D. Morris and Otto A. Davis, "The Sport of Kings: Presidential Preference Primaries" (Paper presented at the American Political Science Association Convention, San Francisco, 1975); Lawrence S. Mayer "Optimal Voting in a Two-Party Primary," *Mathematical Applications in Political Science, VII,* ed. James F. Herndon and Joseph L. Bernd (Charlottesville: University Press of Virginia, 1974); Harvey Zeidenstein, "Presidential Primaries—Reflections of 'The People's Choice'?" *Journal of Politics* 32 (1970); James R. Beniger, "Winning the Presidential Nomination: National Polls and State Primary Elections," *Public Opinion Quarterly* 40 (1970); James I. Lengle and Byron Shafer. "Primary Rules, Political Power, and Social Change," *American Political Science Review* 70 (March 1976): 25-40; and Daniel C. Williams et al., "Voter–Decisionmaking in a Primary Election: An Evaluation of Three Models of Choice," *American Journal of Political Science* 20 (1976). For a more general treatment, see James A. Davis, *Presidential Primaries: Road to the White House* (New York: Crowell, 1967); Donald R. Matthews and William Keech, *Nominating the President* (Washington, D. C.: Brookings Institution, 1975); Richard L. Rubin, *Party Dynamics* (New York: Oxford University Press, 1976); and William J. Crotty, *Political Reform and the American Experiment* (New York: Crowell, 1977), pp. 193-264.

4. Morris and Davis, "Presidential Preference Primaries," and Lengle and Shafer, "Primary Rules."

5. A number of states vied for the honor of enacting the first presidential primary law. In 1901, Florida passed a law allowing party leaders to hold a primary to choose any nominee, including delegates to the Democratic convention. In 1905, the Wisconsin legislature, influenced by Robert M. LaFollette, Sr., enacted a primary law providing for the direct election of delegates, but omitting any provision for a presidential preference primary. Pennsylvania, in 1906, adopted a law allowing delegate candidates to have printed on the ballot their support for a presidential candidate. In 1908, however, no delegate candidate exercised this option. Oregon is usually credited with enacting the first presidential primary law. Oregon's Senator Jonathan Bourne mounted a campaign to convince voters to pass an initiative measure creating a presidential preference primary. The law provided for the expression of a presidential preference and the election of delegates legally bound to support the preference primary victor. The year 1912 marked the beginning of the first broad based usage of presidential primaries. See Davis, *Presidential Primaries, pp. 25-26.*

6. Donald R. Matthews, "Presidential Nominations: Process and Outcome," in *Choosing the President,* ed. James D. Barber (New York: Columbia University Press, 1974), p. 36.

7. See Overacker, *Primary Elections,* pp. 15-22; and Davis, *Presidential Primaries,* pp. 26-28.

8. Less tension is present during the earlier stages of a realignment because the dissatisfied have "realigned" to the other party. As a result, the battle is focused on interparty rather than intraparty politics. Tension mounts when intraparty matters become more divisive during the later stages of a realignment. See James L. Sundquist, *Dynamics of the Party System* (Washington, D. C.: Brookings Institution, 1973), p. 211.

9. Samuel Lubell, *The Future of American Politics,* 2nd ed., revised (Garden City, N.Y.: Doubleday, 1955), p. 217.

10. Davis, *Presidential Primaries,* p. 73.

11. The difference between the number of state laws permitting any kind of presidential primary and the number of states actually holding presidential preference primaries is based on (1) states not exercising their legal option to conduct a preference primary and (2) states holding presidential primaries of a type different from presidential preference primaries. Both factors point to the inability of voters to choose a presidential preference.

    In some cases, an exact count of the number of states permitting presidential primaries was impossible due to the limitations of available data. Two main caveats are therefore necessary: (1) the number of state laws permitting presidential primaries may be slightly understated due to the fact that *Congressional Quarterly's Guide to U.S. Elections,* one of our basic sources, listed only those states in which at least one party held a primary; and (2) the number of state laws permitting presidential primaries may be slightly overstated because *Congressional Quarterly* listed all states holding primaries—not just those with legal, as opposed to party, mandates to do so.

12. See William E. Leuchtenburg, *Franklin D. Roosevelt and The New Deal, 1932-1940* (New York: Harper & Row, 1963), pp. 167-196.

13. Davis, *Presidential Primaries* pp. 72-73.

14. E. E. Schattschneider, *The Semi-Sovereign People* (Hinsdale, Ill.: Dryden, 1960), pp. 62-73.

15. F. Christopher Arterton, "The Strategic Environment of Primaries for Presidential Campaign Organization, 1976" (Paper presented at the New England Political Science Association Convention, Durham, New Hampshire, April 9-10, 1976), Table 1.

16. See Morris and Davis, "Presidential Preference Primaries," pp. 5-10, for a critique of Ranney's method of averaging together both parties' turnout rather than treating them individually.

17. The apparent drop in turnout in 1976 is actually the result of large numbers of unsocialized potential voters entering the primary election universe. See the analysis of Table 6-1 for the effect of first-time primary states on turnout percentages.

18. See Morris and Davis, "Presidential Preference Primaries," pp. 14-18, for an analysis of the relationship between increases in competitiveness and corresponding increases in Democratic primary turnout. Working from an analysis of 108 state presidential primaries held from 1948 to 1976, R. Douglas Rivers found an even higher correlation between competitiveness and turnout than did Morris and Davis. See R. Douglas Rivers, "Turnout and Competition in Presidential Primaries," unpublished paper, (New York: Columbia University Press, 1977).

19. The CBS News primary-day surveys indicate that the Democrats experienced a decrease from 1972 to 1976 in the intensity of internal divisiveness. The issues did not divide the Democratic identifiers as much as in 1972, and Carter was viewed by rank-and-file Democrats as essentially nonideological—receiving support from all ideological groupings. The Republicans, on the other hand, experienced an increase from 1972 to 1976 in the intensity of divisiveness. Republican voters in 1976 were sharply divided in both their opinions on the issues and their choice for the nomination. In 1972, however, they appeared relatively homogeneous regarding both. See the 1972 CBS News Primary Day and National Surveys and the 1976 CBS News/*New York Times* Primary Day and National Surveys.

20. The figure .40 is a Spearman's rank order correlation. See Ranney, *American Presidential Nominations, 1976, p. 33.*

21. For an analysis of the events of the late 1960s and 1970s and their effects on the parties, see Sundquist, *Party System,* pp. 314-331.

22. Michael J. Robinson, "Television and American Politics: 1956-1976," *The Public Interest* 48 (Summer 1977): 3-39; and Robinson's "Media Coverage in the Primary Campaign of 1976: Implications for Voters, Candidates, and Parties," in this volume.

23. Robinson, "Television and American Politics," p. 24.

24. Ibid., p. 15. The fact that middle- and lower-status groups might be aroused to participate does not necessarily imply that television coverage increased their specific knowledge of issues. See Thomas E. Patterson and Robert D. McClure, *The Unseeing Eye* (New York: Putnam, 1976), p. 53.

25. Robinson, "Television and America Politics," pp. 16-25. One example of the changing extent of media coverage of primary elections is the increase, from 1968 to 1976, in primary coverage by CBS News. In 1968, CBS News covered six Presidential primaries; in 1972, CBS News covered seventeen; in 1976, the number of Presidential primaries covered by CBS News rose again, to twenty-nine. The author wishes to thank Warren J. Mitofsky, Director of the CBS News Election and Survey Unit, for making available this and other information.

26. Ranney, *American Presidential Nominations, 1976*. See also Ranney, "Turnout and Representation in Presidential Primaries"; Austin Ranney, "The Representativeness of Primary Electorates," *Midwest Journal of Political Science* 12 (1968): 224-238; and Austin Ranney and Leon D. Epstein, "The Two Electorates: Voters and Non-Voters in a Wisconsin Primary," *Journal of Politics* 27 (1966): 598-616.

27. Most of Ranney's work covers only one or two elections. By limiting the time span of his studies, Ranney misses the secular changes that are evident only when one examines primary data on an extended time dimension.

28. Ranney, *American Presidential Nominations, 1976*, p. 26.

29. Ibid., p. 22.

30. Ranney understates the actual turnout because he does not fully take account of the variations in turnout among his thirteen states. When we weighted by the number of voters per state, the actual number of primary voters increased by 8 percent over Ranney's theoretical figure.

31. Expansion of the general election universe occurred, primarily, as a result of the enfranchisement of eighteen- to twenty-one-year-olds. The primary voting universe, however, expands each time a state holds a presidential primary for the first time. As a result of recent large increases in the numbers of presidential primaries, the potential primary electorate has doubled since 1968.

32. The rounding off of the figures in Table 6-1 obscures an actual increase in turnout of 0.2 percent from 1972 to 1976.

33. Reagan's campaign manager, John Sears, attributed his candidate's failure to contest these organization states to the assumption of Reagan and Sears that it would cost them relatively more money for Reagan to enter the primaries in states with pro-Ford organizations. Sears hoped to shift some delegates from these states into the Reagan column after the primaries were held. See Jules Witcover, *Marathon* (New York: Viking, 1977), p. 416.

34. Lengle and Shafer, "Primary Rules," p. 25.

35. Ibid.

36. Using fifteen pre-California primaries, Lengle and Shafer found that Humphrey would have received more delegates than any other candidate under winner-take-all system; Wallace would have amassed the most delegates under either a proportional or a districted system. Each system also produced different distributions of delegates among the runner-up candidates. Gerald Pomper found, however, that when California was included in the 1972 analysis that McGovern, not Humphrey, would have received more delegates under a winner-take-all system. See "New Rules and New Games in the National Conventions" (Paper delivered at the American Political Science Association Convention, Washington, D. C., 1976).

37. Ibid., p. 35.

38. For example, Carter did poorly in New York, Massachusetts, New Jersey, Rhode Island, and California. In Wisconsin and Michigan, he was able only to eke out slim victories over a weak opponent, Morris Udall.

39. Arterton points out that 41 percent of the 1976 Democratic delegates were elected in districted primaries. A disproportionate share of this 41 percent was contributed by Northern states. The following Northern states used a districted system to elect Democratic delegates: Illinois, New York, Pennsylvania, New Jersey, and Ohio. See Arterton, "Strategic Environment of Primaries," Table III.

40. California used a proportional method within each congressional district; voters in Ohio elected individual delegates within each congressional district; Michigan elected pledged district delegates. See Library of Congress, *Nomination and Election of the President and Vice President of the United States* (Washington, D. C.: Government Printing Office, 1976).

41. See Zeidenstein, "Presidential Primaries— 'The People's Choice?'," pp. 867–872.

42. Alan D. Monroe, "Urbanism and Voter Turnout: A Note on Some Unexpected Findings," *American Journal of Political Science* 21, no. 1 (February 1977): pp. 71–78.

43. See Paul T. David and James W. Caesar, "Operations and Consequences of Proportional Representation in National Convention Delegate Selection, 1976" (Paper presented at the American Political Science Association Convention, Chicago, 1976), p. 37.

44. The data presented in Table 6-3 reflect the author's assumption that few primary voters failed to vote in the general election. This assumption seems reasonable in light of the findings of the Survey Research Center of the University of Michigan. They found that only 1.7 percent of the 1972 primary voters failed to vote in the 1972 general election.

45. Although the survey asked only about union households, the terms "union households" and "union members" will be used interchangeably in this paper.

46. Primary turnout was calculated by the following formula: primary turnout = (percentage of general election voters reporting having voted in the presidential primary) × (percentage of general election turnout). Source: CBS News 1976 General-Election-Day Survey and CBS News/*New York Times* Post-Election Survey.

47. See Angus Campbell, Philip E. Converse, Warren E. Miller, and Donald E. Stokes, *The American Voter* (New York: Wiley, 1964), pp. 42–48, for a discussion of cross pressures.

48. These data are not included in this article but can be found in the appendix (Table 12) of the paper given by the author at the Annual Meeting of American Political Science Association in Washington, D. C., September 1, 1977. The paper given bears the same title as this article.

49. See Rubin, *Party Dynamics*, pp. 50–66, for an analysis of Democratic voting among union members and nonmembers.

7 / The Representativeness of the 1972 Presidential Primaries

Herbert M. Kritzer

I. Introduction

Twenty years ago, V. O. Key suggested that primary elections may fail to represent the views of party followers.[1] While Key was specifically concerned with direct primaries, recent analyses have dealt with both direct primaries involving state contests[2] and indirect primaries that are part of the process of selecting presidential nominees.[3] Despite arguments that presidential primaries are an inconsequential part of the nominating process,[4] the experiences of the 1972 and 1976 nominating contests suggest that primaries can and do play an important role. This makes the question of the representativeness of presidential primary electorates a question of considerable importance.

Past analyses of the representativeness of primary electorates have failed to provide a consistent answer to the question raised by Key. Previous analysts have generally failed to make explicit their standard of representativeness; likewise they failed to state whom the primary electorates should represent. Furthermore, it is doubtful that analyses of state primaries yield generalizations applicable to presidential primaries: presidential primaries are likely to be more salient for voters than state primaries because of the massive media attention they attract. Jacob and Vines report an average turnout of 25.4 percent for state primaries in two-party states[5] compared to an average turnout of 39 percent for presidential primaries as reported by Ranney.[6] Consequently, we do not have a definitive answer as to representativeness of presidential primaries.

This research note examines the representativeness of the Democratic presidential primary electorate in 1972. The question as to whom the primary electorate should represent is both a matter of practical politics and an issue for the theory of representation;[7] one can cite a number of possible groups, such as party activists, party identifiers, and so on.[8] This analysis will compare participants in the 1972 Democratic primaries to four different groups: (1) Democratic identifiers who did not vote in the primaries, (2) politically active Democratic identifiers (that is, those who voted in the 1972 general

Reprinted by permission from *Polity* 10 (Fall 1977), pp. 121-129.

The data used in this analysis were made available by the Inter-University Consortium for Political and Social Research and were originally collected by the Survey Research Center and the Center for Political Studies of the University of Michigan. Neither the original collectors of the data nor the Consortium bear any responsibility for the analyses or interpretations presented here. Computer time for the analysis was provided by Indiana University.

election),[9] (3) all eligible voters regardless of party indentification who did not vote in the Democratic primaries, and (4) persons who supported the Democratic candidate in the 1972 general election. It is left to the reader to answer the question as to whom the primary electorate *should* represent.

II. Data and Analysis

The dataset used in this analysis is the 1972 CPS [Center for Political Studies, University of Michigan] election survey. The analysis is made possible by the large size of the 1972 sample and the increased number of primaries. In 1972 CPS used alternate interview schedules; about half of the 2705 respondents were asked about primary participation. Of these 510 were in states that held presidential primaries[10] and were included in both waves of the survey; these 510 respondents are the basis of this analysis.[11]

The results are shown in Table 7-1. The unitalicized figures in the "party identifiers" panel are the percentage of party identifiers in each category of the independent variable who reported voting in Democratic presidential primaries; the italicized figures are the percentage of identifiers who reported that they had voted in the general election. In the "party supporters" panel, the corresponding figures refer to the percentage of *all* eligible voters participating in the Democratic primaries and the percentage of all eligible voters supporting McGovern in the general election. The tests of significance were computed by means of the Grizzle, Starmer, Koch method of contingency table analysis.[12] The unitalicized chi-squares are tests of whether there are significant differences between primary voters and nonvoters; the italicized chi-squares refer to significant differences between general election voters and nonvoters; and the bold chi-squares test for significant differences between primary voters and general election voters controlling for the average turnout for each type of election.

The table shows three different sets of independent variables: demographic characteristics, measures of political involvement, and attitudes concerning political issues. The comparison of party identifiers who participated in primary elections with those who did not indicates that there are few differences between participants and nonparticipants. Young identifiers (under 25) were less likely to participate, as were weak identifiers and those with a low sense of citizen duty. The only issue on which participants differed from nonparticipants was on amnesty; those supporting amnesty were *less* likely to participate. Comparison of identifiers who voted in the general election show some additional differences; however, those differences are the result of the unrepresentativeness of identifiers who voted in the general election. Controlling for the average level of turnout for the two elections, general election participation was associated with a strong sense of political efficacy and support for amnesty. Overall, one can conclude from this analysis that in 1972 party identifiers who participated in the primaries were generally representative of both party identifiers as a whole and party identifiers who participated in the general election. If the goal of primaries is to represent the views of the party rank and file on political issues and on demographic characteristics, primaries, if we can generalize from the experience of 1972, are effective means of doing so.[13]

Turning to the "party supporters" panel, on only one demographic variable, union membership, did Democratic primary participants differ from all nonparticipants (including Republicans and Independents).[14] While Democratic primary participants were more likely to identify as liberals than nonparticipants, their attitudes on specific issues were

Table 7-1[a] Voting Turnout for Categories of the Independent Variables

Variable	Categories	Party Identifiers Percent Voting					χ²[b]	Party Supporters					χ²[b]
Sex	Male, female	49	51				0.06	26	33				3.26
		92	86				2.40	30	34				0.92
		(92)	(166)				**1.23**	(215)	(295)				**0.49**
Race	White, nonwhite	52	39				2.44	29	34				0.60
		89	86				1.08	28	69				36.75**
		(217)	(41)				**0.51**	(458)	(52)				**19.55**
Union member in	Yes, no	54	48				0.95	37	27				4.88*
		91	89				0.69	42	29				7.87**
		(85)	(172)				**0.19**	(140)	(366)				**0.31**
Socioeconomic status (self-reported)	Working, middle, upper	47	51	67			3.36	27	34	40			4.34
		90	82	89			2.37	33	32	29			0.33
		(157)	(76)	(21)			**5.32**	(324)	(133)	(45)			**4.48**
Income (in thousands)	$0-$5, $5-$10, $10-$15, $15 +	51	46	54	49		1.47	34	28	32	25		2.75
		79	85	93	95		7.83*	32	39	33	30		2.33
		(47)	(66)	(79)	(56)		**4.15**	(76)	(126)	(157)	(133)		**3.36**
Religion	Protestant, Catholic, Jewish, other	50	52	50	40		0.93	27	38	50	28		6.03
		89	86	95	89		0.99	30	28	63	56		12.44**
		(151)	(78)	(8)	(20)		**1.46**	(345)	(119)	(9)	(36)		**11.66**
Age	18-24, 25-34, 35-44, 45-64, 65 & up	35	51	41	61	52	9.68*	25	33	25	33	31	3.15
		92	90	89	91	81	2.29	48	40	30	27	28	12.03*
		(38)	(48)	(44)	(82)	(43)	**10.19***	(61)	(95)	(94)	(170)	(86)	**15.30**
Education (in years)	0-11, 12, some college, BA, post graduate	52	47	52	57	34	2.17	34	25	32	28	29	3.19
		82	89	74	96	95	6.68	26	32	35	39	59	11.58*
		(85)	(81)	(52)	(30)	(9)	**3.79**	(152)	(168)	(97)	(68)	(24)	**13.78**
Citizen duty	Low, high	40	58				8.40**	24	33				5.29*
		83	92				6.78**	33	34				0.01
		(104)	(143)				**1.19**	(202)	(291)				**3.49**
Perceived party differences	Yes, no	51	52				0.04	30	31				0.08
		91	92				0.05	35	31				0.75
		(121)	(97)				**0.00**	(240)	(205)				**0.95**

Table (rotated 90°). Row variable at left, independent-variable category columns (percentages with N's in parentheses), and two chi-square columns at right.

Variable	Categories									χ²ᵃ	χ²ᵃ
Political efficacy	Low, medium, high	32	56	45	34	51	26			1.70	3.19
		81	90	94	35	33	31			8.84**	0.55
		(108)	50	93)	(181)	100	211)			7.61*	**0.80**
Strength of partisanship	Strong, weak, "independent" Democrat (Independent, Republican)	67	48	31	67	48	32	24	07	17.87**	173.53**
		92	86	90	64	42	61	29	07	2.22	187.83**
		(75)	132	51)ᶜ	(75)	132	52)	34	218)	**8.28***	**10.83****
Self-perceived ideology	Liberal, center, conservative	47	48	59	43	28	24			1.57	9.37**
		96	91	86	73	27	10			3.41	143.95**
		(73)	67	36)	(91)	144	140)			**5.20**	**34.54****
Vietnam	Liberal, center, conservative	46	48	57	34	23	28			1.88	5.25
		88	91	94	52	19	10			1.53	99.54**
		(147)	46	45)	(255)	116	132)			**0.54**	**41.40****
End inflation	Liberal, center, conservative	51	49	57	32	25	29			0.24	1.53
		92	94	86	34	26	31			0.65	2.13
		(154)	36	16)	(307)	84	32)			**1.00**	**0.06**
Suppress crime	Liberal, center, conservative	46	47	55	32	27	30			1.68	0.65
		91	89	89	46	39	20			0.24	31.79**
		(94)	50	84)	(155)	93	201)			**2.30**	**22.01****
Help minorities	Liberal, center, conservative	44	52	53	31	34	27			1.70	1.91
		90	91	90	49	34	22			0.02	29.46**
		(94)	50	84)	(146)	129	193)			**1.36**	**16.58****
Improve standard of living	Liberal, center, conservative	56	40	44	33	27	28			2.65	0.94
		95	82	84	35	52	27			3.82	5.30
		(147)	23	14)	(306)	38	29)			**0.05**	**5.67**
Legalize marijuana	Liberal, center, conservative	49	52	47	28	38	30			0.18	2.13
		92	95	85	28	58	37			2.96	17.21**
		(72)	43	51)	(172)	60	79)			**0.38**	**5.25**
Busing	Liberal, center, conservative	62	41	47	46	30	26			2.72	6.01*
		93	92	87	80	60	24			1.25	82.13**
		(29)	15	186)	(41)	23	406)			**1.48**	**22.11****
Amnesty	For, against	42	55		33	28				3.83	0.96
		91	86		61	19				1.41	78.26**
		(93)	138)		(133)	324)				**6.82****	**42.02****

ᵃ See the text for an explanation of the table; numbers in parentheses are the N's upon which the percentages are based.
ᵇ The degrees of freedom for these chi-squares is equal to one less than the number of categories in the independent variable.
ᶜ Only those identifying in some way with the Democratic party were included in this comparison.
* Significant at the .05 level.
** Significant at the .01 level.

significantly more liberal on only one of the eight issues, busing. The major variable distinguishing Democratic primary participants from the rest of the electorate is party identification; the more strongly a person identified with the Democratic party, the more likely he or she would be to vote in a Democratic primary. This overall absence of distinguishing factors is consistent with Kirkpatrick's recent study of representation in the 1972 national conventions in which she found very few differences between the rank and file identifiers of the two parties.[15]

As other studies have shown, there were major differences between McGovern voters and the rest of the voting age population;[16] as a result, the differences between McGovern supporters in November and participants in the Democratic primary were substantial. McGovern voters were more likely to be black, young, well-educated, and non-Christian than either the rest of the electorate or Democratic primary participants. They were also more liberal on all but one of the eight issue-related questions as well as on the self-identified ideology question. Clearly, if the outcome of the nominating process is the nomination of a candidate toward the extreme of the political spectrum rather than toward the middle, there are likely to be sharp cleavages between the primary electorate and the set of voters who support the resulting nominee. However, as a similar analysis of the 1968 California primary showed,[17] if a centrist candidate is the eventual nominee, primary participants will be representative of party supporters in November.

III. Conclusion

In assessing the representativeness of primary electorates, there are a variety of standards which can be used as the basis of comparison. The results of these comparisons and the consequent judgments are dependent upon the contextual factors surrounding the specific elections involved. This analysis indicates that if a broad range of candidate choice is available to the potential primary electorate, the set of voters who turn out will be quite representative of a number of groups of voters, both demographically and in terms of issue attitudes. They will be distinctive primarily in the degree of their partisanship and in their involvement in and commitment to the political process. The electoral campaign of 1972 met this requirement, and the resulting participation in the primaries was highly representative of the party rank and file.

If the major goal of the nominating process is to reflect the wishes of party identifiers, the use of presidential primaries is a good method provided the candidate field is broad enough to reflect the entire spectrum of opinion present in the party. The practical danger of concentrating on this single goal was obvious in the 1972 election. The dominant faction of a party may select a candidate who is repugnant to the rest of the party's supporters; and, if the opposition party selects a candidate who is less repugnant to the defeated segment of the first party, the result is likely to be a wholesale desertion by the unsuccessful faction(s) of that party. While political commentators frequently bemoan the tweedledum-tweedledee character of American political parties, most evidence indicates it is not the party leaders who are tweedledum-tweedledee but the party rank and file, and if one party does offer a "real choice" to the voters, the voters run like mad to the other party.

NOTES

1. V. O. Key, *American State Politics: An Introduction* (New York: Knopf, 1956), p. 165.

2. Austin Ranney and Leon Epstein, "The Two Electorates: Voters and Nonvoters in a Wisconsin Primary," *Journal of Politics* 28 (August 1966): 598-616; Austin Ranney, "The Representativeness of the Primary Electorate," *Midwest Journal of Political Science* 12 (May 1968): 224-238; Andrew DiNitto and William Smithers, "The Representatives of the Direct Primary: A Further Test of V. O. Key's Work," *Polity* 5 (Winter 1972): 209-224; David W. Moore and C. Richard Hofstetter, "The Representativeness of Primary Elections: Ohio, 1968," *Polity* 6 (Winter 1973): 196-222; and William D. Morris, Jeffrey W. Stemple, and Otto A. Davis, "Structural determinants of Turnout in Primary Elections" (Paper presented at the meeting of the Western Political Science Association, San Francisco, California, April 1-3, 1976).

3. Harvey Zeidenstein, "Presidential Primaries—Reflections of 'the People's Choice'?" *Journal of Politics* 32 (November 1970): 856-874; Austin Ranney, "Turnout and Representation in Presidential Primary Elections," *American Political Science Review* 66 (March 1972): 21-37; Herbert M. Kritzer, "Representation in Presidential Primaries: Alternate Approaches" (Paper presented at the meeting of the Northeastern Political Science Association, Buck Hill Falls, Pennsylvania, November, 1973).

4. See William H. Lucy, "Polls, Primaries and Presidential Nominations," *Journal of Politics* 35 (1973): 830-848; Donald Matthews, "Presidential Nominations: Process and Outcomes," in James David Barber, ed., *Choosing the President* (Englewood Cliffs: Prentice-Hall, 1974), pp. 57-60; and William Keech and Donald Matthews, *The Party's Choice* (Washington: Brookings Institute, 1976), pp. 111-156.

5. Herbert Jacob and Kenneth Vines, eds., *Politics in the American States* (Boston: Little Brown, 1965), p. 75.

6. Austin Ranney, "Turnout and Representation," p. 22.

7. See Jeffrey Obler, "Intraparty Democracy and the Selection of Parliamentary Candidates: The Belgian Case," *British Journal of Political Science* 4 (April 1974): 163-186; and Jeane Kirkpatrick, "Representation in the American National Conventions: The Case of 1972," *British Journal of Political Science* 5 (1975): 267-280.

8. Austin Ranney, "Changing the Rules of the Nominating Game," in James David Barber, ed., *Choosing the President*, pp. 75-77.

9. Voters who did not in some way identify with the Democratic party were excluded from comparison with these first two groups even if they reported that they had voted in a Democratic primary.

10. The fifteen states included in this subset of the CPS sample were Florida, Illinois, Wisconsin, Pennsylvania, Massachusetts, Indiana, Ohio, Tennessee, North Carolina, Nebraska, West Virginia, Maryland, Michigan, Oregon, and California.

11. An objection that might be raised to the use of the CPS sample in this way is the time lapse between the primaries themselves and the pre-election interviews in which the primary voting questions were asked; how accurate are the reponses with this kind of a time lag? One indicator of the accuracy of the responses is the degree of overreporting of voting; if the data are inaccurate, on would expect substantial overreporting given the social desirability of voting. The overreporting in this survey is quite low. In the states included in the sample, 21.2 percent actually participated in Democratic presidential primaries as compared to a reported turnout of 28.7 percent; this is well within the normal range of overreporting of voting; see Angus Campbell, et al., *American Voter* (New York: Wiley, 1960), pp. 93-96.

12. James E. Grizzle, C. Frank Starmer, and Gary G. Koch, "Analysis of Categorical Data by Linear Models," *Biometrics* 25 (1969): 489-504; see also Robert G. Lehnen and Gary G. Koch, "A General Linear Approach to the Analysis of Nonmetric Data: Applications for Political Science," *American Journal of Political Science* 18 (May 1974): 283-313; and Herbert M. Kritzer, "NONMET II: A Program for the Analysis of Contingency Tables

and Other Types of Nonmetric Data by Weighted Least Squares," *Behavior Research Methods and Instrumentation* 8 (June 1976): 320–321.

13. This assumes no cross-over voting by those who do not identify with the party.

14. While in the previous analysis, Republicans and nonleaning Independents who reported voting in Democratic presidential primaries were excluded from the analysis, they were included among primary voters in this analysis. Since they only constitute about 14 percent of the voters in the primaries, it is not likely that their inclusion resulted in the similarity of primary participants to the voting age population as a whole.

15. Jeanne Kirkpatrick, "Representation in the American National Conventions," pp. 286–307.

16. Arthur H. Miller, Warren E. Miller, Aldine S. Raine, and Thad A. Brown, "A Majority Party in Disarray: Policy Polarization in the 1972 Election," *American Political Science Review* 70 (September 1976): 753–778.

17. Herbert M. Kritzer, "Representation in Presidential Primaries."

8 / Media Coverage of the 1976 Nominating Process

Rhodes Cook

CBS correspondent Roger Mudd observed on the eve of the Iowa caucuses, the first of the 1976 nominating season:

> The English that is applied to these results is going to be applied by the media and the politicians themselves. It's not exactly the precise figures that will be important, it's whether the media and the politicians agree that this man won and this man lost. [1]

Who won; who lost. This is a judgment the media exercised frequently between January 19, 1976, the date of the Iowa caucuses and June 8, 1976, the final day of the primaries. Instead of acting as a conduit for the exchange of information between the candidates and the voters, the media—particularly the broadcast media—created an ongoing drama with winners and losers, heroes and villians, and a scenario flexible enough to accommodate the most recent primary results.

In the process, the media glossed over the fact that often the most important events in determining the success of a presidential candidate are undramatic—the development of a grass-roots organization, the creation of an effective fund-raising apparatus, and the approval by the states of delegate-selection rules that will shape the contest.

As a partial defense of the media, it must be admitted that they were dealing with a rather new and evolving process. Only since 1960 have primaries been covered closely by the media, and it has only been in the last decade that the importance of the primaries in the nominating process has grown dramatically.

In 1976 there were thirty primaries to cover—a record number. The task was complicated by new delegate-selection rules and an initially wide field of candidates, who themselves adapted their campaigning to gain media exposure.

To its credit, the press in 1976 made a greater effort than in previous years to move beyond the horse-race aspects of much of the earliet reporting on nominating contests. In-depth assessments of voter attitudes, a greater attention to issues, and a more critical self-examination of media's own role in the nominating process characterized media coverage of the 1976 primaries. The press paid more attention to its own impact than ever before, continuing a process of self-examination that had begun four years earlier after President Richard M. Nixon had successfully executed a controlled "rose garden" campaign that barely elicited a whimper from the press.

155

Table 8-1 Selection of Delegates in the Caucus States: Democrats (Boldfaced are steps in the process where national convention delegates are chosen.)

State	Conv. Votes	1st Step	2nd Step	3rd Step	4th Step
Alaska	10	Precinct caucuses—Feb. 10	Judicial district convs.—Mar. 12–Mar.26	**State Conv.**—Apr. 23	
Arizona	25	Presidential preference poll and election of delegates to Cong. Dist. Convs.—Apr. 24	**Congressional Dist. Convs.**—May 8	**State Comm.**—May 5	
Colorado	35	Precinct caucuses—May 3	County convs.—between May 13–June 2	**Congressional Dist. Convs.**—May 22, June 12 and June 25	**State Conv.**—June 26
Connecticut[1]	51	Town caucuses—Apr. 27	Town primaries—May 11	**Congressional Dist. Convs.**—June 12	
Delaware[1]	12	Primary to elect delegates to State Conv.—June 5	**State Conv.**—June 11-12		
Hawaii	17	Precinct caucuses—Mar. 9	**State Conv.**—May 28-30		
Iowa	47	Precinct caucuses—Jan. 19	County convs.—Mar. 6	**Congressional Dist. Convs.**—Apr. 10	**State Conv.**—May 29
Kansas	34	Local unit convs.—Apr. 3	**Congressional Dist. Convs.**—May 1	**State Comm.**—June 5	
Louisiana	41	**Primary** to elect 32 delegates to natl. conv.—May 1	**State Committee**—May 8		
Maine	20	Municipal caucuses—Feb. 1-29	**State Conv.**—May 7-9		
Minnesota	65	Precinct caucuses—Feb. 24	County convs.—between Mar. 13-28	**Congressional Dist. Convs.**—between Apr. 10-May 2	**State Conv.**—June 4-6
Mississippi[2]	24	Precinct caucuses—Jan. 24	County convs.—Feb. 14	**Congressional Dist. Convs.**—Feb. 21	**State Exec. Comm.**—Feb. 29

		...meetings—Apr. 23			...May 23
New Mexico[1]	18	Ward or precinct meetings—Apr. 22	County convs.—Apr. 29	State Conv.—May 15	
North Dakota[1]	13	Precinct caucuses—April 27	Legislative dist. caucuses—by June 14	State Conv.—June 24-26	
Oklahoma	37	Precinct caucuses—Feb. 7	County convs.—Feb. 28	Congressional Dist. Convs.—Mar. 20	State Conv.—Apr. 3-4
South Carolina	31	Precinct caucuses—Feb. 28	County convs.—Mar. 8	State Conv.—Mar. 31	
Utah[1]	18	Voting dist. mass meetings—May 17	County convs.—between May 22-June 2	State Conv.—June 18-19	
Vermont	12	Town caucuses—Apr. 22	**State Conv.—May 22**		
Virginia	54	County, city mass meetings—Apr. 3	**Congressional Dist. Convs.—May 22**		
Washington	53	Precinct caucuses—Mar. 2	County convs.—Apr. 17	Congressional Dist. Convs.—May 22	
Wyoming[1]	10	County mass meetings—Mar. 1-15	**State Conv.—May 8**		Dist. Delegates—June 11
Territories					
Canal Zone	3	Convention—May 1			
Guam[1]	3	Primary to elect national convention delegates—May 1	**State Conv.—Mar. 7**		
Puerto Rico	22	**Dist. Convs.—Feb. 22**			
Virgin Islands[1]	3	**Mass meeting—April 24**			

[1] *Delegate selection plans not approved by Compliance Review Commission by March 1, 1976.*

[2] A primary was created by state law, but both parties announced their intentions to use the caucus system to elect delegates.

[3] In rural Missouri, county mass meetings may be held in place of ward or township meetings.

Table 8-1 (cont.) Selection of Delegates in the Caucus States: Republicans (Boldfaced are steps in the process where national convention delegates are chosen.)

State	Conv. Votes	1st Step	2nd Step	3rd Step	4th Step
Alaska	19	Precinct caucuses—at least 15 days before dist.	State senate dist. Convs.—at least 20 days before state	**State Conv.**—May 22-24	
Arizona	29	County committee meetings—not set	**State Conv.**—Apr. 10		
Colorado	31	Precinct meetings—May 3	County convs.—between May 13—June 2	**Congressional Dist. Convs.**—1st, June 5; others not set.	**State Conv.**—July 9-10
Connecticut	35	Town meetings—Mar. 23-25	Town primaries—May 4	**C.D. Convs.**—July 15	**S.C.**—Mar. 23-25
Delaware	17	Primary to elect delegates to State conv.—June 5	**State Conv.**—June 19		**S.C.**—July 16-17
Hawaii	19	Precinct caucuses—Jan. 27	**State Conv.**—May 15-17		
Iowa	36	Precinct caucuses—Jan. 19	County convs.—Feb. 28	**State Conv.**—June 18-19	
Kansas	34	Precinct caucuses—At least 5 days prior to county convs.	County convs.—March 24-April 8	**Congressional Dist. Convs.**—May 8	**State Conv.**—May 22
Louisiana	41	**Congressional Dist. Mass Caucuses**—May 9-15	**State Conv.**—June 5		
Maine	20	Municipal caucuses—by Mar. 29	**State Conv.**—April 30-May 1		
Minnesota	42	Precinct caucuses—Feb. 24	County convs.—between March 13-31	**Congressional Dist. Convs.**—between Apr. 19-May 15	**State Conv.**—June 24-26

		meetings—Apr. 19-24	between May 8-15		
New Mexico	21	Ward or p.c.—Apr. 25-May 1	County convs.—May 2-8		State Conv.—June 26
North Dakota	18	Legislative dist. caucuses—between May 1-June 14	State Conv.—July 8-10		
Oklahoma	36	Precinct caucuses—April 5	County convs.—April 24	Congressional Dist. Convs.—May 8	State Conv.—May 15
South Carolina	36	Precinct caucuses—Mar. 12-13	County convs.—Mar. 22-27	Congressional Dist. Convs.—Apr. 5-10	State Conv.—Apr. 24
Utah	20	Voting dist. mass meetings—May 17	County convs.—June 1-26		State Conv.—July 16-17
Vermont	18	Town Caucuses—Apr. 22	State Conv.—May 22		
Virginia	51	City, county meetings-not set	Congressional Dist. Convs.—by end of May (exact dates not set)	State Conv.—June 4-5	
Washington	38	Precinct caucuses—Mar. 2	County convs.—Apr. 2-May 18	State Conv.—June 18-19	
Wyoming	17	Precinct caucuses—between Feb. 4-Mar. 5	County convs.—between Mar. 1-15	State Conv.—May 8	
Territories					
Guam	4	Not set			
Puerto Rico	8	Not set			
Virgin Islands	4	Not set			

1 *A primary was enacted by state law, but both parties announced their intention to use the caucus system to elect delegates.*
2 *In rural Missouri, county mass meetings may be held in place of ward and township meetings.*
Source: Reprinted by permission from *Congressional Quarterly.*

The media, nonetheless, approached the first post-Watergate presidential campaign with an unusual degree of cynicism. At the exclusion of more substantive issues, the press preferred to belabor gaffes such as Jimmy Carter's "ethnic purity" statement.

Carter made the remark in an April 2 interview with the *New York Daily News*, saying that he saw nothing wrong with neighborhoods retaining their ethnic purity and would oppose an government action to force racial integration. The statement was not picked up by the national media until several days later, and then it became the center of media attention for much of April.

The press spent much of its time speculating on whether Carter's choice of words would weaken his appeal among blacks and liberals and ultimately destroy his campaign. Speculation on Carter's slippage was conclusively terminated April 27, when the Georgian won a sweeping victory in the Pennsylvania primary.

The press's eagerness to pursue sensational topics stood in contrast to its slowness in researching the background of the candidates, particularly Carter's. Rather than extensively studying Carter's career in Georgia government, the press generally seemed content to label him as an unknown throughout the 1976 primary season. Only the more colorful aspects of Carter's life—such as his "born again" Baptist faith and his faith-healing sister—seemed to draw media scrutiny.

The result in 1976 was a coverage of Carter and other candidates that was both too simplistic and too general, and which seemed to be most enthusiastic when exposing candidate blunders.

The press coverage of specific caucuses and primaries highlighted other problems. Coverage of four of these events in 1976 will be described in some detail because it typifies a definite intrusion into compaigns which colored subsequent events.

The Iowa precinct caucuses on January 19, the first of the events to be discussed, opened the nationwide delegate-selection process and presented the first tangible demonstration of candidate strength. The second event was the New Hampshire primary on February 24, the first of the presidential primaries in 1976 and the initial indication of mass voter appeal. Both the Iowa caucuses and the New Hampshire primary enjoyed an importance far outweighing their delegate counts simply because they came first (see Tables 8-1 and 8-2).

The third event was the April 6 set of primaries in Wisconsin and New York. Delegates chosen in New York outnumbered those in Wisconsin four to one, but the Empire State was virtually ignored by the media because it had a more complex delegate-selection system.

There are two basic types of primaries. New York represented the delegate-selection type, where the contest is strictly for convention delegates elected at the congressional-district level. Wisconsin and most other states have a presidential preference primary, where voters can cast their ballots directly for the candidates; votes are tallied on a statewide basis. The media prefers to focus on this type of primary because of the dramatic, horse-race aspect that can be developed.

The fourth event in which there was a definite media intrusion was the set of climactic primaries on June 8 in California, New Jersey, and Ohio. A questionable interpretation of the results by the media enabled a slumping Carter to lock up the nomination even though he won only one of the three big primaries that day.

Iowa: The First Decision

Iowa and New Hampshire underscored the premise that unlike general election politics, where it is important to peak late in the campaign, in preconvention politics it is more important to score early.

Iowa was significant for three major reasons, none of which actually related to the number of delegates at stake. First, it started the delegate-selection season and gave the first indication of candidate appeal. Second, the media considered it important. In 1972 the media had largely overlooked Senator George McGovern's strong early showing in Iowa against Senator Edmund S. Muskie, which had proved to be an indication of McGovern's grass-roots strength. And third, *since the media considered Iowa important, so did the candidates*—and they were there in force.

Candidates and the media combined to make Iowa a major event, although in actuality what was at stake was publicity, not delegates. The delegates were chosen months later.

The caucus system, as typified by Iowa, is a multitiered process, with meetings scheduled over several months. Meetings at the first level, the precinct caucuses, are the only ones open to mass participation. Participants often discuss both party issues and the selection of delegates to the next step in the process, and meetings frequently last several hours and attract only the most enthusiastic and dedicated party members.

Delegates elected in the precinct caucuses go to county conventions (held on March 10 in Iowa), which in turn elect delegates to the congressional-district and state conventions (April 10 and May 29, respectively). In Iowa, as in most other caucus states, all national convention delegates are elected at the district and state conventions.

But the media focused on the precinct caucuses, and this proved to be a bonanza for Carter. Although he finished 10 percentage points behind "uncommitted," he ran first among the active Democratic candidates and was declared the winner (see Table 8-3).

Carter was the choice of less than 15,000 of the 45,000 participants in the Democratic caucuses, yet he was hailed as the victor and was established as the early front-runner for the nomination. The Iowa results ensured that the Carter campaign would receive serious and intensive coverage from the media.

New Hampshire: The Primary Opener

The heavy media attention given the New Hampshire primary—even more than the Iowa caucus—illustrates an unevenness in delegate-selection coverage, which favors the early events. Although New Hampshire is ideal for the media—a beautiful state with a town-hall tradition and small enough to be covered easily—it is important only because it's primary comes first.

New Hampshire's primary was only one of thirty in 1976, (see Table 8-4) and it sent less than 1.0 percent of the delegates to either convention. Yet this primary was grossly overemphasized by the media. A study by Michael J. Robinson, a political scientist at Catholic University, showed that in their coverage of the presidential campaigns between Thanksgiving in 1975 and late February 1976, the networks devoted 54 percent of their stories to New Hampshire. Major newspapers, the survey continued, devoted about 35 percent of their campaign coverage to New Hampshire. [2]

Table 8-2 1976 Presidential Primary Information (Abbreviations for presidential candidate ballot access: I = Involuntary; nationally recognized candidates placed on ballot by state officials. V = Voluntary; candidate gains place on ballot by own initiative.)

State	Pres. Cand. Ballot Access	Primary Date	Filing Deadline Pres. Cand.	Del. Cand.	Pres. Cand. Withdrawal	Write-ins Permitted	Convention Votes Dem.	Rep.
N.H.	V	Feb. 24	Dec. 26	Jan. 12	May withdraw within 10 days of notification by sec. of state	Yes	17	21
Mass.	I	March 2	Jan. 2	——[1]	Jan. 9	Yes	104	43
Vt.	V	March 2	Feb. 10	——[1]	May withdraw within 10 days of notification by sec of state	Yes	12	18
Fla.	I	March 9	Feb. 10	——[1]	Feb. 15[2]	No	81	66
Ill.	V	March 16	Dec. 29	Jan. 14	No provision	Yes	169	101
N.C.	V	March 23	Feb. 3	——[1]	Failure to give consent = withdrawal	No	61	54
N.Y.	—	April 6	——	Feb. 19	——	Yes	274	154
Wis.	I	April 6	March 2	——[1]	Feb. 29[2]	Yes	68	45
Pa.	V	April 27	Feb. 17	Feb. 17	Feb. 24	Yes	178	103
Texas	V	May 1	Feb. 2	March 1	April 10	No	130	100
Ala.	—	May 4	——	March 1	——	Yes	35	37
D.C.	V	May 4	March 5	March 5	No provision	No	17	14
Ga.	1	May 4	Feb. 10	March 13[3]	Feb. 20[2]	No	50	48
Ind.	V	May 4	March 15	——[1]	March 15	No	75	54
Neb.	1	May 11	March 12	March 12	March 12[2]	Yes	23	25
W. Va.	V	May 11	Feb. 7	Feb. 7	No provision	No	33	28
Md.	1	May 18	March 25	March 9	April 2[2]	No	53	43
Mich.	I	May 18	March 19	——[1]	March 19	Yes	133	84
Ark.	V	May 25	April 6	——[1]	No provision	Yes	26	27
Idaho	I	May 25	April 25	——[1]	No provision	Yes	16	21
Ky.	V	May 25	April 9	——[1]	Failure to pay filing fee = withdrawal	No	46	37
Nev.	I	May 25	April 25	——[1]	No provision	No	11	18
Ore.	I	May 25	March 16	——[1]	No provision	Yes	34	30
Tenn.	I	May 25	April 9	March 25	April 9[2]	Yes	46	43
Mont.	V	June 1	March 23	——[1]	April 22	Yes	17	20
R.I.	I	June 1	Feb. 27	April 12	May 1	No	22	19
S.D.	V	June 1	April 16	April 16	April 16	No	17	20
Calif.	I	June 8	March 26	D: April 16 R: May 9	April 4[2]	Yes[4]	280	167
N.J.	V	June 8	April 29	April 29	May 4	Yes	108	67
Ohio	V	June 8	——	March 25	April 3[5]	Yes	152	97

[1]Delegates chosen outside primary by caucus methods. Ballot filing deadline for national convention delegates does not apply.
[2]Individual must state he is not a presidential candidate and does not intend to become one. (In California, individual only declares non-candidacy.)
[3]Democrats only. Republicans use caucus method.
[4]Write-in campaign must be endorsed by candidate.
[5]Withdrawal deadline for delegate candidates.
Source: Reprinted by permission from *Congressional Quarterly.*

Table 8-3 Caucus Outcomes, 1976 Democratic Presidential Nomination Contest (in percent when greater than 1.0 percent of caucus vote)

	Bayh	Bentsen	Brown	Carter	Church	Harris	Jackson	Humphrey	McCormack	Shriver	Udall	Wallace	Uncommitted
Alaska													
Precinct—2/10[a]	—	—	—	4.0	—	—	6.0	—	—	—	—	—	90.0
District—3/13–3/28	—	—	—	—	—	—	—	—	—	—	—	—	100.0
State conv.—4/23[b]	—	—	—	—	—	—	—	—	—	—	—	—	100.0
(Delegates won)													(10)
Arizona													
Pref. Vote—4/24	—	—	—	10.4	1.6	—	5.4	—	1.1	—	70.8	7.0	3.0
District—5/8	—	—	—	20.0	—	—	—	—	—	—	76.0	4.0	—
State comm.—5/15													
(Delegates won)				(5)							(19)	(1)	
Colorado													
Precinct—5/3	—	—	7.0	23.2	13.5	—	1.0	—	—	—	14.5	—	34.2
County—5/22–6/2[c]	—	—	12.7	21.8	17.5	—	—	1.0	—	—	18.2	—	27.7
District—5/22–6/25	—	—	17.1	34.3	8.6	—	—	—	—	—	14.3	—	25.7
State conv.—6/26													
(Delegates won)			(6)	(12)	(3)						(5)		(9)
Connecticut													
Pref. vote—5/11	—	—	—	33.2	—	—	17.8	—	5.2	—	30.8	—	12.8
District—6/12	—	—	—	37.3	—	—	15.7	—	—	—	31.4	—	15.7
(Delegates won)				(19)			(8)				(16)		(8)
Delaware													
State conv.—6/11[d]	—	—	—	83.3	—	—	—	—	—	—	—	—	16.7
(Delegates won)				(10)									(2)

[a] No official figures tabulated. Based on estimates by state party sources.

[b] National convention delegates were chosen at the district conventions. Their selection was ratified by the state convention.

[c] No statewide figures tabulated. Results are from ten largest counties.

[d] Primary held June 5 to elect delegates to state convention, but races in only three of forty-one legislative districts were contested.

[e] Precinct caucuses were held April 27, but no official figures were tabulated.

Source: *Congressional Quarterly.* Chart is based on information provided by the state committees and wire services.

Table 8-3 (cont.) Caucus Outcomes, 1976 Democratic Presidential Nomination Contest (in percent when greater than 1.0 percent of caucus vote)

	Bayh	Bentsen	Brown	Carter	Church	Harris	Jackson	Hum-phrey	McCor-mack	Shriver	Udall	Wallace	Uncom-mitted
Hawaii													
Pref. vote—3/9	—	—	—	2.4	—	—	2.8	—	—	1.1	4.5	—	85.1
State Conv.—5/28-5/30	—	—	—	—	—	—	5.9	—	—	—	5.9	—	88.2
(Delegates won)							(1)				(1)		(15)
Iowa													
Precinct—1/19	11.4	—	—	29.1	—	9.0	1.1	—	—	3.1	5.8	—	38.5
County—3/6	1.9	—	—	34.2	—	9.1	—	—	—	—	12.9	—	40.9
District—4/10	—	—	—	42.6	—	4.3	—	—	—	—	25.5	—	27.7
State conv.—5/29													
(Delegates won)				(20)		(2)					(12)		(13)
Kansas													
Local unit—4/3	—	—	—	36.1	—	1.8	6.5	—	—	—	4.5	—	50.2
District—5/1	—	—	—	47.1	—	—	2.9	—	—	—	8.8	—	41.2
State comm.—6/5													
(Delegates won)				(16)			(1)				(3)		(14)
Louisiana													
Del. vote—5/1	—	—	—	31.7	—	—	—	—	—	—	—	22.0	46.3
State comm.—5/8													
(Delegates won)				(13)								(9)	(19)
Maine													
Municipal—2/1-2/29	1.0	—	—	25.8	—	3.8	—	—	—	—	3.8	—	64.4
State conv.—5/9	—	—	—	45.0	—	—	—	—	—	—	25.0	—	30.0
(Delegates won)				(9)							(5)		(6)
Minnesota													
Precinct—2/24	—	—	—	—	—	4.2	—	51.4	—	—	1.2	—	41.6
County—3/13-3/28	—	—	—	—	—	4.3	—	55.2	—	—	2.0	—	38.2
District—4/24-5/2	—	—	—	—	—	—	—	73.8	—	—	—	—	26.2
State conv.—6/6													
(Delegates won)								(48)					(17)

	1	2	3	4	5	6	7	8	9	10	11
Precinct—1/24	1.6	14.0		1.1				12.3		43.9	27.5
County—2/14		11.4						10.4		50.1	27.6
District—2/21		20.8						16.7		45.8	16.7
State comm.—2/29											
(Delegates won)		(5)						(4)		(11)	(4)
Missouri											
Mass mtgs.—4/20, 5/11		16.8			2.1	2.4	2.5		5.5	2.1	65.9
District—5/25		54.9			1.4	—	1.4		4.2	—	38.0
State conv.—6/12											
(Delegates won)		(39)			(1)		(1)		(3)		(27)
New Mexico											
Mass mtgs.—4/22		28.5							33.2		37.0
County—4/29		41.8							26.5		31.7
State conv.—5/15		44.4							33.3		22.2
(Delegates won)		(8)							(6)		(4)
North Dakota											
Leg. dist.—4/27, 5/18[e]		2.8					7.4		1.9		65.2
State conv.—6/26		100.0					—		—		—
(Delegates won)		(13)									
Oklahoma											
Precinct—2/7	12.8	18.5		17.0						10.4	40.0
County—2/28		29.0		17.8						5.9	47.3
District—3/20		32.4		18.9						—	48.6
State conv.—4/4											
(Delegates won)		(12)		(7)							(18)
South Carolina											
Precinct—2/28		22.9	—						—	27.6	48.0
County—3/8		30.0	2.5						1.0	28.5	38.4
State conv.—3/31		29.0	3.2						—	25.8	41.9
(Delegates won)		(9)	(1)							(8)	(13)
Utah											
Pref. vote—5/17	9.9	16.4	21.8						8.1		40.6
State conv.—6/19		22.2	27.8						—		50.0
(Delegates won)		(4)	(5)								(9)

Table 8-3 (cont.) Caucus Outcomes, 1976 Democratic Presidential Nomination Contest (in percent when greater than 1.0 percent of caucus vote)

	Bayh	Bentsen	Brown	Carter	Church	Harris	Jackson	Hum-phrey	McCor-mack	Shriver	Udall	Wallace	Uncom-mitted
Vermont													
Town mtgs.—4/22	—	—	4.0	16.2	—	—	—	1.8	—	—	11.1	—	65.3
State conv.—5/22	—	—	16.7	25.0	—	—	—	—	—	—	25.0	—	33.3
(Delegates won)			(2)	(3)							(3)		(4)
Virginia													
Mass mtgs.—4/3	—	—	—	29.9	—	—	—	—	—	—	8.9	2.5	57.8
District—5/22	—	—	—	42.6	—	—	—	—	—	—	13.0	—	44.4
(Delegates won)				(23)							(7)		(24)
Washington													
Precinct—3/2	—	—	—	1.0	—	—	57.5	—	—	—	8.2	1.0	30.3
County, Leg. dist.—4/10, 4/17	—	—	—	—	—	—	60.0	—	—	—	6.5	—	33.1
District—5/22	—	—	—	—	—	—	60.4	—	—	—	13.2	—	26.4
At-large—6/13													
(Delegates won)							(32)				(7)		(14)
Wyoming													
County—3/1	—	—	—	3.7	—	1.4	1.7	—	—	—	5.1	—	87.0
State conv.—5/8	—	—	10.0	10.0	—	—	—	—	—	—	10.0	—	70.0
(Delegates won)			(1)	(1)							(1)		(7)

Table 8-4 1976 Presidential Primaries*

Republican	Votes	%	Democratic	Votes	%
February 24 New Hampshire					
Gerald R. Ford (Mich.)	55,156	49.4	Jimmy Carter (Ga.)	23,373	28.4
Ronald Reagan (Calif.)	53,569	48.0	Morris K. Udall (Ariz.)	18,710	22.7
Others[1]	2,949	2.6	Birch Bayh (Ind.)	12,510	15.2
			Fred R. Harris (Okla.)	8,863	10.8
			Sargent Shriver (Md.)	6,743	8.2
			Hubert H. Humphrey (Minn.)[1]	4,596	5.6
			Henry M. Jackson (Wash.)[1]	1,857	2.3
			George C. Wallace (Ala.)[1]	1,061	1.3
			Ellen McCormack (N.Y.)	1,007	1.2
			Others	3.661	4.8
March 2 Massachusettes					
Ford	115,375	61.2	Jackson	164,393	22.3
Reagan	63,555	33.7	Udall	130,440	17.7
None of the names			Wallace	123,112	16.7
shown	6,000	3.2	Carter	101,948	13.9
Others[1]	3,519	1.8	Harris	55,701	7.6
			Shriver	53,252	7.2
			Bayh	34,963	4.8
			McCormack	25,772	3.5
			Milton J. Shapp (Pa.)	21,693	2.9
			None of the names shown	9,804	1.3
			Humphrey[1]	7,851	1.1
			Edward M. Kennedy (Mass.)[1]	1,623	0.2
			Lloyd Bentsen (Texas)	364	—
			Others	4,905	0.7
March 2 Vermont					
Ford	27,014	84.0	Carter	16,335	42.2
Reagan	4,892	15.2	Shriver	10,699	27.6
Others[1]	251	—	Harris	4,893	12.6
			McCormack	3,324	8.6
			Others	3,463	9.0

* Delegate selection primaries were held in Alabama, New York, and Texas. The figures are not recorded here since there was no presidential preference voting.

[1] Write-in.

[2] Ford unopposed. No primary held.

[3] In addition to scattered write-in votes, "others" include Tommy Klein, who received 1,088 votes in Kentucky.

[4] In addition to scattered write-in votes, "others" include Frank Ahern who received 1,487 votes in Georgia; Stanley Arnold, 371 votes in New Hampshire; Arthur O. Blessitt, 828 votes in New Hampshire and 7,889 in Georgia; Frank Bona, 135 votes in New Hampshire and 263 in Georgia; Billy Joe Clegg, 174 votes in New Hampshire; Abram Eisenman, 351 votes in Georgia; John S. Gonas, 2,288 votes in New Jersey; Jesse Gray, 3,574 votes in New Jersey; Robert L. Kelleher, 87 votes in New Hampshire, 1,603 in Massachusettes and 139 in Georgia; Rick Loewenherz, 49 votes in New Hampshire; Frank Lomento, 3,555 votes in New Jersey; Floyd L. Lunger, 3,935 votes in New Jersey; H. R. H. "Fifi" Rockefeller, 2,305 votes in Kentucky; George Roden, 153 votes in Georgia; Ray Rollinson, 3,021 votes in New Jersey; Terry Sanford, 53 votes in New Hampshire and 351 votes in Massachusettes; Bernard B. Schecter, 173 votes in New Hampshire.

Source: Reprinted by permission from *Congressional Quarterly.*

Table 8-4 (cont.) 1976 Presidential Primaries*

Republican			Democratic		
	Votes	*%*		*Votes*	*%*
March 9 Florida					
Ford	321,982	52.8	Carter	448,844	34.5
Reagan	287,837	47.2	Wallace	396,820	30.5
			Jackson	310,944	23.9
			None of the names shown	37,626	2.9
			Shapp	32,198	2.5
			Udall	27,235	2.1
			Bayh	8,750	.7
			McCormack	7,595	.6
			Shriver	7,084	.5
			Harris	5,397	.4
			Robert C. Byrd (W.Va.)	5,042	.4
			Frank Church (Idaho)	4,906	.4
			Others	7,889	.6
March 16 Illinois					
Ford	456,750	58.9	Carter	630,915	48.1
Reagan	311,295	40.1	Wallace	361,798	27.6
Lar Daly (Ill.)	7,582	1.0	Shriver	214,024	16.3
Others[1]	266	—	Harris	98,862	7.5
			Others[1]	6,315	.5
March 23 North Carolina					
Reagan	101,468	52.4	Carter	324,437	53.6
Ford	88,897	45.9	Wallace	210,166	34.7
None of the names			Jackson	25,749	4.3
shown	3,362	1.7	None of the names shown	22,850	3.8
			Udall	14,032	2.3
			Harris	5,923	1.0
			Bentsen	1,675	.3
April 6 Wisconsin					
Ford	326,869	55.2	Carter	271,220	36.6
Reagan	262,126	44.2	Udall	263,771	35.6
None of the names			Wallace	92,460	12.5
shown	2,234	.3	Jackson	47,605	6.4
Others[1]	583	—	McCormack	26,982	3.6
			Harris	8,185	1.1
			None of the names shown	7,154	1.0
			Shriver	5,097	.7
			Bentsen	1,730	.2
			Bayh	1,255	.2
			Shapp	596	.1
			Others[1]	14,473	2.0
April 27 Pennsylvania					
Ford	733,472	92.1	Carter	511,905	37.0
Reagan	40,510	5.1	Jackson	340,340	24.6
Others	22,678	2.8	Udall	259,166	18.7
			Wallace	155,902	11.3
			McCormack	38,800	2.8
			Shapp	32,947	2.4
			Bayh	15,320	1.1
			Harris	13,067	.9
			Humphrey[1]	12,563	.9
			Others	5,032	.3

Table 8-4 (cont.) 1976 Presidential Primaries*

Republican	Votes	%	Democratic	Votes	%
May 4 District of Columbia[2]					
			Carter	10,521	31.6
			Walter E. Fauntroy (unpledged		
			delegates)	10,149	30.5
			Udall	6,999	21.0
			Walter E. Washington (unpledged		
			delegates)	5,161	15.5
			Harris	461	1.4
May 4 Georgia					
Reagan	128,671	68.3	Carter	419,272	83.4
Ford	59,801	31.7	Wallace	57,594	11.5
			Udall	9,755	1.9
			Byrd	3,628	.7
			Jackson	3,358	.7
			Church	2,477	.5
			Shriver	1,378	.3
			Bayh	824	.2
			Harris	699	.1
			McCormack	635	.1
			Bentsen	277	.1
			Shapp	181	—
			Others	2,393	.5
May 4 Indiana					
Reagan	323,779	51.3	Carter	417,480	68.0
Ford	307,513	48.7	Wallace	93,121	15.2
			Jackson	72,080	11.7
			McCormack	31,708	5.2
May 11 Nebraska					
Reagen	113,493	54.5	Church	67,297	38.5
Ford	94,542	45.4	Carter	65,833	37.6
Others	379	.1	Humphrey	12,685	7.2
			Kennedy	7,199	4.1
			McCormack	6,033	3.4
			Wallace	5,567	3.2
			Udall	4,688	2.7
			Jackson	2,642	1.5
			Harris	811	.5
			Bayh	407	.2
			Shriver	384	.2
			Others	1,467	.8
May 11 West Virginia					
Ford	88,386	56.8	Byrd	331,639	89.0
Reagan	67,306	43.2	Wallace	40,938	11.0
May 18 Maryland					
Ford	96,291	58.0	Edmund G. Brown Jr. (Calif.)	286,672	48.4
Reagan	68,680	42.0	Carter	219,404	37.1
			Udall	32,790	5.5
			Wallace	24,176	4.1
			Jackson	13,956	2.4
			McCormack	7,907	1.3
			Harris	6,841	1.2

Table 8-4 (cont.)   1976 Presidential Primaries*

Republican			Democratic		
	Votes	*%*		*Votes*	*%*
May 18 Michigan					
Ford	690,180	64.9	Carter	307,559	43.4
Reagan	364,052	34.3	Udall	305,134	43.1
Unpledged delegates	8,473	.8	Wallace	49,204	6.9
Others[1]	109	—	Unpledged delegates	15,853	2.2
			Jackson	10,332	1.5
			McCormack	7,623	1.1
			Shriver	5,738	.8
			Harris	4,081	.6
			Others[1]	3,142	.4
May 25 Arkansas					
Reagan	20,628	63.4	Carter	314,306	62.6
Ford	11,430	35.1	Wallace	83,005	16.5
Unpledged delegates	483	1.5	Unpledged delegates	57,152	11.4
			Udall	37,783	7.5
			Jackson	9,554	1.9
May 25 Idaho					
Reagan	66,743	74.3	Church	58,570	78.7
Ford	22,323	24.9	Carter	8,818	11.9
Unpledged delegates	727	.8	Humphrey	1,700	2.3
			Brown[1]	1,453	2.0
			Wallace	1,115	1.5
			Udall	981	1.3
			Unpledged delegates	964	1.3
			Jackson	485	.7
			Harris	319	.4
May 25 Kentucky					
Ford	67,976	50.9	Carter	181,690	59.4
Reagan	62,683	46.9	Wallace	51,540	16.8
Unpledged delegates	1,781	1.3	Udall	33,262	10.9
Others	1,088	.8	McCormack	17,061	5.6
			Unpledged delegates	11,962	3.9
			Jackson	8,186	2.7
			Others	2,305	.8
May 25 Nevada					
Reagan	31,637	66.3	Brown	39,671	52.7
Ford	13,747	28.8	Carter	17,567	23.3
None of the names			Church	6,778	9.0
shown	2,365	5.0	None of the names shown	4,603	6.1
			Wallace	2,490	3.3
			Udall	2,237	3.0
			Jackson	1,896	2.5
May 25 Oregon					
Ford	150,181	50.3	Church	145,394	33.6
Reagan	136,691	45.8	Carter	115,310	26.7
Others[1]	11,663	3.9	Brown[1]	106,812	24.7
			Humphrey	22,488	5.2
			Udall	11,747	2.7
			Kennedy	10,983	2.5
			Wallace	5,797	1.3
			Jackson	5,298	1.2

Table 8-4 (cont.)   1976 Presidential Primaries*

Republican			Democratic		
	Votes	*%*		*Votes*	*%*
			McCormack	3,753	.9
			Harris	1,344	.3
			Bayh	743	.2
			Others[1]	2,963	.7
May 25 Tennessee					
Ford	120,685	49.8	Carter	259,243	77.6
Reagan	118,997	49.1	Wallace	36,495	10.9
Unpledged delegates	2,756	1.1	Udall	12,420	3.7
Others[1]	97	—	Church	8,026	2.4
			Unpledged delegates	6,148	1.8
			Jackson	5,672	1.7
			McCormack	1,782	.5
			Harris	1,628	.5
			Brown[1]	1,556	.5
			Shapp	507	.2
			Humphrey[1]	109	—
			Others[1]	492	.1
June 1 Montana					
Reagan	56,683	63.1	Church	63,448	59.4
Ford	31,100	34.6	Carter	26,329	24.6
None of the names			Udall	6,708	6.3
shown	1,996	2.2	None of the names shown	3,820	3.6
			Wallace	3,680	3.4
			Jackson	2,856	2.7
June 1 Rhode Island					
Ford	9,365	65.3	Unpledged delegates	19,035	31.5
Reagan	4,480	31.2	Carter	18,237	30.2
Unpledged delegates	507	3.5	Church	16,423	27.2
			Udall	2,543	4.2
			McCormack	2,468	4.1
			Jackson	756	1.3
			Wallace	507	.8
			Bayh	247	.4
			Shapp	132	.2
June 1 South Dakota					
Reagan	43,068	51.2	Carter	24,186	41.2
Ford	36,976	44.0	Udall	19,510	33.3
None of the names			None of the names shown	7,871	13.4
shown	4,033	4.8	McCormack	4,561	7.8
			Wallace	1,412	2.4
			Harris	573	1.0
			Jackson	558	1.0
June 8 California					
Reagan	1,604,836	65.5	Brown	2,013,210	59.0
Ford	845,655	34.5	Carter	697,092	20.4
Others[1]	20	—	Church	250,581	7.3
			Udall	171,501	5.0
			Wallace	102,292	3.0
			Unpledged delegates	78,595	2.3
			Jackson	38,634	1.1
			McCormack	29,242	.9

Table 8-4 (cont.)   1976 Presidential Primaries*

Republican			Democratic		
	Votes	*%*		*Votes*	*%*
			Harris	16,920	.5
			Bayh	11,419	.3
			Others[1]	215	—
June 8 New Jersey					
Ford	242,122	*100.00*	Carter	210,655	*58.4*
			Church	49,034	*13.6*
			Jackson	31,820	*8.8*
			Wallace	31,183	*8.6*
			McCormack	21,774	*6.0*
			Others	16,373	*4.5*
June 8 Ohio					
Ford	516,111	*55.2*	Carter	593,130	*52.3*
Reagan	419,646	*44.8*	Udall	240,342	*21.2*
			Church	157,884	*13.9*
			Wallace	63,953	*5.6*
			Gertrude W. Donahey		
			(unpledged delegates)	43,661	*3.9*
			Jackson	35,404	*3.1*
Totals					
Ford	5,529,899	*53.3*	Carter	6,235,609	*38.8*
Reagan	4,758,325	*45.9*	Brown	2,449,374	*15.3*
None of the names			Wallace	1,995,388	*12.4*
shown	19,990	*0.2*	Udall	1,611,754	*10.0*
Unpledged delegates	14,727	*0.1*	Jackson	1,134,375	*7.1*
Daly	7,582	*0.1*	Church	830,818	*5.2*
Others[3]	43,602	*0.4*	Byrd	340,309	*2.1*
	10,374,125		Shriver	304,399	*1.9*
			Unpledged delegates	248,680	*1.5*
			McCormack	238,027	*1.5*
			Harris	234,568	*1.5*
			None of the names shown	93,728	*0.6*
			Shapp	88,254	*0.5*
			Bayh	86,438	*0.5*
			Humphrey	61,992	*0.4*
			Kennedy	19,905	*0.1*
			Bentsen	4,046	—
			Others[4]	75,088	*0.5*
				16,052,652	

New Hampshire jealously guarded its spot in the national limelight. Faced with overtures in 1975 from New England political leaders to join in the formation of a regional primary, New Hampshire legislators responded by enacting a law that automatically moved the state's primary date up one week before that of any other state. The resulting February 24 date for the New Hampshire contest turned out to be the earliest opening ever for the presidential primary season, and just happened to be one week before primaries in Massachusetts and Vermont.

Probably better than any of the other candidates, Carter understood the media payoff for a strong showing in New Hampshire. As in Iowa, he organized early and campaigned often, and consequently ran ahead of the field with about 23,000 of the 82,000 votes cast (see Table 8-4). His share of the vote—less than 30 percent—was hardly overwhelming, but coming in the media fishbowl of New Hampshire, it significantly embellished his growing stature.

The results demonstrated how important media expectations of a candidate are in influencing the interpretation of results. Carter, operating under a set of low expectations, was the big winner in New Hampshire. Ronald Reagan, on the Republican side, was the big loser.

The Developing Republican Contest

Reagan lost to President Ford in New Hampshire by only 1,587 votes out of more than 110,000 cast (see Table 8-4).

Yet, because Reagan was at one point considered a likely winner of the primary, his narrow loss was interpreted by the media as a crippling blow to his campaign. A similar loss in Florida two weeks later nearly ruined Reagan, although at that point only four of the thirty primaries had been held. To his credit, he survived press attempts to bury him, and nearly won the nomination.

Reagan had formally launched his campaign in November 1975, fully hoping to knock Ford out of the race with victories in the early primaries. Reagan strategists expected Ford's powerful advantage of incumbency to be neutralized by the president's status as the first nonelected chief executive and his inexperience in national campaigning.

But Ford's incumbency proved to be a potent asset in organizing and in fund raising, and Reagan narrowly lost the early primaries. Only an upset victory in North Carolina on March 23 kept his campaign afloat. By proving he could win, Reagan survived until May, when his "sun-belt strategy" finally came into play.

In the final weeks of the primary campaign, Ford and Reagan traded primary victories—the President winning in the East and Midwest and his challenger dominating in the South and West. Ford gained a tenuous but permanent lead in the delegate count in late May when he persuaded his technically uncommitted supporters in New York and Pennsylvania—states that Reagan did not seriously contest—to declare for him.

New York and Wisconsin Coverage

Media coverage of the April 6 primaries in New York and Wisconsin raises questions about the press's willingness to try and unravel the meaning of the results of primaries in states with complicated rules. Nearly four times as many delegates were at stake in New York as in Wisconsin, yet the media focused on Wisconsin.

Carter and his major rivals at the time, Senator Henry Jackson and Representative Morris K. Udall, were in both states for the primaries. But because New York had a complex delegate-selection system without a preference vote, the media tended to downplay New York while concentrating on Wisconsin, which had a preference vote (see Table 8-2).

Furthermore, in their primary coverage of the Wisconsin results, the broadcast media showed that network competitiveness can lead to embarrassment. Two networks erringly projected Udall as the primary winner in the early evening, only to have Carter come from behind in the early morning hours to take the victory.

The need for projections is debatable. They emphasize the horse-race, win-lose aspect of the nomination fight, which, as has been argued, can be a disservice. Anyone interested in the results could wait until midnight for something definitive.

The Developing Democratic Contest

Carter scored a landslide victory in Pennsylvania on April 27 that nearly obliterated the field. The loss eliminated Jackson, relegating him to the category of also-rans that already included Senator Birch Bayh, Sargent Shriver, former Senator Fred Harris, and Governors Milton Shapp and George C. Wallace. When Senator Hubert Humphrey announced on April 29 that he would not enter the race, Udall appeared to offer the only active opposition to a Carter sweep.

The competition, though, stiffened in early May when two newcomers—Senator Frank Church and Governor Jerry Brown—began active campaigning. Church scored a surprising upset win over Carter in Nebraska on May 11, beginning nearly a month of problems for the Georgian. Between May 11 and June 1, Carter lost in Maryland, Idaho, Nevada, Oregon, Montana, and Rhode Island, and nearly lost to Udall in Michigan.

Carter's campaign was not fatally hurt by his poor showings for two reasons. First, his regional base in the South provided a cushion strong enough to absorb defeats elsewhere. He had victories on May 25, for example, in Arkansas, Kentucky, and Tennessee that counterbalanced simultaneous losses to Church and Brown in Western states. Second, the Democrats' new rule requiring the proportional division of delegates in caucus states and in most primary states allowed Carter to continue accumulating delegates even in states where he was beaten.

Yet, entering the climactic June 8 primaries, Carter's momentum had faded visibly. He had demonstrated a particularly limited appeal in the West and was still 600 delegates short of the nomination (see Table 8-5).

June 8 Primaries: Media Boosts Carter

To Carter's benefit, the media on election night decided to focus on only one primary, Ohio. Carter's major rival in this primary was Udall, who was underfinanced and still seeking his first primary win. Although Carter had lost by unexpectedly wide margins in California and New Jersey, he did win in Ohio (see Table 8-4).

Actually, it was a mediocre day for Carter, but he was portrayed by the media as virtually invincible. A cascade of political endorsements followed, locking up the nomination a month before the convention.

As in past years, the media played a major role in interpreting the results, narrowing the field, and determining the nominee before the convention even began. It is not coincidental that with such media involvement in primaries, no convention since 1952 has gone beyond one ballot to choose its presidential nominee.

Table 8-5 Delegate Count for Major Candidates During the 1976 Primary Season

		Democrats								Republicans		
Date	Previous Primary	Brown	Carter	Church	Jackson	Udall	Wallace	Others	Uncommitted	Ford	Reagan	Uncommitted
February 28	New Hampshire	—	18	—	4	3	9	3	5	17	4	37
March 6	Massachusettes, Vermont	—	36	—	34	23	32	20	6	53	18	38
March 13	Florida	—	70	—	55	23	58	20	6	96	41	38
March 20	Illinois	—	123	—	55	23	61	115	24	167	53	51
March 27	North Carolina	—	167	—	55	23	86	120	39	206	81	52
April 10	New York, Wisconsin	—	241	1	176	118	104	123	123	251	97	171
May 1	Pennsylvania	—	327	1	195	151	107	162	197	264	137	291
May 8	Texas, Alabama, Washington, D.C., Georgia, Indiana	1	548	1	200	162	140	181	252	292	366	292
May 15	Nebraska, West Virginia	1	572	16	201	183	143	181	302	323	415	361
May 22	Maryland, Michigan	1	682	16	211	258	145	181	317	431	490	391
May 29	Arkansas, Idaho, Kentucky, Nevada, Oregon, Tennessee	17	847	47	236	281	168	212	365	769	620	169
June 5	Montana, Rhode Island, South Dakota	19	869	62	237	291	168	212	395	797	631	172
June 12	California, New Jersey, Ohio	223.5	1,091	69	238	313	168	226	490.5	889	839	244
Convention vote		300.5	2,238.5	19	10	329.5	57	50	3.5[a]	1,187	1,070	1[b]

Needed to nominate: Democrats 1,505; Republicans 1,130.
[a] Three abstentions plus one-half vote for "nobody".
[b] One vote for Elliot.
Source: Based on a tally by Congressional Quarterly published the Saturday after each primary.

175

Ignored by the Media

Two other aspects of media coverage of the delegate-selection process are worth mentioning. First, as in past years, the caucus process was largely ignored, particularly after the primary season began.

With the proliferation of primaries, the number of caucus states has dwindled; yet, in 1976 they still provided about one-third of the delegates to both conventions. Nevertheless, only Iowa, and the late Republican caucuses received notable attention (see Table 8-1).

Second, as Dr. Austin Ranney illustrated in a study for the American Enterprise Institute, caucus participation has always been low and primary turnouts have been declining in recent years.[3] Ranney cited statistics that show that only an estimated 700,000 voters took part in the 1976 Democratic delegate-selection caucuses. (No figures were available for the Republicans.) This was considered to be an all-time high but still represented only 2 percent of the voting-age population in these states.

Ranney's study also showed that in spite of an increase in the number of primaries in 1976, the percentage of voters actually participating declined. In the 1976 primaries, he found that the average turnout of registered voters was 42.9 percent, compared to 46.7 percent in 1972. Ranney noted that even the 1972 turnout percentage represented a decline from the average rate of participation in the previous quarter-century.

The reason behind these dwindling turnouts has so far provoked little discussion in the media. It is a major story in itself why more people do not participate in the nominating process. More emphasis could be paid to nonvoters and the reasons why they stay away from the polls even after party reforms have largely removed roadblocks to their participation.

Conclusion

Most of the problems of media coverage that have been described were not new in 1976. They were present in 1972 and before, and probably will be present in 1980. The media will likely have a major impact on future campaigns whether the present system of caucuses and primaries is maintained or a new system is adopted.

According to one chronicler of recent presidential campaigns, Theodore H. White,

> The power of the press in America is a primordial one. It sets the agenda of public discussion and this sweeping political power is unrestrained by any law. It determines what people will talk and think about, an authority that in other nations is reserved for tyrants, priests, parties and mandarins.[4]

White does not exaggerate, and in the 1976 primaries the media used their enormous power to intrude upon and shape the nomination contests that, ideally, they should have been describing.

The press largely overlooked the essential, but mundane, aspects of the primary campaigns in order to focus on the sensational events that would sustain a dramatic scenario. Candidate gaffes drew the especially close attention of the media. Largely obscured were the less dramatic ingredients of campaigns that are ultimately crucial to success and failure—the state delegate-selection rules, campaign financing, and the development of grass-roots organizations, for example.

At the outset of the 1976 nominating process, the media paid too much attention to the earliest delegate-selection events, Iowa and New Hampshire in particular, thereby giving these states an importance that far outweighed their delegate totals. As the contests developed, it was apparent that the media preferred to focus on presidential preference primaries, largely ignoring significant, but more complex, delegate-selection primaries in states like New York.

Unfortunately, the bottom line throughout the entire primary season was that it was not the voters who had the final say as to who won and who lost; it was the media.

NOTES

1. CBS Television news broadcast, January 19, 1976.
2. See Michael J. Robinson, "Media Coverage in the Primary Campaign of 1976: Implications for Voters, Candidates, and Parties," in this volume.
3. Austin Ranney, *Participation in American Presidential Nominations, 1976* (Washington, D.C.: American Enterprise Institute for Public Policy Research, 1977), pp. 15-22. Ranney's study of the primary turnout omitted states in which there was no statewide record of registered voters, in which there was a primary in only one party, or in which there was no statewide tally of votes for delegates (such as New York). Ranney's turnout percentages were based on twenty-six primaries in 1976 and twelve 4 years earlier. Information on primary turnouts between 1948 and 1968 can be found in Ranney's article, "Turnout and Representation in Presidential Primary Elections," *American Political Science Review* 66 (March 1972): 21-37. See also Richard Rubin's analysis, "Presidential Primaries: Continuities, Dimensions of Change, and Political Implications," in this volume. His interpretation of the available data suggests an increase in primary turnout in recent years. Rubin contrasts his findings with those of Ranney.
4. Theodore H. White, *The Making of the President 1972* (New York: Atheneum, 1973), p. 245.

9 / Media Coverage in the Primary Campaign of 1976: Implications for Voters, Candidates, and Parties

Michael J. Robinson

A former vice-president of the United States once wrote that he pitied "his fellow citizens, who reading newspapers, live and die in the belief, that they have known something of what has been passing in the world in their time."[1]

Were it not for the style of the prose, one might well have attributed that remark to former Vice-President Spiro Agnew and not to its rightful author, former Vice-President Thomas Jefferson.

It was another famous vice-president, Harry Truman, who resurrected Jefferson's somewhat uncharacteristic remark during one of Truman's own frequent disagreements with the press. And it has been almost a matter of faith among vice-presidents, and their bosses, since before Jefferson and well after Truman, that the press does not always offer us reality—that the press, at best, deals in reality. But what the press offers as reality becomes reality for someone, a truth both Agnew and Jefferson could bemoan. In some instances, the media version of reality becomes "reality" for us all.

In the United States, there is the potential for two major media realities—print and television.[2] In this report of news coverage in the 1976 presidential election, we will see that the reality of television and the reality of print can be markedly different in very important circumstances, and that the effects of those differences on public perceptions can actually be documented. We will also see that when the "realities" of print and television diverge, television becomes the medium of record for the public and probably for our political leaders as well.

At base I am offering three things in this report:

1. A comparison between the news coverage provided by network television and that presented by the nation's press vis-à-vis the first three months of the 1976 presidential campaign.

2. An analysis of the effects of that coverage on public perceptions of the campaign.

3. An application of our findings about the coverage of the New Hampshire primary, as a case study, to the analysis of the American political party system.

I freely and gratefully acknowledge the work that Karen A. McPherson did in the original stages of this research. She knows better than anyone that without her help none of this would have happened.

The New Hampshire Study

This comprehensive, quantitative study of the messages provided us by three daily news-papers and three television networks focuses on the period from the end of November 1975 to the end of February 1976, with supplementary analyses of similar periods during the 1972 campaign and during the months of March and April 1976. The project also includes a scientific survey conducted in the Washington, D. C. metropolitan area during the last week in February 1976. Using the New Hampshire presidential primary as the chief example, this section will analyze how the two major media presented it and how the voting-age population responded to their coverage.

The special problems associated with covering the 1976 New Hampshire primary were not new for either network or print journalism. Media coverage in New Hampshire in both 1968 and 1972 had engendered a substantial amount of research and criticism. [3] The major criticisms during both elections centered on the propensity of the media (1) to *overemphasize* New Hampshire presidential politics at the expense of other important politi-cal events, and (2) to declare the losers in New Hampshire to be the *moral victors*—at the expense of the "real" winners.

Memory and videotaped "instant replays" from 1972 suggested that television journal-ism was more susceptible than print journalism to criticism on both counts. By 1972, in fact, network journalists had begun attacking publicly their own performances, and New Hampshire election coverage in general, as both overdone and unjustifiably given to phantom victories.

The journalists' own criticism and my own hunches about the media led me to inves-tigate the extent to which television and print concentrated on New Hampshire news, and the extent to which both media tended to proclaim the literal losers as figurative winners. From the outset it was assumed that television news would demonstrate a greater affinity for both practices than would print. It was also presumed that the differences in the interpretations of reality presented by the two media would filter through to their respec-tive audiences. To test these hypotheses, I conducted two studies: an analysis of the content of television news and printed news, and a public opinion survey.

Content Analysis

The major portion of the analysis spans the seventy weekdays between November 24, 1975, and February 24, 1976. By including each edition of three daily newspapers— the *Washington Post*, the *New York Times*, and the *Columbus Dispatch (Ohio)*—and each edition of the three nightly network newscasts— ABC, CBS, and NBC—I compiled a total of 210 newspapers and 210 news programs from which to work. [4]

Printed items were analyzed directly from the papers themselves; television items from 1975 and 1976 were "coded" from printed summaries obtained from the Television News Archive at Vanderbilt University. [5] I checked these summaries against videotapes of sev-eral programs and found them to be wholly adequate for our purposes. (Eventually I also coded summaries of the 210 television news programs from an analogous time period in 1971 and 1972 so that I could compare coverage in television news over two separate elections.)

For television and print news the coding scheme was identical. I first isolated those items that were regarded as *delegate-selection stories*. These were stories about presidential campaign politics at the state level and covered campaigning in state primaries, state caucuses, and state conventions. I found 185 delegate-selection stories on network television (up markedly from 152 such stories in 1971-1972) and 441 delegate-selection stories in the three newspapers sampled.

The stories were coded on a number of dimensions, most important of which were the principal state and the principal candidate depicted, if any. Most stories could be easily coded for state emphasis, although coding for principal candidate was more problematic.

Washington Area Survey

Committed to linking the findings about content to actual perceptions and beliefs within audiences, I conducted a public opinion survey in the Washington, D. C. metropolitan area during the week following the New Hampshire primary. Drawn from the three area phone directories the original sample included 354 listings, from which interviewers were able to make 258 successful contacts (72.9 percent). Respondents exhibited social, political, and demographic characteristics quite representative of the Washington, D. C. standard metropolitan statistical area. If there was any noticeable difference, it was that the sample seemed more highly educated than the population at large, a finding that was neither unexpected nor altogether damaging to the primary purpose of the survey—to establish a statistical link between the two realities of the early presidential campaign presented by print and television and the "reality" held in the minds of the two separate news audiences.

Findings

The two major basic concerns with media coverage of the campaign explored in this study are overemphasis on New Hampshire and the claiming of moral victory for losing New Hampshire candidates. The data indicate that none of the newspapers and none of the networks made any pronouncements of moral victory in the 1976 New Hampshire primary. Unlike 1972, all six news sources declared the literal winners, Carter and Ford, to be the winners.

More importantly, and predictably, the clarity and accuracy of the message produced an unambiguous clarity and accuracy in public response. A full 80 percent of our respondents, without any prompting, knew that Carter had won the Democratic primary; with prompting, only 2 percent gave the wrong answer. Of the respondents, 86 percent knew, without help, that Ford had won the Republican contest, although 9 percent of all respondents did think that Reagan had won, reflecting the much closer race among the Republicans.

Another important finding is that there was virtually no difference in the accuracy of respondents monitoring the campaign through television and those monitoring it through print. The percent "correct" was quite exactly the same for both groups. Moral victory was *not* directly at issue in the 1976 early presidential campaign. Indirectly, however, it was an issue.

The videotapes and the summaries of the 1972 New Hampshire primary show a marked tendency toward proclaiming moral victory for George McGovern. Although there are no tapes or summaries from 1968, our memory tells us that Eugene McCarthy

Table 9-1 New Hampshire Presidential Primary Voting Statistics

Candidate	Raw vote	Percentage	Absolute Difference in Votes Between Winner and Loser	Percentage Difference in Votes Between Winner and Loser
McCarthy (Dem.), 1968	23,263	41.9	4,257	7.7
McGovern (Dem.), 1972	33,007	37.1	8,227	9.3
Reagan (Rep.), 1976	53,507	49.4	1,317	.8

Source: All figures from *Congressional Quarterly* publications.

was even more a moral victor than McGovern, especially on television. Yet, in 1976, Ronald Reagan was nobody's moral victor despite having fared much better in New Hampshire (in terms of both number and percentage of votes) than did either McCarthy or McGovern. Table 9-1 demonstrates unequivocably Reagan's success vis-à-vis McCarthy and McGovern.

The raw vote separating Ronald Reagan, a private citizen at the time of the balloting, from a then incumbent president, was one-seventh the amount that separated Senator McGovern from Senator Muskie. In terms of percentage, Reagan was nine times closer to plurality than was McGovern in 1972. And Reagan had almost as many popular votes in New Hampshire as McCarthy and McGovern combined!

There are two interpretations for this redefinition of victory. One builds from the notion that the media "learned" from 1968 and 1972 not to play at moral victory anymore. The other sees a partisan attempt by the media, especially the networks, to diminish Reagan's chances for winning the nomination by denying him his moral victory—this because the conservative Reagan was so far removed from the political philosophy of the correspondents and news executives involved.

If our content analysis had not revealed that Reagan actually received two-thirds *more* network coverage than Ford during the early campaign (twenty-seven items for Reagan, eleven for Ford, thirteen for both combined), I might be more willing to accept the view that considers the media as partisan advocates. Because Reagan received more news coverage—print and electronic—one might conclude that the absence of moral victory in 1976, at Reagan's expense, was more an indication of "organizational learning" than of partisan sabotage by the networks. However, a small amount of partisanship may have facilitated the learning by the networks.

Whatever the actual reason for the disappearance of moral victory in 1976, given what I have since learned about the capacity of the media—particularly television—to make the public see moral victory in New Hampshire as the crucial stepping stone to presidential nomination, I feel a certain sympathy for Ronald Reagan. Particularly compelling is his assertion that had the media—especially the networks—chosen to call him the moral victor, he would have won the Republican nomination, and perhaps, the presidency as well.

What has been learned that causes me to have sympathy with such an assertion? I have learned that the emphasis on New Hampshire news is overwhelming in both media. No state primary approaches New Hampshire's in overall news coverage. Figure 9-1

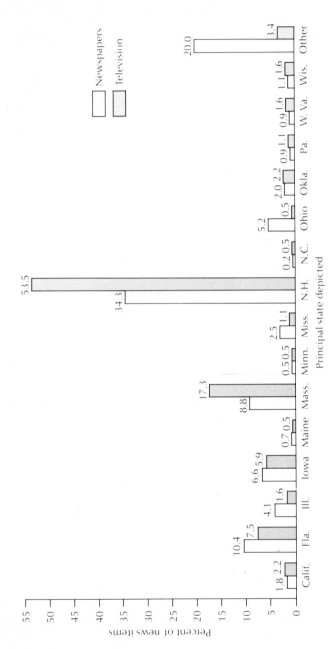

Figure 9-1 Relative frequencies of weekday newspaper and network news coverage for those states receiving coverage in both media, November 24 through February 27, 1976.

presents the percentage of network news items that is devoted to coverage of presidential primaries. The figure documents only those states that received both newspaper and television coverage. Data in the figure are based on statistical evidence from which the following conclusions can be drawn:

- All fifty state primaries combined received 616 news stories; New Hampshire's alone received 250 news stories (41 percent of the total).
- The second most closely covered state primary, that of Massachusetts, received 71 stories, 28 percent of the New Hampshire total.
- All ten nonprimary-states caucuses which began *before* the New Hampshire election received a total of 77 news stories; New Hampshire, alone, received more than three times as many, despite the fact that these ten nonprimary states represented more than 500 delegates to the nominating conventions (more than twelve times as many as New Hampshire).
- The Iowa primary, which by all rights was the first delegate-selection primary, received a total of forty news stories. New Hampshire got more than six times as many.

Perhaps the most notable finding is that the ten pre-New Hampshire states received such miserably little coverage, undercutting the notion that time is the only factor involved in determining coverage. Countering the notion that these data merely reflect the period selected for analysis—the New Hampshire period—I conducted a small-scale content analysis of the television coverage from February 27, 1976 to April 9, 1976. Adding the new figures for states that held primaries between February 27 and April 9 to the early totals, we still find a clear plurality for New Hampshire (see Table 9-2). New York, a state with forty times the population of New Hampshire, merited 30 stories, exactly 30 percent of the final total for New Hampshire.

Furthermore, the results from the New Hampshire primary received the same privileged attention that the day-to-day New Hampshire campaign was given, especially in television news. Nothing makes this more vivid than the differences in news attention given to the results of the primaries in New Hampshire and in New York on network evening broadcasts.

In 1976, New Hampshire Democrats cast a total of 82,381 votes in the New Hampshire primary. On the evening following the state's primary, 2,100 seconds of the news time on the three networks—700 news seconds per network, on the average—were devoted to the results of the primary. New York Democrats, on the other hand, cast 3,746,414 votes in their primary. On the following day, the New York primary received only 560 seconds total evening news time—fewer than 190 news seconds per network.

There were more than forty-five times as many Democrats voting in New York as in New Hampshire. Nevertheless, New Hampshire returns received almost quadruple the coverage time on the evening news. That works out to 170 times as much coverage per vote in New Hampshire as in New York! No matter how one approaches the data, New Hampshire overwhelms New York, and every other state, in news coverage.

For our purposes, however, the more important finding is that television and print did not provide the same emphasis—did not present the same reality. Figure 9-1 shows, among other things, that during our seventy-day analysis:

Table 9-2 Weekday Television Network News Coverage (November 24, 1975 Through April 9, 1976) of Those States That Held Primaries on or Before April 6, 1976

State	Primary Date	Stories	Total Delegates from State	Stories per Delegate	Index of Representation[a]
New Hampshire	February 24	100	38	2.63	1.00
Massachusetts	March 2	52	147	.35	.13
Vermont	March 2	6	30	.20	.08
Florida	March 9	50	147	.34	.13
Illinois	March 16	38	270	.15	.06
North Carolina	March 23.	19	115	.17	.06
New York	April 6	30	428	.07	.03
Wisconsin	April 6	42	113	.37	.14

[a] Ratio of stories per delegate, with New Hampshire used as base.

- Although 34 percent of all campaign stories in print were about New Hampshire, 54 percent of all campaign stories on television were about New Hampshire.
- Although 42 percent of all the campaign news space in print was devoted to New Hampshire, a full 60 percent of the news time on TV was devoted to New Hampshire.
- Although the two most populous states, California and New York, received one-third the attention given to New Hampshire in print (a notable statistic in its own right!), those same two states received only one-twentieth the attention given to New Hampshire on television.

Each network gave more news attention to New Hampshire than any of the three newspapers.

In a number of places I have suggested explanations for the vivid differences between newspapers and news programs.[6] Most revolve around something one might best call the *hoopla imperative*, the tendency for television to be drawn thoroughly toward electoral competition, photogenic environments, human interest, and simplicity of theme. The *hoopla imperative* and the New Hampshire imperative can best be explained as a near inevitable outcome of television's unique need to sustain an audience.

The Media and Public Perception of the New Hampshire Primary

The respondents in our survey indicated that media reality—stated or implied—becomes the public's reality. When both media offered clear and accurate signals about winners, respondents relying on either print or television knew who the winners were. But the perceived *significance* of the victory was quite another matter.

In what was probably the most important series of questions in the interview, respondents were asked what percentage of delegates New Hampshire alone would send to the nominating conventions. The choices were "less than one percent" (the correct choice), "five percent," "ten percent," and "twenty percent." For simplicity's sake, these four possible choices are grouped into two categories: those choices that are regarded as "reasonable" (one or five percent) and those that are regarded as "unreasonable" (the ten or twenty percent).

Next, this new variable—"reasonableness"—is correlated with several other variables, most importantly, the respondent's identification of his principal source of news about the campaign. The supposition underlying the analysis is that the greater the respondent's dependency on television news, the smaller the likelihood of a "reasonable" interpretation of New Hampshire from that respondent.

The fact is that respondents did quite poorly on the quiz, especially considering their rather high level of formal education. Even with guessing, only 42 percent of our respondents gave the correct answer to the question, and a full 37 percent gave what we classified as an unreasonable answer or no answer whatever. Although the public generally does miserably on civics quizzes, [7] this poor showing on so easy a question is, perhaps, best explained by the very considerable emphasis given New Hampshire by *all* mass media. If one were to gauge the literal importance of New Hampshire by its news coverage, twenty percent would have been the reasonable answer. So one should not be a bit surprised to find so large a proportion of our sample taking so exaggerated a view of New Hampshire.

There is one correlational finding from these survey data that tends to support, rather directly, the notions that media-implied reality becomes "reality" for those who pay any attention to the media, and that when two media realities exist, audiences accept the one to which they are more closely attuned. This correlational finding helps substantiate the theory that misperceptions and exaggerations concerning New Hampshire come principally from the mass media, and especially from television.

Remembering that television gave nearly 60 percent of its news emphasis to New Hampshire, I predicted that those who rely on television would be substantially more "unreasonable" in their perceptions of the stakes in New Hampshire than those who rely on print. To test this prediction I correlated the new variable, "reasonableness" about the stakes in New Hampshire, with television dependency and with a number of other variables as well. Although, as expected, none of the correlation coefficients was especially strong, the correlation between television dependency and "unreasonableness" was among the highest that was uncovered, and it was clearly statistically significant (see Table 9-3).

As an indication of the relative importance of the media variable, I point out that where one received his or her information about the presidential campaign—television or newspapers—was as good a predictor of one's accuracy concerning New Hampshire as was one's level of political sophistication. In fact, the only better predictor of "reasonableness" was the respondent's level of education. While I had anticipated that education would be the best predictor in understanding what was going on in New Hampshire, I had not expected "source of news," as a variable, to be quite as prominant as it was.

How important was the news source? Moving from correlation coefficients to percentages one finds that, overall, those who followed the campaign on television were actually twice as likely to be "unreasonable" about the stakes in New Hampshire (22 percent) as those who monitored it through print (11 percent). What's more, this relationship cannot be explained away by simply noting that the more astute citizens generally prefer print. As Table 9-4 indicates, even when holding constant the respondent's level of education or general political knowledge, the correlation between television reliance and misperception (unreasonableness) remains for the bulk of the audience. In fact, for most respondents, the correlations become more pronounced as one breaks the sample into differing levels of education or sophistication. Only college graduates seem immune to these effects. One

Table 9-3 "Reasonableness" in Public Opinion About Stakes in New Hampshire Correlated with Seven Selected Variables (Pearson's R)

Variables	Correlation Coefficient	Significance Level
Education[a]	.37	.001
Political sophistication[b]	.20	.01
News source (tv or print)[c]	.19	.02
Age[d]	.12	.05
Race[e]	.12	NS
Sex[e]	.11	NS
Party identification[e]	.00	NS

[a] Should be read as, "The more formal education the respondent has, the greater the 'reasonableness' (accuracy) concerning New Hampshire."
[b] Should be read as, "The more generally politically sophisticated the repondent, the greater the 'reasonableness' (accuracy) concerning New Hampshire."
[c] Should be read as, "The greater the reliance on newspapers, the greater the 'reasonableness' (accuracy) concerning New Hampshire."
[d] Should be read as, "The older the respondent, the greater the 'reasonableness' (accuracy) concerning New Hampshire."
[e] Not significant at .05 level.

Table 9-4 Sources of Information (Television or Newspaper) and "Reasonableness" Concerning New Hampshire, for Various Levels of Education or Political Sophistication (Pearson's R)

Variable	Correlation Coefficient[a]	Significance Level
Overall correlation	.19	.02
Education		
Less than high school	[b]	NS
High school	.22	.05
College	.01	NS
Political Sophistication		
Low and moderate	.19	.02
High	.05	NS

[a] All read, "The greater the reliance on newspapers, the greater the reasonableness."
[b] Fewer than ten cases.

could well argue that the figures in Table 9-4 imply that a person needs a college degree in order to avoid being confused by the media, especially television.

The correlations presented in Table 9-4 are very important. They imply that television has engendered within viewers, more than any other major medium, misperceptions about the meaning of the New Hampshire primary, and that those misperceptions always exaggerate the importance of that primary. In short, the content of television news influences public perception of reality in a way that clearly reflects the differences in content between the two media.

At base, these figures all suggest that the readers and the viewers came to accept the media "reality" that was offered them, although neither the television nor the newspaper "reality" was accurate. The data also imply that the more emphasis provided by any medium for a political event, the greater its perceived importance, *even if the literal unimportance of the event is mentioned in the message.* The data have also demonstrated that television "reality" is not only less accurate than print "reality," but it also reaches a much larger audience. [8] Taken together, all these facts suggest that television news has played the major role in making New Hampshire the public's most important barometer in predicting who will be the presidential nominee. One could well argue, in fact, that television news has played the crucial role in making New Hampshire the sine qua non of the presidential nominations game for all of the viable candidates.

Although the implications for the candidates are vividly clear, the meaning of all this for the parties themselves is not quite so apparent. But the New Hampshire primary, as it appears on television, does have meaning for the parties—at both the state and national level.

Implications for the Party System

As many of the selections in this volume make clear, one of the most widely shared suppositions among political scientists is that the media—especially television—have played a major role in the continuous decay of the American party system. That is an easy supposition to make, but it is difficult to demonstrate with hard data.

The New Hampshire study does not provide a direct test for the notion that television has weakened the parties. It does not require a great deal of imagination, however, to see the sorry implications for state and national parties, of the network compulsion to cover New Hampshire politics.

State Parties

Like the national party leadership, state party leaders have always considered their role in choosing the party's presidential nominee as one of their most important, and one of their most enjoyable, functions. Since 1968, however, fewer and fewer state party leaders have had control over that major function, as the presidential primary has replaced the state convention and state caucus system as the method for selecting delegates to the national nominating conventions. [9]

Only fifteen states held presidential primaries in 1968 and less than half the delegates at the 1968 conventions came from primary states. In short, up through 1968, party organizations selected the bulk of the delegates—and selected them from party cadres. But in 1968, triggered primarily by Robert Kennedy's death and in part by liberal Democratic frustrations with the nomination of Hubert Humphrey, the primary system began to overwhelm the caucus and convention system of nominating.

Three more general explanations for the collapse of the pre-1968 system are evident: (1) counter-elites, frustrated with party regulars, demanded "reform" of the process; (2) state parties, confused by new national-party guidelines for delegate selection, adopted primaries to absolve themselves from doing wrong; [10] (3) as suggested by our data and intuition, television networks, in what I have called the "Network-New Hampshire syndrome," have developed the tendency to place more and more resources into New Hampshire election coverage with each passing campaign.

As television news reached preeminence as a news medium in the 1960s,[11] and as television began to shift its focus more toward presidential primaries—our data show, for example, that New Hampshire coverage increased on network news by 40 percent between 1972 and 1976!—state legislatures, as a consequence, began adopting presidential primaries. In 1972 there were twenty-one states with presidential primaries; by 1976 there were twenty-nine (twice as many as 1968).

My own personal experience with Democratic leaders in Minnesota and in Iowa—two states that have not, as yet, adopted the presidential primary—persuades me that one of the principal pressures that these leaders feel when deciding whether or not to institute a primary is the pressure to attract television exposure for the state. The pressure to attract television coverage may well be the *major* pressure, in fact.

State leaders sense what our data show. In terms of newsworthiness, primaries overwhelm other methods for selecting delegates. Iowa caucuses in 1976, held four weeks before the New Hampshire primary, received one-ninth the television exposure on the evening news. The Iowa State Democratic Party, in fact, contacted me to find out just how badly their very early caucuses had done in attracting television news. If the state leaders in Iowa really were concerned with gaining news coverage, my data would certainly not lead them to stay with the causus system in 1980.

The pressure to go "early" with a primary is just as intense as the pressure to go "primary" in the first place. In 1975, New Hampshire, threatened in its first-in-the-nation status by a proposal that would have established a New England regional primary, not only refused to cooperate with the other states in the region but also adopted a policy that required the New Hampshire state legislature to do whatever was necessary to ensure that New Hampshire remain first of the nation's primaries. Recently, Puerto Rico, in search of network coverage, adopted legislation that would permit it to be the first primary in the 1980 election, regardless of how early New Hampshire schedules its primary.

The pressure to switch from caucuses and conventions to primaries, and from early primaries to even earlier ones, has produced unintended and deleterious consequences for the state party organizations. Attracting television exposure may well serve to increase tourism or stature among states. But the truth is that the price of that increased exposure is paid principally by state party organizations. Relinquishing the right to select delegates, and relinquishing the chance to send themselves to the national convention, *party leaders have made state party membership and party work less attractive to party activists and to potential party activists.*

At one level, it may seem petty that state party leaders complain that through primaries they lose their chance to go to the big convention. Nevertheless, the problem is a fundamental one. Primaries always take from parties their *raison d'être*, their chance to nominate elective political leaders. And television promotes primaries, especially presidential primaries.

How powerful is the pull toward "the primary presidency" in the age of television news? It is interesting that during the "television era" the rate of increase in presidential primaries has been every bit as great as the rate of increase in the number of primaries during the "reform era," the era that once was regarded as the heyday of primary politics. The coinciding increases in the importance of television news and in the number of presidential primaries are anything but "coincidental."

National Parties

The growing fascination with primaries has probably had as great an impact on national parties as on state parties. The survey data from the New Hampshire study at least imply that television has been causing the public to see the New Hampshire primary as the crucial indicator of who will win the nominations. Candidates believe this at least as firmly as social scientists, and probably more so. Candidate Jimmy Carter said after his nomination that he had always believed that Iowa, New Hampshire, and Florida were the ball game in 1976.

Potential candidates recognize that by winning the early primaries and by using television coverage time they can knock "front-runners" and party favorites off the board quickly. Such a strategy can win the nomination, as it did for both McGovern and for Carter. The immediate result of this phenomenon is a greater number of candidates in New Hampshire with each succeeding election. Seven "serious" Democrats contested the New Hampshire primary in 1976, up by three from 1972.

Simple arithmetic predicts that with more candidates in the field, all else remaining the same, party favorites are less likely to win in New Hampshire, or the nomination itself. So, with the Network-New Hampshire syndrome, the national party stalwarts not only lose some of the legal right to nominate, but they also lose some of the practical advantage they have traditionally had in getting their candidate nominated. We should no longer expect to find very many nominees, other than presidential incumbents, who are party favorites.

Even without television, more primaries and earlier primaries mean more candidates and earlier candidacies. Television is a catalyst in the process, however. Again, the Carter case seems classic. More and earlier primaries, more candidates, and earlier candidacies *all* imply more primary voters—and voters who must decide earlier in the campaign than ever before.

How will primary voters—choosing from among an ever-increasing list of candidates and voting during Superbowl season (or even before Superbowl season by 1980)—decide? It is probable that their exposure to television campaigns and to local and network news images of candidates will affect their decisions: we can expect more and more image voting in the early campaign, and more television-based bandwagon voting in the later stages of the campaign. All this should imply that voters will grow more and more accustomed to voting on grounds *other than party identification*. Therefore, national parties, through the Network-New Hampshire syndrome, lose some of their control of both the nominating process and those who identify with the party.

This has the sound of a vicious circle, and it is precisely that. States, in part seeking to attract television attention, adopt primaries and schedule them at earlier dates. The number of primary voters and the number of image voters is thus increased, and more delegates are selected through extraparty mechanisms. These trends encourage more candidates and, especially, more "maverick" candidates (New Hampshire has proven to be an especially fertile ground for the maverick) to contest the early primaries. This wider field of candidates compels the media, especially television, to cover the early campaign with more intensity and greater resources each succeeding election. We end up at square one, once again, with more states adopting primaries or moving their primary ahead to compete with New Hampshire. The winners in all this are the mavericks, long-shots, and photogenic candidates, the media, and, perhaps, the state's commerical interests. The big losers are the professional party cadres—both state and national.

It is clearly unfair, however, to attribute solely to the Network-New Hampshire syndrome the increase in the number of successful "outsiders" in presidential nominations, the doubling of the number of primaries since 1968, and the growth in political independency as well. It would be a distortion and an exaggeration to claim all that. The parties would not resuscitate themselves even if we were to close down the networks during the three months prior to the New Hampshire primary. But the focus on New Hampshire is probably no more exaggerated in this report than it has been in network television during the last 10 years. And the exaggeration of New Hampshire politics, as practiced by the networks, will probably continue to increase, despite what that may mean for reality, or to the party symbol.

NOTES

1. Thomas Jefferson, *The Writings of Thomas Jefferson*, ed. P. L. Ford (1892-1899), vol. 73, cited in Harry Kranz, "The Presidency v. the Press—Who Is Right?" *Human Rights* 2, no.1 (March 1972).

2. By 1976 only 11 percent of the population relied on media other than television or newspapers as a principal source of news. See *Changing Public Attitudes Toward Television and Other Mass Media, 1959-1976* (New York: Television Information Office, 1977), p. 3.

3. For a concise, journalistic treatment of the problem, see Burns Roper, "Distorting the Voice of the People," *Columbia Journalism Review*, November-December 1975, pp. 28-32.

4. The *Post* and the *Times* were included because they are the prestige press, representing newspapers "of record." The *Dispatch*—hardly a newspaper of record—represents the other world of metropolitan dailies. Being independent, non-Eastern, conservative, and local, in direct contrast with the other two papers, the *Dispatch* served as a control, so to speak. The *Dispatch* proved to be quite similar to both the *Post* and the *Times* in those dimensions of news we chose to consider. Ironically, if there was one main difference it was that the "conservative" *Dispatch* gave more news coverage to Ford than to Reagan, the opposite pattern of that found in the *Post* and the *Times*. Perhaps the *Dispatch* regarded Ford as the "saleable" conservative, while the *Post* and *Times* saw Reagan as curious and, therefore, "good" copy.

5. "Coding," a term used widely by social scientists, is the process by which a story response, or event is broken down into several dimensions and given a score or evaluation for each of those dimensions.

6. Michael J. Robinson and Karen A. McPherson, "Guest Editorial—The Network New Hampshire Symdrome," *Presidential Studies Quarterly* 6 (Fall 1976). Also, Michael J. Robinson and Karen A. McPherson, "Television News Coverage Before the 1976 New Hampshire Primary: The Focus of Television News," *Journal of Broadcasting* 21, no. 2, (Spring 1977): 177-186.

7. A fairly recent set of discouraging figures appears in *Confidence and Concern: Citizens View American Government*, conducted by Louis Harris and Associates, for the Subcommittee on Intergovernmental Relations, Committee on Government Operations of the United States Senate (Washington: Government Printing Office, 1973), pp. 72-77.

8. Our survey shows that clear pluralities received their first news about the results in New Hampshire from television, most of their news about the results from television, and most of their campaign news generally from television.

9. Austin Ranney, "The Democratic Party's Delegate Selection Reforms, 1968-1976," *America in the Seventies: Problems, Policies, and Politics*, ed. Allan Sindler (Boston: Little, Brown, 1977), p. 184.

10. Ibid.

11. By 1963, television had replaced newspapers as the public's primary source of information. By 1976, precisely three-fourths of the public regarded television as the most important source of information about national elections. See *Changing Public Attitudes*, pp. 3-9.

10 / Recruitment and Motives for National Convention Activism: Republican Delegates in 1972 and 1976

Thomas H. Roback

American national party conventions have become an integral part of the tapestry of political culture in the United States. With the advent of continuous television network coverage, the behavior of delegations, candidates, and party officials has become an important agency of political socialization for millions of Americans. Although the disorderly maelstrom of convention activity often inhibits the rational portrayal of events, there is little doubt that this quadrennial event has a certain symbolic importance to those who observe it.

The symbolism of a national convention as an institution grows out of its emphasis on the activity of the party members and candidate organizations who work for months and years to attend the convention and nominate their party's candidate. It is this distinctively human interplay of personal conflict and cooperation among party people that most likely captures the interest of the American voting public. In order to better understand national conventions, it is useful to focus attention on the grass-roots party activists and leaders who attend the convention as delegates.

The identification of the types of people who are selected to attend conventions, and the reasons why they choose to participate in these partisan events, provide excellent opportunities to explain how the American party system operates. It is the contention of this study that studying party activists offers a valuable opportunity to develop a reliable body of data about party behavior. Consequently, this study will examine and compare the recruitment and incentive patterns of two groups of activists who were delegates to Republican national conventions in 1972 and 1976. [1] The obvious benefits of such a study stem from the geographical diversity and varied positions of the groups within the official stratification structure of local, state, and national party organizations.

When studying party activists, it often is useful to focus on some key factors that affect the pool of available organizational recruits. These factors include the participants' social and political background, political socialization experiences, reasons for initial party entry and convention participation, and motives for deciding to remain active in the party after initial recruitment. The findings will be discussed according to candidate preference in 1972 (Nixon delegates) and 1976 (Ford or Reagan delgates).

Political Settings and Methodology

The role of the national convention delegate often represents the culmination of a party activist's career. Frequently, however, this role is conditioned by the particular circumstances surrounding the event itself. It is safe to say that the political settings for the 1972 and 1976 Republican conventions were very different. The 1972 convention was tightly controlled in order to renominate incumbent Richard M. Nixon with as much unanimity and as little conflict as possible. The delegates were in agreement that a competitive convention involving a favored incumbent was unwise, and so they agreed to minimize intraparty conflict. A mild floor debate over delegate apportionment and some complaints about the heavy-handed role of Nixon's Committee to Re-elect the President caused the only instances of conflict. [2]

In 1976, however, the Republicans were a party injured by Watergate and facing further division in a contested convention. The Ford and Reagan race developed into a bitter struggle where ideological purity and unrestrained candidate support tactics were commonplace. The conservative fervor that had been aroused by Goldwater in 1964, and had been muffled in Miami Beach, blared forth at the Kansas City convention. The diverse conditions defining the 1972 and 1976 Republican conventions influenced the pool of party activists available for delegate recruitment and must be recognized when recruitment and motivational patterns are discussed.

The data for this study were gathered by mail survey after both conventions. In 1972, questionnaires were sent to each of the 1,348 Republican delegates, and 828 usable questionnaires were returned, for a response rate of approximately 62 percent. In 1976, questionnaires were sent to each of the 2,259 delegates, and 1,240 completed questionnaires were returned, for a response rate of 55 percent. These response rates compare more than favorably with other national convention surveys. [3] Although the 1976 questionnaire asked some new questions, it contained most of the items used in the 1972 instrument. In both surveys no statistically significant differences were found between the samples and the aggregate social characteristics of both convention delegate populations. Chi-square tests on sex, race, education, age, region, and number of previous conventions attended showed that both samples were not significantly different on these demographic characteristics.

Survey Findings

The belief that national conventions attract the same group of loyal party "insiders" year in and year out is a myth. Most of the delegates only get the opportunity to attend once in their lives, and the turnover from one convention to the next is substantial. For example, almost three-fourths of the Republican delegates in the 1976 sample had never previously attended a convention. Only 10 percent had attended the 1972 Convention, and only about 9 percent had ever attended more than two national conventions. Certain types of party activists, however, will be attracted to the convention by particular candidates or issues in certain presidential years. For example, slightly more than 8 percent of the 1976 delegates also attended the 1964 convention, which nominated Senator Barry Goldwater. This is an unusually high recidivism rate, considering the interval of 12 years.

Quite clearly, this large number of 1964 repeaters was due to the large number of strongly conservative Goldwater supporters who were attempting to nominate Ronald Reagan in 1976.

Social Characteristics

A socioeconomic profile of the delegates provides a basic reference point for data analysis. It has previously been observed that possessing higher social status background makes it easier for citizens to be recruited into a political party. Such people have the necessary educational, occupational, and financial resources to both be attracted by and attractive to the party organization. The identification of the recruitment pool from which such potential party leaders emerge is, therefore, a useful undertaking.

The delegates attending the 1972 and 1976 conventions are quite homogeneous in that they posses a substantial degree of upper-status attributes. Their social profile reflects the widely held Republican stereotype of upper-middle-class affluence. The delegates tended to be white, wealthy, well educated, male and Protestant. They tended to have slightly more than four years of college, to be middle-aged (41–50), and to have annual family incomes between $25,000 and 50,000. They were active in more than one service— fraternal, business, or civic organizations—and were overrepresented in professional or business occupations. [4]

Such Republican homogeneity raises the issue of reforming delegate selection procedures, which has occurred, primarily in the Democratic party, in the early 1970s. There had been some effort between 1968 and 1972 to provide opportunities for more women, blacks, and youth to participate in Republican national conventions. A special committee was formed by the Republican National Committee to study the problem. [5] However, this attempt at wider participation among the groups had no impact on the 1976 Convention. Of the 1,348 delegates in 1972, 35 percent were women. By 1976, apportionment reform increased total delegate representation by almost 40 percent (to 2,259), but female representation slipped to 31 percent. Blacks comprised 3.1 percent of the delegates in both 1972 (a 2 percent increase from 1968) and 1976. Approximately 1 percent of the delegates had Hispanic surnames, and approximately 1 percent were Asian or American Indian. The representation of delegates under the age of thirty increased from 1 percent in 1968 to 7.3 percent 1972. In 1976, this figure declined slightly to 6.7 percent. The effects of Watergate and the nomination struggle in 1976 probably lowered the priority of party-representation reform, or at least severely limited the success of such efforts.

Generally, social background was found to be a poor independent predictor of candidate preference in 1976. Among professionals, however, medical doctors and engineers strongly supported Reagan, whereas lawyers and educators tended to support Ford. The homogeneity of the Republican Party and the probable importance of other variables account for the overall pattern of weak correlation between social background and candidate preference. The only exceptions were among former or current national officials, elected officials, Blacks, and Jews, all of whom gave Gerald Ford overwhelming support (for example, 93 percent of the Black delegates supported Ford [N–24] and twenty-eight of the thirty-two former or current U.S. congresspersons in the sample supported Ford). Governor Reagan was supported by 65 percent of the delegates who were between the ages of eighteen and thirty, and by 66 percent of the delegates who were students.

The degree of generational continuity between the occupations of the delegates and their fathers constitutes another way to examine social background in relation to candidate preference. The occupational status of the delegates is higher than their father's status in all categories.[6] On the average, what is somewhat unexpected is the generally high white-collar occupations of the fathers. Although it is true that the Democratic Party does have stronger support among blue-collar workers, it is still somewhat surprising that so many of the delegates' fathers had an upper-status background. This status continuity reflects, in part, the homogeneous class base upon which the national Republican Party has rested over the last several generations.

The overall pattern according to candidate preference reflects general continuity from 1972 to 1976, but there is a tendency in 1976 for more Ford supporters (66 percent) than Reagan supporters (56 percent) to come from families in which the fathers hold high occupational status. This difference is due primarily to the large number of Reagan delegates' fathers who were farmers, reflecting his support in the South and in the West.

Political Background

The methods by which party activity is established and extended constitute another set of factors that are related to party activism. Comparisons between the 1972 delegates and the Ford and Reagan supporters again will be used to analyze the data. The relationship between socialization and recruitment experiences quite logically begins with family political background. The expectation is that Ford delegates tend to come from families with higher parental political activity than do Reagan delegates. The data in Table 10-1 show little variation among candidate supporters. Parental political activity varied little between 1972 and 1976, and Ford supporters were only slightly more likely to have had activist parents. The fact that only 7 percentage points separate the candidates' supporters provides scant evidence to argue that parental activism will tend to result in support for a "regular" party candidate among offspring. The second part of Table 10-1 presents the party identification of those delegates' parents who had been politically active. These parents tend to be predominantly Republican, but the difference between Reagan and Ford delegates is significant ($C = .23$). Of the Reagan delegates, 36 percent had one or more Democratic parents, as compared with only 16 percent of the Ford delegates and 25 percent of the 1972 Nixon delegates. This finding reflects the fact that Reagan had strong support among Southern delegates, whose parents often were reared in the traditional one-party Democratic South. Finally, it is interesting to note that twice as many Reagan delegates (20 percent) previously supported the Democratic Party as did Ford delegates (9 percent). (These data are not shown on the table.)

Another related hypothesis is that Ford delegates tended to become interested in politics through family, school, or adult peer-group influences, whereas Reagan delegates tended to be socialized by issues and political events. Although the data are not shown on the table, the differences between Ford and Nixon delegates and Reagan delegates are strong. Almost twice as many Ford supporters as Reagan supporters identified family, school, or adult group experiences as their initial source of involvement in politics. On the other hand, 67 percent of the Reagan delegates cited ideological issues and events as their primary agent of socialization. This figure compares with 40 percent for the Ford delegates, and only 31 percent for the Nixon delegates. These findings point to the role of ideological issues as primary socialization agents for those who have become political

Table 10-1 Parental Political Activity and Delegate Support (in percentages)

	Nixon Delegates (1972)	Ford Delegates (1976)	Reagan Delegates (1976)
Parental Political Activity			
Active	38	39	32
Inactive	62	61	68
(N)	(822)	(563)	(629)
		$C = .07, p < .05$	
Party Identification of Active Parents			
Republican	75	84	64
Democrat or bipartisan	25	16	36
(N)	(376)	(215)	(204)
		$C = .23, p < .001$	

activists in the Reagan camp. The pattern among Ford and Nixon supporters, however, suggests the greater importance of earlier, family-based political learning experiences, which lead to a more common pattern of initial activism. In discussing the latter type of socialization, Roback points out that "familial political activity develops positive expectations about the likelihood of political achievement and affiliation within the child [and]. . .that increased visibility and opportunity should lead to a greater probability of eventual recruitment and entrance into the party organization." [7]

Both Ford and Nixon support seem to have been based on this traditional pattern of political learning. The actual issues and group influence cited by the delegates provide a more specific picture of the roots of their political interest. The adult peer groups most often cited were friends who were politically active, regular party officials, and Republican auxiliary group leaders. Of those indicating the latter groups, 70 percent (N = 35) were Ford delegates. The issues with which the Reagan delegates identified their political interest concerned the future of the American economic system and the growth of government. Of the delegates citing such concerns, three-fourths were Reagan partisans, who identified "creeping socialism," "state of the economy," "survival of the free enterprise system," and "excessive growth of government under the Democrats" as the primary factors that got them interested and involved in politics.

National Convention Recruitment and Motivation

The Republican coalitions that supported Gerald Ford and Ronald Reagan can best be differentiated along the dimensions of geography and ideology. Reagan's strength was concentrated in the more conservative states of the South, Southwest and Far West, whereas Ford drew his support from the Midwest, the border South, and the Northeast. While the substantive and operational policy positions of both candidates were really quite similar, Reagan attracted his following on the intensity and purity of his conservatism. The Reagan delegates argued that philosophical principles should not be compromised. Ford's supporters felt that suggesting governmental retreat on many policy problems would repel many American voters who had come to expect governmental

Table 10-2 Party Background Variables by Candidate Preference (in percentages)

	Nixon delegates	Ford delegates	Reagan delegates	V
Years Active in Party				
1- 5	12	9	10	
6-10	23	14	18	
11-15	22	23	33	
Over 15	43	54	39	.15,
(N)	(812)	(571)	(634)	p<.001
Held a Party Office	80	75	70	
(N)	(816)	(564)	(636)	.06
Supported Another Party	18	9	20	
(N)	(812)	(571)	(637)	.16
Supported Goldwater in 1964	68	53	96	
(N)	(758)	(484)	(561)	.58[a]
Delegate at Two or More Conventions	11	14	6	
(N)	(827)	(571)	(634)	.17[a]

[a] Denotes significance at <.01 for the 1976 delegates.

solutions to their problems. While essentially conservative, Ford projected a more moderate image, which focused on pragmatic solutions to policy problems.

Such an orderly configuration of coalitions was jolted at the convention by Reagan's early vice-presidential choice of moderate-liberal Senator Richard Schweiker of Pennsylvania. This bold stroke gained Reagan no increase in delegate strength and was viewed as being too opportunistic by some uncommitted delegates. For a campaign that was predicated on an "anti-Washington" mood, the Schweiker ploy looked like a tactic that a Chicago Democratic ward boss would concoct. In the final analysis, Ford won because enough Republican activists thought that winning the general election would require the nomination of a center-right candidate rather than a far-right candidate.

But what of the differing reasons for convention participation held by delegates forming these coalitions? Such delegate perceptions about convention recruitment experiences and motives have not been closely examined. This section will analyze the relationship between candidate support and a group of variables that often affect convention activism. The upper part of Table 10-2 examines the partisan longevity of the delegates. It is hypothesized that the supporters of President Ford should have been active longer than the more "nonestablishment" Reagan delegates. Of the Ford delegates, 54 percent had been active in the Republican Party for over 15 years, as compared with 39 percent of the Reagan delegates. There are only slight differences among those active 10 years or under. It is interesting that Reagan delegates are more likely (33 percent) than Ford delegates (23 percent) to have served between 11 and 15 years because this time frame corresponds approximately to the time when the Goldwater movement operated. Of the respondents who also were delegates in 1964, however, 84 percent had been active 15 years or longer, indicating that conservative purism of the Goldwater variety probably predated the 1964 candidate. The party longevity of the Nixon delegates tends to fall between that of Ford and Reagan delegates, perhaps reflecting the diverse mixture of Republicans who remained ideologically subdued in 1972.

The lower part of Table 10-2 considers several other party background variables. There are only slight differences among those supporters of Nixon, Ford, Reagan who held formal party office. The Reagan delegates constitute the lowest percentage of officials, but the fact that 70 percent of them were operating within party organizations dispels any notion that the Reagan movement came from outside the regular party structure. The Reaganites may have been amateur in terms of their ideological intensity, but they certainly did not operate from a position of organizational exclusion prior to the convention.

As noted above, 20 percent of the Reagan delegates formerly supported another party as contrasted with only 9 percent of the Ford delegates. Of the 1972 delegates, 18 percent had formerly supported another party. Most of this previous support was on behalf of the Democratic Party. The pattern in 1976 is primarily in response to Reagan's overwhelming support in the heavily Democratic South and Southwest. Of the Southern delegates who were former Democrats, 80 percent supported Reagan ($N = 57$). That represents about one-quarter of the Southern Republicans in the sample, indicating that the Republican Party constituted the first active partisan experience for most of the Southerners.

Studying the preferences of former Goldwater supporters is another way of tracing the ideological roots of the delegates. As expected, the Reagan delegates who participated in 1964 overwhelmingly (96 percent) had supported Barry Goldwater for the nomination; only 53 percent of the Ford delegates had supported Goldwater. It is clear that the same kinds of conservative Republicans who supported Goldwater supported Reagan; Ford probably inherited a good deal of the Eastern and Midwestern moderate support that had opposed Goldwater. Table 10-2 also analyzes previous national convention delegate participation. More than twice as many Ford as Reagan supporters had been delegates at two or more previous conventions. This pattern once again shows that organizational longevity was positively related to Ford support. The 1976 "old guard" clearly supported the established party candidate of the center-right. Of the 119 delegates in the sample who had been delegates at two or more past conventions, 70 percent supported Gerald Ford.

Other important factors in studying convention delegates are the primary sources of preconvention recruitment and delegates' perceptions of their role as representatives at the convention. When the data were examined, it was found that the greatest percentage of delegates in each candidate group felt that the primary factors contributing to their ultimate participation in the convention were not a function of influence attempts by external agents but were self-generated, "internal" decisions. There is a slight tendency for more 1976 delegates than 1972 delegates to not have been approached or influenced by others about becoming a delegate. The lack of controversy at the Miami Beach convention certainly negated several common self-generating stimuli related to ideolgy, factional competition, and party-constituent representation. The differences among delegates who indicated "external" influence attempts are striking in several categories. Of the Nixon delegates, 32 percent were approached by county chairpersons or other party officials; 23 percent of the Ford delegates and only 8 percent of Reagan delegates were so approached. The Reagan delegates apparently did not often have the encouragement of regular organization officials, especially in those states that had close contests and were evenly divided among factions. Where regular party officials were active during the delegate-selection period, they seem to have worked on behalf of President Ford. Of the Reagan delegates, 26 percent were approached by supporters of the candidate who apparently were party co-workers or independent Reagan campaign operatives. This pat-

Table 10-3 Motivation for Convention Participation by Candidate Preference
(in percentage)

Convention Incentives[a]	Nixon Delegates	Ford Delegates	Reagan Delegates
Support issues or ideological position of candidate	20	9	52
Earn reward as recognition of party work	19	14	6
Gain position in party or as elected official	17	18	3
Experience honor and excitement of being a delegate	14	17	7
Represent views of district and state-party members	12	15	10
Desire to support nominee with best chance to win	13	24	21
Act on political ambition and make party contacts	5	3	1
(N)	(731)	(492)	(576)
V = .50, p < .001			

[a] The 1976 delegates were asked, "What were the major reasons why you finally accepted your seat as a delegate." This was a closed question and the delegates were asked to choose the most important reason. In 1972, an open-ended question was used and the responses were coded into the seven categories listed above.

tern is not surprising given the fact Reagan was competing against an incumbent president who had support among many national and state party officials. Such an insurgent candidacy often had to bypass regular organizational channels in order to generate support. At the convention, this culminated in general perception among bitter Reagan supporters that the national committee had rigged many procedural and committee deliberations. One cynical delegate from Massachusetts commented that: "Although the President used the powers of his office to the hilt, it would require an extraordinary President to restrain himself from using his powers, and Ford is certainly *not* extraordinary."

Concerning delegates' conceptions of whom they represented, the major findings are that more than twice as many Nixon delegates as Ford or Reagan delegates indicated that they felt most responsible to their state party organizational leader or elected officials. Once again, the Reagan delegates appear not to conform to the image of the regular party activist. A total of 11 percent of the Reagan delegates (as compared with 6 percent of Ford delegates and only 2 percent of the Nixon delegates) felt most responsible to either their country or directly to their candidate.

The motivations underlying delegate participation at a national convention are presented in Table 10-3. The Republican delegates were asked to cite the reasons most important to their becoming delegates. Concerning support for the issues or the ideology represented by the candidates, the difference between the Reagan delegates and the other delegates is strong. Of the Reagan adherents, 52 percent chose ideological incentives as the prime motivator for their convention participation. In contrast, only 9 percent of the Ford delegates and 20 percent of the Nixon delegates were primarily motivated by ideological incentives. Quite clearly, Reagan supporters were interested in converting their ideological beliefs into concrete action at the convention. The Ford and Nixon delegates had decidedly higher levels of incentive related to group dolidarity and personal material advancement. They cited party or politial position, earned reward for party work, honor and excitement, and political ambition as major reasons for their participation. For example, 18 percent of the Ford delegates, compared with only 3 percent of the Reagan delegates, chose party or political position as their major motivation.

Conclusion

These findings about actual convention recruitment and motivation are substantiated by other data from this study (unreported here) that examine delegate response to organizational incentives for general *party* recruitment and motivation. These data show that the Reagan delegates were more strongly attracted by ideological and impersonal incentives than the Nixon and Ford delegates. The Nixon and Ford supporters tended to rate the more personal and tangible organizational and material incentives higher than the Reagan supporters. Additional findings about whether initial ideological motives develop, over an activist's career, into more "professional" party concerns also substantiate this image of the Reagan supporter. Because of their ideological fervor, the Reagan delegates had a stronger tendency than the Nixon and Ford delegates to sustain their activism on ideological grounds. Reinforcing this view is the widely held public perception (as transmitted by the media) that the Reagan delegates were an ideological "breed apart" that almost pulled off the minor miracle of denying an "incumbent" president his party's nomination.

The 1976 delegates were faced with unavoidable choices to make about the ideological identity of their party and the candidate who could best represent such an identity. I do not share Murray Kempton's view that Republican politics in 1976 belongs to paleontology.[8] Rather, I judge that it is clear that the delegates in Kansas City collaborated in staging an exciting example of the most uniquely American political institution in such a way that it will long be cited by American political scholars. The Republican delegates in 1976 may not have been as ideologically diverse as their Democratic counterparts, but they were hardly predictable or dull.

NOTES

1. See the following studies for examples of the literature that has examined the behavior of party activists and convention delegates: Lewis Bowman and G. R. Boynton, "Recruitment Patterns Among Local Party Officials: A Model and Some Preliminary Findings in Selected Locales," *American Political Science Review* 60 (September 1966): 667–675; Herbert Jacob, "Initial Recruitment of Elected Officials in the U.S.—A Model," *Journal of Politics* 24 (November 1962): 703–716; Lester G. Seligman, "Political Recruitment and Party Structure," *American Political Science Review* 55 (March 1961): 77–86; William J. Crotty, "The Social Attributes of Party Organizational Activists in a Transitional Political System," *Western Political Quarterly* 20 (September 1967): 669–681; Samuel C. Patterson, "Characteristics of Party Leaders," *Western Political Quarterly* 16 (June 1963): 332–352; Jeane Kirkpatrick, *The New Presidential Elite* (New York: Russell Sage, 1976); Thomas H. Roback, *Recruitment and Incentive Patterns Among Grassroots Republican Officials: Continuity and Change in Two States*, vol. 2 (Beverly Hills, Calif.: Sage, 1974); James Q. Wilson, *The Amateur Democrat* (Chicago: University of Chicago Press, 1962); Joseph A. Schlesinger, *Ambition and Politics: Political Careers in the United States* (Chicago: Rand McNally, 1966); M. Margaret Conway and Frank B. Feigert, "Motivation, Incentive Systems, and the Political Party Organization," *American Political Science Review* 62 (December 1968):

1159-1173; Gordon S. Black, "A Theory of Professionalization in Politics," *American Political Science Review* 64 (September 1970): 865-878; Dennis S. Ippolito, "Motivational Reorientation and Change Among Party Activists," *Journal of Politics* 31 (November 1969): 1098-1101.

2. For a more complete discussion of the atmosphere surrounding the 1972 convention, see Thomas H. Roback, "Amateurs and Professionals: Delegates to the 1972 Republican National Convention," *Journal of Politics* 37 (May 1975): pp. 436-486 and Roback's "Reform Attitudes Among Republican Convention Delegates," *Polity*, September 1975, pp. 173-186.

3. For a summary of the response rates of other national convention studies, see John W. Soule and James W. Clarke, "Issue Conflict and Consensus: A Comparative Study of Democratic and Republican Conventions," *Journal of Politics* 33 (February 1971): 75-76.

4. These aggregate statistics were provided by the CBS News Bureau and the Republican National Committee in both years. The demographic attributes of the 1976 delegates in this study almost mirror the findings of an Associated Press survey. See "Survey Clarifies G.O.P. Delegates," *New York Times*, August 8, 1976, p. 31. Coupled with the high response rates, these similarities allow for confidence in the representativeness of the sample; tests of significance will be reported where appropriate.

5. See William J. Crotty, *Political Reform and the American Experiment* (New York: Crowell, 1977), pp. 255-261.

6. Bowman and Boynton found a generally similar pattern but found much less intergenerational difference among local Democratic officials in Massachusetts. See Bowman and Boynton, "Recruitment Patterns," pp. 670-671.

7. Roback, "Amateurs and Professionals," p. 449.

8. Murray Kempton, "Born-Again Republicans," *Harper's*, November 1976, p. 42. Kempton comments, "we do not lard the Cretaceous period with compliments for having outworn the Jurassic."

11 / Recruitment, Representation, and Political Values: The 1976 Democratic National Convention Delegates

John S. Jackson, III, Jesse C. Brown,
and Barbara L. Brown

The 1976 presidential campaign is now history, and in retrospect it is evident that the nomination and election of Jimmy Carter were unusual and unexpected—if not unprecedented. During that campaign several recent historical precedents were shattered and several apparently well-founded empirical generalizations from political science undermined.

Carter, a relative unknown with an unusual personal style, philosophy, and strategy, was clearly outside the mainstream of the nation's political power centers. He was the first politician of the Deep South since 1848 to be nominated by one of the major political parties and subsequently elected to the presidency. He was the first major party nominee in two decades to come from gubernatorial ranks and the first of that element to be elected since Franklin Roosevelt. It should be further noted that, although a governor, Carter lacked the substantial political bases provided these other twentieth-century governor-presidents; both Wilson and F. D. R. presided over industrial states possessing much more political and economic potency than Georgia. Georgia's peanut farmer acquired the nomination as a "dark horse" and largely without the support of many traditionally powerful interest groups in the Democratic Party. Moreover, he entered the presidency absent any prior service in high national office (appointed or elected) having defeated a sitting president, the latter occurring only twice previously in this century. Thus, when measured against U.S. political history, the nomination and election of Carter indeed qualifies as something of an electoral "miracle."

While all these historical precedents are not entirely hoary with age, they combine to present a cumulative picture of Carter's twin victories as something quite out of the ordinary in recent American politics. The Carter victories are sufficiently unique to attempt an explanation of them and to examine the within-party changes that led to the

Reprinted from *American Politics Quarterly*, Vol. 6, No. 1 (April, 1978): 187-221, by permission of the publisher, Sage Publications, Inc.

We wish to thank Professor Robert A. Hitlin of American University for his contributions as co-director of the larger study on which this article is built. Also the Office of Research and Projects at Southern Illinois University, Carbondale, for the financial support of this study.

Democrats recapturing the White House in 1976 after the devastating defeat of 1972. There are two major objectives for this study. The first is to examine the changes in delegate characteristics that have taken place over the span of the 1968 to 1976 conventions.[1] This era was chosen for emphasis because it encompasses an historic period of party change and reform. The second objective focuses on the 1976 convention and the characteristics of the delegates that attended it. Here we will examine the recruitment patterns, group representation, and political values of the delegates and give particular emphasis to the characteristics of the Carter delegates compared to the delegates who supported other candidates. What is it about the delegate selection system used in 1976 and about the characteristics of the delegates that helps explain Carter's unexpected capture of the Democratic nomination?

It is the thesis of this paper that Carter's nomination did not constitute so much a "political miracle" as the outcome of complementary forces within the party and larger society, and that his candidacy only meshed nicely with those forces. The Democrats were "reformed" in 1972 and lost in a landslide. In 1976 the party leaders and middle-level elites wanted to win, and yet to win with a new face untainted by the past and negative connotations of "smoke-filled rooms"; they wanted a reformer who was also safe enough that the party regulars could support him. Carter was the candidate the liberals could support because he was not too conservative, and the conservatives could support because he was not too liberal, and both could support because he could win. Carter was the candidate the South would support because he was one of them and the other sections could support because he was not George Wallace. In short, he was basically the middle course, and the Democratic delegates understood that a move to the middle in 1976 was the route to victory.

This centrist strategy is, of course, the classic prediction about how U.S. parties (i.e., party elites) will behave because they think such behavior will insure electoral success. However, there were many experts who thought it would be difficult if not impossible for the Democrats to adopt the classic centrist strategy in 1976, and there were numerous predictions that the party was about to disintegrate.[2] Also, our thesis concerning Carter's broad-based appeal and the delegates' desire to move toward a unifying candidate is not just the classic argument, because we would not contend that these particular elites would pursue winning at *any* price. Our contention is, rather, that they could pursue both important objectives, i.e., winning and party rectitude, at the same time by voting for Carter. In summary, our thesis is that Carter cut across the major fault lines in the Democratic Party, and in so doing was able to solidify his nomination while at the same time enhancing his chances for victory in the general election by at least temporarily uniting a Democratic Party whose fratricidal destruction had long been predicted. If this thesis is correct, some of the evidence to support it should be available from examining the kind of delegates that supported Carter as compared to those supporting other candidates, and that is the examination offered in this article.

Rules of the Game: Recruitment and Group Representation

When we scratch our collective heads and wonder how Carter ever won, political scientists naturally turn to the rules of the game as one of the possible explanations of the Carter victories. Democratic Party rules governing the selection of national convention delegates changed dramatically between 1968 and 1972. While we do not plan to reproduce a long discussion of the controversies surrounding the post-1968 reform efforts in the Democratic Party, we do intend to examine the outcome of the political process and institutional rules governing the 1976 delegate selection process. The two most important recent rules changes are, first, the new rules on quotas for 1972 and affirmative action for 1974 and 1976 affecting group representation, and, second, the marked increase in the number of primaries. Both changes are the product of pressures created by the reform movement in general and by the McGovern-Fraser guidelines adopted prior to the 1972 convention in particular. In 1964 and 1968 for example, only 15 states held any form of primary. The delegates from the primary states constituted less than 41% of the 1964 delegates and less than 48% of the total delegates in the 1968 national convention. In 1972, the number of primaries increased to 23. In that year, for the first time, more than a majority of the national convention delegates were selected in primaries rather than in conventions or caucuses (Sorauf, 1972: 269-273). The number of primaries increased dramatically again in 1976. This time 30 states plus the District of Columbia held some form of primary. In 1976 almost 75% of the delegates to the national convention were selected in primaries. Our longitudinal data will allow some aggregate-level comparisons of the results of the various selection procedures used in the Democratic Party over the past four national conventions, with particular emphasis on the impact of "quotas" and "affirmative action." Despite major changes in party rules between the 1968 and 1972 conventions, little effort was made in the following years to expand the reform movement. The most significant alteration occurred when the Mikulski Commission in 1973 deleted the "quotas" system and replaced it with the "affirmative action" system. Otherwise, the reform rules of 1972 remained virtually intact for 1974 and 1976 (Democratic National Committee, 1975).

The initial nominating campaign and national convention conducted under the reformed delegate selection rules may have had a significant impact on the nomination of George McGovern in 1972. Like Carter, McGovern proved to be something of a dark horse. As Keech and Matthews (1975) point out, McGovern was the first candidate in 40 years to win his party's nomination without leading the field of contenders at the beginning of the campaign season. Keech and Matthews' analysis leads them to the conclusion that the primaries have not been as crucial as popularly believed; however, the McGovern exception and now the Carter exception lead one to suspect that the primaries are indeed a significant part of the 1972 and 1976 stories. Unlike Carter, McGovern failed dismally in the general election. Some investigations of the 1972 Democratic campaign suggest that novice party rules "stacked" the national convention with the kinds of delegates most likely to support McGovern and that rule changes were very important to his nomination victory. Some experts also maintain that the convention tarnished the nominee's image and made it impossible to unite the party into an effective electoral coalition following the Pyrrhic victory. In reply to these works, Ranney (1974) asserts that the McGovern-Fraser rules were particularly motivated by a desire to maximize the participation of previously disadvantaged groups—especially women, black people, and young people—rather than making the party "combat ready" for November.

Lengle and Shafer's (1976) recent article demonstrates quite explicitly that the rules of the game can have an extremely important impact on candidate fortunes and party fortunes. In this study the authors used the 1972 Democratic Presidential Primary states and examined the impact of winner-take-all plans, proportional plans, and districted plans. They also point out that pure application of any of the three plans would create specific and differential benefits for the ideological wings of the Democratic Party and for the various geographical sections of the United States. Nevertheless, their predictions that the almost exclusive reliance on a districted plan in 1976 would likely have detrimental effect on the chances for a Democratic victory in the general election seem now, with the advantage of 20:20 hindsight, to be curiously wide of the mark. One is left wondering if the rules were somehow of reduced importance in 1976 or if Carter just managed to defy all the rules and win anyway. [3]

In short, there often is posited a close and direct relationship between the rules and the outcome of the game—a proposition of some longstanding tradition in political science as well as sports. Even though that relationship is assumed to be a close one, there has been remarkably little empirical research that indicates which candidates have been advantaged or disadvantaged by the various institutional features of the delegate selection system. This research will allow us to make some progress in specifying some of those empirical relationships.

Representation and Political Preferences

Much of the recent battle in the past 12 years in the Democratic Party has centered on convention representation for various demographic and political groups that compose the party and the larger society. This is a from of what Pitkin (1967) terms "descriptive representation." Descriptive representation is especially evident in the battles over representation for blacks, women, and young people. Others see the quest in more class-oriented terms, and they desire to "open" the party to a greater diversity of occupational, income, and educational groups. For symbolic purposes representation for a demographic group, e.g., women or black people, is important. However, the real payoff in representation comes in the representation of values, in the representation of political, ideological, and party preferences in the convention. Ultimately, it gets down to whether a Carter delegate or a Udall delegate gets to go; whether a Liberal or a Conservative takes the seat. When pushed, most politicians and political scientists would agree that this is the more fundamental payoff question. This is a form of what Pitkin (1967) terms "subjective representation," meaning the representation of values and attitudes rather than demographic groups. We understand, perhaps almost intuitively, that there is probably a linkage between group representation and party and political values among the delegates and that both are probably tied to the recruitment and selection system. [4] However, there is no excess of empirical research showing the systematic connections between the three. The research reported here can bring some new empirical data to bear on some of those connections.

The Study

The empirical basis for this study is a set of data produced by mailed questionnaires sent to the delegates to the 1976 Democratic National Convention. The first wave of questionnaires was mailed in mid-July immediately after the convention ended. A second wave was mailed a month later in mid-August. The questionnaires were mailed to a systematic sample of 985 delegates, and a total of 520 usable questionnaires was received. This constitutes a return rate of 54%, which compares quite favorably with other such studies using mailed questionnaires. A careful comparison between the known characteristics of all the delegates to the national convention and the characteristics of those who returned the questionnaire indicates that there are no systematic biases in our sample. In addition, a similar questionnaire was sent to a random sample of all delegates to the 1974 Democratic Mid-Term Conference, and the methodology and results of that phase of the study have been reported elsewhere (Jackson and Hitlin, 1976). Finally, aggregate data describing the characteristics of all the delegates to the national convention will be presented when they are available.

In the first section we will present the data describing the delegates to the 1976 Democratic National Convention on a number of important characteristics. The data in this section are intended to be descriptive of all the delegates to the national convention.[5] The first analysis presents the changes over time for the most prominent delegate characteristics. In Table 11-1 we see the delegate characteristics of the four most recent Democratic National Conventions, and those conventions include the most crucial reform era.

As can be gathered from the table, 1972 was the high-water mark of representation for young people, women, and black people. The percentages for young people and blacks declined notably for the 1974 Democratic Mid-Term Conference, and the percentages for women declined marginally in 1974. The 1976 convention also represented something of a decline for the women, blacks, and young people in comparison with 1972, but it is evident from Table 11-1 that the decline in their representation did not return to the prereform 1968 levels. The 1976 levels of representation for these groups are much like those achieved in 1974. Thus, the party may well have reached some sort of stasis where representation for these three groups may not change markedly either way without some significant new external impetus. Such an impetus could be provided for women if the National Organization for Women persists in its demand for 50% female delegates in the 1980 convention.[6] Neither women's organizations nor the black caucus are likely to give up more than they did in 1976 in terms of delegate seats gained, and there was considerable pressure raised by both groups in the 1976 Rule Committee deliberations. However, young people are not as well organized, and they may be the group most likely to face erosion in future conventions. Intraparty maneuverings, and particularly the views of President Carter, are likely to be the major determinants of further movement toward or away from representation for these three groups in the 1978 Mid-Term Conference and in the 1980 National Convention. At any rate, Table 11-1 suggests that "Affirmative Action" was not as effective as "Quotas" in producing representation for these three demographic groups in 1974 and 1976, but it was not as big a retreat as its critics often charged.

As was noted earlier, many people see the problem of party reform as a challenge to open the party to more diverse socioeconomic groups having an opportunity to participate in important decisions. In the next section we will present the occupational, educational, and income characteristics of the 1972 delegates as compared to earlier conventions and two indicators of their political/party experience. First, as can be seen in Table 11-2, the occupational and educational characteristics indicate that the delegates for 1976 continued to come from high status backgrounds. Specifically, 68% of the 1976 delegates are engaged in the highest status occupations (technical, professional, and managerial). This result is similar to the 62% attained in 1974 and is little different from the 64% from the highest occupational status in 1972, although there may be an upward movement in 1976. Similarly for education, only 10% of the 1976 delegates had a high school degree or less, and this compares with 11% for 1974 and 17% who had the lowest level of education in 1972. On the other end of the status scale, a total of 71% of the 1976 delegates had a college degree or advanced education beyond a college degree. This compares with 56% of

Table 11-1 Characteristics of Delegates to Recent Democratic National Conventions

	1969[a] %	1972[a] %	(Mid-Term Conference) 1974[a] %	1976[b] %
Age				
Under 30	4	21	7	14
30+	96	79	93	86
Sex				
Male	87	60	64	67
Female	13	40	36	33
Race				
White	95	85	92	84[c]
Black	6	15	8	11

[a] All of the data in this table are characteristics of the total population and not a sample. The 1968 data were from the Democratic National Committee (1970: 26-28). The 1972 data originated with the Democratic National Committee also. See *Congressional Quarterly* (July 8, 1972; 1642). The 1974 data were provided to us by the D.N.C.

[b] The source of these data is a study of the entire population of all 1976 delegates conducted by CBS News, confirmed by a separate study done by the Associated Press. The Democratic National Committee released a study of 25 state delegations before the National Convention began, and that study generally supported the figures above.

[c] 4.5% of the 1976 delegates had Spanish surnames according to the A.P. study.

the 1972 delegates and 61% of the 1974 delegates who had college degrees or post-college education. Not surprisingly, it was estimated by a *Washington Post* (1976, Sec. A: 1) survey that 75% of the delegates had annual incomes of at least $18,000. In summary, the delegates to the national conventions are ordinarily expected to come from upper status backgrounds, and 1976 was no exception. In fact, if there was a trend in the 1972–1976 changes, it was in the direction of a slightly greater upper status educational cast to the 1976 convention.

We also have some data on the number of party and public officials who attended the 1972, 1974, and 1976 conventions. The 1972 convention was widely condemned in some quarters for having excluded too many public and party officials, with Mayor Daley and his Chicago regulars being the most frequently cited case in point, and it is well known that giving party and public officials a role in the nomination is one way to make the party combat-ready for November. The exclusion of Daley was frequently seen as one of the reasons for McGovern's subsequent problems in uniting the party. In 1974 and 1976 there is evidence that the numbers of both party and public officials increased. In 1972, 50% of the delegates either held or had held party office. In 1974 this figure increased dramatically to 77%. In 1976 it dropped somewhat to 63%. Similarly, in 1972 only 26% of the delegates held *public* office; in 1974 37% of the delegates held public office; and in 1976 this total went down slightly to 33%. Thus, the movement in 1974 and in 1976 seemed to be back toward those kinds of delegates that traditionally fare well when the seats are allocated. It is clear that 1974 was the year of some resurgence for the public and

Table 11-2 Occupational and Educational Characteristics of the Delegates to Recent Democratic Conventions

	1972[a] %	1974[b] %	1976[b] %
Occupation			
Technical, professional, mgr.	64	62	68
Clerk & sales	11	12	9
Craftman & operatives	4	3	1
Service	1	1	1
Laborer	0	0.4	4
Farm	1	1	1
Retired	0	1	2
Housewife	13	12	9
Student/unemployed	7	8	5
N =	(2623)	(255)	(499)
Education			
H.S. graduate or less	17	11	10
Some college	27	27	19
College graduate + study beyond college	27	24	30
Prof. or graduate degree	29	37	41
N =	(2641)	(336)	(511)

[a]Data for 1972 based on study by Kirkpatrick (1976: ch. 3)
[b]Data for 1976 based on our sample of delegates. Data for 1974 based on our earlier sample of Mid-Term Conference delegates.

party officials.[7] While there was some attrition in 1976, the officials did not recede to the low levels of representation they suffered in 1972. As we will see again later, it may be surprising that Carter received the nomination from among these delegates, but it is not surprising that this then became an important item in his ability to unite the party.

A final view of the delegates presented in this section will be a characterization of their ideologies. The questions used here were the self-identified ideological positions of the delegates.[8] Table 11-3 presents the comparison between 1972, 1974, and 1976. From Table 11-3 it can be seen that a marked ideological shift took place among the delegates between 1972 and 1976. There was a clear and decided Liberal to Left cant to the 1972 delegation, and, of course, that was a part of the endemic critique of the 1972 convention alluded to earlier. By comparison, 1974 and 1976 represented a shift back to the party's basic center of gravity among the traditional Liberal and Moderate ideological components of the party. The increase in the Moderate category is especially dramatic, and it was accomplished in 1974. We opened with some questions about why Carter was able to do so well in both the nominating process and the general election of 1976. Here we have found one important ingredient of the answer. Later it will be even clearer that the ideological composition of the 1976 delegates was an important factor in Carter's twin victories. From the results presented so far it would appear that the 1974 Mid-Term Conference was an important opportunity for the Democrats to regroup and to make some important progress in solving the party's internal divisions. 1976 then appears as an occasion for consolidation and accepting some sort of operating modus vivendi that had its foundation in Kansas City.

Table 11-3 Ideology of the Delegates to the Recent Democratic
Conventions

	1972 [a] %	1974[b] %	1976 [b] %
Very liberal to radical	49	11	8
Liberal	30	44	43
Moderate	13	41	45
Conservative	6	5	4
Very conservative-right wing	2	0	0.4
N =	(1568)	(340)	(500)

[a] Data from 1972 based on the study done by Kirkpatrick. That study did not use labels that exactly matched the ideological categories used here, but the differences were minor. See Kirkpatrick (1976: 169). We also wish to thank Professor Kirkpatrick for having earlier provided us with access to some of her data.
[b] Ideological self-identification data for 1976 were based on our sample survey. 1974 data based on our earlier sample of Mid-Term Conference Delegates.

This brings us to the second objective of the study, i.e., can it be demonstrated empirically that the rules and the selection of various demographic and party groups makes any difference in the crucial payoff of candidate advantage? If they do not, what variables do really count? In other words, the candidate preferences of the delegates are the ultimate dependent variables in this analysis. The conceptual framework underlying this section and the whole study is presented in Figure 11-1.

Recruitment, Group Representation, and Political Preferences

First we will examine the relationship between the recruitment selection system and the political preferences of the delegates. This will be the direct examination of the question raised earlier, namely, do the official election rules have a differential impact on candidate fortunes? Since the previous evidence of this matter is generally sketchy and inconclusive, we settled for adopting the null hypothesis throughout the paper, in effect

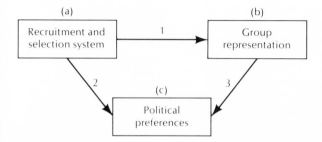

Figure 11-1 Recruitment, representation, and political preferences.

predicting no significant differences between, for example, selection procedures and the delegates' support for various candidates.

The delegates were asked to indicate which candidate they personally favored for the nomination regardless of any official commitment they may have had on the first ballot.[9] Overall, we found that 44% of the delegates said they personally favored Carter. This is very comparable with the percentage of the delegates who were clearly identified by *Congressional Quarterly* (June 5, 1976: 1421) as Carter delegates.[10] Our results indicated that 49% of the delegates selected in the primaries were personally sympathetic to Carter and 51% were sympathetic to other candidates. Alternatively, only 40% of the delegates from the convention/caucus systems were Carter supporters and 60% supported other candidates. These results indicate that the primaries were somewhat more likely to produce Carter delegates than the conventions were, but the differences overall were not statistically significant. While Carter delegates came in very high numbers from both selection channels, there is some indication of an important distinction. It is clear that the primaries were crucial to Carter's nomination strategy, and, just as important, the timing of his primary victories was crucial to his victory. Although Carter won just under of majority of the primary delegates, the opposition was split several ways, with Udall at 14% winning the second highest group of delegates and Brown at 11% winning the third highest group. Carter's victory in winning the nomination was dependent on winning a sufficient number of primaries at the right time to make his nomination inevitable.[11] Although he did not win all the primaries, his strategy worked for the nomination, and his primaty victories were certainly crucial in building the kind of image it took to go on and win the general election as well. This is not to ignore the convention/caucus method, and he won more than any other single candidate that way as well, but there were far fewer delegates to be gained by that route overall. In addition, if Carter had been forced to depend heavily on state convention/caucus victories, as would have been the case in 1968 or before, or if he had won the nomination as a result of a brokered convention, as was widely expected in 1976, he would have been a far different candidate in the general election than he was after coming off his startling series of primary victories. Although the differences were not great, when coupled with total numbers of delegates produced by each method, we can see that the primaries were the major source of Carter supporters, and the convention/caucus systems were disproportionately the source of supporters of the other candidates.

A related finding is the discovery that those who ran "uncommitted" to any candidate were significantly more likely to favor other candidates rather than Carter. This suggests that those with enough political "clout" to get themselves selected without revealing their candidate preferences were not the Carter admirers. We also looked at the primaries and the conventions in terms of whether or not they were held at the state level or at the Congressional District levels. Here we found a pattern which may be rather surprising. That is, the Carter delegates were somewhat more likely to be selected in primaries and conventions at the state level than they were in district level primaries or conventions. The differences were not great, but they were there nevertheless. One could speculate that this result could be a reflection of Carter's having done unexpectedly well in the primaries and conventions and having delegates apportioned to him at this last stage under the party's new proportional representation requirements, but we cannot demonstrate this conclusively.[12]

We turn next to the relationship between group representation and the political preferences of the delegates (arrow 3 in Figure 11-1). In the first section of this paper it was

Table 11-4 The Relationship Between Demographic
Characteristics and Delegate's Presidential Preference

Presidential Preference	Age		
	18-30 %	31-45 %	46+ %
Carter	53	48	36
All others	47	52	64
N =			(494)
x^2 = 9.35			p < .009
Cramer's V		=	.14

Presidential Preference	Sex	
	Male %	Female %
Carter	43	46
All others	57	54
N =		(504)
x^2 = 0.29		Not significant

Presidential Preference	Race	
	Black %	White %
Carter	49	44
All others	51	56
N =		(475)
x^2 = 0.29		Not significant

noted that intense battles have been fought during the last eight years within the Democratic Party over the issue of representation for different groups in the convention. Here we will take that question a step further and ask whether it makes any difference in political terms what groups gain representaion. Specifically, does one candidate benefit and another lose as a result of higher levels of representation for various groups?

First, representation for blacks, women, and young people was examined and those results are presented in Table 11-4. In all three cases the results ran in the same direction. That is, black people, young people, and women were slightly more likely to support Carter than were those who were white, older, and male. However, as is evident from Table 11-4, the differences are statistically significant only in the case of young people. The results for young people are somewhat surprising since Carter was not widely regarded as having any special appeal or support base among the young. One could cautiously infer that Carter benefited overall from the reforms of the past; however, the more important larger result from this table is that Carter's support did not rest exclusively on any traditionally important demographic groupings. He was not exclusively or even markedly the candidate of young people or old people, blacks or whites, men or women, and Carter's strength across the spectrum of delegates is evident. Think for a moment how devastating it could have been to Carter's chances in the nominating process, or in the general election, if most black political elites had opposed him. The broadly based demographic profile of the Carter constituency is already evident in the results provided in Table 11-4, and this was a crucial feature of his being able to unify the party during and after the convention and to go on to victory in November.

The next relationship examined was that between occupation and education and candidate preference. Here we found for occupation that there was a slight tendency for those on the lower end of the occupational prestige ratings (laborers, farmers, and housewives) to favor Carter more often than did those on the upper end of the prestige ratings. This result would be in keeping with the findings for race, age, and sex noted above. On the other hand, the differences found for educational background were minimal. Carter simply scored well with delegates across all educational categories.

In addition, we also looked at the differences between public and party office holders and their presidential preferences, and at the relationship between length of party service and presidential preference. There was only one significant association discovered. Only 37% of the *public* office holders supported Carter compared to 63% who supported all other candidates combined. Here again is a minor indication that party "establishment" groups were somewhat opposed to Carter. However, these differences did not carry over to *party* office holders or those with longer party service. They were as likely to support Carter as they were to support other candidates. This result raises the interesting possibility that those officials Key (1958) called "the-party-in-office" were more opposed to Carter than those from "the party organization."

Finally, for this block of variables, we placed a special emphasis on region in the analysis. No one can look at the map of Carter's 1976 presidential victory without being impressed anew with the indelible imprint of region on American politics. Carter's primary victories also had a decided regional coloration to them. The farther Carter got away from Georgia, the tougher and the fewer the primary victories became. However, unlike most so-called "regional candidates," Carter was able to supersede his regionalism without loosing his power base, and this, too, was one of his strengths. Given all we knew about the impact of region in 1976, it was included as an additional variable.

Table 11-5 demonstrates the relationship between the southern and non-southern delegates and their own personal choices for President. Carter, not surprisingly, was the personal favorite of 72% of the southern delegates. On the other hand, he almost exactly broke even outside the South. It appears from this table that Carter's southern bedrock may have been every bit as crucial to his victory over Brown, Udal, and all the rest in July as it was to become to his victory over Ford in November.

In the final section we will look at the correlations between the ideological and political preferences of the delegates, or, in other words, the correlations among the variables within conceptual block C of Figure 11-1. In Table 11-6 we present the self-identified ideology of the delegates and their preferences for the various candidates.

Here we have two important ingredients of Carter's nomination and general election victories. First, Carter had important strength among *all* the ideological groups within the party. He received large percentages of delegates from each of the ideological groups. A closely related point is that Carter was clearly the candidate of the ideological middle. H

Table 11-5 The Relationship Between Region and
Candidate Choice

	Region	
	Non-South	South
Candidate Choice	%	%
Carter	50	72
Non-Carter	50	28
N =	(339)	(76)

$\chi^2 = 1209.$
$p < .001.$
Phi $= .18.$

got 57% of those who called themselves "Moderates." His closest rival among this crucial centrist group was Jackson, who got 10% of that vote. In comparison, Brown, Udall, and Church were favored by the left side of the party, while none of these three received any support at all from the right side of the spectrum. Alternatively, Wallace, not surprisingly, received all his support from the right side of the party. However, Carter outstripped everybody in all ideological categories except Udall among those delegates who termed themselves as "Left Liberal to Radical," and except Wallace among those delegates who considered themselves "Conservatives or Right-Wing." In addition, among both these groups Carter clearly had the second highest block of delegates.

No other data that have been presented go so far as Table 11–5 in demonstrating clearly why Carter won the nomination and the general election. The Democratic Party is probably the most diverse, broad-based political coalition in the world. It is a vast umbrella under which an extraordinary collection of people take refuge. The candidate who can appeal to a significant proportion of the delegates across this broad ideological spectrum can not only win the Democratic nomination but also emerge from the convention in a formidable position to put it all together for the general election. This is what Carter did, and the foundations of those two victories are clearly evident in Table 11-6.

An additional variable included under the rubric of "party and political preference" has to do with the delegates' concepts of what their role in the convention should be. We chose to tap important intraparty differences between delegates with a group of five items taken directly from Kirkpatrick's (1976) original study of the 1972 delegates. She presented these items as tapping "delegate role perceptions" in general and the "job of the convention delegate" in particular. The question reads:

What do you think are the most important things the convention can do? Below are listed five different functions the convention performs. Please rank them from FIRST through FIFTH most important.

As Kirkpatrick pointed out, there has been serious disagreement within both parties about what the major goals of the parties are and in turn what the convention and thus the delegates should try to accomplish. There are also here clear echoes of the classic debate between the "purist" versus "politician" and "amateur" versus "professional" conceptions of the political parties (Wilson, 1962; Soule and Clarke, 1970; Soule and

Table 11-6   The Relationship Between Ideology and Candidate Choice

Candidate Choice	Delegates' Ideology			
	Left Liberal to Radical %	Liberal %	Moderate %	Conservative to Right Wing %
Carter	16	36	57	23
Jackson	0	1	10	5
Udall	30	27	3	0
Wallace	0	0	3	45
Brown	19	9	6	4
Church	8	6	3	0
Uncommitted	3	3	2	0
Others	24	19	16	23
N =	(37)	(210)	(223)	(22)

Note: Statistics are not reported on this table because of the number of cells with 0 entries.

Table 11-7   Delegate Role Perceptions: The Job of Convention Delegate by Candidate Preference

Role Perception	All Delegates	Carter Delegates	All Other Candidates' Delegates
1. Unifying the party	38%[a]	44%[a]	33%[a]
2. Putting together a winning team	56	58	55
3. Adopt correct issue positions	55	51	58
4. Reforming the party	12	9	15
5. Nominating most deserving candidate	46	47	45
N =	493	215	278

[a] This is the total number of all delegates (or Carter delegates or delegates supporting other candidates) who chose the option as either their first or second choice, and thus the totals do not add to 100%. This data presentation convention here is comparable to that used by Kirkpatrick. See Kirkpatrick (1976: 126-127)

[b] This is the only table where the $\times$ difference between two groups were large enough to be significant at the .05 level.

McGrath, 1975; Roback, 1975; Hofstetter, 1971; Wildavsky, 1965). Table 11-7 provides our results for the 1976 delegates crosstabulated by supporters of Carter and supporters of all other candidates.

When one looks first at the hand column, i.e., the column summarizing the first and second choices for all the Democratic delegates combined, it is clear that the traditional electoral function of "putting together a winning team" is the most popular response, and it is favored by 56% of the delegates as either their first or second choices. It is also somewhat surprising that the second most often selected choice was "adopting the correct issue positions," since our parties have not traditionally emphasized this function. Some authorities maintain that candidate-centered delegates are coming to the fore in the conventions, and some support for this contention is provided by the fact that we found this role to be the third most frequently emphasized by the 1976 delegates. As Kirkpatrick pointed out, items 1 and 2 are the roles ordinarily associated with the "professional" or "politician" view of the conventions and the roles of the delegates, and items 3, 4, and 5 are more often associated with the "purist" or "amateur" conceptions of the role of the delegates. [13] In light of this dichotomy, it is interesting to discover that the two most frequently chosen items include one from the professional and one from the purist domains of delegate roles.

Kirkpatrick (1976) found that these items rather clearly distinguished between the supporters of the 1972 candidates. McGovern and Wallace delegates gave a higher priority to items 3, 4, and 5 (the amateur spirit), while supporters of Muskie and Humphrey (and Nixon) gave higher priority to items 1 and 2. However, as we can see from Table 11-7, the differences between the Carter supporters compared to the supporters of other candidates are not at all great in 1976. Carter delegates did tend to emphasize the traditional electoral and aggregative functions of the conventions a bit more heavily than did the delegates supporting the other candidates. However, the Carter delegates were only slightly less supportive of the roles stressing party reform and issue positions, and there were no essential differences at all on the question of nominating the most deserving candidates. We conclude from this that there were delegates who held the traditional objectives of unifying the party and winning the election in the Carter camp and in almost the same proportions in the other camps. Likewise, there were delegates who sought the newer objectives also in almost the same proportions in the different camps.

This outcome is synonymous with that found for ideology reported in Table 11-6, i.e., Carter's strength lay partially in his broad appeal across a variety of party and demographic groups—although it is also true that he had considerable opposition across many of those same groups. Strategically, if a candidate cannot be loved by everyone, this is probably the next best position from which to gain the nomination in a highly fluid situation because it makes it almost impossible for other candidates to unite in a "stop the front-runner" drive. In addition, strategically, this is probably the next best position from which to unite the party once a genuine contest for the nomination has ended. The time is short and the party's nominee wants to keep traditional leaders and traditional blocks from breaking out of the coalition before the general election. As we have seen, there is a sense that Carter's attaining the nomination was an example of what David, Goldman, and Bain (1960) called a "factional victory"; however, by the time the convention opened, the formerly factious Democrats were remarkably united. While the distributions on ideology and delegate role conceptions do not fully explain Carter's success, they are indicative of the larger truth, and they also fit the pattern established for region.

Conclusion

An overview and strategic assessment of the broad picture is now in order. (Some of the following admittedly takes some license beyond what the empirical data presented will absolutely support.) At the outset we made some assumptions about the importance of the institutional rules of the game. It is widely believed that the electoral rules have a lot to do with advantaging and disadvantaging various groups and candidates. Those rules have been the bone of great contention in the Democratic Party in recent years. The impact of the rules of the game was difficult to demonstrate with empirical data, however. The clearest political impact of the rules was in demonstrating the importance of the primaries in producing the bulk of the Carter delegates. Also, we found evidence in the aggregate data that changing the rules of delegate selection may have contributed to some reduction in the level of minority representation. However, the group and demographic composition of the convention were shown to have only a modest impact on Carter's victory. Our analysis indicates that Carter may have benefited marginally from the inclusion of previously disadvantaged groups, but his benefits were nowhere nearly as salient as those generally believed to have accrued to McGovern in 1972. When one candidate does not derive lopsided benefits, the new rules are more likely to be widely accepted and thus to become institutionalized and then neutral.

In fact, when we looked for variables that really mattered, that actually helped us explain Carter's nomination and general election victories, we discovered what could best be termed some rather straightforward "political" explanations.[14] Specifically, ideology, regionalism, and party orientations help explain Carter's victories better than the rules of the game do. In addition, these variables are not necessarily important because they divide Carter's supporters from others. They are important mostly for what they reveal about the distribution of Carter's support among the party activists. The fact that Carter was strong across a broad spectrum of delegates who themselves divided on a number of traditionally important characteristics is the key to Carter's success. He cut across the important basic cleavages in the party. If Carter had cut along the major fault lines, as McGovern did in 1972, we would now be reading about Ford's dips in the new White House swimming pool or Brown's sleeping on a White House mattress. As it turned out, Carter's strength came from his ability to stand astride those old divisions in a way not equaled since F. D. R. Regionalism came the closest to a cleavage that could have denied Carter either the nomination or the election. However, Carter stood so firmly in the South and east of the Mississippi River that even this major fault line was not fatal, although it could have been in either contest. It will be extraordinarily interesting to see whether Carter proves to be a second Roosevelt for the warring Democrats or whether all the old party fissures will have reappeared by 1980.

NOTES

1. Where the data are available, we will provide 1968 comparisons. Otherwise, the 1972, 1974, and 1976 conventions will be compared.
2. The literature on party realignment and/or "disintegration" is voluminous. For example, see Miller, Miller, Raine, and Brown (1976) and Stewart (1974).
3. See Cavala (1974: 27–42), Lipset and Raub (1973: 43–50), and Center (1974: 325–350). Sullivan and his associates (1974: 22–24) argue that changing the rules was not the major factor in the nomination of George McGovern.
4. For a complete discussion of the recruitment selection process and bibliography, see Prewitt (1970). The emphasis in the present study is on the final filter stage of the selection process.
5. Some of the data are aggregate statistics on the whole population and others are based on random samples. The notes on the tables will delineate the data base being employed.
6. Sullivan et al. (1974: 35) argue that the experience is the major commondity the party gives up when it provides greater representation for such previously disadvantaged groups.
7. Data for 1972 taken from the *Washington Post* article. Data for 1976 taken from the results of the sample survey done for this study. Part of this change can be attributed to reinstituting "ex officio" seats for major party leaders which was done in 1974.
8. While the use of self-identification on ideology can be criticized, this is much less of a problem for political elites than for surveys among the general population. These dele-

gates are, by and large, sophisticated political elites who are accustomed to dealing with the conventional meanings of such common labels as "Liberal" and "Conservative." The completely sensible results in Table 11-6 of this study provide further evidence for the use of self-identification on ideology. Kirkpatrick (1976: 167-168) also uses ideological self-identification and adopts this rationale for its use.

9. We also asked for their official commitment and for whom they voted on the first ballot. There is a high correlation between official commitment and personal sympathy, (Phi = .84). There is a much lower correlation (Phi = .54) between personal commitment and final vote on the first roll-call because, of course, many voted for Carter that did not prefer him or were not committed officially to him. Aggregate data produced by *Congressional Quarterly* (July 17, 1976: 1873) indicate that our survey sample distributions are very close to the population figures. According to *C.Q.*, 74% of the first ballot votes went to Carter, 10% to Udall, and 10% to Brown. Our survey results found 71% who say they voted for Carter on the first ballot, 14% who say they voted for Udall, and 11% who say they voted for Brown.

10. *Congressional Quarterly Weekly Report* (June 5, 1976: 1421) reported that going into the last week of the primaries, Carter had captured 43% of the primary vote and 42% of the delegates from the primary states. *C.Q.* also reported that Carter took only 34% of delegates from the caucuses (*Congressional Quarterly Weekly Report,* July 10, 1976: 1809-1811).

11. Schram (1976). The sense of the importance of timing is especially notable in this account. On the more formal considerations of strategy, see Gamson (1962) and McGregor (1973).

12. For a more thorough discussion of this point about proportional representation, see Lengle and Shafer (1976).

13. We also tapped the "amateur-professional" concept using both the Soule and Clarke (1970) and the Soule and McGrath (1975) scale items. When the original Soule and Clarke "amateur scale" is crosstabulated with candidate preference, the results are the same as those found in the body of this paper, i.e., there were not significant differences between the amateurs and the professionals in their preferences for the candidates. However, these scales have been plagued by the problem of uncertain multidimensionality, and, depending on the items used, the scales seem to subsume from two to four basic factors. For these reasons we chose to report the Kirkpatrick items here.

14. This substantive view is buttressed by the statistical results. More elaborate statistical procedures have been done, but because of space limitations they will not be fully presented. However, Figure 11-1 implies a multiple regression analysis and it substantiates the bivariate results reported here. The multiple regression using all the independent variables (except delegate's role orientations) produced an R^2 of .15. The only independent variables that accounted for significant amounts of variance in candidate choice were ideology $R^2 = .07$ and region $R^2 = .05$, and none of the "rules of the game" or other group variables proved to be important.

REFERENCES

Cavala, W. (1974) "Changing the rules changes the game: party reform and the 1972 California Delegation to the Democratic National Convention." *Amer. Pol. Sci. Rev.* 68 (March): 27-42.

Center, J. (1974) "1972 Democratic Convention reforms and party democracy." *Pol. Sci. Q.* 89 (June): 325-350.

Congressional Quarterly (1976) *Weekly Report.* (June 5): 1421; (July 10): 1809-1811; (July 17): 1873.

David, P. T., R. M. Goldman, and R. C. Bain (1960) *The Politics of National Party Conventions.* Washington, DC: Brookings Institute.

Democratic National Committee (1975) *The Call for the 1976 Democratic National Convention.* Washington, DC: Democratic National Committee.

———— (1970) "Mandate for reform." Report of the Commission on Delegate Selection and Party Structure. Washington, DC: Democratic National Committee.

Gamson, W. A. (1962) "Coalition formation at presidential nominating conventions." *J. of Sociology* 68 (September): 157–171.

Hofstetter, C. R. (1971) "The amateur politician: a problem in construct validation." *Midwest J. of Pol. Sci.* 15 (February): 31–56.

Jackson, J. S. and R. A. Hitlin (1976) "A comparison of party elites: the Sanford Commission and the delegates to the Democratic Mid-Term Conference." *Amer. Pol. Q.* 4 (October): 441–482.

Keech, W. R. and D. Matthews (1975) *The Party's Choice.* Washington, DC: Brookings Institute.

Key, V. O. (1958) *Politics, Parties, and Pressure Groups.* New York: Crowell.

Kirkpatrick, J. J. (1976) *The New Presidential Elite: Men and Women in National Politics.* New York: Russell Sage Foundation.

Lengle, J. I. and B. Shafer (1976) "Primary rules, political power, and social change." *Amer. Pol. Sci. Rev.* 70 (March): 25–40.

Lipset, S. M. and E. Raub (1973) "The election and the national mood." *Commentary* 55 (January): 43–50.

McGregor, E. B. (1973) "Rationality and uncertainty and national nominating conventions." *J. of Politics* 35 (May): 459–478.

Miller, A., W. Miller, A. Raine, and T. Brown (1976) "A majority party in disarray: policy polarization in the 1972 election." *Amer. Pol. Sci. Rev.* 70 (September): 753–778.

Pitkin, H. F. (1967) *The Concept of Representation.* Berkeley: Univ. of California Press.

Prewitt, K. (1970) *The Recruitment of Political Leaders: A Study of Citizen-Politicians.* Indianapolis: Bobbs–Merrill.

Ranney, A. (1974) "Comment on 'changing the rules'." *Amer. Pol. Sci. Rev.* 68 (March): 43–44.

Roback, T. H. (1975) "Amateurs and professionals: delegates to the 1972 Republican National Convention." *J. of Politics* 37 (May): 436–467.

Schram, M. (1976) *Running for President: A Journal of the Carter Campaign.* New York: Pocket Books.

Sorauf, F. (1972) *Party Politics in America.* Boston: Little, Brown.

Soule, J. W. and J. W. Clarke (1970) "Amateurs and professionals: a study of delegates to the 1968 Democratic National Convention." *Amer. Pol. Sci. Rev.* 64 (September): 888–898.

Soule, J. W. and W. McGrath (1975) "A comparative study of presidential nominating conventions: the Democrats 1968 and 1972." *Amer. J. of Pol. Sci.* 19 (August): 501–518.

Stewart, J. G. (1974) *One Last Chance: The Democratic Party, 1974–1976.* New York: Praeger.

Sullivan, D., J. Pressman, B. Page, and J. Lyons (1974) *The Politics of Representation: The Democratic National Convention—1972.* New York: St. Martin's. *The Washington Post* (1976) July 11: 1.

Wildavsky, A. (1965) "The Goldwater phenomenon: purists, politicians, and the two party system." *Rev. of Politics* 27: 386–431.

Wilson, J. Q. (1962) *The Amateur Democrat.* Chicago: Univ. of Chicago Press.

PART ‖‖

THE PARTY AND THE VOTERS

INTRODUCTION

Part III begins with an ambitious and finely executed analysis of changes in the American electorate with which the political parties must contend. Merle Black and George B. Rabinowitz, in "American Electoral Change: 1952–1972 (With a Note on 1976)," evaluate a two-decade period in which the voters' perceptions of the political system and their attitudes toward the parties, candidates, and issues underwent profound change. The implications for the political parties, their ties to their constituents and, of course, their definition of their political role are enormous.

Black and Rabinowitz explore these dimensions of electoral behavior for three groups: Northern whites, Southern whites, and blacks. The analysis is sophisticated and its results indicate an electorate very much in flux. Their conclusions are noteworthy. The authors demonstrate that regionalism continues as a force in American voting behavior, and they show that Southern whites are closer to Republicans than Democrats on many attitudinal dimensions. Despite these findings, they do not forecast, however, a radical digression in future voting patterns for the South.

Black and Rabinowitz diagram the ascent, and to an extent, the descent, of racial concerns as a point of reference for American voters. The authors doubt that these issues will polarize the electorate and contribute to a new party alignment as many feared.

The researchers find that voters are disturbed about their political parties. The positive impressions of party image that tended to reinforce party loyalties appear to be declining. In many cases, voters can think of as many negative as positive things to associate with the parties' performance. If such a decline in esteem continues, and continues to be reinforced by a weakening of psychological ties to the parties (as appears to be happening), then both parties may well be in for difficult times. The authors point out that the greatest dissatisfaction with the parties lies in their inability (as seen by the voters) to address relevant national issues in a meaningful way and to offer adequate solutions.

In assessing the 1976 presidential election, the authors discovered that the Democratic Party's image improved considerably among voters. The effect may be short-run, however, and may simply attest to the volatility of party attitudes. Black and Rabinowitz show, for example, that the relative scope and intensity of support, although high in 1976, was still well below the lowest levels reported for the period of stable party attitudes during the years 1952–1964. The authors conclude that the contrasting perceptions of the two parties made the crucial difference in the presidential election of 1976

The study is an important one. The changes it documents indicate an electorate in transition. At some point, the political parties will have to address directly the problems occasioned by a public whose perception of the parties and what they represent is undergoing a fundamental redefinition.

Joan L. Fee, in "Religion, Ethnicity, and Class in American Electoral Behavior," assesses a related dimension in the changing association between political parties and their constituent groups. She is concerned with the association between religious and ethnic ties and political partisanship. At one time, this concern was a staple of the research on American voting behavior and the findings offered explained much of what both political parties stood for and why they behaved as they did. The emphasis in voting research, however, turned away from examining the established demographic groupings and toward an exploration of the psychological basis for affiliations with the parties and of the attitudinal factors of greatest significance in voter decisionmaking. As a consequence, this strain of research became somewhat neglected. The author helps to reestablish a balanced perspective in the area by exploring the religious bonds between parties and voters. The particular emphasis in the research is on American Catholics.

Fee argues that over the two decades analyzed, religious and ethnic affiliations with the parties remained strong. Some of her findings refute the assumptions of others. For example, it has been argued that Catholics have been undergoing a secular conversion to the Republican Party. It has been claimed that the change has been in progress for generations and that it is tied to economic factors. Fee's analysis indicates this argument may be overly simple. Some groups of Catholics— Irish and Polish Catholics, for example—rival those of the Jewish faith in the continued strength of their allegiance to the Democratic Party. As the author shows, the rise in economic status and the suburbanization of Catholics during the period 1952–1972 did not weaken their support for the Democratic Party. Fee does indicate that education, residence patterns, and the environment in which people live do affect differences within blocs of Catholics, Protestants, Jews, and blacks, the major demographic groupings in the study. The differences can be seen among the various groups in the manner in which they approach politics and how they perceive the political parties. The evidence from this study suggests that the assumptions as to the universality and impact of party identifications across social groupings within the electorate may need rethinking.

Perhaps the greatest amount of speculation concerning the changing shape of the voting universe and its implications for the performance of political parties has centered on the evolution of the New Deal coalition that has explained the partisan division within the electorate since the Great Depression. Michael E. Good and Carl F. Pinkele ("The New Deal Coalition: A Reappraisal") have studied the problem, and although their research is not represented in this volume, their conclusions merit attention. The latter also set the stage for the arguments found in the Ladd selection (below). Good and Pinkele were concerned with tracing social group affiliations within the political parties in presidential and congressional elections over a 24-year period.[1] Their intent was to assess the changing levels of support within the New Deal coalition for the two major political parties. Has the majority party's coalition eroded with time? What types of people and groups support the parties nationally? At what level of intensity? What, if any, redistribution of influence has taken place among groups within the majority party's coalition? The answers to these and related questions aid immeasurably in understanding the present status, group support patterns, and appeals of the parties.

Good and Pinkele found a consistently impressive level of support for the Democratic party in presidential and congressional elections from New Deal groups (blacks, blue collar workers, the economically disadvantaged, urban dwellers, non-Protestants). Blacks emerged as particularly strong in their Democratic affiliation and non-Protestant religious groups were shown to be the most changeable. Southerners were more likely to make a distinction between congressional and presidential elections, favoring the Democratic Party more in one (the congressional races) than in the other.

Good and Pinkele pinpointed what may be at the core of the episodic fortunes of the Democratic Party. While group loyalties generally remained supportive during the period studied, *turnout figures for specific election years varied considerably.* Unpredicted drops in turnout for partisan groups can have decisive consequences for any given contest. The authors showed, for example, that group levels of turnout fluctuated between congressional and presidential elections and from one presidential election year to the next. Overall, they concluded that although individual elections (particularly at the presidential level) demonstrate variations in the levels of group support, the New Deal coalition remained relatively loyal in its affiliations.

An introduction to these findings helps put the next selection in broad perspective. Everett Carll Ladd, Jr.'s interpretation is somewhat different. In a piece represented here, "Liberalism Upside Down: The Inversion of the New Deal Order," Ladd takes another approach in assessing the potency and stability of the coalitions that emerged from the Depression. Ladd employs survey data for the period 1940 to 1974 (and, to a more limited extent, 1976) to trace the change in intensity of support among specific demographic groups of the two parties. His conclusions are thought-provoking.[2]

The appeal of the Republican Party has declined. The Democratic Party, in turn, has undergone what Ladd calls an "inversion" in its patterns of support. In effect, a coalition that was built upon a working-class base has expanded and increased its appeal to middle and upper-class professionals. The shift in the nature of the Democratic coalition is best explained by evolutionary social patterns within the population more generally. It is most unlikely that the Democrats would return to the dominantly working class coalition of the 1930s, or even that they could if they so desired. The redistribution of power within the Democratic coalition has caused an identity crisis of sorts (although Ladd does not call it this) in articulating what precisely the Democratic Party (or either party, for that matter) stands for and whom it represents. The political appeal and policy objectives of the Democratic Party have shifted, and its support groups within the population have been redefined.

Among the most recent changes in politics and political campaigning has been the rise in importance of single-issue interest groups in supporting candidates for election. These new groups have been able to raise large sums of money under the new campaign reform acts and invest these in politics. In fact, the new laws intended to reform campaign expenditures have actually encouraged the rapid proliferation of Political Action Committees (PACs), each with substantial sums to spend on an issue or economic concern it wants taken care of by the government.

The rise of these new groups[3]—some ideological, others more concerned with business and more direct economic rewards—has hurt the political parties. The PACs operate outside the parties, funneling money and support to individuals willing to support their causes. On occasion, they recruit candidates to contest party-endorsed contenders in primaries; their economic resources can be decisive in general elections. The PACs directly, or through funds contributed to favored candidates, foster a reliance on public-relation consultants and high-spending, media-oriented campaigns. The new groups then perform many of the functions once assumed by the parties. They encourage candidates to reach out to nonparty sources for aid and expertise. The very existence of the PACs is a challenge to the parties and the relative degree of unity and within-party cooperation they were able to superimpose on the chaos that is politics.

Selections 15 through 18 deal with these developments. In selection 15, "Organized Labor Takes a Hard Look at Whom It Will Support This Fall," Charles W. Hucker takes a look at a traditionally powerful interest group, organized labor (and specifically, the AFL-CIO) and its strategy in the 1978 elections. Organized labor has a reputation for being the best organized and most powerful interest group within the Democratic coalition. The reputation is well earned.

Yet, the AFL-CIO is not completely satisfied with its role in the coalition, and it promises to be more selective in the future in endorsing and supporting candidates. It wants a discernible commitment, evidenced through a legislative vote, to the causes it holds important.

Organized labor has a great deal of political muscle. It contributed $6 million to congressional candidates in 1974 and $8 million in 1976. Yet, it may not be all that different from other economic issue groups in the pattern of its support.[4] An examination of its pattern of giving in 1976 shows that 75 percent of its funds went to incumbents—those already in power, and those most likely to do it some good.

The "New Right," as it is called, has benefited from the use of the PACs. As Christopher Buchanan illustrates in "New Right: 'Many Times More Effective' Now," the New Right has proved very effective in collecting large sums of money to funnel into campaigns. Such groups as the National Conservative Political Action Committee, the Committee for the Survival of a Free Congress, and Citizens for the Republic have acquired large treasuries through expert solicitation of a highly motivated, politically aware, and economically comfortable clientele. Liberal ideological groups have proved less successful in these regards.

Curiously, it may not be the Democratic Party (at least, initially) that suffers most from the "ideological" money. Many conservative groups have donated large sums to candidates willing to contest Republicans moderates and liberals at the prenomination stage. The strategy has had some success. In 1978, a young, conservative newcomer to politics, Jeffrey Bell, managed to defeat the venerable Clifford Case for the Republican nomination to the U.S. Senate in New Jersey, and another young, conservative newcomer, Avi Nelson, ran the liberal incumbent senator, Edward W. Brooke, a close race in Massachusetts.

The concerns of the corporate PACs are somewhat different from the ideological interest groups. Although the names of the committees are often difficult to distinguish from the broader-based ideological groups (for example, the Nonpartisan Committee for Good Government, a Coca-Cola PAC; or the Nonpartisan Political Support Committee, A General Electric Company PAC), their goals are more specific. In most cases, these PACs are interested in supporting candidates who will aid them directly in some economic way. They "invest" in politics, as Common Cause has contended, with the objective of getting some return on their money.[5]

Charles W. Hucker develops these themes in his selection, "Explosive Growth: Corporate Political Action Committees Are Less Oriented to Republicans Than Expected." Hucker shows, for example, that the contributions of these corporate PACs in 1976 began to rival those of organized labor. Again like organized labor, the bulk (80 percent) of PAC contributions went to incumbents.

The organization of politically-oriented PACs was legalized in the 1974 amendments to the 1971 Federal Election Campaign Act.[6] In effect, the privileges traditionally given to organized labor in this area were extended to business. The growth in the number of PACs has been extraordinary. In 1978, they numbered about 500 and their contributions to, and influence on, campaigns has been (and will continue to be) enormous.

The entrance of new sources of funding has reinforced the move toward a media-oriented politics and the reliance on campaign consultants to provide a wide range of services.[7] Charles W. Hucker, in "Campaign Consultants Portray Candidates as Fiscal Watchdogs," takes a look at the world of the consultant and the problems he faces in an election year. Hucker reviews the efforts of selected consultants and campaign services firms to establish themes and move campaigns in directions that coincide with the voters' mood. Hucker shows how, in an inflation-plagued off-year election, the consultants attempt to take advantage of the current political concerns. As he suggests, the rewards for guessing right can be enormous while mistakes can seriously damage an individual's reputation. In a highly volatile business, new consultants can become celebrities overnight. Success in a highly publicized campaign can mean substantial economic rewards.

Possibly the single greatest recent innovation in campaigning, however, has been the rise in importance of television. In one of their innovative studies of the influence of the medium on political parties and the public, "Television and Voters' Issue Awareness," Thomas E. Patterson and Robert D. McClure report that candidates tailor their campaigns and appeals to the peculiar needs of television.[8] Television is the single most comprehensive medium for reaching a large number of voters; it is also the most expensive.

As the authors note, given the importance of television in campaigns, in reaching voters, providing them with information, and shaping their views on the candidates and issues of the day, it is surprising how little is really known as to the specific impact of the medium in given areas of voter concern. How much and what types of information, for example, do voters assimilate from television as to a candidate's stand on issues? What is most effective in reaching prospective voters and shaping their views—television news reporting or televised campaign commercials? Which alternative provides the better payoff for the candidate? What themes are communicated to the voter (and with what consequences) through televised news programs and through political commercials? These are the types of questions Patterson and McClure explore through an analysis of television in the 1972 presidential campaign.

Not surprisingly, television newscasters were selective in what they reported. They tended to supply only limited information and background materials on candidate positions. This type of reporting does not mesh well with the visual needs and time constraints of a news program. Televised advertising presented both a clearer and more extensive introduction to the policy stands with which the candidates wished to be associated. The substance of the advertising, as was to be expected, was straightforward and created a direct relationship between candidate and issue. The themes conveyed by the televised news programs were more complex and often communicated potentially conflicting messages to the viewer: Richard Nixon is doing a good job with the war in Vietnam; Richard Nixon tolerates political corruption in his administration.

Patterson and McClure find that a regular viewing of television news programs did not increase the viewers' issue awareness. Newspaper reading, on the other hand, tended to substantially increase voters' policy information. Television advertising correlated also with an increase in voters' policy concern. The television commercials had their greatest impact on events peculiar to the election year and were least influential in reshaping voters' response to issues of long-standing controversy.

Patterson and McClure conclude that televised political commercials are important and effective conveyors of candidate messages. They also suggest that the impact of these commercials may be even greater than they can document in their report.

NOTES

1. Michael E. Good and Carl F. Pinkele, "The New Deal Coalition: A Reappraisal" (Paper presented at the Annual Meeting of the Midwest Political Science Association, Chicago, 1977; revised 1978). See also in this regard: Robert Axelrod, "Where the Voters Come From: An Analysis of Electoral Coalitions, 1952–1968," *American Political Science Review* 66 (March 1972); 11–20; and Axelrod, "Communications," *American Political Science Review* 68 (June 1974): 717–720. Other works relevant to the problems discussed are: Everett C. Ladd, Jr., and Charles D. Hadley, *Transformation of the American Party System: Political Coalitions from the New Deal to the 1970's,* 2nd ed., rev. (New York: Norton, 1978); James L. Sundquist, *Dynamics of the Party System* (Washington: Brookings Institution, 1973); and Norman Nie, Sidney Verba, and John Petrocik, *The Changing American Voter* (Chicago: University of Chicago Press, 1976) especially Chaps. 5, 12, 13, and 14.

2. See also Everett Carll Ladd, Jr., *Where Have All the Voters Gone* (New York: Norton, 1978).

3. See William Crotty, *Political Reform and the American Experiment* (New York: Crowell, 1977), pp. 103–137.

4. Ibid., pp. 113–119.

5. Charles W. Hucker, "Explosive Growth: Corporate Political Action Committees Are Less Oriented to Republicans Than Expected," *Congressional Quarterly,* April 8, 1978, p. 850; and in this volume.

6. Crotty, *Political Reform,* pp. 168–190.

7. See "The Party Symbol and Its Changing Meaning," the overview to this volume.

8. The major work by these authors is, Thomas E. Patterson and Robert D. McClure, *The Unseeing Eye* (New York: Putnam, 1976). See also in this regard, Kurt Lang and Gladys Lang, *Politics and Television* (Chicago: Quadrangle, 1968); Harold Mendelsohn and Irving Crespi, *Polls, Television, and the New Politics* (Scranton Pa. Chandler, 1970); John Whale, *The Half-Shut Eye* (London: Macmillan, 1969); and Sig Mickelson, *The Electronic Mirror* (New York: Dodd, Mead, 1972).

12 / American Electoral Change: 1952–1972 (With a Note on 1976)

Merle Black and George B. Rabinowitz

This chapter analyzes partisan change in the United States over the past 20 years. Trends in voting behavior and party identification have been the subjects of many extended analyses; here we wish to expand that focus by including other data sources useful for measuring partisan change over time. In particular, we intend to explore the patterns of likes and dislikes expressed by the electorate toward parties and candidates in presidential elections from 1952 to 1972; the perceptions of the electorate concerning the most important problems facing the government in Washington and the government's abiltiy to deal with these problems; and the trends in public opinion on important national issues. Our objective is to map changing public evaluations of parties, candidates, and issues and to determine how the major stimuli of American politics have been evaluated over time. We will use questions that will take us into the voters' perceptions of the political landscape.

Our analysis will concentrate on three demographic groups: non-Southern (hereafter called Northern) whites, Southern whites, and blacks. The major data source for this paper is the series of presidential election surveys of the U.S. electorate conducted by the Survey Research Center (SRC), and more recently, by the Center for Political Studies (CPS) of the University of Michigan. These are generally recognized as among the best samples of the U.S. electorate, and provide a reasonable number of useful questions asked in essentially similar form over the two decades from 1952 to 1972.

Regional Differences in Historical Perspective

Our analysis of partisan change in the United States begins by sketching the changing nature of sectional differences in presidential voting, congressional voting, and party iden-

This chapter is a condensed version of a paper, presented at the 1974 meetings of the Southern Political Science Association, entitled "An Overview of American Electoral Change: 1952–1972." For those readers interested in a more detailed analysis, we invite them to examine that paper. Our bibliography at the end of this chapter is drawn from the original work. We should also note that since we presented the paper, three books have appeared dealing with substantially similar themes (Asher, 1976; Nie, Verba, and Petrocik, 1976; and Trilling, 1976). We are indebted to Karen Wehrle and Elaine Sharp for their help in organizing the data needed in writing this paper, to Stuart Rabinowitz and the Comparative Politics Discussion Group for useful comments on the manuscript, and to Barbara Higgins for her editorial assistance in condensing and editing the original manuscript. The data on which this paper is based were collected by the Center for Political Studies, which bears no responsibility for our analysis.

tification. Precisely because our survey data cover only a brief time span (1952-1972), it is necessary to view the data in relation to a much longer history of regional differences in party strength (see Figure 12-1).

In the period of classic American sectonalism, roughly 1896-1928, the South always gave a majority of its total vote to the Democratic presidential candidate, while the North never did so. During the Roosevelt era, 1932-1944, both regions supported the Democratic presidential candidate, but substantial percentage differences separated South and North in their degree of enthusiasm. The year 1948 was a critical turning point in Democratic strength within the South. As the role of the South in Democratic Party politics shifted from "a majority faction within a minority party" to a "minority [faction] within the majority [party]" (Potter, 1972:59), Southerners lost their ability to control the party

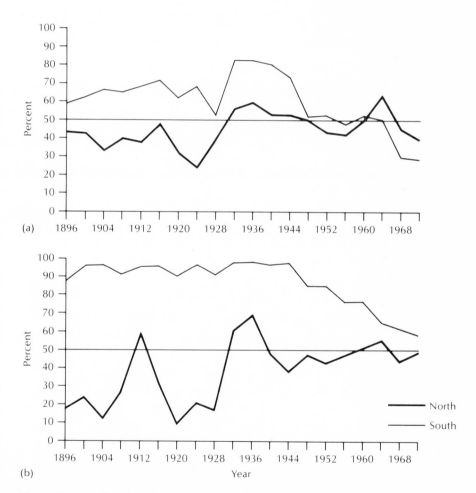

Figure 12-1   (a) Presidential voting, by region (percent Democratic). (b) Congressional voting, by region (percent Democratic). Each point is the Democratic percentage of the total popular vote for president and for the Congress.

and protect the racial interests of the white South. The drop in Southern Democratic support in 1948 produced a virtual convergence with Democratic strength in the North. And although the South was relatively more Democratic than the North during the two Eisenhower elections, the regions again converged in 1960. Since then, an even more interesting shift in the regional strength of the Democratic party has occurred. Beginning in 1964 and persisting through 1972, the North has now become relatively more Democratic than the South in presidential voting. As Ladd (1970: 293–301) and Havard (1972: 710–719) have noted, this regional transformation is of major significance in the contemporary structure of American electoral politics.

Two other indicators of underlying partisan strength are interesting because they lag behind the transformation of regionalism observed at the presidential level. In congressional voting and party identification, trends during the last 20 years show that the North and the South are coming closer together, but not yet converging. In congressional elections, the South has become far less Democratic in its popular vote (Shannon, 1972: 637–687; Wolfinger and Arseneau, 1974: 4), whereas the trend within the North is for increased Democratic strength in congressional elections. In party identification (not shown in Figure 12-1), the regions are closest in their shares of independents (Wolfinger and Arseneau, 1974: 11, f.n. 18), yet substantial differences in the traditional direction separate Democratic and Republican identifiers in the two regions. In party identificaiton, the South is still more Democratic and less Republican than the North.

The data therefore show, over all three indicators, the weakening yet continuing regional differences, the most advanced trend being the reversal of the historical tendency for the South to be more Democratic than the North in presidential voting. Given these patterns of partisan change within both regions, it is necessary to look beyond the acts of voting and the articulation of party loyalties. We need to probe the minds of our respondents to determine how they are evaluating significant political objects. Matthews and Prothro have argued that in a period of electoral change, political scientists ought to pay close attention to the political "images" held by the electorate (Matthews and Prothro, 1966a: 167; 1966b: 377–378, 392–396). How have Americans—Northern whites, Southern whites, and blacks—viewed the parties, candidates, and issues over the last two decades?

Party Images

Since 1952, SRC/CPS election studies have asked respondents a series of open-ended questions about their likes and dislikes concerning the two political parties, thereby providing a detailed data base for longitudinal studies of partisan images in the nation. Although Stokes et al. (1958), Campbell et al. (1960), Stokes (1966), and Kirkpatrick et al. (1974) have published works dealing with party images, none of these studies analyzes in depth the regional similarities or differences in party images. More directly analogous to our interests have been the studies of Matthews and Prothro (1966b), Kessel (1968), and Trilling (1974). Our discussion begins by focusing upon changes over time in the party images of whites within each of the regions, and by examining the trends among blacks across the entire nation. Our analysis is restricted to first responses to the image questions. Through this method, we should obtain a clear overview of the party images within each of these groups.

Among southern whites, there has been a substantial secular decline in the proportion of respondents who could indicate anything they liked about the Democratic Party, a drop from roughly two of three whites in 1952 to only one of three whites in 1972. Yet there has been no secular rise in the expression of discontent about the party among white Southerners; the level of dissatisfaction toward the Democratic Party was higher in 1968 than in 1972. Similarly, there is no evidence of a steadily increasing degree of approval for the Republican Party. Far more important in improving the Republican image has been the declining salience of dislikes about the GOP, from about one of two whites in 1952 to one of three whites in 1972. On balance, Southern whites evaluated the Democratic Party more favorably than the Republicans during the period 1952-1964 (see Matthews and Prothro, 1966b: 377-388), but the advantage in partisan image switched to the GOP during the 1968 and 1972 presidential elections.

Among Northern whites, there has been a fairly steady decline in the expression of approval for the Democratic Party, while dislikes about the party peaked at the end of the Truman and Johnson administrations. In general, Northern whites perceived the Democratic Party favorably until 1968. The partisan image data show no signs of growing Republican strength in the North; the highest level of approval for the party during the entire time series occurred during the Eisenhower administration. Support for the GOP was articulated by only half of the Northern whites in 1968 and dropped to under four of ten whites in 1972. Over the six elections, dislikes about the Republicans have usually been expressed by slightly less than half of the Northern whites. On balance, Northern whites gave an edge to the GOP in the elections of 1952, 1956, and 1968, and to the Democrats in 1960, 1964, and 1972.

Finally, among American blacks, the data indicate some fascinating changes over the six elections. Although blacks have had a favorable image of the Democratic Party during the entire period, the peaks of approval occurred in 1964 and 1968. In 1972, however, the percentage of blacks expressing a particular like about the Democrats dropped below the level of any previous election we have analyzed. Concomitantly, slightly less than one-fifth of the black respondents indicated some dislike about the party. As a consequence, the image of the Democratic Party among blacks, while still overwhelmingly positive, was actually weaker in the 1972 election than in any other election in our time series. Nevertheless, the strongly negative image of the Republican Party among blacks showed little sign of returning to its less negative levels of 1956 and 1960. Since 1964, roughly six of ten blacks have voiced some complaint about the Republican Party, while support for the GOP among American blacks has not regained the modest "heights" of the 1956 and 1960 elections. While blacks may be weakening in their favorable perceptions of the Democrats, they are not becoming more receptive to the Republicans.

Patterns of Partisan Evaluations by Whites Within Regions

There are a variety of situations in which one party can hold a positive lead in its image in comparison with a rival party. Setting aside differences in the magnitude of the advantage, three basic combinations are apparent. First, both parties may be viewed favorably, but one party gains because it is evaluated more favorably than its rival. In this situation, the rival party loses not because its image is composed of more dislikes than likes, but simply because the other party is more popular with the voters. Second, one party may be viewed positively, while the other party is seen negatively. Third, both parties may be evaluated negatively, but one party may gain because it is less disliked than its opponent. In this instance, the winning party benefits not so much from its absolute strength or popularity among the voters, but simply because it is less objectionable than the alternative. An electoral system composed of such parties might well be expected to alienate a large part of the electorate.

Among whites in the North and South, quite striking changes are apparent in the perceptions of the parties over the six elections (see Figure 12-2). Among Northern whites, both parties were basically liked during the period 1952–1960, with only the minor exception of an apparently even balance between likes and dislikes about the Democrats in 1952. The images of the two parties were polarized among Northern whites in 1964 and 1968, while in the 1972 election, both parties evoked more dislikes than likes (-0.5 percent for the Democrats and -6.6 percent for the Republicans). Among Southern whites, the most typical electoral situation has been the positive appraisal of one party in contrast to a negative evaluation of the rival party. This situation has most commonly favored the Democrats (1952, 1956, and 1964), but in 1972 the Republicans were viewed positively, while the Democratic Party was more often disliked than liked. There are single instances of the other two types of evaluative situations among Southern whites. In 1960, both parties were viewed favorably, with an edge to the Democrats; but in 1968, in the face of the Wallace third-party movement, which sloganized that there was "not a dime's worth of difference" between the parties, Southern whites expressed more dislikes than likes about both of the major parties.

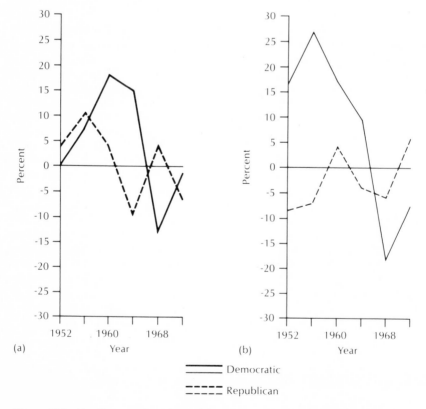

Figure 12-2 Net Democratic and Republican party images, (a) Northern whites. (b) Southern whites.

In only two elections—1968 for Southern whites and 1972 for Northern whites—were both parties viewed negatively. Schreiber (1971) noted the sharp increase in self-proclaimed independents among white Southerners in 1968, and more recently, Wolfinger and Arseneau (1974) showed a steep increase in independents among Northern whites in the 1972 election. The party image data suggest an explanation for the differential timing of the increase in independents among whites in the two regions.

The data also reveal substantial differences in how American mass publics have perceived the parties over the past two decades. Among Northern whites, the rather placid politics of the 1950s and early 1960s is paralleled in the image data; one party wins not because its opponent is unpopular, but because it is simply more favored than its rival. By 1972, however, the Democratic Party appeared to be gaining over the Republicans among Northern whites not because the Democrats were popular in their own right, but because they were less unpopular than the Republicans. Large numbers of Northern whites were apparently being "turned off" by both parties. The Democratic Party's "advantage" in 1972, therefore, was hardly a testimony to its electoral strength.

Among Southern whites, the most impressive structural change is the transformation of the Democratic Party's image from favorable to unfavorable. This trend is consistent from 1956 through 1968. And although the Democratic image among white Southerners recovered somewhat in 1972 from the depths it reached in 1968, it was still substantially negative. The data clearly indicate the waning appeal of the Democratic Party in its former sectional stronghold. However, far less secular change is apparent in the movement of the Republican Party image over the decade. During the period when the Democratic Party suffered its greatest loss in partisan image, 1964–1968, the image of the Republican Party among Southern whites also declined slightly. Although the Republican image was favorable in the 1972 election, no clear trend is apparent, and the past history of unfavorable evaluations of the GOP suggests extreme caution in projecting the persistence, much less further growth, of a favorable Republican image. In short, while the Democrats have endured massive losses of support, there seems considerable skepticism among many Southern whites that the Republicans will provide the type of party alternative they desire.

Continuity and Change in the Substance of Party Images

Thus far our analysis has described the general shape of partisan images without consideration for the substantive content of likes and dislikes. Various coding schemes have been used to organize the open-ended SRC questions. We have coded each response into nine substantive and one miscellaneous subject-matter areas: group benefits, candidate image, domestic policy, general policies, civil rights, party loyalty, foreign policy, government management, and party leaders.

Northern Whites

Considering first the substance of Democratic and Republican images among whites in the North (see Figure 12-3), it is clear that, only one component—the provision of benefits to groups (such as workers, farmers, and common people)—has generated consistently favorable responses to the Democrats and unfavorable ones to the Republicans. The partisan trends on this component are worthy of comment. From 1956 to 1968, there appeared to be an erosion of support for the Democrats, as well as a reduction of Republican liabilities. The 1972 data, however, show a striking reversal of this tendency. The performance in office of the Nixon administration apparently activated a traditional complaint against the GOP and stimulated a more positive appreciation of the Democratic Party's role in providing group benefits. In short, the data show a strong revitalization of a component of partisan images that had been the heart of the Democratic Party's appeal since the New Deal.

Four components of the party images—foreign policy, general policies, government management, and domestic policy—have usually provided gains for the GOP. But only two of these components, foreign policy and general policies, have provided consistent gains sizeable enough to be classified as "moderate." The domestic-policy component appears to have been realigned as a Republican asset in 1960, but the Republican advantage on this component—as in the case of government management—had dissipated by 1972.

Three other components show quite different patterns. Civil rights has had very little impact on the images of the parties among Northern whites. The importance of traditional party loyalty has varied widely, reaching its "peaks" in the landslides of 1956 and 1964. Interestingly enough, however, party loyalty was much weaker in the 1972 landslide— additional evidence (if more were needed) that the Nixon election was not a "party" victory. Finally, there has been enormous variation in the significance, vis-à-vis party images, of the images of specific candidates. Although in every election the Democratic candidate has elicited more negative than positive comments, there is a striking contrast between the positive contribution of the Eisenhower candidacy to the image of the Republican Party and the negative contributions of the Goldwater and Nixon (in 1968) candidacies.

While the Democratic Party's appeal among Northern whites seems largely a residue of its New Deal heritage, the substance of Republican support consists of the foreign-policy and general-policies components. Our analysis does not show the emergence of any new substantive area of GOP appeal, suggesting that the party has failed to align itself with any major set of new issues that could serve as the base for an expanding Republican constituency. Events since 1972 have no doubt further eroded Republican strength in the North.

Southern Whites

Among Southern whites, those components of party images that historically have been most favorable to the Democratic Party—group benefits, party loyalty, and domestic policy—are clearly waning as sources of Democratic advantage (see Figure 12-3). As in the North, the component most favorable to the Democratic Party over the entire time

---

Figure 12-3 Components of net Republican and Democratic party images, Northern and Southern whites. (a) Group benefits. (b) Candidate image. (c) Domestic policy. (d) General policies. (e) Civil rights. (f) Party loyalty. (g) Foreign policy. (h) Government management. (i) Party leaders.

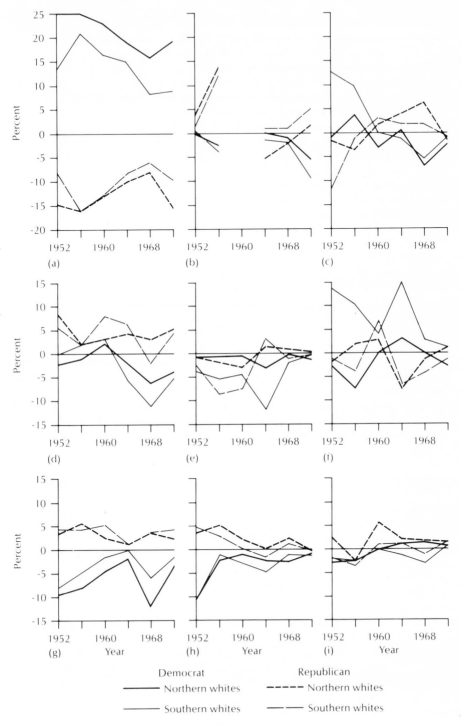

period is group benefits. As in the North, with the exception of the 1972 election, there has been a pronounced secular decline in the salience of this image component, both as an assest to the Democrats and as a liability to the Republicans.

Perhaps even more striking as an example of change in the substance of partisan images is the fading tendency of white Southerners to mention tradtional party loyalty as a reason to support the Democratic party. The last hurrah for this component appears to have been 1964, when the presence of a native white Southerner at the head of the national party ticket apparently reactivated considerable feelings of party loyalty. Matthews and Prothro (1966b: 385-387) have previously emphasized the importance of this image component in 1964, and our analysis documents the subsequent decline of this appeal. As in the North, the domestic-policy component displayed signs of a partial realignment. The partisan advantage arising from the domestic-issues component shifted from the Democrats to the Republicans in 1960; by 1972, however, this component had become neutralized.

Concerning the views of Southern whites toward the Republican Party, it is clear that the favorable substance of the GOP image in the South usually has been composed of the same ingredients we observed in the North: foreign policy, general or "ideological" policies, candidate evaluations, and government management. Of these four components, the most consistent and strongest advantages have usually been based on opinions about foreign and general policies.

Finally, our data highlight the varying impact of racial concerns on party images. The racial policies of both parties have suffered consistently unfavorable evaluations by the white South during the six presidential elections considered, with the single exception of the Republican Party in 1964. The data also show the declining salience of likes and dislikes about racial policies in affecting the images of the parties. We did not anticipate such a marked decline in the expression of racial concerns in the 1968 and 1972 open-ended party-image questions. The party-image data do not indicate that race has been a realigning issue among white Southerners in the sense of producing large numbers of whites who are enthusiastic about the racial policies of the Republicans.

Blacks

Blacks have held, on balance, positive evaluations of the Democrats and negative views about the Republicans over the entire period studied. Before 1964, however, a number of components usually favored the Republican Party: foreign policy, candidate images, government, management and, most importantly, racial policies. Particularly in 1956 and 1960, Democratic strength among American blacks did not rest on civil rights, but rather on the "bread and butter" components—domestic policy, and group benefits—and traditional party loyalty.

The civil-rights activism of the Kennedy and Johnson administrations from 1961 to 1964 sharply clarified, among American blacks, differences between the parties over civil rights. Not until 1964 did references to civil rights by blacks become a source of strong Democratic support. The popularity of the Democratic Party, however, did not rest solely on civil rights. The image data demonstrate the continuation of gains from the components previously favoring the Democrats (group benefits, domestic issues, and party loyalty), as well as the activation of new components (candidate images, general policies, and miscellaneous). Matthews and Prothro's analysis of the impact of civil rights policies upon the party images of Southern blacks seems generalizable to blacks across the nation in 1964 and 1968: "The national Democratic party's record on civil rights was the major cause of the increasingly favorable attitudes of southern Negroes toward the party, but this civil rights record resulted in *generalized approval* of the party and its ways, not just an improved image in the civil rights field" (Matthews and Prothro, 1966b: 388). In 1972, however, as the salience of civil rights declined among American blacks, there was also a drop in the number of nonracial components producing moderate or strong gains for the Democratic Party.

The Convergence of Party Images

To what extent are whites in the two regions converging in their evaluations of the parties? Substantial differences existed between the two groups in the 1950s, with Southern whites more supportive of the Democrats. In 1960, the difference was considerably muted, and Northern whites even appeared to be slightly more pro-Democratic than Southern whites. From 1964 through 1972, there was not a precise convergence in the net image of the two parties, but rather the persistence, in diluted form, of a "new" type of regional cleavage. With the single exception of the 1968 election, when Wallace was also running, the white South became the more Republican of the two groups.

We can further clarify the convergence patterns by looking at the net images of the two parties separately. The net strength of the Democratic party (see Figure 4a) was quite different among Northern and Southern whites before 1960. In the 1960-1972 presidential elections, the image of the Democratic Party was relatively similar for both groups of whites, with the North always more favorably disposed to the Democratic Party. No similar convergence pattern or consistent partisan direction appears in the net evaluations of the Republican Party (see Figure 12-4b). The differences between the regions were large in 1952, 1956, 1968, and 1972. In the former three elections, the GOP was viewed more favorably by Northern whites; Southern whites gave more support to the Republican Party in 1972.

Examining the net patterns of image support provides an overview of regional differences. Any serious examination of convergence, however, must also examine the substance underlying the net figures. Two indices have been used to calculate similarities in how the parties have been perceived over the six presidential elections. One measures the extent to which the general image evaluations of the parties on the ten components correspond, and the other measures the similarity in the specific reasons for liking and disliking the parties, controlling for the net partisanship of the image. *Both indices show a virtually continual convergence over time* (see Figure 12-5). Given the fairly inconsistent pattern in the aggregate images, this result is striking. Examination of the content of the images reveals that regional differences are indeed diminishing.

The reasons for the convergence of the two groups become clear upon analyzing the convergence patterns for each of the nine image components that represent evaluations of the Democratic Party by whites in both regions. In five components—government management, leaders, candidate images, general policies, and foreign policy—the Democratic Party has been perceived similarly by whites in both regions during most of the elections. Three other image components, which had formerly been sources of rather substantial regional differences, were now moving toward or already approximating convergence:

domestic policy traditional party loyalty, and civil rights. Two of these components, domestic policies and traditional loyalty, had formerly favored the Democratic Party among Southern whites more than among Northern whites. On the other hand, the racial issue, which had always hurt the Democratic Party more among Southerners, reached its peak of regional differentiation in 1964 and has since elicited roughly similar evaluations in the two regions. Finally, the single component that had traditionally been more favorable to the image of the party among Northerners—group benefits—was the only substantive area in which sizeable differences between the regions persisted. But even here, both regions gave a decided advantage to the Democratic Party in each year.

In general, convergence tendencies among the components of the Republican partisan image for Northern and Southern whites are less regular than, but generally similar to, those of the Democratic image components. The most interesting developments in the Republican Party image have concerned the evaluations of the party on racial matters and general or "ideological" policies. Typically, Northern whites, in contrast to Southern whites, have not given racial matters much prominence in their evaluations of the GOP. Before the Goldwater candidacy in 1964, Southern whites criticized the Republicans' policies on civil rights. Surprisingly, perhaps Southern whites continued to express more dislikes than likes about Republican racial policies in the 1968 and 1972 elections, although at a greatly reduced level of salience. While considerably more attention needs to be given to the role of racial concerns than we are able to provide in this chapter, the

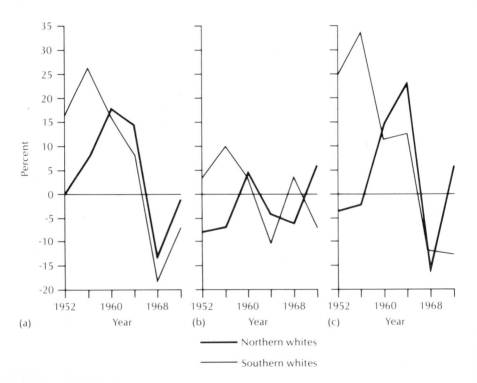

Figure 12-4 Party images, Northern and Southern whites, (a) Net Democratic image. (b) Net Republican image. (c) Total party image.

survey data suggest that references to Republican racial policies have not served as an *explicit* realigning component of the party's image in these two recent elections.

Another surprising development is the shift in the evaluation by Southern whites of the GOP's general policies in 1968. Although white Southerners had been more likely than their Northern counterparts to praise the party for its ideological positions in 1960 and 1964, the Republican Party was actually perceived negatively on this component by Southern whites in 1968. Perhaps the Wallace third-party movement sufficiently undermined the GOP's conservative credentials among white Southerners; in any event, by 1972, whites in the region were once more approving of the party's general or "ideological" policies.

To summarize our analysis, an overall pattern of convergence is apparent between Northern and Southern whites with respect to the substance of party images. There seems to be every reason to believe that the two groups are becoming increasingly alike in the way in which they view evaluate the political parties. Some differences still persist, however, and when we turn to specific issue questions, we shall see that some regional differences remain substantial.

Presidential Candidate Images

We shall now examine trends in the shape and content of candidate images. Since 1952, respondents in each of the SRC/CPS election studies have been asked to express their likes and dislikes about the candidates for president.

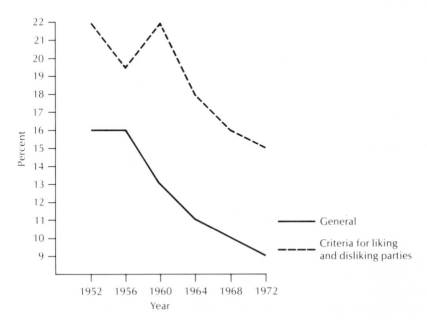

Figure 12-5 Party image convergence for Northern compared with Southern whites.

The previous findings in the literature are of special interest. First, as shown in Figure 12-3, the image of the Republican presidential candidate has typically been much stronger than the image of the Democratic contender—with the obvious exception of 1964 (Stokes, 1966: 22; Kirkpatrick et al., 1974: 11-12). Second, the Republican candidate has usually been evaluated far more favorably than the Republican Party. Third, over the six elections considered, there has been a remarkable divergence, across the nation, in both the partisan advantage of the candidate and the party images. In four elections—1952, 1956, 1960, and 1972—the electorate gave a net advantage to the Democratic Party while simultaneously providing a net advantage to the Republican presidential candidate. Because these findings are based on samples of the entire electorate, we want to determine if these generalizations apply equally to the attitudes of whites within the two regions.

Among Northern whites, the Republican presidential candidate has enjoyed an advantage over his Democratic opponent in every election between 1952 and 1972, with the exception of 1964. Among Southern whites, the only deviation from the national pattern occurred in 1952, when the Democratic candidate held an extremely slim edge. Over the last five elections considered, therefore, whites in both regions have essentially agreed on the more desirable candidate, and have typically evaluated the Republican candidate more favorably than the Republican Party. With the exception of 1964, the gap between Republican candidate image and Republican Party image has been greater among Southern whites than among northern whites.

Figure 12-6 clarifies the electoral situations in which the partisan advantages of the party and candidate images have differed among whites in the two regions. According to our data, only in 1960 and in 1972 have Northern whites diverged in their partisan evaluations of the candidates and parties. In both elections, the Democratic Party held a net advantage, while its presidential candidate suffered a net disadvantage—a difference that was particularly striking in 1972. Among Southern whites, however, partisan divergences in the net advantage of party and candidate images appeared only in 1956 and 1960 (see Figure 12-7). Thus when both party and candidate images are examined according to the attitudes of whites in the two regions, only a single election—1960 Nixon-Kennedy—evoked different partisan advantages in both regions.

Candidate Polarization

Among Northern and Southern whites, there is an increasing tendency to hold polarized views of the candidates: one candidate is appraised positively, while the other candidate is negatively evaluated. The candidate images of white Northerners were polarized in the elections of 1956, 1964, 1968, and 1972. Among Southern whites, the candidate images were polarized during the 1960-1972 presidential elections. The extent of polarization in both regions was particularly striking in the 1972 election. Nixon's commanding lead was not simply a result of McGovern's weakness, but also a function of the incumbent's increasing strength. Moreover, Southern whites evaluated Nixon in 1972 more favorably than any other presidential candidate, Democratic or Republican, in the entire time period.

To probe the structure underlying the candidate images, we examined the substantive content of likes and dislikes by classifying the candidate image responses into the same nine categories we used previously for the party images. The electorate's perception of differences in personal qualities has consistently been the single most important factor in determining which candidate was perceived more favorably. This was especially true in

1956 and 1972 when the Eisenhower and Nixon landslides were heavily based on the electorate's perception of vast differences in the competence and character of the rival candidates. In two other elections, 1960 and 1964, the advantages derived from the candidate qualities component roughly approximated the total advantages of the other eight components. On these eight components, the patterns are, for the most part, muted versions of the trends previously observed for party images, although some minor differences do exist.

Evaluations of Parties' Potential Performance in Resolving the Nation's Most Important Problems

Enduring political change will be founded, at least in part, on real political issues. A vast and impressive literature has developed over the last 10 years, which attests to the substantial role of issues in electoral campaigns (see Kessel, 1972; Miller et al., 1973; Kove-

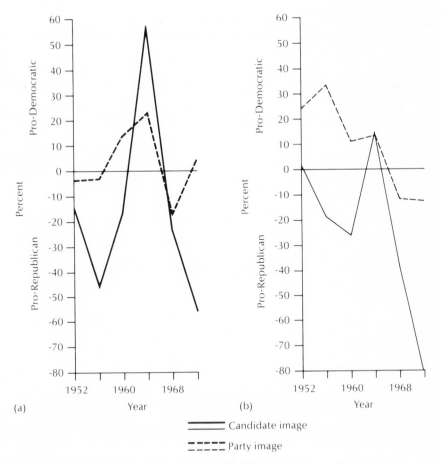

Figure 12-6 Party and candidate images, 1952–1972. (a) Northern whites. (b) Southern whites.

nock et al., 1974; Rabinowitz, 1973; Nie and Andersen, 1974). We shall now consider the effects of political issues on political change in the United States.

In each of the four presidential electoral surveys from 1960 to 1972, respondents were asked to identify the most important problems the federal government should take care of.

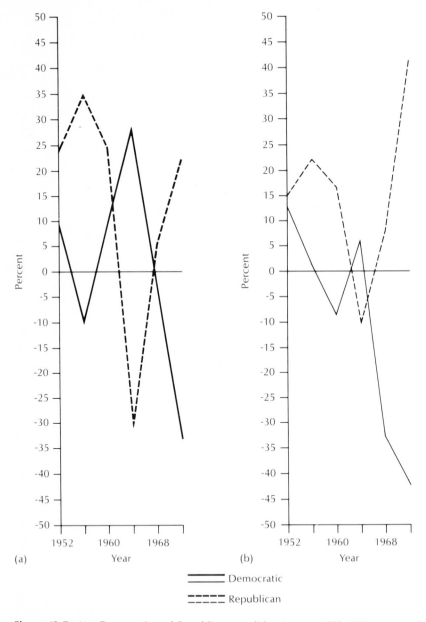

Figure 12-7 Net Democratic and Republican candidate images, 1952–1972. (a) Northern whites. (b) Southern whites.

This question was followed in each survey by a second question asking which party would perform "most like what the respondents wanted." The question has an impressive relation to voting choices and is a very useful vehicle for examining the rise and fall of critical issues and their partisan impact (see Repass, 1971: 389-400). Table 12-1 presents the distribution of responses by white Northerners to these two questions for each of the four elections.

In the table, the columns break down the responses according to the party perceived as best able to cope with the problem. Hence, 10.9 percent of the white Northerners responding to this question identified a social welfare problem as most important and felt that the Democrats were most likely to act on the problem in the preferred manner.

In terms of the net benefits to the parties over the four elections, very sharp swings in partisan strength are apparent. Despite the volatility in partisan strength, there is considerable stability in this picture of overall change. In the last four of the elections considered, only five categories received over 10 percent of the responses: social welfare; racial problems; public order; economic business, and consumer affairs; and foreign affairs. The Democrats have enjoyed an advantage on the social-welfare category in all four surveys. The Republicans have had an advantage on the foreign-affairs question in three of the four surveys, and on the public-order problem in both of the surveys (1968 and 1972) in which public order had any real significance. For economic, business, and consumer affairs, the net advantage to either party has never exceeded 4 percent; on the racial question, the net advantage exceeded 4 percent only in 1964, when the Democrats held a 5.4 percent edge. Overall, the data portend no clear future advantage to either party.

The clearest trend over the entire 16-year period is the general rise of the neutrals— individuals who saw neither party as doing what they wanted. The data are striking and correspond to the rise in negative opinions of the parties we have observed in the analysis of party images. Both the rise of neutrals and the increasingly negative referents to the parties bear a similarity to Miller's findings on governmental trust. Miller has shown that between 1964 and 1972, individual trust in government decreased markedly (Miller, 1974; Converse, 1972). Indeed, if neither party can provide desirable alternative solutions to the problems an individual feels are most important for the government to do something about, it is reasonable for the individual to view the parties unfavorably and lose faith in the government.

The partisan direction of net advantage for white Southerners is identical to that for Northern whites. However, there are substantial differences. In the North, the Democratic advantage increased from 1960 to 1964; in the South, the Democratic advantage decreased over the same time period. In the North, the Republican advantage dropped between 1968 and 1972; in the South, the decline was much weaker. The Nixon administration seems to have been more successful in retaining strength among Southern than among Northern whites. In Figure 12-8, the net partisan strength is plotted over time for each of the three demographic groups. The overall pattern of partisan strength is quite similar to that of party image. In 1964, the South, for the first time, becomes substantially more Republican than the North, a "new" regional difference which has persisted through the 1968 and 1972 elections.

For Southern whites, the same five categories—social welfare; racial problems; public order; economic, business, and consumer affairs; and foreign affairs—received 10 percent or more of the mentions in at least one year. Internal to the categories, however, we again see real differences between the regions. The social welfare category was the main source of Democratic strength in every election in the North. In the South, social welfare was not a source of dependable strength for the Democrats. In both 1960 and 1972, this category

Table 12-1 Most Important Problem: Responses of Northern Whites (in percentages)

Category[a]	Democratic[b]	Neutral	Republican[b]	Democratic-Republican Net[c]
1960				
Social welfare	16.9	10.9	3.9	2.1	8.8
Agricultural and natural resources	7.4	2.5	2.1	2.8	−0.3
Labor and union management	1.2	0.7	0.0	0.5	0.2
Racial problems	0.7	0.3	0.3	0.1	0.2
Public order	0.0	0.0	0.0	0.0	0.0
Economic, business and consumer affairs	5.9	2.6	0.8	2.5	0.1
Foreign affairs	59.5	17.8	18.0	23.7	−5.9
National defense	8.4	2.8	2.0	3.6	−0.8
Functioning of government	0.1	0.0	0.0	0.1	−0.1
Total	100.1	37.6	27.1	35.4	2.2
1964				
Social welfare	25.1	16.2	6.0	2.9	13.3
Agricultural and natural resources	2.3	0.6	1.2	0.5	0.1
Labor and union management	0.9	0.1	0.3	0.5	−0.4
Racial problems	20.9	10.4	5.5	5.0	5.4
Public order	0.2	0.0	0.2	0.0	0.0
Economic, business and consumer affairs	9.4	2.0	3.9	3.5	−1.5
Foreign affairs	33.8	12.5	10.9	10.4	2.1
National defense	5.7	1.3	1.7	2.7	−1.4
Functioning of government	2.0	0.2	0.6	1.2	−1.0
Total	100.3	43.3	30.3	26.7	16.6

[a] Percentage who mentioned category.
[b] Percentage who saw party as most likely to do what they wanted.
[c] Difference between percentage preferring Democrats and percentage preferring Republicans. Positive values indicate a positive association between the variables; minus signs indicate a negative association.

was entirely neutral; in 1968 it generated a very modest 0.4 percent advantage to the Democrats. Only in 1964, when the Democrats had a 4.8 percent advantage, did this category provide any real gain. In every year, the social-welfare category was less salient in the South, and among those to whom it was salient, it was less pro-Democratic; this includes 1960, a year of general Democratic strength in the region. The differences between the regions on this component are of substantial importance. Although other investigators have argued that Southern whites are not significantly different from Northern whites on questions of social welfare (see Key, 1963: 103-105; Hamilton, 1972: 283-286; Rudder, 1974), these data support the opposite view.

No area has received more attention in evaluating Southern political change than race. The data presented here show only a mild net advantage to either party, in any

Table 12-1 (cont.) Most Important Problem: Responses of Northern Whites (in percentages)

	Category[a]	Democratic[b]	Neutral	Republican[b]	Democratic-Republican Net[c]
1968					
Social welfare	9.9	4.0	3.5	2.4	1.6
Agricultural and natural resources	1.8	0.2	0.9	0.7	−0.5
Labor and union management	0.1	0.0	0.1	0.0	0.0
Racial problems	12.1	3.2	5.4	3.5	−0.3
Public order	16.0	1.3	7.5	7.2	−5.9
Economic, business and consumer affairs	6.5	0.5	2.1	3.9	−3.4
Foreign affairs	50.8	9.3	22.2	19.3	−10.0
National defense	1.2	0.1	0.8	0.3	−0.2
Functioning of government	1.7	0.1	0.9	0.7	−0.6
Total	100.1	18.7	43.4	38.0	−19.3
1972					
Social welfare	10.8	4.9	4.6	1.3	3.6
Agricultural and natural resources	3.6	0.6	2.1	0.9	−0.3
Labor and union management	0.2	0.0	0.2	0.0	0.0
Racial problems	7.6	1.9	3.6	2.1	−0.2
Public order	16.9	1.7	10.6	4.6	−2.9
Economic, business and consumer affairs	22.6	7.0	9.1	6.5	0.5
Foreign affairs	32.1	4.9	13.9	13.3	−8.4
National defense	1.6	0.6	0.6	0.4	0.2
Functioning of government	4.7	1.7	1.9	1.1	0.6
Total	100.1	23.3	46.6	30.2	−6.9

year, based on the category of race. Overall, the Southern pattern is quite similar to the Northern one. The exceptions are the greater importance given to this issue by Southerners in 1960 and the greater Republican advantage, based on this issue, among Southerners in every survey since 1964—a trend quite comparable to the one we observed in the party-image data. However, a caveat is in order. The most important question of the survey asked what the respondent feels is "the most important problem for the government in Washington to take care of." It is quite likely that for many Southern whites to whom the racial question is critical, civil rights is an area in which they would *not* like activity on the part of the federal government. Hence the wording of the question is biased against an expression of the opinions of white racial conservatives. When we consider specific issue questions in the following section, we shall confront this problem once again.

In analyzing overall trends among Southern whites, it appears that the South is moving substantially in the Republican direction. In 1960, the Democrats were "preferred to" or "even with" the Republicans in every category. In 1968, they had an advantage only in the social welfare category (0.4 percent), and, in 1972, only in national defense and in functioning of government (1.4 percent and 0.7 percent). Although difficult to predict in an area as potentially volatile as the electorate's perception of the most important problems, it does seem that Southern whites have become substantially pro-Republican. At the least, Southern whites are, and probably will remain—barring unexpected presidential candidacies from either party—more favorably disposed toward the Republicans than are whites in the North.

Finally, Southern whites are similar to Northern whites in their increasing tendency to take a neutral stand—refusing to align with a particular party—on the issues they consider most important. Although the trend in the South was reversed in 1964, the increase was substantial in 1968 and continued in 1972.

For blacks, the data corresponding to most important problem are very similar to the party-image data. Only somewhat Democratic in 1960 (largely because of social welfare), by 1964 blacks were drawn dramatically into the Democratic camp. Since 1964, blacks have remained solidly, though decreasingly, Democratic. Of interest is the rise and fall of the salience of the race issue across the four surveys. For blacks, race was the most critical issue in 1960 and 1964; however, by 1968 racial references had fallen below foreign

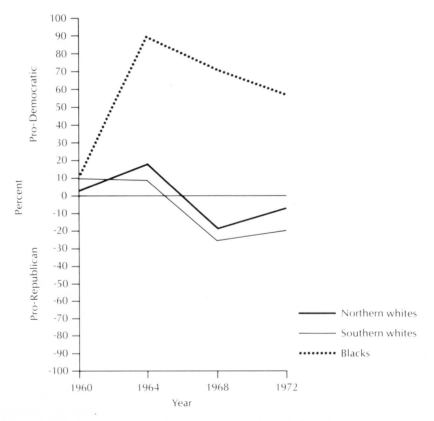

Figure 12-8 Overall partisan advantage on perception of solving important problems.

affairs, and by 1972 below public order; foreign affairs; and economic, business, and consumer problems. The trend of decreasing reference to explicitly racial problems among blacks is similar to that of the nation as a whole (see Figure 12–9) and seems to be of substantial social importance.

Questions on Specific Issues

What are the attitudes of the American public on major political issues and how have these attitudes changed over the past two decades? To answer this question we must turn to the survey questions on specific issues. Seven questions have appeared on at least three of the six SRC presidential election surveys. These all deal with domestic policy, and fall roughly into three categories: social welfare, civil rights, and power of the national government. There are two social-welfare questions: one concerns subsidized medical care, the other federal guarantees of employment. There are three race-related questions, dealing with school integration, fair employment opportunities for blacks, and the rights of blacks to purchase homes. Finally, there are two government-power questions: one deals directly with government power, and the other concerns federal aid to education. During the period from 1952 to 1972, there are no clear trends on either the social-welfare or government-power question. In each instance, we find blacks considerably more supportive of government involvement than either Northern or Southern whites. Among the whites, Northerners are generally more supportive of government actions than Southerners (see Table 12–2).

The most noteworthy trends occur in the civil-rights area. The civil-rights questions, particularly school integration and open housing, do much to illuminate the very delicate nature of the racial issue in American society. It is noteworthy—in light of the marked

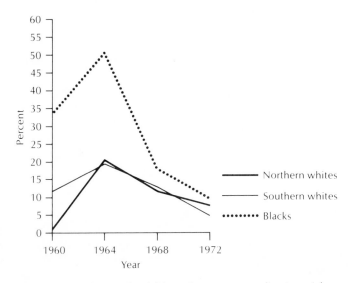

Figure 12-9 Salience of racial issue (percent responding in racial-related category).

Table 12-2 Public Attitudes on Major Political Issues

		White Northerners			White Southerners			Blacks		
		Left[a]	Neutral[a]	Right[a]	Left[a]	Neutral[a]	Right[a]	Left[a]	Neutral[a]	Right[a]
Social Welfare										
Medical	1956	56.7	10.3	33.0	63.9	8.5	27.6	90.7	5.4	3.9
care	1960	63.6	13.9	22.4	60.2	11.8	28.0	96.2	2.6	1.3
	1964	56.2	7.8	36.0	50.9	8.5	40.6	92.1	2.9	5.0
	1968	57.8	7.7	34.5	56.5	5.8	37.7	95.4	1.5	3.1
	1972[b]	46.0	15.3	38.7	31.2	15.0	53.8	71.7	7.1	21.2
Guaranteed	1956	58.8	7.6	33.6	64.4	9.3	26.3	91.0	4.5	4.5
Job	1960	62.4	10.3	27.3	60.5	7.1	32.4	91.8	3.2	5.1
	1964[b]	31.2	14.3	54.6	28.1	11.9	60.0	81.6	6.1	12.2
	1968	31.0	13.1	55.9	25.3	12.8	61.9	82.0	6.8	11.3
	1972	28.1	25.4	46.5	22.0	20.4	57.6	77.4	13.9	8.7
Civil Rights										
School	1956	47.3	7.5	45.2	25.3	5.1	69.6	63.9	9.0	27.0
integration	1960	52.4	7.9	39.8	24.1	7.8	68.1	70.2	7.1	22.7
	1964[b]	49.4	9.7	40.9	20.0	5.5	74.5	81.2	4.5	14.3
	1968	41.7	8.3	50.0	23.3	7.2	69.5	89.9	3.6	6.5
	1972	41.7	8.0	50.3	22.2	7.3	70.5	80.8	6.9	12.2
Open	1964	71.9	—	28.1	35.7	—	64.3	97.9	—	2.1
housing	1968	79.1	—	20.9	50.4	—	49.6	99.3	—	0.7
	1972	86.3	—	13.7	62.4	—	37.6	99.6	—	0.4
Fair	1956	69.4	7.1	23.5	60.6	11.6	27.8	97.1	2.1	0.7
employment	1960	73.5	8.7	17.7	53.0	10.5	36.5	97.6	0.0	2.4
	1964[b]	42.5	9.9	47.6	24.9	5.9	69.2	91.4	3.3	5.3
	1968	40.6	9.3	50.1	30.6	3.9	65.5	88.4	2.2	9.4
	1972	47.2	8.2	44.5	37.5	7.9	54.6	91.0	0.0	9.0
Government Power										
Aid to	1956	73.4	9.6	17.0	71.6	9.4	19.1	88.0	8.3	3.8
education	1960	59.3	10.2	30.5	52.7	18.6	28.7	90.0	6.7	3.3
	1964[b]	36.0	6.4	57.6	25.8	3.9	70.4	70.8	4.4	24.8
	1968	31.2	6.2	62.7	23.0	4.2	72.8	82.6	2.5	14.9
	1972	—	—	—	—	—	—	—	—	—
Government	1964	52.4	4.7	42.9	29.0	4.7	66.3	90.0	0.0	10.0
power	1968	40.5	3.6	55.8	26.4	3.7	69.8	81.6	3.4	14.9
	1972	37.9	5.1	57.0	32.2	5.0	62.8	48.2	5.9	45.9

[a]"Left," "Neutral," and "Right" refer to the proportionate division of respondents along each of the seven item scales, ranging from the most liberal to the most conservative alternative on each of the policy dimensions used in the questions.
[b]Years in which major changes in wording occurred. On only two of the seven questions (open housing and government power) was wording consistent over all surveys. For complete wording of each of the questions in each survey, see Black and Rabinowitz (1974, Appendix).

legal, social, and population (replacement of the aged with the younger segment) changes that have occurred—how little the distribution of the two white groups has changed on the question of school integration over the past two decades. If anything, the data show a decline, among northern whites, in sentiment favorable to school integration. In marked contrast are responses to the open-housing question, which have become dramatically pro-integration among both Northern and Southern whites since that question was first asked in 1964.

Why do these differences appear? The school-integration question deals specifically with the enforcement role of the federal government (see also Campbell, 1971: 129). The open-housing question is largely symbolic, dealing only with rights. It is also likely that the type of activity associated with enforced integration has changed substantially over the time frame, with busing a component by 1972. In addition, to the extent that objections to enforced integration are rooted in perceptions of blacks as lower-class individuals who would detract from the educational quality of the schools, the school-integration question is related to the open-housing question.

The three demographic groups differ more clearly on these civil-rights questions than on questions of either social welfare or government power. Blacks are uniformly more favorably disposed to school integration, open housing, and fair employment than either of the white groups, a fact that is not surprising. Nor is the substantial difference between Northern and Southern whites surprising. It is striking to see how the regional differences have been maintained over the time frame. Only on the open-housing question, where the 1964 difference was 35.8 percent and the 1972 difference was 23.9 percent, do we see any tendency toward convergence. However, 1964 was a year of generally high regional divergence on race-related responses, and Northern whites were starting to approach full consensus on this issue.

The overall picture on the civil-rights question is complex. Other analyses have demonstrated a very consistent liberalization of white attitudes on any measure in which federal enforcement is not a significant component (Greely, 1974: 299-319). Campbell has shown that the most dramatic changes are taking place among the college-educated young. In addition, he has found that changes within this group are resistant to erosion as the individuals age (Campbell, 1971: 54-67). Overall, there seems little doubt that overt racial bigotry is becoming unacceptable to increasing numbers of Americans, a trend that should continue over time. However, the role the federal government should play in encouraging racial equality is still a matter of considerable dispute, and the future of white and black attitudes is difficult to gauge. Clearly, considerable change has taken place; nevertheless, the society is hardly free of racial conflict, and regional differences concerning the status of blacks still persist.

Issues, Vote, and Party Identification

Analysis of trends in public attitudes toward important issues is of interest because it provides a sense of the changing climates of opinion among sets of individuals. To be of political relevance, however, issues must be related to individual political behavior. In this section, we shall examine the relationship between issue positions and presidential voting and party identification for the two white subgroups. We have not analyzed blacks because black attitudes are too homogeneous to allow for meaningful analysis.

Table 12-3 shows the correlations (Tau and Gamma) between each of the seven issues and presidential voting and party identification (the higher the correlations, the stronger the associations). In addition, where data are available, we show the correlations "correcting" for an individual's perception of party positions on the issues. This entailed the use of a second question asking each individual to distinguish between the parties on particular issues. Each individual was assigned to a Democratic, Republican, or neutral category,

Table 12-3 Correlations Between Issues and Party Identification and Vote for Northern and Southern Whites[a]

		Party Identification								Presidential Preference							
		Raw Issue				Proximity Issue				Raw Issue				Proximity Issue			
		Tau C		Gamma		Tau C		Gamma		Tau C		Gamma		Tau C		Gamma	
		N	S	N	S	N	S	N	S	N	S	N	S	N	S	N	S
Social Welfare																	
Medical care	1956	.20	.14	.27	.24	.38	.26	.56	.49	.19	.24	.39	.46	.42	.26	.73	.51
	1960	.18	.10	.27	.15	.40	.24	.51	.34	.17	.31	.32	.52	.48	.50	.71	.78
	1964	.33	.23	.46	.36	.42	.23	.51	.29	.46	.26	.75	.44	.53	.33	.77	.48
	1968	.25	.20	.35	.30	.35	.26	.41	.38	.29	.22	.52	.47	.42	.39	.60	.55
	1972	.23	-.08	.29	-.12	.32	.14	.38	.19	.22	.14	.38	.35	.35	.16	.57	.42
Guaranteed job	1956	.14	.12	.21	.20	.53	.53	.66	.71	.11	.12	.23	.23	.55	.65	.85	.86
	1960	.18	.04	.27	.07	.35	.18	.43	.24	.25	.11	.46	.20	.44	.18	.63	.28
	1964	.19	.20	.26	.32	.20	.03	.25	.04	.25	.22	.48	.39	.23	.17	.37	.26
	1968	.13	.03	.18	.05	.20	.02	.24	.02	.15	.04	.27	.08	.19	.08	.29	.13
	1972	.17	.05	.20	.08	.22	.21	.28	.23	.21	.13	.50	.21	.28	.17	.61	.40

School integration																
1956	.02	.02	.03	.04	.42	.33	.55	.46	.01	.00	.03	.00	.43	.46	.74	.69
1960	−.00	−.06	−.00	−.10	.12	.22	.19	.41	.09	−.09	.16	−.18	.13	.26	.28	.52
1964	.08	.04	.12	.08	.16	.03	.20	.04	.17	.11	.32	.27	.28	.08	.45	.12
1968	.09	.04	.13	.07	.21	.08	.25	.10	.16	.14	.29	.25	.25	.18	.39	.31
1972	.05	−.06	.08	−.10	NA	NA	NA	NA	.17	.07	.32	.22	NA	NA	NA	NA
Open housing[a]																
1964	−.06	−.10	−.10	−.14	NA	NA	NA	NA	.01	.15	.04	.32	NA	NA	NA	NA
1968	+.03	+.03	+.00	+.03	NA	NA	NA	NA	.06	.02	.19	.04	NA	NA	NA	NA
1972	−.06	−.13	−.14	−.17	NA	NA	NA	NA	.01	.11	.06	.38	NA	NA	NA	NA
Fair employment																
1956	.04	−.03	.08	−.05	.41	.38	.56	.59	.05	.01	.12	.02	.43	.48	.76	.77
1960	.04	−.09	.08	−.13	.36	.15	.50	.26	.08	−.04	.19	−.07	.39	.01	.66	.03
1964	.17	−.00	.23	−.01	.20	.01	.24	.01	.21	.12	.38	.28	.25	.15	.42	.23
1968	.12	.04	.17	.06	.17	.03	.20	.04	.18	.13	.30	.27	.20	.11	.31	.18
1972	.06	−.01	.08	−.02	NA	NA	NA	NA	.14	.12	.27	.31	NA	NA	NA	NA
Government Power																
Aid to education																
1956	.09	.01	.24	.02	.45	.41	.60	.59	.09	−.01	.25	−.03	.43	.50	.74	.78
1960	.25	.16	.45	.23	.38	.16	.46	.26	.26	.21	.45	.33	.42	.26	.63	.50
1964	.24	.13	.49	.25	.17	−.06	.20	−.07	.24	.19	.49	.43	.11	−.05	.19	−.07
1968	.19	.02	.42	.04	.00	−.17	.00	−.21	.23	.13	.43	.29	.03	−.05	.05	−.08
Government power																
1964	.37	.22	.52	.40	.40	.19	.47	.24	.49	.43	.80	.76	.44	.25	.64	.36
1968	.22	.29	.33	.53	.20	.16	.24	.19	.26	.44	.48	.74	.26	.20	.41	.31
1972	−.01	.00	−.01	.00	.18	.07	.23	.12	−.09	.01	−.18	.04	.15	.07	.26	.18

[a] Positive values indicate a positive association between the items correlated; minus signs indicate a negative association.

depending on which party most closely approximated his position. Correlations to this variable, which we call "proximity issue," should provide a clearer sense of the relationships between issues and other behavior because the variable takes into account each individual's perceptions.

Issues and Presidential Preference

A common theme running through much of the issue and realignment literature is the critical nature of the 1964 election. Across almost all the issues, the correlations between the respondents' issue position ("raw issue") and their presidential preference peak or approach their strongest relationship in 1964. In the social-welfare area, however, the post-1964 period does not seem very different from the pre-1964 period, at least for Northern whites. In fact, only in the civil-rights area is 1964 clearly critical. Pomper (1972) has shown that in 1964 the public first began to perceive significant differences between the parties on civil-rights issues. The correlations that appear in this year reflect that perception. But if we compare the proximity-issue correlations for civil-rights issues, we see little evidence to suggest that in terms of their own perceptions, people were voting with any greater emphasis on these issues in 1964 than they had previously. Indeed, over the complete set of issues, no evidence is available for any increase in "issue voting" over this entire time frame, if we take individual perception of party stances into account. Without a far more thorough analysis of these proximity items and their relation to party identification we must be circumspect in interpreting the results. Nevertheless, they are interesting and do suggest that the appearance—or nonappearance—of issue voting is heavily dependent on how issue voting is defined.

By 1964, all the "raw issues" show a positive correlation with presidential preference, and yet there are differences between the two regions. Although correlations generally run higher among the Northern than among the Southern white groups, low correlations on the three racial issues, particularly school integration and fair employment, are surprising. One racial issue that does appear more important in the South than in the North is open housing. It is likely that this question, which seems to be entirely irrelevant to presidential choice among Northern whites, does concern the more segregationist Southerners, who vote disproportionately for the Republican candidate. It is only in the face of the 1968 Wallace candidacy that this correlation approaches zero in the South. All in all, the evidence does not suggest that the South has voted in presidential elections as a one-issue region. Race appears to be a single component in an issue cluster, a component which may be more important in the South but which is by no means the sole determinant of vote (see also Matthews and Prothro, 1966b; Converse et al., 1965).

This is not to say that racial issues have not been critical in stimulating Southern political change. Even if racial issues bear no more importance for Southern whites than they do for whites in the North, the electoral consequences in the two regions would be quite different because more Southern voters traditionally take segregationist stands. The partisan clarification of racial position by 1964 does seem the most satisfactory explanation for greater Republican presidential support in the South than in the North since that time. It is nevertheless pertinent to note that race was by no means operating in a vacuum—on every one of the seven issues we analyzed, Southern whites were more conservative than whites in the North. Hence, even if race were not an issue, and if ballots were cast on the basis of any or all of the remaining issues we have analyzed, Southern whites would be more Republican than their Northern counterparts.

Issues and Party Identification

The correlations of raw issues with party identification form a marked contrast to those with presidential preference. Nie and Andersen have noted the declining correlations between issue positions and party identification since 1964 (Nie and Andersen, 1974). The correlations within both regions certainly share this general pattern. In neither region have civil-rights issues become as well located within the partisan structure as the social-welfare or government-power issues. The most striking result is the astonishing lack of order in the partisan identification of Southern whites in 1972. Overall, the correlation pattern suggests that party identification is poorly moored to issues in both regions, and particularly so in the South. In a era in which issues are more salient, and politics is increasingly national in focus, these results suggest a basic instability of the present partisan alignment.

Conclusions

We have systematically explored four sets of variables—the images of the parties, the images of the presidential candidates, the evaluations of the parties on the most important problems of the day, and the distribution of public opinion on several important domestic issues—among whites in both the North and the South and among blacks across the nation. What are the implications of our analysis for the political system of the United States?

First, it seems clear that a basic sectionalism still persists within the nation, although the partisan direction of the regional difference has changed. Southern whites have voted disproportionately for the Republican presidential candidate in the three elections from 1964-1972. In terms of their images of the major parties, their choice of parties to handle the problems they perceive as most important, and their conservatism on major issues of the day, Southern whites are more closely allied with the Republican Party than with the Democratic Party. However, the transition from a Democratic to a Republican region is hardly impending. In terms of congressional voting, state and local officeholding, and party identification, the residue of one-party politics remains.

We are not arguing that white Southerners will necessarily cast the majority of their ballots for Republican presidential candidates in the future. Electoral politics is far too volatile to predict long-term behavior with confidence. Critical issues change from election to election, and administrations vary in their performance in office. Our analysis does suggest that Republicans will fare better among Southern whites than among Northern whites in future presidential elections, unless there are major changes in the policy alternatives or candidates presented to the voters by the two parties. We also anticipate a gradual expansion of Republican electoral strength at the nonpresidential level in the South.

Second, we have seen the rise of racial issues in American politics. The impetus for change in the nation's racial policies came most forcefully from blacks themselves, and the demands in the early 1960s were primarily concerned with abolishing the most blatant forms of racial discrimination in the South. Since that period, civil-rights protest has expanded to include the North. Our data suggest that 1964 was the peak of salience for racial issues in national politics. Since that election, both the party-image data and the most-important-problem responses indicate that racial issues were of declining salience across the entire electorate. Much of the pressure on the federal government for new legislative initiatives specifically for blacks has certainly waned since 1968, and only the school-busing issue remains alive as a white counter-mobilization issue. The potential for a politics of race certainly does exist, but prospects seem reasonably likely that such a polarization will not occur.

Third, despite a 1972 ticket headed by the least personally appealing candidate in the short history of modern survey research, the Democratic Party made a surprisingly strong recovery from the depths of 1968. By 1972, both the general image of the Democratic Party, as well as the electorate's evaluation of the party's ability to cope with the most important problems, had improved substantially. Yet, in 1972, Americans seemed deeply disturbed about their political parties. Each party evoked more dislikes than likes among Northern whites, and only the Republican Party elicited more likes than dislikes among Southern whites. Blacks remained positively oriented toward the Democratic Party, but at lower levels than previously. In addition, over 40 percent of the population saw neither party as able to cope with important national problems. These data—along with other analyses of declining trust in government and of large decreases in the political efficacy of individuals in the society—indicate how inadequately both the party system and the government are perceived to be meeting the demands of the people. It is an interesting paradox that at the very time that the parties are presenting more ideologically distinct alternatives to the electorate, these parties are becoming increasingly less relevant to voters who are disenchanted with the political system's ability to solve important national problems.

Postscript

The analysis for this report was completed before 1976. Since then another presidential election has occurred, and it is interesting to determine how the 1976 results compare with the general patterns of change we have been describing. Three themes run through our analysis: (1) the declining salience of the racial issue, (2) the emergence of the South as a region of relatively greater strength for the Republican Party at the presidential level, and (3) the decreasing tendency of Americans to evaluate positively the two political parties.

Jimmy Carter's ability to appeal to both whites and blacks was demonstrated initially in Southern primary elections, as he effectively destroyed George Wallace as the recognized national spokesman for the South. Carter's victory against Ford in ten of the eleven southern states represents the coming of age of a new generation of Southern politicians, individuals who understand the "new political arithmetic" of the region. Where blacks comprise sizeable proportions of electorates, candidates no longer need a majority of white votes to win. Over the South as a whole, Carter failed to obtain the support of a majority of whites, yet he carried the region because a sufficient minority of whites, plus the overwhelming majority of blacks, voted for him—ample evidence that the racial issue was not salient in 1976.

Table 12-4 Party and Candidate Net Images in 1976 (in percentages)

| | Party Image | | | | | |
| | Democratic | | | Republican | | |
	Positive	Negative	Net	Positive	Negative	Net
Northern whites	44.0	42.1	1.9	36.4	47.7	−11.3
Southern whites	43.6	37.9	5.7	32.1	40.5	−8.4
Blacks	70.8	17.9	52.9	12.1	59.7	−47.6

| | Candidate Image | | | | | |
| | Carter | | | Ford | | |
	Positive	Negative	Net	Positive	Negative	Net
Northern whites	59.1	61.9	−2.8	60.4	55.5	4.9
Southern whites	59.7	51.6	6.1	62.3	48.5	13.8
Blacks	77.3	20.6	56.7	20.1	70.0	−49.9

Turning to trends in party images, a major reversal occurred in 1976. For the first time since 1960, the image of the Democratic Party was stronger among Southern whites than among Northern whites. Does this finding suggest that the South is returning to its traditional role as a stronghold of Democratic support? We think not. The 1976 election was unusual in presenting, as the Democratic presidential candidate, a native white Southerner unencumbered by a long career in Washington. In addition, the Republican Party was particularly vulnerable. Its 1972 standard-bearer had been driven from office in disgrace, the Watergate scandals had embarrassed the party and challenged its reputation for honest and effective management of the government, and the combination of high inflation and high unemployment had led many to question the competence of Republican leaders to guide the economy. Poor performance in office had seriously weakened the Democrats in 1968, and the Republicans faced a similar situation in 1976.

The party and candidate net images for the three demographic groups appear in Table 12-4. Like the Democratic image in 1968, the Republican image declined substantially from 1972 to 1976. In contrast, the image of the Democratic Party, no longer burdened with a weak candidate, continued the improvement we observed in 1972. The most radical change in party image occurred among Southern whites: the net Republican image fell 14.6 percent and net Democratic image rose 12 percent. It would be incorrect, however, to overinterpret this result: the high volatility in the party images of Southern whites is more a reflection of the weak party ties of most white Southerners than a sign of a lasting Democratic resurgence. The strong candidate image achieved by President Ford in the South supports this view; indeed, more Southern whites had favorable comments about Ford than about Carter. In future presidential elections when the Democratic nominee is again a non-Southerner, assuming basic policy positions of the parties are maintained, we suspect that Southern whites will be disproportionately Republican in their presidential voting.

Finally, although 1976 saw the net Democratic image emerge as clearly positive among all three groups, the data show no evidence of a rising interest in parties. In the 1952-1964 period, the lowest percentage of respondents to make favorable responses about the Democrats was 57 percent. In 1976, even with a quite positive net image, only 44 percent of either Northern or Southern whites had favorable comments to make. The improvement of the net image occurred not from a renewed enthusiasm for the Democrats but from a decline in the degree of hostility expressed toward the party.

We concluded the main portion of this chapter by noting a paradox—the parties, while offering more ideologically distinct alternatives, were becoming less relevant to the political behavior of the mass electorate. It seems appropriate to end this postscript by noting another paradox. *In this era of declining party importance, perceptions of the two major parties made the difference in determining the outcome of the 1976 election.* Even a cursory examination of the image data shows that Carter won the election because of strong black support and because he was a Democrat. The 1976 election most closely parallels the 1960 Kennedy-Nixon contest, in which Kennedy actually had a weaker candidate image than Nixon among both white groups. In both 1960 and 1976, a strong party advantage helped make up the difference for the weaker Democratic candidate, suggesting that although political parties were hardly at their high point in 1976, they remained quite potent forces in American electoral politics.

REFERENCES

Abramson, P. R. (1974) "Generational Change in American Electoral Behavior." *American Political Science Review* 68 (March): 93-105.

Asher, H.(1976) *Presidential Elections and American Politics.* Homewoood, Ill.: Dorsey Press.

Beck, P. A. (1974) "Partisan Stability and Change in the American South: 1952-1972." Paper presented at the 1974 Annual Meetings of the American Political Science Association.

Black, M., and G. B. Rabinowitz (1974) "An Overview of American Electoral Change: 1952-1972." Paper presented at the 1974 Annual Meetings of the Southern Political Science Association.

Burnham, W. D. (1970) *Critical Elections and the Mainsprings of American Politics.* New York: Norton.

Campbell, A. (1971) *White Attitudes Toward Blacks.* Ann Arbor, Mich.: Institute for Social Research, University of Michigan.

Campbell, A., P. Converse, W. Miller, and D. Stokes (1960) *The American Voter.* New York: Wiley.

———— (1966) *Elections and the Political Order.* New York: Wiley.

Converse, P. E. (1963) "A Major Political Realignment in the South?" In *Change in the Contemporary South,* ed. A. P. Sindler. Durham, N.C.: Duke University Press.

———— (1972) "Change in the American Electorate." In *The Human Meaning of Social Change,* ed. A. Campbell and P. E. Converse. New York: Sage.

Converse, P. E., A. R. Clausen, and W. E. Miller (1965) "Election Myth and Reality: The 1964 Election." *American Political Science Review* 59 (June): 321-336.

Greely, A. M. (1974) *Building Coalitions: American Politics in the 1970's.* New York: Franklin Watts.

Hamilton, R. F. (1972) *Class and Politics in the United States.* New York: Wiley.

Hammond, J. L. (1974) "Race and Electoral Mobilization: White Southerners, 1952-1968." Paper presented at the 1974 Annual American Sociological Association Meeting.

Havard, W. C., ed. (1972) *The Changing Politics of the South.* Baton Rouge: Louisiana State University Press.

Howard, P. H., M. E. McCombs, and D. M. Kovenock (1974) "Louisiana." In *Explaining the Vote,* Part II, ed. D. M. Kovenock, J. W. Prothro, and Associates. Chapel Hill, N.C.: Institute for Research in Social Science.

Inglehart, R. and A. Hochstein (1972) "Alignment and Dealignment in France and the United States." *Comparative Political Studies* 5 (October): 343-372.

Kessel, J. H. (1968) *The Goldwater Coalition.* Indianapolis: Bobbs-Merrill.

——— (1972) "Comment: The Issues in Issue Voting." *American Political Science Review* 66 (June): 459-465.

Key, V. O. (1963) *Public Opinion and American Democracy.* New York: Knopf.

Kirkpatrick, S. A., W. Lyons, and M. R. Fitzgerald (1974) "Candidate and Party Images in the American Electorate: A Longitudinal Analysis." Paper presented at the 1974 Annual Meeting of the Southwestern Political Science Association.

Kovenock, D. M., J. W. Prothro, and Associates (1974) *Explaining the Vote,* Part II. Chapel Hill, N.C.: Institute for Research in Social Science.

Ladd, E. C., Jr. (1970) *American Political Parties.* New York: Norton.

Matthews, D. R. and J. W. Prothro (1966a) "The Concept of Party Image and Its Importance for the Southern Electorate." In *The Electoral Process,* ed. M. K. Jennings and H. Zeigler. Engelwood Cliffs, N.J.: Prentice-Hall.

——— (1966b) *Negroes and the New Southern Politics.* New York: Harcourt Brace Jovanovich.

Miller, A. H. (1974) "Political Issues and Trust in Government: 1964-1970." *American Political Science Review* 68 (September): 941-972.

Miller, A. H., W. E. Miller, A. S. Raine, and T. A. Brown (1973) "A Majority Party in Disarray: Policy Polarization in the 1972 Election." Paper presented at the 1973 Annual Meeting of the American Political Science Association.

Nie, N. H. and K. Andersen (1974) "Mass Belief Systems Revisited." *Journal of Politics* 36 (August): 540-591.

Nie, N. H., S. Verba, and J. Petrocik (1976) *The Changing American Voter.* Cambridge: Harvard University Press.

Phillips, K. P. (1970) *The Emerging Republican Majority.* Garden City, N.Y.: Anchor.

Pomper, G. M. (1968) "From Confusion to Clarity: Issues and American Voters, 1956-1968." *American Political Science Review* 66 (June): 415-428.

Potter, D. M. (1972) *The South and the Concurrent Majority.* Baton Rouge: Louisiana State University Press.

Rabinowitz, G. B. (1973) *Spatial Models of Electoral Choice.* Working Paper in Methodology No. 7. Chapel Hill, N.C.: Institute for Research in Social Science.

Repass, D. E. (1971) "Issue Salience and Party Choice." *American Political Science Review* 65 (June): 389-400.

Rudder, C. (1974) "State Rights, a Codeword for Racism?" Paper presented at the 1974 Annual Meetings of the Southern Political Science Association.

Schreiber, E. M. (1971) "Where the Ducks Are: Southern Strategy Versus Fourth Party." *Public Opinion Quarterly* 35 (Summer): 157-167.

Shannon, W. W. (1972) "Revolt in Washington: The South in Congress." In *The Changing Politics of the South,* ed. W. C. Havard. Baton Rouge: Louisiana State University Press.

Stokes, D. E. (1966) "Some Dynamic Elements of Contests for the Presidency." *American Political Science Review* 60 (March): 19-28.

Stokes, D. E., A. Campbell, and W. E. Miller (1958) "Components of Electoral Decision." *American Political Science Review* 52 (June): 367-387.

Strong, D. S. (1963) "Durable Republicanism in the South." In *Change in the Contemporary South.* Durham, N.C.: Duke University Press.

Strong, D. S. (1971) "Further Reflections on Southern Politics." *Journal of Politics* 33 (May): 239-256.

Sundquist, J. L. (1973) *Dynamics of the Party System.* Washington, D.C.: Brookings Institute.

Trilling, R. J. (1974) "Party Image and Partisan Change, 1952 to 1972." Paper presented at the 1974 Annual Meeting of the American Political Science Association.

——— (1976) *Party Image and Electoral Behavior.* New York: Wiley.

Wolfinger, R. E. and R. B. Arseneau (1974) "Partisan Change in the South, 1952-72." Paper presented at the 1974 Annual Meeting of the American Political Science Association.

Wright, G. C., Jr. (1974) *Electoral Choice in America.* Chapel Hill, N.C.: Institute for Research in Social Science.

13 / Religion, Ethnicity, and Class in American Electoral Behavior

Joan L. Fee

Although American separation of church and state has prevented a direct connection between religious denominations and political parties, throughout U.S. history the parties have offered differential appeals to voters of various religious convictions.[1] With the advent of survey analysis, the tendency of Catholics and Jews to consider themselves Democrats and of white Protestants to think of themselves as Republicans has been well documented.[2] However, party identification appears to be in a state of flux. Also documented are both the growing number of voters to abandon party identification in favor of an independent stance and the shifting allegiances of the once solidly Democratic South.[3] Perhaps receiving less attention are the changing economic fortunes of religious groups in America. In the years since World War II, Catholic Americans have surpassed white Protestants in median education and income while Jewish Americans continue to maintain their position in the highest socioeconomic slot.[4] This chapter will investigate the relationship between religion and identification with a particular political party, over the last 20 years, paying particular attention to the partisanship of American Catholics.

Before beginning the analysis, it seems appropriate to consider why religious groups would subscribe to different brands of politics. Theoretical justifications assume two main forms: the historical explanations, describing how the religious-political connection begins, and the maintaining theories, showing how the relationship survives over time. In the case of American Catholics, for example, the historical theories take three main tacks.

1. (a) Catholics historically have been an outgroup, low on the social and economic ladder and discriminated against. Thus, they turned to the Democratic Party, which had been dramatized by Roosevelt's egalitarian New Deal.[5]

   (b) Catholics were pushed into the Democratic Party by the belligerent anti-Catholic and pro-Nativist stands of the Whig Republicans, who bequeathed strands of these traditions to the Republican Party.[6]

2. The salient candidacy of Al Smith, occurring at a time of emerging political involvement among immigrants, married Catholics to Smith's party, the Democratic Party.[7]

This chapter is a condensed version of "Political Continuity and Change," in *Catholic Schools in a Declining Church*, eds. Andrew M. Greeley, William C. McCready, and Kathleen McCourt (Kansas City, 1976), pp. 76–102. Reprinted with permission of Sheed, Andrews and McMeel, Inc.

3. (a) At the time of the great immigrant arrivals, the party out of power in the North, where most immigrants settled, was the Democratic Party. In order to gain strength, it appealed to the immigrants through political machines. [8]

(b) Immigrant leaders, excluded from other avenues of advancement, forced their way into the Democratic Party, bringing their followers with them. [9]

Once Catholics have been attracted to the Democratic Party, some mechanism must insure their allegiance over time. There are several theories as to how this might be accomplished.

1. *Historicist causes.* People cling to familiar patterns out of tradition. [10]
2. *Parental socialization.* Catholics adopt the Democratic identification of their parents. [11]
3. *Differential association and group pressures.* Catholics tend to associate with Catholics. Their political conversations reinforce the group trend. [12]
4. *Demographic characteristics.* Religion, in fact, may be a spurious correlate of party identification, passed on because other factors like socioeconomic status remain constant over generations. [13]
5. *Rational choice.* Catholics may continue to consider themselves Democrats because the party seems more sympathetic to the group, including them in leadership positions. [14]

Although we cannot test all of the historical and maintaining theories offered, we hope that our over-time analysis will tend to support or to refute some of these explanations of religious-political association, and the Catholic-Democratic relationship in particular. Part I of the chapter will study changes in political-party identification of American social and religious groups over the last 20 years. The analysis in Part I makes use of an innovative technique, perfected by Kim and Schmidt in their study of party identification using canonical regression techniques. [15] The approach, which correlates groups of variables, is particularly valuable because it allows simultaneous study of two dimensions of party identification: (1) Democratic versus Republican party support and (2) party identification versus independency. [16]

Part II will study the impact of suburbanization on the relationship between religion and politics. It deals most directly with the maintaining theory of differential association and group pressure. As noted, that theory would assert that Catholics maintain their political convictions because they associate with like-minded Catholics. Although Catholic ethnic groups may have acculturated—becoming Americanized—they may retain group characteristics by resisting assimilation, by maintaining a separate ethnic identity. As Catholics move from ethnic pockets of the cities into more heterogenous suburbs, however, their political views may alter.

Indeed, Greer found in a St. Louis study that Catholic suburbanites, although they continued to identify themselves as Democrats, voted more Republican than did their inner-city counterparts. [17] We will note the degree of suburbanization among the various religious groups over the 20-year period under study and will observe the political identification of the groups according to place of residence. Although this forms a rather crude test of assimilation because it does not take into account homogeneity of neighborhood, it will provide some indication of the political impact of suburbanization. Finally, we will compare the party identification patterns of the groups to their scores on a left-right opinion scale.

The data are taken from the Michigan Survey Research Center (SRC) election studies. In order to provide a maximum number of cases for analysis at each point in time, the studies have been grouped into three periods: Time A (1952, 1956, and 1958), Time B (1960, 1962, and 1964), and Time C (1968, 1970, and 1972)—each period containing studies of one congressional and two presidential elections.

Part I: Religious and Ethnic Affiliations with Parties, Over Time

We begin Part I by summarizing our findings concerning religion and party identification in the time span from the 1950s to the 1970s. After introducing the findings, we will illustrate them more fully. The canonical regression of party identification with a variety of social characteristics and of party identification with religion by itself reveals a number of interesting trends.

First, in relation to other characteristics, religion is a fairly important predictor of party identification—distant from other social characteristics. Second, as a predictor of Republican or Democratic party identification, religion remains fairly stable over time, increasing slightly in Time B, the period containing a religiously salient election.

On the second dimension (independency versus partisanship), religion has become a slightly better predictor of partisanship or lack of partisanship over time. A good part of this predictability seems to stem from the growing number of voters who espouse no religion and no party affiliation. Most probably these people are a young cohort of the Vietnam generation voters. We should note, however, that those Americans without a religion have in all time periods been independent. They appear particularly independent in Time B, as compared to those who are affiliated with the major religions and who more steadfastly hold party identifications. What makes these "no-religionists" more important as time goes on is their increasing numbers.

Examination of the partisanship of the various religious groups reveals the following: white Protestants and Catholics remain fairly stable in their over-time partisan commitments, the Protestants maintaining a more Republican identification than the rest of the population, and the Catholics a more Democratic one. As mentioned above, those espousing no religion also demonstrate a stable trend, but one of independency rather than partisanship. From Time A to Time C, the Jews grow slightly less Democratic as compared to the rest of the population, but religion, compared to other social characteristics, becomes a more important predictor of their partisanship. In contrast, nonwhite Protestants dramatically increase their allegiance to the Democratic Party.

The importance of religion as a predictor of party identification is demonstrated in Table 13-1. Table 13-1 notes the correlation of party identification with a full range of demographic variables—religion, race, place of residence, region, and education—and also the correlation of party identification with religion alone.

Party identification and the demographic variables correlate on two statistically significant dimensions: the Democratic versus Republican factor (Dimension I) and the independent versus party identifier factor (Dimension II).[18] We note that there is a moderate relationship between party identification and the social characteristics studied, and that the relationship seems quite stable over the years. Furthermore, given the moderate nature of this relationship, religion is not a bad predictor of party identification. The

Table 13-1 Canonical Correlation of
Party Identification

	Dimension I[a]	Dimension II[b]
With Religion, Race, Place of Residence, Region, and Education		
Time A	.3317	.1198
Time B	.3220	.1178
Time C	.3336	.1504
With Religion		
Time A	.1572	.0421
Time B	.1743	.0813
Time C	.1574	.0833

[a] Democratic versus Republican factor.
[b] Independent versus party-identifier factor.

correlation of religion with party identification is about half of that of party identification with all of the social characteristics taken together. The predictive power of religion in relation to the other social characteristics is rather surprising, given that it does not take race into account. Its power is somewhat diluted by the fact that nonwhite and white Protestants hold such different party allegiances.

Once we have an overall idea of the relationship between religion and party, the question then becomes, "Which groups favor which parties, and how do the relationships change over the years?" Table 13-2 provides the answers. Although the numbers look formidable, they may be easily interpreted using these guidelines:

On Dimension I a positive score indicates a Democratic leaning; a negative score indicates a Republican leaning.

On Dimension II a positive score represents partisanship; negative score represents independency.

For example, on Dimension I Protestants consistently tend toward Republicanism as do noncity dwellers, those of medium and higher education, Northerners, and whites. Consistently Democratic are those of Catholic or Jewish persuasion, blacks, inner-city dwellers, Southerners, and those with little education.

The scores contained in Table 13-2 are mean partisanship scores—the average canonical score of each social or religious group on party identification. The absolute value of the scores have little meaning, but they are expressed in common units making the distance between them meaningful and comparable over the years. The table, in addition to presenting scores for different demographic groupings, offers scores in its final section for a separate ethno-religious category. A word should be said about the peculiar division of Catholics into an Irish and Polish category versus other Catholics. This division results from research done by Petrocik, indicating that between 1952 and 1972 white Protestants, Polish and Irish Catholics, other Catholics, Jews, blacks and Spanish, and a residual category each identify in distinct fashions with political parties.[19]

Table 13-2 also differentiates between "simple" scores (on the left side of the table)—in which one demographic variable is examined at a time to see where the group actually stands on partisanship—and "multiple partial" scores (on the right side of the table)—in which each variable is examined controlling for the other factors. In the first instance, the actual partisan scores of Jews would be examined in relation to, say, the scores of Catholics. In the second instance, the fact that Jews possess higher educational backgrounds and are more likely to live in the city is taken into consideration. Under adjusted, partial scoring, Catholics and Jews are compared in an unreal world, where they possess the same residence conditions and equal educational background, in order to determine the difference in party identification contributed by their religions alone.

Table 13-2 reveals a number of interesting things. First, when the scores have been adjusted, religion (and, in the earlier period, region) appears more important and the other social characteristics decline in value—indicating the consistent importance of religion as a distinct contributor to political views. The other social characteristics, in contrast, tend to reinforce each other. Second, the adjusted religious, racial, and combined ethno-religious scores are noticeably higher and have greater distance between groups than the scores of other categories—indicating greater political differences along religious and ethnic lines than among other educational or residence groupings.

As far as individual religious groups are concerned, the patterns are clear. The Protestant commitment to Republicanism remains fairly steady over the period studied, as does the Catholic commitment to the Democratic Party. The Catholic Democratic score jumps slightly in Time B—a result of the 1960 Kennedy election—and the Catholic independency rate falls slightly during that time period.

Among Jews, interestingly, the actual Democratic commitment seems to have dropped slightly over the years, but the adjusted scores have risen. In other words, the proportion of Democratic Jews in relation to the rest of the population is declining slightly—but with rising educational levels and suburbanization among Jews, the importance of religion as a Democratizing factor is rising.

The "other" religious category forms such a small proportion of the population that the trends here are probably not too reliable, although there seems somewhat of an affinity toward Republicanism and independency among this group. More interesting are the growing number of Americans who express no religious affiliation. These voters show a consistent tendency to choose independency in political affiliation as well as independency in their religious affiliation. Indeed, they represent the most consistently independent group of voters in the United States.

The ethno-religious categories at the bottom of Table 13-2 provide additional information, particularly on the Catholics. The inclination of Irish and Polish Catholics to consider themselves Democrats approaches the Jewish inclination; in fact, their Democratic leanings exceed those of the Jews in the middle period containing the Kennedy election. Blacks, from Time A to Time C, however, evolve from one of the weaker Democratic groups to the most Democratic ethnic grouping. The Catholic groups and the Jews at Time A show the greatest tendency toward independency; by Time C, the differences between the ethno-religious groups seem to have diminished in the area of independency versus partisanship.

In summary, during the 20 years studied, religious and ethnic factors remain important predictors of a voter's brand of politics. We turn now to the question of how suburbanization influences the religio-political relationship.

Table 13-2 Partisanship (Dimension I)[a] and Independency (Dimension II)[b] Scores by Demographic Categories, Times A, B and C

Category	Unadjusted, Simple Scores						Adjusted, Partial Scores					
	Time A (1952-1958) Dimension		Time B (1960-1964) Dimension		Time C (1968-1972) Dimension		Time A (1952-1958) Dimension		Time B (1960-1964) Dimension		Time C (1968-1972) Dimension	
	I	II	I	II	I	II	I	II	I	II	I	II
Religion												
Protestant	-7.6	6.1	-9.1	4.4	-8.3	6.0	-11.4	6.3	-12.8	3.9	-12.4	6.5
Catholic	18.4	-12.6	25.0	-4.9	21.5	-5.6	30.6	-13.3	35.1	-3.2	30.5	-7.4
Jewish	40.7	-19.9	37.2	-30.7	34.3	-25.0	48.7	-26.9	51.1	-29.7	55.9	-25.7
Other	3.7	-25.0	-23.5	0.1	-3.6	-43.8	10.2	-30.3	-21.2	1.3	-7.7	-38.3
None	-4.9	-31.5	10.0	-60.0	4.0	-37.8	-4.7	-33.2	14.9	-58.3	9.7	-38.2
Race												
White	-2.8	-0.1	-3.7	-0.3	-7.5	-1.8	-1.6	0.5	-2.7	0.2	-6.5	-1.4
Black/other	28.5	4.0	36.2	0.5	61.4	14.6	18.6	-5.4	28.7	-2.5	54.4	11.3
Residence Area												
City	16.2	3.6	20.0	-5.5	21.7	9.3	12.9	14.2	14.3	3.1	4.6	1.2

	I	II	I	II	I	II	I	II	I	II	I	II
Not high school graduate	8.5	1.7	14.0	2.6	19.0	−0.6	6.2	1.6	13.3	2.6	15.7	8.4
High school graduate	−4.3	−3.3	−9.3	−2.5	−6.9	−1.0	−1.8	−3.0	−7.7	−2.1	−5.3	−6.6
College graduate	−34.5	4.3	−23.0	−3.7	−31.6	0.2	−30.8	4.2	−24.5	−2.4	−28.4	−0.4
Region												
North/other	−14.5	−3.2	−11.3	−3.9	−9.3	1.6	−17.4	−2.9	−15.1	−2.4	−9.6	3.7
South	36.6	9.0	23.4	7.7	18.8	−3.5	44.8	7.6	32.1	5.1	19.6	−7.5
Ethno-Religious												
White Protestants	−7.9	5.4	−10.1	2.2	−13.6	2.8	−10.0	6.1	−13.7	2.0	−16.0	1.5
Irish, Polish Catholic	20.7	−19.1	45.8	−14.6	29.7	−2.4	32.8	−19.6	53.7	−13.5	37.7	−0.2
Other Catholic	14.2	−13.9	20.3	−1.3	15.1	−11.7	25.0	−14.1	29.1	−0.3	21.5	−2.1
Jewish	40.3	−20.4	37.9	−32.1	32.5	−27.2	44.5	−27.3	46.8	−29.8	46.1	−0.7
Black, Spanish	31.0	5.4	41.7	0	64.7	11.2	14.0	−0.2	25.5	−0.7	52.8	1.3
Others	−23.7	3.1	−21.2	2.4	−26.3	−0.5	−18.1	3.5	−18.3	3.3	−21.8	0.1

[a]A positive score on Dimension I indicates a Democratic leaning; a negative score, a Republican leaning.
[b]A positive score on Dimension II indicates partisanship; a negative score, independency.

Part II: Suburbanization and Religious Affiliation with Parties

As in Part I, we will summarize our findings on the impact of suburbanization before presenting the finer detail. Part II compares the political stances of five racial-religious groups according to both their educational status and their residence patterns. We are especially interested in the impact of a college education and suburbanization on the Democratic Party identification of Catholics, Jews, and blacks. However, we are also interested in how the different racial and religious groups stand on issues. In addition to noting the party with which the groups identify, we indicate each group's score on a liberal to conservative issue scale.

To summarize the findings—similar to their rise in socioeconomic status, the suburbanization of Catholics does not seem to have affected their party identification. Catholic suburbanites are almost as strong Democrats as are Catholics in the inner cities. Within the different ethno-religious groups, however, certain factors do affect partisanship. Among Protestants and Catholics, education seems to determine the direction of party identification. Jews and nonwhite Protestants seem to identify differently according to residence pattern.

Perhaps the most interesting aspect of our study lies in a comparison of party identification with the range of views from left wing to right wing. Although both the most highly educated and the least highly educated groups, white Jews and nonwhite Protestants, respectively, support the Democratic Party, their motives on the surface, seem quite consistent. Each of these groups concomitantly holds the most liberal ideological views. Yet, another highly liberal group, the college-educated "no-religionists," chooses to express its political views in independency. And a more conservative group, American Catholics, also attaches itself to the Democratic Party.

Before turning to the theoretical implications of these findings, let us look at them in more detail. Table 13-3 notes the suburbanization of five racial-religious groups between 1952 and 1972. It reflects the proportion of the population, in each racial-religious group, that lives in the suburbs as a percentage of those located in metropolitan areas. In the case of blacks in Time A, for example, 21 percent of the sample live in the suburbs of large cities (twelve standard metropolitan sampling areas), with the remaining 79 percent inhabiting the inner city.

In each of the time periods under study, the white Protestant group represents the highest proportion of suburbanites. The white Catholics and Jews are suburbanizing at a much more rapid rate than Protestants. The Catholic suburbanization rate, however, has slowed between Times B and C and may be reaching an equilibrium stage. Nonwhite Protestants suburbanized little over the years studied and may even have become more urban. The whites expressing no religion were not represented by enough respondents to offer a stable trend, but they appear somewhat less suburbanized than white Protestants and, possibly, white Catholics.

We now begin a study of Figures 13-1 through 13-4. These figures graph the mean party-identification scores—where 0 equals strong Democrat, 1 equals weak Democrat, 2 equals a Democratic-leaning independent, 3 equals a "pure" independent, 4 equals a Republican-leaning independent, 5 equals a weak Republican, and 6 equals a strong Republican—of the different racial-religious groups according to their educational and residence patterns. The figures possess the advantage of displaying, perhaps more clearly, the trends discussed in Part I. The figures also present evidence of the impact of place of residence on the party identification of religious groups. Unlike the canonical regression

Table 13-3 Suburbanization Patterns Among Different Racial-Religious Groups for Times A, B, and C (Suburbanites as a Percentage, of Those Living in Metropolitan Areas)

Racial-Religious Group	Time A (1952-1958)	Time B (1960-1964)	Time C (1968-1972)	Difference Time A– Time C
White Protestant	64	71	78	
(N)	(969)	(943)	(820)	14
White Catholic	42	60	68	
(N)	(814)	(740)	(774)	26
White Jewish	15	32	49	
(N)	(209)	(218)	(188)	34
White, no religion	62	61	54	
(N)	(42)	(66)	(97)	−8
Nonwhite Protestant	21	23	19	
(N)	(224)	(247)	(216)	−2

scores, however, mean party identification scores do not distinguish between party identifiers and independents. If a group of suburban Catholic Republicans becomes independent and an equivalent group of suburban Catholic Democrats also takes on an independent identification, the mean party-identification score of the group will remain the same. (This was true of the canonical regression technique concerning Democrat-to-Republican [or vice versa] group changes; however, such movement occurs less often than a shift toward independency in these times.) With this caveat in mind, we address the figures.

Figure 13-1 presents the mean party-identification scores of five racial-religious groups—white Protestants, white Catholics, white Jews, those whites who hold no religious affiliation, and black and other nonwhite Protestants—according to their educational backgrounds. The trends shown in Figures 13-1a and b are probably more reliable than those in 13-1c, d, and e because the white Protestant and Catholic groups contain many more people. In these two groups, the difference in mean party-identification scores among the different educational groups is similar. In both cases, across time, the college-educated groups are consistently more Republican or independent in stance, the high-school–educated group slightly more Democratic, and those with less than a high-school education most Democratic of all. A difference exists in degree of Democratic attachment, however, the most educated Catholics showing about the same tendency to call themselves Democrats as the high-school–educated Protestant group. Catholics at all levels of education showed the greatest tendency toward the Democratic Party in the middle time frame containing the Kennedy election.

In contrast to the white Catholics and Protestants, the Jews and nonwhite Protestants seem to be less politically divided on educational lines. Among the Jews, the most educated show the greatest tendency to call themselves Democrats in two of the three time periods. The most Republican and independent Jewish group in all time frames remains the high-school educated. Blacks of all educational levels show a growing Democratic trend over the 20-year period. The Time B fluctuation in the college-educated group may result from the small numbers it contains (N = 15, 28, and 41 in Times A, B, and C, respectively).

Interestingly, those who hold no religious affiliation seem to be fairly cohesive along partisan lines. Again, the fluctuations among the college-educated group probably result from the very few cases the category contains in Times A and B (N = 18, 21, and 62 in Times A, B, and C, respectively). By Time C, the three educational groups had converged in what we know from Part I to be a tendency to independency. In this final time period, the mean party-identification score varies less between educational groupings of the nondenominational than it does among white Catholics and Protestants.

Figure 13-2 compares party-identification scores of racial-religious groups according to place of residence. Interestingly, among white Catholics, and to a lesser degree, white Protestants, place of residence does not distinguish as well as level of education between

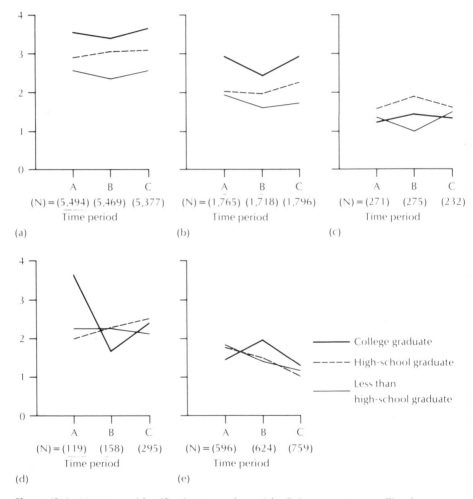

Figure 13-1 Mean party identification scores by racial-religious group, controlling for education (6 = strong Republican; 3 = independent; 0 = strong Democrat). (a) White Protestant. (b) White Catholic. (c) White Jewish. (d) White, no religion. (e) Nonwhite Protestant.

the party-identification tendencies. Catholics, particularly, show almost identical party-identification trends in each of the three residence areas of inner city, suburb, and small city/town/rural area. Among white Protestants (unlike most other groups), those living in small cities, towns, and rural areas are consistently more Democratic than inner-city dwellers.

Among Jews, in contrast, place of residence distinguishes better than educational level between different party-identification patterns, with inner-city residents consistently more Democratic. Small cities, towns, and rural areas—just the opposite of the white Protestant trend—remain consistently less Democratic. Perhaps this tendency of Jews to identify less Democratically in smaller areas and for white Protestants to identify more Democratically

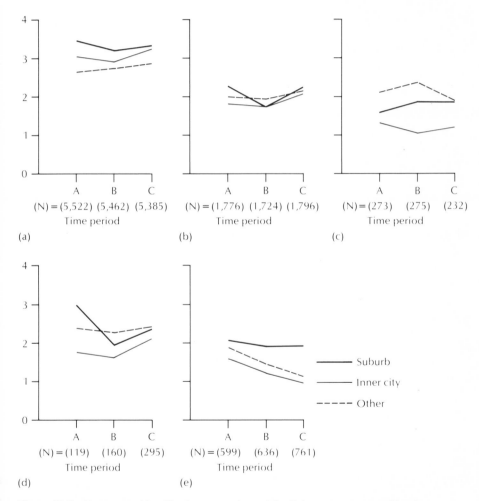

Figure 13-2 Mean party identification scores by racial-religious group, controlling for place of residence (6 = strong Republican; 3 = independent; 0 = strong Democrat). (a) White Protestant. (b) White Catholic. (c) White Jewish. (d) White, no religion. (e) Nonwhite Protestant.

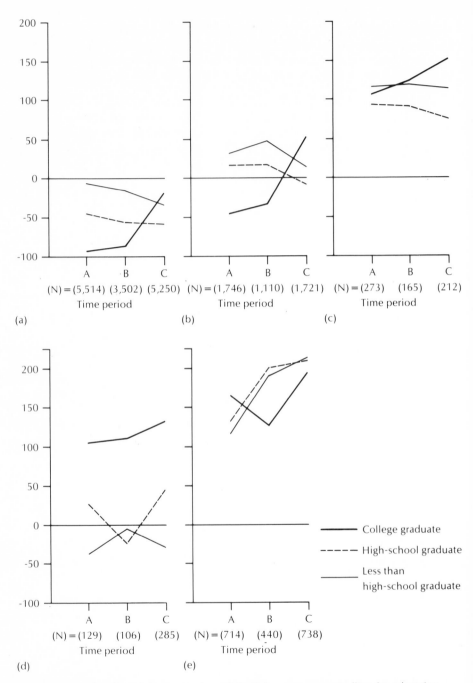

Figure 13-3 Left–right opinion scores by racial-religious group, controlling for education (−300 = very conservative; 300 = very liberal). (a) White Protestant. (b) White Catholic. (c) White Jewish. (d) White, no religion. (e) Nonwhite Protestant.

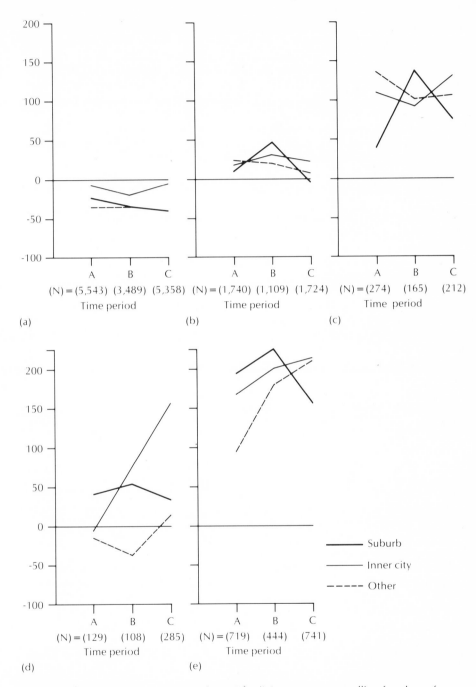

Figure 13-4 Left–right opinion scores by racial-religious group, controlling for place of residence (−300 = very conservative; 300 = very liberal). (a) White Protestant. (b) White Catholic. (c) White Jewish. (d) White, no religion. (e) Nonwhite Protestant.

in the same areas indicates a pressure toward homogeneous political patterns in small towns as opposed to the suburbs.

Blacks show patterns of party identification according to place of residence similar to those corresponding to levels of education; most blacks are becoming more Democratic. Although the number of suburban blacks is fairly small (an average of fifty-one cases per time frame), suburban blacks show a stable party-identification score—seemingly resisting the group pull toward a more Democratic party identification.

Those whites without a religious affiliation demonstrate partisan scores when differentiated by residence similar to those associated with their educational attainment—especially in Time C, which contains the most respondents.

Instead of arraying the various racial-religious groups on a scale of party identification, Figures 13-3 and 13-4 dramatize the different left-right political opinions the various groups hold. Left-right views are measures by a factor-analyzed and weighted scale consisting of five issue areas: black welfare, school integration, economic welfare, size of government, and foreign policy (mostly attitudes toward Communism). The questions under each area are taken from the SRC election files from which the party identification information has come. [20] The left-right opinions of the different groups fall on a scale ranging from 300 (extremely liberal) to −300 (extremely conservative).

Perhaps the most striking feature in Figure 13-3 is the swing toward the left by the college-educated among all religious groups between Times B and C. The Catholic college-educated show the biggest jump, a rise of 80 percentage points between the two time periods. Yet, this changing political ideology does not seem to have sparked, among the well-educated groups, a shift in party identification toward the Democrats. This turning toward liberalism among the college-educated accompanies a slight swing toward conservatism among the less-educated white Protestants, Catholics, and Jews.

Among blacks, education does not seem to affect ideology as much as it does in the other groups. All segments of the black population share quite liberal positions in Time A, and grow more liberal over the years. Again, the downward jump in the pattern of college-educated blacks probably reflects small numbers (N = 15 in Time B, 28 in Time A, and 39 in Time C).

Interestingly, those whites holding no religious affiliation show the greatest difference in ideology between the college-educated and the lesser-educated groups. This may result from a division of the no-religion voters into a group of well-educated agnostics for whom lack of religion is a part of an ongoing ideology, in contrast to a not-as-well-educated group of individuals who have drifted away from religion but who hold political views closer to those of the rest of the population. The first, more highly educated component expresses ideological views similar to those of highly educated Jews; the other, lesser-educated component offers a political ideology more similar to that of white Protestants and white Catholics. Aside from the no-religion whites, the four groups of white Protestants, white Catholics, Jews, and nonwhite Protestants show individually clustered political ideologies which ascend monotonically—spanning the spectrum from the more conservative white Protestants, through the middle shades of white Catholics and Jews, to the most liberal nonwhite Protestants.

Figure 13-4 maps political ideology against residence size. Although white Protestants showed the greatest divergence in party identification between suburban respondents and those in small cities, towns, or rural areas, these two groups espouse similar political ideologies. This fact demonstrates that the translation of ideology into party identification is often a garbled one.

Among white Protestants, Catholics, and Jews alike, the leftward movement in political views among college-educated groups does not spell a liberal swing in the suburbs. In fact, the Catholic and Jewish suburban voters are significantly more conservative than one might expect. This factor indicates a high proportion of suburbanites with less than a college education.

While the number of whites espousing no religion and living in the city remains quite small (N = 16, 26, and 45 in Times A, B, and C, respectively), the extreme upward direction of this line is interesting. The increase might reflect a growing tendency for more radical white, well-educated persons to seek an urban environment. In the 1950s, the differences between the inner city and the suburbs were not so starkly drawn. Today, choosing a suburban residence over an urban one may indicate a more conservative political bent.

If one considers membership in the Democratic Party the more liberal partisan identification, the blacks, of all groups, have evolved most consistently in the 20-year period. From Time A to Time C, they became increasingly Democratic and, at the same time, their political ideology evolved to the left.

Conclusions

At the outset of this paper we proposed to study shifts in party identification among religious groups since the 1950s. We hoped to pay particular attention to the impact of suburbanization on the Catholic population and to see if we could corroborate any of the religious-political theories. We have found that religion continues to exert an impact on party identification over the period studied; and, indeed, the impact seems to be increasing slightly as the distance in partisanship between the religious groups grows. This slight increase results not from a greater commitment by religious groups to particular parties, but rather from an improving ability to predict independency on the basis of religious affiliation (or nonaffiliation).

Furthermore, the connection between religion and party identification does not seem to diminish across groups with changes in socioeconomic status or with suburbanization. For example, the rise in the socioeconomic status of Catholics and their suburbanization between 1952 and 1972 does not diminish their attraction for the Democratic Party. This finding, although it does not totally refute the hypothesis that groups abandon group-held political ties as they assimilate—we do not know, after all, how heterogenous are the environments in which the Catholics live—certainly does not lend weight to the theory.

We do note, however, several within-group partisan differences according to education and residence pattern. White Protestants and Catholics seem to show a similar pattern varying by education, while Jews and nonwhite Protestants identify differently according to the type of environment in which they live. These findings indicate that a general theory on party identification may not always apply to the subsocietal groups within the United States. While parsimony and generalization remain the aims of theory, exceptions to the rule may speak more accurately to the varying experiences of cultural minorities. Besides varying on the best predictor of party affiliation, the groups vary in the ways in which they combine views on issues with the choice of a party. Liberal blacks identify with the Democratic Party; more conservative Catholics feel at home in the same party.

How does one make sense of these choices by religious groupings? One theory that seems to shed light on these political choices is that "outgroups" or "minorities" are attracted to the Democrats. This theory offers a reason why three such diverse groups as white Catholics, Jews, and blacks might find shelter under the same political umbrella. Each group at certain times in U.S. history has been discriminated against by the establishment and thus might continue to shy away from the more establishment-oriented Republican Party.

Our findings seem to support the historical "outgroup" theories of Democratic Party identification. The findings tend to refute the spurious correlate theory that religion is merely a reflection of other demographic characteristics and that as the old ethnic groups suburbanize, the Catholic Democratic ties will diminish. The findings point out the need for more detailed studies of the distinct political patterns of minority groups in our society—a task made difficult by the small numbers of such people encountered in national surveys.

NOTES

1. A concise summary of the relationships between various religious groups and political parties appears in Seymour Martin Lipset, "Religion and Politics in the American Past and Present," in *Religion and Social Conflict,* ed. Lee and Murray (New York, 1964).

2. Beginning with Paul F. Lazarsfeld, Bernard Berelson, and Hazel Gaudet, *The People's Choice* (New York, 1944), most studies touching on religion and politics discuss the attraction of the religions to different parties. A representative sample are: Bernard R. Berelson, Paul F. Lazarsfeld, and William N. McPhee, *Voting* (Chicago, 1954); Angus Campbell et al., *The American Voter,* abridged ed. (New York, 1964); Gerhardt Lenski, *The Religious Factor* (Garden City, N.Y., 1961).

3. See especially, Walter Dean Burnham, *Critical Elections and the Mainsprings of American Politics* (New York, 1970), pp. 91-174; Philip E. Converse, "Possible Realignment in the South," in Angus Campbell et al., *Elections and the Political Order* (New York, 1966), pp. 212-244.

4. See Andrew M. Greeley, "Ethnicity, Denomination and Inequality," *Sage Research Papers in the Social Sciences* 4 (1976).

5. Samuel Lubell, *The Future of American Politics,* 2nd ed. (New York, 1956), p. 41. Campbell et al., *American Voter,* p. 92; also Lipset, "Religion and Politics."

6. Lipset, "Religion and Politics"; also Lawrence Fuchs, "Some Political Aspects of Immigration," in *American Ethnic Politics,* ed. Fuchs (New York, 1968). Fuchs analyzes nativism in American politics, dealing more directly with nationality than with religion. Of course, nationality and religion are often bound up.

7. V. O. Key, Jr., "A Theory of Critical Elections," *Journal of Politics* 27 (1955): 3-18. In "Critical Elections in Illinois, 1888-1958," *The American Political Science Review* 54 (1960): 669-683, Duncan Macrae and James A. Meldrum note the same tendency of Smith's candidacy to wed Catholics to the Democrats and to drive Protestants into Republican ranks; they emphasize, however, that in this state "the more lasting effects of that change seem more closely related to urban-foreign background than to religion as such."

8. Harry A. Bailey, Jr., and Ellis Katz, eds., *Ethnic Group Politics* (Columbus, 1969). This is one of the best readers on religion, nationality, and politics.

9. Ibid.

10. Key and Munger document this tendency among Indiana voters. In essentially similar counties they find continuing *contrasting* partisan attachments over time, "at least to some extent independent of other social groupings." V. O. Key and Frank Munger, "Social Determinism and Electoral Decision: The Case of Indiana," in *American Voting Behavior,*

eds. Burdick and Brodbeck (Glencoe, Ill., 1959), pp. 281-299. Wolfinger's finding that New Haven Italians maintain their support for the Republican Party because of early salient Italian candidacies lends further weight to the theory. Raymond E. Wolfinger, "The Development and Persistence of Ethnic Voting," *The American Political Science Review* 59 (1965): 896-908.

11. H. H. Remmers shows that high school students assume to a great degree the party identification of their parents. H. H. Remmers, "Early Socialization of Attitudes" in *American Voting Behavior,* eds. Burdick and Brodbeck (Glencoe, Ill., 1959), pp. 55-67. See also, M. Kent Jennings and Richard G. Niemi, "The Transmission of Political Values from Parent to Child," *American Political Science Review* 62 (1968): 169-184.

12. The strength of adherence to the group standard depends on the salience of the political issue. Campbell et al., *American Voter,* p. 92, study the Catholic voting patterns vis-à-vis Catholic congressional candidates. For analysis of the 1960 election, see Philip E. Converse, "Religion and Politics: 1960 Election," in *Elections and the Political Order,* ed. Angus Campbell et al. (New York, 1966), pp. 96-124. Berelson and Lenski find a tendency to conform to the group standard of party preference even when the group standard differs from parental party affiliation. Berelson et al., *Voting;* Lenski, *Religious Factor.*

13. When socioeconomic status rises over generations, these "cross pressures" lessen a Catholic's attraction to the Democratic Party. Berelson et al., *Voting.*

14. Peter H. Odegard "Catholicism and Elections in the United States," in *Religion and Politics,* ed. Odegard (Englewood Cliffs, N.J.), pp. 120-121. Odegard observes "under Democratic presidents Franklin Roosevelt and Harry Truman, one out of every four judicial appointments went to a Catholic as against one out of every 25 under Harding, Coolidge, and Hoover."

15. Jae-On Kim and Corwin E. Schmidt, "The Changing Bases of Political Identification in the United States: 1952-1972," *Sociology Working Paper Series,* 74:3 (University of Iowa, Department of Sociology). The authors define canonical regression as a "method of analysis which uses (1) the canonical correlation with dummy variables as a means of quantifying categorical variables, (2) some features of discriminant function analysis as a means of measuring distances between groups, and (3) dummy regression (and MCA) as a means of displaying multivariate relationships."

16. For a fuller explanation of the statistical techniques used in this chapter, see Joan Fee, "Political Continuity and Change," in *Catholic Schools in a Declining Church,* eds. Andrew M. Greeley, William C. McCready, and Kathleen McCourt (Kansas City, 1976), pp. 76-102.

17. Scott Greer, "Catholic Voters and the Democratic Party," *Public Opinion Quarterly* 25 (1961): 611-625.

18. We interpret the two dimensions using the canonical scores contained in Table A.

Table A Canonical Scores for the Partisan and Demographic Categories, Times A, B, and C (Mean = 0; Standard Deviation = 100)

Category	Time A (1952–1958) Dimension		Time B (1960–1964) Dimension		Time C (1968–1972) Dimension	
	I	II	I	II	I	II
Party						
Democrats	98.0	32.7	91.9	43.7	103.0	49.9
Independents	− 42.1	− 179.9	− 21.8	− 183.2	− 28.3	− 141.7
Republicans	− 130.7	86.1	− 142.7	71.5	− 145.4	99.8

19. John R. Petrocik, "Changing Party Coalitions and the Attitudinal Basis of Alignment, 1952-1972" (Ph.D. diss. Department of Political Science, University of Chicago).

20. The intricacies of constructing the scale are described in full in Norman H. Nie, Sidney Verba, and John R. Petrocik, *The Changing American Voter* (Cambridge, 1976).

14 / Liberalism Upside Down: The Inversion of the New Deal Order

Everett Carll Ladd, Jr.

A new class-ideology alignment has taken form over the past decade as part of the transformation of political conflict and hence of the American party system. Since the mid-1960s, there has been an inversion of the relationship of class to electoral choice from that prevailing in the New Deal era. Broadly interpreted, the New Deal experience sustained the proposition that liberal programs and candidates would find their greatest measure of support among lower-class voters and that conservatives would be strongest within the high socioeconomic strata. Now, in many although not all instances, groups at the top are more supportive of positions deemed liberal and more Democratic than those at the bottom. We also see some evidence of an emergent curvilinear pattern, with the top more Democratic than the middle but the middle less Democratic than the bottom.

Table 14-1 reviews the "classic" pattern of class voting as it persisted throughout the New Deal era and into the early 1960s. What had been well established as the "traditional" configuration held neatly for the several sets of groups represented in this table and indeed for all of the various socioeconomic groupings which we can locate with survey data. For example, 38 percent of whites of high socioeconomic status (SES) voted for Democratic nominee John Kennedy in 1960, compared to 53 percent for Kennedy among middle SES whites, and 61 percent of low SES white voters. By 1968, the relationship had changed markedly. For the most part, the top gave the higher measure of backing to the relatively more liberal Democratic nominee than did the bottom. Humphrey was supported by 50 percent of high status whites under thirty years of age, but by only 39 percent of their middle SES age mates and by just 32 percent of young low status electors. The newly emergent conformation was even clearer in 1972, when the somewhat distorting factor of the Wallace candidacy was removed . Among whites—for blacks continued to constitute a "deviating" case of voters disproportionately in the lower socioeconomic strata but overwhelmingly Democratic—those with college training were more Democratic than those who had not attended college; persons in the professional and managerial stratum were more Democratic than the semiskilled and unskilled work force; and so on. McGovern was backed by 45 percent of the college-educated young, but by only 30 percent of their age mates who had not entered the groves of academe. Comparing 1948 and 1972, we see a reversal of quite extraordinary proportions.

Reprinted with permission from the *Political Science Quarterly* 91, no. 4 (Winter 1976-1977): 577-600.

Table 14-1 Democratic Percentage of the Presidential Ballots, White Voters by Socioeconomic Position, 1948-1972

	1948	1960	1968	1972
All				
High SES*	30%	38%	36%	32%
Middle SES**	43	53	39	26
Low SES***	57	61	38	32
Women				
High SES	29	35	42	34
Middle SES	42	52	40	25
Low SES	61	60	39	33
Under 30 Years of Age				
High SES	31	42	50	46
Middle SES	47	49	39	32
Low SES	64	52	32	36
College educated	36	45	47	45
Noncollege	56	49	33	30

*High SES includes persons having upper white collar and managerial occupations who have had college training.
**Middle SES includes persons having lower white collar or skilled manual occupations.
***Low SES includes persons having semiskilled and unskilled occupations, service workers, and farm laborers.
Source: Data are from the following AIPO surveys: for *1948,* #430, 431, 432, 433; *1960,* #635, 636, 637, 638; *1968,* #769, 770, 771, 773; *1972,* #857, 858, 859, 860.

Table 14-1 also suggests, somewhat lightly, the emergence of a curvilinear relationship between class and support for relatively more liberal as opposed to more conservative candidates. McGovern was weakest within the middle strata: among whites holding positions as skilled workers; among women of middle socioeconomic status; among young people holding positions as skilled manual workers. On the whole, McGovern's strength was greatest among those of high status, lowest within the ranks of the middling strata, and somewhat higher again in the lower reaches of the socioeconomic distribution.

Some qualification is in order. While a massive transformation of the relationship of class in voting has obviously occurred, the old pattern has not been obliterated everywhere. If blacks are included, the lower socioeconomic strata still appear more Democratic than the higher cohorts. Even within the white population, some distributions from the 1968 and 1972 presidential contests show the top more Republican than the bottom— although in all cases by a margin markedly reduced from that of the New Deal era. The proportion of professional and managerial whites backing McGovern was 3 percentage points lower than that of blue-collar whites. However, comparing professionals alone (excluding businessmen) to manual workers, we find the former 4 percentage points more Democratic than the latter—the first time since the availability of survey data that this inversion has occurred. And for the first time in the span for which we have survey materials, the college educated in 1972 gave the Democratic nominee a higher percentage of their vote than did the noncollege population. So while there are some exceptions, depending upon how the high and low status publics are defined, an inversion of the New Deal relationship has indeed occurred.

Table 14-2 Democratic Percentage of the Congressional Ballots, White Voters by Socioeconomic Position, 1948-1972

	1948	1960	1968	1972
All				
High SES	33%	46%	42%	48%
Middle SES	49	60	51	49
Low SES	63	66	55	54
Women				
High SES	35	41	42	48
Middle SES	49	57	49	45
Low SES	64	64	55	56
Under 30 Years of Age				
High SES	36	49	46	60
Middle SES	54	54	51	53
Low SES	66	59	54	51
College educated	42	51	46	55
Noncollege	60	55	52	53

Source: Data are from the following AIPO surveys; for *1948*, #430, 431, 432, 433; *1960*, #635, 636, 637, 638; *1968*, #769, 770, 771, 772, *1972*, #857, 858, 859, 860.

Even though this inversion is most notable in presidential voting, the general *direction* of the shift is evident at other levels as well. In Table 14-2, we compare the congressional vote of the several socioeconomic strata for the elections of 1948, 1960, 1968, and 1972. The weakening of traditional class voting can be seen clearly, especially among young voters. In 1947, just 36 percent of high status voters under thirty cast their ballots for Democratic congressional candidates, as against 66 percent of their low status age mates— a margin of 30 percentage points between these two groups. By 1968, the direction was the same—with those of low status more Democratic than their high status counterparts— but the margin had shrunk to just 8 points. in 1972, even the direction had shifted, as 60 percent of the high status young, 53 percent of their age mates of middle status, and only 51 percent of those of low status, cast ballots for Democratic congressional contenders.

For some observers, the 1974 balloting showed the evanescent character of the forces that had contributed to inversion.[1] Yes, issues arose in the 1960s which divided the populace along new lines, different from those of the New Deal years, and thereby scrambled the old class-party relationships. But the conflict of the 1960s lacked staying power, according to this view, and it has faded as quickly as it once arrived. By 1974, issues running coincident with the basic line of cleavage of the New Deal party system had reasserted themselves:

> as soon as Vietnam, race questions, and the social issue gave way to class questions and issues of governmental intervention in the economy, the existing party system [that of the New Deal] took on meaning once again. In 1974, the questions were whether people were going to have jobs, whether their wages would keep pace with the prices in the grocery story, whether oil company projects were too high, who was going to bear the brunt of inflation and of taxes. These aroused class feelings. . . . Sensing that they were threatened, people of traditional Democratic leanings turned instinctively to *their* party. . . .[2]

Table 14-3 Democratic Percentage of the
Congressional Ballots, White Voters by
Socioeconomic Position, 1964 and 1974

	1964	1974
All		
High SES	48%	57%
Middle SES	65	62
Low SES	74	67
Women		
High SES	44	60
Middle SES	64	61
Low SES	74	68
Under 30 Years of Age		
High SES	50	66
Middle SES	70	68
Low SES	74	73
College educated	53	69
Noncollege	71	69

Source: Data are from the following AIPO surveys:
for *1964,* #697, 699, 701, 702; *1974,* #915, 916.

This argument contains a large element of truth—and a fundamental flaw. It fails, in the first instance, to account for what actually happened in the 1974 voting. Examining the data in Table 14-3, we see that the Democrats *did* do exceptionally well among low status voters. Working-class whites, who had deserted McGovern (although not the congressional Democrats) in 1972, overwhelmingly endorsed Democratic candidates for House and Senate, and those running for lower offices, in 1974. Economic worries, together with a Watergate reaction, did in fact submerge the social and cultural issues that were so prominent between 1964 and 1972.[3] Even in this time of economic woe, however when the economic dimension of conflict loomed larger than it had in the preceding years, there was no return to the class-party relationship of the 1930s and 1940s, even to that which persisted into the early 1960s. The Democrats did not do as well among whites of high socioeconomic status in 1974 as among low status whites but, considering the circumstances, they came remarkably close.

The contrast between the 1974 vote distributions and those of 1964—the great congressional landslide a decade earlier—is sharp. The Democrats did no better among middle to lower status voters in 1974 than in 1964, in fact they did not do quite as well, but they bettered their performance markedly within the high status cohorts. While conditions in both elections evoked memories of the New Deal—some said Goldwater wanted to repeal it, and some felt we were entering anew in 1974 the situation that precipitated it—there was no reappearance of class voting in the more recent of the two contests. The "distance" between high and low status voters, immense in 1964, was modest a decade later. Indeed, where noncollege whites under thirty years of age were 18 percentage points more Democratic than their college age mates in the former election, there was no difference at all between the vote of these two groups in 1974.

Nothing in the above commentary offers any comfort to the Republicans. They were badly—almost identically, in the overall percentages—beaten in the 1964 and 1974 congressional contests. The 1974 results actually seem a bit more gloomy for the GOP, since the party lost even its old base among high status voters, a base which had remained relatively secure in the general Goldwater rout. It is essential to note that the Republicans lost *differently* in 1974 than during the New Deal era. The "old New Deal coalitions" were not put back together in the 1974 balloting. Indeed, the only thing that 1934 (or 1964) and 1974 appear to have in common is that Democratic congressional candidates trounced their Republican opponents on each occasion. Can anyone seriously describe a contest in which Democrats secured the support of two-thirds of young college-trained, professional and managerial white voters as a "New Deal type" election?

We have here a basic element in the disruption of the New Deal alignment. In the party system that Franklin Roosevelt built, the top had been decisively more Republican than the bottom. A structure of class voting was erected, remained intact, and became "natural." It was natural in the context of the social group composition and political agenda of the industrial state. It is in no sense natural in postindustrial America. Among its other dimensions, the contemporary party system transformation comprises an inversion of the old class relationship in voting, an inversion first evident at the presidential level but likely to penetrate the entire range of electoral contests where broad policy issues can intrude. The performance of liberal—often but not always Democratic—candidates at the top of the socioeconomic ladder increasingly is approaching, and even surpassing, that at the bottom.

Republican Weakness at the Top

The coin, one side of which is proportionally increased backing for liberal, and thereby often Democratic, candidates among the upper social strata in the United States, has a second surface. Support for conservative, often Republican candidacies within the higher status groups has markedly declined.

Before the New Deal, the Republicans were the party of the American "establishment," although that term was not applied then to the dominant business interests. Even during the New Deal period, the GOP remained the establishment party, in the sense that it held the loyalties of disproportionate numbers of people among those groups who controlled major social institutions, notably the economy. With entry into the postindustrial era, however, two related developments have eroded this Republican position. The *composition* of the establishment has changed with the ascendancy of new political classes, principally of a broad professional stratum—or with substantial overlap and a somewhat different perspective, a massive new intelligentsia. Apart from this altered composition, the ideological proclivity of large segments of the establishment has experienced a major shift.

The Republicans' hold on that loose array of groups and interests which might be said to exercise disproportionate influence in the society has slipped. The intellectual community has grown in numbers and importance. But the Republican position has grown weaker, not stronger, within it. There has been, we know, a long-standing tendency of intellectuals generally to be critics, and of American intellectuals to be socially critical from a liberal perspective.[4] So the GOP, as the more conservative party, has long had good reason not to expect the intellectual community to be one of its strongholds. Still, intellectuals are a variegated group, and they are for the most part among the advantaged rather than disadvantaged segments of the populace. During the New Deal era, there was substantial Republican support within the intellectual stratum. Over the last two decades, this support has declined. In 1948, for example, college faculty were only 6 percentage points less Republican than the electorate generally. The 1972 Republican professorial vote, however, was 18 percentage points below the Republican vote within the electorate at large. [5]

Data on the politics of college students show a similar progression. S. M. Lipset has noted that Harvard University students, generally more liberal and Democratic than their counterparts at other campuses around the country, were solidly Republican in presidential preference up until the 1960s. The respectable straw polls conducted by the *Harvard Crimson* indicated that Thomas Dewey was the choice of 56 percent of the Harvard student body in 1948, while just 25 percent favored Truman. In 1952 and 1956, Adlai Stevenson demonstrated considerable appeal in Harvard Yard, but he still ran behind Eisenhower in the universitywide student balloting. It was not until 1960 that a Democratic presidential nominee was recorded as the choice of a majority of Harvard students, when the *Crimson's* straw poll found Kennedy securing about three-fifths of the student vote. In the elections of 1964, 1968, and 1972 the Harvard student body, so solidly Republican during the New Deal when Harvard alumnus Franklin D. Roosevelt was the popular Democratic standard-bearer, supported the Democratic presidential nominees by overwhelming margins. [6] Harvard is certainly part of the American intellectual establishment—a training ground for so many of the top leaders of government, business, science, the arts, and culture. Throughout the New Deal, its student body was Republican. By the 1970s, Harvard students have become strongly Democratic.

While the absolute distributions are different from campus to campus, the student population of the 1930s and 1940s had been generally Republican, following the normal class distributions of the time: groups of higher socioeconomic status tended to be Republican, and college students were drawn largely from the middle and upper middle classes. During the Eisenhower years, too, students were solidly Republican in presidential politics, supporting Eisenhower by much greater margins than did the general public. [7] By the late 1960s, however, the national college student population was decisively Democratic— or, more precisely, heavily anti-Republican, since large numbers of students were self-described independents consistently voting against Republican presidential nominees. Gallup found a marked drop in Republican allegiance among students continuing during the late 1960s and early 1970s. In 1966, 26 percent of college students described themselves as Republicans, 35 percent as Democrats, and 39 percent as independents; by 1970, Republican identifiers in the student population had declined to 18 percent, compared to 30 percent self-described Democrats, and a massive 52 percent independents; and in 1974, the Republican proportion was at an all time low of 14 percent, as against 37 percent Democratic, and 49 percent in the independent category. [8] Among graduate students, an almost unbelievably low proportion of 9 percent identified with the GOP, while 43 percent thought of themselves as Democrats, and 48 percent as independents. [9] A 1972 CBS election day survey found 54 percent of students in the eighteen to twenty-four age category voting for McGovern, 16 points higher than the proportion among the public at large. [10] Gallup reported in October 1972 that 68 percent of graduate students planned to vote for McGovern, compared to just 31 percent for Republican incumbent Richard Nixon. [11]

These current distributions are really quite extraordinary. Not only are college students an important component of the intelligentsia, but from their ranks will come the bulk of the leadership of the principal institutions in the United States. When only 14 percent of all students and just 9 percent of graduate students profess an affinity for the Republican party, the extent of the latter's decline—and even more, the scope of its potential decline—among the principal political classes becomes evident.

The position of the GOP is even bleaker than these data suggest. Among students at major colleges and universities, Republican electorate support falls below that within the general student population. For both faculty and students, the most prestigious and influential—and most affluent—sectors are the most solidly Democratic. [12]

What we have noted for students and faculty and other segments of the intellectual community applies in all essential regards to the higher and ascendant socioeconomic strata in the United States generally. Data on partisan identification and congressional vote from the New Deal through to the present demonstrate clearly the dramatic decline of Republican backing among the higher status cohorts.

In Figures 14-1 and 14-2, we compare the Democratic and Republican proportions of party self-identification and congressional vote throughout the New Deal era and into the contemporary period, for three groups of high socioeconomic status, all of which have expanded greatly as the society has moved into postindustrialism. The college educated, people employed in professional occupations, and young whites of high socioeconomic status—defined as the college educated employed in professional and managerial positions—are not the only representations of the high socioeconomic strata and the intelligentsia which we could make, but they faithfully illustrate developments occurring in the larger stratum.

One basic fact comes through with absolute clarity from the data presented in these two figures: groups of high socioeconomic status were solidly Republican throughout the New Deal era; sometime in the late 1950s and early 1960s there was a pronounced move toward the Democrats. In 1964, for the first time, Democrats outnumbered Republicans

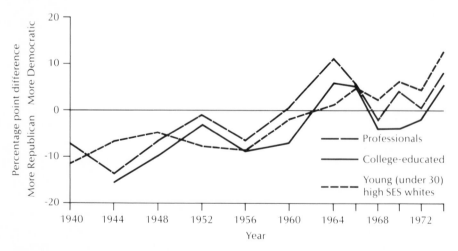

Figure 14-1 Percentage-point difference in the party self-identification of selected social groups, 1940-1974 (+ = more Democratic; − = more Republican). (*Source:* Data are from the following year AIPO surveys: for *1940,* #208, 209; *1944,* #328, 329; *1948,* #430, 431, 432, 433; *1952,* #506, 507, 508, 509; *1956,* #572, 573, 574, 576; *1960,* #635, 636, 637, 638; *1964,* #697, 699, 701, 702; *1966,* #724, 729, 737; *1968,* #769, 770, 771, 773; *1970,* #814, 815, 816, 817; *1972* #857, 858, 859, 860; *1974,* #889, 897, 899, 903, 906.

(in terms of self-identification) throughout many high SES cohorts, and majorities of these groups backed Democratic congressional candidates. While there was some temporary falling off in Democratic support among these groups immediately after 1964, the overall secular progression has not been interrupted. Substantial portions of the high socioeconomic strata in the United States are consistently displaying absolute Democratic majorities in both self-identification and congressional balloting.[13]

Particularly ominous for the long-run prospects of the GOP is the disaffection of young high status whites. During the New Deal era, this group was solidly, indeed massively, Republican. By the mid-1970s, it has become solidly, massively Democratic. These voters will grow older, of course, and perhaps become relatively more conservative, swinging somewhat toward the Republicans apart from what happens as a result of changing issues and changing party positions. But Figures 14-1 and 14-2 make clear that we are dealing with a long-term secular shift, not simply an artifact of Watergate. The Republicans have lost their grip on the American establishment, most notably among young men and women of relative privilege.[14]

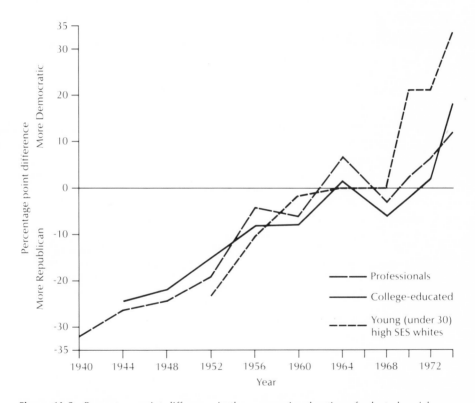

Figure 14-2 Percentage-point difference in the congressional voting of selected social groups, 1940–1974 (+ = more Democratic; − = more Republican). (*Source:* Data are from the following AIPO surveys: for *1940,* #208, 209; *1944,* #328, 329; *1948,* #430, 431, 432, 433; *1952,* #506, 507, 508, 509; *1956,* #572, 573, 574, 576; *1960,* #635, 636, 637, 638; *1964,* #697, 699, 701, 702; *1966,* #724, 729, 737; *1968,* #769, 770, 771, 773; *1970,* #814, 815, 816, 817; *1972,* #857, 858, 859, 860; *1974,* #889, 897, 899, 903, 906.

Sources of the Inversion

The partisan changes thus far described have their origins within broader social and political transformations. Three interrelated arguments form the explanation: (1) The composition of the several broad social classes or strata has changed, and so has their social and political character. (2) The thrusts and meanings of liberalism (and, of course, conservatism) have been altered. (3) Because of this, the high SES cohorts (as now composed) are much more liberal (as now defined) than were their counterparts of times past. Indeed, they often act as the primary sustainers of what now commonly passes as liberalism. This is evident in candidate and party support, as noted, but can be seen as well in stands on issues.

Let us look first to class composition. Entrepreneurial business has largely passed from the scene. It is no longer a major interest collectivity. Managerial business remains an important stratum. But it experiences peculiar fracturings which could not have been contemplated in earlier periods. Increasingly large segments of the broad new upper middle classes, of the professional and managerial community—primarily those at once the most affluent and secure and most closely associated with advanced technology—cease to function as defenders of business values. More to the point, they cease to think of themselves as "business" in the historic sense. They become incorporated into a rising "new class," the intelligentsia, responding to intellectual values and orientations rather than those traditionally associated with business. [15] At the same time, parts of the business community, especially those linked to newer enterprises and the top managers, continue to promote business values and reflect relative conservatism.

The intelligentisa, dramatically enlarged, operates as a distinctive social and political class of postindustrial America. It expresses powerful commonalities. Its members are generally secure in their affluence. More importantly, they share contact with intellectual activity—which does not mean, of course, that they participate in high culture or advanced intellectual pursuits—through that extraordinary nexus of 2500 colleges, 8.8 million college students, 600,000 professors, 900,000 artists, authors, and editors. They are linked by a communications network of unparalleled scope and pervasiveness, an instrument of technology (e. g., television) and wealth and intellectual sophistication. [16]

When we identify upper status groups in the contemporary United States—whether in terms of high educational attainment, the holding of "professional or managerial" occupations, high income, or any combination of such variables—we are not locating primarily a "business class" in the 1930s sense. The upper strata have expanded, become more diverse, assumed a new social coloration.

At the same time, "working class" has taken on a quite different social and political character than it held in the 1930s. Most members of the urban working class were economic "have nots" in the 1930s, who either experienced immediate economic privation or operated with precious little margin over subsistence needs. As such, they supported government-directed changes in the economic order. And the trade union movement, which gathered momentum in the 1930s, organized the "have not" working class and served as one of the principal new claimants for economic betterment and security and influence. These objectives were in large measure attained though governmental intervention and economic growth. The unionized labor force has moved up the socioeconomic ladder. For this group, the victory over economic privation has been won. Producing a wonderfully American semantic contradiction, this segment of the *working class* has become (lower) *middle class*. . . .

The head of the American labor movement, AFL-CIO president George Meany, has spoken insightfully to the transfiguration of labor's place in the postindustrial era. In a 1969 interview with *The New York Times*, Meany was willing to accept both "middle class" and "conservative" as descriptions of the membership of the labor movement.

> Labor, to some extent, has become middle class. When you have no property, you don't have anything, you have nothing to lose by these radical actions. But when you become a person who has a home and has property, to some extent you become conservative. And I would say to that extent, labor has become conservative. [17]

A working class that is middle class and conservative—that ia a distinctive feature of the contemporary social structure.

Conclusions

Over the last decade, a decisive inversion has taken place in the relationship established during the New Deal of class to sociopolitical commitments. The high social strata now consistently provide a greater measure of support for liberal programs and candidates than do the lower strata. This is no temporary phenomenon. No return to the New Deal pattern should be expected. The sources of the inversion lie buried deeply within broad transformations of the society and its political conflict. An understanding of the inversion yields more general insights into the character of contemporary politics.

What we now call liberalism frequently makes the old New Deal majority contributors rather than beneficiaries. Lower-status whites more often feel threatened than encouraged by current extensions of equalitarianism. There has been a significant *embourgeoisement* of the working class. The high socioeconomic cohorts, which had such a distinctive business coloration in the 1930s (and earlier), have changed their social and political character— notably through the growth of the professional stratum. Such developments are central to the inversion described herein.

Nothing in the above requires that the Democrats always find more support at the top than at the bottom. The relationship is between class *and ideology.* The top is more support- ive of the new liberalism than is the bottom, and more inclined to the Democrats only when and to the extent that they are perceived as the partisan instrument of the new liberalism.

* * *

Can the inversion described above be seen in the 1976 balloting and, to the extent that it cannot, why not?

First it should be emphasized that the inverted relationship between class and ideology remains essentially unchanged. Various measures of opinion taken in the course of the 1976 campaign show high-status groups giving more backing than low-status cohorts to programs and policies associated with the contemporary statement of liberalism. And the former continue to show much more positive feeling than do the latter for the symbol *liberal.* To cite one illustration, a national poll conducted by NBC News in mid-September found 40 percent of respondents with advanced degrees calling themselves liberals, com- pared to 35 percent of those with undergraduate training, and just 22 percent and 23 percent respectively among the high school and the grade school educated. [18]

The effects of this relationship were sharply evident in the 1976 Democrat presidential nomination contest. Throughout the primaries, it was a case of the more liberal the contender, the greater the proportion of his overall support drawn from among people of high socioeconomic status. For example, the NBC News survey of Massachusetts Democratic primary voters found that "two candidates—Harris and Udall—seem to be competing at the liberal end of the party spectrum. Both men appeal to upper socioeconomic status voters in the suburbs." [19] Bayh and Shriver occupied intermediate positions, in terms of the perceived extent of their liberalism and the education-occupation-income status of their supporters. Jackson, Carter, and Wallace did best among lower-status Democrats. Other NBC News polls and those of *The New York Times*/CBS News located similar distributions over the winter-spring 1976 primary season. [20]

Various national surveys confirm these state-by-state findings adding, of course, a measure of overall precision. For example, the April 1976 study of Yankelovich, Skelly, and White shows the most prominent Democratic contenders thus arrayed by the self-defined liberalism or conservatism of their supporters (among Democrats and independents): Udall, who had the highest proportion of liberal and the smallest percent of conservative backers; Humphrey; Jackson; Carter; and Wallace, whose backers were decidedly the most likely to think of themselves as conservatives. [21] (The differences in the Humphrey, Jackson, and Carter voter profiles, it should be noted, are modest.) And the candidate array by the socioeconomic status of their adherents is largely the same. Thus 35 percent of the Udall people were from families where the head of the household held a professional or executive position, compared to 26 percent of Carter's backers and 14 percent of Wallace's. An extraordinary 50 percent of those favoring Udall claimed to have completed at least three years of college, the status of 26 percent in the Jackson camp, 25 percent of those supporting Humphrey and Carter, and only 11 percent of the Wallace loyalists.

Much of the commentary immediately following the 1976 general election, however, carried an emphasis quite different from that of this article. It was asserted that Jimmy Carter's victory resulted from a restoration of "the old New Deal coalition"—most notably in a return of the older pattern of class voting. This argument contains a large element of truth—but it has been substantially overstated.

The differences generally in voting patterns between 1976 and, for instance, 1936 are massive. The South was a cornerstone of the New Deal Democratic majority and the region gave the 1976 Democratic nominee his core support. But an exceptional shift has occurred in the underlying structure. During the New Deal era as earlier, blacks were largely disenfranchised in the South and the region voted Democratic because an overwhelming majority of whites were so inclined. In 1976, even with a moderate white Georgian as the party's standard bearer, white southerners appear to have cast a majority of their votes for the Republican nominee. [22] The region went Democratic, then, because relatively recently enfranchised southern blacks returned a heavy Democratic majority.

During the New Deal years, Catholics were heavily and consistently Democratic, in keeping with a pattern of partisan loyalties stretching back to the age of Jackson. in 1976, however, Catholics split their vote evenly between Ford and Carter. [23] Protestants and Catholics voted almost identically in the 1976 presidential balloting—the first time in the period for which we have reliable survey data, and probably the first time in United States history that Catholics have not been notably more Democratic than Protestants.

Even on the matter of class voting, 1976 was hardly a typical New Deal election. According to the NBC election day survey, college students—still a relatively privileged group in social background—continued their recent Democratic ways. The national election day survey conducted by the Associated Press indicates that a large majority of college-educated Americans voted for Democratic House of Representatives nominees.

Fifty-six percent of those with advanced degrees backed Democratic congressional candidates. While persons with a high school education or less were more heavily Democratic than the college-educated groups, the differences, according to the AP survey, were modest, on the order of 6 percentage points. The CBS election day survey found higher-income Americans (with family incomes of $20,000 a year and more) dividing 51–49, Republican and Democratic, in the 1976 congressional balloting. This is hardly the New Deal pattern. The movement toward an inversion noted in voting for U.S. House of Representatives candidates for the elections of the late 1960s and early 1970s was not reversed in 1976.

At the presidential vote level, there *was* a somewhat different pattern in 1976 than we saw in 1968 and 1972—and one more in keeping with the early 1960s. There was a fairly steady increase in the Ford proportion with movement up the socioeconomic ladder, however SES is measured. But any suggestion that class voting was as distinct in the 1976 presidential contest as in those of the New Deal years is, quite simply, wrong. There were clearer differences between high-and low-status voters in 1976 than in 1972 or 1968, but the high- and low-status groups were much less differentiated in 1976 than in the 1936–1948 period.

Louis Harris found, for example, that grade school-educated whites were about 14 percentage points more Democratic in 1976 than were their college-trained counterparts. Whites from families earning less than $5,000 a year were approximately 16 points more for Carter than were whites with family incomes of $15,000 and higher per year. Data made available from the election day "intercept" polls of the *Times*/CBS News and NBC News show similar distributions. In the 1930s and 1940s, by way of contrast, high- and low-status whites were separated by between 30 and 40 percentage points in presidential preference. Robert Reinhold, reporting on the *Times*/CBS News survey noted a related facet of the secular diminution of class voting when he observed that "Mr. Carter succeeded in eating into groups that normally tend to vote Republican. For example, he did better among professional and managerial people than any Democrat in the last quarter century except Lyndon Johnson." [24] Actually, it could be extended to the last half century.

The 1976 Democratic presidential nominee over his long campaign attempted quite successfully to muffle the various social and cultural issues which have been transforming the meaning of liberalism. He did not seek to mobilize—indeed, he sought to avoid mobilizing—a distinctively New Liberal coalition. After eight years in the presidential wilderness and especially because of their overwhelming 1972 defeat, the Democrats generally were willing to follow Carter's lead and sheathed ideological knives in the interests of appeals at once more diffuse and more traditional in their economic emphases. So the 1976 balloting showed some backing away from the inversions of 1968 and 1972. But the relationship described involves, basically, *class* and *ideology*, and the 1976 political experience does not indicate any reversal of the long-term inversion this article has sought to treat.

NOTES

1. See, for example, James L. Sundquist, "Hardly a Two-Party System," *The Nation* (December 7, 1974), 582–586. Sundquist believes the 1974 electoral results support an argument he had developed previously in *Dynamics of the Party System* (Washington, D. C., 1973), that the New Deal alignment remains essentially intact.

2. Sundquist, "Hardly a Two-Party System," p. 385.

3. Gallup has provided survey confirmation of this. See *The Gallup Opinion Index,* 113 (November 1974), especially pp. 1-2, 29-31.

4. For extensive analysis of this subject, see by Everett Carll Ladd, Jr., and S. M. Lipset, *The Divided Academy: Professors and Politics* (New York, 1976).

5. For further data and explanation of faculty voting, see Everett Carll Ladd, Jr., and S. M. Lipset, *Academics, Politics and the 1972 Election* (Washington, D. C., 1973), chaps. 3 and 4. See, also, by the same authors, *The Divided Academy,* chap. 9.

6. For a discussion of the Harvard student straw vote historically, see S. M. Lipset, "Political Controversies at Harvard," in Lipsett and David Riesman, *Education and Politics at Harvard* New York, 1975), chap. 8. There have been changes in the social group composition of the Harvard student body since World War II, of course, but these are not sufficient to account for the partisan shift. The representation of blacks has increased, but blacks remain less than 10 percent of Harvard students. The proportion Jewish is about the same now as in 1948. Harvard students are still an enormously privileged group, in terms of social background, compared to the public at large.

7. For supporting data, see S. M. Lipset and Everett Carll Ladd, Jr., "College Generations From the 1930's to the 1960's, "The Public Interest, no. 25 (Fall 1971), 105-109.

8. *The Gallup Opinion Index,* no. 109 (July 1974), 15.

9. Ibid.

10. CBS News Election Day Survey, data made available to the Social Science Data Center University of Connecticut, courtesy of CBS News.

11. *The Gallup Opinion Index,* no. 88 (October 1972), 3.

12. For supporting data and analysis, see Ladd and Lipset, *The Divided Academy,* chaps. 5 and 9.

13. Not all high SES groups show Democratic majorities, of course. People in the very highest income groups—over $25,000 a year—and business executives, still display Republican majorities, although the extent of the GOP advantage has been reduced even here.

14. Some commentators have insisted that the inversion of the New Deal class-ideology relationship carried with it great opportunities for the Republican party, along with the problems noted above. No one has advanced this argument more persistently and forcefully than conservative journalist Kevin P. Phillips. Large segments of the old working class have in the post-World War II years become middle class and supportive of conservative positions—although not of old-style business conservatism. As the GOP lost ground in an increasingly liberal establishment, it could have more than compensated for its losses by inroads into the massive new bourgeoisie. The populism of the New Deal had a conservative establishment to attack and was directed to the support of liberal programs and policies. The populism of the late 1960s and 1970s, confronting instead a liberal establishment, has led to neoconservative policy responses. But the Republicans have blown this "ideological opportunity of a generation." They have lost ground at the top and have failed to gain in the middle. Phillips, "The Future of American Politics," *National Review,* 24 (December 22, 1972), 1398. See as well his *Mediacracy: American Parties and Politics in the Communications Age* (Garden City, N. Y., 1975). My own views on why the GOP has failed to achieve any widespead, persistent advance as a result of the inversion cannot be covered within the limits of the present article.

15. Public opinion analyst Louis Harris has drawn upon his survey data in developing one aspect of this argument. Noting that in postindustrial America, "at the key executive level, more people [are] employed in professional than in line executive capacities," he stresses the finding that "the one quality that divided most professionals from line executives in business organizations was that professionals felt much more beholden to their outside discipline—whether it be systems engineering, teaching, scientific research, or other professional ties—than to the particular company or institution they worked for. *The Anguish of Change* (New York, 1973). p. 45.

16. College training, an experience shared by more than 35 million Americans, defines the outer boundaries of the intelligentsia. In use *intelligentsia* to include those persons

whose background and vocation associates them directly in the application of trained intelligence. It includes, that is, not only intellectuals—people involved in the creation of new ideas, new knowledge, new cultural forms—but also that larger community whose training gives them some facility in handling abstract ideas, or whose work requires them to manipulate ideas rather than things.

17. "Excerpts from Interview with Meany on Status of Labor Movement." *The New York Times*, August 31, 1969.

18. NBC News, National Poll #55, September 16-18, 1976.

19. NBC News, "The Election Newsletter," February 11, 1976.

20. For reports on these surveys documenting the above conclusion, see Robert Reinhold, "Poll Finds Voters Judging 6 Rivals on Personality, " *The New York Times*, February 13, 1976, pp. 1, 30; R. W. Apple, Jr., "New Political Universe," *The New York Times*, March 3, 1976, pp. 1, 17; Maurice Carroll, "Jackson Won in New York by Narrowly Based Voting," *The New York Times*, April 8, 1976, p. 30; and Robert Reinhold, "Poll Links Udall Strength to Low Vote in Michigan," *The New York Times*, May 20, 1976, pp. 1, 29.

21. These data were made available by Yankelovich, Skelly, and White, and the author wishes to express his appreciation to Ruth Clark, vice-president of that organizaion. Democrats and independents in the April 1976 survey were asked: "If you had to make a choice among Jackson, Carter, Udall, Wallace and Humphrey as the Democratic candidate for the Presidency, whom would you choose?'"

22. The *Times* CBS News election day poll reported a Ford majoirty among white southerners. Working with these data, with data from the Associated Press election day poll, and with actual aggregate voting data from each southern state, I have concluded that Carter received a majority of the white vote only in Georgia, Arkansas, and Tennessee, among the eleven states of the old Confederacy.

23. The various national surveys do not agree exactly on the distribution of the vote of Catholics. According to the Harris survey conducted just before the election (October 29-31), for example, Catholics broke 50-50. The *Times* CBS News election day survey shows Carter with 54 percent of the Catholic vote. The Associated Press survey also indicates Carter won 54 percent of the Catholic vote. All of the major surveys agree that the distribution was very close.

24. Robert Reinhold, "Carter Victory Laid to Democrats Back in Fold, Plus Independents," *The New York Times*, November 4, 1976, p. 25.

15 / Organized Labor Takes a Hard Look at Whom It Will Support This Fall

Charles W. Hucker

Rep. Marilyn Lloyd, a sophomore Democrat whose Tennessee district covers industrial Chattanooga and part of the state's rough eastern hills, is illustrative of a dilemma faced by organized labor's political strategists as they begin to plot their tactics for the 1978 congressional elections.

Although the labor officials rarely mention names, Mrs. Lloyd is among a group of members of Congress, particularly freshman and sophomore Democrats in the House, who have been a disappointment to the unions during the 1977 session of Congress. Labor is angry because these members, despite union support in past elections, did not vote on certain issues as expected. The question now facing labor is what to do about it.

Because of that disappointment nearly all segments of organized labor, which is far from a political monolith vow to take a harder look at voting records and their conformity to labor positions. But there are sharp differences within the union hierarchy over what that closer scrutiny will mean. The sentiment ranges from talk of hit lists to open pledges of withholding support from defecting members to milder reproachments.

Mrs. Lloyd, who received labor endorsements in both of her House races, voted with organized labor on only six of the 10 key issues designated by the AFL-CIO Committee on Political Education (COPE). Two of those anti-labor votes occurred on common-site picketing legislation and the oil cargo preference bill. Losses in the House on those two issues contributed to the widespread view that organized labor had not fared nearly as well as predicted in the first session of the 95th Congress.

Hit List

The Tennessee representative was named in one published report as holding a spot on a union hit list of legislators allegedly targeted for defeat in 1978. But Alexander Barkan, the COPE director and political spokesman for AFL-CIO President George Meany, maintains that "there's no hit list."

Reprinted by permission from *Congressional Quarterly Weekly Report*, Vol. 36, No. 4 January 28, 1978: 193-198. Copyright 1978 Congressional Quarterly Inc.

"The only thing that will be different is that those Democrats who have overall bad records will not be supported," Barkan told Congressional Quarterly. "I'm talking about those supported by COPE in 1974 and 1976."

Although Mrs. Lloyd was more surprised than angered by her mention on a reported COPE hit list, she warned that COPE's strategy could backfire. "It is not going to do any good to threaten people." she said.

Mrs. Lloyd commented that she was satisfied she had good relations with labor unions in her district.

"The concerns of working people in New York state are different from those of working people in the 3rd District of Tennessee," Mrs. Lloyd said. "I don't think this [a COPE endorsement] is going to be decided on a national level; if my labor people want to endorse me, they will."

Although Barkan won't discuss names or even numbers, he clearly is disappointed that some legislators endorsed by organized labor's political action committees had not voted with labor on key issues in 1977. They include labor law revision, minimum wage, common-site picketing and cargo preference legislation. Barkan's current strategy calls for withholding support from certain defectors even if it means the election of more conservative Republicans. Barkan contends that some of the strongest sentiment for this approach comes from the lower ranks of the AFL–CIO.

Barkan began the tough talk in October, saying COPE would consider either (1) opposing "summer-time soldiers," as he likes to call the defecting labor-backed Democrats, or (2) backing independent candidates in general elections, or (3) staying out of a contest by withholding support from the incumbent. His position has softened over the last three months to emphasizing only the last alternative.

Other labor leaders predict further relaxation of the COPE strategy as the 1978 legislative record is compiled and political reality is considered more carefully. The largest doubt expressed in interviews with union officials and members of Congress was whether COPE really intended to sacrifice generally friendly legislators who stray occassionally from the labor line, particulary those from conservative districts such as Mrs. Lloyd. "The question is what is the alternative?" one labor leader stated.

The Barkan strategy is not viewed with universal enthusiam in labor circles. In some quarters, both within and outside COPE, it is believed any punishment tactic toward congressional Democrats would be a mistake. But as one union observer put it, "the concept of closer scrutiny has uniform receptivity."

While organized labor is conceded to be a potent factor in many districts, it is questioned even in some labor quarters whether COPE has the power to alter the outcome in every district where it is unhappy with the Democratic incumbent. In 1976, 262 of 365 COPE-endorsed House candidates won, along with 19 of 28 labor-backed Senate candidates. But an undeterminable number would have won anyway.

Rising Expectations

Barkan's recent line is not the first time that labor has talked tough about supporting its friends and opposing its enemies. But labor's legislative failures in 1977, despite Democratic control of both the White House and the Congress for the first time in eight years, have spawned a nearly unanimous view that congressional voting records must be analyzed more carefully in the future. It is a matter of heightened expectations that were not completely fulfilled.

"Labor expected, with a Democratic President and with Democrats theoretically in control of Congress, this federal government machinery would produce programs which were important to us and legislation on social programs we have been trying to achieve for six or eight years." commented Mikel Miller of the Communication Workers of America. "The feeling was that we had been in a stalemate for eight years because we had a Democratic Congress and a Republican President; theoretically our friends were [now] in charge of the machinery."

But Miller, with a sigh, added: "The dream is often larger than the reality," Still, Miller's group is not interested in taking the hard-line Barkan approach.

Although COPE won its five key Senate votes and eight of its 10 prime House votes in 1977, the current hardline attitude about who to support in the 1978 elections is a direct consequence of labor's record in the first half of the 95th Congress.

Organized labor didn't get it wanted on minimum wage legislation that was passed by Congress and signed by President Carter, for example. Construction and maritime unions were especially upset by the House defeats of the common-site picketing and oil cargo preference bills, particularly since similar proposals had passed in previous sessions. President Ford had vetoed a common-site picketing bill in January 1976 and killed a cargo preference measure with a pocket veto in 1974. But once a more sympathetic President was elected, Congress would not pass the same legislation.

In the 1977 common-site picketing vote, the opposition of 13 freshman Democrats who ran with COPE backing spelled the difference for the bill, which was defeated 205-217.

Jay Foreman, a vice president of the Retail Clerks International Association and administrative assistant to the group's president, said that by the fall of 1977 there was a feeling of "genuine anger" in many union circles following the series of legislative setbacks. Foreman described himself as one of the early exponents of a hit list strategy, but has backed away from that approach because of the political problems he believes it would entail.

Coupled with the labor frustration over Congress's performance is the wary relationship between organized labor and the Carter White House. That was best symbolized by Carter's failure to address the AFL-CIO convention in December 1977. Prior Democratic Presidents routinely had made the trek to the labor conclave. Even Richard Nixon, who never had been considered a friend of organized labor, made that trip.

Privately some labor leaders believe that the hard-line COPE reaction reflects a more fundatmental concern—that organized labor may be seen as a declining political force. "One of the risks is looking impotent," remarked one politically active labor official.

The union difficulties in Congress come at a time when AFL-CIO affiliates have lost 500,000 members over the last two years. They now represent less than a quarter of the country's working population. And those 13,600,000 remaining in unions tied to the AFL-CIO, along with others from outside the federation, are perceived by some as more independent-minded union members, less inclined always to follow obediently the dictates of their leaders.

To some this represents a shakier political base with the danger that the appearance of declining influence may itself lead to further decline.

COPE Approach

Barkan, who stirred controversy because of COPE's decision to remain neutral in the 1972 presidential contest and because of his unhappiness with the Democratic Party's 1974 charter, is leading the labor forces calling for retribution against defecting legislators. Although not known for his eagerness to talk to reporters, Barkan has willingly discussed COPE's unhappiness with some members of Congress labor had counted on for support.

"We want them to understand they can't take our support for granted; we're putting them on notice," Barkan said. "We're criticized that we're parochial. Have you ever heard of the AMA [American Medical Association] supporting someone who favors national health insurance?"

But only in rare instances, Barkan said, will COPE oppose incumbents who had labor support in the past. Rather, COPE is more likely to sit on the sidelines.

"We're not going to go out looking for primary opponents," Barkan stated. "It will take the form of just not supporting, and we will have an educational campaign to explain why when we supported that candidate before."

Other leaders are equally insistent that there is no hit list despite the persistent talk. "There is not a hit list and there are not plans for one," said Foreman of the retail clerks.

But others hold open the door to that option. "There is no hit list," said William J. Holayter, political director of the International Association of Machinists, "but that doesn't mean there won't be one."

The United Steelworkers of America has made public its unhappiness with Rep. Jim Santini (D Nev.), one of the few instances where there is open talk of possibly turning out an incumbent Democrat. "We're not happy with him," said Dean K. Clowes, the steelworkers political activities director. "If we had a good alternative we might oppose him." In any case, Santini definitely will not receive any contributions or an endorsement from the steelworkers political action committee this year.

Washington-based labor political strategists contend that the displeasure expressed by top officials reflects sentiments at the local and state level, where the actual COPE endorsements are made.

"The same voting record that makes us unhappy perhaps makes them more unhappy than us," Barkan said. "Many of them feel a more personal disappointment,"

But if Washington-based labor strategists are interested in dumping Mrs. Lloyd, the Tennessee representative, for example, they won't find ready sentiment for that in her district .

"We haven't agreed with every vote, but I'm not all that displeased with her," said Edward Pierce of the Chattanooga local of the machinists. "She has given us some bad votes and she had given us some good votes," said Charles Dunning of the Chattanooga Building Trades Council, who is inclined to vote for her endorsement although he won't make up his mind until it is known who else is running in Tennessee's 3rd Congressional District.

What Does It Take?

If some organized labor leaders are unhappy, what does it take to please them? Virtually all labor officials insisted they do not expect a 100 percent labor voting record or the legislators they endorsed to be rubber stamps. All labor expects, the union leaders say, is their vote on key issues.

The definition of key vote varies from union to union. Common-site picketing is important to the building trades unions and cargo preference to the maritime unions, but not particularly to the communications workers or the National Education Association or the steelworkers. Even COPE officials currently are undecided how many correct votes on its list of key issues will be necessary to insure another endorsement for an incumbent member.

Labor officials agree that votes during the second session of the 95th Congress easily could change the standing of a member who has perturbed the unions. "Some of these fellows might be able to redeem themselves with one vote," commented Holayter of the machinists.

COPE plans to place greater emphasis on strictly labor issues such as common-site picketing, cargo preference, labor law revision and Hatch Act legislation, than in the past. In its 1977 scorecard on legislators' performance, COPE for the first time segregated votes that directly affect organized labor's interests from more general social issues such as housing development, urban aid and health.

Republican Gain?

Some labor political leaders acknowledge that Barkan's plan to withhold support from defecting Democratic incumbents may aid Republicans.

"That doesn't bother me." declared Barkan. "That is a risk we have to take. We do this with our eyes wide open; we have to take the long view. We'll survive anti-labor Republicans.

"What is the difference between a Democrat who is anti-labor and a Republican who is anti-labor?"

But others are willing to recognize gradations of "anti-laborness."

"Maybe we take the risk and lose a few [Democratic] seats in the House," commented the retail clerks' Foreman. "We wouldn't give up a 60 percenter for a zero percent Republican [on labor issues], but maybe we would give up a 30 percenter."

Part of the COPE approach toward showing congressional Democrats it should not be taken for granted is to detach itself from Democratic Party internal affairs. That detachment was spurred in part by labor defeats at the 1974 mid-term Democratic convention. But despite that effort organized labor has intertwined its congressional fortunes with Democrats. According to the Republican National Political Action Committee, 96.5 percent of the contributions by unions in 1976 to congressional candidates went to Democrats.

Cautious View

Consideration of hit lists or even talk of withholding support is not popular with one segment of organized labor, including the American Federation of State, County and Municipal Employees; the Communications Workers of America; and the United Auto Workers.

FEC's Suits Against Unions

Several labor organizations are preparing for the 1978 elections uncertain of the legality of their political money-handling practices because of suits brought by the Federal Election Commission (FEC).

The commission sued the AFL-CIO on Dec. 16, 1977, charging that the federation had violated federal law by improperly transferring money to the Committee on Political Education (COPE) political contributions fund from the COPE education fund, which is COPE's nonpartisan account within the federation's general treasury. Federal law prohibits the use of dues collected from members, which form the federation's general treasury, for political purposes and requires that contributions to candidates be made from voluntary donations by union members.

The FEC also filed suit against the National Education Association, alleging that the NEA and 18 of its state affiliates had violated federal election law by requiring donations from teachers to NEA political funds.

AFL-CIO Suit

In the AFL-CIO suit, the FEC charges that more than $392,000 had been transferred improperly from the COPE education fund to the COPE political contributions fund since 1970. Federation officials replied that the sum represented a partial repayment of loans, totaling about $704,000, from the political contributions fund to the education fund.

Alexander Barkan, the COPE director, said the system of loans had been approved by the General Accounting Office, which supervised campaign funds before the creation of the FEC. Barkan said the AFL-CIO was willing to accept the FEC's interpretation of the law and stop the loan practices, but first wanted to transfer back to the political contributions fund the remaining $312,000. The FEC would not agree to that, Barkan said.

NEA Suit

Regarding the suit against the NEA, Stanley J. McFarland, NEA director of government relations, said: "We have always maintained that our collection system was legal."

McFarland said that certain sums of money, which he would not disclose, were being held in escrow until the suit was resolved.

The FEC suits against the AFL-CIO and the NEA were based on parts of two complaints filed by the National Right to Work Committee. The actual filing of the suits followed court orders, sought by the right to work committee, directing the FEC to act on the complaints within certain time limits.

Charges

The right to work committee also charged in its complaint against the AFL-CIO that:

> • Registration and get-out-the vote drives during the 1976 presidential campaign, funded by union members' dues, were not actually nonpartisan as required by federal law. Based on that argument, the committee further contended that those activities represented campaign contributions which should have been publicly reported and, because they allegedly were coordinated with the Carter presidential campaign, exceeded contribution limits.

> • The 13.6 million members of the AFL-CIO's affiliated unions are not members of the federation itself and the federation is not permitted to solicit them for political donations. If those individuals are treated as federation members, then the right to work committee alleged that there can be only one COPE contributions fund, not the many now affiliated with the different state AFL-CIOs.

The FEC has notified the right to work committee that investigation of those allegations had been terminated. The FEC apparently concluded there was no wrongdoing on those points because no mention of those charges was made in the FEC suit against the AFL-CIO.

The right to work committee itself was sued Dec. 22, 1977, by the FEC, which asserted that the committee had improperly solicited funds from individuals who were not members of the right to work committee.

Although the public employees group and communications workers are within the AFL-CIO, they often have taken a different view of political strategy than the prevailing one in COPE. For example, they were among nine unions that took part in the Labor Coalition Clearinghouse, which actively recruited delegates to the 1976 Democratic convention, while COPE remained aloof. They also strayed from the COPE line in 1972 by endorsing Sen. George McGovern (D S.D.) in the presidential contest. The UAW is outside the AFL-CIO.

Jerry Wurf, president of the state, county and municipal employees, has called proponents of any kind of punishment strategy guilty of "heavy handedness."

"There is an atmosphere of skepticism and disappointment with traditional Democratic records," commented William Dodds of the United Auto Workers. Although he shares that disappointment, he added, "it is unwise to have a feeling of punishment."

Dodds believes that organized labor is in a shakedown period with the current Congress. "When it doesn't pan out the way you expect there tends to be a looking around, asking who's to blame. There is a downer period." Dodds related. "You have a right to generalities now. Later they [COPE] may still be down, but the question is how to translate that into effective politics."

But the UAW itself will be more "toughly selective" in allocating its resources, Dodds said. "If the UAW is faced with an unexciting Democratic incumbent and an open seat within the same state, we will spend more time with the open seat."

Miller of the communications workers believes it is too extreme to withhold support completely from defectors from labor positions. The communications workers would more likely decrease, but not cut off, support for an incumbent who had a disappointing record in the CWA's view.

Strategy Weaknesses

The critics of the Barkan policy see three major weaknesses in a punishment strategy:

● Even an occasionally defecting Democrat is more likely to favor labor than a Republican.

"It is hard to find a candidate who hasn't helped in some way: besides they are by and large better than their Republican opponents," commented Miller.

● It is not realistic politically to expect to defeat a Democratic incumbent who from time to time is unfriendly, if COPE should attempt that.

Talk of hit lists does not properly account for the advantages of incumbency, Dodds said. "There is an overwhelming tendency to downplay the tremendous power of incumbency."

"If you are going to try to defeat somebody in the primary, you'd better be sure you can do it," warned Miller.

● The plan does not take into account that many labor-backed Democrats run in conservative districts.

Miller noted that some of the offending incumbents have constituencies that are not pro-labor and legislators are very sensitive to political winds in their districts.

"The winds are now blowing harder from the right," Miller observed. "The wind is artificially generated and we have not generated any countervailing wind."

The case of Mrs. Lloyd illustrates some of the difficulties that skeptics see in a hard-line strategy. A Republican alternative to her likely would be clearly anti-labor. Mrs Lloyd's GOP predecessor, LaMar Baker, whom she defeated with 51.1 percent of the vote in 1974, voted with labor only 9 percent of the time that year.

Mrs. Lloyd probably would be difficult to beat in a Democratic primary. She had no primary opposition in 1976 and beat her Republican opponent with 67.5 percent of the ballots.

Mrs. Lloyd also is one of those who has to be concerned about a conservative constituency. Her area once was represented in the House by the late Estes Kefauver (D), but also has been represented by the current Republican national chairman, William Brock.

"It's a conservative district and you must get along with everybody," noted Ray Powell, a vice president of the communications workers local in Chattanooga. "For her district she has a good voting record; if she voted 100 percent [with labor] she wouldn't get elected."

In her first two years in Congress, Mrs. Lloyd voted with the COPE position 65 percent of the time.

Congressional Reaction

Predictably the members of Congress who felt the heat from labor over their 1977 votes are the most sensitive to the early outlines of the COPE strategy.

"This strategy is an emotional reaction," commented Joseph S. Ammerman, a freshman Democrat from Pennsylvania. Ammerman estimated that he received about $15,000 from organized labor for his 1976 campaign. He was one of the 13 freshman Democrats who ran with labor backing that opposed the common-site picketing bill. Pennsylvania building trades unions have registered their unhappiness with him.

"Mr. Barkan impresses me as more intelligent and a better counter than the people who would emotionally take off on this kind of tack," Ammerman said.

The Pennsylvania legislator predicted that hit lists, if they emerge, would backfire by galvanizing anti-labor sentiment among voters. Ammerman represents an area that had not sent a Democrat to the House for 40 years before he was elected in 1976. Ammerman's Republican predecessor had a 26 rating from COPE in his last year in office.

The COPE plans have stirred resentment from several members. "Any group that thinks I am going to be with them 100 percent, they're looking at the wrong person," said John Krebs (D Calif.), who first was elected in 1974.

"If that is not good enough, that's tough." Krebs remarked about his own COPE voting record, which was 87 percent in 1975 and 70 percent in 1976. On COPE's 10 prime issues in 1977, he voted with labor seven times.

In 1974 Krebs defeated Bob Mathias, a Republican who had a COPE rating of 22 that year.

Harold L. Volkmer, a freshman Democrat, has riled construction unions in Missouri with his "no" vote on common-site picketing. Volkmer said he believed that labor expected a 100 percent voting record in return for its support.

"The only thing support ever buys is the basic opportunity to present their point of view; it doesn't buy my vote," commented Volkmer. "If they oppose me in both the primary and general, they will have a hard time getting in the door to talk to me."

In any event, Volkmer does not think he owes a debt of gratitude to organized labor. "They cost me as much as they helped me," he declared. The Missouri representative said he spent an extra $8,000 to $10,000 in his primary campaign in northwest Missouri's 9th District because organized labor was strongly backing a former state labor official in the Democratic primary. Volkmer then received labor assistance in the general election.

Labor's Spending Plans for '78

In 1976 labor union political action committees spent $8.2 million in direct contributions to congressional candidates. Interviews with labor leaders indicate that amount probably will be matched in 1978, but it is unclear whether it will be exceeded.

A more definitive outlook on labor campaign spending will emerge when union political action committees complete their campaign budgeting. The Committee on Political Education (COPE) of the AFL–CIO will begin its campaign budget formulation during a series of regional meetings starting in early February.

According to Common Cause, labor political action committees contributed $8,206,578 to congressional candidates in 1976 (including primaries), compared to $6,315,488 in 1974.

If the 1976 amount is not exceeded in 1978, it will be partly attributable to the more selective labor strategy for the 1978 congressional elections and a desire to build up a reserve for use in the 1980 Democratic delegate selection process.

Contributions by union political committees to candidates must come from voluntary donations from union members. Registration and get-out-the-vote drives may be conducted with union dues.

In soliciting funds from union members for political contributions, Alexander Barkan, the COPE director, is stressing the increased attention of traditional business groups, as well as the New Right, to congressional campaigns.

"It is going very well," Barkan said of COPE's fund raising efforts for the 1978 elections. "There will be a reaction to the right-to-work people. Our people respond when they feel an organized threat."

One employee group faced with an obstacle in its fund raising is the National Education Association. Stanley J. McFarland, NEA director of government relations, said a suit by the Federal Election Commission against the NEA and some of its state affiliates over their fund raising procedures is complicating its budget planning. [See the box on page 293.]

The Communications Workers of America is planning to hold back part of its 1978 receipts from its members to use in the 1980 Democratic delegate selection process. "In 1976 we spent every nickel we had," said Mikel Miller of the communications workers. "In 1978, I don't expect we will do that."

The Retail Clerks International Association will spend about $250,000 in 1978 for direct contributions to congressional candidates. But Jay Foreman of the retail clerks said that amount won't go far. If the retail clerks make contributions in 50 or 60 marginal races and make obligatory donations to 15 or 20 "safe old-timers," Foreman said, its average gift would be less than $500.

Dean K. Clowes of the United Steelworkers of America said his group would contribute about the same amount in 1978 to congressional candidates as it did in 1976 when it gave about $500,000.

In 1976 the top labor contributors to congressional campaigns were the national and state AFL–CIO COPEs, maritime-related unions, the UAW, NEA, the International Association of Machinists and the United Steelworkers.

1976 Labor Contributions

Incumbent/Challenger

Incumbents	$4,666,610
Challengers	1,568,661
Open Seats	1,153,991
	$7,389,262*

Republican/Democrat

House Democrats	$4,842,301
House Republicans	134,740
Senate Democrats	2,318,371
Senate Republicans	93,850
	$7,389,262*

*The amounts represented contributions to candidates who ran in the general election and do not include contributions to primary losers or special election candidates.
Source: Common Cause.

The COPE strategy receives a more sympathetic hearing from Rep. Edward P. Beard (D R.I.), the leader of the 14 member blue collar caucus.

"I would imagine they will not pass out endorsements like bubblegum," Beard, a former house painter, said of the labor unions. "They're saying, 'If you're a fat cat former house painter in Washington, you'd better get off your duff.' "

16 / New Right: "Many Times More Effective" Now

Christopher Buchanan

The organized conservative community seems serious about its promise to "move against Congress in 1978 in a way that's never been conceived of."

A constellation of conservative groups that use the direct-mail services of Richard A. Viguerie and form the nucleus of what is coming to be known as the New Right, already has amassed funds that are far in excess of what it had raised at this point two years ago. New Right groups contributed a bit less than one million dollars to House and Senate candidates in 1976.

Viguerie, one of the New Right's major tacticians, predicts a massive assault on liberal incumbents and says the New Right will be "many, many times more effective" in 1978 than it was two years ago.

A combination of early fund raising drives, which have raised more than $3.5 million already, plus predictions of more to come from the right, have Democrats, labor union, liberals and even some Republicans terribly worried.

"We have the talent and resources to move in a bold, massive way," Viguerie told Congressional Quarterly. "We plan something which is larger than anything that's been done before outside the major two parties."

It is still too early to tell if the prophecy from the man who has been called the political guru and financial wizard of the New Right will come true. But it is already clear that ideological groups on the right, as well as the left, are preparing for an expensive election year.

It is also quite evident that the New Right's activities to date and future plans dwarf anything the liberal organizations and the older, more traditional conservative groups have contemplated.

The so-called New Right is a collection of groups that pledge allegiance to conservative positions on the "social issues," such as abortion, the Equal Rights Amendment and gun control, as well as emotional issues such as ratification of the Panama Canal treaties. There is less emphasis on traditional conservative values of balanced budgets and the free enterprise system. The New Right also makes a point of supporting conservative Democrats as well as Republicans. Most of the groups and their leaders have emerged in the last three or four years.

Reprinted by Permission from *Congressional Quarterly Weekly Report*, Vol. 35, No. 52 (December 24, 1977): 2649-2653. Copyright 1977 Congressional Quarterly Inc.

Viguerie is one of the key figures and certainly the most successful fund raiser in the New Right. From his offices in Falls Church, Va., near Washington, he sends out more than two million letters a week for conservative candidates and half a dozen right-wing organizations.

The most prominent New Right groups include the National Conservative Political Action Committee (NCPAC), the Committee for the Survival of a Free Congress (CSFC), Gun Owners of America (GOA) and the Committee for Responsible Youth Politics (CRYP). All of these groups are planning to be heavily involved in supporting conservative candidates from both parties in next year's primary and general elections.

"We expect to be involved not only in congressional and Senate elections." Viguerie said, "but also legislative, gubernatorial, lieutenant gubernatorial and all kinds of other races as well."

There are several other groups on the right, not connected to Viguerie's operation, that are already active. Ronald Reagan used a million-dollar surplus from his unsuccessful presidential campaign to begin Citizens for the Republic (CFTR). The Fund for a Conservative Majority (FCM) grew out of the Young Americans for Freedom. The oldest of the major right-wing groups, which has raised the least amount of money this year, is the Conservative Victory Fund (CVF), an offshoot of the American Conservative Union.

According to reports filed with the Federal Election Commission in the first 10 months of 1977 these seven groups raised $3,573,824. The four groups utilizing Viguerie's fund-raising machinery have raised two-thirds of the total amount. By contrast the groups which traditionally support liberal candidates, such as the National Committee for an Effective Congress (NCEC), have raised less than half a million dollars in 1977.

Because committees such as these are limited to contributing $5,000 to a candidate for each primary and general election, Viguerie also is planning to do a considerable amount of fund raising directly for candidates. He is confident he can easily raise $250,000 in each of 30 different House elections in 1978. The average cost of a House campaign in 1976 was less than $100,000.

Concern on the Left

The ambitiousness of the conservatives' plans for 1978 have their opponents troubled.

"The right is better organized than they have ever been," worries Russell D. Hemenway, national director of NCEC. "They are beginning to emulate our campaign tactics, which is flattering, but it is also going to make things tougher."

In a speech to the Democratic National Committee Oct. 7, DNC Chairman Kenneth M. Curtis warned that "millions of dollars. . . . will fund a vigorous nationwide effort against progressive Democratic representatives and senators in 1978. I think it is essential," he continued, "to combat the demagoguery of the right wing in any reasonable and feasible way available to us."

Viguerie seems pleased with the apprehension he sees among liberal activists. "I know the left is very bothered, and with good cause." For the last 20 to 30 years, he said, "the liberals have had a free reign." But with the new conservative groups now in place, he predicts, "we are going to give them one gosh awful run for their money."

Viguerie's efforts are not limited to defeating liberal Democrats. "We are not going to ignore some incumbent Republicans if they are a detriment to the interests of the conservative cause," he said.

Several Republican senators are upset by Viguerie's statements and letters being sent on behalf of conservative primary challengers to liberal Republicans.

In a letter to Republican Chairman Bill Brock, eight Republican senators organized by Charles McC. Mathias (Md.) complained that funding primary challenges from the right against incumbent Republicans "is not the kind of healthy competition we should encourage within the Republican Party. It is cannibalism."

Viguerie called the letter hypocritical and asked how three of the senators who signed it could justify demanding party loyalty when they refused to support Sen. Barry Goldwater (R Ariz.) in his 1964 presidential bid.

1978 Game Plans

The political objectives of both the right- and left-wing groups are clear. Conservatives plan to concentrate on ousting House liberals, many of whom were first elected in 1974. They also have targeted for defeat Republican Sens. Clifford P. Case (N.J.) and Edward W. Brooke (Mass.), as well as Rep. John B. Anderson (R Ill.). At the same time the right will support two leading conservative senators, Jesse Helms (R N.C.) and Strom Thurmond (R S.C.), both of whom may face strong Democratic challengers next year.

What Groups Have Spent, Raised

Interest groups have spent more than they have raised during 1977. Expenditures for 1977 include printing and mailing costs both for fund raising and lobbying purposes, as well as salaries, research and general office expenses.

The following figures come from reports filed with the Federal Election Commission, either on a quarterly or monthly basis. Organizations in *italics* usually support liberal candidates. Those in regular type generally support conservative candidates.

Organization	Receipts	Expenditures	Cash on Hand
National Conservative Political Action Committee (NCPAC)	1,002,778	1,167,958	37,109
Committee for the Survival of a Free Congress (CSFC)	757,559	736,466	65,455
Citizens for the Republic* (CFTR)	664,206	790,785	1,484,205
Gun Owners of America (GOA)	616,237	710,314	34,297
Fund for a Conservative Majority* (FCM)	278,877	280,044	7,580
National Committee for an Effective Congress (NCEC)	229,825	240,011	25,664
Conservative Victory Fund (CVF)	199,050	177,041	20,343
Council for a Livable World	161,858	136,807	31,897
Committee for Responsible Youth Politics (CRYP)	55,117	55,361	1,556
League of Conservation Voters	28,346	17,092	13,497

* Includes reports through Sept. 30. All others include reports through Oct. 30.

The liberals see 1978 as a defensive year. NCEC's Hemenway does not expect any gains in the Senate west of the Mississippi River, and said his group's main objective will be holding on to the suburban House districts which NCEC-backed candidates won in 1974 and 1976.

Kathryn Fahnestock, executive director of the League of Conservation Voters, one of the most effective environmental groups involved in supporting candidates said she thought the opposition in the marginal districts would be harder to beat this year.

"In the past couple of elections the candidates who have been put up to oppose pro-environmental incumbents have not been particularly well-suited to the district, which made it easier to re-elect our candidates," she said. But "a lot of folks on the other side have now caught on and will start putting up stonger candidates against these people."

Same Races

The left-and right wing groups will end up targeting their money and support into the same races on opposing sides.

Along with the vigorous Senate campaigns expected to be waged on both sides in North and South Carolina, the re-election effort of Floyd K. Haskell (D) in Colorado will attract a lot of attention on both sides. The chairman of the CSFC, Paul Weyrich, worked for the man Haskell narrowly defeated in 1972, former Sen. Gordon Allott (R 1955-73). Weyrich has a personal reason for seeing Haskell defeated; the Colorado race is "the number-one interest in the country" for his group.

In the House, some liberal two-term members will also see a lot of money poured into their districts from both the left and right. Reps. Timothy E. Wirth (D Colo.) and Abner J. Mikva (D Ill.) are prime targets for CFSC and NCPAC. Both won in 1976 by less than 1 percent. NCEC is committed to helping them resist a strong challenge from the right. Gladys Noon Spellman (D Md.) and Bob Carr (D Mich.) are two prominent NCEC favorites who have appeared on early conservative target lists for 1978.

The primary fund-raising tool for ideological groups on the right and the left, and increasingly for the major political parties as well, is through direct-mail solicitation.

"Without direct mail" says Viguerie, "the conservative cause may not exist today."

Hyperbole

Most direct-mail fund-raising appeals by the right and left use emotional language and hyperbole to get their point across.

NCEC and CSFC frequently use each other's claims to stir up concern among their own supporters over the threat from the other side. An NCEC fund-raising pamphlet used in 1976 began with a bold headline: "There's a new 'enemies-list' and some of your best friends are on it." The list was of 35 liberal House members CSFC had targeted for defeat.

On Oct. 18, NCPAC sent out a letter by first-class postage with "Urgent" stamped in red letters across the envelope. The letter asked readers to "send a $5 or $10 contribution today to help defeat liberal senators who want to give our Panama Canal away."

The letter identified 16 senators—Republicans and Democrats—who "will decide if a Marxist dictator will take both our canal and our money, and then open the canal to

Russian warships—while our Navy is blocked from going through." The four-page, single-spaced letter continued, "What's next on the liberals' agenda? Do we give Alaska back to Russia and pay them at the same time?"

Curtis at the DNC meeting criticized the New Right for their "shrillness, stridency and superficiality." John Buckley, the executive director of the Fund for a Conservative Majority, defended such approaches, saying, "In some cases the shriller you are the more success you have in raising funds."

Although Viguerie denies that direct mail works better for conservatives than liberals, Scott Wolf who has been following the activities of the New Right for the Democratic National Committee, disagrees. He says conservatives have taken advantage of emotional issues that have greater fund-raising appeal. Direct-mail experts concur that the best method for raising money is to conjure up an enemy.

Cost-Effectiveness

Direct mail, however, also has been criticized for not being particularly cost-effective. It has been reported that in North Carolina, of the $1.8 million Viguerie raised for Sen. Helms so far this year, only $200,000 will be used for campaign spending.

In 1976, a Congressional Quarterly study showed that candidates only received 9 cents of each dollar Viguerie raised for three of the largest conservative groups.

Viguerie and other direct-mail advocates respond to the criticism in a number of ways. They argue that the high cost is a result of the initial expense in building up lists of contributors. They promise that the ratio of money spent on campaigns to money raised will be higher in 1978.

The most effective way to raise funds through the mail is to re-solicit past contributors. It is here that Viguerie and the groups he works for have a tremendous advantage. Viguerie maintains current addresses of one and half to two million people who have contributed to right-wing groups or candidates in his files. By contrast, NCEC has a list of 80,000.

Weyrich of the CSFC explains that "prospect mailings" to names on lists of potential contributors may pay for themselves, but will usually not bring in a profit. By contrast, in a mailing to past CSFC contributors, "if it cost 40 cents per name to send out a piece, we might get back as much as $1.75," Weyrich said.

Viguerie's other justification for the high cost of direct mail is that it should not be seen only as a fund-raising apparatus, but also as a means of advertising. "Direct mail is an unbelievably successful advertising medium when properly used," he said. "The people who focus in on direct mail as only a fund-raising vehicle are missing the boat."

Cash vs. Services

Contributions to endorsed candidates are either in the form of direct-cash or in-kind services. The larger organizations tend to favor services rather than contributions because this gives them greater control over how their resources are utilized. Smaller groups without the ability to provide sophisticated services favor direct-cash contributions.

Mac Hansborough, NCEC's chief political consultant, said that it has taken his organization four to five years to develop and refine the in-kind services it now offers. NCEC will provide general campaign consulting, media services, polling information and targeting advice.

On the right, NCPAC and CSFC lean toward services rather than cash. A fund-raising pamphlet from NCPAC says the group "goes beyond 'tossing money into a campaign.' In short, NCPAC has the ability to organize every level of campaign activity."

In 1976, CSFC provided candidates with direct cash support. Weyrich was disappointed with the results—"We threw money away."

"Our particular bag in life is precinct organization," Weyrich said. In 1978 rather than giving cash, CSFC plans to pay the salary of a campaign staff worker in each House district with an endorsed candidate. The staffer's only responsibility will be to conduct the precinct organization campaign. "If he ends up organizing spaghetti dinners and not doing the precinct organization work we will simply stop paying his salary," Weyrich said.

Not every group is as firmly committed to the idea of providing services or having staff people placed in campaigns.

Lyn Nofziger, who runs Reagan's Citizens for the Republic, said his organization would "provide some consultation because we want to know where our money is going, but we probably won't clutter up campaigns with a lot of field men. There just aren't that many good ones around."

Fahnestock of the League of Conservation Voters plans to give cash contributions rather than providing organizational or consultant support. "Most of our candidates reek of organization," she said. "It's the money they need. We don't even tell them how to spend it, but it is usually well spent."

Another environmental group, the Dirty Dozen campaign of Environmental Action, is switching this year to direct-cash contributions. Previously the group campaigned against 12 incumbents it felt had particularly objectionable environmental records by running negative campaigns against them rather than becoming directly involved in the challengers' campaigns. "It was a big hassle with the Federal Election Commission and we incurred a lot of administrative overhead," said Dennis Bass, who coordinates the program. This year he hopes to be able to earmark the group's cash contribution to be used for highlighting environmental issues.

1976 Record

Despite the large amount of money they raised in 1976, the impact of conservative groups on the outcome of the elections was slight.

In the House, CSFC contributed the maximum amount, or close to it, in 17 races. Only three of its endorsed candidates won. NCPAC contributed heavily to 15 House candidates, and only three won. Both groups supported the same three winners, all of whom were Republicans elected to open seats formerly held by Republicans—Eldon Rudd (Ariz.), Robert K. Dornan (Calif.) and Mickey Edwards (Okla.)

Conservative groups fared better in the 1976 Senate elections with NCPAC winning four of eight contests and CSFC winning two of the three where it spent the maximum allowable amount.

Weyrich said several CSFC-supported House candidates lost close elections in 1976 because they did not follow through with the precinct organization plan he advocates. "The theory is that if everything else is in order then a good precinct organization could make the difference in a close election."

Many feel that the high fund-raising costs were responsible for the New Right's poor showing in 1976.

NCEC's Hemenway said, "I'd be embarrassed if I spent 80 cents to raise a dollar." (In 1976, he said, NCEC spent 32 cents on fund raising for every dollar it raised.)

Terry Dolan, chairman of NCPAC, promises that the 1978 costs will not be as high. In 1976, he says it cost 46 cents to raise a dollar. This year's fund raising has cut about 20 cents off the cost. "We're an established group now," says Dolan, "and we are using our own house lists which are much more productive."

Future Plans

Four groups associated with Viguerie—NCPAC, CSFC, GOA and CRYP—except to contribute close to $2 million in 1978 to campaigns ranging from city council races to gubernatorial and senate contests.

Right Active in '77 House Elections

The success rate of right-wing organizations in 1977 special elections has been much better than its 1976 effort. Conservative groups contributed heavily in three of the four special elections held to fill House vacancies this year. Their endorsed candidates won each election.

In Minnesota, Republican Arlan Stangeland received nearly $12,000 from six conservative groups, including $6,552 from NCPAC. Stangeland won the district formerly held by Democrat Bob Bergland, the Secretary of Agriculture, with nearly 58 per cent. *(Minnesota election story, Weekly Report p. 369)*

In Washington, Republican John E. Cunningham upset Democrat Marvin Durning in a traditionally blue-collar Democratic district. Conservatives were active in both the Democratic and Republican primaries. After putting nearly $11,000 into the losing right-wing Democratic primary campaign of John Hemenway, conservatives lined up behind Cunningham, who easily won the Republican nomination. More than $33,000 was contributed to Cunningham's campaign by an array of seven right-wing groups.

NCPAC again was the largest of the groups, contributing $9,000, followed by the Fund for a Conservative Majority with $8,500 and the Gun Owners of America, which gave $7,500. Cunningham also raised more than $250,000 directly through mailings Viguerie sent out across the country on the candidate's behalf.

The Cunningham victory was a boost to the New Right. Supporters said it demonstrated the movement's appeal to blue-collar voters who traditionally were thought to be loyal Democrats. *(Washington election story, Weekly Report p. 995)*

The third special election, in Louisiana, was another surprise victory for a conservative Republican candidate in an historically Democratic district. With the help of $26,772 from six conservative groups, Robert Livingston managed to win the Aug. 27 special election caused by the resignation of Richard A. Tonry (D). A few months after his election Livingston signed a fund-raising letter for the Fund for a Conservative Majority, which donated $5,000 to his campaign. "FCM was instrumental in my upset victory," Livingston wrote. "Without their assistance the election results very easily could have been reversed." *(Louisiana election story, Weekly Report p. 1856)*

In all, major conservative groups contributed more than $80,000 in the three special elections. In each case, they supported winning Republican candidates in races to fill vacancies left by Democratic representatives.

There was no similar effort on behalf of liberal candidates by NCEC or other left wing groups.

NCPAC has the most ambitious plans, expecting to draw on its house list of 150,000 contributors to raise "at least a million dollars" for campaigns, according to Dolan. The organization expects to be involved on a day-to-day basis with about 100 campaigns and will contribute money and campaign services to approximately 200 more.

CSFC plans to contribute between $300,000 and $400,000 in salaries for precinct organization staff workers. Weyrich predicted the group would target 50 liberal House members for defeat and also would be involved in about half of the races for open seats.

H. L. (Bill) Richardson, chairman of the Gun Owners of America, one of the most active groups in 1976, would not disclose how many campaigns the GOA would enter, or how much it would contribute overall. He said the figure would exceed last year's $300,000, which went to state and federal election campaign committees. GOA has a firm rule not to support any incumbents.

One of the smaller organizations by Viguerie standards is the Committee for a Responsible Youth Politics (CRYP). The main task is to train youth coordinators in campaigns, according to Morton Blackwell, who heads CRYP and also is the editor of Viguerie's newsletter, *The Right Report*. CRYP plans to contribute between $75,000 and $100,000 to House and Senate campaigns.

One of the major conservative organizations outside of Viguerie's circle is Reagan's Citizens for the Republic (CFTR). Unlike the Viguerie-related groups, CFTR will only contribute to Republicans. Nofziger, the group's director, refused to speculate on how many campaigns the committee would become involved in, or to what extent.

CFTR's last quarterly filing with the Federal Election Commission covering the first nine months of the year showed it had nearly $1.5 million on hand. But this figure was reduced considerably Nov. 28 when the committee repaid the federal government $611,141 in unused matching funds to Reagan's presidential campaign.

The Conservative Victory Fund, which in recent years has been eclipsed by the efforts of the New Right, hopes to double its contributions to candidates in 1978 and spend close to $200,000. The fund plans to break with its past tradition of only supporting challengers, so that it can help out Sens. Helms, Thurmond and perhaps John G. Tower (R Texas).

The Fund for a Conservative Majority, a descendent of the Young Americans for Freedom, plans to contribute "upwards of $75,000 to $100,000," according to Executive Director John Buckley. The group will concentrate on "a handful of races with solid, hardcore, committee conservatives," Buckley said.

The largest liberal group is the National Committee for an Effective Congress, which has been operating for 29 years. Its 1978 budget calls for spending about $550,000 on campaigns, either through in-kind services or direct and indirect cash contributions. National director Hemenway expects about 35 candidates will receive the maximum support from the committee, and it will endorse another 30 candidates.

17 / Explosive Growth: Corporate Political Action Committees Are Less Oriented to Republicans Than Expected

Charles W. Hucker

The explosive growth of corporate political action committees (PACs), which began in the mid-1970s and continues unabated, is affecting political campaigns in a way not totally expected several years ago.

Not surprisingly, the corporate PAC growth has put business in nearly the same league with organized labor as contributors to congressional campaigns. But what is surprising to some is the difference in the pattern of contributions. Corporate PAC contributions are not as oriented to Repubilcan candidates as labor political contributions are tied to Democratic candidates.

Two years ago some party strategists had predicted—Republicans gleefully, and Democrats fearfully—that the increase in corporate PACs would be a boon to the Republican Party. That was based on the assumption that corporations would favor pro-business, Republican candidates. Instead Democrats in Congress, who pass judgment on business' legislative interests, have attracted substantial business contributions.

Because corporations and labor unions are prohibited by federal law from using corporate and union treasury funds for political contributions, PACs have become a tightly regulated vehicle for political involvement by business and unions. Campaign contributions by political action committees must come from voluntary gifts to the PACs. But corporate and union funds may be used to establish and administer PACs and solicit money for them.

In the wake of the Watergate scandal and the exposure of illegal corporate political contributions, PACs became a clean way for corporations to participate politically. After enactment of the 1974 amendments to the 1971 Federal Election Campaign Act and a 1975 opinion by the Federal Election Commission (FEC), which enforces the act, the number of corporate PACs grew rapidly.

Corporate PACs have more than quintupled in the last three years to greater than 500, while the number of labor committees barely has grown. Contributions by corporate

Reprinted by permission from *Congressional Quarterly Weekly Report*, Vol. 36, No. 14 (April 8, 1978): 849–854. Copyright 1978 Congressional Quarterly Inc.

and business-related trade PACs to all congressional candidates nearly tripled from 1974 to 1976 while labor PAC contributions increased by about 30 percent.

In 1976 corporate and business-related trade PACs gave more than $6.9 million to congressional candidates in general elections, while labor PACs, including teacher associations, gave nearly $8.1 million.

Business Characteristics

According to campaign contribution data compiled by Common Cause, corporate and business-related trade PAC contributions to congressional candidates in the 1976 general elections had the following characteristics:

- 58.9 percent of their contributions went to Republicans, compared to the 96.5 percent of labor contributions that went to Democrats.
- 68.0 percent of the corporate and business-related contributions went to incumbents, compared to the 63.3 percent of labor contributions that were allocated to incumbents.
- Democratic incumbents were favored over their Republican challengers by corporate and business-related PACs by more than a two-to-one margin. [See the table on page 311.]

In 1977 and the first two months of 1978, corporate PAC contributions actually were heavier to Democratic congressional candidates than Republicans. An FEC study shows that corporate PACs gave $499,035 to Democrats and $419,345 to Republicans.

For all of 1977, eight of the top 10 corporate PACs gave more than half of their contributions to Democrats, almost all of them incumbents.

Because of the youth of most corporate PACs, those familiar with them say that their early performance is not necessarily indicative of their future behavior. For example, individuals knowledgeable about corporate PACs expect their contributions in 1978 and in later congressional elections to be less oriented to Democrats and incumbents than they were for the 1976 elections and in 1977.

"The corporate PAC movement is in its infancy," commented Joseph J. Fanelli, president of the Business-Industry Political Action Committee (BIPAC). "It has to mature before you can make valid judgments about how corporate PACs are going to operate."

Maturation of the corporate PAC movement is expected by both its supporters and critics to take at least two or three more congressional elections after 1978.

Critics are worried that by the mid-1980s corporate PACs will dominate congressional politics. Supporters expect corporate PACs to be more sophisticated in their political decisions, more willing to support challengers and more likely to become involved in primary contests in both parties. The last development is watched nervously by Democrats and labor union officials.

Access vs. Philosophy

With Democratic majorities in both chambers of Congress it is not a surprise to some that Democrats receive a significant share of corporate PAC contributions.

Leading Corporate PACs in 1976 Elections
(Contributions made in 1975 and 1976)

	Contributions to Federal Candidates
1. Nonpartisan Political Support Committee (General Electric Co.)	$109,235
2. United Technologies Corporation Political Action Committee (United Technologies Corp.)	90,500
3. Political Awareness Fund (Union Oil Company of California)	86,190
4. Texaco Employees Political Involvement Committee (Texaco, Inc.)	83,300
5. Chrysler Nonpartisan Political Support Committee (Chrysler Corp.)	71,825
6. American Family Political Action Committee (American Family Corp.)	$71,550
7. Nonpartisan Committee for Good Government (Coca-Cola Company)	68,200
8. Southern Railway Tax Eligible Good Government Fund (Southern Railway Company)	66,830
9. North Western Officers Trust Account (Chicago Northwestern Transportation)	64,900
10. Hanson Fund (Tacoma Fund)	62,500

Source: Federal Election Commission.

"This is money of an investment nature, not of an ideological nature," said Fred Wertheimer, Common Cause vice president. "Democrats control the Congress so Democrats get the money."

Wertheimer argues that the contributions to incumbents from all PACs create obligations for the members. "PAC money is tied to lobbying," asserted Wertheimer, who supports public financing of congressional campaigns.

The role of PAC contributions in some cases as a means of gaining access to incumbent members of Congress is acknowledged by business spokesmen. But some would prefer that decisions about corporate PAC contributions be made on philosophy—which candidate most effectively represents a pro-business viewpoint.

"The prevailing attitude is that PAC money should be used to facilitate access to incumbents," remarked Fred Radewagen, director of governmental and political participation programs for the U.S. Chamber of Commerce.

"When a number of them start formulating their contributions," commented the chairman of one large corporate PAC, who asked not to be identified, "they get into using

Leading Corporate PACs in 1977

	Contributions to Congressional Candidates	Per Cent of Funds Given to Democratic Candidates
1. Nonpartisan Political Support Committee (General Electric Co.)	$26,375	63.8%
2. Southern Railway Tax Eligible Good Government Fund (Southern Railway Co.)	22,200	62.8
3. Voluntary Contributors for Better Government (International Paper Co.)	16,637	38.3
4. LTV Corp./Vought Corp. Active Citizenship Campaign (LTV/Vought Corp.)	16,500	68.9
5. Hughes Active Citizenship Fund (Hughes Aircraft Co.)	16,164	60.8
6. Amoco Political Action Committee (Standard Oil of Indiana)	15,600	20.8
7. Lockheed Good Government Program (Lockheed Aircraft Corp.)	15,425	54.5
8. Burlington Northern Employees Voluntary Good Government Fund (Burlington Northern, Inc.)	13,428	80.3
9. United Technologies Corporation Political Action Committee (United Technologies Corp.)	12,025	50.7
10. Nonpartisan Committee for Good Government (Coca-Cola Co.)	12,009	79.1

Source: Federal Election Commission.

their PACs for access purposes rather than for philosophical purposes, which probably was the basis on which it was sold to the employees,"

"They forget philosophy and use it for lobbying purposes," the PAC chairman added.

Radewagen doesn't agree with the emphasis by some corporate PACs on gaining access to incumbents. He says the Chamber is trying to encourage corporate PACs to support non-incumbents who have a free enterprise outlook.

Risk Capital

Radewagen argues that corporate PACs should set aside "risk capital" for contestants in open seats so that in the next decade business can change the complexion of Congress. They also should be willing to support pro-business candidates in Democratic primaries, as well as within the Republican Party, he said.

Radewagen's interest in open seats and primary contests is shared by Stevenson Walker, a PAC specialist for the Public Affairs Council, a Washington-based association that has 325 corporate members. But Walker finds the flow of corporate PAC money to Democratic incumbents understandable.

"It is hard for business, after what has happened on the consumer protection agency, common sites [picketing] and cargo preference [bills], to turn their backs on a number of Democrats who voted with them," Walker said. The business position against the three proposals prevailed in the current Congress.

"On several points Democrats have seen the business point of view," Walker added. "Democrats are not the exclusive property of labor or anyone else. The notion that Democrats are not compatible with business is absurd."

When 69 Democrats joined the unanimous Republicans March 21 to defeat consideration of amendments to the federal campaign finance law in the House, Walker said, "the days of being concerned with a Democratic majority are over" for business.

Despite the call for greater attention by corporate PACs to primary contests and open seats, the tilt toward incumbents remains very strong among some corporate PACs.

"We're inclined to support incumbents because we tend to go with those who support our industry," explained H. David Crowther, treasurer of the Lockheed Good Government Program, the PAC for the Lockheed Aircraft Corporation. "We are not out looking to find challengers. Our aim is not to change the tone of Congress."

In 1977, 54.5 percent of Lockheed PAC's contributions went to Democrats, and Crowther said he expected that percentage to increase in 1978 to reflect the proportion of Democrats in Congress, which is more than 60 percent of the seats in both chambers. But Crowther claimed that Lockheed's PAC contributions weren't designed to increase access to incumbents or to aid the corporation's lobbying efforts. He noted that it is difficult for PACs to know who the good challengers or primary contestants are.

"We have not sought any commitments. All we want is a chance to be heard," said Frank S. Farrell, chairman of the Burlington Northern Employees Voluntary Good Government Fund, which gave 80 percent of its 1977 contributions to Democrats.

Farrell, who was an unsuccessful Republican candidate for the House in 1958 from an open Minnesota seat, said that percentage may decline in 1978 as viable GOP challengers become better known.

Some corporate PACs also tend to support incumbents whose districts include the corporations' facilities.

Incumbent Challenges

Other corporate PACs have not shied away from challengers. For example, Voluntary Contributors for Better Govenment, the International Paper Co. PAC, last year contributed $2,000 to Rep. William S. Cohen, R, who is challenging the re-election bid of Maine Sen. William D. Hathaway, D.

"We had a strong opinion on that race," stated Ralph W. Kittle, chairman of International Paper's PAC. "Sure, it takes a little boldness [to oppose an incumbent]. Someone might think it is against our short-range interest. It probably is. Sometimes you have to take a longer range view. We can't be timid."

Finelli of BIPAC considers it important that corporate PACs be willing to back candidates for philosophical reasons. "To the extent corporate PACs take a long-term look,

1976 Business PAC* Contributions

Republican incumbents	$2,270,598
Democratic challengers	87,594
Democratic incumbents	2,445,352
Republican challengers	1,071,974
Republicans in open seats	741,185
Democrats in open seats	316,221
Total	$6,932,924

*Includes corporate PACs and business-related trade association PACs.
Source: Common Cause.

they will predicate their contributions on a philosophical basis," Fanelli said. "We would like to encourage corporations to take a long-term view."

At the Republican National Committee the large share of corporate PAC money going to Democrats causes chagrin, but not surprise.

"We realize corporations are made up of Republicans and Democrats," said Charles A. McManus Jr., director of the committee's PAC division, which is trying to increase the Republican share of corporate PAC contributions.

In the 1976 elections more than half of the corporate PAC money that was given to GOP congressional candidates went to incumbent Republicans. McManus wants corporate PACs, when giving to Republicans, to shift their emphasis to GOP challengers and candidates in open seats.

McManus is holding seminars for PAC officials to identify strong Republican congressional office-seekers and is working with GOP candidates to make contact with PACs.

Background

The emergence of corporate PACs follow a long period in American political history when corporate political activity was limited severely.

In 1907 the Tillman Act banned corporate gifts of money to candidates for federal elective offices or to committees supporting the candidates. The ban was incorporated in the Federal Corrupt Practices Act of 1925, which extended the prohibition to cover contributions of "anything of value."

The Smith-Connally Act of 1943 and the Taft-Hartley Act of 1947 banned political contributions to federal candidates by unions from their members' dues. The Federal Election Campaign Act of 1971 modified that ban on corporations and unions specifically to allow the use of corporate funds and union treasury money for "the establishment, administration and solicitation of contributions to a separate, segregated fund to be utilized for a political purpose." Those funds now are known commonly as PACs.

But the 1971 act did not make that modification to the ban on political contributions by government contractors. The result was that many corporations held back from forming PACs. Organized labor, which held government manpower contracts, became concerned it would be affected and led a move to have the law changed to permit goverment contractors to establish and administer PACs. That change was incorporated in the 1974 amendments to the federal election campaign law.

The easing of that prohibition opened the way for the formation of corporate PACs. As one campaign finance expert said, "Labor pulled business' chestnuts out of the fire."

Corporations remained skittish about what they were permitted to do until November 1975, when the FEC released an opinion concerning Sun Oil Company's political committee, Sun PAC, reaffirming that corporations could establish and administer PACs. [See the table on page 313.]

But the six-member, bipartisan commission was split on how wide an audience Sun would be allowed to solicit for its PAC. The majority held that Sun could solicit all employees, in addition to stockholders. The two dissenting commissioners argued that Sun could solicit only stockholders.

Under federal law unions are permitted to solicit only their members.

The 1976 amendements to the Federal Election Campaign Act restricted the range of corporate solicitation to a company's management personnel and its stockholders. However, corporations and unions were given the right to solicit the other's group twice a year by mail. That authority is little used.

The 1976 amendments also established restrictions on one company or one labor organization setting up a number of PACs in order to evade the ceiling of $5,000 on contributions by a PAC to a candidate in each election.

Federal law permits an individual to give up $5,000 a year to a PAC. An individual also may give up to $1,000 to a candidate in each election.

For the average union member those limits are well above what he is likely to contribute politically. But for an affluent executive the limits provide several channels for large political contributions. Total political contributions by an individual in one year are not allowed to exceed $25,000.

The evolution of the federal law through 1976 has made PACs more inviting to corporations. No better sign of that is the formation of PACs in 1977 by two business giants—General Motors and American Telephone and Telegraph.

How PACs Operate

Although the law permits corporate PACs to solicit stockholders, very few do. A. U.S. Chamber of Commerce survey in April 1977, found that only 2 percent of the corporate PACs asked stockholders for contributions.

"Stockholders are a broad and very diverse group," commented Farrell of Burlington Northern. "Many of them have differing political complexions and points of view. It's a question of whether it's worth the time and effort."

Management personnel are the main target for the corporate PACs, but corporations vary widely in how low into the management ranks they reach to solicit.

General Electric solicits its 540 top executives and about two-thirds participate, contributing about $70,000 a year. On the other hand, Lockheed solicits its full management group, and approximately 600—about 5 percent of the number solicited—contribute.

The frequency of solicitation also differs greatly among corporations. General Electric and Burlington Northern solicit annually, for example. But others, such as Lockheed, International Paper and Southern Railway Company, solicit less frequently. The meth-

Growth of Nonparty-Related Political Action Committees

	Dec. 31, 1974	*Nov. 24, 1975	**May 11, 1976	Dec. 31, 1976	Dec. 31, 1977
Corporate	89	139	294	433	538
Labor	201	226	246	224	216
Trade, membership and others	318	357	452	489	544
Total	608	722	992	1,146	1,298

*Date of Sun PAC opinion by the Federal Election Commission.
**Effective date of 1976 amendments to the Federal Election Campaign Act.
Source: Federal Election Commission.

ods of solicitation are mail, personal contacts, group presentations and combinations of all three.

Many of the larger corporations use payroll withholding plans for their executives to make contributions. One company that hasn't adopted that approach is General Electric. Stephen K. Galpin, secretary of GE's Nonpartisan Political Support Committee, said he was concerned that the confidentiality of the contributors might be breeched if that information were part of the company's payroll system.

Some corporations permit a PAC contributor to designate which party is to receive his money or to allow the PAC to use it at its discretion. Decisions about which candidates will receive PAC contributions are made by special committees of the PAC in many cases. But in some instances a PAC may not use a formal committee and may leave the decisions up to the PAC chairman, who consults informally with colleagues.

There is less variation in solicitation practices among labor unions. Generally a union business agent or steward will solicit union members in person or in a group on an annual basis.

According to Al Zack, an AFL-CIO spokesman in Washington, very few unions use payroll withholding for voluntary political contributions. If a company uses payroll withholding to collect contributions from its executives, federal law requires that payroll withholding be made available for a union to collect the political contributions of its members who work for the company.

For the AFL-CIO Committee on Political Education (COPE) in each state to make a contribution, Zack said, a candidate must receive a two-thirds vote at a state labor convention or from a body designated by the convention.

Corporate Alternatives

Although corporate funds and union treasury money may not be used for political contributions, federal law allows those funds to be used for non-partisan activities such as voter registration and get-out-the-vote drives. Labor unions have become very skilled in these techniques and those non-partisan efforts often are designed to be of particular help to one candidate, as in get-out-the-vote drives in areas where pro-labor voters predominate.

"Business is 20 years behind labor unions," commented Radewagen of the Chamber of

Commerce about non-partisan methods. Part of the reason for that lag is that union memberships generally are more cohesive and more easily mobilized through phone banks and targeting techniques than a company's executives and its stockholders, who are scattered throughout the country.

In the view of at least one union official, however, corporations are catching up. Corporations "have made more effective use of trade union techniques than union themselves," said William Dodds, national political director for the United Auto Workers.

Interviews with corporate PAC officials revealed no surge in interest in the use of non-partisan political programs as labor unions have employed them. But Walker of the Public Affairs Council noted that there is a gradual rise in sophistication in this area.

Walker predicted that this year about a dozen companies would conduct non-partisan political education seminars for interested executives. He cited one major firm that has hired Republican and Democratic political consultants to instruct executives about voter registration and precinct work. Those executives can become political volunteer workers if they choose.

"The [corporate] PACs are beginning to realize the best way to beat Abner Mikva [D Ill.] is not just to give his opponent $5,000, but to give him 100 trained campaign workers," Walker said. Mikva is regarded as a nemisis by business interests.

Fanelli of BIPAC believes a conservative attitude by many companies about federal election law has put a damper on political training programs and other non-partisan activities.

"There is little experience at it and less appetite for it," Fanelli noted. But he added that if the federal law is changed to put lower limits on PAC contributions to candidates, it would be necessary for corporations to become more actively involved in non-partisan programs.

Partisan Communications

One of the least used political techniques by corporations is partisan internal communications. Under federal law, corporations may spend company funds to send communications to their executives and their stockholders advocating the election or defeat of a candidate. If the costs of those communications exceed $2,000 in one election they must be reported to the FEC. Non-partisan political expenditures by corporations and unions, as well as the cost of administering PACs, do not have to be reported .

Labor unions have a simlar right to use members' dues to send partisan communications to their members. And they have used it much more than corporations.

A study by the FEC shows that in 1976, 66 labor groups spent $2,014,326 for internal partisan communications, while four corporations spent $31,045. One membership group—the National Rifle Association—spent about $100,000.

A majority of the funds was spent in the presidential contest, rather than for congressional races. President Carter was the overwhelming beneficiary. Expenditures in behalf of Carter totaled $1,160,432, while $44,249 was spent advocating the election of former President Ford. None of the funds was spent advocating Carter's defeat, but $43,958 was expended calling for Ford's defeat.

Most of the partisan communication money—87.1 percent—went for direct mailings. Other uses included brochures, phone banks, posters, car stickers and peanuts, according to the FEC.

There is considerable wariness in corporate circles about making partisan communications.

"I question whether it is our business to educate people [stockholders and executives] on behalf of one candidate with stockholder money," commented Galpin of General Electric. "That is a legitimacy question. But there is a credibility problem. Would it do any good?"

18 / Campaign Consultants Portray Candidates as Fiscal Watchdogs

Charles W. Hucker

Campaign consultants are urging many candidates for Congress and for governor this year to document their sympathy with ordinary taxpayers' belief that government is bloated and too costly.

For challengers, political consultants are designing campaigns that portray the candidate as a victim of overreaching government just like the voters he wishes to attract. The same advisers are depicting incumbents as fiscal watchdogs working energetically to eliminate waste and excess bureaucracy.

Congressional Quarterly's [CQ] survey of campaign consultants reveals a common search for ways to build on the sentiment expressed by voters in California, where Proposition 13 has rolled back property taxes. Consultants say their approach to the anti-tax and anti-big government sentiment varies by state and by candidate. But most of those interviewed hope to take advantage of it.

The focus of the 1978 campaigns represents a shift from the last mid-term election, in 1974, when Watergate enveloped almost every state and federal election. Consultants responded then with strategies that generally submerged specific issues in favor of an emphasis on personal traits of honesty and sincerity. This year, however, political consultants are portraying their candidates—particularly non-incumbents—as victims, like the voters, of high taxes and big government.

The approach is illustrated by a sampling of the television ads fashioned by consultants in several states:

- For Democrat Fob James' gubernatorial campaign in Alabama, DeLoss Walker, a Memphis political adviser, designed a television commercial that showed a new school building sitting idle because funds to furnish it with desks had not been appropriated. Walker told CQ that voters are looking for better management of government and that the unused school house demonstrated government waste.
- A television ad for Jane Eskind, candidate for the Democratic Senate nomination in Tennessee, shows a ticking clock and tells the viewers that the federal budget amounts to $765,000 a minute. The John Marttila Consulting firm of Boston is one of Eskind's professional advisers.

Reprinted by permission from *Congressional Quarterly Weekly Report*, Vol. 36, No. 29, (July 22, 1978): 1857-1860. Copyright 1978 Congressional Quarterly Inc.

• Under the tutelage of consultant Walter DeVries, state Sen. Patrick H. McCollough, a Democratic gubernatorial candidate in Michigan, promotes his fiscal conservatism in a 30-minute commerical in which McCollough himself interviews tax experts and discusses tax problems.

• In an advertisement produced by Baltimore consultant Robert Goodman, a Wisconsin butcher complains to U.S. Rep. Robert W. Kasten Jr., a Republican gubernatorial candidate about Democratic Gov. Martin J. Schreiber's initial plan to rebate part of the state surplus.

"Bob, I've never seen anything like it," the white-aproned butcher tells Kasten. "Schreiber overcharges us by more than $400 million and then he says, 'Here, take 20 bucks back.' "

Sounding Credible

As in any year when they mount "low tax, less government" appeals, consultants are concerned about whether advertisements for their candidates are plausible.

"You can say 'more schools, better roads, less taxes,' but that doesn't work," said Matt Reese, who has advised Democratic candidates for nearly 20 years.

"Voters won't buy a demagogic approach," said Republican consultant Goodman. "You can't simply say, 'We're paying too much taxes; throw the rascals out.' "

One method of establising a candidate's credibility is to show him suffering the same plight as all voters. Dan Payne, a partner in the Marttila firm, is using this technique with William R. Ralls, a Democratic candidate for governor in Michigan.

By pointing out that he has never served in the legislature or the governor's office, Payne stated, "Ralls can say 'I have been a taxpayer like you all along.' "

If a candidate is a state legislator aspiring to higher office, he can demonstrate how he has resisted executive branch efforts for higher spending. Republican Assembly leader Perry B. Duryea, a candidate for New York governor, has employed that approach.

One Duryea television ad, produced by Bailey, Deardourff and Associates of Washington, shows one of Duryea's legislative colleagues praising him for leading an effort to cut one of the proposed budgets of former Gov. Nelson A. Rockefeller.

A different technique for capitalizing on resentment against state and federal aloofness is to focus on the virtues of local government. That approach is used by the Rothstein-Buckley consulting firm for South Dakota state Sen. Roger McKellips, who upset the state's lieutenant governor June 6 for the Democratic gubernatorial nomination.

Joe Rothstein, a partner in Rothstein-Buckley, said his firm spent five days filming in McKellips' home town of Alcester, a community of about 700 persons in the southeast corner of the state. The resulting ad focused on McKellips' role in local development. The ads suggested that McKellips as governor could be a catalyst for small South Dakota towns to develop themselves as Alcester had done rather than rely on help from the state level.

"The public has gone through a transition from the '60s where government could do everything to the '70s where government can do nothing," Rothstein said.

No one feels the wrath of anti-government sentiment more acutely than members of Congress and governors running for re-election.

"It is a problem for any incumbent when people see government as too great," remarked Dan Payne. "It is particularly troublesome for liberal Democrats." And Payne's firm deals largely with liberal Democrats.

Incumbents can counter the anti-big government stigma that nags at them by showing voters that they have received their money's worth, Payne said. "People want to feel the incumbent has been working for them and has effective experience; they don't want just seniority."

Two years ago, working for the re-election of Sen. Edmund S. Muskie (D Maine), Rothstein-Buckley produced commercials that depicted how Muskie had solved a community's problem or helped a resident of one of Maine's towns.

This effort to "humanize" government is prominent in 1978. Members of Congress are less likely than in the past to emphasize their connections and influence. One consultant noted that there are fewer mentions of "he's an important man in Washington."

The TV Generation

If the issues change frequently in campaign advertising, the techniques seem to be stabilizing. Since the late 1960s, television has been a crucial tool used by consultants to attract votes.

Most consultants believe that its influence is a permanent factor in statewide campaigns, and that there is decreasing resistance from candidates to using television advertising.

"People of the TV generation are to the age where they are running for office and TV is a comfortable medium with which to communicate," Payne noted.

Payne cited the race of 32-year-old Democratic Rep. Edward J. Markey for an open U.S. House seat from Massachusetts two years ago. In a crowded 12-person primary Markey employed what Payne called "a daring strategy" of allocating 60 percent of his campaign budget for a television blitz in the last two weeks before the election. In the splintered field, Markey won with about 22 percent of the vote.

In 1972 television shared the spotlight with other developing techniques, including direct mail. One principal reason was the Federal Election Campaign Act of 1971 which limited federal candidates to spending no more than $50,000, or 10 cents multiplied by the voting age population of the state or district, whichever was greater, for advertising costs. Of that amount no more than 60 percent could be spent for broadcast advertising.

Those limits also were in effect for the 1974 elections. They were replaced by amendments to the Federal Election Campaign Act, which took effect Jan. 1, 1975, setting overall campaign spending limits with no specific ceilings for any kind of advertising. But before the new amendments could have any impact, they were invalidated by the U.S. Supreme Court in January 1976. The result was that television spending in federal elections in 1976 was not restrained directly by federal law and that is the case this year, also. (*1976 Almanac, p. 459*)

The clearest impact of those events was felt in the presidential elections of 1972 and 1976. More money was spent by the two major presidential candidates for television advertising two years ago than in 1972, even though less money was spent overall in 1976 for the presidential campaigns.

The trend is not as clear in Senate and House races. Political consultants disagree on whether the share of campaign budgets currently allocated for television advertising has remained the same in comparison to the early 1970s or has increased. The Federal Communications Commission no longer compiles separate statistics on political broadcast advertising expenditures.

One factor that restricts television in political campaigns is a requirement, contained in the Federal Election Campaign Act of 1971, that broadcasters charge political candidates seeking advertising time the lowest unit cost available to commercial advertisers for the same time in the weeks immediately prior to an election. Forced to give candidates bargain rates, some broadcasters prefer not to sell them the time.

Political consultants complain that they have had difficulty this year finding all the television advertising time that they want to purchase particularly for 5-minute and 30-minute commercials.

Direct Mail

Direct-mail advertising, used heavily in the 1972 presidential campaigns, has fallen out of favor with some consultants. John Deardourff of Bailey, Deardourff and Associates believes that the market has been nearly saturated with direct-mail political advertising and that it is no longer cost effective.

DeLoss Walker said that he had eliminated the use of direct mail in his campaigns. Walker added that several years ago he could send out direct mail at 13-15 cents a letter and that now the cost is about 30 cents a letter.

In 1972, when the presidential campaigns used direct mail heavily, computers played a key role in producing the letters.

Now that direct mail has declined in some areas as a political advertising method, the role of computers has shifted, although computer-generated direct mail remains the lifeblood of New Right political groups, which primarily use it to raise money.

Computers remain valuable to most consultants primarily for analyzing past election results, reviewing current polling data and storing lists of campaign contributors. Some have used computer analysis to determine the top Democratic, Republican and ticket-splitting precincts in an area.

Computerized telephone banks were hailed in 1972, but are little used this year. The computer telephone banks allowed a voter to receive an individual telephone call, with the candidate making a campaign pitch in a recorded message.

"It is not the kind of personal contact voters want, nor is it persuasive," said Paul Lutzker of Washington-based Hamilton and Staff. "They're offensive," said Matt Reese.

An Unstylish Year

In more than 20 years of televised political advertising, there has been a gradual refinement of technique. No longer are consultants preparing ads as startling or "hot" as the 1964 advertisement in behalf of President Lyndon Johnson which showed an exploding atomic bomb.

Political consultants agree that the current approach to television campaign advertising is "cooler" and stresses realism, often showing a candidate campaigning among voters. Fewer ads are staged.

But beyond that general trend, styles vary from consultant to consultant, although the differences generally are less noticeable to the public than to the professionals. The commercials reflect the influence of several different schools of thought about how political ads should be presented.

"The style this year is unstylish," said one consultant. "You won't find anybody doing anything that comes out of a cookie cutter."

"As an industry, this business has grown and people don't feel locked in to doing what the giants are doing," another said.

Some experts, in fact, believe that the industry is plagued less by faddism and copying than by a tendency for consultants to apply their own individual styles unvaryingly to different candidates, even though the candidates and circumstances vary considerably.

"Most media consultants have a style and fit that style to the candidates," said Michael Kaye of Los Angeles, who produced the television spots for Bill Bradley, Democratic Senate nominee in New Jersey.

Cinema Verite

One influence on political advertising in the 1970s has been the work of Charles Guggenheim, a Washington filmmaker, who popularized the cinema verite style. "Guggenheim was ahead of his time," noted Phyllis B. Brotman, a Baltimore consultant who is president of the American Association of Political Consultants. Guggenheim's cinema verite approach shows candidates moving and talking casually among the voters, with little script and no hard sell.

"As public people, [officeholders] have been picked at and have built up a facade," one consultant said, "The job of the filmmaker is to get behind the facade and show real qualities. Cinema verite involves so much filming that a candidate doesn't know the camera is there and his real qualities emerge."

However, the large amount of filming and high cost involved in cinema verite has troubled some consultants. To obtain, a similar product in less time and at less expense, some professionals have picked selected events to film rather than following a candidate around for days and eliminating most of the footage in the editing room.

A few consultants regard cinema verite as too soft an advertising approach for certain political circumstances, particularly when a not-very-well-known candidate is seeking exposure. But other professionals have adapted cinema verite to 30-minute television advertisements in an effort to gain exposure for candidates unfamiliar to the public.

News Look

Another influence on current political advertising is the "news look." A study of voters after the 1970 Michigan elections by Walter DeVries, a political scientist and professional consultant, led to this approach.

Questioning Michigan voters about the way they made voting decisions, DeVries found that television ads ranked only 24th in influencing undecided voters. Television news ranked first. DeVries' solution to the problem of how to make political ads more influential was to have the commercials resemble television news.

In his 1972 book, *The Ticket-Splitter,* DeVries predicted that political commercials in the 1970s would embody "television newscast formats, mini-documentaries and confrontation situations in simulated press conferences, debates and talk shows."

In this year's Michigan gubernatorial primary, DeVries has applied the technique by having his candidate, Democrat Patrick McCollough, assume a newsman's role. McCollough conducts interviews, with microphone in hand, for the campaign commercials.

The cinema verite and newsroom techniques have been combined in some instances. A Deardourff-produced ad for unsuccessful California gubernatorial candidate Ken Maddy showed two of Ronald Reagan's children seated in chairs in a talk-show arrangement,

---

Bradley & Kaye *vs.* Leone & Garth

In the New Jersey Democratic Senate primary, it was not just a battle between ex-basketball star Bill Bradley and former state treasurer Richard Leone. Also opposing each other were their political consultants—Michael Kaye of Los Angeles and David Garth of New York.

Bradley swamped Leone for the Democratic Senate nomination June 6 and in the process brought increase public attention to Kaye, who designed a package of three 30-second commercials for Bradley. Those three ads showed:

• Bradley addressing viewers about energy problems. Suddenly the screen goes black. Bradley continues speaking. When he finishes, a few seconds later, the slogan "Bradley for U.S. Senate" appears on the dark screen.

• Bradley seated at a desk and talking on the telephone. A narrator describes Bradley's political record. Near the end of the spot, Bradley wads up a piece of paper and shoots it through a small basketball hoop above a wastepaper basket. Kaye described it as a way of reminding people of Bradley's career with the New York Knicks basketball team without having him run up and down a basketball court.

• A man's hands pouring plaster into a mold. When the mold is opened the bust of a man is revealed. The hands use a brush to paint the plaster man and place him on a shelf with other similar busts. A narrator intones that Bradley is not tied to any special interests, but is "cast in a different mold."

The ad infuriated Leone, Bradley's principal primary opponent, although it didn't mention names. In Leone's view, Bradley was unfairly questioning his opponent's political independence.

In a news conference Leone said Bradley's commercials were "an example of bad acting and memorized lines." He also accused Bradley of "insulting Democratic office-holders and politicians with his Hollywood television commercials." Kaye told CQ [Congressional Quarterly] that "the minute my opponent starts attacking my media, I feel very good."

Garth's ads for Leone emphasized his experience in state government and his fights for reform in New Jersey. One of Leone's ads showed him walking on a university campus, knocking on doors and talking to workers, while his credentials were explained.

Garth employed a technique for Leone that a few consultants found disconcerting. In addition to the film of Leone's activity and a written message on the screen, the advertisement also included comments by a narrator that were different from the written message. One competing consultant called this confusing.

making endorsements of Maddy. Behind them a screen showed film clips of their father at the Republican National Convention and of Maddy.

Because some consultants detect a less angry electorate now than in the Vietnam and Watergate eras, less serious settings have been used for some commercials.

"The country isn't anywhere as near uptight as it used to be over Vietnam or Watergate," commented Joe Rothstein. "There are serious problems that people are concerned about, but they don't seem to be the life or death issues that tear the country up." A Rothstein-produced ad for Ed Merdes, Democratic gubernatorial candidate in Alaska, shows Merdes talking to voters on a carnival midway.

One technological innovation in campaign advertising will give political strategists greater flexibility. More television commercial production is using videotape, which can be processed more quickly and in some cases more cheaply than film. "Videotape allows you to respond overnight," John Deardourff said.

Tom Angell, a former Deardourff employee, last year established Interface Video Systems, which has computer-assisted videotape editing facilities that Angell believes provides film-style accuracy in the processing of videotape commercials.

Stars Are Born

With the decline of party organizations and the rise of television over the last three decades, professional campaign consultants have become a central force in statewide elections and in some local contests.

And as the consultants have played a larger role, they have attracted more public attention.

That has been uncomfortable for some professionals in an industry in which standard practice traditionally has been to remain behind the scenes while the candidates occupy the limelight.

"There is a tendency on the part of the new media to treat consultants as they do candidates and celebrities," commented Republican consultant Deardourff (who was named to an "all-star campaign team" by Washingtonian magazine in 1974).

Another consultant remarked that the profession has come to have "a star quality about it."

Each election year seem to bring a new political wizard to the forefront. Frequently he is the consultant linked to the candidate who pulls off the biggest upset of the year, although Deardourff says "the policical advertiser is given too much credit when his candidate wins."

In 1974 John Marttila of Boston occupied center stage, largely because of his role in the special election victory that year by Democrat Richard F. Vander Veen for the Michigan House seat that had been held by Gerald Ford.

In 1976 Deardourff and his partner, Doug Bailey, were hailed when Ford closed a large gap in the polls and nearly defeated Jimmy Carter. In 1977 David Garth was the reigning media wizard when he produced ads for two underdogs who won—Ed Koch in the New York City mayoral election and Brenden T. Byrne in the New Jersey governor's campaign.

"People were starting to believe that if you hired David Garth, you automatically won an election," commented Michael Kaye, a "victor" over Garth this year in New Jersey. *(Weekly Report, p. 1446)*

Garth's services reportedly had been sought by three New Jersey Democrats interested in the U.S. Senate nomination—former state treasurer Richard Leone, ex-basketball star Bill Bradley and U.S. Rep. Andrew Maguire. Garth went with Leone, Bradley hired Kaye and Maguire dropped out of the race. [See the box on page 321.]

Bradley's victory, combined with Kaye's striking advertising campaign, pushed Kaye into public view and generated requests from several candidates for him to do their political commercials.

Kaye has turned down all those invitations, limiting his work to a few campaigns. In addition to Bradley, Kaye is working in the re-election effort of Democratic Sen. Dick Clark in Iowa and in the campaign of U.S. Rep. Yvonne Brathwaite Burke, a Democrat, for California attorney general.

While consultants generally restrict their clients to one party, there are exceptions. Garth, who usually advises Democrats, handled the primary campaign of Richard L. Thornburgh, who is the Pennsylvania GOP gubernatorial nominee. In early July the Thornburgh campaign hired Deardourff to replace Garth. Republican Deardourff also is working for a Democratic candidate for District of Columbia mayor.

Fame in the consulting business can be fleeting. A few crucial losses can damage a reputation and as Deardourff puts it, "There's first place or no place."

19 / Television and Voters' Issue Awareness

Thomas E. Patterson and Robert D. McClure

In today's presidential campaign, television is the primary intermediary between the candidates and most voters. Since 1956, 50 percent or more of America's voters have reported that television is the source of most of their campaign information. [1] There can be little doubt that it is also the focus of the candidates' attention. Their schedules and their actions are tailored to the demands of television news; their financial needs are in great part determined by the high costs of televised political advertising.

The surprising fact is that little is known about the impact of presidential election television. The Twentieth Century Fund Commission on Campaign Costs in the Electronic Era concluded: "We have no accurate measure . . . of the impact of political broadcasting on voters. Yet most informed people believe that the impact is profound, and there is no question that political strategists and political candidates increasingly mold their campaigns around the use of television." [2]

This paper presents some of the first available evidence on the impact of television news and televised political advertising on the American voter. It focuses on television's contribution to voters' awareness of candidates' issue positions during the 1972 presidential election. It does not examine questions nor advance any conclusions regarding television's impact on voters' images of presidential candidates, television's ability to set an election's agenda, and so on. [3]

Data Sources

Our data come from two sources. The first is a panel survey of more than 700 voters, who were interviewed at both the start and conclusions of the 1972 general election. The survey provides information about voters' media exposure and changes in their issue awareness. [4] The second is a content analysis of all weeknight television network newscasts and all televised political ads broadcast during the period September 18 through November 6, 1972. The content analysis provides systematic information on the issue messages that were being communicated to the voters during the general election.

The research presented here was conducted under National Science Foundation grant GS-35408. The support of the Foundation is gratefully adknowledged as is the help provided by our principal assistant, Richard Ender. This article is a revised version of a paper presented at the National Conference on Money and Politics, Washington, D.C., February, 1974.

The Issue Content of Television News

Television can influence voters' issue awareness only on those issues it covers adequately. During the 1972 campaign, television extensively covered a few issues and almost totally neglected most issues.

On their evening newscasts, the television networks gave heavy coverage to only two issues—Nixon's handling of the Vietnam war, and charges of his involvement in political corruption and favoritism (see Table 19-1). This coverage was contained largely in reports on the Paris peace talks and in stories about the Watergate incident and the Soviet wheat deal. An additional four issue positions received at least some attention: Nixon's position on the level of government spending, his handling of inflation, and George McGovern's positions on military spending and Vietnam withdrawal.

Table 19-1 also indicates what was said about the candidates' issue positions—for example, whether news reports indicated that McGovern favored or opposed spending less money on the military. For four of the six heavily covered issue positions, the candidates' stands were unambiguous, as covered on the news. It was claimed that:

- Richard Nixon favored holding down government spending.
- Richard Nixon had done a poor job of handling inflation.
- George McGovern favored spending less money on the military.
- George McGovern favored an immediate withdrawal of troops from Vietnam.

References to Nixon's intention to hold down government spending usually came from announcements about his vetoes of congressional appropriations and his impoundment of appropriated funds. Messages about Nixon's handling of inflation usually were contained in attacks on Republican economic policies by the McGovern camp. References to McGovern's positions on military spending and Vietnam withdrawal came from remarks by McGovern, his spokespersons, or Nixon spokespersons, and were consistent regardless of source.

Network news messages on the other two heavily covered issues were conflicting. On balance, however, the following messages dominated television news time:

- Richard Nixon had done an effective job of handling the Vietnam war.
- Richard Nixon had tolerated political corruption and favoritism in his administration.

On Nixon's handling of Vietnam, the comments favorable to his efforts dominated the last weeks of the campaign, when news from the Paris peace talks was very optimistic. If voters were affected by television news reporting, it was this final barrage of favorable comments that should have been uppermost in their minds. On the corruption issue, the negative comments about Nixon seemed the strongest. They were often buttressed by investigative reports from the *Washington Post* whereas the favorable messages were typically unsupported denials for the *Post's* reports by administration spokespersons.

The Issue Content of Televised Advertising

Televised political advertising, compared with television news, gave both clearer and more extensive coverage to the candidates' issue stands (see Table 19-2). The Nixon and

Table 19-1 Issue Position References[a] on Weekday Evening Television
Network News
(Network Average for September 18–November 6, 1972)

	News Coverage[b]	
	Favorable	Unfavorable
Heavily Covered Issues		
Nixon's position on:		
Vietnam war	12	10
	(10:31)	(5:26)
Eliminating political corruption	6	10
	(2:52)	(6:37)
Holding down government spending	8	1
	(5:10)	(0:26)
Inflation	1	4
	(0:36)	(3:43)
McGovern's position on:		
Spending less on military	5	1
	(3:02)	(0:17)
Immediate withdrawal from Vietnam	7	0
	(3:06)	
Lightly Covered Issues		
Nixon's position on:		
Spending less on military	0	3
		(1:26)
Amnesty for draft evaders	0	3
		(0:56)
More taxes on upper incomes	0	1
		(0:09)
Tougher stand on law and order	1	0
	(0:39)	
Unemployment	2	4
	(0:32)	(0:43)
Putting a stop to busing	3	0
	(0:58)	
China	2	0
	(0:26)	
U.S.S.R.	4	0
	(3:21)	
Honoring foreign commitments	1	0
	(0:08)	
McGovern's position on:		
Amnesty for draft evaders	1	0
	(0:11)	
Eliminating political corruption	1	0
	(0:28)	
More taxes on upper incomes	1	0
	(0:22)	

[a]The coverage by all three networks was added together and then divided by three
to provide average coverage.
[b]Top figures are number of time issues positions were mentioned; bottom figures
(in parentheses) are *total* amount of time (in minutes and seconds) given to issue
position.

Table 19-2 Issue Position References[a] in Nixon and McGovern
Televised Political Spots
(September 18-November 6, 1972, 7-11 p.m.)

	News Coverage	
	Favorable	Unfavorable
Heavily Covered Issues		
Nixon's position on:		
China	34	0
	(27:09)	
U.S.S.R.	34	0
	(14:48)	
Inflation	12	22
	(1:24)	(8:36)
Vietnam war	20	22
	(6:55)	(9:36)
Spending less on military	0	23
		(7:20)
Honoring foreign commitments	10	0
	(6:29)	
Eliminating political corruption	0	20
		(10:58)
McGovern's position on:		
Spending less on military	37	0
	(17:23)	
More taxes on upper incomes	19	0
	(13:40)	
Immediate withdrawal from Vietnam	12	0
	(6:10)	
Lightly Covered Issues		
Nixon's position on:		
Holding down government spending	0	5
		(0:50)
Amnesty for draft evaders	0	0
More taxes on upper incomes	0	6
		(0:42)
Tougher stand on law and order	5	7
	(0:50)	(2:22)
Putting a stop to busing	0	0
Unemployment	0	9
		(2:47)
McGovern's position on:		
Amnest for draft evaders	0	0
Eliminating political corruption	6	0
	(1:00)	

[a]Top figures are number of times positions were mentioned: bottom figures (in parentheses) are *total* amount of time (in minutes and seconds) given to issue position.

McGovern ad campaigns included nine issue positions that were clearly stated and that were awarded reasonably substantial emphasis.

The Nixon ad campaign most frequently communicated four issue stands:

- Richard Nixon favored honoring our commitments to other nations.
- Richard Nixon had done an effective job of handling China.
- Richard Nixon had done an effective job of handling Russia.
- Richard Nixon did not favor spending less money on the military.

There were four issue stands heavily covered by the McGovern ad campaign:

- George McGovern favored an immediate withdrawal from Vietnam.
- George McGovern favored higher taxes on upper-income Americans.
- Richard Nixon had tolerated political corruption and favoritism in his administration.
- Richard Nixon had done a poor job of handling inflation.

And there was one issue stand given heavy coverage by both the Nixon and McGovern campaigns: [5]

- George McGovern favored spending less money on the military.

The issue beliefs for these nine televised advertising messages and the six previously discussed television news messages are the ones on which viewers would be expected to have become better informed during the campaign.

The Effects of Television Exposure

If television news, or advertising, informs its viewers, then those who watch it regularly should become more knowledgeable about the candidate issue positions covered on television during a campaign.

We measured voters' issue information by having our respondents indicate where they thought Richard Nixon and George McGovern stood on a wide range of major political issues. Voters indicated their beliefs by responding to seven-point scales such as the following:

George McGovern favors an immediate pull-out
of all U.S. troops from Vietnam

Likely:——:——:——:——:——:——:——: Unlikely

We had our respondents mark these scales during both an initial interview in September and a final preelection interview in November. Because our respondents indicated their beliefs in both September and November, and because we also measured their exposure to television news and advertising, we can determine whether television viewing was associated with increased awareness of the candidates' positions. Consider, for example, scaled responses to the statement above. It was indicated both on television news and advertising that McGovern favored an immediate withdrawal of U.S. troops. Now, if between September and November, a voter's belief about McGovern's stand moved toward the "Likely" end of the scale, his awareness of McGovern's position increased. But if he moved toward the "Unlikely" end, his awareness decreased.

The tables presented below are based on these changes. To arrive at the figures in the tables, we first added all of the respondents' changes toward the correct end of the scale, and then we added all of the changes toward the incorrect end. We then used these sums in the following formula:

$$\frac{\text{correct change } - \text{ incorrect change}}{\text{correct change } + \text{ incorrect change}}$$

If more change moved toward the correct end of the scale, the resulting number will be positive. If more of it moved toward the incorrect end, the number will be negative. Furthermore, larger numbers indicate sharper change in the correct or incorrect direction, depending on the sign of the number.

Table 19-3 indicates the changes in voters' issue awareness by their exposure to television news. The table demonstrates that regular viewing of television news was not related to gains in voters' issue awareness. Both low and high television news exposure groups had an almost equal change in issue awareness. On those issues emphasized in television news coverage, the average change for an issue was + 29.3 among voters with low news exposure and + 26.8 among those who watched the news regularly. Regular viewers had a greater increase in awareness on only two of the six heavily covered issues—Nixon's handling of inflation and McGovern's stand on Vietnam withdrawal.

For comparison purposes, Table 19-3 also indicates the changes in issue awareness associated with exposure to the daily newspaper. In contrast to television news exposure, newspaper exposure was strongly related to increased issue awareness. On all six of the heavily covered issues, increased newspaper reading resulted in greater gains in issue awareness. The average change among those with low newspaper exposure was + 19.5 compared with a + 33.7 gain among voters with high newspaper exposure.

Because those people who watch the evening news regularly may or may not also read the newspaper regularly, an examination of television news exposure should be accompanied by a simultaneous examination of newspaper exposure. When newspaper exposure is controlled, there is need for a slight modification to the general conclusion that television news contributed nothing to the issue awareness of voters during 1972 presidential general election. Among those who were not regular newspapers readers, and only among that group, the watching of television news was associated with a somewhat higher issue awareness.

Televised political advertising was associated with an increase in voters' issue awareness (see Table 19-4). On those issues heavily covered in ads, the average change was + 31.5 among voters with high exposure to televised political advertising and + 23.7 among those with low advertising exposure.

Advertising effects occurred primarily on issues surfacing during the election year—Nixon's handling of the Soviet Union and China, the two candidates' positions on military spending, and McGovern's tax proposals. Changes on those issues that had been

Table 19-3 Changes in Voters' Issue Awareness for Level of Exposure to Television News and Newspapers

	Low Television News Exposure	High Television News Exposure	Low Newspaper Exposure	High Newspaper Exposure
Heavily Covered Issues				
Nixon's position on:				
Vietnam war	+38	+35	+30	+43
Eliminating political corruption	+22	+11	+10	+17
Holding down government spending	+18	− 7	+ 3	+ 7
Inflation	+ 6	+21	+ 9	+19
McGovern's position on:				
Spending less on military	+63	+52	+43	+64
Immediate withdrawal from Vietnam	+29	+49	+22	+52
Average on heavily covered issues	+29.3	+26.8	+19.5	+33.7
Lightly Covered Issues				
Nixon's position on:				
Spending less on military	+30	+38	+23	+39
Amnesty for draft evaders	+43	+51	+38	+59
More taxes on upper incomes	+16	− 1	+10	+ 5
Tougher stand on law and order	−10	−14	−18	− 7
Unemployment	−19	+ 3	− 8	−10
Putting a stop to busing	+41	+34	+31	+45
China	+33	+30	+13	+48
U.S.S.R.	+24	+27	+ 9	+39
Honoring foreign commitments	+27	+28	+ 7	+50
McGovern's position on:				
Amnesty for draft evaders	+37	+27	+25	+41
Eliminating political corruption	− 5	+ 5	− 5	+12
More taxes on upper incomes	+11	+34	+16	+29
Average on lightly covered issues	+19.0	+21.8	+11.8	+29.2

Note: Each figure represents difference between percentage of voter change in direction of media's message and percentage in opposite direction. Positive figure, therefore, means that more change occurred in direction of media's message. The larger the figure, the greater the amount of change in one direction.

around longer—Nixon's handling of inflation and Vietnam, and McGovern's position on withdrawal from Vietnam—were unaffected by advertising coverage.

We believe that these results probably *underestimate* the effects of televised political advertising. As a group, voters who watch considerable television programming are not particularly informed about politics. If change on the lightly covered issues can be taken as "normal," voters with high ad exposure had less change (+11.8) than those with low exposure (+16.4). *Televised political advertising, by reversing the relationship between change and exposure on the issues it covered in the 1972 campaign, appears to have been a powerful communication channel.*

Televised advertising's effects were concentrated among those people who were not regular followers of the daily news. People who did not read the newspaper regularly, and those who did not watch television news regularly, became substantially better informed

Table 19-4 Changes in Voters' Issue Awareness for Level of Exposure to Televised Political Advertising

	Low Television Ad Exposure	High Television Ad Exposure
Heavily Covered Issues		
Nixon's position on:		
China	+12	+40
U.S.S.R.	+16	+29
Inflation	+14	+11
Vietnam war	+37	+34
Spending less on military	+29	+34
Honoring foreign commitments	+13	+29
Eliminating political corruption	+21	+14
McGovern's position on:		
Spending less on military	+39	+62
More taxes on upper incomes	+17	+26
Immediate withdrawal from Vietnam	+39	+36
Average on heavily covered issues	+23.7	+31.5
Lightly Covered Issues		
Nixon's position on:		
Holding down government spending	+18	−3
Amnesty for draft evaders	+49	+47
More taxes on upper incomes	+13	+4
Tougher stand on law and order	−15	−12
Putting a stop to busing	+51	+31
Unemployment	−16	−6
McGovern's position on:		
Amnesty for draft evaders	+41	+28
Eliminating political corruption	−10	+5
Average on lightly covered issues	+16.4	+11.8

on the issues if they saw many ads than if they saw few. However, among regular followers of the news, whether their medium was television or the newspaper, televised political advertising was not associated with an increase in issue awareness.

Television News on an Information Source

Television news was found to have minimal impact on voters' issue awareness. Certainly, one reason for this is that the networks gave minimal coverage to the candidates' issue positions. Except for coverage of the Paris peace talks and Watergate, television news was largely devoid of this type of content. For example, the average network gave only five minutes total coverage to McGovern's stands on the pocketbook issues of inflation, unemployment, and taxes.

Of course, television news starts with severe limitations as a source of voters' issue information. The words spoken on a television newscast will not fill the space on the front page of a newspaper. Since its coverage of candidates' issue positions necessarily occurs primarily through its audio channel, television news faces considerable difficulty providing extensive coverage of issue positions.

This drawback is compounded by television new's apparent preference for campaign "hoopla" over campaign substance. Considering only stories originating on the campaign trail, television seems more concerned with the crowds and color of the campaign stops, and the closeness of the presidential race, than with what the candidates are saying; at least, the networks spent more time covering these aspects of the 1972 campaign than they did the substantive aspects of the candidacies of McGovern and Nixon.

People's viewing habits also interact with the nature of television news coverage in ways that reduce the informational impact of the medium. Because most people watch television passively and are not deeply involved in what they are viewing, television informs slowly, through repetition and familiarity. Take product advertising as an example. Most people give only passing attention to most televised advertising, and as research has shown, most viewers cannot remember what an ad said even a minute or two after it was shown.[6] People are simply not paying close enough attention to ads. Over longer periods of time, and repeated exposures to ads for the same product, people not only became aware of the product, they may even associate a jingle or catchword with it.

People pay somewhat closer attention to the evening news than they do to product ads, but not all that much. Their limited attention can be seen in their hazy memories of what they have seen. When questioned the following day, only one in three were able to accurately recall a news story. Thus, only recurrent news themes are likely to penetrate viewer awareness. The single news story may attract the viewer temporarily, but its specific impact normally passes as quickly as the next item appears on the screen. There are, of course, dramatic exceptions—such as the attempted assassination of Wallace—that stick in the mind, are thought about, talked about, recalled at a later time. For the most part, however, only news material that appears again and again becomes part of the viewers' political awareness.

Political issues are not in this category. First, most election issues in 1972 were aired only infrequently, being referenced but a few times during the general election. Second, most issue references were so fleeting that they could not have been expected to have much impression on voters; about half the references to candidate issues came in segments of twenty seconds or less. Third, the candidates' issue positions generally were reported in ways that made them elusive. Often, issue references were only contained in the voice-over; the pictures would show the candidate getting off an airplane or performing some other act on the campaign trail.

In sum, television news makes it hard for voters to learn about the issues. When the typical election issue is mentioned infrequently, in a fleeting manner, and in a mix of extraneous news material, the almost certain result is that viewers will learn nothing about it.

These observations are not meant to suggest that television is an unimportant news source. At the outset of this paper, we indicated the standard we would use to judge media impact was precise, but narrow. The narrowness of our initial standard has caused us to ignore the role of the mass media in providing voters contextual information about issues, in aiding voters to develop judgments about a politian's character and leadership capacity, and in forming voter attitudes on policy preferences. In every one of these areas not analyzed here television news may have considerable impact. But using the simple standard we employ, television news is seen as an overrated source of voters' issue informaion. Its content, its format, and its audience simply belie the common, but facile, judgment that television news has a considerable impact on voters' information about candidates' issue positions.

Televised Political Ads as an Information Source

Nearly everyone watches prime-time television sometime during a week. Because political ads are brief and appear during prime-time entertainment shows, they carry their messages to a vast audience.

Moreover, televised ads reach voters who ignore political information in other mass media. Continuous exposure to politics on television news and in newspapers requires a conscious effort from voters. Not surprisingly, a sizeable minority of Americans make no such effort on any regular basis. However, because many of these same Americans watch television's entertainment programming, in which political spots are imbedded, televised ads can provide them with unexpected political information that requires little effort to absorb. Politically inattentive voters are fertile ground for the issue information that ads contain. Before being exposed to ads, these news avoiders are much less likely than news users to already possess the information conveyed by ads. Political spots help reduce this information gap.

Televised ads have been widely criticized, with some justification, for oversimplifying complex campaign issues. But the simple repetitive nature of televised ads enhances their ability to get across their message. Completely controlled by the candidates, ads can be used as frequently as the budget permits to hammer away at certain specific and limited themes. As the findings of mass communication and advertising research make clear, repetition and simplicity play key roles in learning, and political ads stress again and again the same straightforward messages.

Political ads are probably—message-for-message—more effective communicators than either product ads or television news stories. Every four years, a complete absence of ads about presidential candidates gives way to abundant advertising. Television viewers can hardly miss the change. At the campaign's outset, voters appear to be particularly attentive to these intruders on their daily fare. For example, approximately 75 percent of all voters who, responding to unaided recall questions, told us that they could remember seeing a political commercial, could also accurately describe its intended message. This percentage far exceeds the recall of messages intended by product advertising and, as revealed in our analysis of unaided recall of television news stories, far exceeds the remembrance of day-to-day news stories.

Since televised political ads are often considered vehicles for candidate "image" messages, their issue content has been overlooked. Our data, however, indicate that such ads convey a considerable amount of information about candidates' issue positions. In fact, messages about the issue positions of Nixon and McGovern were communicated more frequently through televised advertising than through television news.

This is not to say that televised ads are necessarily a better source of political information in general. In the presentation of another area of political information, ads are weak and network news is strong. Unlike network news, televised ads provide little background or depth to the issue positions they present. They are not a news source and do not contribute continuous information about events underlying political issues. But as cummunicators of statements about issue positions, and of minimal information supporting these positions, televised ads are both heavily laden with, and effective disseminators of, important political information.

NOTES

1. Survey Research Center Election Studies, 1956–1976.
2. *Voter's Time* (New York: Twentieth Century Fund, 1969), p. 6.
3. In this regard, see our book, *The Unseeing Eye* (New York: Putnam, 1976), which explores several areas of television influence, including television's image-making and agenda-setting effects.
4. The data come from a stratified sample of voters who were selected by standard area probability techniques from the Syracuse metropolitan area. During the first wave, September 7–18, 731 respondents were interviewed. In the second wave, October 7–15, 650 respondents were interviewed. In the third wave, October 30–November 6, 650 of our original respondents were contacted again.
5. Nixon's handling of Vietnam was also the subject of both ad campaigns, but the message from the Nixon campaign was favorable and the McGovern message unfavorable. Consequently, it is impossible to assign a pro or a con label to this issue. The issue will be treated as a "lightly covered" issue and will be given favorable direction in keeping with its treatment by television news.
6. Leo Bogart, *Strategy in Advertising* (New York: Harcourt Brace Jovanovich, 1967), p. 139.

PART IV

THE PARTIES AND
THE FUTURE

INTRODUCTION

Part IV concludes the volume by examining the efforts of the political parties to reassess their operations and to modernize their structures and their procedures. Both parties have initiated assessments intended to weigh their contributions to the social order—most would argue that they have made critically important contributions to the evolution of democratic processes over the generations—and to help correct their deficiencies.[1] The intent has been to both mollify the critics skeptical of the parties' value and, in the process, to reform party procedures in such a manner as to better enable them to fulfill their societal responsibilities. The reform movement came at a critical time for the parties. Could they adapt to the changing political and social currents? Could they coopt the emerging emphasis on personalized campaign management and on electronic campaigning to serve their own ends? Could they open their political processes to encourage participation by the greatest number of party identifiers possible, and could they refashion their party councils to better represent rank-and-file interests? Could they, in short, adapt themselves to the needs of a late twentieth century political order and, in the process, redefine their structures and, at least to a degree, their political objectives?

The selections in this part may begin to answer some of these questions. They are concerned with establishing the potential limits of reform possible within a political system with a specialized party arrangement; examining the impact of reform on a national party; and tracing the changing nature of political party operations and the reasons for them.

First, an introductory word on party reform. Most of the analyses of reform concentrate on the Democratic Party. There is a reason for this. The Republican Party did initiate a reform effort principally through the work of two committees, the DO (Delegate and Organization) Committee (1969–1972) and the Rule 29 Committee (1972–1974). However, the reforms recommended by these panels were, for the most part, advisory. Relatively few were enacted and neither the reform committees nor the changes introduced had any major effect on Republican Party operations. [2]

The case of the Democrats is different. After the acrimonious election year of 1968, the Democrats were in the position of needing to adopt changes satisfactory to the major groups in its broad coalition. As it turned out, the reforms advocated and adopted in the period 1968 to 1976 in presidential nominating procedures, national convention operations, and national party structures went far beyond anything anyone was likely to anticipate at the beginning of the reform period.

The most ambitious of the reform committees was the McGovern–Fraser Commission (1969–1972). This group adopted, and then required the national party and each of the state parties to enact, changes in presidential nominating procedures. The McGovern–Fraser "guidelines," as they were called, were meant to insure more open and more impartial rules to protect those participating in the selection of delegates to the national convention. The new rules were also intended to give participants in primaries or caucus-convention systems at the state and local levels a direct voice in chosing their party's presidential nominee.

The McGovern–Fraser reforms can be divided into two categories. First, the nonquota "quotas" advanced by the commission were perceived by the state parties as requiring the proportional representation of blacks, women, and youth in state delegations to the national conventions. (The McGovern–Fraser Commission, however, contended that they were not mandatory.) Another set of rules adopted by the Commission required such things as written party rules, uniform dates within a state for delegate selection, no arbitrary fees or petition requirements, the printing of a potential candidate's preference (or "uncommitted") on ballots, and so on. These rules were intended to ensure that each participant in party primaries or caucuses had an equal and unprejudiced impact on candidate selection. The reforms were extremely ambitious. They were adopted by the state parties and constituted something of a revolution in Democratic presidential nominating practices. [3]

The Democrats went on in the post-1972 period to modify some of the more objectionable qualities in the McGovern–Fraser guidelines. The whole concept of a quota, for example, was dropped and the party attempted to open party structures and practices at all levels (with particular emphasis on the national). It also tried to extend to all party deliberations the due process safeguards implicit in the original McGovern–Fraser recommendations. The Democrats drastically reconstituted their national committee and adopted new procedures for the operation of their national conventions. They instituted midterm conventions, and they went as far as to adopt a party charter—intended as something akin to a party constitution—to codify party law and guide party deliberations. [4]

The reforms were challenged politically and legally. Politically, beginning with the 1972 Democratic convention, the balance of the party supported the new initiatives. Legally, the results were much the same. In a historic case initiated by the Chicago Democratic machine (*Cousins* v. *Wigoda*), decided in January 1975, the Supreme Court backed the national party reforms.[5] In fact, the Court went as far as to emphasize the primacy of national party controls over presidential-delegate selection, even in the face of contradictory state laws. The national party today is perhaps at the peak of its political and legal powers that arose from the reform movement and the unsuccessful political and legal challenges to its newly emergent powers. What the party chooses to do with its newfound authority may well determine the future of parties in this country.

With this as a backdrop, we can approach the essays in this chapter. The section begins with an unusual essay, "A Comparative Analysis of Party Organizations: The United States, Europe, and the World," by Kenneth Janda, which helps to establish the nature of the American parties in comparative perspective. Many have contended that American political parties are rather curious animals, bearing little relationship to their fellow institutions worldwide. While students of political parties have been able to describe some of the distinctive qualities of American parties—their loose organization, decentralized nature, pragmatic and (to a degree) issueless appeal to the voter—no one has been able to adequately compare political parties in the United States with those, say, in European democracies. Given this inability, it is even less surprising that no one has yet been able to compare American parties with a full range of all party types to detail, in empirical terms, where they rank on various structural and operational indices in relation to other parties in democratic and nondemocratic, competitive and controlled political environments.

This is the task Janda has set for himself. The data for the comparisons come from a unique pool of cross-national indices devised by the author. The study is impressive. Professor Janda compares American political parties on four dimensions—degree of organization, centralization of power, coherence, and involvement—to his sample of parties worldwide. He finds that political parties in the United States, when placed in comparative perspective, have more structural differentiation—an articulation of forms and processes at various levels—than commonly assumed. In relation to power distributions, however, American parties rank among the most decentralized in the world. The American parties rank low also on coherence and involvement. Seemingly among the clutter of formal structures and the dispersion of actual power, there is room for improvement.

The second presentation, "Party Reform and Party Nationalization: The Case of the Democrats," evaluates the success of the reformers in their attempts to remedy some of the weaknesses in the parties documented in the Janda analysis. In this selection, Charles Longley traces and then assesses the impact of the party reforms in "nationalizing" the Democratic Party. The author is concerned with reform developments, and their consequences, in five areas: party rules, the party charter, party law, party finance, and party elites.

The party reforms have had a substantial impact on the operations of the national party. But the influence of the national party initiatives varies by area. The national party is unquestionably dominant now in establishing the delegate-selection standards for national conventions. The attempt to extend national party protections to state and local party procedures through the party charter is difficult to assess at this early stage. As Longley points out, the charter is an ambitious document. It does have symbolic importance. More than that, it establishes nationally acceptable criteria for the operation of local and state parties and it does allow for midterm party conferences, a significant departure from previous practices.

Longley analyzes the major recent legal cases dealing with the changing relationship between state and national parties. The national parties may have an increasingly important role in funding local campaigns and in routing funds to state and local party agencies. Changes in national election laws (in, for example, the public funding of presidential elections) and a new assertiveness by the national parties in collecting funds would add to the national parties' influence. Less impressive is the impact of the reforms in changing the representativeness of national committee memberships.

Taken as a package, the impact of the reforms has been impressive. Longley's conclusion, in this regard, is important. He contends that the widely accepted emphasis on the decentralized nature of American political parties may require a reevaluation.

Political parties contribute vital services to contemporary democracy. A further weakening of the institution of the party ultimately could have only adverse effects on the entire political system.

NOTES

1. See "The Party Symbol and Its Changing Meaning," which introduces this volume.
2. The Republican Party's reform efforts are discussed in William Crotty, *Political Reform and the American Experiment* (New York: Crowell, 1977), pp. 255-261; and in Charles H. Longley, "Party Reform and the Republican Party" (Paper delivered at the American Political Science Association Annual Convention, New York, August 31-September 3, 1978).
3. Crotty, *Political Reform*, pp. 238-245; and William Crotty, *Decision for the Democrats* (Baltimore: Johns Hopkins University Press, 1978).
4. Crotty, *Political Reform*, pp. 245-255.
5. For a discussion of the case and the events leading up to it, see William Crotty, "Anatomy of a Challenge: The Chicago Delegation to the Democratic National Committee," in *Cases in American Politics*, ed. R. L. Peabody (New York: Praeger, 1976), pp. 111-158.

20 / A Comparative Analysis of Party Organizations: The United States, Europe, and the World

Kenneth Janda

The Study of Parties and Party Organization

There are major differences in the ways that scholars define a "political party." But according to Riggs's analysis of several different meanings, almost all scholars agree that, at a minimum, a party involves effort on behalf of a "group" or "organization" toward some objective (1973: 6). Although scholars may differ in their identification of the objectives of party activity, they seem united in defining a party in terms of coordinated human effort. Whether this coordinated human effort issues from a group or from an organization in their definitions appears to be due to a terminological rather than a conceptual difference. For our purposes, we will assume that all political parties are organizations with a political objective. Although my personal conceptualization of that political objective is not crucial to the analysis in this paper, I favor a broad conceptualization and define a political party as *an organization that pursues a goal of placing its avowed representatives in government positions.*

The components in this definition bear closer examination. A political party is defined first as an *organization*—implying recurring interactions among individuals with some division of labor and role differentiation. All organizations are acknowledged to have multiple goals; to qualify as a political party, an organization must have as one of its goals that of placing its avowed representatives in government position. The term "placing" should be interpreted broadly to include competing with other parties in the electoral process, restricting the activities of opposing parties, or subverting the political system and installing representatives in government positions by force. Finally, these individuals must be *avowed* representatives of the organization. This requirement eliminates interest groups from consideration as parties. Of course, if interest-group representatives seek office *as* interest group representatives, then the group does qualify as a party. In practical terms, the test is public identification of the representatives with the organization (party) name or label.

The organization of political parties has long held the attention of European scholars.

An earlier version of this paper appeared as "American and European Political Parties Compared on Organization, Centralization, Coherence, and Involvement," prepared for delivery at the 1974 Annual Meeting of the American Political Science Association. It was substantially revised and new data were added for publication in this volume.

Initially, this attention was centered on the distinctiveness of party organization as a social phenomenon. Such concern can be seen in the writings of Ostrogorski and Michels, both of whom stress the invidious consequences of party organization (1902 and 1915). More recently, with the valued acceptance of political parties in representative government, European scholars have turned to studying the differences in party organization, especially as they relate to the parties' roles in governing. Duverger can be cited as the main stimulus for contemporary concern with organizational concepts in parties research. The first paragraph of the first chapter of his classic work, *Political Parties,* emphasizes the importance of party organization:

> it constitutes the general setting for the activity of members, the form imposed on their solidarity: it determines the machinery for the selection of leaders, and decides their powers. It often explains the strength and efficiency of certain parties, the weakness and inefficiency of others. (Duverger, 1963: 4)

Notwithstanding some notable exceptions (e.g., Wilson, 1962; Eldersveld, 1964; Schlesinger, 1965; Crotty, 1968), American scholars have not cultivated the study of party organization as intensively as their European counterparts. Hennessey, in his study of party organization, concludes: "In the most recent general treatments of American political parties, there seems to be little emphasis on the legal-structure aspects of organization, and even in recent editions of the more comprehensive parties-and-politics texts" (1968: 6). Wright agrees that "concern with party organization has been left largely the domain of non-American (mainly European) scholars" and holds that "the largely nonorganizational view of American parties, although understandable in the light of their underdeveloped organizational state, is a main deterrent to the comparative analysis of political parties . . ." (1971: v).

Several reasons can be cited for the neglect of party organization in American scholarship. The most pervasive factor, which has long colored the attitudes of most Americans toward party politics, is a fundamental distrust of political parties (Sindler, 1966: 4–5). Although they recognize the indispensability of political parties to democratic government, Americans have nonetheless been suspicious of parties acting as private organizations in pursuit of the public interest. This has led to the enactment of statutes in virtually every state that prescribe or limit the organization and activity of state parties (Childs, 1967; Crotty, 1974). In both public opinion and law, political parties in the United States are viewed as quasi-public institutions, and there is a general feeling that parties should be responsive to the electorate as a whole rather than to their limited clientele or membership. This view of parties contributes, Schlesinger contends, to the tendency for Americans to neglect party organization in comparison to the Europeans, for whom "the weight of the continental tradition is clearly on the side of parties as organizations to further the interests of their members, particularly in class or economic terms" (1965: 765–766).

Wright has interpreted the normative issue concerning the proper role of party in government in terms of two alternative models: the *Rational-Efficient* model and the *Party Democracy* model. The Rational-Efficient model, which tends to be employed by American social scientists, is summarized briefly by Wright as having "exclusively electoral functions" and being "pragmatically preoccupied with winning elections rather than with defining policy." The Party Democracy model, which is embraced most strongly by European social scientists, is viewed as "more policy-oriented, ideological, and concerned with defining policy in an internally democratic manner involving rank-and-file member participation" (1971: 7). Wright then states, "in the Party Democracy model, organization is of crucial importance; in the Rational-Efficient model, organization is of much less importance" (ibid.: 39-40). Organization becomes important in the Rational-Efficient model only to the extent that it is related to the mobilization of voters at election time and to the winning of elections. In the Party Democracy model, however, members participate continually in party activities and, beyond campaigning, contribute to party policymaking. Party organization then becomes critical in providing for intraparty communications, procedures for reaching decisions, techniques for carrying out party policy, and recruitment of party leaders.

In recent years, the traditional American disinterest in the organization of parties has acquired a different hue: distinct antiorganizational sentiments have begun to enter evaluations of American parties. As Wilson reminds us, "the phrase 'New Left' came to mean, in part, a commitment to political change that would be free of the allegedly dehumanizing consequences of large organizations" (1973: 4). The dogma of "participatory democracy" stifled efforts to trace the organizational consequences of proposed "reforms." These reforms restricted the freedom of parties to determine their composition and their procedures for selecting party officeholders. In Wright's terms, reformers sought to pluck the "intraparty democracy" feature out of the Party Democracy model for transplant into the Rational-Efficient model, with little debate about compatibility and perhaps less about the possible consequences for American politics of further decentralization of power within the parties.

Relatively recent social and technological changes constitute a final factor contributing to the neglect of party organization in the literature. Agranoff notes the new style of campaigning for election:

Party organization no longer has a near-monopoly on campaign communication. The candidate organization, the news event, the computer-generated letter, and most importantly the electronic media are the prevalent means of getting messages across in the modern campaign. The rise of the candidate volunteer and electronic media has enabled the candidate to bypass the party and appeal directly to the voters. (1972: 5)

Agranoff's point is echoed by Wilson:

No one can doubt the tendency of politicians today to build personal followings independent of party organization, to project an image directly to the voters without the mediating influence of legislative involvement or constituency service, and to defer to the perceptions, if not the judgments, of writers, pollsters, and intellectuals rather than of party leaders. (1973: 5)

Given Americans' traditional distrust of political parties and the recent vocalization of antiorganizational attitudes, the established party organizations fell easy prey to technological developments and began to dwindle in importance in the conduct of election campaigns. Wilson finds that "parties, as organizations, have become, if anything, weaker rather than stronger" and concludes that "parties are more important as labels than organizations."

Sometimes the right to use that label can be won by a candidate who participates in no organizational processes at all—as when a person wins a primary election by campaigning as an individual rather than as an organizational representative. (1973: 95)

The undeniable result of these developments is that American parties, particularly at the national level, play only a relatively minor role in the conduct of presidential campaigns. Witness the decidedly subordinate status of both national party organizations in the 1972 and 1976 presidential elections in particular.

If one reads the lesson of Watergate, as I do, to mean that the American national party organizations need *strengthening* rather than "reform," then students of American parties must pay closer attention to party organization and reexamine the organizational consequences of their numerous proposals to change party roles. "Organization," as Wilson argues, "provides continuity and predictability to social processes that would otherwise be episodic and uncertain" (1973: 7). National party organizations have different membership bases and clientele groups than ad hoc coalitions of nonparty professionals and pure mercenaries. As Agranoff says:

> in the new modes of campaigning the party professional has given way to a different type of professional—the advertising and public relations man, the management specialist, the media specialist, the pollster—who performs services for candidates based on the skills he has acquired in non-political fields. (1972: 4)

The socialization of these key actors in a candidate organization differs considerably from the experiences of professional party leaders and officials, who often interact for years with their counterparts in the opposition party. Linked by a network of governmental and social contacts, professionals of opposing parties often develop mutual respect for one another and are more likely than the staff of candidate organizations to view the opposition as "competitors" than as "enemies." The demise of party organizations in the conduct of campaigns, therefore, is likely to be accompanied by a breakdown of constraints on permissible campaign activities, leading to an erosion of standards of fair competition that are so necessary to party politics in a democratic government.

The normative argument of this paper is that American scholars ought to study party organization more intensively than previously to acquire understanding and knowledge helpful to improving the functioning of political parties in U.S. politics, especially at the national level. In paying renewed attention to party organization, however, American scholars must not narrow their focus, as they have in the past, to parochial concerns with the details of American party structures and processes. They must become more broadly analytical, informing their study with party experiences in other countries. In short, the analysis of American parties should be couched in a comparative framework that can accommodate cross-national observations. A comparative orientation is certain to broaden our perspective and stimulate our thinking toward improving the function of parties in the American political system and devising institutional arrangements to serve that purpose.

Comparative Analysis of Party Organization

This paper is intended to stimulate the study of American party organizations along such fresh lines of inquiry. The findings herein are drawn from the analysis of data from the International Comparative Political Parties Project (ICPP),[1] which includes 158 political parties operating from about 1950 to 1962 in fifty-three countries representing all major cultural-geographical regions of the world.[2] The Project scored the parties on nearly 100 variables, each of which served as an indicator of a broader concept in a framework that isolated twelve major concepts in the comparative analysis of political parties. No attempt will be made here to explain the complex methodology of the ICPP Project or to discuss the conceptual framework in its entirety. [3] For the purposes of this analysis, it is sufficient to note that the twelve major concepts were divided into eight that pertained to a party's "external relations" with society and four that pertained to its "internal organization." Despite my belief that a complete analysis of political parties must ultimately consider concepts of "external relations" as well as concepts of "internal organization," my concern in this paper will be limited to only the four internal-organization concepts, which will be described below in detail.

Scholarly concern with party organization, even among European scholars, has not been characterized by conceptual order and clarity. Crotty notes that "party organizational analysis is not new," but he also points out that it is one of the most frustrating lines of inquiry in party research (1970: 281). One source of frustration lies in the hiatus between party research and the literature on organizational theory. Most party scholars have formulated their concepts of party organization without regard to the more general concepts in the organizational theory literature. Anderson's valuable review of concepts in organizational theory identifies six major dimensions of variation in organizational role structure, with special relevance to party research (1968). He labels these "autonomy," "goals," "formalization," "control," "consensus," and "involvement." The first two dimensions, "autonomy" and "goals," are treated in the ICPP conceptual framework as concepts dealing with a party's "external relations" with society. The remaining four dimensions that Anderson identifies appear to embrace, at a higher level of abstraction, most of the specific variables and measures that party scholars have advanced in their treatments of party organization. To facilitate the application of these concepts to the literature on parties I have translated Anderson's labels into terms that figure more prominently in writings about party organization. Thus, the conceptual framework of the ICPP Project seeks to analyze internal party organization according to four general concepts that match with Anderson's dimensions:

Degree of Organization

The degree of organization corresponds to Anderson's "formalization," which he broadly defines as structured patterns of interactions that are prescribed either by formal rules of procedure or by traditions and unwritten rules (1968: 398-399). The more formalized the organization, the more structured the behavior patterns. Because of the tendency within the literature on parties to equate "formal" structure with "legal" structure, I have adopted this broader label for the concept. It appears that differences in the degree of organization are what Duverger means in most of his frequent and diverse references to the structural "articulation" of a party (1963). By equating degree of organization to structural differentiation, similarities to Huntington's "complexity-simplicity" dimension of political institutions also emerge (1965: 399).

Centralization of Power

The concept of centralization of power relates to Anderson's "control" dimension, but specifically to the distribution of control rather than the volume or sources of control. In this sense, the concept is identical with Duverger's concept of "centralization," which, along with decentralization," he says, "define the way in which power is distributed amongst the different levels of leadership" (1963: 52). There is some tendency within the party literature to confuse centralization with organization, or at least to neglect drawing clear distinctions between the two. Duverger cannot be blamed for this conceptual ambiguity, for he takes pains to distinguish between centralization and articulation. Nevertheless, discussions of party politics frequently equate strong party organization with centralization of power. In our analysis, however, the degree of organization of a party and the centralization of power within it are distinctly different concepts.

Coherence

For Anderson, the counterpart dimension of coherence is "consensus," which he defines very broadly as "the degree of congruence in the cultural orientations of various individuals and groups comprising an organization." He then points out that party scholars are interested in the *issues* that obtain consensus, in the *level* of consensus obtained for different issues, and in the *distribution* of consensus across party organs (1968: 396-397). Under this conception, consensus deals primarily with attitudinal agreement among party members. My conceptualization of coherence is somewhat narrower, however, for I focus on the degree of congruence in the attitudes of party members only to the extent that the consensus is expressed in their *behavior*. Thus, coherence in the ICPP framework pertains to the extent of conflict and division among party members. Studies of party "cohesion" and "factionalism" within the party literature would be embraced by our concept of coherence.

Involvement

Involvement pertains directly to Anderson's last dimension of variation in organizational role structure. Anderson does not define involvement but discusses it in terms of the amount and type of participation in the party (1968: 397-398). Duverger places great importance on the amount and type of participation and their relationship to the concept of party membership (1963: 90-132). The more severe the requirements for membership, he argues, the greater the involvement in party activities—ranging from the minimum psychological attachment common to supporters of American parties to the intense psychological and social attachments that characterize Communist Party members. Neumann incorporates similar distinctions in his classification of parties as providing *individual representation* or *social integration* (1956: 404-405). These concerns are incorporated in the ICPP definition of involvement as the degree of behavioral and motivational commitment to the party.

These four concepts have figured prominently in scholarly evaluations of American political parties. Although these studies usually consider at least implicit comparisons with parties in other Western democracies, unfortunately, neither the implicit nor the explicit evaluations of American parties with their European counterparts have been characterized by conceptual rigor, and rarely have they been supported by anything more than impressionistic evidence. Nevertheless, the literature frequently seeks to explain the special character of American party politics in terms of the deviations of U.S. parties from European organizational norms.

Some examples of these evaluations of American national parties have been culled from the literature to illustrate the role of these concepts in scholarly analysis. Following these illustrations, the four concepts presented above will be incorporated into a set of explicit propositions concerning the comparison of American and European parties. The propositions will then be tested with data from the ICPP Project.

On Degree of Organization

Most students of American parties evaluate the degree of party organization quite differently from Samuel Johnson, who states that "major party organization in the United States is more elaborate than in any other country of free politics. It is more consistent, more extensive, and more unified than anywhere else" (1974: 88). Contrary to Johnson, Duverger describes America as having "very weak party articulation" (1963: 45). Similarly, Greenstein contends that "observers are uniformly agreed that the farther one moves from local politics in the United States, the more difficult it is to find evidence of organized party activity" (1970: 43). The prevailing view of American party organization is clearly opposite to Johnson's and much closer to Sorauf's blunt assessment of the situation:

> We have every right to call the party organization by that name, but it is an inescapable fact that the parties, almost alone among our social institutions, have resisted the development of big, efficient, centralized organization.
>
> Even by the standards of the parties of the other democracies, the American party organizations cut an unimpressive figure. . . . Instead of a continuity of relationships and of operations, the American party organization features only improvisatory, elusive, and sporadic structure and activities. And whereas the party organizations of the rest of the Western democracies have had a near permanent, highly professional leadership and large party bureaucracies, the American organizations have generally done without a professional bureaucracy or leadership cadre. (1972: 133)

On Centralization of Power

It would be far more difficult to locate a discordant view of the centralization of power in American parties comparable to Johnson's deviant assessment of party organization, for extreme decentralization of power has often been cited as the major characteristic of the two major parties in the United States. More than 30 years ago, Schattschneider wrote:

> Decentralization of power is by all odds the most important single characteristic of the American major party; more than anything else this trait distinguishes it from all others. Indeed, once this truth is understood, nearly everything else about American parties is greatly illuminated. (1942: 129)

Approximately 15 years later, Ranney and Kendall found that their analysis of leadership and discipline among the various levels of American parties warranted "at least one firm conclusion: *American national parties are decentralized*" (1956: 264, emphasis in original). And recently, Keefe asserted, "There is no lively debate among political scientists concerning the dominant characteristic of American political parties. It is, pure and simple, their decentralization" (1972: 25).

On Coherence

A recurring theme in writings about American political parties is that American parties are coalitions of various interest groups—Greeley refers to the American party as a "super-coalition" (1974: 172)—and that they serve to "aggregate" these diverse interests in the formulation of public policy (Epstein, 1967: 283). One of the manifestations of coalition politics, Lawson notes, is that "there are nearly as many disagreements within as between the two major parties, and this characteristic of our party system is especially marked in Congress" (1968: 156). The study by Turner and Schneier on party pressures in Congress draws some comparisons with European experiences and concludes:

> In the past six to eight decades the major parties in most parliamentary systems have become increasingly more cohesive. American parties, in the same period, apparently have become less significant factors in shaping patterns of roll-call voting behavior. (1970: 37)

As Ozbudun points out, however, the degree of voting cohesion in legislatures is largely a function of systemic factors rather than party attributes (1970: 380). The existence of factions within a party, therefore, promises to be a better indicator of coherence than voting cohesion within the legislature. Most observers would concur with Madron and Chelf, who hold that "factions are a common occurrence in American political parties" (1974: 82). Few, however, venture more explicit comparative statements of factionalism across countries. One who does is Jupp, who believes that the United States demonstrates the conditions that encourage factionalism (1968: 49).

On Involvement

In discussing the involvement of party members in politics in the United States, most scholars begin by recognizing that the term "membership" has no specific meaning. Bone says, "there are no accepted criteria of what constitutes party membership" (1971: 73), and Keefe states:

> The simple fact is that, apart from primary voting in closed-primary states, membership in an American major party is of slight moment. In effect, anyone who considers himself a Democrat is a Democrat; anyone who considers himself a Republican is a Republican. (1972: 49)

For cross-national comparisons, therefore, assessments of involvement in American parties (and other nonmembership parties) must be made for other than party members. One strategy is to limit comparisons of involvement to party militants, whom Barnes defines as those who carry out party activities, regularly attend meetings, or hold formal party positions (1966: 351). The involvement of militants in party activity may be evaluated according to the incentives that spur them in their activism. Clark and Wilson classify incentives as material, solidary, and purposive; this classification has had the most impact on assessing motivation for party workers or militants (1961).

Party militants motivated by purposive incentives would be most deeply and continuously involved in party activities between election campaigns. In a later work, moreover, Wilson argues that material and solidary incentives have declined in importance in the United States, leaving "purpose, principle, and ideology as a major source of incentives for party organizations" (1973: 96). Sorauf's review of the smattering of empirical studies on incentives in American parties also "points to the present dominance of the ideological or issue incentives. Put very simply, the desire to use the party as a means to achieve policy goals appears to be the major incentive attracting individuals to party work these days" (1972: 95-96). But these empirical studies of involvement in American parties have not been done in a comparative framework, leaving little firm basis for cross-national evaluations. Indeed, despite these research findings for American parties, there is a tendency among party scholars to characterize European party militants as being even more motivated by purpose incentives than their American counterparts. Epstein writes:

> In the absence of large-scale patronage, but not necessarily because of only that absence, many European parties developed membership organizations based largely on nonmaterial incentives. These organizations of zealous faithful party adherents had other purposes too, but they have regularly been used to perform the same vote-getting task as the patronage machine. (1967: 111)

And Rossiter contrasts the coolness of American "attitudes toward political parties" with foreign examples:

> Few Americans give to the Democrats or Republicans the deep and encompassing allegiance claimed by parties like the Socialists in Belgium and the Nationalists in South Africa. Even the loose-jointed Conservative and Labour parties of Britain look like armies of dedicated soldiers to the eye of an observer who has watched the ranks and files of the Republican and Democratic parties straggling across our political landscape. (1960: 25)

Propositions to Be Tested

These evaluations of American political parties for degree of organization, centralization of power, coherence, and involvement give rise to the following propositions:

1. American parties tend to rate lower on *degree of organization* than do Western European parties.
2. American parties tend to rate lower on *centralization of power* than do Western European parties.
3. American parties tend to rate lower on *coherence* than do Western European parties.
4. American parties tend to rate lower on *involvement* than do Western European parties.

In these propositions, "American parties" refers only to the Democratic and Republican parties. No differentiation has been made between these parties in the propositions: it is understood that the two U.S. parties are characterized on the national level by very similar internal organizations, although they are considered to be quite different in their external relations with society. The similarity of the Democratic and Republican parties on organizational attributes—and the unquestioning acceptance of this similarity by most American scholars—is itself a significant commentary on party politics in the United States. Discussions of party organization within most European countries, including Britain, must begin by identifying the particular party being described, for organization often varies significantly across parties within the same country. Because European parties display considerable variance in their internal organizations, the above propositions must involve comparisons of the Democrats and Republicans with the mean scores of European parties on these four concepts.

When we acknowledge the existence of diversity in organization among Western European parties, we begin to question the rationale for making comparisons between American and European parties. Granting the scholarly utility of such comparisons in principle, one might ask why limit the comparison to parties in Western Europe? Why not extend the analysis to include competitive parties in other parts of the world? One simple reason for this limitation in the past has been that obtaining appropriate data on non-European parties would probably be difficult. This concern seems justified given the lack of adequate information on European parties. The data from the ICPP Project does extend to other countries; it is therefore advantageous to extend the comparisons that follow to other competitive parties. This will be done by testing an analogous set of propositions comparing the American parties to competitive parties outside of Europe; i.e., Latin America, Africa, Asia, and the remaining Anglo-American countries. These propositions are as follows:

1'. American parties tend to rate lower on *degree of organization* than do non-European competitive parties.

2'. American parties tend to rate lower on *centralization of power* than do non-European competitive parties.

3'. American parties tend to rate lower on *coherence* than do non-European competitive parties.

4'. American parties tend to rate lower on *involvement* than do non-European competitive parties.

No attempt will be made to root these propositions in the party literature. They simply extrapolate the earlier evaluation of American parties into hypotheses to be tested with data on non-European competitive parties. "Competitive parties" are defined here as those for which "an orientation to open competition in the electoral process" plays either the *major role* in the party's overall strategy for placing its avowed representatives in government positions or is the *exclusive* strategy of the party (Janda, 1970).

Carrying the principle of comparative analysis further, one might ask why the comparisons of party organizations are limited to only *competitive* parties throughout the world. Hennessy comments:

> Totalitarian political parties are very different from those typified by Anglo-American parties and centralist parties of western Europe, and it may be . . . that different theories and analyses may be required for two-party systems, multi-party systems, and several kinds of one-party systems. In any case, most of the scholarship by political scientists (as distinguished from political sociologists) has been done on nontotalitarian parties—for better or worse. (1968: 1)

It is my personal belief that the comparative analysis of political parties has been constrained in scope and capacity because of its customary limitation to competitive parties. Therefore, this paper will also refer to findings concerning the degree of organization, centralization of power, coherence, and involvement of noncompetitive parties throughout the world—including not only "totalitarian" parties (i.e., those that restrict competition from other parties) but also subversive parties (i.e., those that use force to achieve their goals).

There seems to be no established scholarly interest in systematic comparisons of American parties to an undifferentiated group of noncompetitive parties across the world; therefore, no formal propositions will be advanced to guide these comparisons. Likely to be of greater interest to scholars is the comparison of American parties to *all* other parties in the world, both competitive and noncompetitive. This approach would provide the broadest and most definitive touchstone for plumbing the special character of party politics in the United States. To formalize our comparison of the Democratic and Republican parties with the central tendencies of all other parties in the world, I propose these propositions:

1″. American parties tend to rate lower on *degree of organization* than do other parties in the world.

2″. American parties tend to rate lower on *centralization of power* than do other parties in the world.

3″. American parties tend to rate lower on *coherence* than do other parties in the world.

4″. American parties tend to rate lower on *involvement* than do other parties in the world.

Presentation of the propositions in this form, I believe, serves a heuristic purpose by keeping them comparable to the two previous sets. On a priori grounds, however, one might fashion quite different propositions when comparing the U.S. parties with all parties in the world rather than with only the more institutionalized parties of Western Europe. But since this comparison is subsidiary to the major purpose of this paper, I have opted for theoretical simplicity and consistency.

Measuring Parties on Internal Organization Concepts

The 158 parties in the study were scored separately for the first and second "halves" of our 1950 to 1962 time period. The time divisions were usually 1950–1956 and 1957–1962, but they varied somewhat from country to country depending on peculiarities of national politics. The data reported in this analysis is drawn only from the 1957–1962 period, which reduces the total sample of parties to 147 because some parties did not exist in both halves of the period and failed to meet the minimum levels of strength and stability required for inclusion in the study.[4]

Each of the four concepts pertaining to the internal organization of political parties was operationalized by scoring the party on a set of indicators of the concept.[5] The four concepts and the indicators for each are as follows:

Degree of organization was indicated by six factors:

1. *Structural articulation.* Scored from 0 to 11, with high scores for numerous national organs with clear functional responsibilities.

2. *Intensiveness of organization.* Scored from 1 to 6, with high scores for smaller units of organization.

3. *Extensiveness of organization.* Scored from 0 to 6, with high scores for thorough coverage of the country.

4. *Frequency of local meetings.* Scored from 0 to 6, with high scores for meetings held monthly or more frequently.

5. *Maintaining records.* Scored from 0 to 16, with high scores for a publishing program, a research division, and accurate membership lists.

6. *Pervasiveness of organization.* Scored from 0 to 18, with high scores for penetrating many socioeconomic sectors and claiming many adherents within each.

Centralization of power was indicated by eight factors:

1. *Nationalization of structure.* Scored from 0 to 6, with high scores for a national committee dealing directly with local party organizations.

2. *Controlling communications.* Scored from 0 to 7, with high scores for the national-level control of influential media.

3. *Administering discipline.* Scored from 0 to 4, with high scores for discipline administered from the national level.

4. *Selecting parliamentary candidates.* Scored from 1 to 9, with high scores for selection by the national level.

5. *Allocating funds.* Scored from 0 to 6, with high scores for national-level collection and allocation.

6. *Selecting the national leader.* Scored from 0 to 8, with high scores for selection by predecessor.

7. *Policy formulation.* Scored from 0 to 7, with high scores for determination of policy by party leader.

8. *Leadership concentration.* Scored from 0 to 6, with high scores for fewest persons who could commit the party to action.

Coherence was indicated by four factors:

1. *Ideological factionalism.* Scored from 0 to 6, with high scores for large factions with some formal organization.

2. *Issue factionalism.* Same as above.

3. *Leadership factionalism.* Same as above.

4. *Strategic or tactical factionalism.* Same as above.

Involvement of party members was indicated by five factors:

1. *Membership requirements.* Scored from 0 to 7, with high scores for severe requirements, e.g., payment of dues and probationary period.

2. *Membership participation.* Scored from 0 to 6, with high scores for most members being militants, i.e., active participants.

3. *Material incentives.* Scored from 0 to 4, with *low* scores for militants motivated by material incentives, e.g., money.

4. *Purposive incentives.* Scored from 0 to 4, with high scores for militants motivated by purposive incentives, e.g., policy.

5. *Doctrinism.* Scored from 0 to 3, with high scores for continued reference to a written body of party doctrine.

The scores assigned to the parties for each set of indicators were standardized and aggregated to form a single score for each concept, such that the mean values tend toward 0.[6] Thus, the *sign* of a party's score on each concept discloses whether it is above or below the average score and its *magnitude* reveals its deviation from the average value of 0.

Comparisons Among the Parties

The data set includes twelve Western democratic countries that featured competitive party politics during the period 1957-1962. A total of forty-four political parties (including the Democrats and the Republicans) in these twelve countries qualified for inclusion in the study and are identified in Table 20-1, where they are listed in conjunction with their scores for each of the scales included in this analysis. Table 20-1, therefore, contains the basic data to be used in testing the propositions dealing with comparisons of American and Western European parties on characteristics of internal organization.

The total number of competitive parties in the study located outside of Western Europe is fifty-seven. Western Europe is, for this analysis, defined rather strictly on a geographical basis. Thus, the nine parties in Australia, Canada, and New Zealand are among the fifty-seven competitive parties representing twenty-three countries outside Western Europe. The remaining noncompetitive parties throughout the world total forty-six and represent thirty different countries, including one Western European nation, Portugal. Because the main focus of this paper is on the comparison of the American and Western European parties, space will not be taken to identify these other 103 parties outside our prime concern. Reference will be made to their scores only through summary statistics.

Degree of Organization

Table 20-2 presents the summary statistics for the degree of organization for each group of parties in the analysis. The small standard deviation for the two U.S. party scores in this table, and in each of the subsequent ones, confirms the assumption, previously noted, that the Democratic and Republican parties are similar in their internal organization. Therefore, their scores have been averaged together and only the means will be used in testing the propositions. The data in Table 20-2 reveal that, in keeping with Proposition 1, American parties tend to score slightly lower on degree of organization than do European parties. But the difference between the two groups is not significant at the 0.05 level according to the t-test of differences between means—the test used in this paper for the level of significance and the model of evaluation for all references to statistical significance[7]—and thus the American parties should be regarded as similar to the European parties on degree of organization. Propositions 1' and 1'' are also unsupported by the data in Table 20-2. If anything, the American parties tend to be more structurally differentiated than both competitive parties outside Europe and all other parties combined, although these differences are also not statistically significant.

Centralization of Power

The data in Table 20-3 lend powerful support to Proposition 2, for the American parties are strikingly less centralized than European parties and the difference is statistically

352

Table 20-1   American and Western European Political Parties Scored for Degree of
Organization, Centralization of Power, Coherence, and Involvement[a]

ID#	Country and Party	Organization	Power	Coherence	Involvement
1	United States Democratic	.14	−1.37	−.80	−.77
2	United States Republican	.01	−1.41	−.73	−.77
11	British Labour	.32	.21	−.77	.20
12	British Conservative	.51	.41	.62	−.20
51	Irish Fianna Fail	−.47	.52	.88	−.69
52	Irish Fine Gael	−.38	−.05	.88	−.49
53	Irish Labour	−.45	.23	.88	−.10
101	Austrian Peoples	.64	−.41	−.72	−.43
102	Austrian Socialist	.59	.07	−.39	−.14
103	Austrian VDU-FPO	−1.18	−.30	−1.14	.34
111	French MRP	.79	−.42	.08	.55
112	French Radical Socialist	−.45	−.70	−.72	−.65
113	French SFIO	.15	−.14	−.65	.38
114	French Gaullist	−.67	.22	−.54	−.36
115	French Communist	.97	.34	.74	.95
121	West German CDU	1.10	.07	.22	−.02
122	West German SPD	1.15	−.27	−.29	1.35
123	West German FDP	.56	−.16	.11	.55
141	Greek Liberal	−2.70	.20	−1.81	−1.08
142	Greek EPEK	−2.27	−.18	.41	−1.08
143	Greek Rally-ERE	−1.53	.52	.45	−.67
145	Greek EDA	.52	.63	.61	.83
201	Danish Social Democrat	.84	.09	.91	.40
202	Danish Venstre	.35	.20	.15	.40
203	Danish Conservative	.64	.20	.88	.40
204	Danish RAD Venstre	.25	.29	.42	.40
221	Iceland Independence	−.17	.39	.84	−.77
222	Iceland Progressive	.18	.10	.70	−.68
223	Iceland Peoples Union	.59	.52	.14	.97
224	Iceland Social Democrat	−.42	.33	−.99	−.11
241	Swedish Social Democrat	.92	−.69	.23	−.17
242	Swedish Center	.49	−1.21	.55	.10
243	Swedish Liberal	−.26	−1.22	.44	.04
244	Swedish Conservative	−.24	−.99	.19	.20
261	Dutch Catholic Peoples	.58	−.46	−.41	.07
262	Dutch Labor	.95	−.39	−.36	.24
263	Dutch Liberal	.32	−.77	−.25	−.05
264	Dutch ARP	.79	−.21	.16	.09
265	Dutch CHU	.01	−.67	−.93	−.10
266	Dutch Communist	.57	.74	−.17	.78
271	Luxembourg Christian Social	−.29	−.34	.45	−.10
272	Luxembourg Socialist Labor	−.41	−.45	.14	.40
273	Luxembourg Democratic	.22	−.12	.35	−.34
274	Luxembourg Communist	.44	.45	.83	1.69

[a]The values in the table are the parties' scale scores, reported to two decimal places, for each of the concepts. The scale scores on each dimension are developed from the items presented in the text. A more complete discussion of the scaling techniques used can be found in my *Comparative Political Parties: A Cross-National Survey* (New York: Free Press, forthcoming) and *Political Parties: Their Internal Organization and External Relations* (New York: Free Press, forthcoming).

Table 20-2 Comparison of Parties on Degree of Organization

Party Grouping	Mean Value	Standard Deviation	(N)
United States	.075	.09	(2)
Western European competitive	.08	.84	(42)
Non-European competitive	−.37	.80	(54)
Noncompetitive	−.08	.80	(46)
All parties outside United States	−.14	.82	(142)[a]

[a]Three parties could not be scored on degree of organization.

Table 20-3 Comparison of Parties on Centralization of Power

Party Grouping	Mean Value	Standard Deviation	(N)
United States	−1.39	.03	(2)
Western European competitive	−.08	.49	(42)
Non-European competitive	−.09	.81	(56)
Noncompetitive	.37	.62	(47)
All parties outside United States	.06	.70	(145)

significant at the 0.05 level. Note also that the European parties themselves tend to be below the world mean for centralization of power. As a group, the most centralized parties are the noncompetitive parties, reflected in the extremely high scores of the seven ruling Communist parties in our study. Of course, Propositions 2′ and 2″ are also supported by these data, and the differences are even more striking when the U.S. parties are compared to all the parties combined.

Coherence

Proposition 3, which states that American parties are less coherent than European parties, is also borne out by the data in Table 20-4, and the difference is again statistically significant. The same is true of Propositions 3′ and 3″; American parties tend to rate lower on Coherence than competitive parties outside of Europe and lower than all the parties in the world taken as a group, but this last comparison is only marginally significant.

Involvement

The tendency for activists to be less involved in American parties than in European parties, which is the thrust of Proposition 4, is supported by the data in Table 20-5 and the test for significance. Propositions 4′ and 4″ are also supported, although the difference

Table 20-4 Comparison of Parties on Coherence

Party Grouping	Mean Value	Standard Deviation	(N)
United States	−.76	.05	(2)
Western European competitive	.07	.66	(42)
Non-European competitive	−.07	.83	(55)
Noncompetitive	−.06	.69	(43)
All parties outside United States	−.02	.74	(140)[a]

[a]Five parties could not be scored on coherence.

Table 20-5 Comparison of Parties on Involvement

Party Grouping	Mean Value	Standard Deviation	(N)
United States	−.77	.00	(2)
Western European competitive	.07	.60	(42)
Non-European competitive	−.16	.74	(55)
Noncompetitive	−.03	.88	(45)
All parties outside United States	−.05	.75	(142)[a]

[a]Three parties could not be scored on involvement.

in involvement between American and non-European competitive parties barely achieves significance and might fail under an alternative statistical model.

Our findings and the results of the statistical tests as they bear on our propositions are easily summarized. The proposition that characterizes the American parties as being low on degree of organization is not supported in any of its three variants. All of the other propositions are supported. American parties do tend to rate lower on centralization of power, coherence, and involvement than do competitive parties in Western Europe, than competitive parties outside of Europe, and parties worldwide that are not differentiated as to their goal orientation.

Conclusions

The most striking finding of this analysis is, of course, its failure to demonstrate that American parties are lacking in degree of organization in comparison with Western European parties. Perhaps the fault lies either with my conceptualization of "organization" or my attempt to operationalize the concept through the selection of indicator variables. But a conceptualization of organization in terms of "structured behavior patterns" and "structural differentiation" seems to be in accord with the concept in the organizational theory literature, and many of my indicator variables have sprung directly from the party literature. I leave it to others to redefine and remeasure the parties in retesting the proposition. I believe that the discrepancy between the literature's evaluation of American parties and the finding of this study is more likely to be the result of notions of "organization" which involve judgments of the distribution of authority within a structure than structural differentiation per se. In point of fact, American political parties do tend to have as much if not more in the way of formal structure than most other parties in the world, and the previously cited statement by Johnson on the elaborate nature of American party organization, although certainly extreme, appears to be more accurate than the prevailing wisdom in our textbooks.

The prevailing wisdom of our textbooks, however, is supported conclusively by the next most striking finding of this analysis. American parties are clearly less centralized than the European norm, and they are certainly among the most decentralized parties in the world. None of the Western European parties in the sample had a lower score on the centralization of power than did U.S. parties. Moreover, when the entire sample of the world's parties is considered, the American parties outrank only the Blancos and Colorados of Uruguay—which some scholars would contend are not parties but coalitions, or groupings of parties—and the Social Action Party of Chad, which terminated in 1962, at the end of our time period.

The other major findings of the study, that American parties tend to feature less coherence and less involvement than do Western European parties and other parties throughout the world, conform largely as expected to most evaluations within the literature. Although these two concepts pertain to important aspects of party organization and aid in understanding the operation of the parties in American politics, they are perhaps of less relevance for those who seek to alter the function of the parties because they are not easily manipulable. Although some scholars argue for a realignment of the parties on issues and ideology such that more coherence among American parties would result, there is no clear procedure for forcing such a realignment. Similarly, there is no observable mechanism for instilling in party activists a greater degree of commitment to their work, which makes involvement an equally unwieldly variable for planned change.

The two aspects of party organization that afford the most opportunity for induced change are, of course, degree of organization and centralization of power. Because of our finding that American parties are not as deviant as claimed in the extent of their structural differentiation, there appears to be less capacity for change in American politics through further elaboration of party structure. Instead, the prime avenue for moving U.S. politics by means of its parties is through an increase in the centralization of power at the national level, which would tend to retard the ominous growth of personalized politics in both parties and return control to more broadly-based organizations of responsible professionals. Strengthening the national committees by designating them as the prime agencies for collecting and dispersing campaign funds, for example, would certainly deflate the role of personal candidate organizations in presidential elections. The desirability of this particular change ought to be the subject of careful analysis and informed debate. But the lessons from recent years should be clear. It is time to inquire whether American government and politics are best served by national political parties that are so extremely decentralized that they stand virtually alone among comparable institutions in Western Europe and throughout the world.

NOTES

1. The ICPP Project was established with support from the National Science Foundation (grants GS-1418, GS-2533, and GS-27081). NSF support terminated in 1971. The Foreign Policy Research Center in Philadelphia also supported my work on the project while a Visiting Fellow in 1970-1971. The American Enterprise Institute in Washington, D.C., kindly sponsored my writing for one quarter in 1973.

2. The areas and countries represented in ICPP studies of political parties are as follows. *Anglo-American:* United States, Great Britain, Canada, Ireland, Rhodesia and Nyasaland Federation, and India; *West Central Europe:* Austria, France, Federal Republic of Germany, Greece, and Portugal; *Scandinavia and the Benelux Countries:* Denmark, Iceland, Sweden, Netherlands, and Luxembourg; *South America:* Ecuador, Paraguay, Peru, Uruguay, and Venezuela; *Central America and Caribbean:* Cuba, Dominican Republic, El Salvador, Guatemala, and Nicaragua; *Asia and the Far East:* Burma, Cambodia, Indonesia, North Korea, and Malaya; *Eastern Europe:* Albania, Bulgaria, German Democratic Republic, Hungary, and the U.S.S.R.; *Middle East and North Africa:* Sudan, Tunisia, Lebanon, Iran, and Turkey; *West Africa:* Dehomey Ghana, Guinea, Upper Volta, and Togo; *Central and East Africa:* Central African Republic, Chad, Congo-Brazzaville, Kenya, and Uganda.

3. The ICPP Project is thoroughly described in Janda (1968, 1969, 1970, and 1975). The data from the ICPP Project have been deposited with the Inter-University Consortium for Political and Social Research.

4. It was easier to specify minimum levels of strength and stability as requirements for inclusion in the project for legal parties than for illegal ones. Legal parties had to win at least 5 percent of the seats in the lower house of the legislature at least twice during our time period. For illegal parties, we accepted estimates of support by at least 10 percent of the population over a 5-year period. In certain cases, especially in Africa, we departed from these standards to include some parties but not to exclude any.

5. Reliabilities for all the scales were calculated with the use of Cronbach's *alpha* (Bohrnstedt, 1970). The reliabilities were 0.72 for the coherence scale, 0.78 for involvement, 0.82 for degree of organization, and 0.83 for centralization of power.

6. The mean scores did not actually equal zero due to the impact of missing data for some of the indicators. Parties were assigned scores for each concept based on the indicators for which they could be scored.

7. There is room for disagreement over the statistical test that would be the most appropriate for testing these propositions with these data. For example, the sampling units in this study were not parties but nations—or, if you will—party systems. This complicates matters because the sample is not strictly speaking a random sample of parties. By and large, I have ignored this distinction in the statistical tests, and I have also ignored the fact that the United States, Canada, and Great Britain were not drawn in the original sample but were added later. Furthermore, there is the issue of conceptualizing the populations that the parties represent under the t-test model. My interpretation, with which others might differ, is that the test is conducted to determine the probability that American parties and the counterpart party groupings consititue random samples from either the same population or ones with equal means. In applying the t-test, moreover, there is the problem of wide differences in sample variances and, for the American group, a very small sample size ($N = 2$). Although the t-values were calculated with both separate estimates of the population variance and a pooled estimate, with the appropriate values chosen on the basis of a homogeneity of variance test, the very small sample size can produce inefficient variance estimates. Although a correction for degrees of freedom was employed for such instances (Blalock, 1960:175–176), the t-test is still thought to be somewhat unstable under the circumstances.

    An alternative approach to evaluating the statistical significance of these comparisons would be to assess the position of the American parties in the probability distribution of parties for each of the groups to be compared. This would be done most accurately with reference to probability density functions generated for each distribution. Because the referent distributions did not depart dramatically from normality—all had kurtosis values under 1.0 and all but one had skewness values under .8—this approach was executed instead by calculating the deviations of each American party from the group mean in terms of the group standard deviation and estimating the probability of occurrence with reference to areas under the normal curve. When the *joint* probabilities for both parties were calculated, the results confirmed the t-test procedure in every instance. I have employed the t-test approach in the text because of its greater familiarity to most readers. I wish to thank Mark Levine for raising some issues in the statistical analysis, which caused me to probe further and place the analysis on firmer ground.

REFERENCES

Agranoff, R. (1972) *The New Style in Election Campaigns.* Boston: Holbrook Press.

Anderson, L. (1968) "Organizational Theory and the Study of State and Local Parties." In *Approaches to the Study of Party Organization,* ed. W. J. Crotty. Boston: Allyn and Bacon.

Barnes, S. H. (1966) "Participation, Education, and Political Competence: Evidence from a Sample of Italian Socialists." *American Political Science Review* 69 (June): 348–353.

Blalock, H. M. (1960) *Social Statistics.* New York: McGraw-Hill.

Bohrnstedt, G. W. (1970) "Reliability and Validity Assessment in Attitude Measurement." In *Attitude Measurement,* ed. G. F. Summers. Chicago: Rand McNally.

Bone, H. A. (1971) *American Politics and the Party System.* New York: McGraw-Hill.

Burns, J. M. (1963) *The Deadlock of Democracy.* Englewood Cliffs, N.J.: Prentice-Hall.

Childs, R. S. (1967) *State Party Structures and Procedures.* New York: National Municipal League.

Clark, P. D. and J. Q. Wilson (1961) "Incentive Systems: A Theory of Organizations." *Administrative Science Quarterly,* 6 (September): 129–166.

Crotty, W. J., ed. (1968) *Approaches to the Study of Party Organization.* Boston: Allyn and Bacon.

——— (1970) "A Perspective for the Comparative Analysis of Political Parties." *Comparative Political Studies* 3 (October): 267–296.

——— (1974) *Presidential Nominating Procedures. A Compendium of Election Practices in 1972.* 2 vols. New York: National Municipal League.

Duverger, M. (1963) *Political Parties.* New York: Wiley. First published (1951) *Les Partis Politiques.* Paris: Armand Colin.

Eldersveld, S. J. (1964) *Political Parties: A Behavioral Analysis.* Chicago: Rand McNally.

Epstein, L. D. (1967) *Political Parties in Western Democracies.* New York: Praeger.

Greeley, A. M. (1974) *Building Coalitions.* New York: New Viewpoints.

Greenstein, F. I. (1970) *The American Party System and the American People.* Englewood Cliffs, N.J.: Prentice-Hall.

Hennessy, B. (1968) "On the Study of Party Organization." In *Approaches to the Study of Party Organization,* ed. W. J. Crotty. Boston: Allyn and Bacon.

Huntington, S. (1965) "Political Development and Political Decay." *World Politics* 17 (April): 386–430.

Janda, K. (1968) "Retrieving Information for a Comparative Study of Political Parties." In *Approaches to the Study of Party Organization,* ed. W. J. Crotty. Boston: Allyn and Bacon.

——— (1969) "A Microfilm and Computer System for Analyzing Comparative Politics Literature." In *The Analysis of Communication Content,* eds. G. Gerbner, et al. New York: Wiley.

——— (1970) "A Conceptual Framework for the Comparative Analysis of Political Parties," *SAGE Professional Papers in Comparative Politics,* 01-002. Beverly Hills, Calif.: Sage Publications.

——— (1971a) "Conceptual Equivalence and Multiple Indicators in the Cross-National Analysis of Political Parties." Paper delivered at the Workshop on Indicators of National Development, sponsored by the International Social Science Council, UNESCO, and ECPR and held in Lausanne, Switzerland.

——— (1971b) "A Technique for Assessing the Conceptual Equivalence of Institutional Variables Across and Within Culture Areas." Paper delivered at the 1971 Annual Meeting of the American Political Science Association, Chicago, Illinois.

——— (1971c) "Diversities among Political Parties in Industrialized Societies." Paper delivered at the 1971 Symposium on Comparative Analysis of Highly Industrialized Societies, sponsored by the International Social Science Council and held in Bellagio, Italy.

——— (1975) "A World-Wide Study of Political Parties." In *Personalized Data Bases,* eds. B. Mittman and L. Borman. New York: Wiley.

——— (in press) *Comparative Political Parties: A Cross-National Survey.* New York: Free Press.

——— (forthcoming) *Political Parties: Their Internal Organization and External Relations.* New York: Free Press.

Johnson, S. A. (1974) *Essentials of Political Parties.* Woodbury, N.Y.: Barron's Educational Series.

Jupp, J. (1968) *Political Parties.* New York: Humanities Press.

Keefe, W. J. (1972) *Parties, Politics, and Public Policy in America.* New York: Holt, Rinehart and Winston.

Lawson,K. (1968) *Political Parties and Democracy in the United States.* New York: Scribner.

Madron, T. W. and C. P. Chelf (1974) *Political Parties in the United States.* Boston: Holbrook.

Michels, R. (1915) *Political Parties: A Sociological Study of the Oligarchical Tendencies of Modern Democracy.* London: Jarrold and Sons. Also published in 1949. New York: The Free Press.

Neumann, S., ed. (1956) *Modern Political Parties.* Chicago: University of Chicago Press.

Ostrogorski, M. (1902) *Democracy and the Organization of Political Parties.* 2 vols. New York: Macmillan. Also published in 1964. Garden City, N.Y.: Anchor.

Ozbudun, E. (1970) "Party Cohesion in Western Democracies: A Causal Analysis," *SAGE Professional Papers in Comparative Politics,* 01-006. Beverly Hills, Calif.: Sage Publications.

Ranney, A. and W. Kendall (1956) *Democracy and the American Party System.* New York: Harcourt Brace Jovanovich.

Riggs, F. W. (1973) "Parties and Legislatures: Some Definitional Exercises." Paper delivered at the 1973 International Political Science Association Meetings, Montreal, Canada.

Rossiter, C. (1960) *Parties and Politics in America.* Ithaca, N.Y.: Cornell University Press.

Schattschneider, E. E. (1942) *Party Government.* New York: Rinehart.

Schlesinger, J. A. (1965) "Political Party Organization." In *Handbook of Organizations,* ed. J. G. March. Chicago: Rand McNally.

Sindler, A. P. (1966) *Political Parties in the United States.* New York: St. Martin.

Sorauf, F. J. (1972) *Party Politics in America.* Boston: Little, Brown.

Turner, J. and E. V. Schneier (1970) *Party and Constituency: Pressures on Congress.* Baltimore: Johns Hopkins Press.

Wilson, J. Q. (1962) *The Amateur Democrat.* Chicago: University of Chicago Press.

——— (1973) *Political Organizations.* New York: Basic Books.

Wright, W. E. (1971) *A Comparative Study of Party Organization.* Columbus: Merrill.

21 / Party Reform and Party Nationalization: The Case of the Democrats

Charles Longley

The traditional description of American political parties emphasizes the decentralized and largely autonomous character of the party system. The national parties, as such, "have little power vested in them and possess no real authority over state and local party organizations or elected officials."[1] Or, as V. O. Key concluded over 20 years ago, "there are no national parties, only state and local parties."[2] And when attention is directed specifically to the national party committees, Cotter and Hennessy propose that they are

> large groups of people variously selected who come together now and then to vote on matters of undifferentiated triviality or importance, about which they are largely uninformed and in which they are often uninterested.[3]

In short, we are left with the impression that the national party organization is little more than a hodgepodge of disparate state party organizations.

Some suggest, however, that the usual characterization of national party organization is no longer wholly accurate. Austin Ranney, for example, notes that the McGovern–Fraser Commission reforms constituted an "unprecedented national intrusion" into the bailiwick of state parties.[4] And although Jewell and Olsen observe that state party vagaries persist, the recent national Democratic Party rules reforms have had a "nationalizing effect" and a concomitant "organizational strengthening."[5] The net result of recent events, suggests another author, has been the emergence of the Democratic Party as a "truly national association."[6] Clearly then, it is appropriate to appraise the contemporary ties that bind the national and state party organizations. Of particular concern is the extent to which the national Democratic Party has assumed a more authoritative role with respect to the conduct of state party affairs. Five dimensions will be considered here: (1) party rules, (2) the Democrat's party charter, (3) party "law", (4) party finances, and (5) party elites.

This is a revision of a paper originally delivered at the Annual Meeting of the Midwest Political Science Association, April 29–May 1, 1976. Ellen Goldstein, Susan Smith, and Sheila Hixson of the Democratic National Committee provided helpful background material. Professor Patricia Longley provided thoughtful criticism, and Alexa Longley assisted with numerical computations.

Party Rules

As Saloma and Sontag have argued, the period between 1968 and 1972 saw the first serious attempt at reform since the Progressive era.[7] To be sure, the Democratic Party had implemented other reforms just before this time, such as the imposition of "loyalty oaths" to protect the party's presidential nominee and the adoption of antidiscrimination provisions following the 1964 national convention. Nevertheless, it was mandated at the 1968 convention that state parties afford "all Democratic voters . . . a full, meaningful and timely opportunity to participate" in the range of activities associated with the delegate-selection process.[8] To implement the convention's mandate the Democratic National Committee (DNC) appointed a Commission on Party Structure and Delegate Selection. This panel, chaired initially by Senator George McGovern and later by Representative Donald Fraser, reviewed existing delegate-selection procedures and, in 1969, promulgated a series of guidelines.[9] The McGovern–Fraser Commission's proposals constituted an unprecedented intrusion into the affairs of state and local parties. In some instances the commission required action by state parties, and in other cases action was merely urged. For the first time, a uniform set of party rules, adopted by a national party commission, was imposed on the party's subnational units. Failure to comply with the new rules could result in the unseating of state delegations to the national convention or, ultimately, result in the withdrawal of recognition of the state party as the legitimate agent of the national party, as was done in 1968 with respect to the "regular" Mississippi Democratic Party.[10]

The McGovern–Fraser guidelines required state parties to, among other things, adopt party rules for delegate selection, adopt procedural safeguards (such as proscriptions on unit rule and proxy voting, requirements for adequate public notice and uniform meeting times in publicly convenient places, and elimination of mandatory party assessments for delegates), as well as ban such current party practices as closed slatemaking meetings, preferential treatment for endorsed candidates, and ex officio membership in a delegation. State parties were also instructed to afford "reasonable representation" for women, youth, and minority-group members based on their presence in the state's population. Where state law conflicted with the commission's guidelines, the state parties were to "make all feasible efforts to repeal, amend, or otherwise modify" the contrary provisions. In other words, the national Democratic Party clearly asserted its authority over state parties and state statutes that might impede the realization of the commission's guidelines.

Compliance with the McGovern–Fraser rules did not come easily. The 1972 convention was confronted with an unprecedented number of credentials challenges and a rash of lawsuits contesting the rules themselves as well as their implementation. Even so, as Austin Ranney noted, there was substantial compliance.[11] Even more important, as Ranney observes,

> the point to be emphasized here is what they [the rules] have done to revive *national* party agencies' power over state affiliates. The commission was mandated by a *national* convention, appointed and encouraged by a *national* chairman and given real clout by a *national* committee. The guidelines required state parties to make radical changes in many of their accustomed ways of doing things, and the state parties all got into line.[12]

In 1972, the national convention extended the party's commitment to rules reform. A second party commission was established and, after a series of public meetings, the "Mikulski Commission" (so named after Baltimore city councilwoman Barbara Mikulski, who chaired the panel) issued a series of recommendations that were subsequently adopted by the DNC in early 1974. [13] Although some of the original McGovern–Fraser guidelines were revised, the Mikulski commission perpetuated the authority of the national party to set the standards for delegate selection. For example, statewide winner-take-all primaries were banned, the presidential preference of delegate candidates was to be identified on the ballot, participation in the delegate-selection process was to be limited to Democrats, and a party watchdog (the Compliance Review Commission) was established to monitor and assist state party compliance with the 1976 delegate-selection rules. At the same time, the Mikulski guidelines recognized the importance of state and local parties by increasing the ceiling for state-committee-appointed delegates from 10 percent to 25 percent and substituting affirmative action programs for the reasonable-representation "quotas" of 1972. That the Mikulski Commission revised some rules should not obscure the more central consideration: the rules of the game were again defined by a national party panel affirmed by the party's national committee, with implementation overseen by a national party unit. The recognition that subnational party units may well bear the immediate responsibility for implementation in no way detracts from the nationalization of party rules that has occurred. Should there be insufficient compliance with the rules the DNC's executive committee is now empowered to establish the entire delegate-selection procedure for a state! Admittedly, this prospect may be remote (as the party's accession to Wisconsin's open primary in 1976 would suggest) but the telling point remains: the authority of the national Democratic Party to tell state parties what to do with respect to delegate selection is now a given. The Democratic Party's third reform commission, chaired by Morley Winograd of Michigan, promises to expand even further the role of the national party. [14]

The Party Charter

Before the 1972 national convention, the Democratic Party had attempted to codify the party's rules and practices, leading to the adoption of a written constitution. Under the leadership of Representative James O'Hara (chair of the 1972 convention rules committee) a draft charter was drawn up which, according to one critic, would "Europeanize" the Democratic Party, much to the detriment of state and local units. [15] Deferring action on the proposed charter, the 1972 convention instead passed a resolution calling for

> the formation of a charter commission and mandating the Democratic Party to meet in conference in 1974 to adopt a charter from the commission's draft and discuss issues: a Democratic Conference on Party Organization and Policy. [16]

Former North Carolina Governor Terry Sanford was named to chair the charter commission. Following a series of open meetings conducted across the country, delegates to the "mini-convention" met in Kansas City in December 1974. [17]

Just before the conference, one long-time observer of national politics suggested that

> the stilted phrases spelling out the trade-offs between centralized guarantees of free access to party decisionmaking and a reaffirmed commitment to a federalized party structure mark the terms of agreement which the diverse elements of the nation's oldest party will accept as the ground rules for their own cooperation and fraternal combat. [18]

Upon conclusion of the conference, the twelve-article charter eventually adopted did in fact constitute a series of "trade-offs," but the document also constituted the Democratic Party's first written constitution. It was, in fact, the first time any major American political party accepted such a document. In this sense the charter thus marks a significant step toward making formal the practices and rules of the past that were once subject to the whim of passing majorities on a variety of organizational levels.

The charter's contents can be summarized as follows:

Article I provides a detailed description of and standardized rules for presidential nomination procedures.

Article II spells out the formulation of the DNC and its procedures, asserting the primacy of national rules over contrary state rules or laws.

Article III defines DNC membership, apportionment and responsibilities.

Article IV establishes an executive committee.

Article V defines the role of the national chairperson.

Article VI provides for an optional midterm convention on party policy.

Article VII prescribes a judicial council to oversee delegate selection and resolve intra-party conflicts.

Article VIII establishes a national finance council.

Article IX establishes a national educational and training council to further the objectives of the party.

Article X contains antidiscrimination clauses and mandates openness in all party affairs through establishment of affirmative action programs.

Articles XI and XII contain general provisions and provide for amendments, bylaws, and rules.

The charter admittedly is but a scrap of paper. Nonetheless, the document does contribute to the evolution of a nationalizing Democratic Party in several important respects. Uniform standards for delegate selection, guarantees of access to all party affairs, and affirmative action programs became required for state parties. Moreover, the structure of the national organization was clarified through the creation of new party components with detailed responsibilities. The size of the DNC, expanded in 1972, was pegged to the party's national constituency instead of to a "state-sovereignty" model with equal representation for each member unit. Additionally, specific reference was made to the need for a membership attuned to the demographic shape of the Democratic constituency.

Those advocating a "cadre-like" party, however, were not altogether successful; members, according to the new charter, would be neither "dues paying" nor "card carrying." A midterm policy conference to "discuss the issues" and heighten the party's policy consciousness, although optional, was not in fact mandated. From this perspective, then, the actual language of the charter may be seen as a blunt recognition of the "prevailing federalism of American politics."[19] To stop here, however, would be in error. Adoption of the party's first constitution also represents a symbolic gain. Intraorganizational relationships were made formal; a charter was, after all, adopted. Austin Ranney notes that with the adoption

it will no longer be accurate to describe the national party, as most scholars have in the past, in terms like "a ghost party" or a loose alliance of [state and local parties] to win . . . the presidency.[20]

The party charter should be recognized in symbolic as well as in more tangible terms. In a sense, what the charter actually states may well be less important than what the charter represents: confirmation of a national Democratic Party.

Party Law

Recent Democratic reforms have also spawned a series of legal contests and given rise, as John Quinn notes, to two sets of constitutional issues.

> The first set of conflicts involves the relationship of *state* election laws governing delegate selection to national political party delegate selection rules such as those promulgated by the Democratic Party under mandate of the 1968 and 1972 presidential nomination conventions. . . . [The second set of conflicts] arises between the parties' interests in delegate selection and the individual voter's interest in representation protected by the due process and equal protection clauses of the Constitution. [21]

Legal niceties aside, one prominent Democratic state chairperson, also a member of the Compliance Review Commission and former head of the Association of the Democratic State Chairmen, stated the problem more bluntly:

> Now a state party puts itself in one hell of a difficult political situation when it pays attention to party rules and not the state law. Now if you want to run in a bad atmosphere, you run where your party has apparently with deliberate intent ignored or violated a state law in order to adhere to a party rule. You will find in most of the states in this country you are going to just catch hell. [22]

The Democratic Party conflicts between national party rules and state law have been particularly nettlesome. Most of the legal suits have arisen from contests surrounding the seating of national convention delegates. The resolution of "who wins?" obviously bears heavily on the extent to which the national party can dictate party rules to its subnational units. Repeated judicial recognition of the authority of the central organization may well promote state party compliance in the face of prolonged, expensive and, more than likely, unsuccessful litigation. From the perspective of political parties, the First Amendment affords a guarantee of free association. This freedom thus ensures that parties can organize and conduct their business without the restraint of contrary state law.

Credentials challenges arising out of the 1972 Democratic nomination process are particularly instructive in setting forth the contrasting points of view. The unseating of delegations from Chicago and California, selected through each state's primary process, led to the filing of lawsuits contesting the decision of the credentials committee. [23] At the district-court level the suits were dismissed on the grounds that the questions posed were not appropriate for judicial resolution; they were nonjusticiable matters. Upon appeal, the Court of Appeals in Washington, D.C., reversed the lower court and in so doing denied relief to the unseated Chicago delegates. It also overturned the decision of the party's credentials committee and ordered the original California delegates be reseated. Meeting in special session, the U.S. Supreme Court issued a *per curiam* opinion. Its decision was handed down less than three days before the national convention was scheduled to begin. In its opinion, the Supreme Court stayed the action of the appellate court and thereby returned the ultimate power of decision to the convention itself. The reasoning behind the court's action sheds considerable light on the constitutional relationship between national party rule and state law.

The Supreme Court noted initially that the questions presented were in fact novel. The problems encountered, it indicated, also were exacerbated by the imminence of the convention. Nevertheless, the court observed that although there was little germane precedent, parties were generally free to resolve their own internal disputes.

> No case is cited to us in which a federal court has undertaken to interject itself into the deliberative processes of a national political convention; no holding up to now gives support for judicial intervention in the circumstances presented here, involving as they do relationships of great delicacy that are essentially political in nature. [24]

In so saying, the Supreme Court obviously took cognizance of the fact that the outcome of the contested challenges could weigh heavily on the eventual decision of the convention concerning the party's presidential nominee. This position was further developed in the following:

> It has been understood since our national parties came into being as voluntary associations of individuals that the convention itself is the proper forum for determining intra-party disputes as to which delegates should be seated. [25]

The court opinion concluded by observing,

> If this system is to be altered by the federal courts in the exercise of their extraordinary equity powers, it should not be done under the circumstances and time pressures surrounding the actions brought in the District Court and the expedited review in the Court of Appeals and this Court. [26]

The importance of this ruling in establishing the authority of the national party is clear enough. It is a national party body that is left with the power of decision. The party could choose to reseat (or to unseat again) delegates, and its determination would not be colored by existing state law.

The Chicago challenge also gave rise to a second case, which refocused judicial attention on the problem of state law versus national party rule. [27] Having lost in federal court, the unseated Chicago delegates sought and obtained a state court injunction barring the successful challengers from sitting at the convention. Upon recognition by the convention, the challengers did so anyway and were subsequently convicted of contempt of court. Upon return from the Miami convention, judicial relief from the contempt conviction was sought on the basis that the injunction was improperly granted.

The Illinois Court of Appeals forcefully upheld the lower court's action. Among other things, the court ruled the following: the 1972 reforms "in no way take precedence . . . over the Illinois Election Code"; [28] "the law of the State is supreme and party rules to the contrary are of no effect"; [29] the state's right to protect the right to participate in a primary "is superior to whatever other interests the party might wish to protect"; [30] and— if that was not sufficient—the convention could not impose delegates on the people of Illinois because "such action is an absolute destruction of the democratic process of this nation and cannot be tolerated." [31] In other words, the Illinois court took issue not only with the action of the convention but with the party reforms as well!

The U.S. Supreme Court, hearing *Cousins* v. *Wigoda* on appeal, decided otherwise. The rationale set forth by the majority for granting certiorari was that it would contribute to the decision on

> the important question presented whether the Appellate Court was correct in according primacy to state law over the National Political Party's rules in the determination of the qualifications and eligibility of delegates to the party's national convention. [32]

In reversing the contempt citation, the Supreme Court concentrated on the subject of free political association shielded by the First Amendment. This right, the court held, was superior to the state's concern with protecting the integrity of participation in a primary. Of particular concern to the court was the fact that involved here was delegate selection to a party's national convention. Thus, according to the court,

> consideration of the special function of delegates to such a Convention militates persuasively against the conclusion that the asserted state interest constitutes a compelling state interest. [33]

State parties, after all, are affiliated with a national party and "the states themselves have no constitutionally mandated role in the great task" of selecting a party's presidential and vice-presidential nominees. [34]

The court then speculated on the implications of an arrangement whereby states could set the boundaries for delegate selection and concluded with the following observation:

> If the qualifications and eligibility of delegates to the National Political Party Conventions were left to state law . . . each of the 50 states could establish the qualifications of its delegates to the various party conventions without regard to party policy, an obviously intolerable result. [35]

However improvident it may be to generalize from a single case, the Supreme Court's holding in this instance constitutes a landmark ruling. Clearly, state parties are put on notice that the national party organization is preeminent in matters concerning the conduct of party business. Of greater significance, the national party can proceed with relative assurance that its further ventures at defining the rules of the game will enjoy juridicial approval stemming either from the courts' reticence to become engaged in "political matters" or from their reliance on precedent.

The extent to which the national party might seek to impose its will on state parties can also be illustrated by reference to the 1976 delegate-selection rule restricting participation to "Democrats only." State parties were required to make "all feasible efforts" to ensure that Republicans (or independents) did not dabble in Democratic politics and thereby skew the presidential preference of Democratic voters. A case in point was Wisconsin's "open primary" where, in 1972, an estimated 20 percent of the primary voters "crossed over." The state party argued that prevailing state law did not in fact require voters to publicly avow their party preference as a precondition for primary participation and asked that the offending rule be held invalid. Attorneys for the DNC, however, argued that the Wisconsin state party was attempting to "avoid the unambiguous holding of the Supreme Court in *Cousins* v. *Wigoda,* which asserted national party authority in such matters. [36] The District Court eventually dismissed the case (it was "premature" for judicial intervention) and the Compliance Review Commission subsequently granted an exemption for the 1976 Wisconsin primary. But the waiver in this instance was conferred by the national party and did not come at judicial direction. In other words, the principle of national party dominance in the area was continued even though the open primary was held as originally scheduled.

The cases cited thus far have focused on the Democratic Party. Contests involving the Republican Party have also contributed to the nationalization of party authority. Here, however, the court has rejected challenges to the national party based on alleged violation of the Fourteenth Amendment's equal protection clause. One suit, noteworthy alone for the fact that it spanned a period of 5 years and two Republican national conventions, challenged the "bonus delegates" provision of the GOP's rules. In essence, the Ripon Society argued that a flat grant of bonus delegates was contrary to the court's rulings that representative bodies be apportioned on population. The Ripon position gained support at the district-court level, but subsequent appeal overturned the finding. The Appeals Court for the District of Columbia noted that delegate allocation might be subject to the Fourteenth Amendment, but

> the public and private interests in making decisions through some other scheme of representation outweigh the interests served by numerically equal apportionment. [37]

And although the right to vote is allied with the nomination process, "between that right and the right of free political association, the latter is more in need of protection in this case." [38]

According to the court, it is up to a party to decide on how best to gain electoral success; it is not the judiciary's role to hold one method more or less rational than another. Similarly, the court rejected attempts to have the winner-take-all 1976 Republican presidential primary in California declared unconstitutional. The extent and manner to which voters participate in the delegate-selection process, and the manner in which that participation is reflected in national convention representation, said the Supreme Court, "are matters for the political parties themselves to determine, and, if the parties permit it, for the states." [39]

The evolution of party law would thus appear to augur well for national party authority. There is, admittedly, the ever present prospect that practical "political" considerations will reveal internal contradictions (such as was true for the Wisconsin open primary), but this likelihood should not obscure the more central concern. In light of judicial reluctance to intervene, and in the context of prior decisions, balky state parties will continue to "just catch hell."

Party Finance

Most of the research on "money and politics" is directed toward analyzing campaign finances. Common Cause, for example, has made this topic more visible by scrutinizing the sources of revenues as well as how the money is spent. [40] More academic inquiry has long been a concern of the Citizen's Research Foundation. [41] And the financial scandals associated with Watergate have done much to raise the issue of campaign finances more generally and to encourage appropriate federal legislation. To date, however, there has been little explicit attention given to the subject of party organization funding. [42] And, for the national Democratic Party, the recent balance sheets have been impressive only in a negative way. There is some evidence, however, that the party's financial plight may well be lessening and that financial adversity has, in fact, contributed to innovative fund raising by the national party. Moreover, the extent to which the national organization can acquire a firmer financial footing may well determine the prospects for expanded efforts by the party.

The implications of a revision in party financing have not passed totally unrecognized. Herbert Alexander, for example, commented,

> if the money is given to the national committee this could significantly change power balances within the parties. I do not say it is necessarily wrong to give it to the national committee if you recognize that you are thereby strengthening the national committee vis-à-vis senatorial and congressional committees. . . . [43]

In another context, Alexander suggested that

> direct national fundraising weakens the power of state and local organizations to the degree that they cannot claim credit as the chief source of the party's wealth, or the federal candidates' resources. . . . When national funds are ample, only the power of the ballot remains as the bastion of local power. [44]

It is doubtful, perhaps, that the Democratic Party's funds will soon be "ample." It is true, however, that the national organization has reduced its sizeable outstanding debt and also has moved to solidify its financial ties with candidates and state parties. Together these developments contribute to the need for change in the relations between national and state parties.

The data in Table 21-1 portray the financial status of the party over a 10-year period. As recently as 1971 the national party was laboring under a debt largely incurred following the 1968 primary efforts of Senators Kennedy and Humphrey. That this debt has been substantially diminished is obvious, although some reduction came through negotiations with party creditors on a "reduced-cents-per-dollar" basis. At the same time, the annual budget has increased from approximately $200,000 in 1972 to nearly $340,000 in 1975. Two additional developments also promise to facilitate a more promising fiscal future for the party.

First, with the election of Jimmy Carter, the national Democratic Party is obviously blessed with a feature attraction on the fund-raising circuit. During 1978, for example, the President was scheduled to speak at a minimum of five gatherings intended to generate funds for the national organization. Second, the DNC successfully petitioned the Federal Elections Commission for a waiver on the ceiling for single-year contributions to the national party for debts incurred prior to the enactment of campaign reform legislation. [45] In other words, the monies owed from 1968 to American Airlines and A.T.&T. (being amortized at the rate of $50,000 per month), as well as debts to individuals, could be eliminated without running afoul of current legislation. In concert, these prospects can only be thought encouraging.

The national party has also initiated novel fund-raising techniques to further the effort at debt reduction as well as generate revenues for state parties. Most noteworthy among these efforts is the telethon, which features party officials and popular entertainment figures. The data in Table 21-2 indicate the results of three telethons sponsored to date.

Table 21-1 Democratic National Party Finances,
1968-1977 (in dollars)

1968-1971	
1968 Presidential campaign deficit	6,000,000
1968 Humphrey primary debt assumed	1,500,000
1968 Kennedy primary debt assumed	1,000,000
Operating losses, 1968-1971	800,000
Total deficit, 1968-1971	9,300,000
Deficit, 1972	5,000,000
Deficit, 1973	3,000,000
Deficit, 1974	2,600,000
Deficit, 1975	2,800,000
Deficit, 1976 (Carter campaign debt included)	3,600,000
Deficit, 1977	1,800,000

Source: Data obtained from DNC.

Overall, the telethon netted more than $3,000,000 for state parties and nearly $2.4 million for the DNC. The California state party realized nearly $500,000 alone, while the state party mean was approximately $73,000. Profits were allocated by a formula that prorated each state's share in accordance with monies received from that state; a fixed percentage after expenses was allotted to the DNC. In contrast to early fears that the telethons would merely siphon off money that would have been contributed to the party in any event, subsequent analysis revealed that nearly two-thirds of the contributors were first-time donors. [46] Additionally, the states were provided with a list of the names of the donors from their states. Thus, state parties acquired new names to approach for funds at a later date as well as a potential source for regular party activities.

The national party also can play a more substantive electoral role as a result of reformed campaign finance legislation. As noted by Adamany and Agree when commenting on the 1974 Federal Elections Campaign Act, the state or national party committee was authorized

> to spend up to the greater of two cents times the voting age population of $20,000 to support senatorial candidates . . . and up to $10,000 to support each House candidate. [47]

The DNC can also engage in unlimited expenditures for electoral activities such as voter registration and mobilization. The extent to which these programs are actually realized may be in dispute, but from the candidate's perspective, "the trend will be to shift these functions to party committees to allow the candidate to use his full quota for final appeals to the voter." [48] In 1978, the DNC's treasurer projected spending a total of $1.7 million on House and Senate races. [49] Amounts of this magnitude obviously promote the visibility of the national organization in a most direct manner. [50]

This discussion of party finance has suggested: (1) the debts of the past are being relieved, (2) the national party has sought to assist state parties, and (3) recent campaign finance reform has carved out a particularly attractive role for party organizations. It would be an overstatement, however, to conclude that all is well with the party's fortunes,

Table 21-2 Democratic National Committee Telethon Finances (in dollars)

	1973	1974	1975	Total
Income	4,215,215	5,403,672	3,700,000[a]	13,318,887
Expenses	2,273,237	2,555,839	2,751,336	7,580,412
Net	1,941,978	2,847,833	1,009,272	5,798,903
State share	1,100,000	1,815,086	504,636	3,419,722
DNC share	841,987	1,032,747	504,636	2,379,370

[a]Estimated.
Source: Data provided by Ms. Kitty Halpin, DNC Telethon Coordinator.

even with a Democrat in the White House. The lingering debt has curbed the size of the national committee's staff, and meeting the payroll persists as a major Democratic headache. [51] By the same token the fiscal health of the national party is more sound now than in any time in the recent past.

Party Elites

One goal of the 1972 reform effort was to make the national committee more numerically representative of the Democratic "presence" in the electorate as a whole. Traditionally, seats on the DNC were apportioned equally, with each state being represented by a committeeman and a committeewoman. The net result of this arrangement was to give the same number of votes to Alaska and Delaware as to California and New York. Following the 1972 convention, membership on the DNC was increased to over 300, with state delegations ranging from a minimum of four (including the state party chairperson) to eighteen members. Provision was also made for a limited number of elected party and public officeholders. Up to an additional twenty-five members were authorized to help "balance" demographic composition in accord with newly adopted affirmative action guidelines. The "new" DNC was thus structured to achieve a more proportionally equitable popular and demographic representation. [52]

An examination of DNC membership both before and after the onset of reform provides a final basis from which to assess party nationalization. In particular, we can compare the party elites along a series of descriptive dimensions under the assumption that DNC composition may well be important in shaping the agenda and role of the national party. Indicators to be employed are age, race/ethnicity, education, religion, party service, and public officeholding.

Age

Table 21-3 contains available age data for the prereform and postreform DNC members. The postreform committee reflects the presence of younger members, with nearly 20 percent under 40 years of age. The earlier committee counted but 12 percent in this category. By the same token, there are over twice as many members over 60 years of age in the earlier period (25 percent) than in the later period (12 percent). For both committees, however, the dominant group is between 40 and 49 years of age, and nearly two-

Table 21-3 Democratic National Committee Age Distribution
(in percentages)

Age	Prereform (August 1970)	Postreform (November 1975)
30 or younger	0	2
30–39	12	18
40–49	37	37
50–59	26	31
60–69	17	10
70 or older	8	2
(N)	(92)	(220)

thirds of both committees fall between the ages of 40 and 59. The distributional data obscure the finding that the average age for the prereform group is 50, whereas the postreform DNC membership averages 48 years of age. There is, therefore, some change between the two committees, but nothing of major proportion.

Race/Ethnicity

Following 1972, the DNC was subject to affirmative action guidelines. The data on racial diversity are presented in Table 21-4. The postreform committee does, in fact, reflect an increased proportion of nonwhite members. Blacks more than double their share of the seats, jumping from 6 percent to 13 percent. Hispanic delegates increase from 1 percent to 5 percent on the later DNC. Although, percentage gains are noteworthy themselves, the gains in numbers are also important. (On the earlier DNC there were six black members and one Hispanic. For the postreform committee there were forty-three blacks and sixteen Hispanics.) With a greater number of members, the prospects for more influence and an effective caucus activity are enhanced.

Not to be overlooked, however, is the fact that the DNC is largely composed of white members, thus raising the prospect that the change is more symbolic than tangible. Even so, the postreform DNC does differ from its predecessor, acquiring a racial composition closer to national demographic characteristics.

Education

The educational background for both sets of DNC members is contained in Table 21-5. In contrast to the earliest period, the level of education for members of both 1970 committees is high. In each case, however, the change largely occurs for members with less than a college education. Although the postreform DNC appears to have somewhat less formal education, this could be explained by lack of appropriate information for 15 percent of the delegates. When "unknowns" are eliminated, 60 percent of both the pre- and postreform DNCs hold a college degree. The postreform DNC, however, is characterized by more extensive education beyond the bachelor's degree. Of the postreform members, 12 percent hold M.A. or Ph.D. degrees, whereas only 3 percent of the prereform DNC held compa-

Table 21-4 Democratic National Committee Racial Diversity
(in percentages)

Race/Ethnicity	Prereform (August 1970)	Postreform (November 1975)
White	92%	81%
Black	6	13
Hispanic	1	5
Other	1	1
(N)	(102)	(323)

rable degrees. The percentage of members with a legal education also varies, with 27 percent of the prereform members so trained as against 24 percent of the postreform members. Overall, these two sets of party elites appear well educated in contrast to the general population, which, in 1975, included but 13 percent with a college education. The differences in educational level between the two committees are more in degree than in kind.

Religion

The religious preference of DNC members is indicated in Table 21-6. Most notably, Protestant affiliation declines in the postreform committee by approximately 8 percent. Jewish identifiers increase slightly from 8 percent to 10 percent on the later committee. Catholic membership remains steady at slightly less than 25 percent. When compared to the 1948-1963 period examined by Cotter and Hennessy, the representation of Jews shows the most marked change, up from the 2.3 percent of those years. The expanded DNC does not, however, suggest a radical restructuring in terms of the members' religious affiliations.

Party Service

Some observers feel that the most recent party-reform effort was a reaction to the events surrounding the 1968 Democratic presidential nominating contest.[53] In many instances the charge was made that the party's councils and processes were not open to "full, meaningful and timely" participation.[54] Consequently, we might expect that the prereform committee was composed of mainly party "regulars," those whose background encompassed extensive party service. In this context, for example, Cotter and Hennessy noted that "many members are selected because they are already important in the state party."[55]

> To them that have shall be given. The most common reason for selection as a national committee member is simply the fact that the individual is already a successful and visible party or governmental leader in the state. More than any other way, national committeemen and -women get the job because they are governors or mayors or congressmen or state legislators or party committee chairmen (state or local) and vice chairmen.[56]

Table 21-5 Democratic National Committee Education Levels (in percentages)

Education	1948-1963	Democrats	
		Prereform (August 1970)	Postreform (November 1975)
High school or less	16	10	9
Some college	20	28	24
College	53	58	52
Unknown	11	4	15
(N)	(306)	(102)	(323)

Table 21-6 Democratic National Committee Religious Preference (in percentages)

Religion	Prereform (August 1970)	Postreform (November 1975)
Protestant	53	45
Catholic	24	23
Jewish	8	10
Other	3	3
Unknown	12	19
(N)	(102)	(323)

To what extent do the postreform committee personnel differ from their prereform counterparts in terms of party service? Does the latter period evidence the presence of individuals with a lesser degree of subnational party experience and hence suggest that the party's national council is more "open"? The assumption here is that the postreform era would in fact be characterized by a greater proportion of party "irregulars"—those whose involvement was neither as traditional in the sense of moving through the local and state levels of party hierarchy nor as extensive in terms of the number of party offices held. Given that the 1972 national convention was marked by an unusual number of "first-timer's," whose presence was attributed to the McGovern-Fraser reform guidelines, we might also expect to see a greater percentage of so-called "amateur" Democrats on the reformed national committee.[57] Tables 21-7 and 21-8 enable us to pursue this line of inquiry.

There is little overt difference in the entry levels of members of the two DNC committees. The postreform group does evidence less initial local party officeholding, yet this is largely offset by more extensive state-level entry. If we assume that traditional recruitment patterns encompass both local and state formal party experience, the reform-era members might be characterized as less "regular." Of greatest interest, however, is the finding that over 70 percent of both groups have held local and state party responsibilities. (Democrats functioning at the national level are less visible in both instances.)

Table 21-7 First Recorded Party Office Held Before Democratic National Committee Service (in percentages)

Entry Level	Prereform (August 1970)	Postreform (November 1975)
Local	57	51
State	17	20
National	19	20
None	0	2
Unknown	8	7
(N)	(102)	(323)

When state party chairpersons and vice-chairpersons are eliminated from the data (because they sit on the postreform DNC ex officio) the results are somewhat different. In this situation, nearly half again as many later members (24.9 percent versus 18.6 percent) began their partisan tenure at the national level. Additionally, fewer of the postreform members were veterans of local party councils (49.8 percent versus 56.8 percent). Nonetheless, it appears that DNC members of both eras are practiced party politicians. Moreover, whatever increase in "amateur" Democrats might have taken place was offset by the increased size of the DNC with ex officio memberships given to state chairpersons.

In Table 21-8, the extent to which national committee members have held party office is reported. In addition to expecting that the later DNC clientele would include national-level entrants, it might also have been projected that the postreform committee would reflect less traveled party members. Such does not appear to be the case. The membership's party background is generally comparable for both periods along the dimension of subnational party service. The only notable difference is that the later group has fewer state and local officeholders, which is possibly a function of their younger age.

The information pertaining to party service suggests that DNC membership, although not permanently fixed, does adhere to a general pattern. Admittedly, time and financial constraints, as noted by Cotter and Hennessy, enter in, but an expectation that the reformed DNC would differ substantially along this dimension is not realized. [58]

Public Officeholding

One additional descriptive indicator can be assessed in contrasting the committees before and after the reform. Cotter and Hennessy also note that national committee members occasionally sat on the DNC by virtue of holding elective office during the 1948–1963 period. [59] Table 21-9 provides the data on public officeholding for the two periods compared here. Overall, the postreform period is characterized by somewhat less officeholding (23 percent versus 30 percent). The greatest discrepancy occurs on the national level. State and local officeholding are the more typical incubators for national committee membership in both instances, although state officeholding is slightly less pronounced in the later period. Of greater interest is the finding that public officeholding, like party service, remains generally constant. This would suggest that the nationalization move-

Table 21-8 Previous Subnational Party Office of Democratic
National Committee Members (in percentages)

Party Office	Prereform (August 1970)	Postreform (November 1975)
Local	10	12
Local and State	48	42
State	16	18
Other, unknown	26	28
(N)	(102)	(323)

Table 21-9 Highest Office Held Before Democratic National
Committee Service (in percentages)

Public Office	Prereform (August 1970)	Postreform (November 1975)
Local	7	9
State	18	15
National	6	2
None, Unknown	69	74
(N)	(102)	(323)

ment in the party had very little effect on the public service background of its constituents. For most members, holding electoral office is still unrelated to their presence on the party's council.

Party Elites and Party Nationalization

The reformed DNC does differ from its prereform counterpart, but not radically so. Postreform DNC members, as a group, are slightly younger; formally, somewhat less educated; and certainly more racially diverse. Data on religious affiliation shows a decrease in Protestant members, but an increase in Jewish members. In terms of party entry and service, however, both national committees are composed of individuals with substantial experience. Election to public office prior to committee service has remained stable, retaining a state and local cast more than a national one. By and large, national committee membership does not appear to have changed substantially.

On Party Nationalization

The party-reform effort initiated at the 1968 national convention led to the emergence of a more authoritative national Democratic Party organization. Most notably, the adoption of uniform delegate-selection standards, which in turn sparked a series of court tests, have clearly established the supremacy of national party rules over state party practices and state law. Additionally, the Democratic Party charter both codified and symbolized the preeminent role of the national party (while still allowing, of course, state and local parties considerable autonomy and discretion). Although the national organization has become financially more self-sufficient and supportive of state parties, the latter must continue to fund the bulk of their own operations. Membership on the DNC is now more demographically diverse than in the prereform period, but national committee members continue to evidence substantial experience in state and local party councils.

What might be concluded from the current investigation, quite simply, is that the traditionally accepted party decentralization perspective is no longer wholly accurate. To overstate the case, however, would be just as much an error as to ignore the changes that have occurred. The national party is increasingly permeating all levels of party organization. This much is clear. It is particularly dominant in those procedural areas involving delegate selection. Nevertheless, there is little evidence to suggest that the national organization can either dictate presidential recruitment per se (as the case of Jimmy Carter would surely attest) or recruitment below the presidential level. Furthermore, there is little reason to expect that in the foreseeable future the party's central committee is likely to serve as the primary source of party policy or that it will seek to "punish" errant party officeholders. Allegiance to the Democratic Party will likely remain a matter of self identification, not a matter of card-carrying or dues-paying.

The extent to which further party nationalization might be expected, much less realized, is difficult to assess. American political parties operate in a context of separation of powers and federalism. These two factors obviously impose structural constraints on the development of a uniform and unified national party. [60] Consider also that the organizational changes identified here were initiated in a period marked by particularly salient national issues and spurred by reform-oriented activists who worked through newly created party commissions. Moreover, between 1968 and 1976 the Democratic Party did not occupy the White House. With the election of Jimmy Carter and his ex officio assumption of the role of "head of party," however, the manner in which the president promotes or opposes party nationalization will be of major importance. [61]

It should also be recognized that the American political party, *sui generis,* currently confronts a shrinking electorate that increasingly calls itself "independent," splits its ballots, and responds to candidate and issue cues as well as to party labels. For some observers, the United States is in a period of "party decomposition." [62] It is easier, however, to identify the changes of the past than to predict the future. But Democratic Party reform has occurred, and with it has come a significant move away from party politics as usual. To paraphrase Alexander Bickel, the reforms may yet belie the Jeremiahs while still disappointing the revolutionaries. [63]

NOTES

1. Joyce Gelb and Marion Leif Palley, *Tradition and Change in American Party Politics* (New York: Crowell, 1975), p. 211.

2. V. O. Key, *Politics, Parties and Pressure Groups,* 4th ed. (New York: Crowell, 1958), p. 361.

3. Cornelius Cotter and Bernard C. Hennessy, *Politics Without Power* (New York: Atherton, 1964), p. 3.

4. Austin Ranney, *Curing the Mischiefs of Faction* (Berkeley: University of California Press, 1975), p. 2. See also William Crotty, *Political Reform and the American Experiment* (New York: Crowell, 1977), pp. 238-261; and Crotty, *Decision for the Democrats* (Baltimore: Johns Hopkins University Press, 1978), chaps. 2, 3, and 4.

5. Malcolm E. Jewell and David M. Olsen, *American State Political Parties and Elections* (Homewood, Ill.: Dorsey, 1978), p. 301 and p. 324.

6. Gerald Pomper et al., *The Election of 1976* (New York: McKay, 1977), p. 7.

7. John S. Saloma and Frederick H. Sontag, *Parties: The Real Opportunity for Citizen Politics* (New York: Knopf, 1972).

8. Quoted in Commission on Party Structure and Delegate Selection, *Mandate for Reform* (Washington, D.C.: Democratic National Committee, 1970), p. 9. Hereafter cited as *Mandate*.

9. *Mandate*, pp. 38-48; and Crotty, *Decision*, chap. 3.

10. The 1964 national convention conditioned "the seating of delegations at future conventions on the assurance that discrimination in any State Party affairs on the grounds of race, color, creed or national origin did not occur." Cited in *Mandate*, p. 39. In January 1968, the DNC adopted six antidiscrimination standards and at the 1968 convention it was ruled that the Mississippi Democratic Party had not complied with these standards. Consequently, recognition as the official agent of the national party in Mississippi was given to the "loyalist" faction of the Mississippi party, headed by Aaron Henry.

11. Ranney, *Curing*, p. 184; and Crotty, *Decision*, chap. 4.

12. Ranney, *Curing*, p. 185 (emphasis added).

13. Commission on Party Structure and Delegate Selection, *Democrats All* (Washington, D.C.: Democratic National Committee, 1973). See also Crotty, *Political Reform*, pp. 245-247; and Crotty, *Decision*, chap. 7.

14. See Report of the Commission on Presidential Nomination and Party Structure, *Openness, Participation and Party Building: Reforms for a Stronger Democratic Party* (Washington, D.C.: Democratic National Committee, 1978); and Crotty, *Decision*, chap. 8.

15. Ben J. Wattenberg, "When You 'Quota' Somebody In, Somebody Is Booted Out," *Los Angeles Times*, December 1, 1974.

16. Cited in R. M. Koster, "Surprise Party," *Harper's Magazine*, March 1975, p. 24.

17. See, for example, "We the Democrats of the United States . . . 'In Mini-Convention Assembled,' A Report on the Kansas City Charter Conference," *Democratic Review*, February/March 1975, pp. 27-43. One dissenting assessment of the conference, for its failure to take issue positions, is offered by Ronnie Dugger, "Fast Shuffle at Kansas City," *The Progressive*, February 1975, pp. 22-25. See also, Dennis G. Sullivan, Jeffrey L. Pressman, and F. Christopher Arterton, *Explorations in Convention Decision Making* (San Francisco: Freeman, 1976); Crotty, *Political Reform*, pp. 247-255; and Crotty, *Decision*, chap. 7.

18. David S. Broder, "Democrats Ready to Adopt Charter," *Washington Post*, December 1, 1974, p. A1.

19. Broder, "Democrats Adopt Charter," p. A16.

20. Ranney, *Curing*, p. 187.

21. John Quinn, "Presidential Nomination Conventions: Party Rules, State Law, and the Constitution," *Georgetown Law Journal* 62, no. 6 (July 1974): 1621-1622.

22. Transcript of the Compliance Review Commission, May 31, 1975, p. 205A.

23. See *Keane* v. *National Democratic Party*, Civil No. 1320-72 (D.D.C. July 3, 1972) and *Brown* v. *O'Brien* 469 F.2d 563 (D.C. Cir.), respectively. For a case study of the Chicago challenge, see William Crotty, "Anatomy of a Challenge: The Chicago Delegation to the Democratic National Convention," in *Cases in American Politics*, ed. Robert L. Peabody (New York: Praeger, 1976), pp. 111-158.

24. 409 U.S. 4 (1972).

25. Ibid.

26. 409 U.S. 4 (1972).

27. *Cousins* v. *Wigoda*, 95 S. Ct. 541 (1975).

28. 14 Ill. App., 3d 460, 302, N.E. 2d, 625.

29. Ibid., 627.

30. Ibid., 629.

31. Ibid., 631.

32. 95 S. Ct. 545 (1975).

33. 95 S. Ct. 548 (1975).

34. 95 S. Ct. 549 (1975). (But note, too, that Justices Burger, Stewart, and Rehnquist do not concur with this.)

35. Ibid.

36. From the Democratic Party's brief filed in the Wisconsin suit, p. 20.

37. Cited in "Politics: The GOP," *Ripon Forum,* 11 (October 1975): 1. The case is *Ripon Society* v. *National Republican Party, 1975.*

38. Ibid., p. 2.

39. *Graham* v. *March Fong Eu et al.,* as quoted in Leslie Oelsner, "Supreme Court Upholds the Winner-Take-All Role for California's Republican Presidential Primary," *New York Times,* January 26, 1975, p. 17.

40. See also, *Dollar Politics* (Washington, D.C.: *Congressional Quarterly, 1974).*

41. See, for example, John F. Bibby and Herbert E. Alexander, *The Politics of National Convention Finances and Arrangements,* Study No. 14, (Princeton, N.J.: Citizens Research Foundation, 1968) and Thomas L. Pahl, *The Minnesota Republican Neighbor to Neighbor Drive: Successful Small Gift Solicitation,* Study No. 19, (Princeton, N.J.: Citizens Research Foundation, 1971). See also, Crotty, *Political Reform,* pp. 103–190.

42. But see David Adamany, *Financing Politics: Recent Wisconsin Elections* (Madison: University of Wisconsin Press, 1969); and David Adamany, *Campaign Funds as an Intra-Party Political Resource: Connecticut 1966–68* (Princeton, N.J.: Citizens Research Foundation, 1972).

43. Quoted in Delmar Dunn, *Financing Presidential Campaigns* (Washington, D.C.: Brookings Institution, 1972), p. 77.

44. Herbert Alexander, *Money in Politics* (Washington, D.C.: Public Affairs Press, 1972), p. 95.

45. These funds must of course be raised. A substantial portion of the 1968 debt is in the form of personally held notes. The waiver thus raises the prospect of a tax write-off approach to eliminate the debt.

46. Art Kosatka, "Behind the Scenes at the Democratic Telethon," *Democratic Review,* June/July 1975, p. 41.

47. David W. Adamany and George E. Agree, *Political Money* (Baltimore: Johns Hopkins University Press, 1975), p. 58.

48. Ibid., p. 59.

49. This projection has subsequently been modified downward.

50. Consider, for example, that the Republican national committee, in 1977, spent more than $100,000 in state and local elections and projects a multimillion dollar program for 1978.

51. In early 1978, the size of the DNC professional staff was reduced from ninety to sixty members, and further staff cuts were not ruled out. At the time of his resignation as DNC chairperson, Kenneth M. Curtis lamented the difficulties imposed by the remaining debt. See, "Curtis Says Money Was Top Headache as DNC Chairman," *Washington Post,* December 9, 1977, p. A20.

52. For one discussion of representativeness at the 1972 convention see, Jeanne Kirkpatrick, "Representation in the American National Conventions: The Case of 1972," *British Journal of Political Science* 5 (July 1975): 265–322. For the current study of the DNC, source materials include *Who's Who in American Politics* (New York: Bowker, n.d.), bibliographic files of the DNC, and a variety of secondary sources. Excluded from this analysis are ex officio members of the DNC, with the exception of state chairpersons and territorial representatives.

53. See Saloma and Sontage, *Parties: The Real Opportunity,* pp. 13-29, for one assessment. See also Crotty, *Decision,* chap. 1.

54. *Mandate,* pp. 17-32, details shortcomings of the 1968 delegate-selection process.

55. Cotter and Hennessy, *Politics Without Power,* p. 53.

56. Ibid., pp. 53-54.

57. The phrase is taken from James Q. Wilson, *The Amateur Democrats* (Chicago: University of Chicago Press, 1962). See also Denis R. Sullivan et al., *The Politics of Representation: The Democratic Convention 1972* (New York: St. Martin, 1974), for a discussion of "amateurs" and "professionals" at the 1972 Convention.

58. Cotter and Hennessy, *Politics Without Power,* p. 54.

59. Ibid.

60. For a discussion of this point, see Kenneth Janda, "A Comparative Analysis of Party Organizations: The United States, Europe, and the World," in this volume.

61. See William Crotty, "The National Committees as Grass-roots Vehicles of Representation," in this volume.

62. For a summary statement, see Walter Dean Burnham, "American Parties in the 1970's: Beyond Party?", in *The Future of Political Parties,* eds. Louis Maisel and Paul Sacks, *Sage Electoral Studies Yearbook,* vol. 1 (Beverly Hills: Sage, 1975), pp. 238-277.

63. Alexander Bickel, *The New Age of Political Reform: The Electoral College, the Convention, and the Party System* (New York: Harper & Row, Harper Colophon Books, 1968), p. 52.